13th Global Wordnet Conference (GWC 2025)

Pavia, Italy
27-31 January 2025

ISBN: 979-8-3313-3283-9

Printed from e-media with permission by:

Curran Associates, Inc.
57 Morehouse Lane
Red Hook, NY 12571

CURRAN ASSOCIATES INC.
proceedings
.com

Some format issues inherent in the e-media version may also appear in this print version.

Printed with permission by Curran Associates, Inc. (2026)

For permission requests, please contact the Association for Computational Linguistics at the address below.

Association for Computational Linguistics
209 N. Eighth Street
Stroudsburg, Pennsylvania 18360

Phone: 1-570-476-8006
Fax: 1-570-476-0860

acl@aclweb.org

Additional copies of this publication are available from:

Curran Associates, Inc.
57 Morehouse Lane
Red Hook, NY 12571 USA
Phone: 845-758-0400
Fax: 845-758-2633
Email: curran@proceedings.com
Web: www.proceedings.com

TABLE OF CONTENTS

GWC 2025

Proceedings of the 13th Global Wordnet Conference

Chiara Zanchi, Luca Brigada Villa, Erica Biagetti, Alexandre Rademaker, Francis Bond & German Rigau (Eds.)

27–31 Jan, 2025

University of Pavia

Italy

With the support of:

Foreword

The Global WordNet Conference 2025 (GWC2025) brought together scholars and practitioners to discuss the latest advancements in lexical semantics and the development of WordNet-like lexical resources. The event addressed diverse topics, including multilingual WordNet expansion, the integration of Large Language Models into semantic frameworks, and the applications of WordNets in historical linguistics and cultural studies.

The initiative to host GWC2025 at the University of Pavia was inspired by the PRIN project *Linked WordNets for Ancient Indo-European Languages* (PRIN_2022 2022YAPFNJ; PIs Chiara Zanchi and Riccardo Ginevra), based in the Department of Humanities. This project, in collaboration with the Università Cattolica del Sacro Cuore in Milan, focuses on developing WordNets for Latin, Ancient Greek, and Sanskrit, thereby advancing the inclusion of ancient languages in computational linguistics, Natural Language Processing, and language resource creation. In alignment with these goals, the 2025 edition of the Global WordNet Conference featured a panel on ancient languages, examining WordNet architecture and applications for languages both within and beyond the project's scope, such as Old English and Coptic.

The conference featured three keynote speakers who shared their expertise in the development, implementation, and application of WordNets, as well as their reflections on the role of WordNets in society in the era of Linked Data and Large Language Models:

- In her talk 'Towards a Cultural WordNet: From Words to Meanings to Cross-Cultural Nuances', Rada Mihalcea (University of Michigan) discussed the creation of a Cultural WordNet and its applications.
- Marco Passarotti (Università Cattolica del Sacro Cuore) explored interoperability and linked data approaches for the Latin WordNet in a talk entitled 'WordNet in the Net. Making it all Interact'.
- Piek Vossen (Vrije Universiteit Amsterdam) presented '30 Years Embracing and Abandoning Wordnets', a talk on the evolution of WordNets over three decades since the original creation of the Princeton English WordNet.

The conference was preceded by a teach-in delivered by Angela Caiazza (NTT DATA Italia) on the transformative impact of Large Language Models on modern business strategies. This reflected an ongoing collaboration between the Department of Humanities at the University of Pavia and NTT DATA, established through a recently signed framework agreement, to promote outreach initiatives, internships, collaborative projects, workshops, and seminars.

As detailed in the program, the conference featured over thirty presentations, two-thirds of which were delivered by international scholars. Beyond attracting global researchers, GWC2025 fostered synergy among institutions that contribute to the cultural life of the city of Pavia: not only the University but also the Municipality of Pavia – particularly the Department of Public Education and Professional Training – as well as the Almo Collegio Borromeo and Collegio Ghislieri. The event's scientific significance was recognized globally by the Global WordNet Association and nationally by AILC, the Italian Association for Computational Linguistics. Two scholarships were made available to support student presenters in their participation in the conference. Moreover, participants were able to enjoy the city of Pavia through a rich social program, which offered numerous opportunities for informal exchange and community building.

Conference Chairs

- German Rigau (HiTZ Center, University of the Basque Country UPV/EHU)
- Francis Bond (Palacký University)

Local Organizing Chairs

- Chiara Zanchi (University of Pavia)
- Erica Biagetti (University of Pavia)
- Luca Brigada Villa (University of Pavia)
- Claudia Roberta Combei (University of Rome Tor Vergata)
- Tullio Facchinetti (University of Pavia)
- Stefano Rocchi (University of Pavia)
- Silvia Zampetta (University of Pavia)

Program Committee

- Verginica Barbu Mititelu (Romanian Academy Research Institute for Artificial Intelligence)
- Erica Biagetti (University of Pavia)
- Francis Bond (Palacký University)
- Luca Brigada Villa (University of Pavia)
- Paul Buitelaar (University of Galway)
- Claudia Roberta Combei (University of Rome Tor Vergata)
- Valeria de Paiva (Samsung Research America and University of Birmingham)
- Tullio Facchinetti (University of Pavia)
- Christiane Fellbaum (Princeton University)
- Greta Franzini (Eurac Research - Institute of Applied Linguistics)
- Riccardo Ginevra (UCSC Milan)
- Hugo Gonçalo Oliveira (University of Coimbra)
- Ales Horak (Masaryk University)
- Shu-Kai Hsieh(National Taiwan Normal University)
- Eleonora Litta (UCSC Milan)
- Silvia Luraghi (University of Pavia)
- Francesco Mambrini (UCSC Milan)

- Claudia Marzi (Institute for Computational Linguistics - National Research Council)
- John Mccrae (National University of Ireland, Galway)
- Verginica Barbu Mititelu (Romanian Academy Research Institute for Artificial Intelligence)
- Ludovica Pannitto (University of Bologna)
- Marco Passarotti (UCSC Milan)
- Bolette Pedersen (University of Copenhagen)
- Maciej Piasecki (Wroclaw University of Science and Technology)
- Alexandre Rademaker (IBM Research and EMAp/FGV)
- German Rigau (HiTZ Center, University of the Basque Country UPV/EHU)
- Stefano Rocchi (University of Pavia)
- Rachele Sprugnoli (University of Parma)
- Fabio Tamburini (University of Bologna)
- Piek Vossen (Vrije Universiteit Amsterdam)
- Silvia Zampetta (University of Pavia)
- Chiara Zanchi (University of Pavia)

Student Helpers

- Eleonora Carmen Canneto
- Annachiara Clementelli
- Beatrice Marchesi
- Lorenzo Reina

Organizing Secretariat

- Marta Daffara - Pragma Congressi

Using digital resources to study semantics and word formation in a historical language: FEAR and TREMOR in the Latin WordNet and Word Formation Latin

Giorgio Carboni,° Riccardo Ginevra,* Eleonora Litta*

°Università per Stranieri di Siena, *Università Cattolica del Sacro Cuore, Milano
g.carboni@dottorandi.unistrasi.it, riccardo.ginevra@unicatt.it,
eleonoramaria.litta@unicatt.it

Abstract

The paper aims to show how the semantics and word formation of an historical language like Latin may be investigated by means of digital resources. We focus on words pertaining to the semantic field FEAR and study them using the Latin WordNet and Word Formation Latin. We describe and analyze how these lemmas' semantics patterns with their morphology, and which relations occur between them.

1 Introduction

The combined study of semantics and morphology can be greatly enhanced by using digital resources developed by computational linguistics. For Latin, two resources appear to be particularly useful to this purpose: the Latin WordNet (LWN) and Word Formation Latin (WFL). The former is a lexical resource which represents the lexicon in a relational way and "is built around the idea of synonymy in the broad sense" (Mambrini et al. 2021: 17). Originally created by translating English and Italian data into Latin within the MultiWordNet framework (Minozzi 2008), the LWN has been refined, extended, and further developed first within the ERC project "LiLa: Linking Latin"[1] and now within the PRIN 2022 project "Linked WordNets for Ancient Indo-European languages".[2] In the LWN, word senses are associated to lexical entries as synsets, i.e. sets of cognitive synonyms, each expressing a distinct concept, so "that [the synonyms within a synset] are interchangeable in some context without changing the truth value of the proposition in which they are embedded".[3] The process of annotation in LWN consists in the association of lemmas with the synsets of the Princeton WordNet (PWN; Fellbaum 1998) that can best represent the senses of each Latin lemma; by using synsets from the PWN, the LWN can take advantage of information that is already available in the PWN, such as the lexical domains to which each synset belongs (e.g. synsets dealing with feelings like fear belong to the lexical domain Emotion). As for Word Formation Latin (Litta et al. 2019), it is a derivational morphology resource for Classical Latin, where lemmas are analyzed into their formative components, and relationships between them are established on the basis of Word Formation Rules.

The aim of this paper is to argue for the use of the LWN for investigations that focus not only on the semantics of Latin, but also on its word formation processes. In our study, we show that a WordNet-based analysis allows us to identify semantic affinities and differences between words, while a WFL-based analysis helps us explore how meanings pertaining to different lexical domains seem to pattern according to word formation.

[1] https://lila-erc.eu.

[2] https://sites.google.com/unipv.it/linked-wordnets/home-page?authuser=0.

[3] Quoted from the glossary of the Princeton WordNet: http://wordnet.princeton.edu.

The semantic field chosen for this pilot study is that of FEAR[4] in the lexical domain of Emotion. As detailed in Section 2, we find FEAR to be a concept with close (arguably trivial) links to other concepts belonging to different lexical domains, such as the concepts for TREMOR in the domains Body and Motion (due to the trembling and visible movements of the body that the sentiment of fear can induce). As described in Section 3, the manual annotation of selected lemmas from a specific semantic field allowed us to identify a specific pattern of polysemy, as well as to analyze this pattern from the perspective of word formation processes. The results are summarized in Section 4.

2 Annotation of the semantic field FEAR in the LWN with the aid of WFL

Many words related to the semantic field of FEAR are attested in Latin. The lemmas initially selected for the annotation task are listed in Table 1. This first selection was grounded on the information provided by standard Latin dictionaries of synonyms (e.g. Döderlein 2010), but further words not listed by these dictionaries were also selected for annotation, whereas other words were excluded even if listed in the dictionaries (e.g. *vereor*, whose semantics seems to be closer to the concept REVERENCE than to FEAR, being used when someone does not wish something to happen or to indicate respect for another person, usually someone with some kind of authority, rather than to refer to actual fear and dread).

Lemma	Meaning[5]	Part of Speech
formido	'dread'	Noun
horreo	'to stand on end, to be terrible'	Verb
metus	'fear'	Noun
paveo	'to be struck by fear'	Verb
terreo	'to struck'	Verb
timeo	'to fear'	Verb
tremo	'to quiver'	Verb

Table 1: Lemmas initially selected for the LWN annotation task.

The selection was then expanded by taking into consideration not only the single FEAR lemmas, but their entire derivational families. We used WFL to

Figure 1: Derivation graph of *metuo* 'fear' in WFL.

extract all derivatives of each lemma, e.g. for the noun *metus* 'fear' we extracted the denominative (N-To-V) verb *metuo* 'to fear' and the prefixed verb *praemetuo* 'to fear beforehand' (Figure 1).

The extraction provided us with a total of 141 lemmas, which were then semantically annotated in LWN and associated with a total of 518 synsets from PWN. The annotation resulted in 39 lemmas sharing two or more common synsets, and 41 lemmas associated with synsets pertaining to quite different lexical domains, namely Emotion, Body, and Motion.

The analysis that follows focuses on word families whose members are often annotated with synsets linked to both concepts FEAR and TREMOR, as our data allow for the identification of a frequent and close link between the two. This seems to be the case for the verbs *horreo*, *paveo*, and *tremo*, as well as for most of their derivatives, for a total of 41 lemmas (Table 3 in the Appendix). As for *formido*, *metus*, *timeo*, and their derivatives, they do not attest this polysemy pattern, and thus lie beyond the scope of this analysis.

In what follows we briefly describe the three synsets that are most relevant to this study (Table 4 in the Appendix), evoked by words associated with the concepts FEAR, TREMOR, or both.

2.1 Synset 201784021

The definition of this PWN synset is "be afraid or scared of; be frightened of". It pertains to the PWN lexical domain of Emotion and denotes primarily the state of BEING AFRAID (OF). It is well suited for the meaning of the verbs *horreo, paveo, tremo*, and of several of their derivatives. Its pairing with lemmas from the *tremo* derivational family is particularly interesting here, given that the primary

[4] Small capitals are conventionally used in the paper to mark semantic concepts in general and, for practical purposes, used as shortcuts in place of complex synset IDs or synset glosses.

[5] Meanings of Latin lemmas are taken from Lewis and Short (1879) and Glare (2016).

sense of *tremo* mainly denotes a type of motion (see below) and not necessarily an emotion. A total of 16 lemmas have been annotated with this synset.

2.2 Synset 200014027

The definition of this PWN synset is "move with or as if with a tremor". It pertains to the PWN lexical domain of Body and it is always associated with the derivatives of the verb *tremo*, as it denotes the act of TREMBLING. It is also associated with a number of derivatives of *horreo* and *paveo*, to denote the physical TREMOR that is often linked with FEAR. A total of 19 lemmas have been annotated with this synset.

2.3 Synset 201892939

The definition of this PWN synset is "tremble convulsively, as from fear or excitement". Its PWN lexical domain is Motion, and it may thus denote the act of TREMBLING FOR FEAR. This synset is associated with derivatives of all three verbs, and may thus be considered a link between the previous two synsets. A total of 19 lemmas have been annotated with it.

3 Semantics and word formation: FEAR, TREMOR, and the *-sc-* suffix

The three synsets above, henceforth labelled BEING AFRAID (OF) (2.1), TREMBLING (2.2), and TREMBLING FOR FEAR (2.3) respectively, co-occur in the LWN annotation of several lemmas, which may thus be described as polysemous.

In many cases all three synsets appear to be associated with the same lemma. Out of 22 polysemous verbs that are annotated with at least two of these three synsets, a total of 15 lemmas attest all three of them: *horreo*, *paveo*, *tremo*, and 12 of their derivatives (listed in Table 2). More than half of the latter (8; underlined in Table 2) are *-sc-* verbs, which are currently regarded to be dynamic/intransitive counterparts of stative/transitive base verbs or inchoative verbs referring to the beginning of a situation (Budassi et al. 2019: 240). Furthemore, in 6 of these lemmas, the *-sc-* suffix is combined with a preverb as well.

As for the 7 polysemous verbs taken into account that are not associated with all three synsets in the LWN, they can either be exclusively prefixed (*adhorreo*, *inhorreo*, *contremo*, *praetremo*, *intremo*) or both prefixed and suffixed (*cohorresco*, *intremesco*). The 2 verbs derived exclusively through the *-sc-* suffix (*horresco*, *tremesco*) are instead both characterized by this polysemy.

Base	Derivative
horreo	<u>*abhorresco*</u>, *exhorreo*, <u>*exhorresco*</u>, <u>*horresco*</u>, <u>*inhorresco*</u>, *perhorreo*, <u>*perhorresco*</u>
paveo	*pavito*
tremo	*attremo*, <u>*contremesco*</u>, <u>*pertremisco*</u>, <u>*tremesco*</u>

Table 2: Bases and derivatives that attest the triple polysemy.

In the case of the derivatives of *horreo*, verbs with the suffix *-sc-* seem to be those that best attest the triple polysemy (5 out of 8) – the highly polysemous verbs *horresco*, *abhorresco*, *exhorresco*, *inhorresco*, and *perhorresco* are all formed through this suffix –, but the same triple polysemy is also found with *exhorreo* and *perhorreo*, 2 verbs that are derived exclusively through a preverb. Given that their base *horreo* is a dynamic verb that already attests the triple polysemy, it is not surprising that the latter so frequently occurs among its derivatives. It must be noted, however, that 2 derivatives of *horreo* (*adhorreo*, *cohorresco*) do not seem to attest it.

As for *paveo* and its derivatives, no *-sc-* verbs from this derivational family seem to attest this polysemy. According to WFL, *paveo* has 3 *-sc-* derivatives (*pavesco*, *compavesco*, *expavesco*), but each of them has been annotated exclusively with the synset for BEING AFRAID (OF). This is exactly paralleled by *timesco* 'to fear', which, although a *-sc-* derivative, does not attest any TREMBLING sense, most likely because its base verb *timeo* did not have any semantic trait related to movement. Correspondingly, the *-sc-* derivatives of *paveo* may have been created when their base had not yet acquired any dynamic TREMBLING senses (like *timeo*), as opposed to the *horreo* derivatives, for which the TREMBLING sense may have been the primary one.

This may indeed be the case for *tremo* and its derivatives, which seem to often attest this polysemy, especially when they present the *-sc-* suffix (*contremesco*, *pertremisco*, *tremesco*), but also without it (*attremo*), perhaps because their (already polysemous) base *tremo* was a verb with a primary dynamic sense TREMBLING in the first place. According to Haverling (2000: 51), "the suffixed verb indicates that something trembles at something, i.e. when something happens [...], whereas the unsuffixed verb describes the action more generally"; our data, however, does not seem to allow for this generalization, as both the base verb and its *-sc-* derivatives attest the polysemy.

The presence of a prefix, although very frequent in our list of verbs, does not seem to be the most frequent trigger of the triple polysemy. If the latter's triggering factor did involve word formation, it may rather have been the *-sc-* suffix, as exemplified by the verbs *adhorreo* and *horresco*, ultimately both derived from the highly polysemous *horreo*. The prefixed verb *adhorreo* simply means 'to shudder' and has been annotated with the synsets for TREMBLING and TREMBLING FOR FEAR, while *horresco* may mean 'to be frightened of', 'to shudder' and 'to shake with fear', and has thus been annotated with all three synsets for BEING AFRAID (OF), TREMBLING, and TREMBLING FOR FEAR. The fact that the polysemy of *horreo* is retained by *horresco* may thus be linked to the presence of the *-sc-* suffix, as opposed to its lack in *adhorreo*.

A further interesting case is that of *contremo*, mentioned above as one of the 4 prefixed verbs that do not attest the triple polysemy, whose *-sc-* counterpart *contremesco*, however, actually does attest all three synsets. In general, among the 22 polysemous verbs analyzed here, the only derivational category (however small) that always attests the triple polysemy seems to be the one consisting of the two non-prefixed *-sc-* verbs, *horresco* and *tremesco*.

In brief, our data seem to support the impression of a link between the *-sc-* suffix and the attestation of all three synsets BEING AFRAID (OF), TREMBLING, and TREMBLING FOR FEAR. It must be noted, however, that a few verbs that are both prefixed and *-sc-* suffixed (e.g. *cohorresco* 'to shake' and *intremesco* 'to tremble') do not attest the triple polysemy, prompting the question if in such cases the presence of a prefix may have neutralized the effect of the *-sc-* suffix.

4 Conclusions

The origin of the triple polysemy discussed in this paper is most likely to be traced back to the close and visible link between the act of BEING AFRAID (OF) and that of TREMBLING in human experience, which ultimately combine in TREMBLING FOR FEAR. This association may sound trivial to our ears; however, the co-occurrence of these three synsets is not attested in the LWN anywhere outside of the derivational families taken into account here, namely those of *horreo, paveo, tremo*, and their derivatives. Within the FEAR semantic field, no further LWN lemmas show such a constant and precise connection between FEAR and TREMOR. For instance, at least 3 further LWN lemmas – *mico, moveo, trepido* – may be annotated with at least one of the three synsets discussed here, but none of them (or their derivatives) attests traces of this triple polysemy.

As noted above, quite often the verbs that attest the triple set of synsets are either *-sc-* derivatives or derivational bases of such verbs. It may thus be worth noting that, according to WFL, the verb *mico* 'to quiver' does not attest any *-sc-* derivatives (but it attests prefixed derivatives such as *praemico* 'to glitter very much'), and the same is true for *moveo* 'to move' or *formido* 'to fear'. A connection between the *-sc-* suffix and the triple polysemy discussed here may thus be worth being pursued further in future studies, which may investigate if the derivation through this suffix could indeed have been a triggering factor for the broadening (or the retaining, as in some cases above) of the synsets associated to each lemma.

This study has shown some possibilities of an analysis of a historical language that is based on digital resources like LWN and WFL. The inquiry conducted through the annotation in LWN of synsets associated to Latin bases and derivatives belonging to specific derivational families (collected through WFL) may help us detect quite consistent patterns. We have found that words related to the semantic field of FEAR are more likely to become – or remain, if their bases already were – polysemous when they are derived through the suffix *-sc-*, as this kind of derivation (at least when it is not combined with prefixation) is the only one that consistently attests the triple polysemy described above. Even though the association of these three concepts (BEING AFRAID (OF), TREMBLING, and TREMBLING FOR FEAR) is obviously grounded in human experience, it does not occur frequently outside of the specific lexical families discussed here.

References

Budassi, Marco, Litta Modignani Picozzi, Eleonora, M. G., and Passarotti, Marco. 2019. What's beyond 'inchoatives'? Derivation types on the basis of *-sc-* verbs, in Holmes, N., Ottink, M., Schrickx, J., Selig,

M. (ed.) *Lemmata Linguistica Latina*. Volume I: Words and Sounds, De Gruyter, Berlin: 240-257.

Döderlein, Ludwig von; Taylor, Samuel Harvey; Arnold, Henry Hamilton (translator). 2010. *Döderlein's Hand-Book of Latin Synonymes by Ludwig von Doederlein.* Edited by Hope L. & Spehar I. Gutenberg project, URL: http://www.gutenberg.org/ebooks/33197 [Accessed 10 October 2024]

Fellbaum, Christiane. 1998. *WordNet: An Electronic Lexical Database*. MIT Press: Cambridge, MA.

Glare, P.G.W. (ed.). 2016. *Oxford Latin Dictionary.* Clarendon Press: Oxford.

Haverling, Gerd. 2000. *On -sco- verbs, prefixes and semantic functions: a study in the development of prefixed and unprefixed verbs from early to late latin.* Acta Universitatis Gothoburgensis: Göteborg.

Lewis, Charlton, T, Short, Charles. 1879. *Latin-English Lexicon*. Oxford University Press: Oxford.

Litta Modignani Picozzi, Eleonora, M. G., Passarotti, M. C. 2019. (When) inflection needs derivation: a word formation lexicon for Latin, in Holmes, N., Ottink, M., Schrickx, J., Selig, M. (ed.) *Lemmata Linguistica Latina*. Volume I: Words and Sounds, De Gruyter, Berlin: 224- 239.

Mambrini, Francesco, Passarotti, Marco, Litta Modignani Picozzi, Eleonora and Moretti, Giovanni. 2021. Interlinking Valency Frames and Wordnet Synsets in the Lila Knowledge Base of Linguistic Resources for Latin. *Zenodo*, 2021. 16-28.

Minozzi, Stefano. 2008. La costruzione di una base di conoscenza lessicale per la lingua latina: Latin Wordnet. in G. Sandrini (ed.) *Studi in onore di Gilberto Lonardi*. 243-258

A Appendices

Table 3 presents all the lemmas linked to FEAR and TREMOR and their generic meaning.

Lemma	Meaning
abhorresco	to tremble or shudder greatly at
adhorreo	to shudder
attremo	to tremble at a thing
cohorresco	to shudder
contremebundus	trembling
contremesco	to tremble to be afraid of
contremo	to tremble greatly, to quake
contremulus	trembling
exhorreo	to tremble or shudder exceedingly at
exhorresco	to tremble or shudder exceedingly, to be terrified
horrentia	a shuddering, horror
horreo	to stand on end
horresco	to tremble or shudder greatly at
horrifer	that brings trembling or terror
horrificus	that causes tremor
horripilation	a bristling of the hair
horripilo	to bristle with hairs, be shaggy
horror	a standing on end a terror
inhorreo	to stand on end
inhorresco	to send forth sharp points to tremble
intremefactus	shaken
intremesco	to tremble
intremo	to tremble
intremulus	shaking
paveo	to be struck with fear
pavidus	trembling, quaking
pavitatio	a trembling
pavito	to tremble or quake with fear
pavor	a trembling
perhorreo	to tremble or shudder greatly at
perhorresco	to tremble or shudder greatly
pertremisco	to tremble greatly at
praetremo	to tremble beforehand
tremebundus	trembling
tremefacio	to cause to shake
tremesco	to begin to shake
tremidus	trembling
tremipeda	with trembling feet
tremo	to shake, quake
tremor	a shaking
tremulus	shaking

Table 3: Lemmas linked to FEAR and TREMOR

Table 4 contains the lemmas associated with the synsets presented in sections 2.1, 2.2, and 2.3.

Synset ID	Definition	Lemmas
#201784021	be afraid or scared of; be frightened of	*horreo, exhorreo, inhorreo, perhorreo, horresco, exhorresco, inhorresco, perhorresco, paveo, pavito, tremo, attremo, praetremo, tremesco, contremesco, pertremisco*

#200014027	move with or as if with a tremor	*horreo, adhorreo, exhorreo, inhorreo, perhorreo, horresco, exhorresco, inhorresco, perhorresco, paveo, pavito, tremo, attremo, contremo, intremo, tremesco, contremesco, intremesco, pertremisco*
#201892939	tremble convulsively, as from fear or excitement tremble convulsively, as from fear or excitement	*horreo, adhorreo exhorreo,inhorreo perhorreo, horresco, abhorresco, cohorresco, exhorresco, inhorresco, perhorresco, paveo, pavito, tremo, attremo, tremesco, contremesco, intremesco, pertremisco*

Table 4: Lemmas associated with the synsets presented in sections 2.1, 2.2, and 2.3

Renovating the Verb Hierarchy of English Wordnet

John P. McCrae
Insight Centre and ADAPT Centre
University of Galway
john@mccr.ae

Abstract

English Wordnet's hierarchy of senses is a key feature that enables the resource to be used for a wide range of analysis, however, it is only complete for nouns and not for other parts of speech. In this work, we propose an improvement of the hierarchy of verbs, such that all verbs are connected to one of eight top synsets. We evaluate this resource in terms of improved connectivity and in comparison to SimVerb-3500, and show that this hierarchy makes the resource more useful. We extensively discuss further improvements that would make English Wordnet more practical for a wide range of applications and bring it closer in line with other lexical resources for verbs.

1 Introduction

English Wordnet is still the primary resource for lexical semantic analysis in computational linguistics and its model of links between words has proved invaluable to a wide range of experiments (Jin et al., 2024; Stanisz et al., 2024). The nouns in English Wordnet form a complete hierarchy with a single root element, however, there is no such complete hierarchy for other part-of-speech values. In this paper, we look at the verbs of English WordNet editions, including the Princeton WordNet (Miller, 1995; Fellbaum, 2010, PWN) and the more recent Open English Wordnet versions (McCrae et al., 2019)[1]. We firstly examine the nature of hypernymy and troponymy in wordnets and develop guidelines for the establishment of links between verbal synsets. We then use these principles to 'renovate' the verb hierarchy of English WordNet leading to a far more complete hierarchy of verbs. We examine how this improves the hierarchy in terms of connectedness and compare this with a semantic similarity resource. This new hierarchy is also released as part of the 2024 edition of Open English WordNet.

We then discuss some of the challenges with the verb hierarchy in English Wordnet, in particular, related to the representation of frame information in the wordnet, as well as how this can relate to other frame resources, such as FrameNet (Baker et al., 1998). Finally, this paper will look at some perspectives for the improvement of verb modelling in WordNet in particular through the establishment of new relations that would further connect verbs together.

2 Related Work

Classifications of verbs have been investigated from a number of directions based on their syntactic and semantic properties (Levin, 1993) and this has led to the development of a number of resources such as VerbNet (Schuler, 2005), FrameNet (Baker et al., 1998) and PropBank (Kingsbury and Palmer, 2002). These resources are focused on the use of frame semantics (Fillmore, 1976), which is complementary to the graph structure used by wordnets and as such, there has been much interest in linking these resources with English Wordnet in order to provide a complete description of verb semantics. One of the first of these efforts was by Shi and Mihalcea (2005), who linked FrameNet, VerbNet and WordNet and this was further extended by Laparra and Rigau (2010). Similar mappings were developed by Tonelli and Pighin (2009) and (Ferrández et al., 2010) and this lead to the creation of SemLink (Palmer, 2009), later extended with the inclusion of OntoNotes (Hovy et al., 2006) to SemLink+ (Palmer et al., 2014). Similarly, other resources such as Predicate Matrix (Lopez de Lacalle et al., 2014) and the conceptual descriptions of Stoyanova and Leseva (2023) have produced large-scale resources that combine these resources. In particular, Leseva et al. (2018)'s classification used the hypernymy structure of English Word-

[1]We use the term 'English Wordnet' to cover releases by both projects

net to provide a joint classification of verbs. They found that the majority of verbs could be accommodated in the classification, but noted that there was a large amount of semantic mismatch between the hypernyms in WordNet and the hierarchy of FrameNet.

Other approaches to the classification of verbs have focused on other features such as the morphosyntax of verbs, for example by examining the morphosyntactic derivations (Šojat and Srebačić, 2014) or by noun derivations (Mititelu et al., 2021), which would allow the verb relations to be connected to the noun hierarchy. Finally, other attempts have classified verbs through ontological categories, such as events (Puşcaşu and Mititelu, 2008) using TimeML or through upper ontologies such as SUMO (Chow and Webster, 2007).

More recently, VerbAtlas (Di Fabio et al., 2019) has introduced a large-scale resource that organises all the WordNet synsets into semantic frames, however, it still has substantial quality issues.

3 Verb Hierarchy

Verbs in English Wordnet form a hierarchy based on a 'is a manner of' relationship known as *troponymy* as introduced by Fellbaum and Miller (1990). In contrast to the noun hierarchy, verbs are much more polysemous and their senses are not as sharply distinct as the nouns' senses. Still verbs, like nouns, follow a substitution test using a template such as "if someone/thing Xs (someone/thing), then something must also Y (someone/thing)", for example "if someone nibbles something, then someone must also eat something". Substitution is a necessary condition for a verb hypernym but it may cause issues as outlined by Fellbaum and Miller (1990) if not phrased well. Secondly, there may be differences in the morphosyntax of verbs that make it hard to properly apply the substitution as such some other changes should be allowed.

- Changing the preposition used to mark a particular argument in a frame or changing a direct object to a prepositional argument, e.g., 'punish (somebody with something)'[02505278-v] to 'impose (something on somebody)'[00750288-v];
- Replacing a direct object or prepositional argument with 'something' or 'someone', e.g., 'do (something)'[02566500-v] to 'act'[02372362-v];
- Dropping a direct object, e.g., 'observe (a holiday)'[02584595-v] to 'behave'[00010428-v].

Importantly, the subject must have the same semantic role, as this always makes a sense distinction, as discussed below.

For noun definitions, most definitions in WordNet follow a *genera-differentia* style of definition where a noun (the *genera*), which is generally the hypernym, is further differentiated by other criteria (the *differentia*) to give the specific sense. For verbs, the form of the definition does not generally follow this principle, instead, verb meaning is given by a verbal phrase with some arguments or adjuncts. As such, it is less often the case that a hypernym occurs within the definition. For some cases, when the definition contains a verb with a simple adverb or adjunct this can hold, for example, 'behave unnaturally or affectedly' (dissemble, pretend, act)[01725433-v] was marked with 'behave'[00010428-v] as the hypernym in OEWN 2024. However, for many other cases this does not hold, for example, 'render unable to see' (blind)[02172999-v] does not imply any 'rendering' takes place, and instead this verb was mapped to the hypernym of 'alter'. Another issue is that frequently the main verb of the definition is a light verb, such as in 'come to a halt' (stop, halt)[01864781-v] which cannot be mapped to the corresponding sense of the verb 'reach or enter a state, relation, condition, use, or position' (come)[00543200-v], as the substitution test would fail ('if something stops, it must also come'). A more extreme example of this is the copula 'be'[02610777-v], which is given as the hypernym of 138 verbs in Princeton WordNet 3.1. This seems to be a misunderstanding of the concept of troponymy as many of these senses represent passive constructions ('be composed of' (comprise, consist)[02639437-v]), adjectival constructions ('be loyal to' (stick, adhere, stand by, stick by)[02644714-v]) or other constructions ('be the reason or explanation for' (account for)[02641114-v]). These don't generally pass the substitution test as above[2].

4 Methodology

The goal of this work is to improve the verb hierarchy and eliminate isolated verb senses, which are not connected to any other verbs in the resource.

[2] 'Something consists of X' does imply 'something is of X', however, there is a different synset of 'be'[02626667-v] that is relevant for this case

As such, we focused on the verb synsets of OEWN 2023, which did not have a hypernym, which consists of 591 synsets. We then also included all verbs whose hypernym is the copula sense of 'be', due to the fact that we concluded that these senses were nearly all erroneous, which added a further 139 synsets to the analysis, leading to our analysis covering 730 verb synsets (5.2% of all verbs in OEWN 2023).

Initially, we attempted to find an automatic method to help find an initial mapping for these hypernyms. The first approach was to use the first verb mentioned in the definition and apply word sense disambiguation to find the first sense. However, this was found to be highly inaccurate and misleading, firstly as a lot of definitions used the copula 'be', light verbs or the verb 'cause'. An analysis of 100 random verb synsets showed that the hypernym verb only occurs in 35 out of 100 verb definitions. We also considered using a large language model to suggest the hypernyms, however, initial chats with ChatGPT indicated that these systems were not good at this task, frequently suggesting synonyms such as 'merit' for 'deserve' or 'perplex' for 'confuse' or words that are hard to relate, for example, 'owe' for 'obligate'. It is possible that a more refined model such as TaxoLlama (Moskvoretskii et al., 2024), may have performed better.

Given the difficulty of the task, it was decided that this was best conducted by a single highly expert annotator through a simple spreadsheet interface to suggest the most appropriate hypernym and the relevant sense of the hypernym. ChatGPT was used to suggest hypernyms in some cases, however as noted above, these were not frequently found to be useful. While this lacks natural validation, given the challenge of the task, it was concluded that this was the best way to implement the model development. In addition, a number of smaller related issues were discovered with the verbs in OEWN and these were created as issues on the GitHub of the OEWN project[3]. The verbs that were marked as troponyms of the copula 'be' were annotated using the same procedure and only one verb synset was deemed to truly be a hypernym of the copula, namely the verb 'stand'[02617408-v] in sentences such as 'I stand corrected.'

4.1 Top Verb Synsets

The following verbs were not judged to have a hypernym, and as such can be seen as top concepts for the verb hierarchy:

act ('perform an action')[02372362-v] - 12976 children - This hierarchy is shown in more detail in Figure 1. This sense covers all actions that are carried out by an agent and have some temporal scope.

happen, occur, ... ('come to pass')[00340744-v] - 43 children - This is used for events not initiated by a causal agent.

exist, be ('have an existance')[02609706-v] - 438 Children - Covering most stative verbs.

have, have got, hold ('have or possess, either in a concrete or an abstract sense')[02208144-v] - 233 children - A stative verb of possession. One significant child is 'keep, hold on'[02207166-v] with 145 children.

know, cognize, cognise ('be cognizant or aware of a fact or a specific piece of information')[00596016-v] - 55 children - Stative verbs relating to knowing a fact

relate, pertain, ... ('be relevant to')[02681865-v] - 153 children - Stative verbs that relate two entities.

miss, lack ('be without')[02638434-v] - 6 children - The antonym of 'have', indicating not having.

be ('have the quality of being; (copula, used with an adjective or a predicate noun)')[02610777-v] - 1 child - The copula sense of the verb to 'be'.

As we have noted before, there does not seem to be a single verb sense that covers all verb meanings, however as we can see from the size of the graph, the verb 'act' covers the large majority of verbs (93.2%). We also distinguish between event verbs with a causal agent and non-causal events and this is due to the requirement that the subject is not changed by hypernymy. For most causal verbs, the causal agent is the subject, whereas for non-causal verbs the event is the subject. The other top verbs are all stative verbs and these are distinguished between most intransitive verbs under

[3]Issue numbers: #1034, #1035, #1036, #1037, #1038, #1039, #1041, #1042, #1043, #1056

- act, move[02372362-v] [12976 children]
  - ↪ interact[02382049-v] [1353 children]
    - ↪ treat, handle, do by[02519853-v] [126 children]
    - ↪ communicate, intercommunicate[00742582-v] [1097 children]
      - ↪ inform[00833312-v] [698 children]
        - ↪ tell[00954556-v] [489 children]
          - ↪ impart, leave, give, pass on[02301114-v] [419 children]
            - ↪ convey[00930591-v] [418 children]
              - ↪ express, show, evince[00945869-v] [394 children]
                - ↪ express, verbalize, verbalise, utter, give tongue to[00942415-v] [263 children]
                  - ↪ state, say, tell[01011267-v] [183 children]
      - ↪ talk, speak, utter, mouth, verbalize, verbalise[00944022-v] [160 children]
  - ↪ move[01835473-v] [336 children]
  - ↪ travel, go, move, locomote[01839438-v] [751 children]
  - ↪ learn, hear, get word, get wind, pick up, find out, get a line, discover, see[00600349-v] [204 children]
    - ↪ perceive, comprehend[02110960-v] [197 children]
      - ↪ feel, experience[01775456-v] [138 children]
  - ↪ think, cogitate, cerebrate[00630153-v] [721 children]
    - ↪ evaluate, pass judgment, judge[00672179-v] [374 children]
  - ↪ change[00109468-v] [1441 children]
    - ↪ change integrity[00139943-v] [169 children]
    - ↪ change state, turn[00145958-v] [202 children]
    - ↪ change magnitude[00169459-v] [218 children]
      - ↪ increase[00156409-v] [151 children]
  - ↪ remove, take, take away, withdraw[00173351-v] [201 children]
  - ↪ touch[01208838-v] [197 children]
  - ↪ cover[01335412-v] [189 children]
  - ↪ connect, link, tie, link up[01357376-v] [267 children]
    - ↪ attach[01299048-v] [170 children]
  - ↪ induce, stimulate, cause, have, get, make[00772482-v] [4717 children]
    - ↪ make, create[01620211-v] [754 children]
      - ↪ re-create, recreate[01622373-v] [135 children]
    - ↪ change, alter, modify[00126072-v] [3770 children]
      - ↪ move, displace[01854282-v] [1242 children]
        - ↪ put, set, place, pose, position, lay[01496967-v] [216 children]
        - ↪ separate, disunite, divide, part[01559703-v] [132 children]
        - ↪ transfer[02236972-v] [279 children]
          - ↪ convey, transmit, communicate[02236443-v] [258 children]
            - ↪ communicate, pass on, pass, pass along, put across[00744289-v] [257 children]
              - ↪ request, ask for, bespeak, call for, quest[00754770-v] [232 children]
                - ↪ ask[00754499-v] [171 children]
                  - ↪ request[00755473-v] [169 children]
                    - ↪ order, tell, enjoin, say[00748704-v] [133 children]
      - ↪ affect, impact, bear upon, bear on, touch on, touch[00137133-v] [151 children]
      - ↪ better, improve, amend, ameliorate, meliorate[00206293-v] [129 children]
      - ↪ transfer[02225243-v] [469 children]
        - ↪ give[02204104-v] [386 children]
          - ↪ supply, provide, render, furnish, offer[02332196-v] [157 children]
  - ↪ get, acquire[02215637-v] [242 children]

Figure 1: Verb hierarchy of action verbs, including all verbs with more than 120 children

'exist' and relations expressed by 'pertain', with the idea of possession and cognition as top concepts. Finally, not having ('lacking') is a top concept as the opposite of 'having' and the copula is treated as a separate verb.

4.2 Evaluation

As the annotation was conducted by a single annotator, it is important to validate the quality of the proposed hierarchy. We do this by comparison with a resource that is specialised in the semantics of verbs, namely SimVerb-3500 (Gerz et al., 2016). We also present some general comparisons of the hierarchy of PWN with the new hierarchy proposed for Open English Wordnet 2024.

4.2.1 Connectedness

A key goal of this work is to create connected components in the graph to ensure that algorithms that use the wordnet structure can capture information. As such, we present the size of the connected components in versions of English Wordnet in Figure 1. We measure the components in terms of the number of components considering only **troponymy** (hypernymy) relations, including other **synset** relations (antonymy and similar) and considering sense level relations such as morphological **derivation** (principally between verbs and nouns). We also state the size of the largest connected component in the graph. As we can see Priceton WordNet versions and previous versions of OEWN have been well-connected in general with most verbs in a large connected component, and only about 80 verbs completely disconnected from any other synset. This work has allowed us to completely connect all the verbs (with morphological derivations) improving the connectedness and usability of the resource.

4.2.2 SimVerb-3500

SimVerb-3500 (Gerz et al., 2016) is a large dataset designed for measuring the semantic similarity between pairs of verbs. It contains 3,500 verb pairs, each annotated with a similarity score that reflects how closely related the meanings of the two verbs are. SimVerb-3500 extends other lexical similarity datasets like WordSim-353, by focusing exclusively on verbs, providing a specialized resource for research in verb semantics, compositionality, and lexical relations. The similarity scores were generated through human judgments.

In order to examine the effectiveness of the new hierarchy we compared the Spearman's correlation of wordnet-based similarity metrics to the SimVerb-3500 correlation scores. We examined two metrics the Wu-Palmer metric (Wu and Palmer, 1994) and path distance. We selected only these two metrics out of our analysis as the other metrics either could not easily be applied to verb similarity, as they relied on a single super-concept, which does not exist for verbs, (Leacock-Chodorow (Leacock et al., 1998)) or on information content (such as Resnik (Resnik, 1995)), which is largely incomplete for verbs[4].

The results of the analysis are presented in Table 2, where the correlations are presented according to each resource. Surprisingly the correlations for the new hierarchy were actually not different to the original hierarchy, slightly decreasing for path similarity and increasing for Wu-Palmer similarity. This was in spite of the fact that the scores for the new hierarchy were far more informative, for example, for the PWN hierarchy 1,196 (34.2%) of the scores were zero indicating that the terms had no connection whereas the new hierarchy only 84 (2.4%) of scores were zero. To further examine this we examined the classification of the verb relations given in SimVerb-3500, which are based on the relations in PWN, in this case, we see the new hierarchy improving on many of these classes[5]. Of particular importance to note is the antonym class where the previous hierarchy had no correlation and the new hierarchy has a negative correlation. This is due to the instruction of the dataset to assign low scores to antonyms, and the negative correlation can be seen as an improvement in the new hierarchy. As clarified by the authors of the dataset "evaluation based on Spearman's ρ may be problematic ... with antonyms." (Gerz et al., 2016), and a quick examination of the 'none' category in the data indicates that there are many antonyms not identified by PWN or OEWN that have a low score in this resource. As such, we can say that overall the similarities in the new hierarchy are more useful in most situations.

5 Discussion

This work on verbs has highlighted a number of directions that could further improve the verb hier-

[4] In all cases, we used the implementation provided by the WN library `https://wn.readthedocs.io/en/latest/api/wn.similarity.html`

[5] Note we excluded synonyms as they did not have meaningful correlations in either resource

Resource	Troponym Components	Synset Components	Deriv. Components	Largest Component
PWN 3.0	540	207	86	13,421
PWN 3.1	545	210	87	13,423
OEWN 2019	545	210	87	13,423
OEWN 2020	552	214	88	13,494
OEWN 2021	552	216	89	13,478
OEWN 2022	552	216	89	12,481
OEWN 2023	542	211	83	13,475
OEWN 2024	8	4	1	14,010

Table 1: Analysis of the size of the connected components in the graphs of WordNet versions

Method	Co-hyponyms	Antonyms	Hypernyms	None	All
		Princeton WordNet 3.0			
Wu-Palmer	0.226	-0.01	0.244	0.165	0.483
Path	0.205	-0.03	0.281	0.166	0.487
		Open English WordNet 2024			
Wu-Palmer	0.215	-0.117	0.278	0.188	0.485
Path	0.224	-0.105	0.279	0.167	0.473
Size	190	111	800	2093	3500

Table 2: Pearson Correlation of metrics using OEWN 2024 and PWN 3.0 hierarchy with SimVerb-3500

archy and as such we consider some ways in which the organisation of verbs could be further improved in future versions of wordnets

5.1 Frames

Princeton WordNet introduced syntactic frames to each of the verbs that indicate whether a verb has a transitive or intransitive usage and other kinds of arguments such as prepositional or clausal arguments. In addition, it is indicated whether the subject and direct object of the frame can be animate or inanimate. Many lexicographic resources, for example, Merriam-Webster, sort verbs into intransitive and transitive frames before indicating different senses of the verbs. OEWN currently has 1,466 verb senses, which have both a transitive and intransitive frame. We distinguish two types of relationships between the senses of transitive and intransitive verbs:

Object-Drop Verbs In this case, the intransitive sense of the verb has the same meaning as the transitive sense, with the object replaced with an existential word. For example, "X eats" ⇒ "X eats something"

Labile Verbs Here the intransitive sense of the verb has a similar meaning except that the object of the transitive verb becomes the subject of the intransitive verb. For example. "X changes Y" ⇒ "Y changes".

We analysed the case where two verb senses (with the same lemma) exclusively use either transitive or intransitive frames and found 10,088 such pairs. We analysed a random sample of 500 of these pairs and found that 475 senses were not related (95.0%), 22 were labile verbs (4.4%), 2 had errors in the frame data and only 1 instance was an object-drop verb (namely 'spat'[01240625-v] and 'spat'[02763140-v]). As such, we conclude that the current modelling in WordNet separates labile verbs but not object-drop verbs.

We also observed a number of labile verb pairs of senses of verbs that are normally object-drop due to a systematic polysemy. An example of this is the verb 'clean', which is primarily an object-drop verb, but has a sense[02747835-v] defined as 'be cleanable' and with 'This stove cleans easily' as an example, which is a labile verb of the most frequent sense of 'clean'. It is not clear if these

Resource	Same Lexfile	Diff. Lexfile	Percent
PWN Verbs	11637	1619	12.2%
OEWN Verbs	11824	2040	14.7%
OEWN Nouns	2527	76002	3.2%

Table 3: Number of hypernym links between synsets in different lexicographer files

senses should be included in the resource or if they could be included under the primary sense.

5.2 New Relations

In order to further increase the density of the connections between verbs in the resource, it would be good to include more links between synsets. This could be done by adding new relation types that better capture the semantics of verbs. The following have been frequently observed in the resource

Labile verb As discussed above, labile verbs are common in the resource and connecting these would help to associate verbs together

Transitive Causative Alternations This is the case where two transitive verb senses have an alternation like a labile verb, but the subject and object are reversed.

Adjectival Links Quite a few senses are defined as simply 'be ADJ', for example, 'fall (be due)'[02667093-v] or 'press (be open)'[02728657-v]. It would be good to introduce a link between verbs and adjectives where the meaning is directly connected like this.

Causes The cause relation is already present for some verbs, however, there are many verbs that are defined as 'cause to VERB' but there is no connection, e.g., 'protuberate (cause to bulge out or project)'[02720606-v].

5.3 Supersenses

The lexicographer files are used to group the senses of words into broad categories and were part of the annotation process in the creation of Princeton WordNet. These lexicographer files, thus provide broad semantic categories that can be used to group the senses of words. For verbs, the following lexicographer files exist:

Body 552 Synsets

Change 2,393 Synsets

Cognition 698 Synsets

Communication 1,563 Synsets

Competition 459 Synsets

Consumption 247 Synsets

Contact 2,204 Synsets

Creation 699 Synsets

Emotion 346 Synsets

Motion 1,411 Synsets

Perception 465 Synsets

Possession 849 Synsets

Social 1,112 Synsets

Stative 758 Synsets

Weather 80 Synsets

These lexicographer files for verbs are quite varied in size and moreover as shown in Table 3 a substantial number of these verbs are not in the same lexicographer file as their hypernym, which is not the same as the lexicographer file as the hyponym. This is markedly higher than the nouns and the hierarchy introduced in this paper further increases the number of cross-lexicographer-file hypernyms. To further examine this we looked at the verbs that were declared to be 'stative' verbs, which are verbs that describes a state rather than an action and should correspond to most of the top verbs in Section 4.1, except for 'act'[02372362-v] and 'happen'[00340744-v] which are dynamic verbs, and 'have'[02208144-v] and 'know'[00596016-v], which are stative but associated with `possession` and `cognition` lexicographer files. We found 36 verb synsets that were in the `stative` lexicographer but were not stative verbs, of these 34 were better suited to the `social` lexicographer file, one to `change` and one to `possession`. Most of these verbs were indicated as hyponyms of the copula sense of the verb 'be'. We also found 37 verbs that were hyponyms of one of the stative top-level verbs but were not in the `stative` lexicographer file. We observed that 6 of them had incorrect hypernyms (in PWN 3.1) and have been changed in the OEWN 2024 release. The remaining 32 synsets (86.5%) were in fact stative verbs and should probably be included in this lexicographer file.

The lexicographer files defined are mostly well-mapped to the hierarchy in Figure 1, with several of our top-level verb synsets mapping well to lexicographer files, e.g., 'know'[00596016-v] corresponding strongly to the `cognition` verbs. Most of the significant verbs in the new hierarchy are strongly

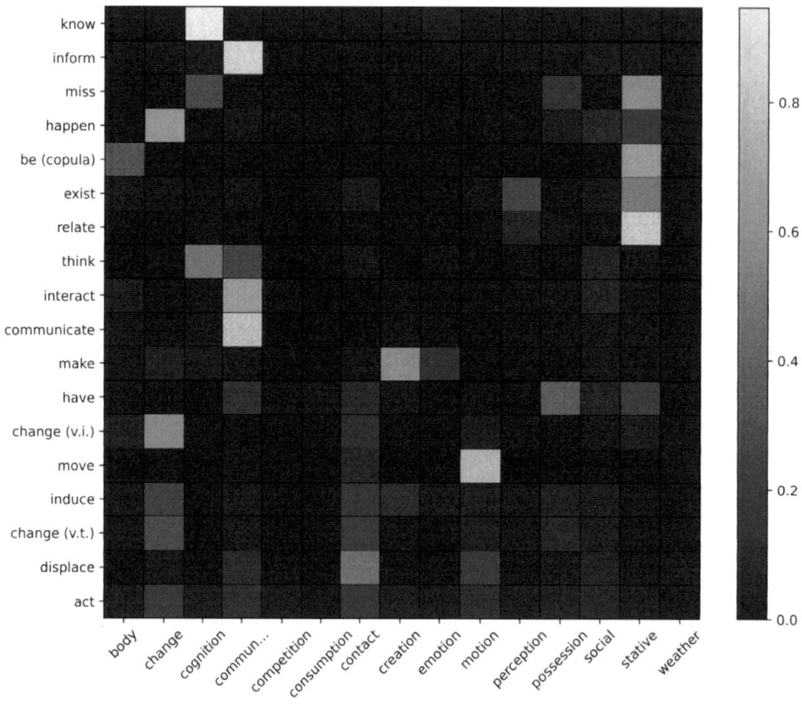

Figure 2: The relative distribution of children of the most significant[6] synsets between lexicographer files

associated with a single lexicographer file. However, we do also note that some lexicographer files do not seem to be strongly associated with any top-level verbs, in particular, the files for `competition`, `consumption` and `weather` are probably not useful categorisations and are also among the smallest files.

5.4 Comparison to Frame Resources

The improvement of the verb hierarchy would be helpful in the organisation of frames and help to bring English Wordnet closer to frame resources such as FrameNet, VerbNet or PropBank. While this work does not attempts to merging the efforts of VerbNet similar projects with English Wordnet, subcategorization is considered as described in Section 5.1. Current mappings between English Wordnet and frame reosources such as SemLink have only a few mappings and these are mostly to high-level concepts and as such there are only minor improvements possible. We also analysed the resource relative to VerbAtlas (Di Fabio et al., 2019), which covers nearly all the English Wordnet synsets, however, we were surprised to find that the majority of hypernyms were in different frames in VerbAtlas (6,766/13,186, 51.3%) in OEWN 2023 and this new hierarchy further increased this (7,244/13,738, 52.7%). This is surprising as the organisation of VerbAtlas claims to group verbs which have similar meanings into frames. We analysed the reason on 50 randomly chosen synsets for this and it was concluded that in most cases (54%) the wordnet sense was incompatible with the key sense in VerbAtlas and in only 6% of the cases the error was in English Wordnet; the remainder of the cases involved co-hyponyms or ambiguous senses.

6 Conclusion

In this work, we have connected the English Wordnet verb hierarchy by defining top-level synsets for verbs and linking up over 600 verbs that were isolated in the Princeton WordNet hierarchy. This has led to a resource that is more connected and we showed that this is useful for semantic similarity and potentially for applications based on this. In this work, we have used SimVerb-3500 to measure this, however we note that the calculation of similarity without context could be misleading and a more comprehensive approach using corpora and subcategorization resources would further improve the verb hierarchy. As such, we have still not reached a resource that has a broad-coverage and high-accuracy description of English verbs and there is a need for more kinds of links and more robust representation of frames to produce a resource that can serve linguistic data science applications. This work provides a step in this direction by improving on the previous hierarchies in English Wordnet.

Acknowledgements

John P. McCrae is supported by Research Ireland under Grant Number SFI/12/RC/2289_P2 Insight_2, Insight SFI Centre for Data Analytics and Grant Number 13/RC/2106_P2, ADAPT SFI Research Centre.

References

Collin F. Baker, Charles J. Fillmore, and John B. Lowe. 1998. The Berkeley FrameNet Project. In *36th Annual Meeting of the Association for Computational Linguistics and 17th International Conference on Computational Linguistics, COLING-ACL '98, August 10-14, 1998, Université de Montréal, Montréal, Quebec, Canada. Proceedings of the Conference*, pages 86–90. Morgan Kaufmann Publishers / ACL.

Ian C. Chow and Jonathan J. Webster. 2007. Integration of linguistic resources for verb classification: Framenet frame, wordnet verb and suggested upper merged ontology. In *Computational Linguistics and Intelligent Text Processing*, pages 1–11, Berlin, Heidelberg. Springer Berlin Heidelberg.

Andrea Di Fabio, Simone Conia, and Roberto Navigli. 2019. VerbAtlas: a novel large-scale verbal semantic resource and its application to semantic role labeling. In *Proceedings of the 2019 Conference on Empirical Methods in Natural Language Processing and the 9th International Joint Conference on Natural Language Processing (EMNLP-IJCNLP)*, pages 627–637, Hong Kong, China. Association for Computational Linguistics.

Christiane Fellbaum. 2010. *WordNet*, pages 231–243. Springer Netherlands, Dordrecht.

Christiane Fellbaum and George A Miller. 1990. Folk psychology or semantic entailment? Comment on Rips and Conrad (1989). *Psychological Review*, 97(4):565–570.

Óscar Ferrández, Michael Ellsworth, Rafael Muñoz, and Collin F. Baker. 2010. Aligning FrameNet and WordNet based on semantic neighborhoods. In *Proceedings of the Seventh International Conference on Language Resources and Evaluation (LREC'10)*, Valletta, Malta. European Language Resources Association (ELRA).

Charles J. Fillmore. 1976. Frame semantics and the nature of language. *Annals of the New York Academy of Sciences*, 280.

Daniela Gerz, Ivan Vulić, Felix Hill, Roi Reichart, and Anna Korhonen. 2016. SimVerb-3500: A large-scale evaluation set of verb similarity. In *Proceedings of the 2016 Conference on Empirical Methods in Natural Language Processing*, pages 2173–2182, Austin, Texas. Association for Computational Linguistics.

Eduard Hovy, Mitchell Marcus, Martha Palmer, Lance Ramshaw, and Ralph Weischedel. 2006. OntoNotes: The 90% solution. In *Proceedings of the Human Language Technology Conference of the NAACL, Companion Volume: Short Papers*, pages 57–60, New York City, USA. Association for Computational Linguistics.

Haibo Jin, Ruoxi Chen, Andy Zhou, Jinyin Chen, Yang Zhang, and Haohan Wang. 2024. Guard: Role-playing to generate natural-language jailbreakings to test guideline adherence of large language models. *arXiv preprint arXiv:2402.03299*.

Paul R. Kingsbury and Martha Palmer. 2002. From TreeBank to PropBank. In *Proceedings of the Third International Conference on Language Resources and Evaluation, LREC 2002, May 29-31, 2002, Las Palmas, Canary Islands, Spain*. European Language Resources Association.

Egoitz Laparra and German Rigau. 2010. eXtended WordFrameNet. In *Proceedings of the Seventh International Conference on Language Resources and Evaluation (LREC'10)*, Valletta, Malta. European Language Resources Association (ELRA).

Claudia Leacock, Martin Chodorow, and George A Miller. 1998. Using corpus statistics and WordNet relations for sense identification. *Computational Linguistics*, 24(1):147–165.

Svetlozara Leseva, Ivelina Stoyanova, and Maria Todorova. 2018. Classifying verbs in wordnet by harnessing semantic resources. *Proceedings of CLIB*, pages 115–125.

Beth Levin. 1993. *English verb classes and alternations: A preliminary investigation.* University of Chicago Press.

Maddalen Lopez de Lacalle, Egoitz Laparra, and German Rigau. 2014. Predicate matrix: extending SemLink through WordNet mappings. In *Proceedings of the Ninth International Conference on Language Resources and Evaluation (LREC'14)*, pages 903–909, Reykjavik, Iceland. European Language Resources Association (ELRA).

John P. McCrae, Alexandre Rademaker, Francis Bond, Ewa Rudnicka, and Christiane Fellbaum. 2019. English WordNet 2019 – an open-source WordNet for English. In *Proceedings of the 10th Global Wordnet Conference*, pages 245–252, Wroclaw, Poland. Global Wordnet Association.

George A. Miller. 1995. Wordnet: a lexical database for english. *Commun. ACM*, 38(11):39–41.

Verginica Mititelu, Svetlozara Leseva, and Ivelina Stoyanova. 2021. Semantic analysis of verb-noun derivation in Princeton WordNet. In *Proceedings of the 11th Global Wordnet Conference*, pages 108–117, University of South Africa (UNISA). Global Wordnet Association.

Viktor Moskvoretskii, Ekaterina Neminova, Alina Lobanova, Alexander Panchenko, and Irina Nikishina. 2024. TaxoLLaMA: WordNet-based model for solving multiple lexical semantic tasks. In *Proceedings of the 62nd Annual Meeting of the Association for Computational Linguistics (Volume 1: Long Papers)*, pages 2331–2350, Bangkok, Thailand. Association for Computational Linguistics.

Martha Palmer. 2009. SemLink: Linking PropBank, VerbNet and FrameNet. In *Proceedings of the Generative Lexicon Conference*, pages 9–15. GenLex-09, Pisa, Italy.

Martha Palmer, Claire Bonial, and Diana McCarthy. 2014. SemLink+: FrameNet, VerbNet and event ontologies. In *Proceedings of Frame Semantics in NLP: A Workshop in Honor of Chuck Fillmore (1929-2014)*, pages 13–17, Baltimore, MD, USA. Association for Computational Linguistics.

Georgiana Puşcaşu and Verginica Barbu Mititelu. 2008. Annotation of WordNet verbs with TimeML event classes. In *Proceedings of the Sixth International Conference on Language Resources and Evaluation (LREC'08)*, Marrakech, Morocco. European Language Resources Association (ELRA).

Philip Resnik. 1995. Using information content to evaluate semantic similarity in a taxonomy. In *Proceedings of the Fourteenth International Joint Conference on Artificial Intelligence, IJCAI 95, Montréal Québec, Canada, August 20-25 1995, 2 Volumes*, pages 448–453. Morgan Kaufmann.

Karin Kipper Schuler. 2005. *VerbNet: A broad-coverage, comprehensive verb lexicon*. University of Pennsylvania.

Lei Shi and Rada Mihalcea. 2005. Putting pieces together: combining framenet, verbnet and wordnet for robust semantic parsing. In *Proceedings of the 6th International Conference on Computational Linguistics and Intelligent Text Processing*, CICLing'05, page 100–111, Berlin, Heidelberg. Springer-Verlag.

Krešimir Šojat and Matea Srebačić. 2014. Morphosemantic relations between verbs in Croatian WordNet. In *Proceedings of the Seventh Global Wordnet Conference*, pages 262–267, Tartu, Estonia. University of Tartu Press.

Tomasz Stanisz, Stanisław Drożdż, and Jarosław Kwapień. 2024. Complex systems approach to natural language. *Physics Reports*, 1053:1–84. Complex systems approach to natural language.

Ivelina Stoyanova and Svetlozara Leseva. 2023. Expanding the conceptual description of verbs in WordNet with semantic and syntactic information. In *Proceedings of the 12th Global Wordnet Conference*, pages 284–294, University of the Basque Country, Donostia - San Sebastian, Basque Country. Global Wordnet Association.

Sara Tonelli and Daniele Pighin. 2009. New features for FrameNet - WordNet mapping. In *Proceedings of the Thirteenth Conference on Computational Natural Language Learning (CoNLL-2009)*, pages 219–227, Boulder, Colorado. Association for Computational Linguistics.

Zhibiao Wu and Martha Stone Palmer. 1994. Verb semantics and lexical selection. In *32nd Annual Meeting of the Association for Computational Linguistics, 27-30 June 1994, New Mexico State University, Las Cruces, New Mexico, USA, Proceedings*, pages 133–138. Morgan Kaufmann Publishers / ACL.

An Abstract Multilingual WordNet

Krasimir Angelov
Chalmers University and University of Gothenburg / Sweden
krasimir@chalmers.se

Abstract

We present a variant of WordNet for 265 languages where the primary constituents of the synsets are abstract identifiers, rather than language specific lexemes. The identifiers are then verbalized to each language through a grammar. Currently, for most of the languages, the grammar only provides lemmas, but for 28 of them, there is also, full morphology and syntax. We review the bootstrapping methodology, evaluate the quality, and show-case applications.

1 Introduction

WordNets exist and are being created for several languages, but more importantly, equivalent synsets across languages are kept linked together. This makes WordNets not just into valuable language-intrinsic resources but also into useful cross-lingual translation dictionaries.

The latter, however, is not without problems. To start with, by going from a particular word sense, in the synset for one language to a synset in another language we lose information and introduce unnecessary ambiguity. For example, for most plant and animal species, the corresponding synset contains both the colloquial name as well as the Latin name of the species. This means that, if one starts from the colloquial word "apple" and goes to another language, they will be forced to accept that "Malus pumila" is a possible translation, despite that most languages have a more reasonable translation.

The above is an extreme example but there are plenty of more subtle cases. For instance, in English, the words "marihuana" and "cannabis" share the same synset, and both words have their cognates in many other languages. If we just go through the linked synsets, then one could freely translate "marihuana" to "cannabis" and vice versa. In this case the semantic difference is not so clear, but if we want to stay close to the original text, it is preferable to use cognates when they exist.

Other synonyms exist for historical reasons, e.g. Thailand vs Siam or Cambodia vs Kampuchea, and using one or the other depends on the sociopolitical context.

In the next section we present the design of an Abstract WordNet, where in addition to synsets with semantic relations between them, we also preserve the translation relation. Obviously, this can be done in many ways, but the particular choice makes the resource compatible with Grammatical Framework (Ranta, 2011). The model has also been tried for a smaller set of languages already in Angelov (2020).

Grammatical Framework is a formalism centered around the concept of abstract syntax. In short, the abstract syntax is a collection of functions with fixed types, where the functions themselves are implemented in different ways for different languages. For example adjectival modification on an abstract level can be:

```
AdjCN : AP -> CN -> CN
```

i.e. it is a function which takes an adjective phrase and a common noun and returns a new common noun. The word order, the agreement and the possible inflections are defined separately for each concrete language.

Words are functions with no arguments, e.g.:

```
apple_1_N : N
apple_2_N : N
```

may represent the two senses of "apple" (the fruit and the tree).

2 Design for an Abstract WordNet

While the synsets of a traditional WordNet (Princeton, 2006) are language specific and contain lemmas, we choose to make them abstract – each synset contains names of functions which are defined separately in the grammar for each language.

By design, the words that we choose to represent a function in each language should be as close as possible, meaning that they must share as many senses as possible. This also makes the choice robust in translation – when going from one language to another, the chosen translations will remain valid for as many senses as possible. This is advantageous since even if the model cannot pick the exact sense, the translation is still likely to remain correct. When relevant, these should be cognates or borrowed words, but only if these have not changed meanings or register.

For example, "house" and "hus" (Swedish) are good translation equivalents regardless of the sense. On the other hand, "familj" (Swedish) is not a good translation despite that "house" and "family" share one sense in English (a social unit living together). The word "family" should rather translate as "familj". As it happens both examples are also cognates.

Obviously, a tight one-to-one alignment between languages will be problematic. For instance, there are words which simply cannot be translated to another language. In that case we represent the gap by just leaving the corresponding function undefined. In other cases, a word may translate to a multiword expression. That is supported, since the abstract functions can also generate complex phrases. Finally, some languages provide more ways to express a concept than others. In that case, we either use the same word to represent several functions, or we leave some functions undefined.

Since all the data is initially automatically generated, we also store the current status per language. First of all, a definition might be missing either because there is a lexical gap, or because we simply do not have enough data. We cannot know the difference without consulting a native speaker.

When we do know the definition, it is either already **validated**, **unchecked** or **guessed**. The difference between the last two is that for an unchecked definition we know that it represents the right sense but maybe it is not the best translation. On the contrary, guessed definitions are possible translations but not necessarily for the same sense. The unchecked definitions come from existing monolingual WordNets, e.g. we used the Open Multilingual WordNet (Bond and Foster, 2013) extensively. On the other hand, guessed definitions are extracted from translation dictionaries.

Another notable difference is that while a typical WordNet contains only lemmas, in our implementation each function normally computes a full inflection table. This is necessary, if we want the definitions to be usable in combination with the existing syntactic combinators provided by the framework. Currently full morphology is only provided for 28 languages, but we aim at extending that to all of the languages.

3 Data Collection

The creation of the initial Abstract WordNet was reported in Angelov (2020), where the focus was on Swedish, Bulgarian and English, and the compatibility with Grammatical Framework. In the process existing resources for the two languages (Borin et al., 2013; Viberg et al., 2002; Borin et al., 2008; Kann and Hollman, 2011; Simov and Osenova, 2010) were also absorbed. At the time, lexicons for 11 other languages were also bootstrapped from PanLex (Kamholz et al., 2014) by using the method in Angelov and Lobanov (2016). Since then, 10 more languages were added, and the data has been incrementally cleaned up. As we will see in Section 5, the status per language is still varying.

Here we want to extend the lexicon with as many languages as possible, and we even include some low-resource languages. Since we rely on translation dictionaries, the quality of the existing data affects the quality of the new translations. The cleanup for the original languages is therefore beneficial when adding new languages.

The main source for both the old languages and the new ones is PanLex - a collection of translation dictionaries for thousands of language pairs. The problem with PanLex is that although we get translation pairs, we cannot know in what sense the translation is appropriate. This is partly resolved by using Wikidata - a collaborative taxonomy created by the Wikimedia community which has labels in many languages and a partial mapping to WordNet.

While the previous work relied on self-made links from WordNet synsets to English articles in Wikipedia, here we switched to Wikidata. The advantages are several. First of all Wikidata contains structural information rather than plain text. Furthermore, it is a direct hub between different Wikipedia editions which makes it easier to query for labels in different languages. Finally, Wikidata has entities with no corresponding English articles, and those can still be linked with WordNet.

Wikidata has the property P8814 which is its way to link to WordNet. To these links, we added new ones by projecting the Wikipedia links created in Angelov (2020). In the process the number of links almost doubled and many mistakes were fixed on both sides. Currently there are 30416 links. Unfortunately, since Wikidata only consists of concepts, the links point only to nouns in WordNet.

To compensate for that we also used Wiktionary, which we accessed through the Wiktextract tool (Ylonen, 2022) which reads the raw markup and extracts structured data. The data contains both morphology and translations, but like for PanLex, the senses for which the translations apply are not linked to WordNet. We created our own mapping.

Each abstract function, we verbalized in English and matched it to an entry in the Wiktextract data with the same lemma and part of speech tag. So far, this means that different WordNet senses will map to the same entry. After that we check the glosses. For example, for "apple" in Wiktionary we have four glosses: *fruit*, *tree*, *wood* and *apples and pears*. Obviously the first two must correspond to the identifiers apple_1_N and apple_2_N above (Page 1). To find the best match, we computed the SBERT similarity (Reimers and Gurevych, 2019) between the possible WordNet and Wiktionary glosses.

When we printed the candidate matches in the order of the descending score, the candidates at the top matched very well, while the candidates at the bottom had nothing in common. Unfortunately, there is no clear cut-off point. We started looking at the matches from bottom to top. At score 0.3148 we observed that 3 out 5 candidates are correctly matched. At score 0.4 we got 4 out of 5. Finally, at level 0.45, 10 out of 10 candidates were correctly matched. We used that as a cut-off point and discarded everything with a lower score. We realize that we discarded a lot of useful data in this way but at the same time we are pretty sure that what we retained is very well matched.

In the rest of the data, it is still possible that an abstract function maps to several Wiktionary glosses. In that case, we just retained the highest scoring match. The exception is when the two top-most scores are very similar, in that case SBERT cannot make good distinctions. For that purpose, if the difference is less than 0.005 points, we looked manually at the two candidates. There were only 312 of those. At the end we got 40652 relations from abstract functions to Wikitionary glosses which unlike Wikidata contain different parts of speech.

4 Finding New Translations

From the content of the existing WordNet, PanLex and Wikidata, we construct the matrix T which represents the abstract lexicon together with the translations in all languages. Here for every function f and every language l, the element T_{fl} is a set of items of the form:

$$\langle \text{lemma}, s, w, l, c, d \rangle$$

where we have the language specific lemma followed by a number of scores. For the definition of the scores, it is also useful to define the set:

$$C_{fl} = \{\text{lemma} \mid \langle \text{lemma}, s, w, l, c, d \rangle \in T_{fl'}, l' \neq l\}$$

i.e. all lemmas for the same function but for a different language l'. The scores are:

s (status) is 0 if the verbalization is already validated, 1 if unchecked and 2 if guessed

w (wiki) is 0 if the verbalization appears in Wikidata and 1 otherwise

l (languages) is the number of sources in PanLex which claim that the current lemma is a translation for one of the lemmas in C_{fl}.

c (co-occurences) is the number of pairs of linked synsets for two different languages in which the current lemma co-occurs together with a lemma in C_{fl}

d (distance) is the shortest Levenshtein distance between the current lemma and any other lemma in C_{fl}.

The matrix is constructed by first inserting all existing translations in the current WordNet. For those we retrieve the current status s. If Open Multilingual WordNet has data for a language, we insert that as well with $s = 1$. After that we add translations from Wikidata, for these w is always 0, and $s = 2$ unless the translation was already added in the previous step with a different status. Finally we add translations from PanLex with $s = 2, w = 1$ unless the translation was already added with different scores.

Once we have collected all the data, we compute the scores l, c and d for all lemmas by looking at the lemmas in C_{fl}. Since here we compare the candidate lemmas for a new language with the already existing ones, it pays off if there are already many existing and well cleaned up languages.

Here it is also crucial that we work with abstract functions and not complete synsets. If we were using the synsets, this would add too many ambiguities when considering all possible synonyms in all possible languages.

Score l helps us to select translations which are recommended in most dictionaries. By looking at several languages and intersecting their dictionaries, we narrow down the right new lemma, even if the existing lemmas in some of the languages are ambigous. The efficiency of this criteria is obviously limited by the existance of multiple dictionaries and the number of already present lemmas.

Score c is higher for robust translations like the examples "house-hus" and "family-familj" in Section 2. Finally d helps us to put together cognates which often look similar. The later is especially relevant for closely related languages.

The best translation for each function f and language l is selected by sorting the set T_{fl} by the key $(s, -c, -l, w, d)$ in descending order. In other words, we prefer translations that are possibly validated (the s score), and robust (the $-c$ score), are cited by more translation dictionaries (the $-l$ score), and if possible are mentioned in Wikidata. Finally, since we also sort by the d score, we select candidates which look the most like a translation in another language if all of the previous criteria are the same.

From the sorted list we always pick the first lemma and we compute its new status as follows:

- if $s = 0$, the lemma retains its status as validated. This rule is useful when a language is regenerated to take into account new external data. In that case we want to keep already validated translations.
- if $s = 1$ and $l > 1$, the lemma is marked as validated. The intuition is that previously, we only knew that a lemma had the right sense but now we also found more than one translation dictionaries which also list it as a good translation.
- if $w = 0$ and $l > 1$ then the lemma is also marked as validated. This happens when the lemma is used as a label for a Wikidata entity. Since those are linked on the sense level, $w = 0$ has the same semantics as $s = 1$, i.e. the lemmas share the same sense but maybe are not good translations. If on the other hand the label is also confirmed by more than one translation dictionary, then we can accept it.
- if $w = 0$ and $s = 1$ then the lemma is confirmed to have the right sense by both Wikidata and an existing WordNet for the language. Since here we have a synergy of two independent semantic sources, we mark those entries as validated although we cannot be completely sure that this is the best translation.
- if $s = 1$ the lemma remains unchecked.
- in all other cases, we treat the lemma as guessed.

5 Evaluation

We started with the evaluation of the existing languages by comparison with Wiktionary. The statistics are on Table 1.

We first looked at already validated abstract identifiers and compared them with existing Wiktionary lemmas. The first two columns on the table show the number of such cases as well as how often the two definitions match. As we expected, there is no perfect agreement but nevertheless it is quite high.

When we looked manually at cases where there is a disagreement, we observed examples where there is more than one possible translation and none is a better choice than another. This means that naturally, when the grammars and the lexicon are used for translation or natural language generation, the choices that we made will carry a particular style. This is not dissimilar from human translators who tend to use certain words more frequently than others.

After that we focused on abstract identifiers that are not validated yet. Again, we counted how often the two lemmas match, and we show the statistics in the columns "Confirmed" and "Not Confirmed". As we can see there are many WordNet definitions which have not been checked yet, but by comparing with Wiktionary we can confirm that they were indeed correct. In other cases, we cannot confirm the validity of the translations yet. They may be wrong, but they may also be just alternatives choices. In any case, after the evaluation we changed the status of all confirmed definitions to validated, but choose not to remove the unconfirmed yet.

Finally, there are cases where Wiktionary has a translation, but we do not. In that case we just inserted those in our data set. The number of cases is shown in the last column. There we have the absolute number of insertions as well as the percentage of holes that we filled in in that way.

Figure 1 shows the overall status of the lexicon before and after the update. There, green color corresponds to validated definitions, yellow unchecked, and red guessed. The height of the column shows the relative number of definitions. For each language there are two bars. The first one represents the status before the comparison with Wiktionary, and the second the status after the update.

Now we turn our attention to the newly added languages. All languages and their absolute sizes are shown on Table 3. The already existing languages are marked with an asterisk after the name. For them the percentage of validated items is generally much higher.

For all other languages the entries are simply extracted by using the algorithm from Section 4, and we have not done any manual validation yet. For those languages, we only have the lemma, the morphology and syntax are not integrated yet.

As we can see the sizes of the lexicons vary widely, and it is dependant on how much data we can find. In the collection, we only included languages for which we can find at least 5000 lemmas. The percentage after every language shows how many of the translations that we selected match the entries in Wikidata or Wiktionary. The number depends on both the quality of the selection and the actual size of Wikidata and Wiktionary for a particular language. In general, we expect that many more translations are correct but at the moment we have nothing else to compare those against.

6 Applications

Apart from semantic tasks where the main issue is the semantic interrelations between words inside the same language, the Abstract WordNet can also be used in translation and natural language generation. The key ingredient here is the integration with syntax. A recent example is Angelov et al. (2024) where Wikipedia articles for countries were automatically generated from information in Wikidata.

This is done by automatic generation of abstract syntax trees which are then verbalized to each language. The lexicon comes from the WordNet while the syntax from the libraries.

Since there are still mistakes in the lexicons, the initial draft of each article contained errors. On the other hand, we get a rapid prototype for multiple languages with no extra cost. The evaluation of the prototype is reflected on Table 2, which we copied from Angelov et al. (2024). As we can see the BLEU scores vary and roughly reflect the age of the resources. Swedish and Bulgarian have the highest scores, but they are also the oldest languages. On the other hand, Russian is only a recent addition.

After only fixing a few words the BLEU scores rappidly go to over 80%. Changing only the lexicon is often not enough to go to 100% since there are also idiomatic uses of the language which are not captured in the shared abstract syntax. The only exception here is English but this is only because the initial program was made to generate correct English to start with. The final gap is closed only by producing slightly different abstract expressions for every language.

By incorporating more languages, we aim to make this kind of rapid prototyping of language applications, accessible for all languages, even for low-resource ones. This also aligns with the goal of Abstract Wikipedia (Vrandečić, 2020) which aims to make Wikipedia more widely accessible.

7 Conclusion

We showed an alternative design for a WordNet which is integrated with a multilingual grammar, and which can be used for translation and natural language generation. We also show how the lexicon can be extended to hundreds of languages.

For the new languages we used Wiktionary only for evaluation, but it can be utilized better if we also used it during the selection of translations just like we used Wikidata. This will potentially increase the lexicon sizes for some languages and will validate more entries. On the other hand, if we do this then we will have nothing to evaluate against. We leave that therefore as a future work.

Only 28 languages are currently integrated with the corresponding grammars although the framework provides a library with more than 40 languages. For the integration it is crucial that we add morphology as well, which is necessary for the syntactic combinators that must inflect the words in the right way.

The existing grammars provide a morphological API which given one or more forms constructs the rest of the inflection table. The accuracy of the API depends on the language and on how irregular a particular word is (Détrez and Ranta, 2012). A key

	Existing								Inserted	
	Matching		Conflicting		Confirmed		Not Confirmed			
Africans	699	(91.97%)	61	(8.03%)	1627	(71.80%)	639	(28.20%)	248	(7.57%)
Bulgarian	9730	(62.60%)	5814	(37.40%)	1976	(34.67%)	3723	(65.33%)	1518	(6.67%)
Catalan	8783	(86.26%)	1399	(13.74%)	3318	(46.58%)	3805	(53.42%)	333	(1.89%)
Chinese	216	(67.71%)	103	(32.29%)	53	(0.78%)	6770	(99.22%)	8826	(55.27%)
Dutch	7624	(84.33%)	1417	(15.67%)	4274	(43.71%)	5505	(56.29%)	277	(1.45%)
Estonian	2729	(86.91%)	411	(13.09%)	1942	(54.50%)	1621	(45.50%)	100	(1.47%)
Finnish	17737	(61.12%)	11285	(38.88%)	428	(25.99%)	1219	(74.01%)	654	(2.09%)
French	13151	(74.73%)	4446	(25.27%)	3468	(42.56%)	4680	(57.44%)	532	(2.02%)
German	7304	(78.54%)	1996	(21.46%)	9205	(50.98%)	8850	(49.02%)	472	(1.70%)
Italian	9477	(83.85%)	1825	(16.15%)	4391	(42.68%)	5896	(57.32%)	394	(1.79%)
Korean	1865	(93.02%)	140	(6.98%)	4276	(51.46%)	4034	(48.54%)	180	(1.72%)
Maltese	153	(80.10%)	38	(19.90%)	1330	(73.64%)	476	(26.36%)	142	(6.64%)
Polish	7621	(86.60%)	1179	(13.40%)	4307	(48.93%)	4496	(51.07%)	2951	(14.36%)
Portuguese	12526	(69.00%)	5627	(31.00%)	3114	(53.08%)	2753	(46.92%)	402	(1.65%)
Russian	2958	(87.98%)	404	(12.02%)	16537	(71.59%)	6561	(28.41%)	345	(1.29%)
Slovenian	3924	(64.64%)	2147	(35.36%)	542	(50.89%)	523	(49.11%)	163	(2.23%)
Somali	69	(84.15%)	13	(15.85%)	139	(39.60%)	212	(60.40%)	102	(19.07%)
Spanish	10062	(81.05%)	2353	(18.95%)	6458	(50.96%)	6215	(49.04%)	361	(1.42%)
Swahili	39	(76.47%)	12	(23.53%)	539	(67.46%)	260	(32.54%)	3366	(79.84%)
Swedish	10182	(78.94%)	2717	(21.06%)	2693	(56.83%)	2046	(43.17%)	1416	(7.43%)
Thai	2087	(70.48%)	874	(29.52%)	475	(19.02%)	2022	(80.98%)	866	(13.69%)
Turkish	3388	(85.45%)	577	(14.55%)	3709	(47.78%)	4054	(52.22%)	332	(2.75%)

Table 1: Evaluation on Existing Languages

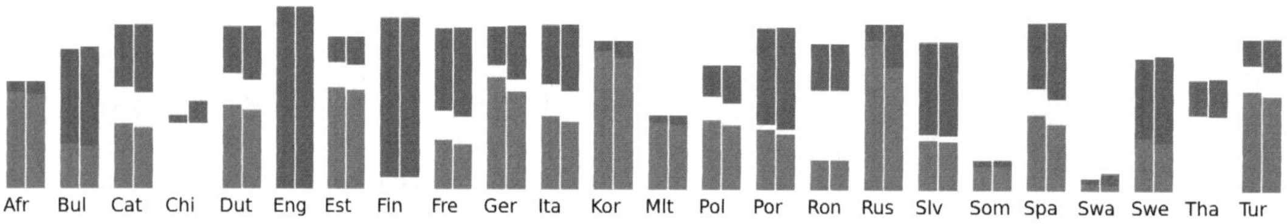

Figure 1: Status of the different languages before and after the validation with Wiktionary

	Initial Draft				Improved Draft			
	1-gram	2-gram	3-gram	4-gram	1-gram	2-gram	3-gram	4-gram
Bulgarian	80.04	72.94	67.05	**61.12**	99.17	98.88	98.65	**98.41**
English	94.08	93.13	92.19	**91.19**	100.00	100.00	100.00	**100.00**
French	64.43	53.94	44.80	**38.01**	95.60	93.45	91.10	**88.75**
Russian	43.21	26.01	17.28	**11.77**	93.12	88.82	85.68	**83.28**
Spanish	73.57	62.48	52.82	**44.75**	96.13	93.75	91.10	**88.31**
Swedish	81.82	76.44	71.67	**67.01**	99.26	98.94	98.75	**98.57**

Table 2: BLEU scores for the generated articles after each phase.

aar	Afar	9846	7%	abk	Abkhazian	13057	10%	ace	Achinese	6002	22%
ady	Adyghe	9304	12%	afr	Afrikaans*	70320	13%	als	Albanian (Tosk)	67430	4%
alt	Southern Altai	13788	3%	amh	Amharic	18565	13%	ang	Anglo-Saxon	42773	6%
arc	Aramaic	6906	19%	arg	Aragonese	44459	6%	ary	Arabic (Moroccan)	7380	21%
arz	Arabic (Egyptian)	31153	14%	asm	Assamese	23934	6%	ast	Asturian	60580	13%
ava	Avaric	26089	5%	aym	Aymara	22969	6%	azb	South Azerbaijani	10482	24%
azj	North Azerbaijani	52518	11%	bak	Bashkir	34063	12%	bam	Bambara	30442	4%
ban	Balinese	11438	16%	bar	Bavarian	14240	14%	bcl	Central Bicolano	10551	15%
bel	Belarusian	73977	13%	ben	Bengali	69110	9%	bul	Bulgarian*	94691	67%
bis	Bislama	12827	9%	bjn	Banjar	5443	19%	bod	Tibetan	22449	8%
bre	Breton	63208	9%	bos	Bosnian	45965	9%	bxr	Buriat	12127	12%
cat	Catalan*	97751	44%	cha	Chamorro	36070	3%	che	Chechen	31269	10%
chu	Old Church Slavonic	17400	7%	chv	Chuvash	26044	11%	ceb	Cebuano	36381	13%
ces	Czech	103625	12%	cho	Choctaw	6634	11%	chr	Cherokee	18943	6%
chy	Cheyenne	17770	6%	ckb	Central Kurdish	46370	6%	cmn	Chinese*	110165	13%
cor	Cornish	45052	6%	cos	Corsican	26614	8%	csb	Kashubian	18794	8%
crh	Crimean Tatar	27799	6%	cym	Welsh	73184	13%	dan	Danish	86194	24%
deu	German*	105914	33%	diq	Dimli	13296	16%	div	Divehi	8122	16%
dsb	Lower Sorbian	38371	6%	dzo	Dzongkha	31461	3%	ell	Greek	98997	19%
eng	English*	114563	100%	epo	Esperanto	93748	20%	est	Estonian*	98839	19%
eus	Basque	88130	26%	ewe	Ewe	17656	6%	ext	Extremaduran	8183	18%
fas	Persian	90365	14%	fao	Faroese	56735	8%	fin	Finnish*	112469	86%
fij	Fijian	11680	10%	fra	French*	106546	53%	frc	French, Cajun	9057	9%
frp	Franco-Provençal	25660	7%	frr	Northern Frisian	13301	19%	fry	Western Frisian	53486	8%
fur	Friulian	39397	6%	gle	Irish	78437	17%	gag	Gagauz	8292	16%
gan	Gan	9734	11%	gcr	Guianese	37803	1%	gla	Gaelic	62484	13%
glg	Galician	86233	22%	got	Gothic	12563	11%	grc	Ancient Greek	37803	6%
gsw	Alemannic	14891	12%	guj	Gujarati	71884	5%	glv	Manx	78691	5%
hau	Hausa	36862	6%	hak	Hakka Chinese	37624	5%	hat	Haitian Creole	39155	8%
haw	Hawaiian	52008	3%	heb	Hebrew	76553	13%	hin	Hindi	92061	9%
hrv	Croatian	90951	21%	hsb	Upper Sorbian	30878	9%	hun	Hungarian	96184	21%
hye	Armenian	80531	15%	ibo	Igbo	22518	5%	ido	Ido	74231	12%
ile	Interlingue	52695	4%	ina	Interlingua	74901	7%	ind	Indonesian	82157	23%
iii	Sichuan Yi	22938	3%	iku	Inuktitut	20087	6%	ilo	Iloko	24153	7%
inh	Ingush	12935	9%	isl	Icelandic	79210	11%	ita	Italian*	103916	41%
jam	Jamaican Creole	24284	5%	jav	Javanese	22267	12%	jbo	Lojban	24144	5%
jpn	Japanese	102801	35%	kaa	Karakalpak	7765	19%	kat	Georgian	73174	15%
kab	Kabyle	28291	5%	kal	Kalaallisut	6912	19%	kan	Kannada	23651	17%
kau	Kanuri	6282	11%	kaz	Kazakh	63718	10%	kbd	Kabardian	7346	13%
kcg	Tyap	5083	5%	kik	Kikuyu	8854	11%	kin	Kinyarwanda	26479	4%
khm	Khmer	43396	8%	kor	Korean*	95411	13%	krc	Karachay-Balkar	17052	6%
ksh	Colognian	19661	5%	koi	Komi-Permyak	11219	9%	kur	Kurdish	52224	6%
kpv	Komi-Zyrian	10880	12%	kir	Kyrgyz	45678	10%	lad	Ladino	6514	21%
lao	Lao	39200	6%	lat	Latin	74951	8%	lav	Latvian	71512	10%
lbe	Lak	25298	4%	lez	Lezghian	28201	5%	lfn	Lingua Franca Nova	58802	3%
lin	Lingala	19252	8%	lit	Lithuanian	71903	16%	lim	Limburgish	31220	7%
ltz	Luxembourgish	44917	10%	lug	Luganda	24644	3%	lij	Ligurian	35554	5%
lld	Ladin	26685	8%	lmo	Lombard	11674	19%	ltg	Latgalian	13349	9%
lzz	Laz	5558	13%	mah	Marshall	28233	3%	mal	Malayalam	41816	10%
mar	Marathi	65326	6%	mcn	Masana	7245	0%	mdf	Moksha	40323	5%
mhr	Eastern Mari	59020	3%	min	Minangkabau	6051	24%	mkd	Macedonian	70062	15%
mlg	Malagasy	18860	16%	mnw	Mon	7650	1%	mon	Mongolian	71589	6%
mrj	Western Mari	5838	24%	mlt	Maltese*	52795	12%	mwl	Mirandese	9496	15%
mya	Burmese	33043	10%	myv	Erzya	41797	4%	mzn	Mazanderani	7821	24%
nan	Min Nan Chinese	17795	19%	nav	Navajo	29752	9%	nap	Neapolitan	31818	5%
nau	Nauru	6692	18%	nds	Low German	18514	11%	nep	Nepali	21344	10%
nld	Dutch*	101817	34%	nno	Norwegian Nynorsk	53446	18%	nob	Norwegian Bokmål	90040	17%
nov	Novial	26373	5%	nya	Nyanja	11727	8%	oci	Occitan	11891	30%
ori	Oriya	9334	15%	oss	Ossetian	33339	9%	pag	Pangasinan	10459	9%
pap	Papiamento	47770	4%	pam	Pampanga	12181	12%	pcd	Picard	37787	4%
pli	Pali	12311	9%	pms	Piedmontese	14957	15%	pnb	Western Panjabi	10070	29%
pol	Polish*	99392	25%	por	Portuguese*	101483	64%	prg	Prussian	10926	7%
pus	Pushto	8651	20%	que	Quechua	11782	18%	rmy	Vlax Romani	12100	10%
roh	Raeto-Romance	34172	4%	ron	Romanian*	96712	32%	rue	Rusyn	7171	21%
run	Rundi	10561	7%	rup	Aromanian	26719	7%	rus	Russian*	109088	26%
sag	Sango	6360	13%	sah	Sakha	29653	8%	san	Sanskrit	47117	4%
sco	Scots	30370	14%	scn	Sicilian	51852	8%	sgs	Samogitian	9997	18%
shi	Tachelhit	10449	9%	shn	Shan	9061	12%	sin	Sinhalese	22048	13%
srd	Sardinian	31002	9%	snd	Sindhi	10598	15%	sma	Southern Sami	15527	6%
sme	Northern Sami	52119	6%	sms	Skolt Sami	11825	11%	slk	Slovak	91588	20%
slv	Slovenian*	87577	68%	smo	Samoan	12791	10%	smn	Inari Sami	13721	11%
sna	Shona	22913	7%	som	Somali*	22279	21%	spa	Spanish*	105949	46%
sqi	Albanian	54189	11%	srp	Serbian	59483	12%	srn	Sranan	29389	4%
sot	Southern Sotho	9226	10%	stq	Saterland Frisian	12528	12%	sun	Sundanese	18926	10%
swa	Swahili*	10349	82%	swe	Swedish*	99623	55%	szl	Silesian	9065	28%
tam	Tamil	69361	8%	tah	Tahitian	14139	7%	tat	Tatar	33533	8%
tel	Telugu	70048	9%	tet	Tetum	27917	4%	tgk	Tajik	39981	12%
tha	Thai*	102483	23%	tgl	Tagalog	60739	10%	tir	Tigrinya	26006	4%
tsn	Tswana	26531	3%	ton	Tonga	25382	4%	tpi	Tok Pisin	29355	5%
tur	Turkish*	95333	22%	tuk	Turkmen	52711	6%	tyv	Tuvinian	32380	4%
udm	Udmurt	21349	8%	uig	Uighur	23474	8%	ukr	Ukrainian	80760	16%
urd	Urdu	71483	9%	uzb	Uzbek	42173	14%	vec	Venetian	36120	10%
vep	Veps	14417	14%	vie	Vietnamese	97153	11%	vls	West Flemish	9407	17%
ven	Venda	14057	6%	vol	Volapük	38529	14%	vro	Võro	12109	13%
wln	Walloon	32361	9%	war	Waray	16651	22%	wol	Wolof	19317	8%
wuu	Wu Chinese	11813	27%	xal	Kalmyk	18634	9%	xho	Xhosa	11767	10%
xmf	Mingrelian	5658	39%	yid	Yiddish	53512	8%	yor	Yoruba	46988	4%
yue	Yue Chinese	54050	9%	zsm	Standard Malay	80181	24%	zul	Zulu	29660	1%

Table 3: List of languages with lexicon size and per cent of validated word senses

feature of the API is that it can always produce the right inflection but for irregular cases it will require more forms as input. By using it in combination with the inflection tables that Wiktionary provides, we can find how to use the API in the best way.

There are still more than 200 languages for which we do not have any grammars. We started looking into how the morphology can be learned automatically by using the inflection tables in Wiktionary as examples. Albanian, Kazakh and Macedonian are three pilot languages where we first attempted that. At least some of the syntactic combinators are easy to learn as well. This is definitely future work that we want to pursue.

The extracted lexicons are available on GitHub: https://github.com/GrammaticalFramework/gf-wordnet and can be queried through the search interface here:
https://cloud.grammaticalframework.org/wordnet/

References

Krasimir Angelov. 2020. A parallel WordNet for English, Swedish and Bulgarian. In *Proceedings of the 12th Language Resources and Evaluation Conference*, pages 3008–3015, Marseille, France. European Language Resources Association.

Krasimir Angelov, Andrea Carrión del Fresno, Ekaterina Voloshina, and Aarne Ranta. 2024. Leveraging grammatical framework and wordnet for natural language generation from wikidata.

Krasimir Angelov and Gleb Lobanov. 2016. Predicting translation equivalents in linked wordnets. In *The 26th International Conference on Computational Linguistics (COLING 2016)*, page 26.

Francis Bond and Ryan Foster. 2013. Linking and extending an open multilingual wordnet. In *In 51st Annual Meeting of the Association for Computational Linguistics: ACL-2013*, pages 1352–1362, Sofia.

Lars Borin, Markus Forsberg, and Lennart Lönngren. 2008. The hunting of the BLARK - SALDO, a freely available lexical database for Swedish language technology.

Lars Borin, Markus Forsberg, and Lennart Lönngren. 2013. SALDO: a touch of yin to WordNet's yang. *Language Resources and Evaluation*, 47(4):1191–1211.

Grégoire Détrez and Aarne Ranta. 2012. Smart paradigms and the predictability and complexity of inflectional morphology. In *EACL*, pages 645–653. The Association for Computer Linguistics.

David Kamholz, Jonathan Pool, and Susan Colowick. 2014. Panlex: Building a resource for panlingual lexical translation. In *Proceedings of the Ninth International Conference on Language Resources and Evaluation (LREC'14)*, Reykjavik, Iceland. European Language Resources Association (ELRA).

Viggo Kann and Joachim Hollman. 2011. Slutrapport för projektet Folkets engelsk-svenska lexikon.

Princeton. 2006. WordNet 3.0 Reference Manual. http://wordnet.princeton.edu/doc.

Aarne Ranta. 2011. *Grammatical Framework: Programming with Multilingual Grammars*. CSLI Publications, Stanford. ISBN-10: 1-57586-626-9 (Paper), 1-57586-627-7 (Cloth).

Nils Reimers and Iryna Gurevych. 2019. Sentence-BERT: Sentence embeddings using Siamese BERT-networks. In *Proceedings of the 2019 Conference on Empirical Methods in Natural Language Processing*. Association for Computational Linguistics.

Kiril Simov and Petya Osenova. 2010. Constructing of an ontology-based lexicon for Bulgarian. In *Proceedings of the Seventh International Conference on Language Resources and Evaluation (LREC'10)*, Valletta, Malta. European Language Resources Association (ELRA).

Åke Viberg, Kerstin Lindmark, Ann Lindvall, and Ingmarie Mellenius. 2002. The Swedish WordNet project. In *Proceedings of Euralex*, pages 407–412.

Denny Vrandečić. 2020. Architecture for a multilingual Wikipedia. *Preprint*, arXiv:2004.04733.

Tatu Ylonen. 2022. Wiktextract: Wiktionary as machine-readable structured data. In *Proceedings of the 13th Conference on Language Resources and Evaluation*, pages 1317–1325.

Misalignment of Semantic Relation Knowledge between WordNet and Human Intuition

Zhihan Cao
Institute of Science Tokyo
cao.z.ab@m.titech.ac.jp

Hiroaki Yamada
Institute of Science Tokyo
yamada@comp.isct.ac.jp

Simone Teufel
University of Cambridge
simone.teufel@cam.ac.uk

Takenobu Tokunaga
Institute of Science Tokyo
take@c.titech.ac.jp

Abstract

WordNet provides a carefully constructed repository of semantic relations, created by specialists. But there is another source of information on semantic relations, the intuition of language users. We present the first systematic study of the degree to which these two sources are aligned. Investigating the cases of misalignment could make proper use of WordNet and facilitate its improvement. Our analysis which uses templates to elicit responses from human participants, reveals a general misalignment of semantic relation knowledge between WordNet and human intuition. Further analyses find a systematic pattern of mismatch among synonymy and taxonomic relations (hypernymy and hyponymy), together with the fact that WordNet path length does not serve as a reliable indicator of human intuition regarding hypernymy or hyponymy relations.

1 Introduction

Semantic relations represent how the senses of two lexical items are related. These relations structure the vocabulary of natural languages (Miller and Fellbaum, 1991; McNamara, 2005; Saeed, 2015), making them essential for both human language comprehension and production. On the practical side, the performance of a wide range of natural language processing (NLP) tasks improves when incorporating information about semantic relations, including text simplification, paraphrasing, natural language inference, and discourse analysis (Tatu and Moldovan, 2005; Madnani and Dorr, 2010; Glavaš and Štajner, 2015; Alamillo et al., 2023). Therefore, semantic relations are not only important in analyzing languages but also a crucial piece of lexico-semantic information for NLP even in the current era of large language models.

In order to afford the analysis of the lexical semantics and the evaluation of whether large language models properly recognize semantic relations, we need a good resource of semantic relations at hand. Such a resource should contain only valid items and have as wide a coverage as possible.

Experts' introspection can guarantee the validity. An example of such resources is WordNet (Miller, 1995). The core object of WordNet is the *synset*, a set of synonymous lexical items which represents a word sense. Semantic relations are then defined on a pair of synsets[1]. WordNet was constructed in the 1980s by lexicographers and successively updated until 2006, with version 3.1 as the final release.

WordNet encompasses diverse semantic relations: hypernymy, hyponymy, holonymy, meronymy, antonymy, synonymy, and some others. However, a well-known drawback of WordNet (other than the fact that the project has stopped and has therefore not been updated for years) is that semantic relations are not treated equally; synsets are constructed on the basis of synonymy and the WordNet hierarchical structure is built by hypernymy and hyponymy links between the synsets. Other relations, such as antonymy, holonymy, and meronymy, are documented less. Hence, there is an imbalance in the number of synset pairs in different semantic relations [2], indicating the coverage of WordNet is limited.

Language users' intuition is an orthogonal resource of semantic relation knowledge that we can tap into. A body of research has shown that such intuition can be used to augment or modify WordNet. For example, Veale and Hao (2008) introduce the modifier–modifiee relation into WordNet,

[1] Antonymy is the exception. It is defined on a pair of synset-disambiguated lexical items, or *lemmas* in the WordNet terminology.

[2] Among all 82,115 nominal synsets, more than 90% are linked to at least one hypernym. However, only 25% of synsets have at least one holonym. For meronymy, it is merely 12%.

which is a relation between an adjective and a noun and expresses their cultural association. To do so, they mine real-world similes online, based on the construction *"as* ADJECTIVE *as* NOUN*"*. Word sense disambiguation is performed afterwards in order to establish connections to WordNet. Their evaluation compares the modifier adjectives mined online with adjectives extracted from the WordNet glosses. They find improved performance in determining the sentiment of the modifiee noun when using the adjectives mined. McCrae et al. (2019, 2020) also use human intuition to improve WordNet. Their methodology is based on collecting explicit feedback from WordNet users. Using that methodology, they have detected missing or wrong lexical items in a synset, lack of synsets, lack of relations, and inappropriate relations.

Previous approaches offer refined but pointwise modifications: data-mining methods are prone to frequency biases, often resulting in suboptimal performance for low-frequency terms; feedback-based approaches rely on incidental discoveries by a self-selected group of NLP practitioners. In order to build the best possible repository of semantic relations, it becomes efficient and effective if we integrate refined and systematic approaches.

Developing systematic augmentations requires a holistic understanding of WordNet. As a preliminary step, this study aims to achieve such an understanding by carefully investigating the alignment between language users' intuition and expert opinions regarding semantic relations. Our results reveal a general misalignment across various semantic relations, with distinct patterns emerging from deeper analyses. The data collected in this work is made available at `https://github.com/hancules/HumanElicitedTriplets`.

2 Method

The fundamental question of the present study is to what extent semantic relation knowledge documented in WordNet [3] aligns with the knowledge held by language users. We include six relations: hypernymy (HYP), hyponymy (HPO), holonymy (HOL), meronymy (MER), antonymy (ANT), and synonymy (SYN). We study the alignment separately for each relation.

[3]We use the modified WordNet version by McCrae et al.

2.1 Elicitation

The main unit we work with is the triplet consisting of a target word w, a relation r and a relatum v. The sentence *"an orange is kind of a fruit"* that expresses a hypernymy relation would then be translated into (*"orange"*, HYP, *"fruit"*). We use the triplets to compare the information in WordNet and the relational knowledge of language users. We collect triplets from language users by elicitation, a well-established methodology in linguistics (McKinley and Rose, 2019) (the procedure will be explained in Section 3).

2.2 Match Status

Some elicited triplets already exist in WordNet with the same direct relation (i.e. not related through transitivity); such elicited triplets are called **matched triplets**. Another type of elicited triplets is the **missing triplet**, where no direct relation between the target word and relatum is documented, although both individually exist in WordNet. It can also happen that the target word and relatum in elicited triplets are both found in WordNet but in a different relation. We name these **mismatched triplets**. The existence of matched triplets confirms our confidence in WordNet's information, and the missing and mismatched triplets are potential resources for the improvement of WordNet.

2.3 Analysis Objectives

We start with two analyses that intend to capture the general picture of alignment. If WordNet aligns with language users' intuition, there should be more matched triplets and fewer missing and mismatched triplets. Our first analysis investigates the distribution of three match statuses.

Some triplets may be elicited commonly from language users. We can calculate the *elicitation frequency* for each triplet. Elicitation frequency is an indicator of how intuitive the corresponding triplet is to the language users. A good alignment should also result in a monotonic increase relationship between the elicitation frequency and the intuitiveness of matched triplets. Our second analysis looks at whether highly intuitive triplets are more likely to be documented in WordNet.

For mismatched triples, we measure *mismatch likelihood*, which indicates how likely an elicited triplet is documented as a different relation in WordNet. By comparing mismatch likelihoods of different relations for each elicited relation, we can figure out whether it occurs particularly for certain relations. One possible reason for a high mismatch likelihood is that words could be polysemous, where the senses are related to each other. The related nature between senses introduces a high mismatch likelihood between certain elicited and documented relations. For example, if a word is a metonym, as it can form both synonymy and meronymy with another word, a high mismatch likelihood between synonymy and meronymy might be observed.

Missing triplets have been defined based only on direct relations so far. For transitive relations such as hypernymy and hyponymy, some missing triplets might be found in WordNet through transitivity. For those *indirectly matched triplets*, we consider the path length between the target word and relatum and calculate the correlation of path length against elicitation frequency. Through this analysis, we can gain insights into the relation between the WordNet structure and human intuition.

3 Data

3.1 Template-based Elicitation

The elicitation is carried out using templates (Ettinger, 2020). We first verbalize a relation by a template, such as a hypernymy template *"a* [TARGET] *is a type of* [RELATUM]*"*. After [TARGET] is specified, the elicitation can be carried out as a cloze task: participants are asked to fill in slot [RELATUM] with up to five words as relata, and we construct elicited triplets.

For all relations, we hand-craft templates. Particularly for hypernymy and hyponymy, we design some of our templates based on lexico-syntactic patterns by Roller et al. (2018) [4]. Such templets for hypernymy are *"a* [TARGET] *is a kind of a* [RELATUM]*"* and *"a* [TARGET] *is a specific case of a* [RELATUM]*"* while for hyponymy, *"a* [TARGET]*, such as a* [RELATUM]*"*. Examples of other templates follow.

> **HYP:** the word [TARGET] has a more specific sense than the word [RELATUM],
>
> **HPO:** the word [TARGET] has a more general sense than the word [RELATUM],
>
> **HOL:** a [TARGET] is contained in a [RELATUM],
>
> **MER:** a [TARGET] contains a [RELATUM],
>
> **ANT:** a [TARGET] is the opposite of a [RELATUM],
>
> **SYN:** a [TARGET] is similar to a [RELATUM].

In total, we use nine templates for antonymy, seven for hypernymy, holonymy, and synonymy, six for meronymy, and four for hyponymy. The full list of templates can be found in Appendix A.

3.2 Target Words

We need target words to elicit relata from participants. Proper target words need at least one possible relatum for the relation of interest. Therefore, target words cannot be randomly sampled.

We exploit two existing human-confirmed corpora of triplets (Vulić et al., 2017; Overschelde et al., 2004) to obtain valid target words. We use only target words from these two resources but do not use their triplets as is. This is because 1) none of them include all five relations of interest and 2) their size is too limited (1,347 triplets in total).

We first remove triplets from the above corpora where either target word or relatum is not a noun or is not in the intersection of vocabularies of BERT (Devlin et al., 2018), RoBERTa (Liu et al., 2019), and ALBERT (Lan et al., 2020)[5]. Target words are then extracted from the resulting triplets, and augmented as follows. For symmetric relations antonymy and synonymy, we extract both target words and relata in the current triplets as the target words for elicitation. For each of the other relations, we extract the target words in triplets of the relation and the relatum in the triplets of the reverse relation. Meronymy and holonomy are reversed to each other, and so are hyponymy and hypernymy. We remove any duplicates from the extracted target words.

This procedure results in 713 target words for hypernymy, 319 for hyponymy, 195 for holonymy, 146 for meronymy, 105 for antonymy, and 218 for synonymy[6]. These target words and templates yield a total of 10,979 task sentences used in the elicitation experiment.

3.3 Collection of Elicited Triplets

We use the Amazon Mechanical Turk (MTurk) crowdsourcing platform in order to collect relata

[4]Their patterns are extracted in the same fashion as Hearst (1992).

[5]This is a design decision made in conjunction with an experiment reported in Cao et al. (2024).

[6]This amounts to 1,304 unique target words; note that some target words are associated with more than one relation.

Relation	# Target Words	# Templates	# Triplets	(# Hapaxes)
HYP	713	7	11,739	(6,329)
HPO	319	4	5,721	(3,646)
HOL	195	7	3,496	(1,870)
MER	146	6	2,997	(1,568)
ANT	105	9	1,447	(804)
SYN	218	7	3,094	(1,589)
TOTAL	1,696 (1,304 unique)	40	28,494	15,806

Table 1: Target words, templates, and the numbers of elicited triplets, with the numbers of hapaxes in brackets.

from language users. Participants are restricted to those who have the Mturk Master qualification and whose answers are approved more than 500 times at an approval rate beyond 95%, and who additionally currently live in either the United States, the United Kingdom, Australia, or Canada.

We split the 10,979 task sentences into 276 subsets of around 37.8 sentences on average, making sure that no subset contains more than one sentence with the same relation and the same target word. We collected responses from four participants for each subset.

In total, 48 qualified participants were recruited. We explicitly instructed participants that they could use nouns and could not use multi-word expressions. The time limit for responding to each sentence is three minutes. Participants each answered 22 subsets on average. We collected 30,193 elicited triplets.

3.4 Identification of Match Status

The identification of the documented relation for an elicited triplet follows this procedure. For all synsets of the target word and relatum, we first check if they are documented directly in any relation of interest. If none, the triplet is identified as a missing triplet. If the documented relation matches the elicited relation, it is then identified as a matched triplet. In all other cases, the triplet is identified as a mismatched triplet.

Due to our treatment of word senses, some elicited triplets may include word pairs that stand in multiple relations in WordNet. However, it is very rare and there are only 456 out of 30,193 elicited triplets. We exclude such triplets. We also exclude triplets whose relatum can not be found as a noun in WordNet (there are 1,243 of these). This results in 28,494 triplets, out of which 12,688 are hapaxes, observed only once (cf. Table 1).

Although each template is designed specifically for only one relation, in reality, it is possible that the template might unintentionally evoke another relation for participants, according to their interpretation. In such case, the relata elicited may not be related to the target word in the intended relation, resulting in invalid relata; for each relation, we therefore measure the association between the distributions of relata coming from different templates. The higher the association is, the more confidently we can say that the templates successfully express that relation.

To calculate the association among templates within each relation, we use two association metrics: Cramér's V (1946) and the generalized Jensen-Shannon divergence (GJSD) (Fuglede and Topsoe, 2004). Cramér's V quantifies the association between multiple nominal samples. It ranges from 0 to 1, where higher means more strongly associated. GJSD extends the Jensen-Shannon divergence so that it is able to compare multiple distributions. GJSD ranges from 0 (similar) to 1 (dissimilar).

Relation	GJSD	Cramér's V
HYP	0.22	0.49
HPO	0.24	0.66
HOL	0.22	0.49
MER	0.21	0.52
ANT	0.21	0.43
SYN	0.22	0.47

Table 2: Association between templates per relation.

Table 2 shows the average metric scores over different target words per relation. We observe that the average GJSD are around 0.20 across relations, indicating a high similarity of relata distributions that come from different templates within a relation. The mean Cramér's V are above 0.40 for all relations, which is generally interpreted as a strong association (Kotrl, 2003; Akoglu, 2018). We conclude that the templates within relations overall express the same relation.

3.5 Metrics

3.5.1 Elicitation Frequency

The elicitation frequency $\mathcal{F}$ of a triplet (w, r, v) is defined as follows.

$$\mathcal{F}(w, r, v) = \frac{f(w, r, v)}{\sum_i f(w, r, v_i)} \quad (1)$$

where $f(w, r, v)$ is the number of times v was elicited in relation r to w across templates.

One of our analysis objectives is to observe whether highly intuitive triplets are more likely documented. To do so, we create a curve of the elicitation frequencies and match rates. Match rates are obtained as follows. For a relation r and a frequency threshold in a range of $[0, 1]$, we retain triplets (w, r, v) that have an elicitation frequency above it, and then the match rate is the proportion of matched triplets among them. The curve of elicitation frequency and match rate is then generated by plotting each threshold and the match rate.

3.5.2 Mismatch Likelihood

The mismatch likelihood $\mathcal{L}$ measures to what extent an elicited relation r is likely to be documented as a different relation s in WordNet. It is the normalized sum of frequencies of mismatched triplets whose elicited relation is r and documented relation is s. T_s^r denotes a set of such mismatched triplets. A mismatch likelihood of s given r is defined as follows.

$$g(s; r) = \sum_{(w,r,v) \in T_s^r} \mathcal{F}(w, r, v) \quad (2)$$

$$\mathcal{L}(s; r) = \frac{g(s; r)}{\sum_{R \setminus \{t\}} g(t; r)} \quad (3)$$

where $R \setminus \{t\}$ denotes the relation set with the relation t excluded. The mismatch likelihood is defined within the interval $[0, 1]$. For a given elicited relation, the mismatch likelihoods of the remaining five relations sum to one. It enables a comparison of the five relations, allowing us to find out for which documented relation, the mismatch is most likely to occur.

4 Results

4.1 Distribution of Triplet Categories

Figure 1 displays the distributions of match statuses for each relation. Missing triplets dominate: more than 60% of triplets are not found in WordNet. This tendency holds for both hapax and non-hapax triplets[7]. It indicates a large misalignment between language users and WordNet concerning semantic relation knowledge.

There are more matched than mismatched triplets for hyponymy and meronymy, while they are comparable for hypernymy and holonymy. In addition, the proportion of matched triplets is particularly low for hypernymy and holonymy, both below 10%. Hypernymy and holonymy are two relations that require abstraction for the generic form (hypernym) and for the whole (holonymy). We might hypothesize that abstraction, a cognitively expensive process, pushes the proportion of matched triples lower.

Antonymy has the lowest mismatch rate of 4%. It shows a different behavior from synonymy, which has a very high mismatch rate at 20%. Antonymy triplets are most unlikely, whereas synonymy triplets are most likely, to be mismatched as other relational triplets. This result can be explained by their definition. Antonymy is the only relation discussed here that is based on mutual exclusion between the target word and relatum. On the other hand, synonymy is based on inclusion, which is a property that hypernymy, hyponymy, holonymy, and meronymy also share to different degrees (Joosten, 2010). Hence, there is a clear line between antonymy and all other five relations, resulting in a low mismatch rate of antonymy.

4.2 Dynamics of Elicitation Frequency and Match Rate

Let us consider how match rates are related to the elicitation frequency (intuitiveness) of triples. Figure 2 shows the relation between the elicitation frequency and the match rate per relation. If the more intuitive triplets are more likely documented in WordNet, we would expect two distinct patterns: 1) a monotonic increase in match rates against elicitation frequency, and 2) eventual convergence of the curves to a match rate of one.

However, not all curves exhibit a consistent monotonic increase. While there is a rapid initial

[7]The distribution of hapax and non-hapax triplets can be found in Appendix B.

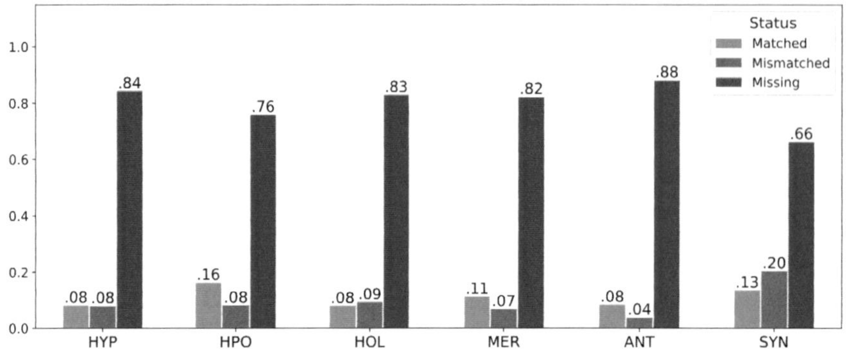

Figure 1: Match status distribution per relation.

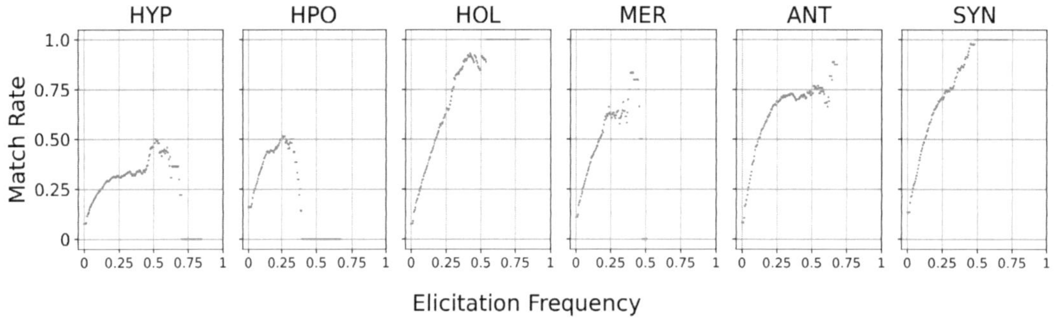

Figure 2: Human elicitation frequency vs. match rate.

increase in match rates across all relation types, only the synonymy curve continues to increase, ultimately converging to a match rate of one. The other relations stop increasing at a certain point, roughly halfway between zero and the largest elicitation frequency. In other words, the match rate increases only at lower elicitation frequencies.

Apart from synonymy, holonymy and antonymy also reach a match rate of one. For hypernymy, hyponymy, and meronymy, the curves even drop to a match rate of zero. This suggests that some very intuitive triplets with maximal elicitation frequency for these three relations are not documented in WordNet.

To sum up, the intuitiveness of triplets can hardly explain the match rate, as the two variables do not align in the expected manner.

4.3 Mismatch Likelihood Matrix

After a glance at the overall landscape, we will now look at mismatched triplets. Figure 3 presents the mismatch likelihood matrix between the human-elicited relations and the WordNet-documented relations. The vertical axis shows the documented relation s, and the horizontal axis

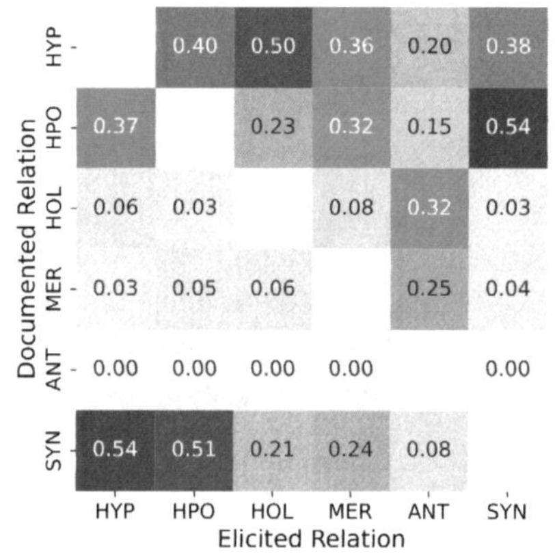

Figure 3: Mismatch likelihood matrix.

shows the elicited relation r, where each cell gives the mismatch likelihood $\mathcal{L}(s; r)$. Likelihoods in the same columns sum up to one.

For antonymy, the mismatch likelihood is highest for holonymy and meronymy. Readers may recall that the mismatch rarely happens for antonymy, as we have seen in Figure 1. When it happens, antonymy triplets are most likely to be documented as either holonymy or meronymy.

This mismatch often happens when a word is a metonym and involves temporal duration. For example, (*"day"*, ANT, *"night"*) is documented in meronymy. *"Day"* can be interpreted as *"time for Earth to make a complete rotation on its axis"* and *"the time after sunrise and before sunset while it is light outside"*, according to WordNet. This first sense contains the second, resulting in both meronymy and antonymy between *"day"* and *"night"*.

For other elicited relations than antonymy, elicited triplets are likely to be documented as hypernymy, hyponymy, and synonymy (high values in the first, second, and last rows). This tendency is particularly strong when the elicited relation is either hypernymy, hyponymy, or synonymy. It is extremely rare for triplets elicited for antonymy to be mismatched with other relations (low values in the fifth row).

Furthermore, the semantic characteristic of words may influence the mismatch likelihood as well, and we may need an augmentation method that is sensitive to such characteristics. For example, mismatch likelihoods could be higher for words that refer to an abstract concept rather than a physical entity (abstract or physical word, in short). Abstract words are often more context-dependent, making them more polysemous than physical words [8]. Because of the relatively strong polysemous nature of abstract words, we expect them to result in higher mismatch likelihoods.

We find 6,723 triplets, whose target word and relatum are abstract words and 6,555 physical triplets. Mismatch likelihoods are calculated for each. For mismatch likelihood of hypernymy given hyponymy, the abstract triplets show a higher value than the physical triplets (0.43 vs. 0.28). For likelihoods of hyponymy given hypernymy, the abstract triplets also exceed the physical triplets (0.43 vs. 0.31), aligning with our expectations.

4.4 Distance of Matched Triplets

We now include indirectly matched hypernymy and hyponymy triplets in the analysis. We define the distance of matched triplets as the length of the shortest path between the target word and relatum in the WordNet hierarchy; directly matched triplets have a distance of one.

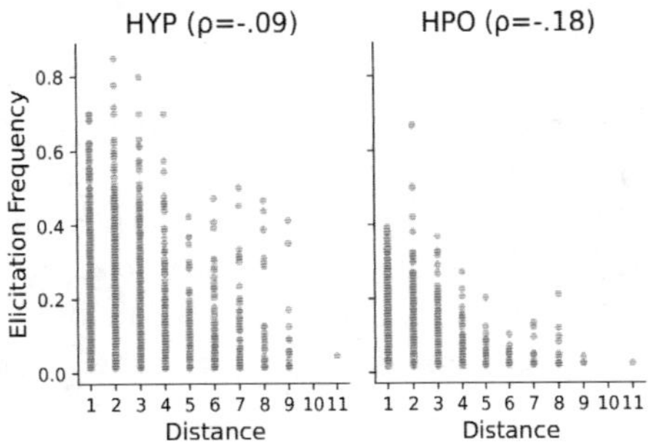

Figure 4: Distances of matched triplets.

We find that 1,895 indirectly matched triplets out of 9,890 (19%) missing hypernymy triplets and 1,331 out of 4,338 (30%) missing hyponymy triplets. They are more than the directly matched 932 hypernymy triplets and 922 hyponymy triplets.

Figure 4 shows the relation between the elicitation frequency and the distance of both directly (with a distance of one) and indirectly (with a distance above one) matched triplets for hypernymy and hyponymy. More than 50% of the indirectly matched triplets have distances between two and four (1,541 for hypernymy and 1,187 for hyponymy). For both relations, triplets with a distance of less than four have similar ranges of elicitation frequency.

We calculate the Spearman'ρ between the distance and elicitation frequency of the triplets. The ρ values are -0.09 for hypernymy and -0.18 for hyponymy, indicating a negligible correlation between WordNet path length and language users' intuitiveness. We conclude that the WordNet path length is not an indicator of language users' intuition on hypernymy and hyponymy triplets. Previous literature reports a related phenomenon: humans tend to find indirect hypernymy or hyponymy triplets more intuitive compared to direct triplets (Vulić et al., 2017).

5 Conclusion

In the present work, we provide a straightforward and flexible methodology of comparison between language users' intuition and WordNet as the preliminary step of systematic augmentation of WordNet. Our findings suggest that a misalignment exists between them; it can be observed from the

[8] We define abstract words as those whose all synsets are a descendent of *"abstraction.n.06"*. Physical words are those whose all synsets are a descendent of *"physical_entity.n.01"*. In our data, abstract target words have more synsets (3.2 on average) than physical target words (2.3 on average). The difference is statistically significant by a Mann-Whitney U test with a significance level of 5%.

following aspects. First, the majority of elicited triplets are overall missing in WordNet, regardless of relations; even highly intuitive triplets could be missing in WordNet. Second, for some word pairs, there is a mismatch between the elicited relation and the WordNet-documented relation. Finally, WordNet path length is not an indicator of language users' intuition. This misalignment suggests the needs and directions of augmentation.

6 Future Work

WordNet has rich and fine-grained lexico-semantic information, which may facilitate mining missing relations. For example, previous work (Boyd-Graber et al., 2005; Maziarz and Rudnicka, 2020) uses WordNet glosses to establish evocation relations, which are semantic associations where a lexical item brings another to mind. We hypothesize the glosses might also be useful in recognizing the semantic relations that we discussed in the present work. As a preliminary experiment, we explore whether the similarity between glosses can differentiate related (matched and missing) and unrelated triplets.

We calculate the gloss-based similarity of word pairs in matched, missing, and unrelated triplets and compare the similarities among triplet groups. The gloss-based similarity for triplets is defined as the maximum BERTScore (Zhang et al., 2020) computed across all possible gloss pairs between the target word and relatum. The gloss-based similarity ranges between zero and one, with higher values indicating a greater degree of similarity between the glosses of two words.

We use non-hapax triplets for matched and missing triplets (15,806 in total). 30,000 unrelated triplets are sampled from WordNet, guaranteeing both the target word and relatum in the triplets appear in the human elicitation data. A Mann-Whitney U test at a significance level of 5% is then performed between the unrelated triplets against matched or missing triplets within every relation. We additionally apply the test between matched and missing triplets. We expect the gloss-based similarity for matched and missing triplets to be higher than that of unrelated triplets.

Figure 5 shows the results. For all relations, both matched and missing triplets yield significantly higher gloss-based similarities than the unrelated triplets (UNR), aligning with our expectations. For matched triplets, the highest

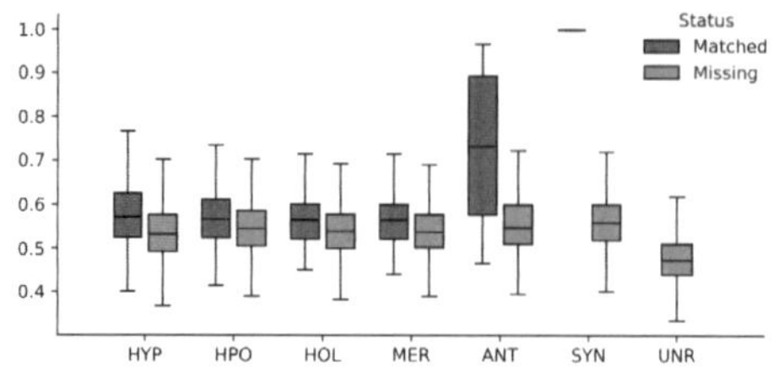

Figure 5: Gloss-based similarity of triplets per relation. UNR means unrelated triplets.

mean gloss-based similarities are observed for synonymy (1.00) and antonymy (0.74). As two synonyms share the same gloss by definition, their similarity always marks the full value. Two antonyms differ in only a few specific semantic features while sharing other features, leading to similar glosses.

However, the missing triplets, which are the focus of augmentation, show significantly lower similarities than the matched triplets across all relations. It indicates the difficulty in mining missing triplets at the same level of confidence as for the matched triplets. Moreover, the mean gloss-based similarities for all relations range narrowly between 0.54 and 0.57. It suggests that distinguishing these relations based solely on the gloss-based similarity is difficult.

In summary, glosses can be useful in recognizing semantic relatedness and hence it is possible to augment WordNet. However, relying solely on glosses is insufficient to determine whether two words have a relation, nor to identify the relation type. To achieve an effective augmentation, it is essential to employ other information in WordNet.

7 Limitation

In the present study, we employed only four participants for each template. Their backgrounds and experiences could influence their responses, resulting in a potential bias in the experimental results. The small number of participants we employed might not be sufficient to rule out annotator bias completely.

Acknowledgments

This work was supported by JST SPRING, Grant Number JPMJSP2106. The third author was supported by Institute of Science Tokyo (formerly Tokyo Institute of Technology)'s World Research Hub Program.

References

Haldun Akoglu. 2018. User's guide to correlation coefficients. *User's guide to correlation coefficients*, 18:91–93.

Asela Reig Alamillo, David Torres Moreno, Eliseo Morales González, Mauricio Toledo Acosta, Antoine Taroni, and Jorge Hermosillo Valadez. 2023. The analysis of synonymy and antonymy in discourse relations: An interpretable modeling approach. *Computational Linguistics*, 49:429–464.

Jordan Boyd-Graber, Christiane Fellbaum, Daniel Osherson, and Robert Schapire. 2005. Adding dense, weighted connections to wordnet. In *3rd International Global WordNet Conference, Proceedings*, pages 29–35, Jeju Island, Republic of Korea. Masaryk University.

Zhihan Cao, Hiroaki Yamada, Simone Teufel, and Takenobu Tokunaga. 2024. A comprehensive evaluation of semantic relation knowledge of pretrained language models and humans. *Preprint*, arXiv:2412.01131.

Harald Cramér. 1946. *Mathematical Methods of Statistics*. Princeton University Press, Princeton.

Jacob Devlin, Ming-Wei Chang, Kenton Lee, and Kristina Toutanova. 2018. Bert: Pre-training of deep bidirectional transformers for language understanding. *Proceedings of the 2019 Conference of the North American Chapter of the Association for Computational Linguistics: Human Language Technologies, Volume 1 (Long and Short Papers)*, 1:4171–4186.

Allyson Ettinger. 2020. What bert is not: Lessons from a new suite of psycholinguistic diagnostics for language models. *Transactions of the Association for Computational Linguistics*, 8:34–48.

B. Fuglede and F. Topsoe. 2004. Jensen-shannon divergence and hilbert space embedding. In *International Symposium on Information Theory 2004 Proceedings.*, pages 30–30. IEEE.

Goran Glavaš and Sanja Štajner. 2015. Simplifying lexical simplification: Do we need simplified corpora? In *Proceedings of the 53rd Annual Meeting of the Association for Computational Linguistics and the 7th International Joint Conference on Natural Language Processing (Volume 2: Short Papers)*, volume 2, pages 63–68. Association for Computational Linguistics.

Marti A Hearst. 1992. Automatic acquisition of hyponyms from large text corpora. In *COLING 1992 Volume 2: The 14th International Conference on Computational Linguistics*, pages 539–545.

Frank Joosten. 2010. Collective nouns, aggregate nouns, and superordinates. *Lingvisticae Investigationes*, 33:25–49.

Joe W. Kotrl. 2003. The incorporation of effect size in information technology , learning , and performance research. *Information Technology, Learning, and Performance Journal*, 21:1–7.

Zhenzhong Lan, Mingda Chen, Sebastian Goodman, Kevin Gimpel, Piyush Sharma, and Radu Soricut. 2020. ALBERT: A lite BERT for self-supervised learning of language representations. In *8th International Conference on Learning Representations, ICLR 2020, Addis Ababa, Ethiopia, April 26-30, 2020*. OpenReview.net.

Yinhan Liu, Myle Ott, Naman Goyal, Jingfei Du, Mandar Joshi, Danqi Chen, Omer Levy, Mike Lewis, Luke Zettlemoyer, and Veselin Stoyanov. 2019. Roberta: A robustly optimized BERT pretraining approach. *CoRR*, abs/1907.11692.

Nitin Madnani and Bonnie J. Dorr. 2010. Generating phrasal and sentential paraphrases: A survey of data-driven methods. *Computational Linguistics*, 36:341–387.

Marek Maziarz and Ewa Rudnicka. 2020. Expanding wordnet with gloss and polysemy links for evocation strength recognition. *Cognitive Studies*.

John P. McCrae, Alexandre Rademaker, Francis Bond, Ewa Rudnicka, and Christiane Fellbaum. 2019. English WordNet 2019 – an open-source WordNet for English. In *Proceedings of the 10th Global Wordnet Conference*, pages 245–252, Wroclaw, Poland. Global Wordnet Association.

John Philip McCrae, Alexandre Rademaker, Ewa Rudnicka, and Francis Bond. 2020. English WordNet 2020: Improving and extending a WordNet for English using an open-source methodology. In *Proceedings of the LREC 2020 Workshop on Multimodal Wordnets (MMW2020)*, pages 14–19, Marseille, France. The European Language Resources Association (ELRA).

Jim McKinley and Heath Rose. 2019. *The Routledge Handbook of Research Methods in Applied Linguistics (1st ed.)*. Routledge.

Timothy P. McNamara. 2005. *Semantic Priming*. Psychology Press.

George A. Miller. 1995. Wordnet. *Communications of the ACM*, 38:39–41.

George A. Miller and Christiane Fellbaum. 1991. Semantic networks of english. *Cognition*, 41:197–229.

James P Van Overschelde, Katherine A Rawson, and John Dunlosky. 2004. Category norms: An updated and expanded version of the battig and montague (1969) norms. *Journal of Memory and Language*, 50:289–335.

Stephen Roller, Douwe Kiela, and Maximilian Nickel. 2018. Hearst patterns revisited: Automatic hypernym detection from large text corpora. In *Proceedings of the 56th Annual Meeting of the Association for Computational Linguistics (Volume 2: Short Papers)*, pages 358–363, Melbourne, Australia. Association for Computational Linguistics.

John I Saeed. 2015. *Semantics*. Hoboken, NJ: Wiley-Blackwell.

Marta Tatu and Dan Moldovan. 2005. A semantic approach to recognizing textual entailment. In *Proceedings of Human Language Technology Conference and Conference on Empirical Methods in Natural Language Processing*, pages 371–378. Association for Computational Linguistics.

Tony Veale and Yanfen Hao. 2008. Enriching wordnet with folk knowledge and stereotypes. In *Proceedings of Global WordNet Conference*, pages 453–461, Szeged, Hungary.

Ivan Vulić, Daniela Gerz, Douwe Kiela, Felix Hill, and Anna Korhonen. 2017. Hyperlex: A large-scale evaluation of graded lexical entailment. *Computational Linguistics*, 43:781–835.

Tianyi Zhang, Varsha Kishore, Felix Wu, Kilian Q. Weinberger, and Yoav Artzi. 2020. Bertscore: Evaluating text generation with BERT. In *8th International Conference on Learning Representations, ICLR 2020, Addis Ababa, Ethiopia, April 26-30, 2020*. OpenReview.net.

A All Templates

Relation	Template
HYP (7)	a [TARGET] is a type of a [RELATUM] a [TARGET] is a kind of a [RELATUM] the word [TARGET] has a more specific meaning than the word [RELATUM] a [TARGET] is a [RELATUM] a [TARGET] is a specific case of a [RELATUM] a [TARGET] is a subordinate type of a [RELATUM] the word [TARGET] has a more specific sense than the word [RELATUM]
HPO (4)	my favorite [TARGET] is a [RELATUM] a [TARGET], such as a [RELATUM] the word [TARGET] has a more general meaning than the word [RELATUM] the word [TARGET] has a more general sense than the word [RELATUM]
HOL (7)	a [TARGET] is a component of a [RELATUM] a [TARGET] is a part of a [RELATUM] a [TARGET] is contained in a [RELATUM] a [TARGET] belongs to constituents of a [RELATUM] a [TARGET] belongs to parts of a [RELATUM] a [TARGET] belongs to components of a [RELATUM] a [TARGET] is a constituent of a [RELATUM]
MER (6)	constituents of a [TARGET] include a [RELATUM] components of a [TARGET] include a [RELATUM] parts of a [TARGET] include a [RELATUM] a [TARGET] consists of a [RELATUM] a [TARGET] has a [RELATUM] a [TARGET] contains a [RELATUM]
ANT (9)	it is not likely to be both a [TARGET] and a [RELATUM] a [TARGET] is the opposite of a [RELATUM] the word [TARGET] has an opposite sense of the word [RELATUM] it is impossible to be both a [TARGET] and a [RELATUM] the word [TARGET] has a meaning that negates the meaning of the word [RELATUM] it is a [TARGET] so it is not a [RELATUM] the word [TARGET] has an opposite meaning of the word [RELATUM] if something is a [TARGET], then it can not also be a [RELATUM] the word [TARGET] has a sense that negates the sense of the word [RELATUM]
SYN (7)	a [TARGET] is also known as a [RELATUM] a [TARGET] is often referred to as a [RELATUM] the word [TARGET] has a similar meaning as the word [RELATUM] a [TARGET] is similar to a [RELATUM] the word [TARGET] means nearly the same as the word [RELATUM] a [TARGET] is indistinguishable from a [RELATUM] a [TARGET] is also called a [RELATUM]

Table 3: All templates used in data collection are presented by relation.

B Distributions of hapax and non-hapax triplets.

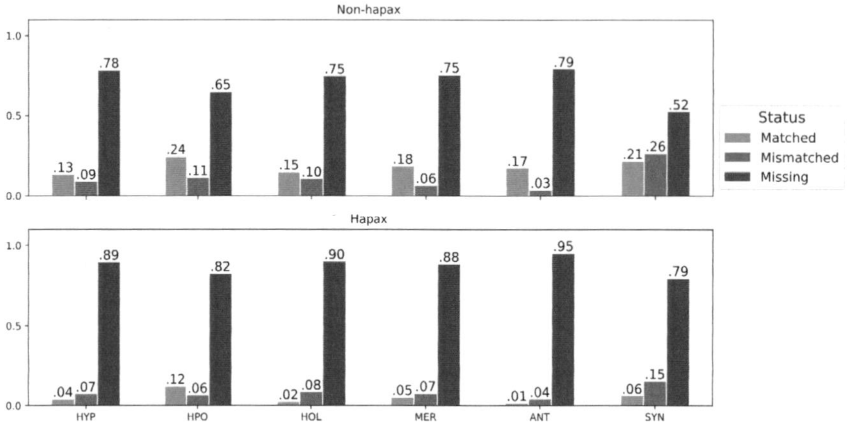

Figure 6: Match status distribution per relation, distinguishing hapax and non-hapax triplets.

Expanding WordNet Based on Glosses: Methodology and Applications

Yicheng Sun and Jie Wang
Richard Miner School of Computer and Information Sciences
University of Massachusetts, Lowell, MA 01854, USA
Correspondence: Jie_Wang@uml.edu

Abstract

We introduce a method called AI-WordNet for expanding WordNet using only glosses. Given a lemma and its gloss, AI-WordNet predicts the corresponding lexname for the gloss, decides whether a new synset should be created for the lemma, finds the best hypernym for the new synset, and updates the corresponding hypernym-hyponym relationships. We demonstrate a low-cost implementation of AI-WordNet for noun lemmas using PWN 3.0 as the training dataset. Intrinsic evaluations show that AI-WordNet achieves a high F1 score of 94.6% for lexname prediction, and 64.8% direct hits on true hypernyms with an average distance of 1.374 from the predicted hypernyms to the true hypernyms. We apply AI-WordNet to generate distractors for cloze-question creation on answer keys containing new lemmas not yet included in PWN 3.0, using glosses extracted from Wiktionary. Extrinsic evaluations confirm the high quality of the generated distractors.

1 Introduction

Using WordNet to complete an NLP task offers the advantage of achieving a controllable and explainable solution. For instance, WordNet has been used to automate the generation of distractors for constructing cloze questions based on an answer key derived from a given text. Cloze questions are fill-in-the-blank exercises where each blank is accompanied by multiple options, including distractors—incorrect but plausible choices—alongside the correct option known as the answer key. In this approach, distractors are constructed from lemmas in WordNet that are semantically related to the lemmas in the answer key within a specified distance. This ensures a clear rationale for their selection by leveraging the semantic relationships between the lemmas in the answer key and those in the distractors.

However, not all lemmas of interest are included in WordNet. Therefore, an effective and low-cost solution for inserting new lemmas into WordNet is highly desirable, ensuring that the existing system for completing the NLP task can continue to function seamlessly.

Adding a new lemma to WordNet requires information about its gloss, as well as its gloss's lexname, synset, hypernyms, and hyponyms. While this can be achieved by curating authoritative digitized dictionaries or datasets with predefined lexical relations, emerging lemmas are often not yet included in these sources. Even when they are present, they are typically represented as standalone entries without systematic semantic connections or with relationships tied to broader lemmas rather than being specifically linked to their glosses.

Addressing these issues, we present a method called AI-WordNet to facilitate the insertion of new lemmas into WordNet using only their glosses. These glosses can be easily sourced from Wiktionary or other publicly available databases, enabling a streamlined and efficient approach to expanding WordNet's lexical coverage.

AI-WordNet performs the following tasks: It first predicts a lexname for the gloss. If the lemma is new but the gloss already exists in WordNet, it joins the lemma to the appropriate synset. Otherwise, it creates a new synset for the lemma. To find a hypernym synset for the newly created synset, it predicts a path of inherited hypernyms. It then checks whether any of these predicted hypernyms are already in WordNet. If a match is found, it selects the best-matched hypernym synset. Otherwise, it searches for the closest matching hypernym gloss among existing glosses and maps it to its corresponding hypernym synset. Finally, It updates the relevant hypernym-hyponym relationships to incorporate the newly created synset.

We demonstrate a low-cost implementation of AI-WordNet for noun lemmas using various open-source pre-trained small models (PLMs) fine-tuned on datasets constructed from PWN 3.0 (Princeton WordNet v3.0), which can be run on a commonplace GPU server.

We show through intrinsic evaluations that AI-WordNet achieves a high F1 score of 94.6% for lexname prediction, and 64.8% direct hits on the true hypernyms with the average distance of 1.374 from the predicted hypernyms to the true hypernyms. Additionally, we apply AI-WordNet to generate controlled and explainable distractors using the cloze-question-generation system (Sun and Wang, 2023) on texts containing new lemmas with glosses extracted from Wiktionary. Extrinsic evaluations confirm the high quality of the generated distractors, as errors in lexname predictions and hypernym identifications, as long as they remain within a reasonable range of the ground truth, are acceptable for distractor generation without compromising overall effectiveness.

2 Related Work

Sun and Wang (Sun and Wang, 2023) presented a system called Cloze Question Generator (CQG) for constructing cloze questions from a given article, with a particular emphasis on generating multigram distractors using the semantic structure of WordNet. This approach allows users to control how distractors are generated and provides explanations for the appropriateness of the generated distractors based on the WordNet structure.

In particular, given an answer key for a stem (a sentence with blanks to fill in), CQG first segments the answer key into a sequence of instances. For each instance, it generates instance-level distractor candidates using a transformer and sibling synsets in WordNet, and ranks them based on contextual similarities, synset relations, and lexical relatedness. Distractor candidates are then formed by selectively replacing instances with the top-ranked instance-level candidates, which are subsequently checked for legitimacy as phrases. Finally, CQG selects the top-ranked distractor candidates as distractors based on contextual semantic similarities to the answer key. This process is controllable, and the selection of distractors can be explained based on the WordNet structure, specifically by examining how semantically distant the distractors are from the answer key.

Intrinsic evaluations demonstrated that CQG significantly outperforms previous methods, and extrinsic evaluations also confirmed the high quality of the generated distractors.

To the best of our knowledge, no published work has reported automatic insertions of new lemmas into WordNet using glosses as the sole source of information, although the white papers of both BabelNet (Navigli and Ponzetto, 2012) and ConceptNet (Speer et al., 2016) indicate that new entries can be added automatically. However, the methods employed remain undisclosed. On the other hand, Koeva (Svetla, 2021) demonstrated how to expand WordNet using conceptual frames.

On a separate note, cloze questions can be generated from a given text using pre-trained general-purpose large language models (LLMs), such as GPT-4. However, this approach functions as a black box, offering limited control over the generation of distractors and minimal explainability regarding the rationale behind their selection. Furthermore, when answer keys contain lemmas absent from the training dataset of the underlying LLM, the model is unable to generate suitable distractors. Resolving this issue often requires retraining the model, a process that is both astronomically expensive and time-consuming.

3 AI-WordNet Overview

For emerging terms or phrases, such as new Internet slang or academic terminology that have not yet been included in any authoritative dictionary, we classify them as lemmas.

In what follows, unless otherwise stated, direct hypernyms will be referred to simply as hypernyms. Direct hypernyms, as well as any hypernyms beyond the direct hypernym level—such as hypernyms of hypernyms—are collectively referred to as inherited hypernyms.

AI-WordNet consists of six components (Fig. 1):

(1) The **Lexname Predictor** predicts a lexname L for the gloss g.

(2) The **Synset Identifier** identifies an appropriate synset for (l, g). If l is in WordNet and there is an existing synset for l with a gloss that has the same meaning as g, then it drops (l, g). Otherwise, it checks if there is a synset S for which $l \notin S$, but with a gloss that shares the same meaning as g. If so, place l in S. If not, create a new synset $S_{l,g}$.

Note that the lexname predicted for g by the

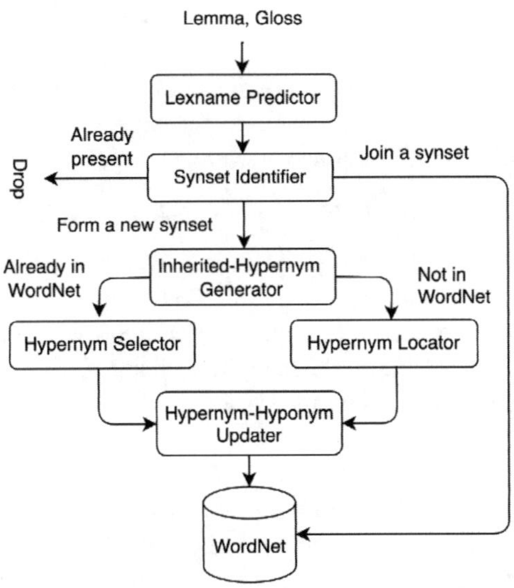

Figure 1: Schematic of AI-WordNet and data flow

Lexname Generator reduces the search space to only include synsets with the same predicted lexname for (l, g). This is the reason for the Lexname Predictor to precede the Synset Identifier.

(3) The **Inherited-Hypernym Generator** generates a hypernym h for the new synset $S_{l,g}$. Depending on whether h is in WordNet, the system goes to the Hypernym Selector or the Hypernym Locator.

(4) The **Hypernym Selector** determines, for the given h, an appropriate synset from (possible) multiple synsets of h contained in WordNet.

(5) The **Hypernym Locator** locates the best a synset in WordNet as g's hypernym.

(6) The **Hypernym-Hyponym Updater** updates the hypernym-hyponym structure of WordNet when new synsets are inserted.

4 Implementation

Nouns and phrasal nouns are the most relevant as answer keys for constructing cloze questions. We present a low-cost implementation of AI-WordNet for noun lemmas using small open-source PLMs that can be fine-tuned.

Implementations for lemmas of other parts of speech, such as verbs and phrasal verbs, can be carried out using the same approach.

4.1 Fine-tuning Through OpenPrompt

We fine-tune PLMs directly for various generation tasks and indirectly for various classification tasks using the OpenPrompt (OP) platform (Ding et al., 2021). OP uses the mechanism of Verbalizer to enhance fine-tuning.

Let M be a PLM supported by OP. Denote by OP/M a fine-tuned model of M through OP over a dataset and Verbalizer with the following general prompt template (PT):

> [text] {'place_holder': text_1}, ..., [text] {'place_holder': text_n}. [text] [mask] [text].

Here {'place_holder': text_k} represents a variable and [text] a text segment without variables, which could be empty. A Verbalizer includes terms positively or negatively associated with the target to be predicted.

On a training dataset, OP automatically replaces the variables with data entries in the dataset one at a time, and uses M to predict what is in the place of the [mask]. The predicted term, if not in the Verbalizer, is first mapped to a term in the Verbalizer through a neural network and then mapped to a target term through another neural layer.

In what follows, we choose T5 as the default PLM due to its strong performance and its availability as a no-cost, open-source model.

4.2 Datasets

The primary dataset, denoted by WordNet-N, consists of all noun synsets in PWN 3.0 together with lexnames, glosses, hypernym synsets, and hyponym synsets. It contains a total of 82,061 data entries, which are organized into 26 classes corresponding to the 26 lexnames for noun synsets.

We will later construct various datasets from WordNet-N, which maintain the same proportion across classes to ensure consistent class distribution. Each dataset will be named using the abbreviation of its corresponding component followed by "DS." For instance, the dataset for training and testing the Lexname Predictor will be named LP-DS. These datasets are published on github [1]. Each dataset will be split following the standard 80-20 ratio for training and testing.

4.3 Lexname Predictor (LP)

The LP-DS dataset consists of all gloss-lexname pairs extracted from WordNet-N, except the lexname 'noun.Tops', which represents the highest category for any noun glosses.

Fine-tuning T5 and OP/T5 uses, respectively, the following PTs:

[1] https://github.com/wordneter/dataset

What is the lexname of the given gloss?
GLOSS: {gloss}.
{'place_holder': gloss}. The lexname for the gloss is [mask].

The Verbalizer specified for each of the 25 lexnames consists of just the suffix. For example: the Verbalizer for lexname 'noun.person' is {'person'}.

LP first predicts a lexname L for g via the fine-tuned T5. If L is a suffix of a noun lexname, use 'noun.L' as the lexname for g. Otherwise, use the fine-tuned OP/T5 to predict a lexname for g.

4.4 Synset Identifier (SI)

The SI-DS dataset is constructed as follows: For each gloss in WordNet-N, identify the corresponding gloss with the same meaning from a digitized Oxford Dictionary. Use the low-cost GPT-3.5-Turbo to generate glosses with different wordings that express the same meaning, and glosses that express different meanings with various degrees of differences. Select independently at random 10,000 pairs of glosses that convey the same connotations (meaning) and label them as 1. Similarly, select independently at random 10,000 pairs of glosses that have different connotations and label them as 0.

SI is an OP/T5 binary classifier fine-tuned on SI-DS using the following PT:

Sentence 1: {gloss 1}.
Sentence 2: {gloss 2}.
The meanings of sentence 1 and sentence 2 are [mask].

For the label 1, the Verbalizer includes {'synonymous', 'equivalent', 'identical', 'interchangeable', 'coincident', 'matching'}. For the label 0, it includes {'disparate', 'divergent', 'distinct', 'dissimilar', 'unalike', 'incompatible', 'varied'}. Note that the word 'alike' is not precise enough for label 1, whereas 'unalike' is acceptable for label 0.

Note that we might be tempted to directly use cosine similarity of sentence embeddings for glosses to identify whether g is similar to an existing gloss. However, different glosses can have a cosine similarity score close to 1 under BERT embeddings as the following example shows: The glosses 'United States actor; son of Maurice Barrymore and Georgiana Barrymore (1878-1954)' and 'United States actor; son of Maurice Barrymore and Georgiana Barrymore (1882-1942)' for Synset(barrymore.n.01) and Synset(barrymore.n.03) have a cosine similarity of 0.999 under BERT embeddings. Setting the threshold this high would result in incorrectly identifying certain glosses with the same meaning as different, rendering this approach unsuitable.

4.5 Inherited-Hypernym Generator (IHG)

The IHG-DS dataset is constructed as follows: Initially, for each synset in WordNet-N, use its gloss as the source and the path of its inherited hypernyms as the target, where the path starts from the direct hypernym of the synset.

Glosses can be categorized into two types: those containing inherited hypernyms and those that do not. Specifically, 83.4% of glosses in WordNet-N fall into the first category, with 73.5% of them containing direct hypernyms. This imbalance between the two types causes a model trained on the initial dataset to favor extracting nouns or phrasal nouns from glosses as hypernyms, negatively impacting the generation of hypernyms for glosses in the second category, as none of the extracted terms is an appropriate hypernym.

To achieve a better balance, we use GPT-3.5-Turbo to generate, for each gloss, three differently articulated versions, and add these generated glosses to the training dataset if they contain no inherited hypernyms. This improves the ratio of the first and the second categories from 87:13 to 63:37. Note that this data augmentation is performed exclusively on the training dataset.

Note that all paths of inherited hypernyms for noun lemmas eventually converge at the same root node, 'entity', which has the lexname 'noun.Tops'. As a result, a model trained on the initial dataset tends to extract a lemma from the path closer to the root as the hypernym. To mitigate this issue, we extract the initial k nodes of the hypernym path as the target text, and we refer to it as a k-gram.

Fine-tuning OP/T5 uses the following PT on the augmented training dataset:

Generate {k} inherited hypernyms for a given gloss. Sort them based on their proximity to the gloss in terms of meaning, separated by symbol $\rightarrow$. GLOSS: {gloss}.

The first lemma in the k-gram is designated as the *predicted hypernym* of the underlying gloss. For example, for the lemma-gloss pair ('apple', 'fruit with red or yellow or green skin and sweet to tart crisp whitish flesh'), IHG outputs the following path:

'edible fruit $\rightarrow$ fruit $\rightarrow$ produce',

where 'edible fruit' is the predicted hypernym.

We found that the predicted hypernym may vary depending on the values of k. We select $k = 3$ based on the experiments we conducted with various values of k, ranging from 1 to the full path length, which indicates that $k = 3$ maximizes the probability of the predicted hypernym being the true hypernym.

Let h be the predicted hypernym in the 3-gram. If it is in WordNet-N, then pass it to the Hypernym Selector. Otherwise, branch to the Hypernym Locator.

4.6 Hypernym Selector (HS)

Let L be the predicted lexname by LP, $S_{l,g}$ be either a new synset or an existing synset identified by SI, and h be what is passed by IHG. If h appears in only one synset, then this synset is the hypernym synset of $S_{l,g}$. If h appears in multiple synsets $S_{h,1}, \ldots, S_{h,m}$ with $m > 1$ and $S_{h,i}$ having gloss g_i, we use HS to select an appropriate synset S_{h,g_i} as the hypernym synset of $S_{l,h}$.

HS is a fine-tuned ESCHER (Barba et al., 2021) model on the HS-DS dataset, where ESCHER is a transformer-based model for extractive sense comprehension with superior performance over similar word-sense-disambiguation (WSD) tools.

Each data entry in HS-DS consists of three components: input text, target location, and ground truth. The input text is a sentence that combines the hypernym and the target gloss using the following template:

[hypernym] is a hypernym of the gloss:
[target gloss].

The template provides the model with the necessary context for understanding the relationship between the gloss and its hypernyms. The target location specifies the location of the hypernym within the input text for the model to identify and focus on the relevant part of the input text during fine-tuning. The ground truth is the actual synset name of the hypernym of the underlying gloss.

HS takes h, g, and g_i's as input and returns the gloss that is the closest to the hypernym of g. For example, let g be 'Fruit with red or yellow or green skin and sweet to tart crisp whitish flesh with h being 'fruit'. The lemma 'fruit' appears in three synsets with glosses being, respectively, 'The ripened reproductive body of a seed plant', 'An amount of a product', and 'The consequence of some effort or action'. The gloss 'The ripened reproductive body of a seed plant' is the closest to g determined by HS, which is returned as the output.

4.7 Hypernym Locator (HL)

HL is branched if the predicted hypernym is not in WordNet-N. In this case, it is still possible that the true hypernym of the gloss g, denoted by h, exists in WordNet-N. This would mean that there is another gloss g' in WordNet-N with h being its hypernym, indicating that h is not a leaf node. Thus, g' can be identified by traversing all glosses in WordNet-N and applying an embedding-based method, such as BERT embeddings, to find the gloss most similar to g based on cosine similarity. The hypernym of g' would then be designated as the hypernym of g.

Unfortunately, h could also be a leaf node in WordNet-N, then g' is likely h itself, as g' may likely be the most similar to g. In such a scenario, running the above algorithm assigns h's hypernym h' as g's direct hypernym (see Fig. 2). This should be avoided to preserve the correct hierarchical structure.

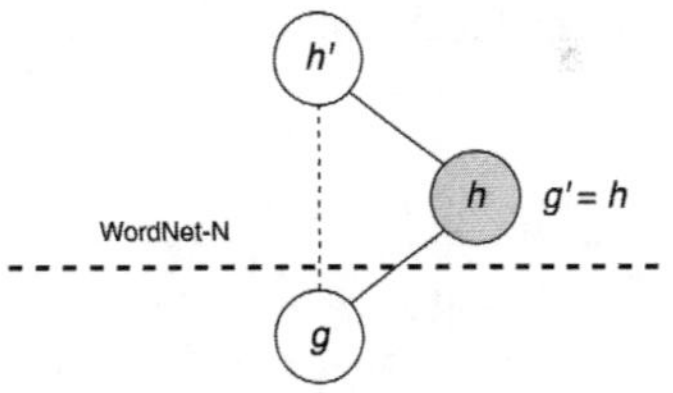

Figure 2: Assigning h' as the direct hypernym to g should be avoided, where the shaded node h is a leaf node in WordNet-N

To address this issue, HL uses LLM-Embedder (Zhang et al., 2023) fine-tuned on the HL-DS dataset. LLM-Embedder is an embedding method with a specifically pre-trained LLM through contrastive learning and knowledge distillation.

Each data point in the HL-DS dataset consists of (1) a gloss in WordNet-N; (2) an instruction to find the best hypernym gloss for the given gloss; (3) the synset for the true hypernym gloss of the given gloss called the query synset; (4) a set of glosses that are not direct hypernyms of the query synset; and (5) a set of glosses connected to the query synset with a distance at most 2, excluding direct hypernym glosses.

HL, on input g, searches from the set of all

glosses in WordNet-N that have the same lexname as that of g for the best hypernym gloss of g, using the same instruction as in the training dataset with g being the gloss for the query synset. In particular, HL first combines the instruction and the query to create an augmented query, which is transformed into an embedding vector by LLM-Embedder. It generates concurrently embedding vectors for each gloss in the underlying set of glosses. Next, HL computes the cosine similarity between the embedding vector of the augmented query and the embedding vector of each gloss in the gloss set. The gloss with the highest similarity score is deemed the best hypernym gloss for the input gloss g. HL outputs the synset of this gloss.

4.8 Hypernym-Hyponym Updater (HHU)

After a new synset $S_{l,g}$ is inserted into WordNet-N, if an original synset $S_{l',g'}$ becomes a sibling of $S_{l,g}$, and both glosses g and g' share a common lemma, yet $S_{l,g}$ did not select $S_{l',g'}$ as its hypernym, then it would mean that $S_{l,g}$ should become the direct hypernym of $S_{l',g'}$. This situation can be illustrated using the following example:

Suppose that the following new lemma l with the gloss g is added to WordNet, with 'platform' identified as its direct hypernym, where

> $l =$ 'social media platform'.
>
> $g =$ 'an online digital space that allows individuals and groups to connect, interact, and share content with each other. These platforms enable users to create profiles, share text, photos, videos, and other multimedia forms, and partake in various communication and networking modes'.

Now, assume that prior to this insertion, the lemma $l' =$ 'TikTok' with the gloss $g' =$ 'a social media platform that allows users to create, share, and discover short-form videos' was already inserted, and 'platform' was identified as its direct hypernym. Now $S_{l',g'}$ becomes a sibling of $S_{l,g}$. Since g and g' share the same lemma 'platform', the fact that $S_{l,g}$ did not select $S_{l',g'}$ as its hypernym implies that $S_{l,g}$ (for 'social media platform') is a more specific hypernym of $S_{l',g'}$ (for 'TikTok'). Hence, it is necessary to perform this update to ensure that the hypernym-hyponym relationships are properly restored, maintaining consistency in the semantic network (see Fig. 3).

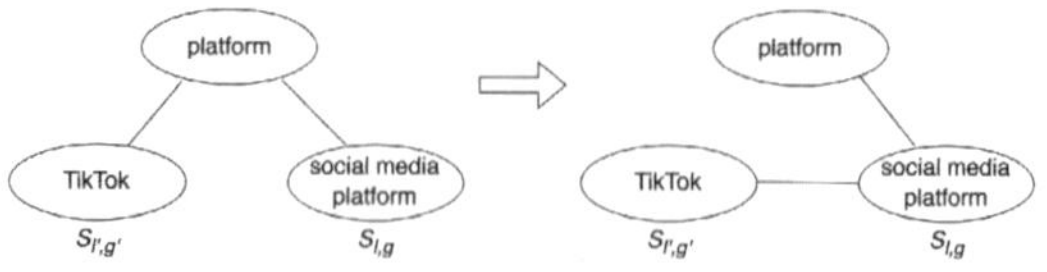

Figure 3: An illustration of updating hypernyms

HHU rectifies the hypernym-hyponym associations as follows: After a new synset $S_{l,g}$ is inserted, check for each sibling synset $S_{l',g'}$ whether g and g share a common lemma. If yes, then set $S_{l,g}$ to be the direct hypernym of $S_{l',g'}$. Otherwise, no changes are made.

5 Evaluations

AI-WordNet takes about 3 seconds in the worst case to insert a new lemma into WordNet with a given gloss on a machine equipped with an A6000 GPU and an i9 CPU. We evaluate the accuracy of AI-WordNet through both intrinsic and extrinsic evaluations.

5.1 Intrinsic Evaluations

Intrinsic evaluations use the standard metric of **F1 score** to assess the performance of the classification task in predicting lexnames. For the generation task in predicting hypernyms, two metrics are used: **direct hits** on the ground truth, which measures exact matches; and **distance** from the ground truth, which accounts for how far the predicted hypernyms deviate from the correct ones.

Specifically, the metric of direct hits is the percentage of predicted hypernyms that exactly match the true hypernyms of glosses, denoted by $H(1, 1)$. The metric of distance is the length of the shortest path between the predicted hypernym and the true hypernym of the underlying gloss in the test set. Thus, a distance of 0 means a direct hit, the distance of 1 means the predicted hypernym is a hypernym of the true hypernym, and a distance of 2 means the predicted hypernym is either a sibling or the grand-hypernym of the true hypernym (see Fig. 4).

Let H-AvgD denote the average distance between the predicted hypernyms and the true hypernyms, with smaller values indicating better performance.

Table 1: Intrinsic evaluations of AI-WordNet

Lexname F1	$H(1,1)$	**H-AvgD**
0.946	0.648	1.374

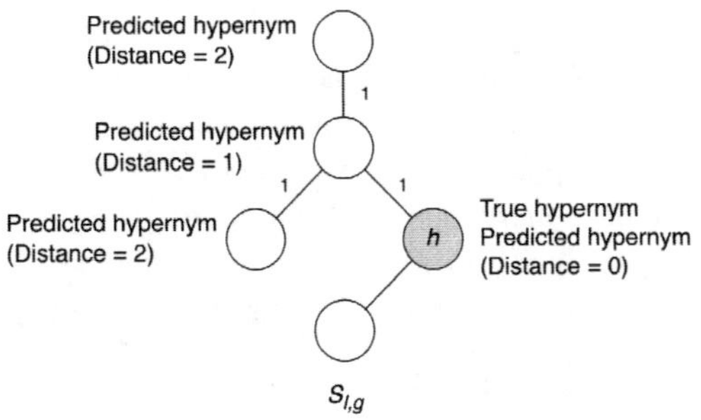

Figure 4: Distance illustration; the shaded node is the true hypernym

It can be seen from Table 1 that the low-cost implementation of AI-WordNet achieves a high F1 score on lexname predictions, and 64.5% direct hits with an average distance of 1.374, indicating that the predicted hypernyms are closely related to the corresponding true hypernyms.

5.2 Extrinsic Evaluations

Observe that the distance falls within a small range. These minor discrepancies would unlikely negatively impact the generation of reasonable distractors (Section 5.3 provides more information).

We randomly select 8,000 noun entries from Wiktionary at `https://www.wiktionary.org/` that are not included in WordNet-N, and insert them using AI-WordNet. Each entry consists of a lemma-gloss pair, where the gloss is the definition provided in Wiktionary. Instead of manually verifying whether these entries are correctly integrated into WordNet, a process that demands advanced linguistic and domain expertise beyond our scope, we assess the contextual appropriateness of the distractors generated for the new lemmas within the answer keys of the constructed cloze questions.

Specifically, we select independently at random 300 of the constructed cloze questions using the CQG system (Sun and Wang, 2023), where the stem sentences for the cloze questions are extracted from the history section of Wiktionary, which includes the corresponding lemmas.

Three human judges were recruited to evaluate the reliability and plausibility of distractors generated by CQG using the following rubric. They have all written exam questions with at least three years of teaching experience at the college level.

- **Reliability**: A distractor receives a score of 1 if placing it in the blank space of the stem results in a contextually appropriate and grammatically correct, yet logically incorrect, sentence. If it fails to meet these criteria, it receives a score of 0.
- **Plausibility**: Distractors are assessed on a 3-point scale. 0 points: The distractor is obviously wrong. 1 point: The distractor is somewhat confusing. 2 points: The distractor is highly confusing, making it difficult to determine the correct answer.

The judges were presented with the cloze questions, where each cloze question consists of a stem, the correct answer, and three distractors, together with the definition of the correct answer. Table 2 shows the evaluation results.

Table 2: Human valuations of the quality of the generated distractors

	Reliability	Plausibility
Judge 1	0.9600	1.7300
Judge 2	0.9878	1.6922
Judge 3	0.9801	1.7234
Avg	0.9760	1.7152
Stdev	0.0117	0.0164

The high average reliability score of 0.976 indicates that the vast majority of distractors are contextually appropriate and grammatically correct, yet logically incorrect in the context of the question to be true distractors. The average plausibility score of 1.7152 is closer to 2 than 1, which indicates that the distractors are sufficiently confusing, making it challenging for examinees to immediately identify the correct answer.

These results further demonstrate that AI-WordNet meets the requirements for generating high-quality distractors in the creation of cloze questions.

5.3 Predicted and True Hypernyms

If the predicted hypernym does not align with the true hypernym, the predicted hypernym may still suffice for generating distractors in cloze questions. In such cases, the primary requirement is for the distractors to create enough confusion within the same contextual space, rather than achieving perfect linguistic accuracy. Below are several examples of lemmas, synset names and the corresponding glosses extracted from PWN 3.0, accompanied by explanations that demonstrate why the predicted hypernym, despite not being perfectly accurate, still leads to effective distractor generation.

(1) For the synset 'diabetes.n.01' with the gloss 'a polygenic disease characterized by abnormally high glucose levels in the blood; any of several

metabolic disorders marked by excessive urination and persistent thirst', the true hypernym is 'polygenic_disorder.n.01'. AI-WordNet generates 'metabolic_disorder.n.01' as its hypernym synset, which aligns with the characteristic of diabetes as a metabolic disease. Thus, it is deemed adequate for generating distractors.

(2) For the synset 'seven_seas.n.01' and the gloss 'an informal expression for all of the oceans of the world', the true hypernym is 'body_of_water.n.01'. AI-WordNet generates 'ocean.n.01' as its hypernym synset, which is deemed adequate for generating distractors, although it should logically be considered a hyponym rather than a hypernym.

(3) For the synset 'cold_turkey.n.01' and the gloss 'a blunt expression of views'[2], the true hypernym is 'expression.n.03'. AI-WordNet generates 'opinion.n.01' as its hypernym synset, correlating to the expression of views to some extent and so is deemed adequate for generating distractors, although it doesn't capture the full essence of the term.

(4) For the synset 'south_pacific.n.01' and the gloss 'that part of the Pacific Ocean to the south of the equator', the true hypernym is 'part.n.03'. AI-WordNet generates 'pacific.n.01' as its hypernym synset, correctly recognizing the part-whole geographic relationship, and so is deemed adequate for generating distractors.

(5) For the synset 'company.n.09' and the gloss 'a unit of firefighters including their equipment', the true hypernym is 'unit.n.03'. AI-WordNet generates 'fire_department.n.01' as its hypernym synset, which is contextually relevant in the firefighting context. Thus, it is deemed adequate for generating distractors, even though it fails to convey the concept of 'company.n.09' as a unit.

These examples demonstrate why using AI-WordNet in generating distractors achieves high reliability and plausibility, even though AI-WordNet only achieves 64.8% exact match of the hypernyms in PWN 3.0.

On the other hand, the current implementation of AI-WordNet may generate hypernyms for certain short glosses that are not contextually appropriate. For example, for the synset 'pipa.n.01' with gloss 'type genus of the Pipidae', AI-WordNet outputs 'bird_genus.n.01' as its hypernym, which is entirely incorrect. This issue likely arises due to the brevity of the gloss, where the only available information is the term 'Pipidae' without further description. As a result, the underlying models fail to fully grasp the meaning. Such issues can be mitigated by enhancing the knowledge base of the underlying models.

5.4 Hypernym Extraction vs. Generation

As mentioned in Section 4.5, over 80% of glosses in WordNet-N contain inherited hypernyms. Exploring how to directly identify and extract these hypernyms from the glosses faces the following challenges: (1) Distinguishing between glosses that contain inherited hypernyms and those that do not is challenging. Glosses may not explicitly mention their hypernyms, making it hard to categorize them accurately. (2) Even if we can determine that a gloss contains an inherited hypernym, extracting it is not straightforward. Glosses are often abstract or formulated in a way that doesn't explicitly convey the hypernym. For instance, the gloss for the synset 'idleness.n.01' is 'having no employment', but its hypernym synset is 'inactivity.n.03'. Extractive methods might mistakenly identify 'employment' or 'no employment' as the hypernym, which is incorrect.

Overcoming these challenges requires more sophisticated approaches, potentially combining extractive techniques with deeper semantic analysis to capture the correct hypernyms.

We note that certain hypernyms predicted by AI-WordNet, which do not align with the ground-truth hypernyms, could potentially be resolved more effectively through extractive methods. For example, for the synset 'adenopathy.n.01', its gloss is 'a glandular disease or enlargement of glandular tissue', and its true hypernym is 'glandular disease', which is explicitly mentioned in the gloss. AI-WordNet, however, predicts 'pathology.n.01' as its hypernym synset, which, although contextually acceptable for generating distractors, is not as accurate as an extractive approach.

This observation suggests that integrating both generative and extractive methods may offer substantial improvements in hypernym prediction, warranting further investigation.

6 Conclusions and Final Remarks

AI-WordNet represents our initial effort to expand existing lexical datasets based solely on glosses,

[2]This lemma has another synset 'cold_turkey.n.02' in PWN 3.0 with gloss 'complete and abrupt withdrawal of all addictive drugs or anything else on which you have become dependent'.

aiming to address the specific requirements of generating controllable and explainable distractors for cloze questions. This approach is particularly useful in today's rapidly evolving lexicon, where new lexemes frequently emerge. We demonstrated the utility of AI-WordNet in generating high-quality distractors for cloze question generation from a given text.

Similarly, AI-WordNet can be applied to create controllable and explainable distractors for various types of multiple-choice questions within the framework of AI-oracle machines. AI-oracle machines use a combination of PLMs as oracles and conventional algorithms to perform complex tasks by breaking them into manageable subtasks, guiding query formulation, and ensuring alignment with predefined requirements (Wang, 2024). By integrating AI-WordNet into this framework, it becomes possible to generate distractors that are not only contextually relevant but also transparent in their derivation, thereby enhancing the quality and reliability of multiple-choice assessments.

Moreover, AI-WordNet can be used to create a specialized WordNet from scratch for lemmas in a specific domain, such as a particular area of medicine or a new field in the sciences, as long as they are in the same language as the models trained on the existing WordNet and their glosses are available. Whether expanding an existing WordNet or creating a new one from scratch, AI-WordNet can be used to provide an initial version for domain experts to refine and build upon.

For an under-resourced language lacking an extensive WordNet, such as PWN 3.0 for English, AI-WordNet can be employed to construct a version of WordNet within the framework of transfer learning, based on the premise that all human languages share a common root set of synsets, as represented in PWN 3.0. This can be achieved by identifying a moderate number of critical synsets unique to the language, along with their lexical names and hypernym-hyponym relations, and using this information to fine-tune models initially trained on PWN 3.0. Note that this gloss-based approach can be used to create a parallel language with a different vocabulary, which might be useful for generating a secret code to transmit messages, similar to the Code Talker project undertaken by the US military during WWII, which used the Navajo language spoken by Native American tribes for secure communications.

To improve the direct-hit ratio of the predicted hypernyms, we may explore the combination of generative and extractive methods, enhance the underlying PLMs and devise new gloss-sense discerning techniques that go beyond traditional word-sense disambiguation methods.

As a closing remark, we experimented with replacing the underlying PLMs with GPT-3.5-Turbo, out-of-the-box and fine-tuned. Unfortunately, we find that this approach performs significantly worse on our tasks compared to specialized smaller models. This finding demonstrates that for certain tasks, properly fine-tuned smaller models can deliver better performance while being more cost-effective.

Acknowledgment. This work was supported in part by Librum Technologies, Inc.

References

Edoardo Barba, Tommaso Pasini, and Roberto Navigli. 2021. ESC: Redesigning WSD with extractive sense comprehension. In *Proceedings of the 2021 Conference of the North American Chapter of the Association for Computational Linguistics: Human Language Technologies*, pages 4661–4672, Online. Association for Computational Linguistics.

Ning Ding, Shengding Hu, Weilin Zhao, Yulin Chen, Zhiyuan Liu, Hai-Tao Zheng, and Maosong Sun. 2021. Openprompt: An open-source framework for prompt-learning. *Preprint*, arXiv:2111.01998.

Roberto Navigli and Simone Paolo Ponzetto. 2012. Babelnet: The automatic construction, evaluation and application of a wide-coverage multilingual semantic network. *Artificial Intelligence*, 193:217–250.

Robyn Speer, Joshua Chin, and Catherine Havasi. 2016. Conceptnet 5.5: An open multilingual graph of general knowledge. *CoRR*, abs/1612.03975.

Yicheng Sun and Jie Wang. 2023. Generate cloze questions generatively. In *Proceedings of the International Joint Conference on Neural Networks (IJCNN 2023)*. IEEE and the International Neural Network Society.

Koeva Svetla. 2021. Towards expanding WordNet with conceptual frames. In *Proceedings of the 11th Global Wordnet Conference*, pages 182–191, University of South Africa (UNISA). Global Wordnet Association.

Jie Wang. 2024. AI-oracle machines for intelligent computing. *Preprint*, arXiv:2406.12213.

Peitian Zhang, Shitao Xiao, Zheng Liu, Zhicheng Dou, and Jian-Yun Nie. 2023. Retrieve anything to augment large language models. *Preprint*, arXiv:2310.07554.

SHACL4GW: SHACL Shapes for the Global Wordnet Association RDF Schema

Anas Fahad Khan
Istituto di Linguistica Computazionale
Consiglio Nazionale delle Ricerche
Pisa, Italy
fahad.khan@ilc.cnr.it

John P. McCrae
Insight Centre and ADAPT Centre
University of Galway
Galway, Ireland
john@mccr.ae

Abstract

In this article, we introduce SHACL Shapes for Global Wordnet RDF (SHACL4GW), a new resource which uses the Semantic Web SHACL standard for the validation of RDF files using the Global Wordnet Association RDF format. We begin by giving a motivation for the creation of such a resource, continue by describing the resource itself and end with our plans for future work.

1 Introduction

In the current article, we introduce a new resource for the validation of RDF wordnets produced using the Global Wordnet Association (GWA) RDF format; as we will see this resource, **SHACL Shapes for Global Wordnet RDF** (SHACL4GW), follows the well-known SHACL standard (Knublauch and Kontokostas, 2017) for validating RDF graphs. In what follows, we begin by introducing the Global Wordnet formats, this will give us a broad overall context for the current work; next, we will give an outline of the SHACL standard and describe why it is so useful, both in general and in the particular case of the GWA RDF format. We will also see how it relates to and complements the existing RDF schema for wordnets that has been made available by the Global Wordnet Association.

2 Global WordNet Formats

The Global Wordnet formats were proposed by the Global Wordnet Assocation (Vossen et al., 2016) and further extended by McCrae et al. (2021) in order to provide a common format for the inclusion of wordnets in the Collaborative Interlingual Index (Bond et al., 2016, CILI). The format supports three-plus serialization formats with the primary format being XML, based on the Kyoto-LMF model (Soria et al., 2009). In addition, the formats support serialization in JSON (with a JSON-LD schema) and an RDF data model that can be serialized in any RDF serialization format, including Turtle (Carothers and Prud'hommeaux, 2014). Note that, in the rest of the paper, we will refer to the serialization in RDF as GWA RDF (and the primary Kyoto-LMF format as GWA LMF). As with LMF and OntoLex-Lemon (Cimiano et al., 2016; McCrae et al., 2011), the main elements of the RDF data model are the *lexical entry* and the *synset* (equivalent to the lexical concept in OntoLex-Lemon). The model fully supports the relations used in Princeton WordNet (Miller, 1995; Fellbaum, 2010)as well as relations introduced by later projects such as EuroWordNet (Vossen, 2004). In addition, extra features such as pronunciation information used by resources such as Open English WordNet (McCrae et al., 2019) are also supported.

The following is a simple example of an XML entry in the GWA LMF format.

```
<LexicalEntry id="example-w1">
  <Lemma writtenForm="grandfather"
         partOfSpeech="n"/>
  <Sense id="example-sense1"
         synset="example-synset1"/>
</LexicalEntry>
...
<Synset id="example-synset1" ili="i90287"
        partOfSpeech="n"
        members="example-w1">
  <Definition>
    the father of your father or mother
  </Definition>
  <SynsetRelation relType="hypernym"
                  target="example-synset2"/>
</Synset>
```

Listing 1: Part of Speech Information

This describes a single entry, 'grandfather' which is linked to a synset with an associated definition. The members of the synset are given allowing their order to be specified. In addition, an ILI identifier is given to allow this resource to be included in the CILI (Bond et al., 2016). The synset is described with a definition and a hypernym link to another synset.

3 The Shapes Constraint Language

The **Shapes Constraint Language (SHACL)** is a W3C standard which provides a standard way of validating RDF graphs with respect to user-defined sets of constraints; such constraints, in SHACL parlance, are known as *shapes*. Thanks to its usability and flexibility SHACL has become an important component of the Semantic Web stack, complementing other well-known Semantic Web technologies such as RDF, RDFS and OWL. In this regard, it is worth noting that, in contrast with OWL and its adoption of the open world assumption, SHACL makes it simple to impose closed world constraints on RDF data – something which is often vital for the purposes of data validation. SHACL also allows for the generation of informative reports in the course of the validation of a graph which highlight and describe the violations of constraints and can also grade violations according to their seriousness (as determined by users themselves). The use of SHACL facilitates an extra level of integration and interoperability of RDF datasets in addition to that offered by other RDF technologies, standards and best practices – along with (not unrelatedly) helping to ensure a high level of data quality of RDF data. Moreover, as well as being very expressive, SHACL shapes are also reasonably simple to create, at least for those familiar with RDF syntax, thanks to the fact that they are defined using RDF triples.

The current work is novel for introducing the use of SHACL shapes in a linguistic linked data context. Although SHACL has been widely used for semantic data validation in other domains, with numerous online tutorials and tools available for working with the language[1], there are few (publicly available) resources that show the use (and usefulness) of SHACL in the context of linguistic linked data. The GWA RDF format presents an excellent case study for demonstrating the utility of SHACL for validating RDF language resources. This additional means of validating RDF wordnets provides an extra, much needed level of interoperability to such resources – over and above that offered by the OntoLex-Lemon ontology (on which the GWA RDF format is based) and the wordnet-specific RDF vocabulary wn made available by the Global Wordnet Association[2] – and thus helps to contribute to the growth of the Global Wordnet Grid[3]. Up until now only the DTD schema[4], made available by the GWA, has offered this functionality and only for the GWA LMF XML format; the use of SHACL shapes for GWA RDF will allow for the direct validation of RDF files (that is, without the need to first convert RDF graphs to the LMF XML format). Moreover, it does this by using standard Semantic Web technologies in a way that is easily shareable and can be easily built upon in the case of extensions to the GWA schema. The idea of the present work is both to argue for the *use* of SHACL shapes for validating GWA RDF graphs, as well to propose *a specific set of* SHACL shapes, which we describe below and which can be downloaded at the following link: `https://github.com/anasfkhan81/SHACL4GW`.

4 Creating SHACL shapes for GWA RDF

4.1 SHACL4GW

In the rest of this article, we will describe the SHACL "Shapes Graph" which we have developed for GWA RDF and which we refer to as SHACL4GW; this graph is available at `https://github.com/anasfkhan81/SHACL4GW`. It can be used to validate individual GWA RDF files via the excellent SHACL playground site[5]. In particular, we will explain some of the thinking behind the design decisions we have taken.

It is important to emphasise that the work we present here (SHACL4GW) is intended as a proposal to be shared and discussed with the wider wordnet community[6] with a view to gathering feedback and, if needed, modifying our proposal in collaboration with others. In a number of cases, we have left things open since we were not aware of there being a settled best practice for how to represent such cases in RDF (this is most notably the case with *LexicalResource*, see below), with the intention once again to open a discussion with the wider community as to what the best approach might be.

We began the process of putting together our

[1]SHACL is also the subject of a forthcoming book by Veronika Heimsbakk `https://veronahe.wordpress.com/shacl-for-the-practitioner/`

[2]`https://globalwordnet.github.io/schemas/wn#`

[3]`http://globalwordnet.org/resources/global-wordnet-grid/`

[4]`https://globalwordnet.github.io/schemas/WN-LMF-1.3.dtd`

[5]`https://shacl-playground.zazuko.com/`

[6]The Global Wordnet Conference is obviously an excellent venue for this.

SHACL graph by analysing the original DTD file for the GWA LMF format. Several of the declarations in the DTD could, it turned out, be easily converted into SHACL shapes using classes and properties from the wn vocabulary and the OntoLex vocabulary on which it is based. In other cases the conversion wasn't so straightforward, as we shall see. In general, the DTD was our primary guide to which elements should be obligatory and which to make optional. Our priority throughout was to maintain interoperability between formats, and indeed to make it even simpler to convert, and to 'roundtrip', between the different GWA formats (LMF XML, JSON, and RDF). In addition, we also sought to emphasise interoperability between wordnets in RDF without making the constraints overly restrictive.

4.2 Methodology

One fairly indicative example of the kinds of decisions we had to make in drafting our SHACL graph is given by cases in which we associate language metadata with individual URI resources. This is required (obligatory) in the case of the *Lexicon*, but implied (non-obligatory) in the case of *Definition*. Here we decided to limit the user to the choice of two linked data properties the `dc:language` property or the OntoLex lime metadata module property `lime:language` using the SHACL `sh:or` logical constraint. This choice allows a certain level of flexibility, since the DC property is very frequently used in general, but the *lime* property is commonly used in the context of OntoLex; at the same time this limitation helps to make GWA RDF graphs much more interoperable than otherwise.

```
sh:or  ([
       sh:name "Language" ;
       sh:description "Ensure there is one 
            single language assigned to the 
            Wordnet , via DC:language" ;
       sh:path dc:language ;
       sh:minCount 1 ;
       sh:maxCount 1 ;
       sh:nodeKind sh:IRIOrLiteral ;]
    [  sh:name "Language" ;
       sh:description "Ensure there is one 
            single language assigned to the 
            Wordnet , via lime:language" ;
       sh:path lime:language ;
       sh:minCount 1 ;
       sh:maxCount 1 ;
       sh:nodeKind sh:Literal ;])
```

Listing 2: Use of logical sh:or constraint.

We now look at some of the main classes covered in SHACL4GW. In this first version of our graph, we decided not to create constraints corresponding to the *LexicalResource* declaration in the original DTD since there isn't a standard way of representing a Lexical Resource defined container for one or more lexicons in OntoLex[7]. A number of elements in the original DTD have the same set of Dublin Core metadata elements as potential attributes. Instead of adding these to individual shapes, we created a `MetadataElementShape` which is associated with individual classes via the property `sh:TargetClass`.

Lexicon

When it came to creating shapes for the Lexicon class, there were no major surprises (except possibly for the addition of a `sh:or` clause for language information as mentioned above) and the conversion from the DTD was fairly straightforward. We defined a `sh:NodeShape` called `LexiconShape` with target class `lime:Lexicon`, in addition to creating property shapes using the following properties and classes to add relevant constraints regarding label, email, license, version, URL, citation, status, note and confidence information: `rdfs:label`, `schema:email`, `cc:license`, `owl:versionInfo`, `wn:status`, `wn:note`, `wn:confidenceScore` respectively.

Lexical Entry

The creation of the shape corresponding to *LexicalEntry*, `LexicalEntryShape`, was, once again, fairly straightforward. We associate each *LexicalEntry* with exactly one lemma by making use of `ontolex:canonicalForm` and targeting the `FormShape` node (described elsewhere in the file) in order to ensure that this has the correct shape. Similarly, we make sure that senses have the correct shape via another property shape with path `ontolex:sense` and which targets the `SenseShape` node (which again is described elsewhere in the file). Part-of-speech information (obligatory for *LexicalEntry* elements) is described by the following shape:

```
sh:property [
sh:name "Part of Speech" ;
    sh:path wn:partOfSpeech   ;
    sh:minCount 1 ;
    sh:maxCount 1 ;
sh:in (wn:noun wn:verb wn:adjective wn:adverb
      wn:adjective_satellite wn:named_entity
wn:conjunction wn:adposition wn:other_pos wn:
    unknown_pos ) ;
]
```

Listing 3: Part of Speech Information

[7] One possible candidate for a class corresponding to LexicalResource could be the Data Catalog Vocabulary class *dataset*. However, it may also be that there is no need to explicitly cover this in our SHACL graph.

Note how SHACL allows us to guarantee that each Lexical Entry has exactly one part of speech as well as specifying what values this can have. Although we can encode similar information as axioms in OWL, it is complicated to use such axioms for the purposes of validation because of the Open World Assumption.

Senses and Sense Relations

For the *Sense* element, we were able to formulate SHACL constraints that corresponded fairly closely to almost all of the declarations in the DTD, aside, that is, from those referring to the lexicalized status of a *Sense* element and adjposition information (adjectival position); we couldn't find elements in standard pre-existing RDF vocabularies corresponding to these declarations[8]. For the rest, we were able to make use of OntoLex and `wn` vocabularies to determine our shapes. In order to ensure that *SenseRelations* belonged to the list found in the `wn` vocabulary we used the `sh:in` property as follows:

```
sh:targetClass vartrans:SenseRelation ;
sh:property [
sh:name "Category" ;
sh:description "Make␣sure␣the␣Sense␣Relation␣
    belongs␣to␣the␣correct␣category" ;
    sh:path vartrans:category ;
    sh:minCount 1 ;
    sh:maxCount 1 ;
    sh:in (wn:antonym wn:also wn:participle
        wn:pertainym wn:derivation wn:
        domain_topic wn:has_domain_topic wn:
        domain_region wn:has_domain_region
        wn:exemplifies wn:is_exemplified_by
        wn:similar wn:other wn:
        simple_aspect_ip wn:
        secondary_aspect_ip wn:
        simple_aspect_pi wn:
        secondary_aspect_pi wn:feminine wn:
        has_feminine wn:masculine wn:
        has_masculine wn:young wn:has_young
        wn:diminutive wn:has_diminutive wn:
        augmentative wn:has_augmentative wn:
        anto_gradable wn:anto_simple wn:
        anto_converse)];
```

Listing 4: Part of Speech Information

Synsets and Synset Relations

Finally, in this brief summary, we will look at the constraints which we have defined for senses and synsets, the latter of which, it should be noted, are encoded in GWA RDF using the OntoLex class `LexicalConcept`. As for senses, we were able to capture all of the constraints found in the DTD declarations apart from those pertaining to the so called 'lex file', since we were unable to find relevant pre-existing vocabularies to encode this in RDF. With regards to the relationships between synsets, encoded in the GWA LMF format as *SynsetRelations*, we define a `ConceptualRelationShape` which allows us to restrict the relationships between synsets to those proposed by the GWA.

```
ex:ConceptualRelationShape a sh:NodeShape ;
sh:targetClass vartrans:ConceptualRelation ;
sh:property [
sh:name "Category" ;
sh:description "Make␣sure␣the␣Synset␣Relation␣
    belongs␣to␣the␣correct␣category" ;
    sh:path vartrans:category ;
    sh:minCount 1 ;
    sh:maxCount 1 ;
    sh:in (wn:agent wn:also wn:attribute wn:
        be_in_state wn:causes wn:
        classified_by wn:classifies wn:
        co_agent_instrument wn:
        co_agent_patient wn:co_agent_result
        wn:co_instrument_agent wn:
        co_instrument_patient wn:
        co_instrument_result wn:
        co_patient_agent wn:
        co_patient_instrument wn:
        co_result_agent wn:
        co_result_instrument wn:co_role wn:
        direction...  wn:ir_synonym wn:
        similar)];
```

Listing 5: Part of Speech Information

5 Summary and Conclusions

In this paper, we have discussed the creation of a SHACL shapes graph for the GWA RDF format. We have motivated the need for such a resource and detailed our first (and fairly comprehensive) attempt at such a graph. In summary, we have covered the following classes mentioned in the original LMF DTD:

- *Lexicon, Lexical Entry, Form, Pronunciation, Tag, Definition, ILI Definition, Example, Sense, Synset, Sense Relation, Synset Relation*

In addition we have partially covered *SyntacticBehaviour*. The following classes that are present in the original LMF are not explicitly covered as we were not aware of a settled best practice for representing this information in RDF using the OntoLex vocabulary and, moreover, this information is not common in wordnet resources:

- *Lexicon Extension, Requires, Extends, External Lexical Entry, External Lemma, External Form, External Sense, External Synset*

In the case of the External prefixed elements (e.g. External Lexical Entry), it may turn out that given the linking mechanism in RDF there is no need to define specific shapes here. In any case we have managed to to cover all of the commonly used parts of the schema used by the Global Wordnet Association.

[8]Note that in Ontolex, senses lexicalize concepts rather than being lexicalized themselves.

Acknowledgements

John P. McCrae is supported by Research Ireland under Grant Number SFI/12/RC/2289_P2 Insight_2, Insight SFI Centre for Data Analytics and Grant Number 13/RC/2106_P2, ADAPT SFI Research Centre.

References

Francis Bond, Piek Vossen, John McCrae, and Christiane Fellbaum. 2016. CILI: the collaborative interlingual index. In *Proceedings of the 8th Global WordNet Conference (GWC)*, pages 50–57, Bucharest, Romania. Global Wordnet Association.

Gavin Carothers and Eric Prud'hommeaux. 2014. RDF 1.1 Turtle. W3C recommendation, W3C.

Philipp Cimiano, John P. McCrae, and Paul Buitelaar. 2016. Lexicon model for ontologies: Community report. W3C community report.

Christiane Fellbaum. 2010. *WordNet*, pages 231–243. Springer Netherlands, Dordrecht.

Holger Knublauch and Dimitris Kontokostas. 2017. Shapes constraint language (SHACL). W3C recommendation, W3C.

John McCrae, Dennis Spohr, and Philipp Cimiano. 2011. Linking lexical resources and ontologies on the semantic web with lemon. In *Proc. of the 8th Extended Semantic Web Conference*, pages 245–249.

John P. McCrae, Michael Wayne Goodman, Francis Bond, Alexandre Rademaker, Ewa Rudnicka, and Luis Morgado Da Costa. 2021. The GlobalWordNet formats: Updates for 2020. In *Proceedings of the 11th Global Wordnet Conference*, pages 91–99, University of South Africa (UNISA). Global Wordnet Association.

John P. McCrae, Alexandre Rademaker, Francis Bond, Ewa Rudnicka, and Christiane Fellbaum. 2019. English WordNet 2019 – an open-source WordNet for English. In *Proceedings of the 10th Global Wordnet Conference*, pages 245–252, Wroclaw, Poland. Global Wordnet Association.

George A. Miller. 1995. Wordnet: a lexical database for english. *Commun. ACM*, 38(11):39–41.

Claudia Soria, Monica Monachini, and Piek Vossen. 2009. Wordnet-LMF: fleshing out a standardized format for wordnet interoperability. In *Proceedings of the 2009 International Workshop on Intercultural Collaboration*, pages 139–146.

Piek Vossen. 2004. EuroWordNet: a multilingual database of autonomous and language-specific wordnets connected via an inter-lingualindex. *International Journal of Lexicography*, 17(2):161–173.

Piek Vossen, Francis Bond, and John McCrae. 2016. Toward a truly multilingual GlobalWordnet grid. In *Proceedings of the 8th Global WordNet Conference (GWC)*, pages 424–431, Bucharest, Romania. Global Wordnet Association.

Wordnet and Word Ladders: Climbing the abstraction taxonomy with LLMs

Giovanni Puccetti[1], Andrea Esuli[1], Marianna Bolognesi[2]

[1]Istituto di Scienza e Tecnologie dell'Informazione "A. Faedo"
[2]ABSTRACTION Research Group – Università di Bologna,
Correspondence: giovanni.puccetti@isti.cnr.it

Abstract

WordNet has long served as a benchmark for approximating the mechanisms of semantic categorization in the human mind, particularly through its hierarchical structure of word synsets, most notably the IS-A relation. However, these semantic relations have traditionally been curated manually by expert lexicographers, relying on external resources like dictionaries and corpora. In this paper, we explore whether large language models (LLMs) can be leveraged to approximate these hierarchical semantic relations, potentially offering a scalable and more dynamic alternative for maintaining and updating the WordNet taxonomy.

This investigation addresses the feasibility and implications of automating this process with LLMs by testing a set of prompts encoding different sociodemographic traits and finds that adding age and job information to the prompt affects the model ability to generate text in agreement with hierarchical semantic relations while gender does not have a statistically significant impact.

Token: *parallelogram*
Abstraction Ladder: thing, object, shape, polygon, quadrilateral, *parallelogram*, rectangle, rhombus, square

(a) **Parallelogram**

Token: *creationism*
Abstraction Ladder: idea, theory, belief, philosophy, worldview, *creationism*, theism, monotheism, biblical, fundamentalist, young-earth

(b) **Creationism**

Figure 1: Examples of LLM-generated ladders for a concrete concept (a): **parallelogram** and an abstract one (b): **creationism**.

1 Introduction

The advent of large language models (LLMs) has revolutionized the landscape of Natural Language Processing (NLP), providing new avenues for exploring linguistic structures and semantic relations. One area of interest is the hierarchical organization of word meanings, captured by the semantic relation IS-A represented in WordNet. This paper aims to investigate the capacity of LLMs to understand this semantic relation by inspecting their ability to construct word *ladders* based on it. A word ladder is a sequence of words ordered by hypernym/hyponym relation, that include an initial given word and that go from a more generic term to a more specific one, as shown in Figure 1. In this perspective, word ladders represent the "branches" of WordNet, spanning from highly specific words (e.g., "chihuahua") to highly general ones (e.g., "living creature"). By analyzing how LLMs construct these hierarchies of hypernyms/hyponyms, we explore mechanisms that govern conceptual categorization and sense-making processes for different types of words, namely: concrete and abstract ones. Additionally, we will explore the sensitivity of the word ladders produced by LLMs to sociolinguistic factors, manipulating the sociodemographic "profile" that the LLM is prompted to play.

Our study explores the following key questions:

1. What type of categorizations do LLMs rely upon, when generating word ladders?

2. Can they organize hypernym/hyponym semantic relations for concrete as well as for abstract concepts?

3. Can LLMs approximate different types of

Category	Variants
job	linguist, researcher, teacher, poet, writer
age	8, 12, 15, 18, 22, 25, 30, 40, 50, 70
gender	not specified, male, female

Table 1: Sociodemographic variants encoded in different system prompts.

speakers, hence generating different types of word ladders? What type of speaker better approximates the categorizations encoded in WordNet?

Overall, through this analysis, we aim to contribute to a deeper understanding of the interaction between linguistic structures and model behavior, shedding light on the implications for both NLP applications and theories of human cognition.

2 Theoretical Background

Word taxonomies, such as WordNet (Miller, 1995), provide a structured representation of the paradigmatic relationships between words, labelling semantic relations like hypernymy (generalization) and hyponymy (specialization). These relations in turn shed light on the conceptual mechanisms of conceptual categorization, a core property of human cognition (Murphy, 2024), which is facilitated by language (Rissman and Lupyan, 2023). The construction of word ladders, which depict the progression from general to more specific terms, as shown in Figure 1, is a valuable task for assessing the semantic (paradigmatic) competence of large language models (LLMs). This approach allows us to evaluate their ability to abstract and generalize across different levels of word meaning.

As a matter of fact, LLMs in recent years have demonstrated remarkable abilities in natural language generation, based on these models' incredible accuracy in predicting and adjusting predictions on upcoming words in context, therefore on a syntagmatic level. Their architecture enables them to produce contextually appropriate responses in various domains (Brown et al., 2020), nevertheless crucial differences with human performance persist. Recent studies have specifically focused on the ability of LLMs to perform semantic categorizations and abstractions. For instance, (Samadarshi et al., 2024) examined the performance of state-of-the-art large language models (LLMs) against expert and novice human players in the New York Times Connections word game, a game in which players have to group words together to form semantically coherent ad-hoc categories. The authors found that even the top model, GPT-4o, can only fully solve 8% of the games. The results show that human players, especially experts, significantly outperform even the most advanced LLMs in tasks involving categorization and abstraction, which rely on paradigmatic relationships in the lexicon. In other words, while LLMs can typically generate coherent and cohesive text by inserting plausible words within syntagmatic contexts, their grasp of deeper paradigmatic, semantic relationships often falls short of aligning with established linguistic frameworks (Radford et al., 2019). In another recent example, Arora et al. (2023) highlight the limitations of LLMs in recognizing nuanced semantic distinctions, indicating that while these models can engage in categorization, their performance varies depending on the complexity of the task and the dataset used. To mitigate these limitations, Moskvoretskii et al. (2024) show that LLMs' understanding of semantic relations benefits from training on WordNet-like data.

ladder	Specificity	Position
thing	1.25	1
object	0.5	2
shape	1.25	3
polygon	1.5	4
quadrilateral	1.75	5
parallelogram	2.0	6
rectangle	2.25	7
rhombus	2.25	8
rhomboid	2.2	9
	Quality	0.89

Table 2: Example ladder with specificity scores calculated for each word. The Quality is measured as the Pearson correlation coefficient between the specificity and the position columns.

While several works stress that the difference with humans is significant, there are clues that, through training on in-domain data, LLMs can understand taxonomy-like relations (Moskvoretskii et al., 2024).

Constructing word ladders of hypernyms and hyponyms presents distinct challenges when dealing with concrete versus abstract concepts. Concrete concepts, such as "banana," generally exhibit

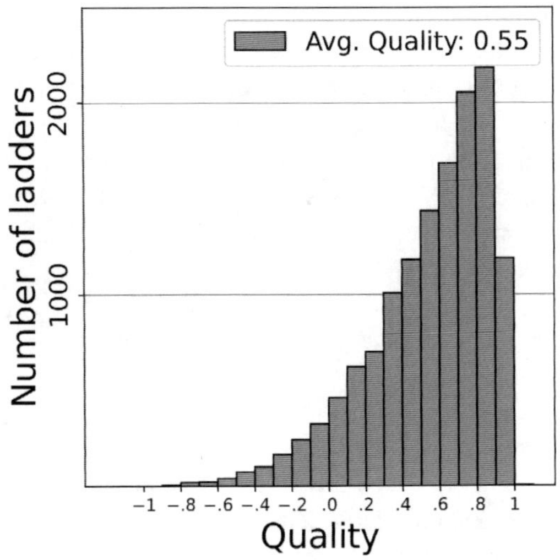

Figure 2: Distribution of the ladders' Quality for the *expert linguist prompt.*

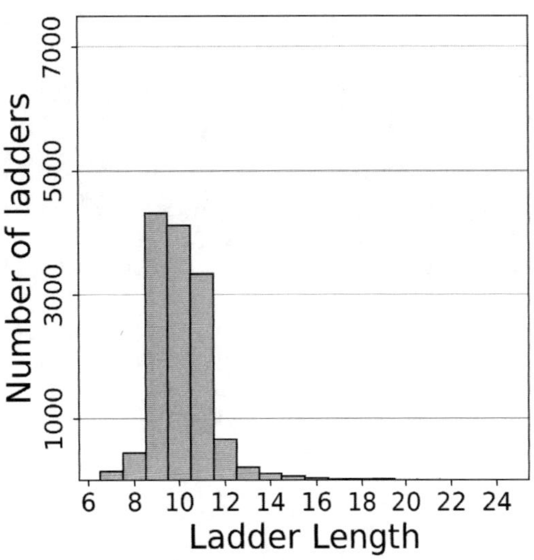

Figure 3: Distribution of the ladders' length for the *expert linguist prompt.*

clearer hierarchical relationships (Murphy, 2004; Mervis and Rosch, 1981), especially in domains like plants and animals, which are often structured by Linnaean taxonomies. For example, a "banana" is readily classified as a "fruit," which belongs to the broader category of "plant," and ultimately "living organism". In contrast, abstract concepts, like "belief", are more difficult to categorize due to their less tangible nature and variability in interpretation across contexts (Borghi et al., 2017b). Abstract concepts often involve multifaceted meanings that depend on cultural, social, and cognitive factors, making it harder to construct clear hierarchical relationships (Barsalou, 2008). This complexity can lead to ambiguity in determining appropriate hypernyms or identifying precise subcategories, as the boundaries between abstract concepts are more fluid than for concrete entities (Borghi et al., 2017a).

Finally, from a sociolinguistic perspective, research shows that sociodemographic factors significantly influence the types of categorizations performed by speakers, when using language (Labov, 1964; Milroy and Milroy, 1992; Barbieri, 2008; Wieling et al., 2011; Holmes, 2013). In the computational domain it has been shown that including demographic information such as age and gender significantly enhances the performance of text-classification tasks across multiple languages (Hovy, 2015). Ideally, by imposing sociodemographic profiles on LLMs, we can investigate how these factors influence the construction of word ladders and the resulting semantic relationships. Furthermore, we can correlate the specificity of words extracted from the generated ladders with that from WordNet, to infer which sociodemographic profiles better approximate the IS-A semantic relations encoded in WordNet. This approach not only enhances our understanding of LLM behavior but also aids in comprehending the peculiarities and potential limitations of WordNet, which is often used as a benchmark for evaluating various tasks, assuming that its cognitive underpinnings make it a suitable comparison to approximate any type of speaker (Bolognesi et al., 2020, inter alia).

To summarize, this study aims to systematically analyze the paradigmatic, hypernym/hyponym semantic relations encoded in the word ladders generated by LLMs. We will assess the accuracy and reliability of the categorizations produced, identify common challenges faced by the models, and explore how variations in sociodemographic profiles influence the semantic output.

3 Method

To explore the ability of LLMs to generate meaningful ladders in an open and replicable manner, we focus on *Llama 3.1 405b*, a highly performing open source LLM, which competes with proprietary models such as ChatGPT in several tasks.[1] A comparative study involving different models will be reserved for future research.

[1] https://huggingface.co/open_llm_leaderboard

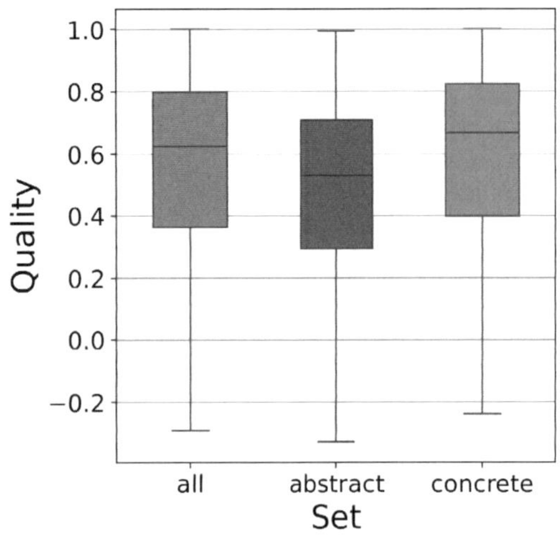

Figure 4: Boxplot of ladders Quality for the *expert linguist prompt*, comparing distribution when considering the full set (left), abstract nouns (center) and concrete nouns (right).

3.1 Ladders Generation

LLMs use two different prompts when generating text, a *system prompt* and a regular *prompt* (Dubey et al., 2024). The system prompt sets the overall behavior of the model, allowing it to adopt specific roles or tones. For instance, it might be instructed to act as "a lawyer specializing in maritime law" or "a cheerful person who frequently uses emoticons." This shapes the model's general response style but doesn't specify the particular task it should perform. The regular prompt, on the other hand, defines the specific task we want the model to execute. In our approach, we use the system prompt to simulate different sociodemographic profiles, while the regular prompt will guide the model to generate content aligned with our specific interests.

We instruct *Llama 3.1 405b* to generate ladders by using the following prompt: *Construct a list of single word concepts around the word: {word}. The bullets before the word {word} have to be increasingly more generic while those after the word {word} increasingly more specific. Make it look like one list.* In the instruction, *{word}* is replaced every time by a specific word. As the words for starting the ladder generation we use a list of 13,518 tokens, which are the items classified as nouns in the dataset of concreteness ratings collected by Brysbaert et al. (2014).

We explore two dimensions in sociodemographic profiles, age and job. We define 10 age values and 5 jobs (Table 1, see Appendix A for the complete list of all the system prompts), producing 15 system prompts: *You are a teenager of 18 years old learning in college*, *You are an expert linguist analysing the abstraction and concreteness of words.* We also generate 30 additional system prompts with an explicit specification of gender (male or female): *You are a young woman of 22 years old learning in university.* As a result we generate 13,518 × 45 = 608,310 ladders.[2]

3.2 Ladders Evaluation

We evaluate the ladders generated by LLM by calculating the Specificity of each word inserted in a ladder and correlating this measure with the order they have in the ladder. We use the measure of word specificity from Bolognesi et al. (2020). This metric is based on WordNet 3.0, which is available in the Natural Language Toolkit (NLTK, version 3.2.2) Python library (Bird et al., 2009). The measure is based on the distance of a word from the root node of the WordNet hierarchy, where the root is the most general concept, i.e., *entity*:

$$\text{Specificity}(w) = \frac{1+d}{20}$$

where d is the number of nodes between the word w and the root node, and 20 is the longest distance between the root node and a leaf in WordNet.

We define the quality of a ladder as how much the order of words in the ladder correlates with their order by Specificity measured using WordNet. Formally, if $W = \{w_i\}_{i=1}^n$ is a ladder composed of n words w_i and $X = \{x_i\}_{i=1}^n$ are their Specificity scores measured in WordNet, e.g. $x_i = \text{Specificity}(w_i)$, we define the quality of the ladder as:

$$\text{Quality}(X) = personr(X, N)$$

where $N = \{1, \dots, n\}$ are the integers between 1 and n.

This *Quality* metric goes from -1 to 1, and it assigns scores close to 1 to the ladders where the words are sorted according to the Specificity measured in WordNet, 0 to those that ordered randomly and -1 to those that have a reverse order compared to their Specificity.

Table 2 shows an example of a ladder with the Specificity scores for each word and the Quality of

[2]We release this dataset and the code used to create it in anonymized form here `https://anonymous.4open.science/r/abstract_llm-6B9A/README.md`.

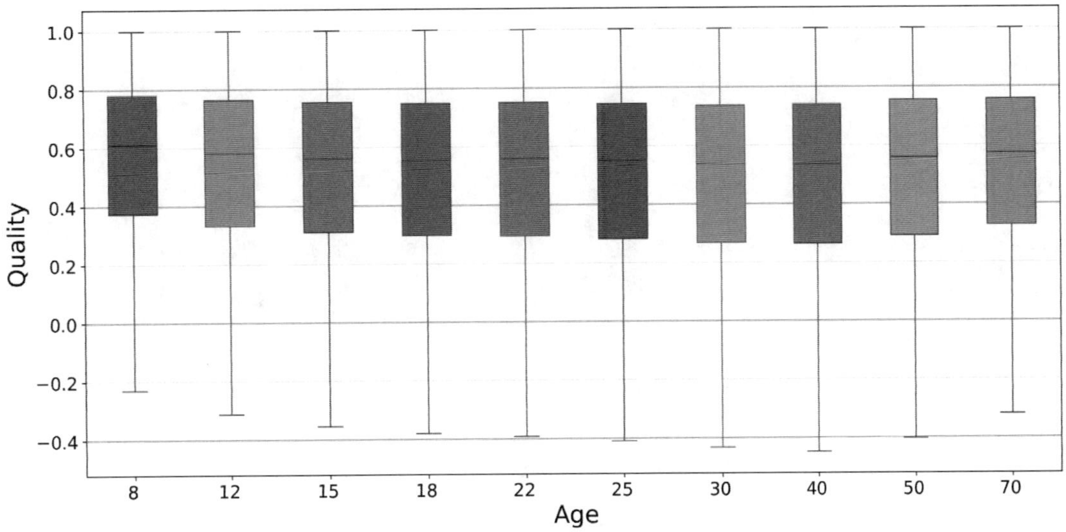

Figure 5: Boxplot of ladders Quality for all ages studied.

the ladder. In the example, the words are almost perfectly sorted and the Quality is high, however, there are two exceptions, *object*, which has a lower Specificity than *thing* and should therefore come first and *rhomboid* that has a lower Specificity than *rectangle* and *rhombus* and should therefore come before them, thus Quality is lower than 1.

4 Results

Before exploring separate sociodemographic roles, we want to understand how well the model is able to generate coherent and well ordered ladders, to do this, we initially focus on the ladders generated by the model when prompted as an expert linguist.

Figure 2 shows the distribution of Quality for all the ladders generated by the linguist prompts, there is a noticeable correlation between the Specificity of the entities in the ladder and their position, showing that they are well sorted. Notice how the average of 0.55 is relatively high in $[-1, 1]$ range, indicating a good degree of correlation. There are only a few ladders that have a negative Quality index, underlining that the model is rarely misaligned with WordNet, and therefore general commonsense.

Looking at the distribution of the lengths of the generated ladders, Figure 3 shows that the model spontaneously generates ladders mostly of length 9, 10, 11 although we don't ask for this explicitly in the prompt.[3]

[3]Indeed, the examples we provide in Figure 1 have length 9 and 11.

Abstractness and Concreteness: can the model generate ladders for both, abstract as well as concrete words? To answer this question we measure the Quality of the ladders on two subsets of the Brysbaert nouns, one containing more concrete examples and one containing more abstract ones, both built using WordNet (Bolognesi et al., 2020). Specifically, the former contains all the synsets that have the node "physical entity" as an ancestor, and the latter contains all the synsets that have the node "abstraction" as an ancestor.

Figure 4 shows the box plots for ladders Quality for the full set (green), only abstract nouns (blue), and only concrete nouns (orange). When compared to the full set of nouns, the Quality is higher for the concrete nouns, which have higher median, and lower for abstract nouns. This is coherent with human behaviour (Mervis and Rosch, 1981).

We conducted Mann-Whitney U tests to reject the null hypothesis that the medians of the concrete and abstract groups are the same. The tests returned very low p-values (of the order of 10^{-80}). This finding suggests that the difference in Quality among ladders constructed starting from abstract and concrete prompts is reflected in the LLMs. This is comparable to human behavior, where humans display more difficulties in creating taxonomic relations for abstract vs. concrete concepts.

5 A Multifaceted Perspective

WordNet was developed by a team of experts in linguistics, cognitive science, and lexicography.

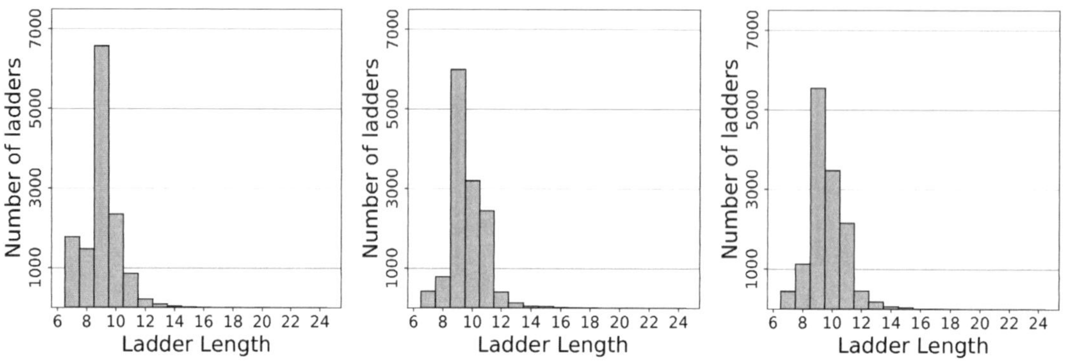

(a) Child: 8 years old. (b) Adult: 30 years old. (c) Senior: 70 years old.

Figure 6: Distribution of ladders length for all nouns, for three different system prompts, (a) for a 8 years old child, (b) for a 30 years old adult, and (c) for a 70 years old senior.

Accordingly, our previous analyses prompted the LLM to mimic this type of speaker. We now extend our investigation to explore how the results change when the LLM is used to replicate the behavior of different sociodemographic groups.

In the analyses hereby reported we manipulate three sociodemographic factors, namely: Age, Profession, and Gender. We observe how these variables impact ladders construction.

Age: how does the age encoded in the system prompt affect the generated ladders? When prompting the model with different ages, we experimented with a wide range of ages: 8 years old, 12, 15, 18, 22, 25, 30, 40, 50, and 70. We used a finer categorization for younger ages and a coarser one for older ages, based on the assumption that during developmental and schooling years, more noticeable changes in language use occur compared to adulthood.

Figure 5 shows the distribution of quality of the ladders generated by the model when prompted to act like a person of different ages. We can see a *U-shape*, where the Quality appears to be higher, i.e., better correlated with WordNet-based Specificity, for young and old ages, while lower for ages between 22 and 50. We can thus conclude that the model is more aligned to WordNet when prompted as a child or as an older person.

This finding is somewhat counterintuitive, and we hypothesized that the model would generate shorter ladders when prompted with a "child" or "senior" profile, based on the idea that both these groups might find it harder to generate longer ladders. Figure 6 shows the distribution of ladders length (number of words inserted in a ladder) for system prompts where the age is set to 8 years old (fig. 6a), 30 years old (fig. 6b) and 70 years old (fig. 6c). The model tends to generate ladders of length 9, 10 and 11, for all ages. Note that we did not specify the length in the prompt, the model spontaneously keeps the lengths in this range. However, when prompted to mimic the behavior of a child or senior, ladders appear to be shorter than when prompted to mimic the behavior of an adult. To ensure that we are not seeing a spurious difference among different ages, we performed a one-way ANOVA test on the ladders length for the different ages, the test returned a p-value of the order 10^{-44} indicating that the difference is significant and the post-hoc Tukey test also returns only significant p-values with the highest of the order of 10^{-10}.

Profession: how strongly does encoding the job in the system prompt affect ladders generation? To investigate the effect of different expertise, we compare prompts that ask to act like a person with a specific job. We use the following jobs, all involving intellectual work: *linguist*, *poet*, *teacher*, *writer*, *researcher*.

Figure 7 shows the box plots of the ladders Quality for each job. Interestingly, the two roles involving more creative work (poet and writer) are the ones with the lower Quality, while the more analytical roles, i.e. linguist, researcher and teacher, have higher Quality. These results are coherent with WordNet systematicity, favoring more analytical writing, and also with the inherent fuzziness of the concept of specificity which becomes harder to understand when used in more creative writing.

To test the significance of the differences among

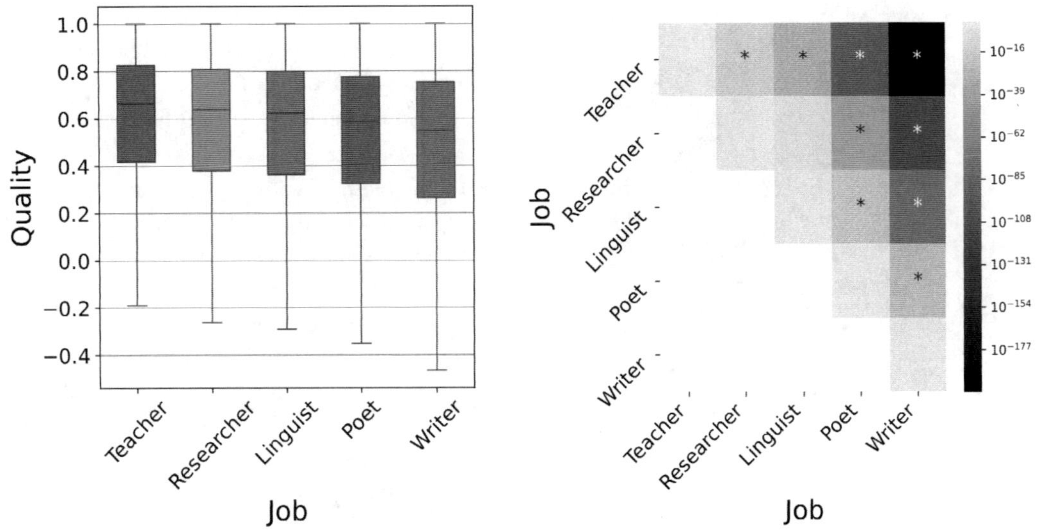

(a) Boxplot of ladders concreteness for all jobs studied.

(b) P-values for pairwise MannWithney U tests.

Figure 7: Study of the Quality distribution for all the jobs studied. In (a) the boxplot of the Quality for each job and in (b) a heatmap reporting the p-values for pairwise Mann-Whitney U tests (the * indicates p-values lower than 0.05).

the distributions, we performed pairwise Mann-Whitney U tests (McKnight and Najab, 2010) among the ladders of each pair of prompts. This test determines whether two distributions are the same or not. In our case, when given two sets of ladders, we aim to answer the question: "Do these two sets of ladders reflect an equal ability to understand the concepts of specificity?" Performing the Mann-Whitney U test between the characteristics of two sets of ladders generated from different system prompts allows us to address this question. We also apply the Bonferroni correction (Dunn, 1961) to adjust for multiple comparisons.

Through this approach we want to understand if prompting the model to behave according to different sociodemographic classes generates significantly different ladders and what type of sociodemographic profile approximates the word specificity encoded in WordNet.

Figure 7b shows the p-values for the Mann-Whitney U tests. The only non-significant p-value (above 0.05 after applying Bonferroni correction) relates to the comparison between Linguist and Researcher, which are interestingly very close types of profession, with the profile "Teacher" being associated with the highest ladders Quality.

Gender: how strongly does encoding gender in the system prompt affect ladders generation? To understand how gender affects the Quality of the generated ladders, we had the model generate responses using the same prompts as for age, with an added description of the character as either female or male. For example, we used "boy/girl" for younger ages, "man/woman" for middle ages, and "male/female" for older ages. We compared all the ladders generated across all ages. Similarly to how we compared different jobs, we used a Mann-Whitney U test with Bonferroni correction to determine whether adding different genders to the system prompts affects the generated ladders.

Figure 8 shows the pairwise p-values for the Mann-Whitney U tests of the null hypothesis that the distribution of qualities is the same between pairs of system prompts. The squares marked with an asterisk indicate that the null hypothesis is rejected, meaning there is a significant difference between the distributions of the two groups. While this is true for most comparisons, there are interesting exceptions.

Most notably, male and female ladders generated at the same ages are not significantly different from each other, this is shown in the upper diagonal starting at the intersection between the rows "8 female" and "8 male" and marking all intersections between prompts with the same age, showing that gender alone does not change the overall ability of the model to generate coherent ladders. [4]

[4] We made the same test also for the specification of jobs

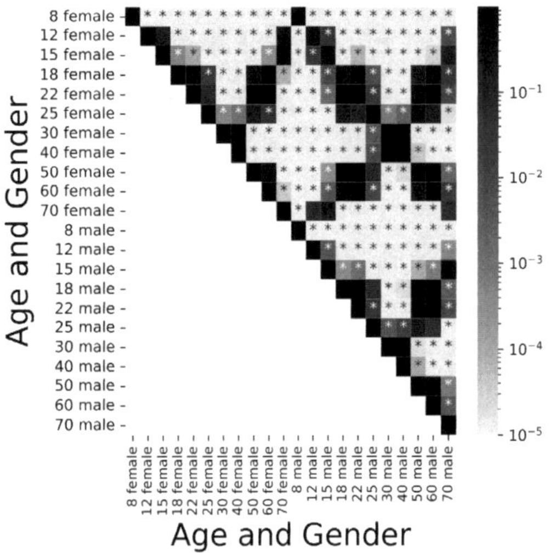

Figure 8: P-values for the Mann Withney U tests to measure if the distribution of qualities is significantly different across prompts, the * indicates p-values below 0.05 (The heatmap uses log-scale for more understandable coloring, while * are based on the actual p-values).

Figure 8 also reveals that the "U - shape" shown in Figure 5, indicating how the higher Quality is seen for younger and older ages, appears even if we are diversifying by gender. Indeed, we see that outside the upper diagonal the only non significant p-values are of the kind younger female or male against older female or male. Indicating a degree of similarity between the qualities of younger and older characters.

Note that the high number of significant tests (even when using Bonferroni correction) is reasonable given the large sample size of the populations (of ladders) we are comparing, returning small p-values also with small distribution shifts.

6 Discussion and Conclusions

This study is focused on the ability of Large Language Models (LLMs) to replicate the hierarchical structure of word meaning representations found in WordNet and summarized in the semantic relation IS-A. This relation connects more specific terms (hyponyms) to more general categories (hypernyms). We explored to what extent do LLMs are able to reproduce this paradigmatic semantic relation, and in particular their ability to do so for concrete and for abstract concepts. Moreover, we explored how different sociodemographic profiles prompted to the LLM approximate the categorizations encoded in WordNet.

We can summarize the main results as follows:

- LLMs overall replicate humans' difficulties in constructing word taxonomies for abstract concepts compared to concrete ones.
- When prompted to impersonate different jobs LLM generate significantly different ladders resulting in varying Quality. More analytical jobs generate ladders that are more aligned with WordNet, while more creative roles generate ladders with lower Quality;
- Age plays a relevant role when prompting LLMs to use their understanding of specific and generic concepts and we identify a "U - pattern" where younger and older ages result in higher Quality, we speculate this is due to simpler ladders that are more easily aligned with WordNet architecture;
- Gender does not play a major role in the generation of ladders, since adding male or female attributes to the prompts doesn't significantly affect the Quality of ladders.

We also acknowledge the main limitations of this study: 1. While we compared the ladders generated by the LLM to those from WordNet, we are unable to make direct comparisons with human-generated ladders due to the absence of such data; 2. Although we tested several system prompts, there is potential for further exploration with more complex and diverse sociodemographic profiles. We plan to address all these points in future research.

In conclusion, this study sheds light on our understanding of both the capabilities and limitations of Large Language Models (LLMs) in categorizing and abstracting knowledge based on semantic lexical relations. By analyzing the ability of LLMs to generate word ladders that mirror WordNet's IS-A hierarchies, the research helps us understand how these models handle complex semantic structures.

The findings will not only help identify where LLMs excel or fall short in replicating human-like categorization but also highlight the nuanced challenges they face, particularly in distinguishing between concrete and abstract concepts.

and we obtained the same result, i.e., gender specification has no significant impact in the characteristics of the generated ladders.

Acknowledgments

Financed by the European Union - NextGenerationEU through the Italian Ministry of University and Research under PNRR - PRIN 2022 (2022EPTPJ9) "WEMB: Word Embeddings from Cognitive Linguistics to Language Engineering and back", and by the European Union (GRANT AGREEMENT: ERC-2021-STG-101039777). Views and opinions expressed are however those of the author(s) only and do not necessarily reflect those of the European Union or the European Research Council Executive Agency. Neither the European Union nor the granting authority can be held responsible for them.

References

Daman Arora, Himanshu Singh, and Mausam. 2023. Have LLMs advanced enough? a challenging problem solving benchmark for large language models. In *Proceedings of the 2023 Conference on Empirical Methods in Natural Language Processing*, pages 7527–7543, Singapore. Association for Computational Linguistics.

Federica Barbieri. 2008. Patterns of age-based linguistic variation in american english. *Journal of Sociolinguistics*, 12(1):58–88.

Lawrence W. Barsalou. 2008. Grounded cognition. *Annual Review of Psychology*, 59(1):617–645.

Steven Bird, Ewan Klein, and Edward Loper. 2009. *Natural Language Processing with Python*. O'Reilly Media, Beijing.

M. Bolognesi, C. Burgers, and T. Caselli. 2020. On abstraction: decoupling conceptual concreteness and categorical specificity. *Cognitive Processing*, 21(3):365–381.

Anna M. Borghi, Laura Barca, Ferdinand Binkofski, and Luca Tummolini. 2017a. Abstract concepts, language and sociality: From acquisition to inner speech. *Topics in Cognitive Science*, 9(3):673–693.

Anna M. Borghi, Ferdinand Binkofski, Cristiano Castelfranchi, Felice Cimatti, Claudia Scorolli, and Luca Tummolini. 2017b. The challenge of abstract concepts. *Psychological Bulletin*, 143:263–292.

Tom B. Brown, Benjamin Mann, Nick Ryder, Melanie Subbiah, Jared Kaplan, Prafulla Dhariwal, Arvind Neelakantan, Pranav Shyam, Girish Sastry, Amanda Askell, Sandhini Agarwal, Ariel Herbert-Voss, Gretchen Krueger, Tom Henighan, Rewon Child, Aditya Ramesh, Daniel M. Ziegler, Jeffrey Wu, Clemens Winter, Christopher Hesse, Mark Chen, Eric Sigler, Mateusz Litwin, Scott Gray, Benjamin Chess, Jack Clark, Christopher Berner, Sam McCandlish, Alec Radford, Ilya Sutskever, and Dario Amodei. 2020. Language models are few-shot learners. *Preprint*, arXiv:2005.14165.

Marc Brysbaert, AB Warriner, and V Kuperman. 2014. Concreteness ratings for 40 thousand generally known english word lemmas. *BEHAVIOR RESEARCH METHODS*, 46(3):904–911.

Abhimanyu Dubey, Abhinav Jauhri, Abhinav Pandey, Abhishek Kadian, Ahmad Al-Dahle, Aiesha Letman, Akhil Mathur, Alan Schelten, Amy Yang, Angela Fan, Anirudh Goyal, Anthony Hartshorn, Aobo Yang, Archi Mitra, Archie Sravankumar, Artem Korenev, Arthur Hinsvark, Arun Rao, Aston Zhang, Aurelien Rodriguez, Austen Gregerson, Ava Spataru, Baptiste Roziere, Bethany Biron, Binh Tang, Bobbie Chern, Charlotte Caucheteux, Chaya Nayak, Chloe Bi, Chris Marra, Chris McConnell, Christian Keller, Christophe Touret, Chunyang Wu, Corinne Wong, Cristian Canton Ferrer, Cyrus Nikolaidis, Damien Allonsius, Daniel Song, Danielle Pintz, Danny Livshits, David Esiobu, Dhruv Choudhary, Dhruv Mahajan, Diego Garcia-Olano, Diego Perino, Dieuwke Hupkes, Egor Lakomkin, Ehab AlBadawy, Elina Lobanova, Emily Dinan, Eric Michael Smith, Filip Radenovic, Frank Zhang, Gabriel Synnaeve, Gabrielle Lee, Georgia Lewis Anderson, Graeme Nail, Gregoire Mialon, Guan Pang, Guillem Cucurell, Hailey Nguyen, Hannah Korevaar, Hu Xu, Hugo Touvron, Iliyan Zarov, Imanol Arrieta Ibarra, Isabel Kloumann, Ishan Misra, Ivan Evtimov, Jade Copet, Jaewon Lee, Jan Geffert, Jana Vranes, Jason Park, Jay Mahadeokar, Jeet Shah, Jelmer van der Linde, Jennifer Billock, Jenny Hong, Jenya Lee, Jeremy Fu, Jianfeng Chi, Jianyu Huang, Jiawen Liu, Jie Wang, Jiecao Yu, Joanna Bitton, Joe Spisak, Jongsoo Park, Joseph Rocca, Joshua Johnstun, Joshua Saxe, Junteng Jia, Kalyan Vasuden Alwala, Kartikeya Upasani, Kate Plawiak, Ke Li, Kenneth Heafield, Kevin Stone, Khalid El-Arini, Krithika Iyer, Kshitiz Malik, Kuenley Chiu, Kunal Bhalla, Lauren Rantala-Yeary, Laurens van der Maaten, Lawrence Chen, Liang Tan, Liz Jenkins, Louis Martin, Lovish Madaan, Lubo Malo, Lukas Blecher, Lukas Landzaat, Luke de Oliveira, Madeline Muzzi, Mahesh Pasupuleti, Mannat Singh, Manohar Paluri, Marcin Kardas, Mathew Oldham, Mathieu Rita, Maya Pavlova, Melanie Kambadur, Mike Lewis, Min Si, Mitesh Kumar Singh, Mona Hassan, Naman Goyal, Narjes Torabi, Nikolay Bashlykov, Nikolay Bogoychev, Niladri Chatterji, Olivier Duchenne, Onur Çelebi, Patrick Alrassy, Pengchuan Zhang, Pengwei Li, Petar Vasic, Peter Weng, Prajjwal Bhargava, Pratik Dubal, Praveen Krishnan, Punit Singh Koura, Puxin Xu, Qing He, Qingxiao Dong, Ragavan Srinivasan, Raj Ganapathy, Ramon Calderer, Ricardo Silveira Cabral, Robert Stojnic, Roberta Raileanu, Rohit Girdhar, Rohit Patel, Romain Sauvestre, Ronnie Polidoro, Roshan Sumbaly, Ross Taylor, Ruan Silva, Rui Hou, Rui Wang, Saghar Hosseini, Sahana Chennabasappa, Sanjay Singh, Sean Bell, Seohyun Sonia Kim, Sergey Edunov, Shaoliang Nie, Sharan Narang, Sharath Raparthy, Sheng Shen, Shengye Wan, Shruti Bhosale, Shun Zhang, Simon Vandenhende, Soumya Batra, Spencer

Whitman, Sten Sootla, Stephane Collot, Suchin Gururangan, Sydney Borodinsky, Tamar Herman, Tara Fowler, Tarek Sheasha, Thomas Georgiou, Thomas Scialom, Tobias Speckbacher, Todor Mihaylov, Tong Xiao, Ujjwal Karn, Vedanuj Goswami, Vibhor Gupta, Vignesh Ramanathan, Viktor Kerkez, Vincent Gonguet, Virginie Do, Vish Vogeti, Vladan Petrovic, Weiwei Chu, Wenhan Xiong, Wenyin Fu, Whitney Meers, Xavier Martinet, Xiaodong Wang, Xiaoqing Ellen Tan, Xinfeng Xie, Xuchao Jia, Xuewei Wang, Yaelle Goldschlag, Yashesh Gaur, Yasmine Babaei, Yi Wen, Yiwen Song, Yuchen Zhang, Yue Li, Yuning Mao, Zacharie Delpierre Coudert, Zheng Yan, Zhengxing Chen, Zoe Papakipos, Aaditya Singh, Aaron Grattafiori, Abha Jain, Adam Kelsey, Adam Shajnfeld, Adithya Gangidi, Adolfo Victoria, Ahuva Goldstand, Ajay Menon, Ajay Sharma, Alex Boesenberg, Alex Vaughan, Alexei Baevski, Allie Feinstein, Amanda Kallet, Amit Sangani, Anam Yunus, Andrei Lupu, Andres Alvarado, Andrew Caples, Andrew Gu, Andrew Ho, Andrew Poulton, Andrew Ryan, Ankit Ramchandani, Annie Franco, Aparajita Saraf, Arkabandhu Chowdhury, Ashley Gabriel, Ashwin Bharambe, Assaf Eisenman, Azadeh Yazdan, Beau James, Ben Maurer, Benjamin Leonhardi, Bernie Huang, Beth Loyd, Beto De Paola, Bhargavi Paranjape, Bing Liu, Bo Wu, Boyu Ni, Braden Hancock, Bram Wasti, Brandon Spence, Brani Stojkovic, Brian Gamido, Britt Montalvo, Carl Parker, Carly Burton, Catalina Mejia, Changhan Wang, Changkyu Kim, Chao Zhou, Chester Hu, Ching-Hsiang Chu, Chris Cai, Chris Tindal, Christoph Feichtenhofer, Damon Civin, Dana Beaty, Daniel Kreymer, Daniel Li, Danny Wyatt, David Adkins, David Xu, Davide Testuggine, Delia David, Devi Parikh, Diana Liskovich, Didem Foss, Dingkang Wang, Duc Le, Dustin Holland, Edward Dowling, Eissa Jamil, Elaine Montgomery, Eleonora Presani, Emily Hahn, Emily Wood, Erik Brinkman, Esteban Arcaute, Evan Dunbar, Evan Smothers, Fei Sun, Felix Kreuk, Feng Tian, Firat Ozgenel, Francesco Caggioni, Francisco Guzmán, Frank Kanayet, Frank Seide, Gabriela Medina Florez, Gabriella Schwarz, Gada Badeer, Georgia Swee, Gil Halpern, Govind Thattai, Grant Herman, Grigory Sizov, Guangyi, Zhang, Guna Lakshminarayanan, Hamid Shojanazeri, Han Zou, Hannah Wang, Hanwen Zha, Haroun Habeeb, Harrison Rudolph, Helen Suk, Henry Aspegren, Hunter Goldman, Ibrahim Damlaj, Igor Molybog, Igor Tufanov, Irina-Elena Veliche, Itai Gat, Jake Weissman, James Geboski, James Kohli, Japhet Asher, Jean-Baptiste Gaya, Jeff Marcus, Jeff Tang, Jennifer Chan, Jenny Zhen, Jeremy Reizenstein, Jeremy Teboul, Jessica Zhong, Jian Jin, Jingyi Yang, Joe Cummings, Jon Carvill, Jon Shepard, Jonathan McPhie, Jonathan Torres, Josh Ginsburg, Junjie Wang, Kai Wu, Kam Hou U, Karan Saxena, Karthik Prasad, Kartikay Khandelwal, Katayoun Zand, Kathy Matosich, Kaushik Veeraraghavan, Kelly Michelena, Keqian Li, Kun Huang, Kunal Chawla, Kushal Lakhotia, Kyle Huang, Lailin Chen, Lakshya Garg, Lavender A, Leandro Silva, Lee Bell, Lei Zhang, Liangpeng Guo, Licheng Yu, Liron Moshkovich, Luca Wehrstedt, Madian Khabsa, Manav Avalani, Manish Bhatt, Maria Tsimpoukelli, Martynas Mankus, Matan Hasson, Matthew Lennie, Matthias Reso, Maxim Groshev, Maxim Naumov, Maya Lathi, Meghan Keneally, Michael L. Seltzer, Michal Valko, Michelle Restrepo, Mihir Patel, Mik Vyatskov, Mikayel Samvelyan, Mike Clark, Mike Macey, Mike Wang, Miquel Jubert Hermoso, Mo Metanat, Mohammad Rastegari, Munish Bansal, Nandhini Santhanam, Natascha Parks, Natasha White, Navyata Bawa, Nayan Singhal, Nick Egebo, Nicolas Usunier, Nikolay Pavlovich Laptev, Ning Dong, Ning Zhang, Norman Cheng, Oleg Chernoguz, Olivia Hart, Omkar Salpekar, Ozlem Kalinli, Parkin Kent, Parth Parekh, Paul Saab, Pavan Balaji, Pedro Rittner, Philip Bontrager, Pierre Roux, Piotr Dollar, Polina Zvyagina, Prashant Ratanchandani, Pritish Yuvraj, Qian Liang, Rachad Alao, Rachel Rodriguez, Rafi Ayub, Raghotham Murthy, Raghu Nayani, Rahul Mitra, Raymond Li, Rebekkah Hogan, Robin Battey, Rocky Wang, Rohan Maheswari, Russ Howes, Ruty Rinott, Sai Jayesh Bondu, Samyak Datta, Sara Chugh, Sara Hunt, Sargun Dhillon, Sasha Sidorov, Satadru Pan, Saurabh Verma, Seiji Yamamoto, Sharadh Ramaswamy, Shaun Lindsay, Shaun Lindsay, Sheng Feng, Shenghao Lin, Shengxin Cindy Zha, Shiva Shankar, Shuqiang Zhang, Shuqiang Zhang, Sinong Wang, Sneha Agarwal, Soji Sajuyigbe, Soumith Chintala, Stephanie Max, Stephen Chen, Steve Kehoe, Steve Satterfield, Sudarshan Govindaprasad, Sumit Gupta, Sungmin Cho, Sunny Virk, Suraj Subramanian, Sy Choudhury, Sydney Goldman, Tal Remez, Tamar Glaser, Tamara Best, Thilo Kohler, Thomas Robinson, Tianhe Li, Tianjun Zhang, Tim Matthews, Timothy Chou, Tzook Shaked, Varun Vontimitta, Victoria Ajayi, Victoria Montanez, Vijai Mohan, Vinay Satish Kumar, Vishal Mangla, Vítor Albiero, Vlad Ionescu, Vlad Poenaru, Vlad Tiberiu Mihailescu, Vladimir Ivanov, Wei Li, Wenchen Wang, Wenwen Jiang, Wes Bouaziz, Will Constable, Xiaocheng Tang, Xiaofang Wang, Xiaojian Wu, Xiaolan Wang, Xide Xia, Xilun Wu, Xinbo Gao, Yanjun Chen, Ye Hu, Ye Jia, Ye Qi, Yenda Li, Yilin Zhang, Ying Zhang, Yossi Adi, Youngjin Nam, Yu, Wang, Yuchen Hao, Yundi Qian, Yuzi He, Zach Rait, Zachary DeVito, Zef Rosnbrick, Zhaoduo Wen, Zhenyu Yang, and Zhiwei Zhao. 2024. The llama 3 herd of models. *Preprint*, arXiv:2407.21783.

Olive Jean Dunn. 1961. Multiple comparisons among means. *Journal of the American statistical association*, 56(293):52–64.

Janet Holmes. 2013. *An Introduction to Sociolinguistics*. Routledge.

Dirk Hovy. 2015. Demographic factors improve classification performance. In *Proceedings of the 53rd Annual Meeting of the Association for Computational Linguistics and the 7th International Joint Conference on Natural Language Processing (Volume 1: Long Papers)*, pages 752–762, Beijing, China. Association for Computational Linguistics.

William Labov. 1964. *The social stratification of English in New York City*. Ph.D. thesis, Columbia University. Ph.D. thesis.

Patrick E McKnight and Julius Najab. 2010. Mann-whitney u test. *The Corsini encyclopedia of psychology*, pages 1–1.

Carolyn B. Mervis and Eleanor Rosch. 1981. Categorization of natural objects. *Annual Review of Psychology*, 32:89–115.

George A. Miller. 1995. Wordnet: a lexical database for english. *Commun. ACM*, 38(11):39–41.

Lesley Milroy and James Milroy. 1992. Social network and social class: Toward an integrated sociolinguistic model. *Language in Society*, 21(01):1–26.

Viktor Moskvoretskii, Alexander Panchenko, and Irina Nikishina. 2024. Are large language models good at lexical semantics? a case of taxonomy learning. In *Proceedings of the 2024 Joint International Conference on Computational Linguistics, Language Resources and Evaluation (LREC-COLING 2024)*, pages 1498–1510, Torino, Italia. ELRA and ICCL.

Gregory L. Murphy. 2004. *The big book of concepts*. MIT Press.

Gregory L. Murphy. 2024. *Categories We Live By: How We Classify Everyone and Everything*. The MIT Press, Cambridge, MA.

Alec Radford, Jeffrey Wu, Rewon Child, David Luan, Dario Amodei, and Ilya Sutskever. 2019. Language models are unsupervised multitask learners. *Preprint*, arXiv:1901.11117.

Lauren Rissman and Gary Lupyan. 2023. The power of the lexicon: Eliciting superordinate categories with and without labels. *PsyArXiv*. Preprint.

Prisha Samadarshi, Mariam Mustafa, Anushka Kulkarni, Raven Rothkopf, Tuhin Chakrabarty, and Smaranda Muresan. 2024. Connecting the dots: Evaluating abstract reasoning capabilities of llms using the new york times connections word game. *arXiv preprint arXiv:2406.11012v2*. Cs.CL.

Martijn Wieling, John Nerbonne, and R. Harald Baayen. 2011. Quantitative social dialectology: Explaining linguistic variation geographically and socially. *PLOS ONE*, 6(9):e23613.

A Prompts

Table 3 shows that full list of prompts used to generate the ladders.

Generic Prompts
You are a child of 3 years old learning about the world. You are a child of 5 years old learning about the world. You are a child of 8 years old learning in elementary school. You are a child of 12 years old learning in middle school. You are a teenager of 15 years old learning in high school. You are a teenager of 18 years old learning in college. You are a young adult of 22 years old learning in university. You are a young adult of 25 years old learning in graduate school. You are a young adult of 30 yearnewpages old learning in a professional setting. You are a middle-aged adult of 40 years old learning in a professional setting. You are a middle-aged adult of 50 years old working in a professional setting. You are a middle-aged adult of 60 years old working in a professional setting. You are a senior of 70 years old who is now retired.
You are a teacher explaining the concept of abstraction and concreteness to a class of 5th grade students. You are a researcher studying the concept of abstraction and concreteness in language. You are an expert linguist analysing the abstraction and concreteness of words.
You are a poet trying to find the perfect words to describe a feeling. You are a writer trying to find the perfect words to describe a scene.
Female Prompts
You are a girl of 3 years old learning about the world. You are a girl of 5 years old learning about the world. You are a girl of 8 years old learning in elementary school. You are a girl of 12 years old learning in middle school. You are a female teenager of 15 years old learning in high school. You are a female teenager of 18 years old learning in college. You are a young woman of 22 years old learning in university. You are a young woman of 25 years old learning in graduate school. You are a young woman of 30 years old learning in a professional setting. You are a middle-aged woman of 40 years old learning in a professional setting. You are a middle-aged woman of 50 years old working in a professional setting. You are a middle-aged woman of 60 years old working in a professional setting. You are a senior woman of 70 years old who is now retired.
You are a female teacher explaining the concept of abstraction and concreteness to a class of 5th grade students. You are a female researcher studying the concept of abstraction and concreteness in language. You are a female expert linguist analysing the abstraction and concreteness of words.

You are a female poet trying to find the perfect words to describe a feeling. You are a female writer trying to find the perfect words to describe a scene.
Male Prompts
You are a boy of 3 years old learning about the world. You are a boy of 5 years old learning about the world. You are a boy of 8 years old learning in elementary school. You are a boy of 12 years old learning in middle school. You are a male teenager of 15 years old learning in high school. You are a male teenager of 18 years old learning in college. You are a young man of 22 years old learning in university. You are a young man of 25 years old learning in graduate school. You are a young man of 30 years old learning in a professional setting. You are a middle-aged man of 40 years old learning in a professional setting. You are a middle-aged man of 50 years old working in a professional setting. You are a middle-aged man of 60 years old working in a professional setting. You are a senior man of 70 years old who is now retired.
You are a male teacher explaining the concept of abstraction and concreteness to a class of 5th grade students. You are a male researcher studying the concept of abstraction and concreteness in language. You are a male expert linguist analysing the abstraction and concreteness of words.
You are a male poet trying to find the perfect words to describe a feeling. You are a male writer trying to find the perfect words to describe a scene.

Table 3: Prompts used to generate the ladders.

B Ladders statistics for all ages

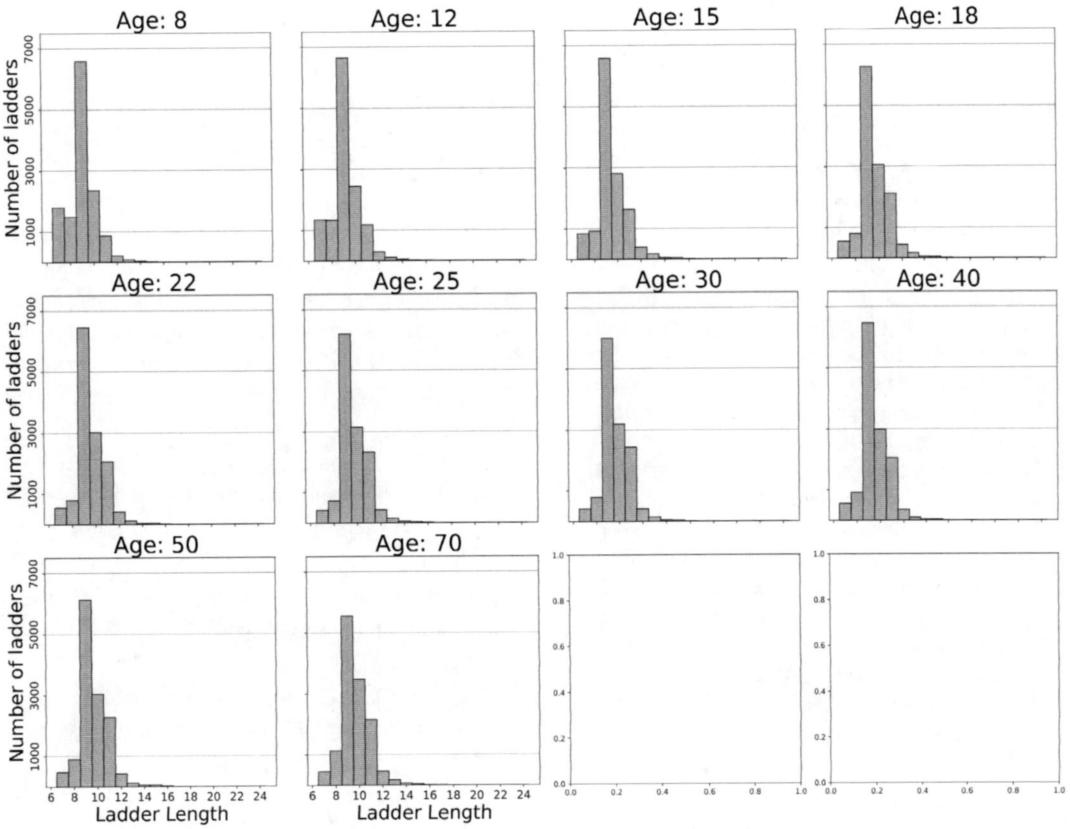

Figure 9: Ladder length distribution for all ages tested.

Exploring Latin WordNet synset annotation with LLMs

Daniela Santoro[1], Beatrice Marchesi[1], Silvia Zampetta[1], Marco Del Tredici[4], Erica Biagetti[1], Eleonora Litta[2], Claudia Roberta Combei[3], Stefano Rocchi[1], Tullio Facchinetti[1], Riccardo Ginevra[2], Chiara Zanchi[1]
[1]Università degli Studi di Pavia, [2]Università Cattolica del Sacro Cuore,
[3]Università degli Studi di Roma "Tor Vergata", [4]Independent Researcher, Spain
{daniela.santoro01, beatrice.marchesi03, silvia.zampetta01}@universitadipavia.it
{erica.biagetti, stefano.rocchi,
tullio.facchinetti, chiara.zanchi01}@unipv.it
{eleonoramaria.litta, riccardo.ginevra}@unicatt.it
marcodeltredici@gmail.com
claudia.roberta.combei@uniroma2.it

Abstract

This study explores the application of Large Language Models to populate synsets in the Latin WordNet, keeping a human-in-the-loop approach. We compare zero-shot, few-shot, and fine-tuning methods against an English baseline. Quantitative analysis reveals significant improvements from zero-shot to fine-tuned approaches, with the latter outperforming the baseline. Qualitative assessment indicates better performance with verbs and polysemous lemmas. While results are encouraging, human oversight remains crucial for accuracy. Future research could focus on improving performance across different parts of speech and degrees of polysemy, potentially incorporating etymological information or cross-linguistic data.

1 Introduction

The paper explores the use of Large Language Models (LLMs) to populate synsets of the Latin WordNet (LWN) and to evaluate the extent to which these models can contribute to this task. WordNets are lexical databases that organize word meanings in a network. The original WordNet was designed for English (Miller et al., 1990) as a psycholinguistic project. Over time, it lost its psycholinguistic focus, and shifted toward computational lexical semantics, leading to the development of similar databases for other languages, including ancient ones such as Latin, Ancient Greek, Sanskrit, and Old English (Minozzi, 2009; Bizzoni et al., 2014; Hellwig, 2017; Khan et al., 2022).

The building blocks of WordNet architecture are synsets, i.e. sets of cognitive synonyms accompanied by a brief definition and an ID-number. For instance, Latin nouns such as *absentia*, *carentia*, *deliquio*, *deliquium*, *desiderium*, *defectus*, *egestas*, etc. belong to the synset n#14472871 'the state of needing something that is absent or unavailable', meaning that they are partly synonymous. Furthermore, lemmas can be assigned to multiple synsets, which indicates polysemy: this is the case of Latin *absentia* which, besides belonging to synset n#14472871 above, is also assigned to the synsets n#13984260 'the state of being absent' and n#01236910 'failure to be present'.

The Latin WordNet (LWN) was first developed in 2004 following the Expand Method (Vossen, 2002), automatically translating English and Italian data from the MultiWordNet (Bentivogli et al., 2002) into Latin through the help of bilingual dictionaries. The resulting database contained 9,378 lemmas and 8,973 synsets. However, this approach led to an over-reliance on modern English and Italian, resulting in some anachronistic and inaccurate senses, particularly in the context of technical terminology (Minozzi, 2017). Later on, Franzini et al. (2019) proposed to refine the Latin WordNet by manually removing the modern terms and adding the missing senses.[1]

[1]At Exeter University, the LWN was further expanded to 70,000 lemmas using a gloss-ranking method to assign synsets (Exeter University, 2023). This method assigns greater weight to the translation equivalents that occur more frequently across glosses in the reference dictionaries, thus reducing the impact

A further effort to clean and expand on the original LWN was started and is currently still under way in the context of the LiLa project (Passarotti et al., 2019; Mambrini et al., 2021), which consists in the construction of a Knowledge Base of interlinked resources for Latin using Linked Open Data standards. The annotated and cleaned portion of the LWN currently amounts to 18,227 synsets associated to 10,449 lemmas. The work on the Latin WordNet continues in the framework of the project *Linking WordNets for Ancient Indo-European Languages*, whose aim is to extend and harmonize three WordNets for Latin, Ancient Greek and Sanskrit (Biagetti et al., 2021).

Although several methods for automatically populating synsets have been tested, the results typically required manual evaluation. The first such method exploits morphosyntactically annotated corpora to learn syntactic patterns for automatic hypernym discovery (Snow et al. 2005). Another method uses parallel corpora, by inducing sense clusters in new languages using multilingual semantic spaces (Apidianaki & Sagot 2014). Finally, models of distributional semantics have been used to automatically identify relations missing in the WordNets (on word embeddings for Ancient Greek, see Singh et al. 2021 with references; on Sanskrit, Sandhan et al. 2021; on Latin, Mehler et al. 2020). Since manually populating all synsets is a very time-consuming process, this work aims to speed this task up by developing a human-in-the-loop pipeline aided by LLMs.

Our experiment is based on Mistral-7B (Mistral AI, 2023), which was selected for its optimal balance between performance and efficiency. The architectural features of Mistral-7B, built upon the original Transformer architecture (Vaswani et al., 2017), enable high performance with limited computational resources (Ainslie et al., 2023; Touvron et al., 2023). The demonstrated adaptability of the model, achieved through efficient fine-tuning techniques like Low-Rank Adaptation (LoRA) (Hu et al., 2021a; Zhang et al., 2024), along with its multilingual capabilities (Jiang et al., 2023), provided a solid foundation for adaptation to this task.

This paper is organized as follows. In Section 2 we describe our data and methodologies. In particular, in Section 2.1 we present the dataset used in our experiment; in Section 2.2 we discuss the zero-shot experiment, followed by the few-shot experiment in Section 2.3. The final phase of our experiment, which involved fine-tuning using the LoRA technique, is detailed in Section 2.4. In Section 3, we report the results of the experiments, providing both a quantitative (Section 3.1) and a qualitative (Section 3.2) analysis. Section 4 contains the conclusions.

of outliers. The ranking method produced better results than those achieved by Minozzi (2017), especially expanding the scope of lemmas with precise synset assignments. However, in other cases the results have been ambiguous, requiring a careful manual review.

2 Data and methodologies

This section outlines the data and methodologies employed in applying LLMs to automatically enrich LWN synsets through Natural Language Generation (NLG). Our experiment progressed through three methodological phases of increasing complexity:

1. Implementation of zero-shot (ZS), through the application of prompt tuning techniques on a smaller batch of lemmas, and few-shot learning (FS).

2. Development of a validation approach in English, to establish a methodological baseline (EB = English baseline).

3. Fine-tuning (FT), optimizing the model for populating the synsets of the LWN.

This progression enabled a systematic evaluation of the effectiveness of different model adaptation strategies, analyzing the contribution of each approach in improving performance in the automatic generation of Latin synsets.

Sections 2.1-2.4 detail the composition of the Latin dataset obtained from the LiLa LWN (Mambrini et al., 2021), focusing on the current state of the available training data, the selection criteria for the testing dataset, and the development of our experiment.

2.1 Datasets

The data used in our experiments were entirely extracted from the LWN. Our testing dataset was constructed by selecting 80 synsets, divided into two main categories to ensure a balanced and representative evaluation:

- 40 relatively well-populated synsets, each containing 15 chiefly polysemous lemmas, hence labelled as "polysemy dataset".

- 40 less populated synsets containing at least two monosemous lemmas, hence labelled as "monosemy dataset".

Thus, in spite of the assigned labels, neither subset exclusively comprises polysemous or monosemous lemmas: such datasets would have required an artificial selection of synsets, not grounded on the actual composition of the LWN. Overall, the "polysemy dataset" comprises 28 verbs and 12 nouns, while the "monosemy dataset" includes six verbs, 27 nouns, and eight adjectives.

For the subsequent fine-tuning, we employed the entire LWN updated as of May 2024, excluding the data selected for testing. This training dataset included a total of 9,345 lemmas distributed across 16,529 synsets, broken down as: 2,726 verbs in 4,601 synsets; 983 adjectives in 1,955 synsets; 5,313 common nouns in 9,463 synsets; 233 adverbs in 419 synsets; 90 proper nouns in 91 synsets.

It is important to highlight the methodological significance of using LWN itself as the source of training data. This decision creates a feedback loop where the model, initially trained on structured data, is subsequently used to generate new data of the same nature. This methodology explores not only LLMs' potential to enrich linguistic resources but also examines a potential bidirectional interaction between language models and lexical databases.

To establish a methodological benchmark, we also created an English baseline dataset. This choice aligns with established practices in NLP, where validation in a high-resourced language provides an essential reference point for assessing innovative approaches in low-resourced languages (Bender, 2011; Joshi et al., 2020; Bird et al., 2009; Navigli and Ponzetto, 2012). The English dataset was built following the same structural criteria used for the Latin dataset, ensuring a consistent evaluation framework across the two languages. Through word-by-word translation from Latin into English, we created two parallel sets of synsets.

2.2 Zero-Shot Approach

For both the English and the Latin datasets, a zero-shot experiment was first conducted. This technique, well-documented in the literature (Brown et al., 2020; Perez et al., 2021), leverages the ability of LLMs to tackle new tasks without specific training or providing any example, relying solely on the knowledge acquired during pre-training through a small set of instructions. This step also offered an opportunity to evaluate the inherent understanding and the implicit knowledge Mistral-7B has of Latin vocabulary. We developed our first set of prompts – one for English and one for Latin generation – after a series of testing on a smaller batch that comprised 10 lemmas, equally distributed from both our monosemy dataset and our polysemy one, which through trial and error and various tests led us to find the best approach to instruct our model for the task keeping in mind its limitations (see Appendix A).

2.3 Few-Shot Approach

Following the zero-shot experiment, we developed a few-shot learning strategy. This approach, as described by Brown et al. (2020), allows the model to learn from a limited number of examples provided in the prompt, potentially improving its performance on specific tasks without fine-tuning. As noted by Liu et al. (2021), the effectiveness of few-shot learning heavily depends on the quality and representativeness of the provided examples, to leverage the LLM's general linguistic knowledge, adapting it – in our case – to the specificities of the target language. Perez et al. (2021), suggested that few-shot learning can be particularly effective in specialized domains or for low-resourced languages. For this reason, we developed a set of prompts that maintained the basic structure used in the zero-shot approach but integrated a series of 15 examples with an almost equal distribution of lemmas from our monosemy dataset (7) and from the polysemy one (8). In the initial phases of this approach, we still needed to refine our prompts. Using our prompt testing dataset (see Section 2.2), we conducted a series of 10 tests. These examples provided valuable insights, allowing us to improve our instructions with each iteration and move closer to achieving the desired output. Examples extracted from the final prompt can be seen in Appendix A.

2.4 Fine-Tuning with LoRA

The final phase of our experiment involved fine-tuning using the LoRA technique (Hu et al., 2021b), which introduces low-rank matrices trained in parallel to the original model weights. This allows for targeted adaptation without modifying most of the original parameters, addressing challenges such as computational cost and "catastrophic forgetting" (McCloskey and Cohen, 1989).

We implemented LoRA using Google Colab

with access to an NVIDIA A100 GPU. The LoRA configuration was set with a low-rank matrix dimension (r) of 8 and a scale factor (lora_alpha) of 32. We targeted the query and value projections (q_proj and v_proj) within the model's attention mechanism for adaptation. A dropout rate of 10% was applied for regularization following standard practices (Srivastava et al., 2014). Performance monitoring included metrics such as accuracy, precision, recall, and F1-score (Goutte and Gaussier, 2005). An early stopping mechanism with a patience of one epoch was implemented to prevent overfitting (Prechelt, 1998).

Initially, the training was set for 10 epochs. However, we observed overfitting at the fifth epoch. In response, we recalibrated the process, empirically determining that four epochs provided an optimal balance between task-specific learning and overfitting prevention.

The training process over four epochs revealed insightful trends in both training and validation loss. The training loss showed consistent improvement, decreasing from 2.055000 in the first epoch to 1.629100 in the final epoch. This progressive reduction indicates that the model was effectively learning from the training data, refining its ability to generate Latin synonyms. The validation loss started at 2.05 and reached 1.949 in the final epoch, showing a slight increase from the previous epoch. This behavior aligns with Prechelt (1998) observations on learning dynamics and the risk of overfitting. The final divergence between training and validation loss suggests that the model reached an optimal balance point, as described by Goodfellow et al. (2016). The use of LoRA allowed us to adapt the model to the specific task efficiently, taking into account our limited computational resources and while maintaining its general language understanding capabilities.

3 Results and discussion

This section presents a comprehensive evaluation of our experiment in Latin synonym generation using various approaches of LLMs. Our analysis is twofold, combining quantitative metrics with qualitative observations to provide a bird-eye view of the models' performance and of generated synonyms. The process of annotation and validation of the model's results involved two annotators who worked on assessing the presence in the output of potential synonyms, i.e. lemmas that are semantically similar and may thus be considered for inclusion in the same LWN synset. The quantitative analysis offers a detailed examination of the performance metrics across four distinct approaches: an EB, as well as ZS, FS, and FT models for Latin. We evaluated these approaches using standard metrics such as precision, recall, and F1 score, providing insights into the models' accuracy and efficiency in relation to the final goal of our task. Complementing the statistical evaluation, our qualitative analysis focuses on the linguistic considerations regarding the potential synonyms generated.

3.1 Quantitative analysis

As discussed in section 2, our experiment encompassed different approaches. In this subsection, we will discuss the results of the model output at each stage in order to assess its weaknesses and improvements.

	Overall			Polysemy			Monosemy		
	F1	P	R	F1	P	R	F1	P	R
EB	.169	.287	.120	.196	.372	.133	.138	.208	.103
ZS	.078	.094	.066	.069	.115	.049	.096	.074	.139
FS	.175	.215	.148	.159	.254	.116	.212	.170	.280
FT	.336	.487	.256	.373	.670	.258	.221	.200	.247

Table 1: Compact performance metrics (F1: F1-score, P: Precision, R: Recall | EB: English Baseline, ZS: Zero-Shot, FS: Few-Shot, FT: Fine-Tuning)

As shown in Table 1, the EB achieved an overall F1-score of 0.169, setting our initial performance benchmark. Interestingly, it showed better performance on lemmas from the polysemy dataset, achieving an F1-score of 0.196, while for lemmas from the monosemy dataset the F1-score was 0.138. This baseline demonstrates the inherent challenges in synonym generation, even in a high-resourced language like English.

The ZS approach showed a significant drop in performance compared to the EB. It achieved an overall F1-score of 0.078, with a precision of 0.094 and a recall of 0.066. Out of 500 generated predictions, only 47 were correct against the 710 ground truth synonyms. This approach struggled particularly with the polysemy dataset (F1-score: 0.069; precision: 0.115, recall: 0.049) compared to the monosemy dataset (F1-score: 0.096; precision: 0.074, recall: 0.139).

The FS method demonstrated a marked improvement over the ZS approach, achieving an overall F1-score of 0.175 – with a precision of 0.215 and a recall of 0.148 – which is comparable to the EB.

Out of 530 predictions, 114 were correct against the 771 ground truth synonyms. Unlike the EB, this approach performed better on the monosemy dataset (F1-score: 0.212) compared to the polysemy one (F1-score: 0.159). This suggests that even a small number of examples can significantly enhance the model's ability to generate Latin potential synonyms, bringing its performance closer to that of the EB.

The FT approach using LoRA showed the most substantial improvement, surpassing both the EB and the former FS approach to Latin with an overall F1-score of 0.336. It achieved a precision of 0.487 and a recall of 0.256. Out of 464 predictions, 226 were correct against the 882 ground truth synonyms. Notably, this approach demonstrated a significant boost in performance for the polysemy dataset (F1-score: 0.373; precision: 0.669, recall: 0.258) compared to the monosemy one (F1-score: 0.221; precision: 0.200, recall: 0.247).

Across all approaches, we observed a general trend of lower recall compared to precision, suggesting that the models were more conservative in their predictions but relatively accurate when they did generate potential synonyms. The fine-tuned model showed the most balanced precision-recall trade-off, particularly for the polysemy dataset (precision: 0.669, recall: 0.258).

The progression from the EB through the various approaches to Latin reveals several interesting trends in synonym generation performance. The ZS generated a similar number of predictions (500) compared to the EB (499), but it experienced a significant drop in accuracy, with precision (0.094) and recall (0.066) both falling well below the baseline. This indicates the difficulty of transferring general language knowledge to a specialized task in an ancient language without task-specific adaptation. The FS method marked a substantial improvement over the ZS approach, bringing the performance close to, and in some aspects surpassing, the EB. With 530 predictions and 114 potential synonyms, it demonstrated that even a small number of examples could enhance the model's ability to generate Latin synonyms. The performance on the monosemy dataset (F1: 0.212) surpassed the one on the polysemy dataset (F1: 0.159), contrasting with the baseline's trend. The fine-tuned model, however, demonstrated the most significant improvement. Despite generating fewer predictions (464) than the other approaches, it produced the highest number of potential synonyms (226). This efficiency is reflected in its greater precision (0.487) and recall (0.256), both outperforming the EB and the previous approaches to Latin (ZS and FS). The fine-tuned model's performance on the polysemy dataset was particularly impressive, with an F1-score (0.373) nearly doubling the performance on the monosemy dataset (0.221), indicating a nuanced understanding of multi-meaning Latin lemmas.

In addition, the disparity in performance between the polysemy and the monosemy datasets is particularly interesting from a linguistic perspective, as it gives insights into the model's ability to navigate semantic complexity. The superior performance on the polysemy dataset (F1-score 0.373 vs 0.221 for the monosemy one) suggests that the model effectively leverages the broader semantic variation associated with polysemous words to generate more potential synonyms; also, as we will further discuss in Section 3.2, it is worth noting that in the polysemy dataset rather common and more frequent lemmas (which we can assume the model has already encountered in its pre-training) are more likely to occur. On the other hand, most of the monosemous terms are rare and less frequent, but at the same time their limited semantic variation seems to constrain the model's ability to generate diverse potential synonyms, resulting in lower recall. These findings align with previous research on the challenges of word sense disambiguation and synonym generation in NLP (Navigli, 2009; Ide and Véronis, 1998). The task of accurately identifying and generating synonyms requires not only a deep understanding of semantic relationships but also the ability to discern subtle nuances in word meanings and usage contexts, which remains a significant challenge for current language models (Camacho-Collados and Pilehvar, 2018).

3.2 Qualitative analysis

The results described in the previous section will now be discussed from a qualitative perspective, in order to better understand how the model actually performed in each phase, highlighting challenges such as hallucinations, task misalignment, and differences between the monosemy and polysemy datasets.

Table 2 provides two examples, illustrating the progression of word generation across the ZS, FS, and FT approaches for both monosemy and poly-

Dataset	Word	ZS	FS	FT
Monosemy	pinna	auris, pinne, pinnulae, pilae, pars alaris externa, caudum, crus	pinnula, remigium	penna, ala, vexillum
Polysemy	abundantia	abundare, copiosus, affluere, plenitudo, primoresprimos, summosmaximioptimom	copiositas, plenitudine, proceritate, opulentas, abundans, affluentias	copiositas, opulentia, uber, ubertas, sufficitentia

Table 2: Examples of Latin Word Generation

semy datasets. This progression demonstrates how the model's performance changes with different levels of task-specific training.

3.2.1 Zero-Shot and Few-Shot

Starting from the ZS approach, the model performed well below the baseline (see Section 3.1). Despite the explicit instructions given in the prompts (see Appendix A), the generations include inadequate results such as English words, multi-word expressions, inflected Latin forms and pseudo-words. These pseudo-words are a byproduct of hallucinations. Hallucinations in LLMs are a well-documented phenomenon whereby the model generates content that is factually incorrect or nonsensical, yet presented confidently (Ji et al., 2022). In the context of this task, hallucinations manifest as the generation of plausible-sounding but non-existent Latin words. This behavior aligns with observations in other studies where LLMs produce fluent but inaccurate responses, especially in specialized domains or low-resourced languages (Maynez et al., 2020). An example of a zero-shot generation for lemmas of the monosemy dataset is given in (1), while (2) exemplifies the results for lemmas of the polysemy dataset:[2]

1. ELOCUTILIS: **eloquens**, *eloquentior*, *etiam loquax*, **verbosus**, *atque fluentissimus*, *fluidores*. Score: 2/6

2. ADHORTATIO: *exhortationem*, **admonitio**, *monitus esto*, *instigare*, *provocatum esse*. Score: 1/5

Another factor that negatively affects the results is the tendency of the model to generate words with a different part of speech (POS) than the input, which does not meet the target of the task. This phenomenon, often referred to as "task misalignment" or "goal misgeneralization", occurs when the model fails to fully grasp or adhere to the specific requirements of the given task (Shah et al., 2022). In our case, the model's propensity to generate words with incorrect POS suggests a failure to maintain consistent morphosyntactic constraints across the input-output pairs.

Comparing these results to the English baseline, some common issues emerge, specifically, the mismatch of POS between the input and the generations and the inclusion of multi-word expressions, pseudo-words and inflected forms in the results. An example from the baseline monosemy dataset is shown in (3) and one from the baseline polysemy dataset in (4):

3. PRUNING: **trimming**, *cutting back*, prune, *a plant*, *cut off branches from*. Score: 1/5.

4. CHAINING: strolling, marching, treading, wandering, ambling, *saunters*, striding, joyfully. Score: 0/8

These examples highlight the complexity of the task of populating synsets, even in a high-resourced language like English. The model struggles with consistently returning one-word items, often providing verbal phrases (e.g., "cutting back") or definitions (e.g., "cut off branches from"). Moreover, the inclusion of inflected forms (e.g., "saunters") and words that are completely misaligned to the POS of the target word (e.g., "joyfully" for CHAINING) further illustrates the difficulty of the task. This complexity is additionally evidenced by our quantitative analysis of the English baseline, discussed in 3.1. These results highlight the inherent challenges in automated synonym generation. However, such issues are much more frequent in the Latin synonym generation task, thus having a greater impact on the results.

It is interesting to note that the results of the zero-shot approach sometimes include portions of text that are unrelated to the task, such as instructions given in the prompts, as in (5), and texts probably retrieved from the data used for the training of the model, as in (6), in which what seems to be glosses and morphological tags are reported in the generation:

5. ACCIO: *exigere*, *esse*, *your response should*

[2]The examples present the input lemma in capital letters, while the generations are thus marked: potential synonyms are bolded (e.g. **admonitio**), existing Latin lemmas that are not valid synonyms are rounded (e.g. actio), and generations corresponding to English words, multi-word expressions, inflected Latin forms or pseudo-words are reported in italics (e.g. *to mix, etiam loquax, eloquentior, fluidores*).

be a json object containing an array of strings. Score: 0/3

6. AGO: *person singular indicative active present tense neuter nominative case*, *agit*, *declension noun*, actio, *accusative plural feminine case*, *actiones*. Score: 0/6

Outputs such as (6) suggest the presence of Latin linguistic data in the model's pre-training corpus. The inclusion of grammatical terms and inflected forms suggests that the model has been exposed to Latin grammatical descriptions and dictionary entries during its training phase. It should be mentioned that our use of the zero-shot method served as a litmus test, allowing us to gauge the extent of Latin knowledge already embedded in the model. The model's tendency to reproduce fragments of linguistic descriptions rather than providing simple synonyms indicates that, while the model has some knowledge of Latin, it struggles to apply this knowledge appropriately within the specific context of our task.

Coming now to the few-shot approach, this methodological turn seems to have a positive effect on the results, which is confirmed by the quantitative analysis. In particular, the presence of English lemmas and multi-word expressions in the generations decreases significantly, while pseudo-words and inflected forms remain frequent. Examples are offered in (7), presenting the generations for a lemma from the monosemy dataset, and (8), which contains the results for a lemma from the polysemy dataset:

7. SUAVILOQUENS: *dilatabiliter*, *loquebatur*, *modestius*. Score: 0/3

8. ACCUMULATIO: **acervus**, *agglomeratum*, **caterva**, *congestion*, **copia**, **grex**, **massa**, mulier, *monte*, *pecuie*, *plebe*. Score: 5/11

The mismatch between the POS of the input and that of the results is an issue that also affects the generations obtained through this approach. Overall, the performance of the model increases compared to the zero-shot approach, showing a greater adherence to the task and to the prompts. This means that the few-shot approach proves useful in adapting the model's performance to a low-resourced language such as Latin (as highlighted in 3.1).

3.2.2 LoRA Fine-Tuning

Moving on to the results of fine-tuning, one can acknowledge great improvements, both for monosemous lemmas, as (9), and for polysemous lemmas, like (10):

9. COGITAMENTUM: **meditatio**, cognomen, *cognomentum*, nomen. Score: 1/4.

10. ABSCONDO: **abscido**, delego, delicio, **detraho**, effingo, extinguo, **pello**, **occulto**, **praeservo**, **servo**, **tego**. Score: 7/11

The occurrence of English lemmas and multi-word expressions in fine-tuning results is close to none, while inflected forms and pseudo-words are still present, though less frequently than in the results of the previous approaches. Furthermore, the correspondence between the POS of the input and that of the results is higher.

An interesting observation stems from example (9), in which *meditatio* is validated as a potential synonym of *cogitamentum*. Currently, in the LWN, *meditatio* and *cogitamentum* are not considered synonyms as they do not share any common synsets. However, these two lemmas both appear in Latin dictionaries with the definition 'a thought' (Glare 1968, s.v. *meditatio*; Lewis and Short 1879, s.v. *cogitamentum*). This instance thus proves the potential of the approach adopted in this work in assisting humans in the annotation process by identifying synonymy relations which might not have been encoded in the WordNet.

It should be mentioned that the model produced empty outputs on three occasions during the synonym generation task: once for a monosemous lemma (*commisereor*) and twice for polysemous lemmas (*carpo*, *circumscriptio*). This phenomenon has otherwise been observed only once, specifically with the zero-shot approach on the monosemy dataset (*actutum*). While the generation of an empty output is inconclusive for the task at hand, at the same time it might be a sign of improvement and adaptation of the model, showing a preference for generating an empty output instead of unrelated results.

Interestingly, the fine-tuning approach shows more encouraging results in generating potential synonyms for verbs as opposed to other POS. The model also performs better with polysemous rather than with monosemous lemmas. This improved performance with polysemous lemmas can be partially attributed to the nature of the generation process itself. As the model's output is based on stochastic prediction, polysemous lemmas offer a broader semantic space from which to generate potential synonyms, increasing the likelihood of producing correct responses. This phenomenon aligns with several studies in the field of NLP and cognitive science. Pilehvar and Camacho-Collados (2019) discuss how word sense disambiguation benefits from the rich semantic space of polysemous lemmas in vector space models, which is analogous to our observation in synonym generation. Similarly, Ethayarajh (2019) demonstrates that contextual word embeddings capture more information for polysemous lemmas due to their varied usage contexts. These studies collectively support the idea that the richer semantic variation of polysemous lemmas can lead to improved performance in various language tasks, including, as we observe, synonym generation with language models.

While this trend toward better performance with polysemous lemmas neatly emerges from our results, a closer examination reveals an interesting pattern specific to our dataset. The model's performance appears to be particularly better with verbs. This pattern persists despite the makeup of our training data (cf. 2.1): even though nouns nearly double the number of verbs in the training data, the model still performs better with verbs. This observation may be partially explained by the composition of our dataset: verbs are much more represented in the polysemy than in the monosemy dataset (28 vs 6 verbs). This unbalance is probably due to the fact that verbs are inherently more polysemous than other POS. For instance, Gentner and France (1988) demonstrated that verbs are more likely to extend their meanings in novel contexts compared to nouns. Similarly, Fellbaum (1990) showed that verbs have a higher degree of polysemy in the Princeton WordNet compared to nouns. On the other hand, the difference in performance might be explained considering the lemmas that constitute the monosemy dataset: the majority seems to be rare words, often associated with a very specific meaning and few synonyms. The issues with monosemous lemmas can thus be explained by the fact that they are under-represented in the pre-training dataset on account of their low frequency and also by the fact that they have few synonyms because of the specificity of their meaning. This hypothesis is backed up by the obtaining a satisfactory performance with frequent monosemous lemmas that have numerous synonyms, such as (11) and (12):

11. ASPORTATIO: *abductionem*, **captura**, carnificina, *furta*, **rapina**, *stulcium*, *ueneficiam*, **latrocinium**, *strage*, pugna, bellum, *luparium*, *saeculariua*, nex, *mordebatio*, *praedae*, **spoliatio**. Score: 4/17

12. POLLICITATIO: **votum**, **fides**, **foedus**, **pactum**, sancimentum, **testamentum**. Score: 5/6.

In conclusion, the experiment – and particularly the fine-tuning approach – has revealed complex patterns that go beyond simple performance differences based on the monosemy-polysemy opposition. Furthermore, the challenges encountered with monosemous lemmas, and especially with particularly rare terms with highly specific meanings, highlight the importance of considering word frequency and semantic specificity in model training and evaluation.

4 Conclusions

This study investigated the use of LLMs to enrich the LWN through automated synonym generation, specifically by comparing ZS, FS and FT approaches. The results provide several important insights and suggest potential paths for advancing the use of LLMs in enriching lexical resources for ancient and low-resourced languages such as Latin. First, we found that the zero-shot approach offers an initial baseline for Latin synonym generation, but it lacks accuracy, showing the difficulty of directly applying LLMs to ancient languages without task-specific adaptation. The few-shot approach shows a significant improvement in the synsets population, suggesting that even a small number of task-specific examples can significantly improve the model's performance. The most important results were achieved by the FT approach using the LoRA technique. This approach produced better results than ZS and FS approaches, particularly in the generation of potential synonyms for polysemous lemmas. Overall, this study not only advances our understanding of automatic synonym generation for Latin, but also provides insights into the broader challenges of processing ancient languages and dealing with semantic complexity in NLP. Furthermore, the results obtained with our fine-tuned model can be used to partially automate the synset annotation process, providing substantial support to annotators.

Future research could explore the development of models that result in a better performance across different parts of speech and degrees of polysemy, potentially incorporating etymological information or using cross-linguistic data from related languages. Also, it could be interesting to further evaluate the results related to the addition of new data – such as other dictionaries – and a possible revision of the current dataset – taking into account the findings of this experiment on rare lemmas – to fine-tune and ground the model even more, with the ultimate goal to improve overall performance and reduce hallucination. In addition, investigating whether and how the approaches we employed apply to other ancient languages could contribute to understanding the universality of these semantic processing patterns in computational linguistics.

Acknowledgements

This project is funded through the European Union Funding Program – NextGenerationEU – Missione 4 Istruzione e ricerca - componente 2, investimento 1.1 "Fondo per il Programma Nazionale della Ricerca (PNR) e Progetti di Ricerca di Rilevante Interesse Nazionale (PRIN)" progetto PRIN_2022 2022YAPFNJ "Linked WordNet for Indo-European Languages" CUP F53D2300490 0001 - Dipartimento Studi Umanistici (Università di Pavia) and CUP J53D23008370001 – Dipartimento di Filologia classica, Papirologia e Linguistica storica (Università Cattolica del Sacro Cuore, Milano).

References

Ainslie, J., Aneja, J., Cowan, B., Eltanbouly, A., Gillick, D., Goldberg, Y., Gopalakrishnan, K., Jiang, A., King, M., Martens, J., et al. (2023). Grouped query attention for long context large language models. *arXiv preprint arXiv:2305.13245*.

Apidianaki, M. and Sagot, B. (2014). Data-driven synset induction and disambiguation for wordnet development. *Language Resources and Evaluation*, 48:655–677.

Bender, E. M. (2011). *Linguistic fundamentals for natural language processing: 100 essentials from morphology and syntax*. Morgan & Claypool Publishers.

Bentivogli, L., Forner, P., Magnini, B., and Pianta, E. (2002). Revising the wordnet domains hierarchy: semantics, coverage and balancing. In *Proceedings of the Workshop on Multilingual Linguistic Resources*, pages 101–108.

Biagetti, E., Zanchi, C., and Short, W. M. (2021). Towards a gold standard for a latin wordnet: Setting evaluation standards from ancient to modern languages. In *Proceedings of the 11th Global Wordnet Conference*, pages 47–57.

Bird, S., Klein, E., and Loper, E. (2009). *Natural language processing with Python: analyzing text with the natural language toolkit*. O'Reilly Media, Inc.

Bizzoni, Y., Boschetti, F., Del Gratta, R., Diakoff, H., Monachini, M., and Crane, G. (2014). The making of ancient greek wordnet. In *Proceedings of the Ninth International Conference on Language Resources and Evaluation (LREC'14), Reykjavik, Iceland*, pages 1140–1147. European Language Resources Association (ELRA).

Brown, T., Mann, B., Ryder, N., Subbiah, M., Kaplan, J. D., Dhariwal, P., Neelakantan, A., Shyam, P., Sastry, G., Askell, A., et al. (2020). Language models are few-shot learners. *Advances in neural information processing systems*, 33:1877–1901.

Camacho-Collados, J. and Pilehvar, M. T. (2018). From word to sense embeddings: A survey on vector representations of meaning. *Journal of Artificial Intelligence Research*, 63:743–788.

Ethayarajh, K. (2019). How contextual are contextualized word representations? comparing the geometry of bert, elmo, and gpt-2 embeddings. In *Proceedings of the 2019 Conference on Empirical Methods in Natural Language Processing and the 9th International Joint Conference on Natural Language Processing (EMNLP-IJCNLP)*, pages 55–65.

Exeter University (2023). Expansion of the latin wordnet at exeter university. Unpublished work.

Fellbaum, C. (1990). English verbs as a semantic net. *International Journal of Lexicography*, 3(4):278–301.

Franzini, G., Peverelli, A., Ruffolo, P., Passarotti, M., Sanna, H., Signoroni, E., Ventura, V., and Zampedri, F. (2019). Refining the latin wordnet. In *Proceedings of the Sixth Italian Conference on Computational Linguistics*.

Gentner, D. and France, I. M. (1988). The verb mutability effect: Studies of the combinatorial semantics of nouns and verbs. In *Lexical ambiguity resolution*, pages 343–382. Morgan Kaufmann.

Glare, P. G. W., editor (1968). *Oxford Latin Dictionary (OLD)*. Oxford University Press, Oxford.

Goodfellow, I., Bengio, Y., and Courville, A. (2016). *Deep learning*. MIT press.

Goutte, C. and Gaussier, E. (2005). A probabilistic interpretation of precision, recall and f-score, with implication for evaluation. In *European conference on information retrieval*, pages 345–359. Springer.

Hellwig, O. (2017). Coarse semantic classification of rare nouns using cross-lingual data and recurrent neural networks. In *Proceedings of the 12th International Conference on Computational Semantics (IWCS)*, volume 137, pages 3934—-3941. European Language Resources Association (ELRA).

Hu, E. J., Shen, Y., Wallis, P., Allen-Zhu, Z., Li, Y., Wang, S., and Chen, W. (2021a). Lora: Low-rank adaptation of large language models. *arXiv preprint arXiv:2106.09685*.

Hu, E. J., Shen, Y., Wallis, P., Allen-Zhu, Z., Li, Y., Wang, S., Chen, W., et al. (2021b). Lora: Low-rank adaptation of large language models. *arXiv preprint arXiv:2106.09685*.

Ide, N. and Véronis, J. (1998). Introduction to the special issue on word sense disambiguation: the state of the art. *Computational linguistics*, 24(1):2–40.

Ji, Z., Lee, N., Frieske, R., Yu, T., Su, D., Xu, Y., Ishii, E., Bang, Y., Madotto, A., and Fung, P. (2022). Survey of hallucination in natural language generation. *ACM Computing Surveys*, 55(12):1–38.

Jiang, Z., Chen, Y., Tu, K., Wang, W., Qin, B., and Li, T. (2023). Multilingual language models are better zero-shot learners. *arXiv preprint arXiv:2309.07445*.

Joshi, P., Santy, S., Budhiraja, A., Bali, K., and Choudhury, M. (2020). The state and fate of linguistic diversity and inclusion in the nlp world. *arXiv preprint arXiv:2004.09095*.

Khan, F., Minaya Gómez, F. J., Cruz González, R., Diakoff, H., Diaz Vera, J. E., McCrae, J. P., O'Loughlin, C., Short, W. M., and Stolk, S. (2022). Towards the construction of a wordnet for old english. In *Proceedings of the Thirteenth Language Resources and Evaluation Conference, Marseille, France*, volume 137, pages 3934–3941. European Language Resources Association (ELRA).

Lewis, C. T. and Short, C. (1879). *A Latin Dictionary (LS)*. Clarendon Press, Oxford.

Liu, P., Yuan, W., Fu, J., Jiang, Z., Hayashi, H., and Neubig, G. (2021). Pre-train, prompt, and predict: A systematic survey of prompting methods in natural language processing. *arXiv preprint arXiv:2107.13586*.

Mambrini, F., Passarotti, M., Litta, E., and Moretti, G. (2021). Interlinking Valency Frames and WordNet Synsets in the LiLa Knowledge Base of Linguistic Resources for Latin. In *Further with Knowledge Graphs*, volume 53 of *Studies on the Semantic Web*, pages 16–28.

Maynez, J., Narayan, S., Bohnet, B., and McDonald, R. (2020). On faithfulness and factuality in abstractive summarization. *arXiv preprint arXiv:2005.00661*.

McCloskey, M. and Cohen, N. J. (1989). Catastrophic interference in connectionist networks: The sequential learning problem. *Psychology of learning and motivation*, 24:109–165.

Mehler, A., Jussen, B., Geelhaar, T., Trautmann, W., Sacha, D., Schwandt, S., Glądalski, B., Lücke, D., and Gleim, R. (2020). The frankfurt latin lexicon: From morphological expansion and word embeddings to semiographs. *Studi e Saggi Linguistici*, 58(1):121–155.

Miller, G. A., Beckwith, R., Fellbaum, C., Gross, D., and Miller, K. J. (1990). Introduction to wordnet: An on-line lexical database. *International journal of lexicography*, 3(4):235–244.

Minozzi, S. (2009). The latin wordnet project. In *Latin Linguistics Today. Akten des 15. Internationalem Kolloquiums zur Lateinischen Linguistik*, volume 137, pages 707–716. Innsbrucker Beiträge zur Sprachwissenschaft.

Minozzi, S. (2017). Latin wordnet, una rete di conoscenza semantica per il latino e alcune ipotesi di utilizzo nel campo dell'information retrieval. *Umanistica Digitale*, 1(1).

Mistral AI (2023). Mistral 7b. `https://github.com/mistralai/mistral-src`. Accessed: 2023-10-11.

Navigli, R. (2009). Word sense disambiguation: A survey. *ACM computing surveys (CSUR)*, 41(2):1–69.

Navigli, R. and Ponzetto, S. P. (2012). Babelnet: The automatic construction, evaluation and application of a wide-coverage multilingual semantic network. In *Artificial Intelligence*, volume 193, pages 217–250. Elsevier.

Passarotti, M., Cecchini, F. M., Franzini, G., Litta, E., Mambrini, F., and Ruffolo, P. (2019). Lila: Linking latin. risorse linguistiche per il latino nel semantic web. In *Umanistica Digitale*, volume 3(5).

Perez, E., Kiela, D., and Cho, K. (2021). True few-shot learning with language models. *Advances in Neural Information Processing Systems*, 34:11054–11070.

Pilehvar, M. T. and Camacho-Collados, J. (2019). Wic: the word-in-context dataset for evaluating context-sensitive meaning representations. In *Proceedings of NAACL-HLT 2019*, pages 1267–1273.

Prechelt, L. (1998). Early stopping-but when? *Neural Networks: Tricks of the trade*, pages 55–69.

Sandhan, J. K., Adideva, O., Komal, D., Modani, N., Naik, A., Muthiah, S. K., and Kulkarni, M. (2021). Evaluating neural word embeddings for sanskrit. `https://arxiv.org/pdf/2104.00270.pdf`. Accessed: [Insert access date here].

Shah, R., Al-Shedivat, M., Carbonell, J., and Gu, A. (2022). On the pitfalls of goal misgeneralization in learning diverse action sequences. *arXiv preprint arXiv:2206.01222*.

Singh, P., Rutten, G., and Lefever, E. (2021). Pilot study for bert language modelling and morphological analysis for ancient and medieval greek. In *Proceedings of the 5th Joint SIGHUM Workshop on Computational Linguistics for Cultural Heritage, Social Sciences, Humanities and Literature*, pages 129–135, Punta Cana, Dominican Republic (online). Association for Computational Linguistics.

Snow, R., Jurafsky, D., and Ng, A. Y. (2005). Learning syntactic patterns for automatic hypernym discovery. In *Advances in Neural Information Processing Systems*, volume 17, pages 1297–1304. MIT Press.

Srivastava, N., Hinton, G., Krizhevsky, A., Sutskever, I., and Salakhutdinov, R. (2014). Dropout: a simple way to prevent neural networks from overfitting. *The journal of machine learning research*, 15(1):1929–1958.

Touvron, H., Lavril, T., Izacard, G., Martinet, X., Lachaux, M.-A., Lacroix, T., Rozière, B., Goyal, N., Hambro, E., Azhar, F., et al. (2023). Llama 2: Open foundation and fine-tuned chat models. *arXiv preprint arXiv:2307.09288.*

Vaswani, A., Shazeer, N., Parmar, N., Uszkoreit, J., Jones, L., Gomez, A. N., Kaiser, Ł., and Polosukhin, I. (2017). Attention is all you need. In *Advances in neural information processing systems*, pages 5998–6008.

Vossen, P. (2002). Eurowordnet: general document. In *EuroWordNet: A multilingual database with lexical semantic networks*, pages 1–39. Springer.

Zhang, K., Luo, Y., Qin, Y., Zhang, S., Wu, Y., Xu, R., and Fu, Q. (2024). Lora: Low-rank adaptation of large language models. *arXiv preprint arXiv:2106.09685.*

A Prompts Used in the Experiment

This appendix contains the full prompts used in our experiment for both Latin and English.

A.1 Latin Prompt

```
latin_prompt = f"""You are a powerful AI
    ↪ assistant trained in semantics.
You are a Latin native speaker. The only
    ↪ language you speak is Latin.
Your task is to provide a bullet list of
    ↪ Latin synonyms for a user-chosen
    ↪ word.
Observe the following instructions very
    ↪ closely:
[INST]
- Generate only Latin synonyms.
- Provide single-word expressions only.
- Do NOT generate long phrases.
- ABSOLUTELY AVOID including any
    ↪ additional explanations or
    ↪ comments in your output.
- VERY IMPORTANT: DO NOT translate the
    ↪ words.
- VERY IMPORTANT: Use LATIN exclusively.
- For NOUNS generate only the NOMINATIVE
    ↪ CASE, as shown in the examples
    ↪ below.
- For VERBS generate only the FIRST-
    ↪ PERSON SINGULAR of the INDICATIVE
    ↪ , as shown in the examples below.
- List each Latin word separately with
    ↪ proper formatting.
## Note
Note that the examples provided may
    ↪ predominantly feature words
    ↪ starting with specific letters by
    ↪ chance and should not influence
    ↪ the generation process to favor
    ↪ those letters.
Ensure that the generated Latin synonyms
    ↪ start with a wide range of
    ↪ letters from the alphabet.
### Examples
(...)
[/INST]
'{word}':
Synonyms:
"""
```

A.2 English Prompt

```
english_prompt = f"""You are a powerful
    ↪ AI assistant trained in semantics
    ↪ .
Your task is to provide a bullet list of
    ↪ English synonyms for a user-
    ↪ chosen word.
Observe the following instructions very
    ↪ closely:
[INST]
- Generate only English synonyms.
- Provide single-word expressions only.
- Do NOT generate long phrases.
- IMPORTANT: Do NOT any additional
    ↪ explanations or comments in your
    ↪ output.
- List each English word separately with
    ↪ proper formatting.
### Examples
(...)
[/INST]
'{word}':
Synonyms:
"""
```

A.3 Examples from the Final Prompt

```
word: 'asparagus'
synonyms: ['bracchium', 'cacumen', '
    ↪ flagellum', 'frutex', 'pertica',
    ↪ 'planta',
            'propago', 'sagitta', '
                ↪ sarmentum', 'semen', '
                ↪ stirps', 'suboles',
            'suffrago', 'uirga', 'uitis']

word: 'ordo'
synonyms: ['protelum', 'series', 'uersus
    ↪ ']
```

Constraining constructions with WordNet: pros and cons for the semantic annotation of fillers in the Italian Constructicon

Flavio Pisciotta
University of Salerno
fpisciotta@unisa.it

Ludovica Pannitto
University of Bologna
ludovica.pannitto@unibo.it

Lucia Busso
Aston University
l.busso@aston.ac.uk

Beatrice Bernasconi
University of Turin
beatrice.bernasconi@unito.it

Francesca Masini
University of Bologna
francesca.masini@unibo.it

Abstract

The paper discusses the role of WordNet-based semantic classification in the formalization of constructions, and more specifically in the semantic annotation of schematic fillers, in the Italian Constructicon. We outline how the Italian Constructicon project uses Open Multilingual WordNet topics to represent semantic features and constraints of constructions.

1 Introduction

In Construction Grammar (CxG, Hoffmann and Trousdale, 2013), the basic units of linguistic description are constructions (cxns), which are conventionalized pairings of form and function (Goldberg, 1995, 2006). Crucially, cxns can vary in complexity and schematicity, including not only words, but also more complex and/or abstract units such as predicative structures, idioms, and word formation processes. CxG, as other usage-based approaches, assume that cxns are not stored as a mere list, but as a structured network (the *Construct-i-con*) in which cxns are linked by different kinds of relationships (Diessel, 2019, 2023).

Despite traditional research in CxG not focusing much on language as a system, recent years have seen a growing interest in *Constructicography*, a blend of "Practical Lexicography" and CxG (Boas et al., 2019). That is, the notion of "Constructicon" has acquired an additional meaning. Beside relating to the structured inventory of all constructions in a language, it has come to indicate a linguistic resource that aims at representing and formalising the network of constructions in a given language (Lyngfelt et al., 2018b).

Constructicography, therefore, is the research field that aims to build Constructicons, that is, to develop repositories of cxns that consistently and coherently describe the grammar (and thus the constructional network) of a specific language. Constructicons already exist for a number of languages (e.g., Janda et al. 2018; Lyngfelt et al. 2018a; Torrent et al. 2018), and are often linked to the FrameNet enterprise (Baker et al., 1998). In fact, Frame Semantics is considered a "sister" framework to CxG - as both theories stem from Fillmore's work on semantic roles (Fillmore, 1968) - and is typically used to represent semantic aspects of constructions (Borin and Lyngfelt, forthcoming).

Despite Constructicography being a fast-growing research area in many languages, Italian has so far been at the periphery of it. Not only there is no Constructicon, but there is also no published Italian FrameNet, although there have been several attempts at developing such a resource (Tonelli et al., 2009; Lenci et al., 2010; Basili et al., 2017). The present contribution introduces the Italian Constructicon (ItCon) project (Masini et al., 2024). This project aims to bridge this gap by building an open and collaborative resource that is designed to be interoperable with existing resources for Italian (treebanks, lexical databases, corpora). Crucially, we outline how we use WordNet-based semantic classification to represent the semantic layer of Italian constructions.

As it stands, the resource is still in its infancy. Therefore, the primary goal so far is to develop a solid theoretical and operational background for the project. In this contribution, we focus specifically on how to constrain the generative power of cxns with respect to the semantic productivity of the open slots of semi-specified cxns (Suttle and Goldberg, 2011; Perek, 2016), and how this problem can be addressed operationally through the integration of data from WordNet(s) available for Italian (Roventini et al., 2000; Pianta et al., 2002) in our annotation format. We will proceed by briefly describing the architecture of ItCon and the annotation format of constructional entries (Section 2), and then we discuss how our annotation scheme can benefit from the connection with WordNet, as well as the possible limitations of such proposals

```
#cxn-id = 171
#cxn = fare Npsych
#function = cause to feel ref:B

ID  UD.FORM  LEMMA  UPOS  FEATS        HEAD  DEPREL
A   _        fare   VERB  _            0     root
B   _        _      NOUN  Number=Sing  A     obj

REQUIRED  WITHOUT               SEM.FEATS             ADJACENCY  IDENTITY
1         _                     _                     _          _
1         CHILDREN:DEPREL=det   OntoClass=feeling     _          _
```

Listing 1: Example of CoNLL-C annotation for the light verb cxn *fare* $N_{feeling}$ 'make feel $N_{feeling}$' (lit. do $N_{feeling}$) (Pisciotta and Masini, forthcoming). Since this construction only occurs with a psychological noun in the singular form, the features of the noun are specified with "number=sing", and the semantic layer uses the topic of "feeling" to constraint the nouns that can occurr in the second slot of the construction.

(Sections 3 and 4).

2 Architecture of the Italian Constructicon

ItCon consists of three linked structures:

- a **database of cxns**;
- the **graph of cxns**, where each node represents a cxn in terms of the set of constraints that it expresses and edges represent horizontal and vertical links holding between cxns;
- a body of **annotated examples** in CoNLL-U format (Nivre et al., 2016), incrementally built by annotating instances of a specific cxn (i.e., constructs) in texts by means of a specific feature in the `MISC` field.

In the **database of cxns**, each entry describes a cxn through a number of text fields and tags. They serve the purpose of specifying information about the properties and behavior of the constructs, as well as linking the database entry to a node in the **graph of cxns** and to a subset of the **annotated examples**.

Each node in the graph of cxns consists of a columnar formalization customized for cxns representation, based on CoNLL-X format (Buchholz and Marsi, 2006) and therefore named CoNLL-C (Masini et al., 2024), that can be converted into a Grew query (Guillaume, 2021) in order to match occurrences of the cxn in CoNLL-U annotated corpora, i.e., Universal Dependencies (UD, Nivre et al. 2016) treebanks. The generative power of the cxn gets constrained at this level, as it is necessary to narrow down the possible set of matched occurrences. This is done through a set of fields specifying formal and functional constraints, which we briefly describe.

2.1 The CoNLL-C format

The CoNLL-C format is a UD compatible format[1]. As shown in Listing 1[2], each formalized cxn is described by a set of metadata (i.e., the lines prefixed by #) that specify holistic properties of the cxn (such as its *semantic function*), and by a number of fields, containing a token-by-token description of the cxn components. The first 7 fields (`ID`, `UD.FORM`, `LEMMA`, `UPOS`, `FEATS`, `HEAD`, `DEPREL`) can be mapped on the matching fields in CoNLL-U format. Since one of the aims of such formalization is to match the relevant constructs in UD-annotated corpora, some other fields were added to formally constrain the queried pattern. They include information such as whether a token is necessarily expressed (`REQUIRED`), the possibility of intervening material within the cxn (`ADJACENCY`), any excluded values (`WITHOUT`), as well as the need for sharing of some features between two tokens (`IDENTITY`).

Taking into account the aforementioned fields, the formalization in Listing 1 can be rewritten in Grew query language (Guillaume, 2021) (Listing 2):

Listing 2: Formalization of *fare* $N_{feeling}$ as Grew query.

```
pattern {X1 [lemma='fare'];
         X2 [upos=NOUN, Number=Sing];
         X1 << X2;
         X1 -[obj]-> X2}
without {X2 -[det]-> X3}
```

However, such formalization can only partially constrain the set of matching patterns. For instance, by searching the PoSTWITA-UD treebank (Sanguinetti et al., 2018) applying such a query, we

[1] For a comprehensive description of the format and the relevant fields, see (Pannitto et al., 2024).

[2] The columnar format was split in two lines for space reasons.

obtain both patterns corresponding to *fare* $N_{feeling}$ 'make feel $N_{feeling}$' cxn (1), as well as false positives (2):

(1) *fare schifo* 'to disgust', *fare paura* 'to frighten', *fare piacere* 'to please'

(2) *fare demagogia* 'to be demagogic', *fare parte* 'to be part', *fare cassa* 'to make profit'

Patterns in (2) are not instances of the cxn we want to match: they do not express a causative nor a psychological semantics (since they do not involve nouns expressing psychological states). For such reasons, we added the `SEM.FEATS` field, where semantic features of the tokens filling the empty slots can be specified.

As for now, the semantic features include the semantic class (`OntoClass`) for nouns and verbs, and Aktionsart (`Aktionsart`) for verbs only. Given the need for interoperability with other resources, however, cross-linguistically and cross-resource shared annotation schemes are needed for such features. In the following section, we show how we intend to employ WordNet data to annotate the `OntoClass` semantic feature in our cxns, discussing the advantages and limitations of such an approach.

3 WordNet for semantic classification

As mentioned, one of the semantic features we included in the formalization is `OntoClass`. In this category, we annotate the semantic classes of slots in our cxns using Open Multilingual WordNet (OMW) topics (Bond and Foster, 2013), as currently mapped onto Italian MultiWordNet (Pianta et al., 2002). These topics are the Lexicographer files used by Princeton WordNet (Fellbaum, 1998), and correspond to the top nodes used to build the hierarchy of the four WordNet categories: noun, verb, adjective, and adverb (Miller et al., 1990). Currently, we decided to employ the tagset only for nouns (26 classes) and verbs (15 classes).

We chose to employ OMW topics over developing an original classification for several reasons. Firstly, using OMW topics provides ItCon with an annotation scheme that is cross-linguistically interoperable, and a shared standard. Even though at the moment of writing (January 2025) no other Constructicon annotates semantic constraints on fillers of cxns, we hope that in the future using OMW will provide an easy and theoretically-grounded way to link constructicons.

Secondly, OMW topics have been already used as a semantic classification in sense-tagged corpora[3], which potentially makes ItCon interoperable with other, not CxG-related sense-tagged or WordNet-related resources.

Another advantage of using OMW's ontology is that it includes the hierarchy of synsets, which allows for flexibility in determining the level of granularity needed in tagging semantic constraints case by case, while still relying on a relatively small number of tags[4].

As for now, we found ourselves resorting to such a semantic classification in constraining the matching process of our cxns. Although a more systematic testing is needed, we present here two preliminary steps for an evaluation of tagset. First, we test how helpful the tag set can be in the matching process (Section 3.1): we do this by proposing an algorithm to exploit OMW Topics, and by applying it to constrain instances of *fare* $N_{feeling}$ cxn. Then, we present a first evaluation of the coverage of Italian Treebanks lexicon (Section 3.2), to assess to what extent Italian MultiWordNet can be exploited in ItCon formalization.

3.1 Case study: *fare* light verb construction

In Section 2.1, we introduced as an example *fare* $N_{feeling}$ cxn, pointing at the high number of potential false positives in the matching process of its instances (cf. 1-2). Ideally, by applying the OntoClass tag `feeling`, referred to the OMW Topic `noun.feeling` (Listing 1), we should be able to exclude most of the false positives in our sample:

(3) Instances of *fare* $N_{feeling}$:

a. *fare* ***schifo***
do.INF disgust.SG
noun.feeling

b. *fare* ***paura***
do.INF fear.SG
noun.feeling

c. *fare* ***piacere***
do.INF pleasure.SG
noun.feeling

(4) False positives:

a. *fare* ***demagogia***
do.INF demagogy.SG
noun.communication

[3]See, for instance, SemCor (Miller et al., 1994) and the subsequent work on multilingually aligning sense-tagged corpora (Bentivogli and Pianta, 2005; Attardi et al., 2010).

[4]The lower number of tags is the reason why we chose OMW topics over EuroWordNet (Rodríguez et al., 1998) top nodes (n = 63).

b. *fare* ***parte***
do.INF part.SG
noun.group

c. *fare* ***cassa***
do.INF cash.SG
noun.quantity

However, performing this step is not trivial, since to our knowledge, there are no Super Sense Taggers available for Italian[5]. Thus, for this first evaluation, we elaborated a simple algorithm (Algorithm 1) to filter the occurrences extracted from Grew according to the Ontoclass tag included in the CoNLL-C formalization.

```
forall occurrences do
  if filler_lemma in omw-it 1.4 then
    find filler lemma synsets;
    forall filler lemmas' synsets do
      | find lexname of synset
    if OntoClass tag in lexnames then
      | tag occurrence as cxn
    else
      | tag occurrence as not_cxn
```

Algorithm 1: Pseudocode for the semantic matching algorithm.

We extracted all the occurrences of *fare* $N_{feeling}$ (n = 426) from Italian treebanks[6], by applying the Grew query in Listing 2. We applied Algorithm 1 to the resulting occurrences, by using NLTK[7] in Python to access omw-it 1.4 data. Then, we manually checked the results for the evaluation. The results are shown in Table 1.

		Real labels	
		cxn	not_cxn
Output	cxn	54	17
	not_cxn	2	353

Table 1: Performance of the algorithm.

As shown by the table, the results are encouraging, even if manual check of the annotation is needed. In particular, the accuracy of the annotation is quite high (0.95). This is mainly due to the high number of true negatives. In fact, most of the occurrences were correctly excluded from the sample, and only two potential examples (two occurrences of *impressione* 'repulsion') were incorrectly discarded. Thus, it seems that in this case we could safely discard occurrences identified as negatives, without losing too much information. However, the generative power of the formalization is not completely constrained. In fact, precision is a bit lower (0.76): this is because some lemmas can have an emotion-related secundary meaning (e.g., *fuoco* 'fire', *fede* 'faith'), but are not actually exploited to create psych-predicates with *fare*. Nonetheless, we are confident that a finer-grained approach could yield better results.

Thus, while manual checking is still needed, these preliminary results suggest that employing OMW topics can represent a meaningful and powerful way to semantically constrain our constructions. Further evaluations on a larger sample of cxns will show to what extent this approach can be generalized to our database.

3.2 Coverage of Italian Treebanks lexicon

Since the primary aim of our formalization is to map cxns in ItCon to UD-annotated corpora, as a preliminary evaluation of our tagset we checked how many lemmas and how many forms in Italian UD treebanks are associated to at least one synset (and thus, at least one OMW topic) in Italian MultiWordNet. We extracted the frequency lists for noun and verb lemmas from Italian treebanks, and selected the lemmas with frequency higher than 5 (n = 5273). We then extracted all the synsets and the associated *lexnames* (OMW topics) for each lemma using NLTK.

Though not all the lemmas in Italian Treebanks have a corresponding OMW topic, the results are encouraging (Appendix A). Only 10% of the noun lemmas (n = 394) and 12.7% of the verb lemmas (n = 173) are not assigned any semantic tags (Table 4). Moreover, the percentage of untagged nouns and verbs in Italian Treebank gets lower if we look at the forms count (obtained by adding together the frequencies of the lemmas). Namely, only 3.5% of the forms (both for the verbs and for the nouns) is not associated to any topics (Table 5).

Although a broader coverage of the Italian treebanks would be desirable, also considering that we set a strict frequency threshold, these results are

[5]There have been proposals and evaluations of Super Sense Taggers for Italian (Picca et al., 2008; Attardi et al., 2010), including an EvalIta campaign in 2011 (https://www.evalita.it/campaigns/evalita-2011/tasks/super-sense-tagging/). However, at the moment, there are no freely available resources published.

[6]https://universaldependencies.org/#italian-treebanks with the exception of Italian-Old (Corbetta et al., 2023), as it is actually a treebank of old Italian, containing Dante Alighieri's *Divine Comedy*.

[7]https://www.nltk.org/

promising. In fact, they suggest that a substantial number of constructs can be identified using our semantic annotation.

3.3 Limitations

Nonetheless, using OMW topics as semantic tags can bear some limitations. Firstly, a pre-defined classification does not necessarily include all needed semantic classes, as opposed to a bottom-up classification[8]: using an existing widely used ontology makes adding new, *ad hoc* semantic tags impossible, as it would hinder interoperability with other WordNet-connected resources. Secondly, the semantic classification is only available for nouns and verbs, since there are no top nodes for adverbs and only three top nodes for adjectives (`all`, `participial`, `pertainyms`). Currently, the choice of the semantic tagset for adjectives and adverbs stands as an open challenge: while at least for adjectives some classifications exist (e.g., Dixon 2004), also in the context of some WordNets (e.g., GermaNet, Hamp and Feldweg 1997), they are not mapped onto Italian resources. Thus, while they could be used for descriptive purposes, it would be difficult to employ them consistently in the matching process.

4 Future steps: annotation of inter-slot semantic relations

A challenge for our formalization is represented by the cases in which constraining the fillers of a single slot is not enough in order to match the instances of a cxn. As a matter of fact, the idiosyncratic behaviour of some syntactic and multiword cxns consists in the semantic interdependence of their slots (Desagulier, 2016). Some examples include:

(5) Oxymorons (La Pietra and Masini, 2020)

a. *l'* *ingiustizia* *della* *giustizia*
DET.F.SG injustice.SG of.DET.F.SG justice.SG
noun.attribute noun.attribute
'the injustice of justice'

b. *allegria* *triste*
joy.SG sad.SG
noun.feeling adj.all
'sad joy'

(6) Cognate cxns (Melloni and Masini, 2017; Busso et al., 2020)

a. *vivere* *la* *vita*
live.INF DET.F.SG life.SG
verb.stative noun.state
'to live life'

b. *danzare* *una* *danza*
dance.INF DET.F.SG dance.SG
verb.motion noun.act
'to dance a dance'

For instance, in (5) the two slots are filled by antonymic words, while in (6) the verb and the object are derivationally or semantically related. In such cxns, acknowledging the paradigmatic or semantic relationship between the fillers is necessary in order to define the cxns and to distinguish such instances from other formally similar cxns. Such relations can take place between same-POS fillers (5a) but also between different-POS fillers (5b, 6).

A possible solution could be to use the network structure of WordNet. As a matter of fact, OMW topics are only taken as a semantic classification, since they are top nodes of the hierarchy and no semantic relation is specified among them (let alone cross-POS relations). It should therefore be quite straightforward to constrain the possible fillers by checking if a specific semantic relation between two fillers exists in WordNet's database. This can be implemented through the `IDENTITY` field in the CoNLL-C formalization.

Normally, we employ the `IDENTITY` field to specify if two or more fillers' fields should have the same value for a given feature. For instance, Table 2 shows how this field is employed in the case of discontinuous reduplication cxns N_i *non* N_i 'N not N' (e.g. *sapone non sapone*, lit. soap not soap, meaning 'soap-free detergent') (Masini and Di Donato, 2023).

ID	UD.FORM	LEMMA	UPOS	...	IDENTITY
A	_	_	NOUN	...	_
B	non	non	ADV	...	_
C	_	_	NOUN	...	UD.FORM=A

Table 2: Partial CoNLL-C formalization of N_i *non* N_i 'N not N' cxn.

However, `IDENTITY` can easily be adapted to represent same-POS relations by making reference to WordNet relations between synsets: for instance, in a oxymoronic N_1 Prep N_2 cxn such as (5a), the synsets of the two nouns are linked by an `antonym` relation. This relation could be formalized, so as to remain queryable in WordNet, as:

LEMMA=`antonym`:N_1

[8]See for instance the approach taken in Jezek et al. (2014).

Problems arise in case of different-POS fillers, such as in *Cognate Object cxns*, where the verb and the object are semantically (and often derivationally) related, the object being a shadow argument of the verb. While MultiWordNet does not encompass cross-POS relations, ItalWordNet (Roventini et al., 2000) includes a number of cross-POS relations, inherited from EuroWordNet (Vossen, 1998)[9].

However, by consulting the most recent OMW-compliant version of ItalWordNet[10] (Quochi et al., to appear), such relations seem to be employed only partially. Nonetheless, the behaviour of the constructs in (6) is captured in ItalWordNet: *danzare* 'to dance' is in a `similar` relation with *danza* 'dance', pointing that the two synsets express similar meanings[11], and the same holds for *vivere* 'to live' and *vita* 'life'.

While being ideally very powerful for our formalization, such an approach needs a wide and consistent coverage of the Italian lexicon and its relations in WordNet. This is needed in order to avoid filtering out possible instances of the cxns if a semantic relation is absent in WordNet. For instance, quite common examples of Cognate cxns (7-8) would be filtered out since the verb and the object bear no relation in ItalWordNet:

(7) *Sara* ***ha*** ***dormito*** *un* ***sonno***
Sara AUX.3SG sleep.PST DET.M.SG sleep.SG
di piombo
of plumber.SG
'Sara slept a deep sleep.' (Busso et al., 2020)

(8) ***Ho*** ***sognato*** *un*
AUX.1SG dream.PST DET.M.SG
bel ***sogno*** *stanotte.*
beautiful.M.SG dream.SG last_night
'Last night, I dreamed a beautiful dream.'
(adapted from Melloni and Masini 2017)

Nonetheless, for the moment this annotation can still be useful at the descriptive level, since it provides us with a consistent way to annotate constructional properties of our entries in a fine-grained fashion, and will be hopefully exploited in the future for the matching process.

[9] See Alonge et al. (1998) and Roventini et al. (2000) for a description of the relations.

[10] `https://github.com/valeq/IWN-OMW/`

[11] Actually, the `similar` relation was not defined in EuroWordNet, but is part of the Princeton WordNet relations (`https://globalwordnet.github.io/schemas/#rdf`).

5 Conclusions

The present contribution has outlined how the Italian Constructicon project aims at making lexical and constructional resources interoperable in a fruitful manner. We have shown how WordNet's network structure can be employed to flexibly describe the idiosyncratic behaviour of constructions. The biggest limitations of this approach are practical in nature. In fact, this protocol would work properly only with a greater coverage of OMW semantic classification, together with Italian corpora annotated with (super)senses. Moreover, as ItCon is committed to include morphological (i.e., word-formation) cxns, an unanswered question is whether this semantic classification will prove to be adequate for the annotation of semantic constraints in morphological cxns as well (as for now it has been employed for multiword and syntactic constructions). Despite these open questions, and despite the ItCon project still being in its infancy, we have shown how using Open Multilingual WordNet to represent cxns' semantic features is a fruitful way to link different types of language resources, making them interoperable cross-linguistically.

6 Data and code

Data and code for the paper are available at: `https://github.com/LaboratorioSperimentale/adoc/tree/main/publications/GWC2025/data`.

References

Antonietta Alonge, Nicoletta Calzolari, Piek Vossen, Laura Bloksma, Irene Castellon, Maria Antonia Marti, and Wim Peters. 1998. The linguistic design of the EuroWordNet Database. In Piek Vossen, editor, *EuroWordNet: A multilingual database with lexical semantic networks*, pages 19–43. Springer Netherlands, Dordrecht.

Giuseppe Attardi, Stefano Dei Rossi, Giulia Di Pietro, Alessandro Lenci, Simonetta Montemagni, and Maria Simi. 2010. A resource and tool for Super-sense Tagging of Italian Texts. In *Proceedings of the Seventh International Conference on Language Resources and Evaluation (LREC'10)*, Valletta, Malta. European Language Resources Association (ELRA).

Collin F. Baker, Charles J. Fillmore, and John B. Lowe. 1998. The Berkeley FrameNet project. In *36th Annual Meeting of the Association for Computational Linguistics and 17th International Conference on Computational Linguistics, Volume 1*, pages 86–90, Montreal, Quebec, Canada. Association for Computational Linguistics.

Roberto Basili, Silvia Brambilla, Danilo Croce, and Fabio Tamburini. 2017. Developing a large scale FrameNet for Italian: the IFrameNet experience. In Nissim Malvina Basili Roberto and Satta Giorgio, editors, *Proceedings of the Fourth Italian Conference on Computational Linguistics CLiC-it 2017*, page 59–64. Accademia University Press.

Luisa Bentivogli and Emanuele Pianta. 2005. Exploiting parallel texts in the creation of multilingual semantically annotated resources: the MultiSemCor corpus. *Natural Language Engineering*, 11(3):247–261.

Hans C. Boas, Benjamin Lyngfelt, and Tiago Timponi Torrent. 2019. Framing constructicography. *Lexicographica*, 35(2019):41–85.

Francis Bond and Ryan Foster. 2013. Linking and extending an open multilingual WordNet. In *Proceedings of the 51st Annual Meeting of the Association for Computational Linguistics (Volume 1: Long Papers)*, pages 1352–1362, Sofia, Bulgaria. Association for Computational Linguistics.

Lars Borin and Benjamin Lyngfelt. forthcoming. FrameNets and ConstructiCons. *The Cambridge Handbook of Construction Grammar*.

Sabine Buchholz and Erwin Marsi. 2006. Conll-X shared task on multilingual dependency parsing. In *Proceedings of the tenth conference on computational natural language learning (CoNLL-X)*, pages 149–164.

Lucia Busso, Alessandro Lenci, and Florent Perek. 2020. Valency coercion in Italian: An exploratory study. *Constructions and Frames*, 12(2):171–205.

Claudia Corbetta, Marco Passarotti, Flavio Massimiliano Cecchini, and Giovanni Moretti. 2023. Highway to Hell. Towards a Universal Dependencies Treebank for Dante Alighieri's Comedy. In *Proceedings of CLiC-it 2023: 9th Italian Conference on Computational Linguistics, Nov 30 — Dec 02, 2023, Venice, Italy*.

Guillaume Desagulier. 2016. A lesson from associative learning: asymmetry and productivity in multipleslot constructions. *Corpus Linguistics and Linguistic Theory*, 12(2):173–219.

Holger Diessel. 2019. *The Grammar Network: How Linguistic Structure Is Shaped by Language Use*. Cambridge University Press.

Holger Diessel. 2023. *The Constructicon: Taxonomies and Networks*. Elements in Construction Grammar. Cambridge University Press.

Robert M. W. Dixon. 2004. Adjective Classes in Typological Perspective. In Robert M. W. Dixon and Alexandra Y. Aikhenvald, editors, *Adjective Classes: A Cross-Linguistic Typology*. Oxford University Press.

Christiane Fellbaum. 1998. *WordNet: An Electronic Lexical Database*. The MIT Press.

Charles J. Fillmore. 1968. The case for case. *Universals in Linguistic Theory*.

Adele Goldberg. 1995. *Constructions: A construction grammar approach to argument structure*. University of Chicago Press.

Adele Goldberg. 2006. *Constructions at Work: The Nature of Generalization in Language*. Oxford University Press.

Bruno Guillaume. 2021. Graph matching and graph rewriting: GREW tools for corpus exploration, maintenance and conversion. In *Proceedings of the 16th Conference of the European Chapter of the Association for Computational Linguistics: System Demonstrations*, pages 168–175, Online. Association for Computational Linguistics.

Birgit Hamp and Helmut Feldweg. 1997. GermaNet - a lexical-semantic net for German. In *Automatic Information Extraction and Building of Lexical Semantic Resources for NLP Applications*.

Thomas Hoffmann and Graeme Trousdale, editors. 2013. *The Oxford Handbook of Construction Grammar*. Oxford University Press.

Laura A. Janda, Olga Lyashevskaya, Tore Nesset, Ekaterina Rakhilina, and Francis M. Tyers. 2018. A constructicon for Russian: Filling in the gaps. In Benjamin Lyngfelt, Lars Borin, Kyoko Ohara, and Tiago Timponi Torrent, editors, *Constructicography: Constructicon development across languages*, page 165–182. John Benjamins Publishing Company.

Elisabetta Jezek, Bernardo Magnini, Anna Feltracco, Alessia Bianchini, and Octavian Popescu. 2014. T-PAS; a resource of typed predicate argument structures for linguistic analysis and semantic processing. In *Proceedings of the Ninth International Conference on Language Resources and Evaluation (LREC'14)*, pages 890–895, Reykjavik, Iceland. European Language Resources Association (ELRA).

Marta La Pietra and Francesca Masini. 2020. Oxymorons: a preliminary corpus investigation. In *Proceedings of the Second Workshop on Figurative Language Processing*, pages 176–185, Online. Association for Computational Linguistics.

Alessandro Lenci, Martina Johnson, and Gabriella Lapesa. 2010. Building an Italian FrameNet through semi-automatic corpus analysis. In *Proceedings of the Seventh International Conference on Language Resources and Evaluation (LREC'10)*, Valletta, Malta. European Language Resources Association (ELRA).

Benjamin Lyngfelt, Linnéa Bäckström, Lars Borin, Anna Ehrlemark, and Rudolf Rydstedt. 2018a. Constructicography at work: Theory meets practice in the Swedish constructicon. In Benjamin Lyngfelt,

Lars Borin, Kyoko Ohara, and Tiago Timponi Torrent, editors, *Constructicography: Constructicon development across languages*, pages 41–106. John Benjamins Publishing Company.

Benjamin Lyngfelt, Lars Borin, Kyoko Ohara, and Tiago Timponi Torrent, editors. 2018b. *Constructicography: Constructicon development across languages*. John Benjamins Publishing Company.

Francesca Masini, Beatrice Bernasconi, Claudia Borghetti, Lucia Busso, Maria Pina De Rosa, Claudio Iacobini, M. Silvia Micheli, Ludovica Pannitto, Flavio Pisciotta, and Fabio Tamburini. 2024. Towards an Italian Constructicon. In *The 13th International Conference on Construction Grammar (ICCG13)*, Göteborg (Sweden), 26–28 August 2024.

Francesca Masini and Jacopo Di Donato. 2023. Non-prototypicality by (discontinuous) reduplication: the N-*non*-N construction in italian. *Zeitschrift für Wortbildung / Journal of Word Formation*, 7(1):130–155.

Chiara Melloni and Francesca Masini. 2017. Cognate constructions in Italian and beyond: A lexical semantic approach. In *Contrastive Studies in Verbal Valency*, page 220–250. John Benjamins Publishing Company.

George A. Miller, Richard Beckwith, Christiane Fellbaum, Derek Gross, and Katherine J. Miller. 1990. Introduction to WordNet: An On-line Lexical Database*. *International Journal of Lexicography*, 3(4):235–244.

George A. Miller, Martin Chodorow, Shari Landes, Claudia Leacock, and Robert G. Thomas. 1994. Using a semantic concordance for Sense Identification. In *Human Language Technology: Proceedings of a Workshop held at Plainsboro, New Jersey, March 8-11, 1994*.

Joakim Nivre, Marie-Catherine De Marneffe, Filip Ginter, Yoav Goldberg, Jan Hajic, Christopher D Manning, Ryan McDonald, Slav Petrov, Sampo Pyysalo, Natalia Silveira, et al. 2016. Universal dependencies v1: A multilingual treebank collection. In *Proceedings of the Tenth International Conference on Language Resources and Evaluation (LREC'16)*, pages 1659–1666.

Ludovica Pannitto, Beatrice Bernasconi, Lucia Busso, Flavio Pisciotta, Giulia Rambelli, and Francesca Masini. 2024. Annotating Constructions with UD: the experience of the Italian Constructicon. In *Uni-Dive 3rd general meeting*, Hungarian Research Centre for Linguistics, Budapest (Hungary), 29–30 January 2025.

Florent Perek. 2016. Using distributional semantics to study syntactic productivity in diachrony: A case study. *Linguistics*, 54(1):149–188.

Emanuele Pianta, Luisa Bentivogli, and Christian Girardi. 2002. MultiWordNet: developing an aligned multilingual database. In *Proceedings of the First International Conference on Global WordNet*, pages 293–302, Mysore, India. Global WordNet Association.

Davide Picca, Alfio Massimiliano Gliozzo, and Massimiliano Ciaramita. 2008. Supersense tagger for Italian. In *Proceedings of the Sixth International Conference on Language Resources and Evaluation (LREC'08)*, Marrakech, Morocco. European Language Resources Association (ELRA).

Flavio Pisciotta and Francesca Masini. forthcoming. A paradigm of psych-predicates: unraveling the constructional competition between light verb constructions and derived verbs in italian. In Anna Riccio and Jens Fleischhauer, editors, *Light verbs: synchronic and diachronic studies*. Düsseldorf University Press.

Valeria Quochi, Roberto Bartolini, and Monica Monachini. to appear. ItalWordNet goes open. In *LiLT Special Issues on Open Multilingual WordNets*. CSLI Publications.

Horacio Rodríguez, Salvador Climent, Piek Vossen, Laura Bloksma, Wim Peters, Antonietta Alonge, Francesca Bertagna, and Adriana Roventini. 1998. The Top-Down strategy for building EuroWordNet: vocabulary coverage, base concepts and top ontology. In Piek Vossen, editor, *EuroWordNet: A multilingual database with lexical semantic networks*, pages 45–80. Springer Netherlands, Dordrecht.

Adriana Roventini, Antonietta Alonge, Nicoletta Calzolari, Bernardo Magnini, and Francesca Bertagna. 2000. ItalWordNet: a large semantic database for Italian. In *Proceedings of the Second International Conference on Language Resources and Evaluation (LREC'00)*, Athens, Greece. European Language Resources Association (ELRA).

Manuela Sanguinetti, Cristina Bosco, Alberto Lavelli, Alessandro Mazzei, Oronzo Antonelli, and Fabio Tamburini. 2018. PoSTWITA-UD: an Italian Twitter treebank in Universal Dependencies. In *Proceedings of the Eleventh International Conference on Language Resources and Evaluation (LREC 2018)*, Miyazaki, Japan. European Language Resources Association (ELRA).

Laura Suttle and Adele Goldberg. 2011. The partial productivity of constructions as induction. *Linguistics*, 49(6):1237–1269.

Sara Tonelli, Daniele Pighin, Claudio Giuliano, and Emanuele Pianta. 2009. Semiautomatic development of FrameNet for italian. In *Proceedings of the FrameNet Workshop and Masterclass, Co-located with the Seventh International Workshop on Treebanks and Linguistic Theories (TLT8)*, Milan, Italy. EDUcatt.

Tiago Timponi Torrent, Ely Edison da Silva Matos, Ludmila Meireles Lage, Adrieli Laviola, Tatiane da Silva Tavares, Vânia Gomes de Almeida, and Natália Sathler Sigiliano. 2018. Towards continuity between the lexicon and the constructicon in FrameNet Brasil. In Benjamin Lyngfelt, Lars Borin, Kyoko Ohara, and Tiago Timponi Torrent, editors, *Constructicography: Constructicon development across languages*, page 107–140. John Benjamins Publishing Company.

Piek Vossen, editor. 1998. *EuroWordNet: A multilingual database with lexical semantic networks*. Springer, Dordrecht, Netherlands.

A Coverage

class	n. lemmas	n. forms
noun.Tops	58	9153
noun.artifact	1744	31035
noun.act	1566	45486
noun.person	1338	22933
noun.communication	1211	40686
noun.attribute	862	25920
noun.cognition	805	35952
noun.state	714	24911
noun.group	525	30015
noun.event	366	9797
noun.substance	279	3809
noun.location	267	13602
noun.possession	261	12188
noun.animal	251	3457
noun.object	237	5300
noun.feeling	235	4024
noun.body	231	6398
noun.quantity	215	7920
noun.food	208	1651
noun.time	203	14581
noun.plant	200	1559
noun.phenomenon	141	5869
noun.relation	116	5561
noun.process	112	3314
noun.shape	89	2408
noun.motive	20	1329
verb.change	552	16761
verb.communication	550	20294
verb.contact	477	11470
verb.social	414	15671
verb.motion	291	10265
verb.cognition	273	12995
verb.possession	260	11749
verb.stative	259	15682
verb.creation	210	8864
verb.body	168	4437
verb.emotion	158	3547
verb.competition	119	4594
verb.consumption	80	4099
verb.perception	27	6782
verb.weather	27	397

Table 3: Count of lemmas and forms (nouns and verbs only) for each OMW topic (a lemma can belong to more than one topic).

POS	0	1	2	3	4	5	6	7	8	9	11	Total
noun	394 (10,1%)	1882 (48,2%)	913 (23,4%)	429 (11,0%)	172 (4,4%)	83 (2,1%)	18 (0,5%)	9 (0,2%)	4 (0,1%)	3 (0,1%)	0 (0%)	3907 (100,0%)
verb	173 (12,7%)	503 (36,8%)	369 (27,0%)	159 (11,6%)	89 (6,5%)	43 (3,2%)	20 (1,5%)	4 (0,3%)	3 (0,2%)	1 (0,1%)	2 (0,2%)	1366 (100,0%)
Total	567 (10,8%)	2385 (45,2%)	1282 (24,3%)	588 (11,2%)	261 (5,0%)	126 (2,4%)	38 (0,7%)	13 (0,3%)	7 (0,1%)	4 (0,1%)	2 (0,0%)	5273 (100,0%)

Table 4: Counts and percentages and of noun and verb lemmas by number of OMW topics in Italian Treebanks.

POS	0	1	2	3	4	5	6	7	8	9	11	Total
noun	5388 (3,5%)	49610 (31,9%)	40024 (25,8%)	23757 (15,3%)	18327 (11,8%)	12270 (7,9%)	2263 (1,5%)	1340 (0,9%)	850 (0,6%)	1483 (1,0%)	0 (0%)	155312 (100,0%)
verb	2449 (3,5%)	14439 (20,4%)	15196 (21,4%)	12276 (17,3%)	8663 (12,2%)	4161 (5,9%)	3529 (5,0%)	1197 (1,7%)	2995 (4,2%)	416 (0,6%)	5595 (7,9%)	70916 (100,0%)
Total	7837 (3,5%)	64049 (28,3%)	55220 (24,4%)	36033 (15,9%)	26990 (11,9%)	16431 (7,3%)	5792 (2,6%)	2537 (1,1%)	3845 (1,7%)	1899 (0,8%)	5595 (2,5%)	226228 (100,0%)

Table 5: Counts and percentages of noun and verb forms by number of OMW topics in Italian Treebanks.

Metonymy is more multilingual than metaphor: Analysing tropes using ChainNet and the Open Multilingual Wordnet

Francis Bond
Dept. of Asian Studies; Sinofon Project
Palacký University
bond@ieee.org

Rowan Hall Maudslay
Dept. of Computer Science & Tech.
University of Cambridge
rh635@cam.ac.uk

Abstract

The senses of a word are often systematically related to each other, either by metaphor or metonymy. Because speakers of different languages share the same basic cognitive common ground, it is possible that the same metaphors and metonyms will appear across different languages. In this paper, we investigate the extent to which English metaphors, metonyms, and homonyms are evidenced across different languages. To achieve this analysis we use ChainNet and the Open Multilingual Wordnet. ChainNet provides detailed annotations of figurative sense relations such as metaphor and metonymy in English, while the Open Multilingual Wordnet aligns multilingual synsets across more than 30 languages. We find that metonyms are more universal than metaphors, and that both metaphors and metonyms are much more universal than homonyms. Further work is needed to determine which metaphors or metonyms are more universal than others.

1 Introduction

Words exhibit multiple senses that are semantically related. This phenomenon is known as **polysemy**. Polysemy can be decomposed into two distinct categories: metaphor and metonymy (Jakobson, 1956). A **metaphor** is a language usage which frames one thing in terms of another which is analogically similar. As an example, consider these two usages of the word *death*:

(1) a. News of her *death* moved him deeply.
    b. The *death* of Rome was now inevitable.

In (1a), the word *death* is used literally to refer to the end of a life, while in (1b) it is used metaphorically to refer to the end of an empire's hegemony.

A **metonym**, on the other hand, is a language usage in which a word stands in for another meaning based on some understood association or contiguity. Senses which are metonymically related are often very similar, but are of different semantic types (Pustejovsky, 1995). For example, consider these two usages of the word *apple*:

(2) a. The *apple* was delicious.
    b. He watered the *apple* in the garden.

In (2a) the word *apple* refers to a fruit, while in (2b) the word *apple* refers to a tree which bears this fruit. These senses are metonymically related because they refer to different semantic types (fruit and tree), but they share a close association.

Metaphor and metonymy are collectively known as **tropes**. Tropes are productive processes, and it is therefore possible for the same tropes to occur in different languages. For example, the metaphor in example (1) also occurs in Catalan (with the word *mort*) and in Slovene (*smrt*), and the metonym in example (2) also occurs in French (*pomme*) and in Chinese (苹果).

In contrast to polysemy, words can also exhibit senses which are semantically unrelated. This is known as **homonymy**. Consider these two usages of the word *bat*:

(3) a. I hit the ball with my *bat*.
    b. I could hear a *bat* in the darkness.

In (3a), *bat* refers to a wooden implement used in ball games, while in (3b) *bat* refers to a nocturnal mammal that uses echolocation. In this case, homonymy has arisen because these senses have distinct etymological origins: the sense of *bat* in (3a) comes from Old French, while the sense of *bat* in (3b) has a Scandinavian origin. Homonymy is widely thought to be a coincidence of a language's development, and it is therefore unlikely that a particular homonym will appear in different languages which have developed independently. Indeed, the two senses of *bat* in example (3) are realised using different wordforms in many languages, including Chinese, French, Croatian, Indonesian, and so on.

In this paper, we investigate to which extent the metaphors, metonyms, and homonyms in English appear in other languages. Because metaphor and metonym are productive, it is impossible to enumerate every metaphor or metonym that exists in a language (e.g. Black, 1962, 1977). For this reason, we choose to focus specifically on conventionalised metaphors and metonyms. These are the metaphors and metonyms that are widely used by a language community, including those in examples (1) and (2). To analyse whether conventional metaphors and metonyms in English appear across languages, we exploit two lexical resources. The first resource is the Open Multilingual Wordnet (OMW: Bond and Foster, 2013), which is a multilingual lexicon in which different languages are aligned using the same inventory of word senses. The second resource is ChainNet (Maudslay et al., 2024), which identifies metaphors, metonyms, and homonyms in the English component of the OMW.

The remainder of this paper is organized as follows. In Section 2, we describe the lexical resources used in our study. In Section 3, we detail the methodology we employed to analyse the presence of metaphors, metonyms, and homonyms across languages. We present the numerical results, highlighting the stronger cross-linguistic presence of metonymy compared to metaphor. In Section 4, we look at how we can use the synonyms and translations to further specify the metaphor and metonymy links. In Section 5, we discuss the implications of our findings, including challenges related to wordnet construction and the potential role of large language models (LLMs) in future studies. Finally, in Section 6, we summarise our conclusions and propose directions for future research, particularly regarding the application of our findings to sense-tagged corpora and the systematic annotation of figurative tropes across languages.

2 Lexical resources

Effective cross-linguistic analysis depends on reliable lexical resources. In this section, we detail the two key resources which form the backbone of our study: ChainNet and the Open Multilingual Wordnet We additionally briefly introduce UniMet and the Italian Metaphor Database, which are existing resources that are closely-related to our work.

2.1 The Open Multilingual Wordnet

A **wordnet** (Miller, 1995) is a type of lexicon with two special properties. The first is that multiple different wordforms can be associated with the same concept, if those wordforms are synonymous. For example, in the Princeton English WordNet (PWN: Fellbaum, 1998) the words *dessert*, *sweet*, and *afters* are all associated with the concept glossed by "a dish served as the last course of a meal". For this reasons, in a wordnet a concept is known as a **synset** (synonym set). The second property is that synsets and senses in a wordnet are linked to each other by different semantic and lexical relations. For example, in PWN the synset given above is connected to the synset which has the gloss, "part of a meal served at one time", by the "is a" relation.

The OMW is a collection of wordnets for different languages. These languages are linked through the collaborative interlingual index (CILI; Bond et al., 2016), which is a language-neutral list of concepts. The combined wordnets include English (Fellbaum, 1998), Albanian (Ruci, 2008), Arabic (Elkateb et al., 2006), Chinese (Huang et al., 2010), Danish (Pedersen et al., 2009), Finnish (Lindén and Carlson., 2010), French (Sagot and Fišer, 2008), Hebrew (Ordan and Wintner, 2007), Indonesian and Malaysian (Nurril Hirfana et al., 2011), Italian (Pianta et al., 2002; Toral et al., 2010), Japanese (Isahara et al., 2008), Norwegian Bokmål and Norwegian Nynorsk (Lars Nygaard, personal communication 2012), Persian (Montazery and Faili, 2010), Portuguese (de Paiva and Rademaker, 2012); Polish (Piasecki et al., 2009), Thai (Thoongsup et al., 2009), and Basque, Catalan, Galician and Spanish (Gonzalez-Agirre et al., 2012). We used version 1.4 of the OMW from `https://github.com/omwn/omw-data`, accessed through the python **wn** module (Goodman and Bond, 2021).

2.2 ChainNet

The OMW identifies the senses of words in different languages, but it does not identify if and how these senses are related. Consider the nominal senses of the English word *tear* in the Open English Wordnet (OEWN: McCrae et al., 2019):

tear$_1$	[*teardrop*] a drop of the clear salty saline solution secreted by the lacrimal glands, e.g. "his story brought tears to her eyes"
tear$_2$	[*rip, rent, snag, split*] an opening made forcibly as by pulling apart
tear$_3$	[*bust, binge, bout*] an occasion for excessive eating or drinking
tear$_4$	the act of tearing, e.g. "he took the manuscript in both hands and gave it a mighty tear"

The senses of *tear* exhibit metaphor, metonymy, and homonymy, but this structure is not identified in the OEWN. ChainNet addresses this by identifying how senses are related to one another. In ChainNet, every nominal sense is either a prototype, or is linked to another sense by metaphor or metonymy. Homonyms are implicitly those senses which are not connected to each other, directly or indirectly.

An example of ChainNet annotation for the word *tear* is shown in Figure 1. The sense $tear_2$ (a hole made by ripping) is a prototypical sense, which is extended by metonymy to $tear_4$ (the act of ripping) and by metaphor to $tear_3$ (a binge). The sense $tear_1$ is a separate prototype, which is disconnected from the other senses, indicating that it is a homonym. ChainNet is also also annotated with "feature transformations" (not shown here), where specific characteristics of a sense are either retained, lost, or altered when the sense is extended through metaphor; we do not use these feature transformations in this paper.

ChainNet was created using manual annotation. Of the 15,234 polysemous nouns in the OEWN, 6,500 were annotated, for a total coverage of 22,178 senses. By far the majority of words with more than three senses have been annotated (>90%). This makes ChainNet the first dataset to systematically capture inter-sense relations at scale. The data and tagging guidelines are available at `https://github.com/rowanhm/ChainNet`.

2.3 UniMet: Universal Metonymy

Khishigsuren et al. (2022) have created a resource with metonymy tropes using wordnet concepts from the Universal Knowledge Core (UKC: Giunchiglia et al., 2017, 2018, 2023), another wordnet-like multilingual lexicon. Khishigsuren et al. identified metonyms in a top down manner. More specifically, they first identified 26 metonymy patterns based on pairs of UKC domains, such as `body part` and `person`. These domain pairs were then used to extract synset pairs, such as "the upper part of the human body" → "a person who is in charge". A total of 51,000 candidate synset pairs were filtered to 4,900 pairs. Every possible lexicalisation of these pairs from the UKC was extracting, yielding a total of 20,000 instances of metonymy from 189 languages. All parts of speech were included, and therefore the cases of metonymy in this data include pairs of senses of different parts of speech (e.g. noun–verb pairs).

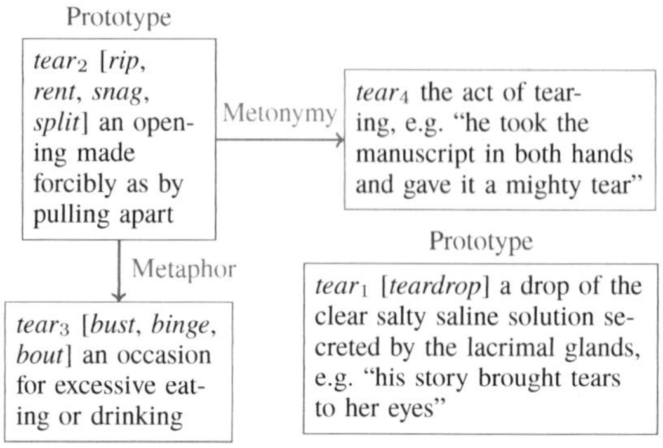

Figure 1: Complete annotation for *tear* in ChainNet

Cases are also included that consist of different wordforms: Khishigsuren et al. distinguish between what they call "morphological metonymy", in which a pair consists of different wordforms that are morphologically related (such as French *garde–garder*) and "lexicalised metonymy", which are pairs in which both wordforms are the same.

Considering only lexicalized metonymy between nouns in English, there are 3,298 pairs in Khishigsuren et al.'s data. By contrast, there are 6,116 metonymy pairs in ChainNet, and 7,521 metaphors. Only 265 pairs are shared by both resources, although for these 96 are in different directions in the two resources.

There are 20 metonymy pairs in UniMet which are classified as examples of metaphor in ChainNet. Of these, 9/20 are cases of generalisation, for example a shift from the definition of the word *kale* as "a hardy cabbage with coarse curly leaves that do not form a head" → any "coarse curly-leafed cabbage", or equivalently the shift of *enamel* from "a colored glassy compound fused to the surface of metal or glass or pottery" → "any smooth glossy coating". Generalisation was considered a subtype of metaphor in the ChainNet annotation guidelines, and is not commonly considered to be a type of metonymy. Of the remaining 11 cases, six appear to be mistakes with UniMet (i.e. clear cases of metaphor) while five appear to be mistakes with ChainNet (i.e. clear cases of metonymy). Examples of mistakes with UniMet include a pair of definitions for *muscle*, "one of the contractile organs of the body" → "a bully employed as a thug or bodyguard", as well as a pair of definitions for *mouth*, "the opening through which food is taken in and vocalizations emerge" → "a spokesperson" (the latter being evoked in sentences such as "the *mouth* of the organisation"). Of the five mistakes in ChainNet, one is an example of specialisation (*essence*: "any substance possessing to a high degree the predominant properties of a plant or drug or other natural product from which it is extracted" → "a toiletry that emits and diffuses a fragrant odor"), three are for artefacts made from a specific material (e.g. *brass*: "an alloy of copper and zinc" → "a memorial made of brass"), and one is a plant–food alternation (*broccoli*: "plant with dense clusters of tight green flower buds" → "branched green undeveloped flower heads".

2.4 The Italian Metaphor Database

Alonge (2006) described the construction of a database of Italian Metaphors built through a study of a corpus and linked to the Italian Wordnet, but we have not found any release of the data.

3 Analysing tropes across languages

Having outlined our primary lexical resources, we now investigate how English metaphors and metonymy are used cross-lingually. We start off by investigating how likely it is that two different senses of an English word (in the OEWN) will both be translated using a single word in different languages (in the OMW). We conduct this investigation for three different types of sense pairs, based on ChainNet annotation: those which are linked directly linked by metaphor, those which are directly linked by metonymy, and those which are not directly linked. Our hypothesis is that sense pars which are linked are more often translated using the same word.

As an example, consider the English word *head*, which can refer to either a body part or metaphorically to a person in charge. This is also true in Japanese (頭 *atama*), Italian (*capo*), and many other languages. In English the word *head* is also used to count animals, as in the sentence "200 *head* of cattle". This metonymic extension of *head* is also a possibility in Japanese (頭 *tou*) and Italian (*capo*). However, not every extension will be shared by all languages. For example, in English a third common extension of the word *head* is a metaphor to refer to the main part of a grammatical constituent, as in the sentence "the *head* of an NP is N". This extension does not exist in Japanese, where the main part of a grammatical constituent is translated as 主要語 (*shuyougo* "main element") or 主辞 (*shuji* "main appendant"). We show the relevant senses of *head* from ChainNet in Figure 2.

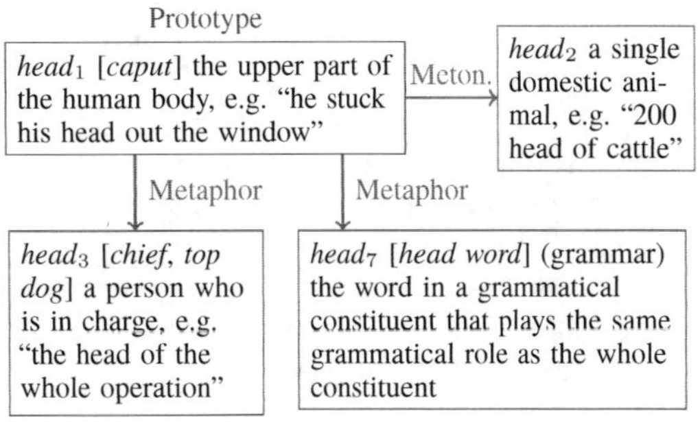

Figure 2: ChainNet-style annotation for *head*

When we evaluate whether tropes appear across different language, it is important to test across multiple wordnets produced by different groups using different methodologies. One of the reasons for this is because we need to consider the possibility that a wordnet has been constructed by naïvely translating an English wordnet. This could result in the situation where the senses of an English word also occurred together in another language, even if speakers of that language did not use these senses in that way.

To evaluate whether another language has the same tropes as English, we use the following procedure:

1. For every English word $w \in \mathcal{W}$ that has been annotated in ChainNet:

   For each pair of senses s_1, s_2 from w:
   - Look up all the translations of each sense, yeilding two sets of words, $\mathcal{W}_1, \mathcal{W}_2 \subset \mathcal{W}$.
   - Measure the overlap between $\mathcal{W}_1$ and $\mathcal{W}_2$ using the Jaccard index, which is defined as size of the intersection of two sets over the size of their union:
   $$\text{jaccard}(\mathcal{W}_1, \mathcal{W}_2) = \frac{|\mathcal{W}_1 \cup \mathcal{W}_2|}{|\mathcal{W}_1 \cap \mathcal{W}_2|}$$
   - Store the overlap and note if the senses are linked (and if so how they are linked).

2. Compute the average overlap considering only the pairs of senses which are unlinked, only the pairs sense which are linked by metaphor, and only the pairs of senses which are linked by metonymy.

3. Normalise the overlap scores by dividing them by the average overlap of all sense pairs.

Language	Code	Unlinked	Metaphor	Metonomy	All	Translated
Albanian	sq	0.74	1.27	2.38	0.009	822
Basque	eu	0.82	1.30	1.80	0.102	5,562
Bulgarian	bg	0.73	1.54	2.11	0.007	380
Catalan	ca	0.83	1.23	1.84	0.101	6,000
Croatian	hr	0.81	1.22	1.98	0.051	3,576
Danish	da	0.74	1.46	2.09	0.007	332
Dutch	nl	0.79	1.38	1.90	0.032	2,991
Finnish	fi	0.82	1.35	1.76	0.106	7,971
French	fr	0.94	1.10	1.25	0.294	18,975
Galician	gl	0.70	2.13	1.55	0.004	271
Greek	el	0.72	1.30	2.45	0.025	1274
Hebrew	he	0.69	1.58	2.31	0.011	472
Icelandic	is	0.73	1.51	2.13	0.005	388
Indonesian	id	0.87	1.21	1.58	0.123	9,803
Italian (IWN)	it	0.79	1.46	1.80	0.018	968
Italian (MWN)	it	0.80	1.39	1.81	0.065	4,614
Japanese	ja	0.89	1.11	1.55	0.088	8,130
Lithuanian	lt	0.63	1.46	2.86	0.010	692
Mandarin Chinese	cmn	0.74	1.57	1.97	0.016	1,347
Norwegian Bokmål	nb	0.73	1.49	2.12	0.008	339
Norwegian Nynorsk	nn	0.73	1.52	2.10	0.008	340
Polish	pl	0.75	1.43	2.07	0.024	1,326
Portuguese	pt	0.80	1.26	1.96	0.083	5,414
Romanian	ro	0.83	1.30	1.71	0.108	6,429
Slovak	sk	0.73	1.35	2.31	0.025	2,067
Slovenian	sl	0.81	1.41	1.74	0.111	6,243
Spanish	es	0.85	1.17	1.79	0.095	5,915
Standard Arabic	arb	0.74	1.28	2.38	0.016	1,337
Standard Malay	zsm	0.87	1.22	1.60	0.126	10,272
Swedish	sv	0.70	1.71	2.10	0.012	417
Thai	th	0.80	1.48	1.71	0.038	2,336
Mean		0.78	1.39	1.96	0.056	3,774.3

Table 1: Differences in the translation overlap by language

Results are shown in Table 1. For Italian, there are two results, which are computed from the Ita-WordNet (IWN: Toral et al., 2010) and the Multi-WordNet (MWN: Pianta et al., 2002) respectively. Our hypothesis clearly holds: over all languages, unlinked senses share the fewest translations (0.78 overlap), while metaphors share more (1.39) and metonyms share the most of all (1.96).

The wordnets in OMW are of vastly different sizes, so the number of sense pairs that have a translation ("Translated" in Table 1) varies from as few as 271 for Galician to as many as 18,975 for French. The average score of all those sense pairs that have a translation ("All" in Table 1) is also wildly different, ranging from 0.004 for Galician to 0.294 for French. Only Galician has the score for metaphor (2.13) larger the score for metonymy (1.55), which we hypothesise is due to data sparsity, rather than some language specific property: we would expect it to behave much like Portuguese (which has a metaphor/metonym overlap of 1.26/1.96).

Several of the wordnets are made semi-automatically, by translating the English wordnet and then correcting the translations (French, Indonesian, Romanian, Slovenien, Standard Malay). In these wordnets, a high proportion of senses with translations were identified (all >0.1, while

Sense	Mandarin	Japanese	Finnish	Italian	Portuguese
cherry$_1$ (wood)	樱桃木	桜, 桜材	kirsikkapuumetsä	ciliegio	cerejeira
cherry$_2$ (tree)	樱桃树	桜, 櫻	kirsikkapuu	ciliegio	cerejeira
cherry$_3$ (fruit)	樱桃	桜桃, 桜ん坊	kirsikka	cerasa , ciliegia	ginja , cereja
cherry$_4$ (colour)	樱桃红	桜ん坊色	kirsikanpunainen[2]	ciliegia	cereja

Table 2: Translations of the senses of *cherry* in other languages

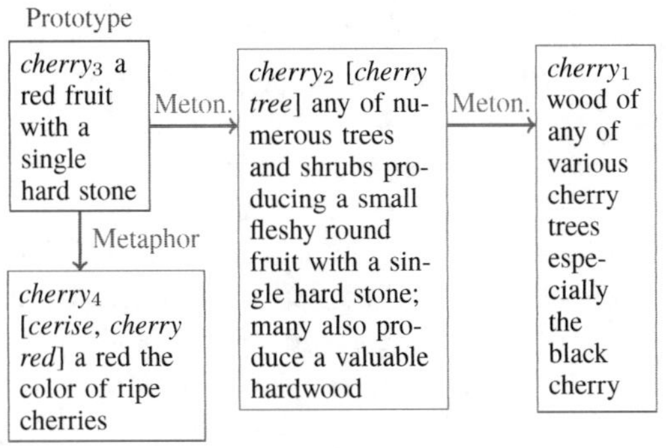

Figure 3: Complete annotation for *cherry* in ChainNet

the average is only 0.056), suggesting that the construction method that is used for a wordnet affects the overlap scores.

In order to measure perfectly how well tropes carry over between languages, we would need to mark metonymy and metaphor systematically for each language, and make sure all synsets have all relevant translations. Even so, it is striking how uniform our results are, even for very different resources and different languages. Without exception, senses linked by tropes are more likely to have an identical translation that those senses which are not linked. With one exception, metonymy is more likely to have an identical translation then metaphor. We therefore conclude that the same metonyms and metaphors appear in different languages, to varying degrees.

4 Using translations to specify tropes

Even when a pair of senses is not translated with the same word, it is often translated by a derivationally-related word (like morphological metonymy, §2.3). As an example, consider the four senses of the English word *cherry*, which are shown in Figure 3. The word *cherry* has a single prototype, *cherry*$_3$ (fruit). The sense is extended by metaphor for *cherry*$_4$ (colour), and by metonymy for *cherry*$_2$ (tree); the cherry tree sense is then itself extended by metonymy by *cherry*$_1$ (wood). Example translations of these senses are shown in Table 2. We added some translations which were missing from the OMW; those that we added are shown underlined. In each of the shown languages, different wordforms are used for the different senses. However, there is some relation between these wordforms. In Mandarin, the word for the tree, wood, and colour is the same as the word for the fruit but with the word for tree, lumber, or colour attached to the end.[1] Japanese has a special word for the cherry fruit, 桜ん坊 (*sakuranbō* "cherry"), with the etymological origin probably being 桜 (*sakura* "cherry tree") + の (*no* "of") + 坊 (*bō* "monk"), because the cherry fruit resembles the shaved head of a monk. The word sense can be built compositionally, by adding 材 (*zai* "lumber") to 桜 (*sakura* "cherry tree"). Finnish also adds a suffix word for tree (*puu*) and other compounds.[2] Finally, Italian and Portuguese both describe the fruit and colour using the same wordform, and the tree and wood another wordform. In both cases, there is a clear relation between these two wordforms (*ciliegia* vs. *ciliegio* for Italian and *cereja* vs. *cerejeira* for Portuguese).

The *cherry* example demonstrates that even if the translations are not identical, sometimes different translations still share some semantic link. We can address this by analysing other synonyms in the same language, or translations in another language. For example, the metonymically-linked senses *cherry*$_3$ (fruit) and *cherry*$_2$ (tree) both share the same wordform in English, *cherry*. However, *cherry*$_2$ also has the synonym, *cherry tree*. The difference between them (`+tree`), can be used to classify this metonym as specifically a metonym which connects something to a tree. If we do this for all tropes, we find the same patterns repeated. Consider, for example, the first four senses of *chestnut*

[1] This is also possible for English, and indeed the OEWN contains the synonym *cherry tree* for *cherry*$_2$ and *cherry red* for *cherry*$_4$ (but not *cherry wood* for *cherry*$_1$).

[2] We think there may be a mistranslation for the cherry wood: *kirsikkapuumetsä* means "cherry forest" which could also be "cherry wood". This would suggest a problem with the wordnet.

in the OEWN:

chestnut$_1$	wood of any of various chestnut trees of the genus Castanea
chestnut$_2$	[*chestnut tree*] any of several attractive deciduous trees yellow-brown in autumn; yield a hard wood and edible nuts in a prickly bur
chestnut$_3$	edible nut of any of various chestnut trees of the genus Castanea
chestnut$_4$	the brown color of chestnuts

These senses each correspond to one of the four senses of *cherry*, and they show the same relation patterns of metonymy (*chestnut*$_3$ $\rightarrow$ *chestnut*$_2$ $\rightarrow$ *chestnut*$_1$) and metaphor (*chestnut*$_3$ $\rightarrow$ *chestnut*$_4$). Additionally, they have the same differences in synonym wordforms between *chestnut*$_3$ and *chestnut*$_2$ (`+tree`). When we look across the entire dataset, we find this and many other patterns repeating.

One interesting difference we have found in these patterns is that the direction in ChainNet is different for the same relation, depending on which parts of a tree are culturally important. For trees like cherry, chestnut and walnut, which are most widely used for their fruit, the metonymy chain goes: fruit → tree → wood. However, for trees used mainly for their wood, such as teak or mahogany, the metonymy goes from wood → tree.

The data and scripts to recreate these findings are available at `https://github.com/bond-lab/chainnet-xling`.

4.1 Different languages mark different things

One point of interest in Table 2 is that different languages mark different alternation patterns. For example, Japanese explicitly marks the colour sense with 色 (*iro* "colour"), Mandarin and Finnish explicitly mark the tree sense, and Mandarin and Japanese explicitly mark the wood sense. By building up a collection of these rules, it would be possible to predict how a language would accommodate new senses, and to specify which patterns are marked or unmarked in a particular language. For example, Japanese marks fields of study with 学, but English does not mark fields of study: the word *history* refers to both the past, and to the study of the past. We can therefore use information from Japanese to subtype the unmarked relation in English, for pairs like *accounting*$_3$ (defined as "the occupation of maintaining and auditing records and preparing financial reports for a business") and *accounting*$_2$ ("a system that provides quantitative information about finances"), which in Japanese are 会計 and 会計学 respectively. The same is true for the sense *history*$_5$ ("all that is remembered of the past as preserved in writing; a body of knowledge"), which in Japanese is 歴史 or 史, and *history*$_3$ ("the discipline that records and interprets past events involving human beings"), which in Japanese is 歴史学 or 史学.

To facilitate investigation into derivation marking, we have created a database that link pairs of concepts (using CILI) to differences between them. This database is linked to the OMW so that the information is accessible in any wordnet, and makes it possible to search based on concepts, tropes, words, or differences. This database makes it easy to find, for example, all metaphors connected with the CILI concept i77824 (defined as "a red fruit with a single hard stone"), or to lookup all tropes linked by `+tree`. This effectively makes it possible to identify subregularities in WordNet senses. For example, a search for metonyms with `-spot` identifies all senses of the form "a playing card or domino or die whose upward face shows n pips", where n is *one*, *four*, *five*, *six*, *seven*, *eight*, *nine*, and *ten*.[3] Many of these subregularities are already captured in the wordnet hierarchy: all of these concepts are all children of the {*spot*, *pip*} synset, defined as "a mark on a die or on a playing card (shape depending on the suit)".[4]

In future work, we intend to use the difference links and tropes to identify regular patterns, and then to use these patterns to generate all possible exemplars. Using this method, it would be possible to identify missing items in the OMW. However, as language is not completely regular, this will require manual checking of the results.

4.2 Limitations

While the findings point to significant cross-linguistic patterns, several limitations need to be addressed to refine the analysis. Currently we only look for prefixes and suffixes. Because of this, more complicated morphology or substitution (e.g. 树/木 "tree"/"wood" in Chinese) will be missed. In future work, we may consider other patterns. Moreover, some of the difference links we find are just spelling variants (e.g. `+te`, evidenced in *toilet*/*toilette* or *sextet*/*sextette*. These can be explicitly marked as spelling variants in the GWA LMF format for wordnets (McCrae et al., 2021),

[3] Strangely, the OEWN is missing *two-spot* and *three-spot*.

[4] The exception is *one-spot*, which is likely the result of an annotation error in the OEWN.

but this has not yet been done systematically for English. We intend to highlight these as suggested improvements to the upstream wordnets when we find them.

5 Discussion and future work

The findings of this study have far-reaching implications for our understanding of figurative language across languages. By demonstrating that metonymy is more widely shared across languages than metaphor, we show a measurable difference between the relations. This indicates that metonymy, as a form of meaning extension based on association and contiguity, is more grounded in universal cognitive processes, possibly related to human categorization and object-referencing behaviours. In contrast, metaphor, which often requires analogical reasoning and cultural framing, appears to be more language-specific or culturally nuanced. These finding fit well with existing discussion in metaphor research. For example, Lakoff and Johnson (1980, p. 39) argue that "the grounding of metonymic concepts is in general more obvious than in the case with metaphorical concepts, since [metonymy] usually involves direct physical or causal associations".

A trope could be shared across multiple languages for several different reasons. One possibility is that the same trope arose independently in different languages, because speakers of different languages share some basic cognitive common ground, and the trope builds on some common cultural context. For example, the metaphor for *death* in example (1) and the metonym for *apple* in example (2) both appear in multiple languages: these tropes could have arisen independently in different speaking communities, because death is a universal part of the human experience, and apples have been grown around Eurasia since antiquity. Alternatively, it is also possible that the same trope appears in multiple languages because it was imported into one language from another. For example, the presence of the *death* metaphor in Catalan and Slovene could be because they are both Indo-European languages, which share a common ancestor. However, even if the same metaphor entered different languages from a common origin, the fact that the metaphor persists today is still of note. Many historical homonyms have presumably not had the same staying power, as otherwise we would expect the "unlinked" scores in Table 1 to be higher for languages which are more closely related in terms of their typology.

At a practical level, our results provide valuable insights for constructing multilingual lexical resources. The fact that metonymy exhibits more cross-linguistic consistency suggests that resources like wordnets can benefit from prioritizing metonymic links when constructing multilingual synsets. Future research could explore how languages with different cultural and historical backgrounds handle metonymy and metaphor differently, in order to enrich linguistic databases with finer-grained semantic distinctions. We would also like to conduct a detailed analysis of possible sense extension along the lines of Peters (2003) and Alonge and Lönneker (2004). Looking at a small subset of metonymical relations in three languages from EuroWordnet (Dutch, English and Spanish), Peters (2003) investigated how metonymy can be used to suggest missing senses, while Alonge and Lönneker (2004) did the same for metaphors. It should also be noted that in many cases a relationship could be described as metaphor or metonymy, depending on the perspective of the analyst and whether they are highlighting contiguity or similarity (Steen, 2005, p. 5).

Finally, we would like to add the metaphor/metonymy links to the WordNet LMF as new sense-level links. If this were done, it would then be possible to add the ChainNet links to the Open English WordNet (OEWN). ChainNet's detailed annotations of metaphor and metonymy offer a structured view of inter-sense relationships that is currently missing from OEWN. By integrating these links directly into OEWN, researchers and developers could benefit from a unified resource in which figurative sense extensions are directly accessible. This would make OEWN not only a more comprehensive lexical resource but also an essential tool for studying lexical polysemy and figurative language at scale. In addition, it would make it possible to keep the ChainNet data synchronised with the OEWN as new synsets and senses are added or deleted.

6 Conclusions

In this study, we have demonstrated that metonymy is more consistently multilingual than metaphor across over 30 languages. This finding underscores the importance of recognizing metonymy as a fundamental cognitive process that transcends cultural and linguistic boundaries, whereas metaphor seems to be more contextually bound to individual languages and cultures. Our use of ChainNet and the Open Multilingual Wordnet has allowed us to systematically explore these patterns and provide new insights into the structure of polysemy.

The results point to a greater need for linguistic resources that reflect these differences in how figurative language operates cross-linguistically. As linguistic researchers, we should continue to probe how and why certain figurative relations hold across languages while others do not. Future research should expand the dataset and explore these phenomena across more languages, ultimately deepening our understanding of the interplay between language, cognition, and culture.

In order to continue research such as this, it is essential to continue expanding wordnets and enhancing their searchability. Expanding these resources and linking them to sense-tagged corpora will unlock even deeper insights into the nature of polysemy and figurative language across cultures.

References

Antonietta Alonge. 2006. The Italian metaphor database. In *Proceedings of the Fifth International Conference on Language Resources and Evaluation (LREC'06)*, Genoa, Italy. European Language Resources Association (ELRA).

Antonietta Alonge and Birte Lönneker. 2004. Metaphors in wordnets: From theory to practice. In *Proceedings of the Fourth International Conference on Language Resources and Evaluation (LREC'04)*, Lisbon, Portugal. European Language Resources Association (ELRA).

Max Black. 1962. *Models and Metaphor*. Cornell University Press.

Max Black. 1977. More about metaphor. *Dialectica*, pages 431–457.

Francis Bond and Ryan Foster. 2013. Linking and extending an open multilingual wordnet. In *51st Annual Meeting of the Association for Computational Linguistics: ACL-2013*, pages 1352–1362, Sofia.

Francis Bond, Piek Vossen, John McCrae, and Christiane Fellbaum. 2016. CILI: The collaborative interlingual index. In *Proceedings of the 8th Global Wordnet Conference (GWC 2016)*, pages 50–57.

Valeria de Paiva and Alexandre Rademaker. 2012. Revisiting a Brazilian wordnet. In *Proceedings of the 6th Global WordNet Conference (GWC 2012)*, Matsue.

Sabri Elkateb, William Black, Horacio Rodríguez, Musa Alkhalifa, Piek Vossen, Adam Pease, and Christiane Fellbaum. 2006. Building a wordnet for Arabic. In *Proceedings of The fifth international conference on Language Resources and Evaluation (LREC 2006)*.

Christine Fellbaum, editor. 1998. *WordNet: An Electronic Lexical Database*. MIT Press.

Fausto Giunchiglia, Khuyagbaatar Batsuren, and Abed Alhakim Freihat. 2018. One world-seven thousand languages (best paper award, third place). In *International Conference on Computational Linguistics and Intelligent Text Processing*, pages 220–235. Springer.

Fausto Giunchiglia, Khuyagbaatar Batsuren, and Gabor Bella. 2017. Understanding and exploiting language diversity. In *Proceedings of the Twenty-Sixth International Joint Conference on Artificial Intelligence, IJCAI-17*, pages 4009–4017.

Fausto Giunchiglia, Gábor Bella, Nandu C. Nair, Yang Chi, and Hao Xu. 2023. Representing interlingual meaning in lexical databases. *Artificial Intelligence Review*, page 11053–11069.

Aitor Gonzalez-Agirre, Egoitz Laparra, and German Rigau. 2012. Multilingual central repository version 3.0: upgrading a very large lexical knowledge base. In *Proceedings of the 6th Global WordNet Conference (GWC 2012)*, Matsue.

Michael Wayne Goodman and Francis Bond. 2021. Intrinsically interlingual: The Wn Python library for wordnets. In *11th International Global Wordnet Conference (GWC2021)*.

Chu-Ren Huang, Shu-Kai Hsieh, Jia-Fei Hong, Yun-Zhu Chen, I-Li Su, Yong-Xiang Chen, and Sheng-Wei Huang. 2010. Chinese wordnet: Design and implementation of a cross-lingual knowledge processing infrastructure. *Journal of Chinese Information Processing*, 24(2):14–23. (in Chinese).

Hitoshi Isahara, Francis Bond, Kiyotaka Uchimoto, Masao Utiyama, and Kyoko Kanzaki. 2008. Development of the Japanese WordNet. In *Sixth International conference on Language Resources and Evaluation (LREC 2008)*, Marrakech.

Paul Jaccard. 1901. Étude comparative de la distribution florale dans une portion des alpes et des jura. *Bulletin de la Société vaudoise des sciences naturelles*, 37:547–579.

Roman Jakobson. 1956. The metaphoric and metonymic poles. In Roman Jakobson and Morris Halle, editors, *Fundamentals of Language*. Mouton de Gruyter.

Temuulen Khishigsuren, Gábor Bella, Thomas Brochhagen, Daariimaa Marav, Fausto Giunchiglia, and Khuyagbaatar Batsuren. 2022. Metonymy as a universal cognitive phenomenon: Evidence from multilingual lexicons.

George Lakoff and Mark Johnson. 1980. *Metaphors we live by*. University of Chicago Press.

Krister Lindén and Lauri Carlson. 2010. Finnwordnet — wordnet påfinska via översättning. *LexicoNordica — Nordic Journal of Lexicography*, 17:119–140. In Swedish with an English abstract.

Rowan Hall Maudslay, Simone Teufel, Francis Bond, and James Pustejovsky. 2024. ChainNet: Structured metaphor and metonymy in WordNet. In *Proceedings of the 2024 Joint International Conference on Computational Linguistics, Language Resources and Evaluation (LREC-COLING 2024)*, pages 2984–2996, Torino, Italy. ELRA and ICCL.

John P. McCrae, Michael Wayne Goodman, Francis Bond, Alexandre Rademaker, Ewa Rudnicka, and Luís Morgado da Costa. 2021. The global wordnet formats: Updates for 2020. In *11th International Global Wordnet Conference (GWC2021)*.

John P. McCrae, Alexandre Rademaker, Francis Bond, Ewa Rudnicka, and Christiane Fellbaum. 2019. English WordNet 2019 —an open-source wordnet for English. In *Proceedings of the 11th Global Wordnet Conference (GWC 2019)*.

George A. Miller. 1995. WordNet: A lexical database for English. *Commun. ACM*, 38(11):39–41.

Nurril Hirfana Mohamed Noor, Suerya Sapuan, and Francis Bond. 2011. Creating the open Wordnet Bahasa. In *Proceedings of the 25th Pacific Asia Conference on Language, Information and Computation (PACLIC 25)*, pages 258–267, Singapore.

Mortaza Montazery and Heshaam Faili. 2010. Automatic Persian wordnet construction. In *23rd International conference on computational linguistics*, pages 846–850.

Noam Ordan and Shuly Wintner. 2007. Hebrew wordnet: a test case of aligning lexical databases across languages. *International Journal of Translation*, 19(1):39–58.

Bolette Sandford Pedersen, Sanni Nimb, Jørg Asmussen, Nicolai Hartvig Sørensen, Lars Trap-Jensen, and Henrik Lorentzen. 2009. DanNet — the challenge of compiling a wordnet for Danish by reusing a monolingual dictionary. *Language Resources and Evaluation*, 43(3):269–299.

Wim Peters. 2003. Metonymy as a cross-lingual phenomenon. In *Proceedings of the ACL 2003 Workshop on the Lexicon and Figurative Language*, pages 1–9, Sapporo, Japan. Association for Computational Linguistics.

Emanuele Pianta, Luisa Bentivogli, and Christian Girardi. 2002. Multiwordnet: Developing an aligned multilingual database. In *Proceedings of the First International Conference on Global WordNet*, pages 293–302, Mysore, India.

Maciej Piasecki, Stan Szpakowicz, and Bartosz Broda. 2009. *A Wordnet from the Ground Up*. Wroclaw University of Technology Press. (ISBN 978-83-7493-476-3).

James Pustejovsky. 1995. *The Generative Lexicon*. MIT Press, Cambridge, MA.

Ervin Ruci. 2008. On the current state of Albanet and related applications. Technical report, University of Vlora. (`http://fjalnet.com/technicalreportalbanet.pdf`).

Benoît Sagot and Darja Fišer. 2008. Building a free French wordnet from multilingual resources. In *Proceedings of the Sixth International Language Resources and Evaluation (LREC'08)*, Marrakech, Morocco.

Gerard Steen. 2005. Metonymy goes cognitive-linguistic. *Style*, 39(1):1–11.

Sareewan Thoongsup, Thatsanee Charoenporn, Kergrit Robkop, Tan Sinthurahat, Chumpol Mokarat, Virach Sornlertlamvanich, and Hitoshi Isahara. 2009. Thai wordnet construction. In *Proceedings of The 7th Workshop on Asian Language Resources (ALR7), Joint conference of the 47th Annual Meeting of the Association for Computational Linguistics (ACL) and the 4th International Joint Conference on Natural Language Processing (IJCNLP),*, Suntec, Singapore.

Antonio Toral, Stefania Bracale, Monica Monachini, and Claudia Soria. 2010. Rejuvenating the italian wordnet: upgrading, standardising, extending. In *Proceedings of the 5th International Conference of the Global WordNet Association (GWC-2010)*, Mumbai.

Analysis of Anachronistic Lemmas and Semantic Fields in Ancient Greek WordNet

Gianluca Scatigno
Alma Mater Studiorum Università di Bologna, Bologna - Italy
Piazza San Giovanni in Monte, 2
gianluca.scatigno@unibo.it

Abstract

The Ancient Greek WordNet is a valuable resource for classical studies, but its accuracy is compromised by the presence of anachronistic semantic fields and lexical entries. This study conducts a comprehensive analysis to identify and categorize these anachronisms within the WordNet framework. The study systematically reviews and critiques semantic and lexical elements that are misaligned with the linguistic, cultural, and historical context of the ancient Greek world.

1 Ancient Greek WordNet

Over the past decade, there has been a significant proliferation of semantic-lexical resources for various languages, both modern and ancient, based on the WordNet relational model. This growth can be attributed not only to the crucial role of WordNets in linguistic studies but also to advances in artificial intelligence, particularly in Natural Language Processing (NLP), where many tasks take benefit of these databases[1].

The need to develop such resources has been especially critical for ancient languages like Latin and Ancient Greek[2]. For the latter, the Ancient Greek WordNet was created, and its structure will be briefly described here.

The Ancient Greek WordNet (AGWN) was modeled after the Princeton WordNet (PWN), following the same structure of synsets—groups of synonymous nouns, verbs, adjectives, and adverbs—organized in a hierarchical framework. This relational model captures semantic relations like hypernymy and hyponymy[3].

In AGWN, hyponymy and hypernymy are represented through semfields, which group synsets into broad macrocategories. These are defined using a numbering system based on the Dewey Decimal Classification (DDC), a general knowledge organization system commonly used in libraries and archives. The well-defined categories and extensive network of relationships within the DDC make it universally applicable across languages[4].

The backbone structure of AGWN consists of ten numbered classes, subdivided into ten divisions, which are further broken down into more specific sections. For example, class 100 (Philosophy & Psychology) includes divisions such as 110 (Metaphysics) and 120 (Epistemology), which can be further detailed into more specific categories. AGWN adopts this nested hierarchical structure to provide an adequate conceptual coverage, along with robust data organization[5].

Despite its strengths, AGWN has limitations in representing Ancient Greek, particularly due to anachronisms. Occasionally, lemmas may be associated with definitions that are completely out of context for classical antiquity.

These issues primarily stem from the data sources and the construction process of AGWN. Firstly, relying on Greek-English bilingual dictionaries may fail to capture the subtleties of ancient Greek semantics and polysemy, resulting in errors like the one previously mentioned. Additionally, the alignment with Princeton WordNet (PWN), which is based on contemporary English, may introduce anachronisms and errors that undermine semantic coherence[6].

Moreover, the classification system used in AGWN reflects modern knowledge organization schemes, which may not align with historical frameworks[7]. The Dewey system is not free from

[1] Bizzoni et al. 2014, 1140.

[2] Bizzoni et al. 2014, Minozzi 2009.

[3] Fellbaum 2005, 665-667.

[4] Bentivogli et al. 2014, 96.

[5] The Dewey Decimal Classification has been employed within the WordNet Domains Hierarchy project, which aimed to reorganize WordNet content across languages (vd. Bentivogli et al. 2014).

[6] Bizzoni et al. 2015, 47.

[7] Dewey published the classification in 1876 and it has

bias, rooted in the Eurocentric and colonial context in which it was developed. This, combined with Dewey's strong Christian orientation, has influenced the classification approach, leading to a predominant representation of Christianity and a neglect of other religions, which are consequently perceived as irrelevant and marginal[8].

In the end, the representation of semantic relations in ancient lexicons can differ significantly from modern conceptualizations.

My work on synsets is part of the PRIN 2022 "Resilient Septuagint". This project addresses the issue of intertextuality within the Biblical tradition, which is characterized by textual granularity and variety[9]. Its main goal is the development of a semantic search engine capable of managing this complexity and detecting Biblical citations within Greek texts. In this context, the semantic fields that we focus on are killing, healing, dream, and vision.

Synsets are crucial for capturing all relevant conceptual nuances, managing the granular and plural nature of Biblical texts—which never circulated in a single form—and understanding their relationship with other texts, such as early Christian commentaries.

2 Methodology

Inaccurate synsets can compromise NLP tasks, distorting model results and reducing coherence. When synsets are imprecise, NLP algorithms may misclassify or misinterpret textual data, resulting in erroneous outputs.

Consider a scenario where a lemma such as *apotheke* is mistakenly associated with a modern concept like "baseball" due to an erroneous synset definition. In this case, the model might misinterpret references to "storerooms" or "repositories" in ancient texts as related to contemporary concepts like "baseball". This mismatch could lead the model to inaccurately link unrelated passages or misrepresent the thematic content of the texts. For example, a passage discussing the storage of agricultural goods might be incorrectly connected to a text about sports.

been updated periodically since then to reflect changes in knowledge and terminology; M. Dewey (1876), *Classification and Subject Index for Cataloguing and Arranging the Books and Pamphlets of a Library [Dewey Decimal Classification].* Project Gutenberg, 2004. Retrieved July 15, 2024 from https://www.gutenberg.org/files/12513/12513-h/12513-h.htm

[8]Igwe - Ayandokun 2024, 214-227.

[9]Dainese - Mambelli 2024, 40-41.

An attempt to improve the precision of the Ancient Greek WordNet was made by Bizzoni et al. in 2015, focusing on a subset of lemmas based on the Homeric lexicon. This effort utilized distributional semantics to identify and correct lexical relationships through automated analysis of aligned corpora. [10]. However, manual refinement was also necessary to achieve the desired level of accuracy and reliability.

While a complete manual cleanup of the synsets—by assigning each lemma the most accurate definition—is theoretically possible, it is cost-effective due to time constraints. A practical approach is to begin by trimming down semfields, eliminating those that are completely out of context or anachronistic.

The elimination of the anachronistic categories was carried out in blocks of 100, based on the DDC, and evaluating the historical coherence of each with respect to the ancient Greek world. Once this step was completed, I conducted a general review, focusing on semfields that were similar or intersecting, and selecting the least misleading one.

This type of cleanup was performed across the entire database. To further refine the data regarding our fields of interest, I worked on a smaller group of lemmas selected by the philologists Laura Bigoni and Fabio Tutrone. For each lemma, which had previously been assigned several synsets of varying degrees of coherence by AGWN, I retained three synsets that best reflected the semantics of the lemmas, respecting their polysemy.

In this paper, I have focused mainly on the first part, relating to the analysis of semfields. Below, some examples of the semfields that could be removed from WordNet will be presented and discussed.

3 Anachronisms

Certainly, it is possible to identify and eliminate semfields that are clearly anachronistic. However, some semfields, while including modern and contemporary concepts, may still contain references to the ancient culture.

Semfields that can be safely eliminated are those related to modern and contemporary entities, institutions, and geopolitical concepts with no continuity with the ancient world, in order to mantain contextual and historical relevance. For example, many semantic fields in class 900 (Geography and

[10]Bizzoni et al. in 2015, 47-50.

History) pertain to modern states such as those in North, South, and Central America, or Oceania. This includes categories related to American culture and the New World, such as 897 (Native North American literatures) and 817 (American humor and satire in English). The same applies to other modern languages and their literary works, including Spanish, French, Italian, and Russian.

Additionally, semfields describing modern and contemporary historical events tied to these geopolitical entities, such as 940.2 - covering the historical period from 1453 onward, the early modern period - should also be excluded[11].

Another macro group includes objects, tools, technologies, and artistic or scientific techniques that have no equivalent in Ancient Greece. The most evident examples pertain to the digital and virtual worlds, such as the semantic fields 770 (Photography, computer art, cinematography, videography), 384.5 (Wireless communication), and everything related to IT and computing, primarily found in class 000 (Computer science, information, and general works).

This group also includes concepts tied to modern or contemporary inventions, such as 384.6 (Telephone), 358.1 (Guided missile forces and warfare), and 686 (Printing and related activities), which presuppose the invention of telephone communication, guided missile warfare, and printing[12].

Other examples come from the world of music, with semfields related both to musical genres, such as 784.5 (Pop Music), and to musical instruments that have no counterpart in ancient culture, such as 786.7 (Electrophones, electronic instruments).

However, more generic categories might still encompass elements relevant to both the ancient and modern worlds, such as 784.1 (General principles, musical forms, instruments) or semfields related to specific types of instruments that already existed in antiquity, like string, wind, and percussion instruments.

This demonstrates that some semfields can indeed contain elements useful for analyzing ancient languages. For instance, music is a form of artistic and cultural expression documented since antiquity. A similar argument could be made for philosophy. Perhaps more than any other intellectual discipline, philosophy spans centuries, continually exploring themes and questions rooted in ancient thought. It would not be surprising, therefore, to connect the term *episteme* to the epistemological doctrines of Kant and Wittgenstein, just as *psyche* relates to the ideas of Freud and Jung[13].

In other cases, elements consistent with the Hellenic context can also be found in categories related to much more modern concepts. I have found that this holds true mostly for disciplines and sciences that have a modern status but address issues that were already subjects of inquiry in ancient times.

Examples of this type can also stem from the already mentioned term *psyche*, with its various diachronic nuances. Indeed, some of the most interesting entries relate to the semantic field of perception, movement and vision, or even to subfields concerning the subconscious and altered states of mind. These are all psychological aspects that Greek language can describe meticulously with its rich and polysemous lexicon.

Just consider the variety of verbs used to indicate actions related to sight. The verb *horaw* alone encompasses a wide range of visual experiences, from simple sight to perceiving something with understanding, while *skeptomai* is entrusted with indicating careful observation and examination, and *theaomai* carries a connotation of contemplation and admiration. In contrast, *blepo* refers to a more active and direct form of observation[14].

Clearly, not all the categories of this section can be applicable or useful in ancient studies. The semfield 152.8 Quantitative threshold, discrimination, reaction-time studies, for example, refers to modern studies involving specific concepts and methodologies, that have no ancient equivalent.

Another emblematic case is the section 610-619, which covers 'Medicine and Health.' Undoubtedly, semfields like 612 Human Physiology and 616 Diseases will provide fundamental lemmas such as *kardia, soma, nous* or *nosos, ousia* and *algos*.

Similarly, categories related to wounds and injuries, as well as surgical, pharmacological, and therapeutic techniques in general, are relevant. While these categories may include many references to modern technologies—such as MRI or contemporary surgical methods—that lack ancient counterparts, eliminating these semfields entirely

[11]940.2 includes historical events up to 1814.

[12]Although specific technologies and weapons similar in terms of action and effect were employed, one cannot speak of "guided missile forces" in Ancient Greece; Partington 1999, XVI considers Greek fire and gunpowder represent «pre-modern forms of "scientific" knowledge».

[13]Wright - Potter 2000, 1-11; Brunschwig 2008, 229-240.

[14]Bran 2014, 216-222.

could result in the omission of important lemmas. These might include terms for body parts, types of wounds or cuts, various forms of trauma, and specific terminology related to military or scientific contexts, particularly those characteristic of Hippocratic medicine[15].

Whithout a doubt, it makes sense to handle semfields related to more general categories (e.g., 617 Surgery I& Related Medical Specialties) with greater caution and to disregard those that are more specific (e.g., 617.9 Geriatric, Pediatric, Military, Plastic Surgery, Transplantation of Tissue and Organs, Anesthesiology). Other examples may shed light on this approach.

In the case of engineering, which falls under sections 620-629, it is clear that we will find unequivocally anachronistic semfields related to advanced technologies, such as 629 Aerospace Engineering, or to modern concepts and inventions, like 621 Applied Physics and 626 Highway Engineering. In other cases, however, we will find semfields applicable to multiple historical periods, such as 623 Civil Engineering, or very general ones, such as 620.1 General Principles of Engineering.

If we take a semfield like 658.3 Personnel Management, the situation is different. We are dealing with a category that is already very specific and narrow in semantic and cognitive terms. Undoubtedly, the concept of personnel management - and even less so that of human resources - was not formalized as it is today. However, forms of it did indeed exist, from armies to state bureaucracy to public construction. It is certainly not difficult to imagine that within such a semfield, prominent lemmas like *hegemon, logistes* or *therapon* could be included, as they denote specific social roles.

Moreover, personnel and human resource management is a complex and interdisciplinary domain: it spans various disciplines, both ancient and modern, including sociology, philosophy, and economics. Moreover, many administrative and organizational aspects—although general in nature—are not in contradiction with the ancient world. This is true for processes such as selection and recruitment, for example of soldiers, or for training, such as that of future politicians[16].

Due to its less formalized nature compared to modern practices and its adherence to a different societal context, it is clear that this particular semfield will, in most cases, contain terms related to the modern world. Given that the semfield is already quite specific and narrowly defined, if the decision is not to eliminate it entirely, it would be advisable to manually clean the individual lemmas by associating them with the correct synsets.

On the other hand, it is quite plausible that some lemmas might appear in multiple semantic fields[17]. For example, to simplify, the lemma *psyche* could be relevant both to philosophical contexts and to modern psychological concepts.

This requires a careful evaluation of lemmas' applicability across different semantic fields. When a lemma appears in more than one field, it may be advantageous to assess which semantic field provides the most historically accurate and contextually appropriate representation, and to retain that one while disregarding the other. Given the large number of lemmas in AGWN, automating this process can be very useful.

4 Conclusion

Refining the Ancient Greek WordNet (AGWN) necessitates a careful balance between historical accuracy and semantic preservation. It is crucial to prioritize the removal of clearly anachronistic material. Simultaneously, retaining synsets and semfields that accurately reflect ancient contexts—despite potential overlaps with modern interpretations—is essential. This is particularly relevant for broader categories, which are more likely to contain diachronically valid and less specific elements.

Manual refinement is vital for detailed fields where anachronistic and historically accurate terms coexist; this is where biases can be most pronounced. Terms related to modern technologies or concepts without ancient counterparts must undergo rigorous review and be aligned with appropriate synsets[18]. This meticulous process minimizes the risk of misrepresentation and enhances the semantic accuracy of the database. Moreover, cross-checking problematic lemmas ensures that they are

[15]Until the last century, Greek medicine was often regarded as the foundation of modern biomedical science, celebrated for its rationality and clinical observations. Although this idealized view constrained a deeper understanding, it highlights a fundamental connection between ancient and modern medicine, demonstrating significant continuity and influence; van der Eijk 2005, XIV-XVI.

[16]Finley 1973, 17-34.

[17]By the way, a single lemma can be associated with multiple synsets; Biagetti et al. 2021, 259.

[18]Lemmas can be manually associated with other definitions, but typically WordNets, including AGWN, also provide the option to create new synsets and definition.

not confined solely to misleading semantic fields, thereby preserving valuable material.

The improvements in AGWN offer scholars more reliable tools for exploring ancient texts performing NLP tasks more accurately. They enable more nuanced insights into the semantic and intertextual relationships that have shaped the Greek literary traditions.

Moreover, this study highlights the theoretical importance of scrutinizing how modern frameworks can inadvertently impose contemporary biases on ancient knowledge. In doing so, it calls for a more critical use of digital resources in the study of antiquity, ensuring that the tools we rely on reflect the historical realities they aim to represent.

5 References

Luisa Bentivogli, Pamela Forner, Bernando Magnini, and Emanuele Pianta. 2014. Revising the Wordnet Domains Hierarchy: semantics, coverage and balancing. In *Proceedings of the Workshop on Multilingual Linguistic Resources*, pages 94-101.

Erica Biagetti, Chiara Zanchi and William Michael Short. 2021. Toward the creation of WordNets for ancient Indo-European languages. In *Proceedings of the 11th Global WordNet Conference 2021*, pages 258–265.

Yuri Bizzoni, Federico Boschetti, Riccardo Del Gratta, Harry Diakoff, Monica Monachini, and Gregory Crane. 2014. The making of Ancient Greek WordNet. In *Proceedings of the Ninth International Conference on Language Resources and Evaluation (LREC'14)*, pages 1140-1147.

Yuri Bizzoni, Riccardo Del Gratta, Federico Boschetti, and Marianne Reboul. 2015. Enhancing the Accuracy of Ancient Greek WordNet by Multilingual Distributional Semantics. In *Proceedings of the Second Italian Conference on Computational Linguistics CLiC-it*, pages 47-50.

Răzvan Bran. 2014. From Sight to Thought. A Diachronic View On the Greek Verbs of Cognition. *Research and Science Today* 2(8):216-222.

Jacques Burschwig. 2008. The epistemological turn. In *The Cambridge History of Hellenistic Philosophy*, pages 29-41.

Davide Dainese and Anna Mambelli. 2024. Intertestualità tra Bibbie e antichi commentari cristiani: l'esempio di simul nel De Genesi ad litteram di Agostino. *Lexicon Philosophicum. Internationl Journal for the History of Texts and Ideas* 11:40-65.

Melvil Dewey. 2004. Classification and Subject Index for Cataloguing and Arranging the Books and Pamphlets of a Library [Dewey Decimal Classification], *The Project Gutenberg EBook*.

Philip van der Eijk. 2005. *Medicine and Philosophy in Antiquity*. Cambridge University Press, Cambridge, UK.

Christiane Fellbaum. 1998. *WordNet: An Electronic Lexical Database (Language, Speech, and Communication)*, MIT Press, Cambridge, Ma.

Christiane Fellbaum. 2005. WordNet and Wordnets. In *Encyclopedia of Language and Linguistics*, pages 665-670.

Kingsley N. Igwe and Ahmed Abayomi Ayandokun. 2024. Review of the treatment of religion and religious works in the library of congress and Dewey decimal classification schemes for knowledge organization in libraries. *Samaru Journal of Information Studies* 24:214-227.

Stefano Minozzi. 2009. The Latin WordNet Project. In *Proceedings of the Fourth International Global WordNet Conference. GWC 2008 (Szeged, Hungary, 22nd-25th January 2008)*, pages 707-716.

Moses Israel Finley. 1973. *The Ancient Economy*, University of California Press, Berkeley, California.

James Riddick Partington. 1999. *A History of Greek Fire and Gunpowder*, The John Hopkins University Press, Baltimore, Maryland.

John Paul Wright and Paul Potter. 2000. *Psyche and Soma: Physicians and Metaphysicians on the Mind-Body Problem from Antiquity to Enlightenment*, Oxford University Press, New York.

Some Updates on the Development of an Historical Language Wordnet

Fahad Khan[1], Daniel Prado Aranda[2], Francesca Romana Cammisa[3], Michele Cavallaro[4], Maria Francesca Carmela Giusy Germanà[4], Federica Misino[4], Chiara Tenti[4], Javier E. Díaz-Vera[2], Francisco Javier Minaya Gómez[2], Francesca Frontini[1]

[1]Istituto di Linguistica Computazionale "Antonio Zampolli", Italy,
[2]Universidad de Castilla-La Mancha, Spain,
[3]University of Bologna, Italy,
[4]University of Siena, Italy

Correspondence: fahad.khan@ilc.cnr.it

Abstract

In this article, we give an update on an ongoing initiative to build an Old English Wordnet (OldEWN). The initial phase of this initiative was dedicated to the compilation of an emotion lexicon for Old English intended to function both as a stand-alone resource as well as a part (a sub-wordnet) of what will eventually be a wordnet covering the entire lexicon. In this phase, we worked with a pre-existing research dataset in the area of Old English emotions and re-used public domain lexicographic works as the basis of our lexicon. Another interesting aspect of this phase of our work was that it was a collaboration between researchers from the Istituto di Linguistica Computazionale, the Universidad de Castilla-La Mancha and a number of interns from the University of Siena. This initial phase is now over, and we are currently preparing to publish the wordnet in RDF format as well as to host it on a triple store. In this report we will give background on the process of creating this part of our wordnet and the challenges we faced, as well as describing the dataset itself.

1 Introduction

The term *Old English* (OE) refers to a set of related West Germanic dialects spoken in Great Britain from the 5th until the 12th centuries and which were the predecessors of modern English. OE has a corpus of surviving texts dating from the period c. 650 to c. 1150 CE, after which the language was essentially overshadowed by French for well-known historical reasons (Magennis, 2011). Although the development of computational resources for Old English has tended to lag behind that of other ancient languages, notably Ancient Greek and Latin, there has, nonetheless, been real progress on this front in the last few decades. Perhaps the most significant project in this regard has been the compilation and publication (in instalments) of a contemporary, scholarly dictionary for the language, the *Dictionary of Old English* (DOE)[1], first made available in an electronic edition as a CD-ROM and then via a web interface. In addition, the DOE project has also made a corpus available in TEI containing most surviving works in OE[2]. The DOE was intended to supersede previous legacy Old English lexicographic works, most notably the *Bosworth-Toller Anglo-Saxon Dictionary*[3] and *A Concise Anglo-Saxon Dictionary* by J. R. Clark Hall (we will refer to this latter work as CAS in what follows), both of which were first published in the 19th century and both of which have editions which are freely available in the public domain (at the time of writing). Notwithstanding the DOE's status as the single most comprehensive OE lexicon currently available – one that is informed by the latest contemporary scholarship in the field – both the Bosworth-Toller and CAS remain valuable resources and in particular for students of Old English. This is largely due to the DOE's status as a closed resource that can only be accessed from behind a paywall, but also because at the time of writing the DOE is still unfinished (although it does cover the majority of the letters in the OE alphabet). Another important electronic lexical resource for Old English is the *Thesaurus of Old English* (TOE), a lexico-semantic network whose organisational principles have been heavily inspired by Roget's Thesaurus[4] and which is also navigable via a graphical graph-based interface[5].

We have presented a very short (and incomplete) summary of the situation as regards OE language resources in order to give some background to the work which is to be described in the rest of the article in which we detail an ongoing initiative to build another kind of lexical resource for Old English,

[1]https://doe.artsci.utoronto.ca/
[2]http://hdl.handle.net/20.500.12024/2488.
[3]https://bosworthtoller.com/
[4]https://oldenglishthesaurus.arts.gla.ac.uk/
[5]http://evoke.ullet.net/app/#/view?source=toe

namely a wordnet. It is worth noting that this initiative was inspired by (and shares numerous aims in common with) previous work on the construction of Latin[6] and Ancient Greek wordnets[7]. In our particular case, however, the plan is to proceed by focusing on specific semantic fields (trying, whenever possible, to integrate the latest research on these semantic fields and the OE lexicon into our work). This will result in a number of different domain-specific wordnets, each of which is intended to be used both as a stand-alone resource and to be eventually integrated into a more comprehensive wordnet covering the whole OE lexicon (and containing those, more general concepts which weren't included in the component wordnets), this is the Old English Wordnet *(OldEWN)*. The present work is concerned with the forthcoming publication of a wordnet covering the OE emotion lexicon – that is, that part of the OE vocabulary which is dedicated to the expression and/or description of the emotions and other related concepts (an introduction to the OldEWN project in general is given in (Khan et al., 2022)). In the following section, Section 1.1, we will expand upon the specific motivations behind this work as well as the approach which we have taken while working on this part of the Old English Wordnet (OldEWN) project. In section 2 instead we give a detailed description of the resource itself.

1.1 Constructing An Old English Wordnet for Emotions

One strong impetus behind the current work was the desire to see how wordnets could be used to compare conceptualisations in a given semantic field across languages, or across different stages of the same language. In the case of emotion terms, we were originally interested in comparing Old English with Latin in order to track the influence of cultural exchanges and language contact on the conceptualisation of emotions, as well as making comparisons between Old English and Modern English, to see how stable certain distinctions were over time. Note that, although the work presented in the current paper remains within the framework of the standard wordnet schema, we are planning on enriching and extending this schema to allow for more sophisticated descriptions of linguistic and historical relationships between senses and between languages; see (Khan et al., 2023).

[6]https://latinwordnet.exeter.ac.uk

[7]https://greekwordnet.chs.harvard.edu

When it comes to actually putting together the lexicon our approach throughout the whole OldEWN project has been based on the use of pre-existing lexicographic resources as a means of bootstraping our resource (an approach which isn't uncommon in the creation of wordnets for historical and under-resourced languages). Primary among these pre-existing resources is Clark-Hall's Concise Anglo-Saxon dictionary (CAS) which is the foundation of our attempts to construct OldEWN thanks to its fairly authoritative lemma list[8], the relative brevity of its definitions (making them easier to process and work with), and of course the fact that it is now in the public domain. In the case of the emotion lexicon, we also based our efforts on a research dataset previously compiled by one of the co-authors of the current work, Javier Díaz-Vera, and which gives a comprehensive description of the emotion lexicon of OE from a cognitive linguistics point of view. Although our initial choice of OE words was based on the list in this dataset, the CAS supplied us with the exact form of each lemma, as well as an initial list of senses for each entry (including those senses that weren't in Díaz-Vera's original research dataset). We used the definitions in the CAS to assign synsets to senses by matching them to glosses from the Open English Wordnet [9] (McCrae et al., 2019, 2020) and then deriving synsets on the basis of shared ILI (Interlingual Index) identifiers. This process wasn't always straightforward, and often the CAS defintions were only a starting point, to be modified according to our original research dataset and augmented with other lexicographic material, including definitions from the Bosworth Toller. In view of these difficulties we decided to carry out the whole process manually. However, the experiences gained during this stage will help us in future experiments on automating this process.

In order to add an extra layer of conceptual organisation to our wordnet, and to make it easier to navigate, we adopted the classification of the emotions proposed by the Geneva Wheel of Emotions (GWE) (Scherer, 2005). This classification can be found in Table 1. Here we summarise the procedure we used to generate the OldEWN emotion lexicon:

[8]The orthography used in the CAS is followed by other resources such as the DOE and the TOE, something which can be vital in a language such as OE with such a varied orthography.

[9]https://en-word.net

- *Generating a list of lexical entries*: the list of entries was taken from the Díaz-Vera dataset classifying emotion words in Old English (see (Khan et al., 2023) for more details on this dataset and its relationship with the OldEWN), this list was subsequently added to on the basis of the CAS and the BT,
- *Establishing a list of lemmas and senses*: lemmas (i.e., the canonical forms of the words chosen in the last step) were taken from a public domain OE lexicon (CAS); where possible the senses for these terms were based on the definitions for the entries in CAS (even if our senses don't always correspond to those listed as individual, separate senses in the dictionary); sometimes we modified and/or added senses when they were in our original dataset but not in the CAS,
- *Mapping synsets to senses*: next, we searched for the Open English Wordnet synset gloss that best matched the meaning of each of the senses derived in the previous step (we compared synset glosses with the senses and their definitions as determined in last stage) and assigned senses Interlingual Index ILI identifiers (Bond et al., 2016) accordingly; in many cases there wasn't a synset gloss that matched exactly, so we we looked for potential hyponyms; in future work we intend to propose new interlingual index concepts using the pre-existing Global Wordnet Association workflow on the basis of our observations in this stage,
- Finally we generated new Old English synsets based on those senses that are mapped to the same ILI.

It is worth noting that the work described here was the fruit of a collaboration between three different institutions, and in particular of researchers from the the Istituto di Linguistic Computazionale «A. Zampolli» and the University of Castilla-La Mancha who worked along side student interns from the *Lingue e comunicazione interculturale e d'impresa* BA of the University of Siena. A large part of the success of the work being described here can be attributed to the success of this collaboration.

2 Resource Description

The output of the work described in the last section is a lexical resource describing the whole emotion vocabulary of Old English (as well as related words) with the senses of words organised in synsets according to the standard wordnet schema. We intend to publish this resource as an RDF dataset with an open licence (CC-BY) both in a triple store, making it available via a public SPARQL endpoint, as well as depositing it in a CLARIN repository. We also plan to continue working on other parts of the OE lexicon in the near future. In addition to this, we plan to enrich the emotion lexicon by integrating information on semantic shifts and adding etymological links to modern English words. The current version of the resource can be found here: `http://lari-datasets.ilc.cnr.it/OldEWN_Emotions#`

2.1 The Old English Lexicon of Emotions: A First Version

We decided to generate our lexicon directly as an RDF dataset in the turtle format[10]; this is one of the formatting/publication choices recommended by the Global Wordnet Association[11]. One of the main motivations behind this choice was that it made it easier to make our data publically available for querying using the powerful SPARQL query language, and for eventually linking to other datasets. For instance, we can easily extract the list of lemmas in the lexicon with the following simple query:

```
SELECT ?f
    WHERE
    {
        ?l ontolex:writtenForm ?f .
    }
    ORDER BY ?f
}
```

Listing 1: Simple SPARQL Query.

In effect then, with this dataset we have created a linguistic knowledge graph of Old English emotion words in which lexical semantic information is organised using the wordnet schema. The initial work of compiling the data was carried out using Google sheets, we subsequently downloaded each sheet in the TSV format and which we then converted to RDF using an adhoc Python script that made use of the Python library RDFLib. In particular we modelled our data using the OntoLex-Lemon vocabulary[12] as well as the specialised wordnet RDF vocabulary[13] which has been made available by the

[10]https://www.w3.org/TR/turtle/
[11]https://globalwordnet.github.io/schemas/
[12]https://www.w3.org/2016/05/ontolex/
[13]https://globalwordnet.github.io/schemas/wn

GWA for the purpose of publishing and exchanging wordnets as linked data (we will refer to this latter vocabulary as wn in what follows). After carrying out the conversion and following an initial data cleaning process we ended up with a lexicon consisting of 1522 Old English lexical entries, along with 2358 lexical senses and 1021 synsets. Our senses are tagged for the emotional semantic fields featured in Table 1 and taken from the GWE.

Emotion (GWE)	**Senses**	**Examples**
General Emotions	136	*brēostwylm*
Involvement-Interest	51	*georn, ellen*
Amusement-Laughter	24	*gamen, ārǣran*
Pride-Elation	86	*þrútian*
Joy-Happiness	167	*hyht, drēam*
Enjoyment-Pleasure	70	*bliss*
Tenderness-Feeling Love	71	*lufu, lufian*
Wonderment-Feeling Awe	78	*āblycgan, ege*
Feeling Disburdened-Relief	12	*līhtan*
Astonishment-Surprise	15	*styltan, ofwundrian*
Longing-Nostalgia	164	*gītsung*
Pity-Compassion	18	*efensārgung, frōfornes*
Sadness-Despair	228	*biter*
Worry-Fear	804	*sēoðan*
Embarrassment-Shame	215	*scamu*
Guilt-Remorse	68	*gylt, scyld*
Disappointment-Regret	64	*hrēow, bētan*
Envy-Jealousy	24	*æfeste, anda*
Disgust-Repulsion	151	*fēogan, hatian*
Contempt-Scorn	30	*forsēon*
Irritation-Anger	126	*irisian, irre*

Table 1: Emotion, Number of Entries, and Example Words

We use the wn property `note` to associate this information with individual senses. One can easily write a SPARQL query to count the number of senses belonging to each category:

```
SELECT (COUNT(?s) AS ?triples)
WHERE {
?s a ontolex:LexicalSense ;
    wn:note "Involvement-Interest"@en .
  }
```

Listing 2: Ontolex-Lemon example in turtle.

In what follows, we will look at the word *bliss* from the Enjoyment-Pleasure semantic field to show how the OldEWN is structured. The lexical entry with its three senses is as follows:

```
:BLISS_N a ontolex:LexicalEntry ;
    lexinfo:gender lexinfo:masculine ;
    ontolex:canonicalForm :BLISS_N_lemma ;
    ontolex:sense [
                a ontolex:LexicalSense ;
                skos:definition "'bliss,'␣
                    merriment,␣happiness"@en ;
                ontolex:isLexicalizedSenseOf :
                    olde_924 ;
                wn:note "Enjoyment-Pleasure"@en,
                "Joy-Happiness"@en
                ],
                [
                a ontolex:LexicalSense ;.
                skos:definition "kindness,␣
                    friendship,␣grace,␣favour"
                    @en ;
                ontolex:isLexicalizedSenseOf :
                    olde_468 ;
                wn:note "Enjoyment-Pleasure"@en,
                "Joy-Happiness"@en
                ],
                [
                a ontolex:LexicalSense ;
                skos:definition "cause␣of␣
                    happiness"@en ;
                wn:note "Enjoyment-Pleasure"@en,
                "Joy-Happiness"@en
                ];
    wn:partOfSpeech wn:noun .
```

Listing 3: Example Entry.

The first of these senses is associated with an Old English synset with the identifier `old_924`. This latter synset is defined as follows. Note the link to the ILI concept with identifier i110442.

```
:olde_924 a ontolex:LexicalConcept ;
    skos:inScheme <http://example.org/olde/> ;
    wn:definition [ rdf:value "a state of extreme
        happiness"@en ] ;
    wn:ili ili:i110442 ;
    wn:partOfSpeech wn:noun .
```

Listing 4: Synset

Again one of the most important advantages of making our resource available in RDF is that we can use the SPARQL language to create queries such as the following which lists all the senses belonging to the same synset.

```
SELECT DISTINCT ?s
WHERE {
?l ontolex:sense ?s .
?s ontolex:isLexicalizedSenseOf :olde_294 .
?s  skos:definition ?d .
  }
```

Listing 5: SPARQL Query

2.2 Conclusions and Future Work

In this submission we have given an update on the development of a wordnet for Old English, focusing on the publication of that part of the resource which describes emotion terms in Old English and which is now complete. Aside from beginning to work on other semantic fields we have listed a number of future aims throughout the paper (in particular enhancing our resource with information on semantic shifts). To these we add the following:

- Adding links to other relevant resources. This includes linking to Old English entries for the words in our wordnet (where they exist) in the linked data version of Wiktionary, DBnary[14] (Sérasset, 2015); we would also like to add

[14] https://kaiko.getalp.org/about-dbnary/

etymological links from our wordnet to Open English Wordnet[15].

- Another goal is to add new concepts derived from the vocabulary of Old English to the Collaborative Interlingual Index (CILI). This latter serves as a bridge between different wordnets, facilitating cross-linguistic comparisons. We aim to enhance the representation of ancient and historical languages in global wordnet resources in collaboration with other researchers working on wordnets for e.g., Latin and Ancient Greek, making it easier for researchers to draw connections between Old English and other languages represented in the CILI. (Vossen et al., 1999; Bond et al., 2016)

References

Francis Bond, Piek Vossen, John Philip McCrae, and Christiane Fellbaum. 2016. Towards a universal index of meaning. In *Proceedings of the 8th Global WordNet Conference (GWC)*, pages 50–57.

Fahad Khan, John P. McCrae, Francisco Javier Minaya Gómez, Rafael Cruz González, and Javier E. Díaz-Vera. 2023. Some considerations in the construction of a historical language WordNet. In *Proceedings of the 12th Global Wordnet Conference*, pages 101–105, University of the Basque Country, Donostia - San Sebastian, Basque Country. Global Wordnet Association.

Fahad Khan, Francisco J. Minaya Gómez, Rafael Cruz González, Harry Diakoff, Javier E. Diaz Vera, John P. McCrae, Ciara O'Loughlin, William Michael Short, and Sander Stolk. 2022. Towards the construction of a WordNet for Old English. In *Proceedings of the Thirteenth Language Resources and Evaluation Conference*, pages 3934–3941, Marseille, France. European Language Resources Association.

Hugh Magennis. 2011. *The Cambridge Introduction to Anglo-Saxon Literature*. Cambridge University Press.

John P. McCrae, Alexandre Rademaker, Francis Bond, Ewa Rudnicka, and Christiane Fellbaum. 2019. English WordNet 2019 – An Open-Source WordNet for English. In *Proceedings of the 10th Global WordNet Conference – GWC 2019*.

John Philip McCrae, Alexandre Rademaker, Ewa Rudnicka, and Francis Bond. 2020. English WordNet 2020: Improving and Extending a WordNet for English using an Open-Source Methodology. In *Proceedings of the Multimodal Wordnets Workshop at LREC 2020*, pages 14–19.

[15]https://en-word.net

Klaus R. Scherer. 2005. What are emotions? and how can they be measured? *Social Science Information*, 44(4):693–727.

Gilles Sérasset. 2015. Dbnary: Wiktionary as a lemon-based multilingual lexical resource in rdf. *Semantic Web*, 6(4):355–361.

Piek Vossen, Wim Peters, and Julio Gonzalo. 1999. Towards a universal index of meaning. In *Proceedings of ACL-99 workshop, Siglex-99, standarizing lexical resources*, pages 81–90.

Enhancing Lexical Resources: Synset Expansion and Cross-Linking Between ItalWordNet and MariTerm

Lucia Galiero[1], Federico Boschetti[2], Riccardo Del Gratta[2], Angelo Mario Del Grosso[2], Monica Monachini[2]
[1]Università di Bologna, Forlì, Italy
[2]Istituto di Linguistica Computazionale "Antonio Zampolli", Consiglio Nazionale delle Ricerche (ILC-CNR), Pisa, Italy
lucia.galiero@studio.unibo.it
{federico.boschetti, riccardo.delgratta, angelomario.delgrosso, monica.monachini}@ilc.cnr.it

Abstract

This paper outlines the first operation towards a full update of MariTerm, a WordNet-like resource on maritime terminology developed and maintained by CNR-ILC, in preparation for future compliance with FAIR principles (Wilkinson et al., 2016). The project focused on expanding and linking synsets between ItalWordNet (IWN), a general lexical database for Italian, and MariTerm to enrich IWN with maritime concepts. A semi-automatic pipeline was developed to facilitate this process, prioritizing critical semantic relations and automatic evaluation. Key outcomes include an enriched ItalWordNet with links to MariTerm concepts and a revised MariTerm with connections to IWN synsets. While further refinement is needed, this work marks a significant step toward integrating maritime terminology into ItalWordNet.

1 Introduction

In the last twenty years, research best practices in Digital Humanities have integrated the effective organization and representation of knowledge with the need of making data available for long-term preservation and re-use. In this regard, leveraging legacy resources can contribute to save them from being consigned to oblivion, but also enriches modern resources (Frontini et al., 2016).

The project hereafter described takes measures in this direction with a work involving two key lexical resources for the Italian language: ItalWordNet[1], a comprehensive and generalized lexical database, and MariTerm (Marinelli and Spadoni, 2007), a specialized resource for maritime terminology.

As for the task, the main objectives of the project were the expansion of ItalWordNet, and the linking of relevant synsets from ItalWordNet to MariTerm and vice versa. For further clarification, the concept of "expansion" here refers to updating ItalWordNet synsets with missing semantic information (mostly critical semantic relations and synsets) from MariTerm. The term of "linking" should instead be intended the creation of systematic links between related synsets across the two resources.

The remainder of this contribution is organized as follows: Section 2 illustrates previous work, Section 3 provides a brief overview of the lexical resources involved, Section 4 will delve into the major setbacks encountered, Section 5 will discuss the implemented approach, and finally Section 6 will discuss and summarize results, as well as possible advancements of the present work and specifications on distribution of produced data.

2 Related Work

Previous work in linking a specialized resource to a general WordNet has been provided with the case of the GeoNames ontology (Frontini et al., 2016). The resource was originally issued in English and was already available as Linked Open Data (LOD) in RDF. Its content was later integrated to Princeton WordNet 3.0 (PWN) (Fellbaum, 1998) and to IWN. The most recent LOD WordNet resource for Italian provided by the ILC-CNR is represented by

[1]See for more: `https://www.ilc.cnr.it/progetti/italwordnet-2/`

IWN 2.0[2], which was created in compliance with the WordNet 2.0. specifications[3].

Another case for a cross-linked lexical resource is provided by Ancient Greek WordNet, (Bizzoni et al., 2014), whose content has also been released in LOD and matched English-Greek concepts have been mapped to PWN. Within the creation of AGWN, PWN has also been implemented as a pivot to link Greek concepts to several other languages covered by the project, mainly Croatian and Latin. This cross-lingual linking model that implements PWN as pivot network is also known as MultiWordNet (MWN) (Pianta et al., 2002). However, as we will illustrate in the upcoming paragraph, ItalWordNet builds relations with other WordNets through another model.

3 The Resources

3.1 ItalWordNet

ItalWordNet (Roventini et al., 1998), was initially developed the late 1990s and the early 2000s as part of the EuroWordNet project (Vossen, 1998)[4], which created WordNets for several European languages, and the Italian national project SI-TAL[5]. IWN organizes Italian words into synsets, i.e., sets of groups of synonyms that share a common meaning and are interchangeable in certain contexts, capturing internal lexical-semantic relationships. In all its versions, IWN is designed to align with Princeton WordNet, and has been upgraded and enlarged over time (Niero, 2006; Bocco et al., 2003). Nevertheless, IWN has always been developed independently form other WordNets, resulting in different sets of semantic relations and in potential loss of information when converting the resource to new formats (Quochi et al., 2017).

3.2 MariTerm

Developed in the mid-2000s in collaboration with the Port of Livorno, MariTerm is a lexical-semantic database focusing on maritime terminology, based on the Word-Net model. While it perfectly mirrors IWN's WordNet-like structure, the MariTerm ontology maps maritime terms to their specific concepts of nautical science and maritime transport. Although lacking the extensive coverage of generalized lexicon seen in IWN, it represents an invaluable resource for specialized terminology.

3.3 Resource architecture

Both ItalWordNet and MariTerm can be marshalled in eXtensible Markup Language, and their structures are both based on the EuroWordNet model (Vossen, 1998). Specifically, alignment to EWN for multilingual application is achieved via the InterLingual Index (ILI). Thus, these two resources for Italian are not directly aligned to the PWN, as it was in the case of AGWN (Bizzoni et al., 2014) and GeoNamesWordNet (Frontini et.al., 2016). Nonetheless, the shared overlapping representation of synsets in both IWN and MariTerm ensures rich semantic connectivity, facilitating the cross-resource linking. **Error! Reference source not found.** summarizes the content and the extension of all resources involved[6]. It should also be noted that, at the time of the writing, both original resources were available in XML format but did not comply to any of the Global Wordnet standards[7]. Moreover, since MariTerm does not have an updated version in LOD to date (see Section 5 for more), it was decided to implement a version of IWN that was not converted to a LOD representation for the sake of suitability. Regarding the scope of this work, neither the resulting resources have been updated to the aforementioned standards in order to reflect the structure of the originals.

[2]Available at: http://hdl.handle.net/20.500.11752/ILC-66.

[3]WN 2.0. Specifications available at https://www.w3.org/2006/03/wn/wn20/

[4]More info also at: https://archive.illc.uva.nl/EuroWordNet/

[5] More at: https://www.ilc.cnr.it/progetti/tal-2/

[6] Both original resources contained duplicate synsets. Specifically, 809 were found in IWN and 27 in Mariterm, and were identified by means of the same numerical ID and first word form listed. Numbers remained consistent through all the phases of the work presented in this contribution, and no significant information was lost. Although these duplicates were retained in all resources, the numbers in Table 1 and Table 3 reflect only the unique items, excluding duplicates.

[7]See for more: https://globalwordnet.github.io/schemas/

4 Major Setbacks

The overarching structure of both IWN and MariTerm showed total overlap. However, this shared feature did not suffice from the earliest stages of developing a pipeline, and other potential issues gradually accumulated.

One key issue was that synsets in each resource had different unique identifiers, making a direct alignment impossible. Furthermore, even in cases where lemma (word form) and sense attributes matched for a couple of synsets, semantic relations often diverged, leading to inconsistencies in meaning. This other type of mismatch made it even more impractical to rely solely on these attributes for updating and linking the two resources. For instance, it was observed that each of the matched synsets for the word "navigare" (EN: "*to sail*") corresponds to different sense numbers. This might be a possible result of IWN and MariTerm being developed as independent resources, but also a result of the word "navigare" (EN: "*to sail*") having multiple sense variants in both lexical databases.

Further ambiguity was introduced by the presence of multiple lemmas within a single synset, a common feature in both resources but that could lead to redundant or wrong alignments altogether.

Most importantly, neither resource seemed to feature a suitable attribute or section for cross-resource linking. Notably, the MariTerm introductory paper (Marinelli and Spadoni, 2007) stated the presence of a section for cross-resource linking, which was still nowhere to be found upon further inspection. Specifically, the links provided in such sections were represented by plug-in relations, a type of semantic relations that connects synsets across specialized and general WordNets (Niero, 2006). In their turn, plug-in relations can be identified as upward (if linking a specific term to a general one), downward (if vice versa) and horizontal (if connecting synsets by any other type of relation). The two former kinds of links were the most used for this work due to the semantic relations that were chosen as object of focus.

On a minor note, discrepancies in definitions between corresponding synsets increased the challenges. In fact, some synset couples displayed different definitions, which posed a problem as to which definition should be used in the final output files. In other cases, definitions were missing from at least one of the two resources, with the risk of losing crucial information for synset comparison and evaluation. One example for actual definition discrepancy comes from the synsets for the word "pagaia" (EN: *"paddle"*):

- IWN definition: "remo a pala larga con il quale si voga senza appoggiarlo alla falchetta."

  (EN: "wide-bladed oar with which one rows without resting it on the sickle.")

- MariTerm definition: "remo con le due estremità a pala che si maneggia tenendolo al centro con entrambe le mani si usa sulle canoe e su altri natanti di tipo fluviale o balneare".

  (EN: "paddle-like ends that is handled by holding it in the middle with both hands – it is used on canoes and other watercraft of the river or bathing type")

Following is instead a case for missing definition from a resource, taken from the synset for the word "azimut" (EN: "*azimuth*"):

- IWN definition: *missing*

- MariTerm definition: "nella navigazione astronomica indica l'arco di cerchio compreso tra il nord e la verticale dell astro stesso."

  (EN: "in astronomical navigation, the arc of a circle between north and the vertical of the star itself.")

5. Expansion and Linking stages

This work focused on critical semantic relations such as near-synonymy, hyponymy, hyperonymy, and their variants for synsets belonging to different parts of speech (i.e., "xpos_near_synonym" etc.).

5.1 Preliminary candidate extraction

The expansion and linking process we developed consisted of two main phases, each implemented in a dedicated Jupyter Notebooks using Python[8]. The

[8] Notebooks and data available at: `https://drive.google.com/drive/folders/1mJLIS16qRkAp8UobGEkoxtSfsq8-p1o6`

first one focused on extracting shared synsets as follows: extraction of all synsets from both XML files, identification of shared ones, and saving the output in a CSV file for further analysis.

Within this context, the first problem that was solved was the presence of multiple lemmas inside synsets across resources. Specifically, the Python script was designed to match synsets only if the first lemma listed was the same, and such a logic would be implemented for this and all subsequent portions of the pipeline[9].

5.2 Scoring, matching synsets and expanding IWN

5.2.1. The similarity score framework

The second phase centred on the expansion and linking process. Once the transitory resource with preliminary candidates was refined, it was necessary to build a scoring metric between synsets across resources to ensure that only the best match of synsets was picked up, thus identifying and preventing incorrect updates and ambiguities from early on.

The first step towards calculating similarity for synset pairs was vectorization, which was applied to all definitions inside the datasets, including both definitions for a given main synset and its possible target synsets. Albeit mainly used on large collections of texts rather than lexical databases, the TF-IDF approach still yielded consistent results in a time-efficient way, due to it being applied only to definitions. Without looking at the data and assuming that all synsets and target words linked to a semantic relation featured a definition in both resources, the amount of sentences reaches up to a potential 200.000 total sentences of different lengths. Definition redundancy, in a way, provides another major advantage for the use of TF-IDF. As a matter of fact, definitions for target words tend generally to be the same as the one for the synset they point to. Such consistency allows TF-IDF to better capture uniqueness of words across the definition pool, leading to more nuanced results.

The resulting vectors were then compared via cosine similarity. The rest of the scoring metric is based on two main calculations: similarity of synset definitions and weighted relation similarity. The former compares the definitions (also known as "glosses") of synsets with the same lemma in both resources. In its own regard, relation similarity compares the definitions of target synsets in both databases, multiplying scores obtained by target synset definitions by a weight that reflects the importance of the semantic relation (e.g., hyperonymy, hyponymy). Weights for hyperonymy and hyponymy amount to 0.82 and 0.7 respectively, with both values being based on an existing work by Tülü et al. (2019) which assigned weights for semantic relations inside WordNet 3.0. On the other hand, weights for all other relations at the core of this project were not presented in the work described by Tülü et al. (2019), probably due to IWN inheriting all its semantic relations from EuroWordNet, thus presenting a notable structural difference with WordNet 3.0. Therefore, weights for relations that were not mentioned by Tülü et al. (2019) were manually assigned, with near synonymy being awarded 0.6. All others were given a baseline of 0.5. The abovementioned structural differences with WordNet 3.0 present an argument as to why advanced pipelines for automated weight assignment for WordNet semantic relations like SemSpace (Ohran and Tülü, 2021) were deemed unsuitable for the extent of the present work.

The scores for definition similarity and weighted relation similarity are then summed together. Shared relations between synsets were awarded bonuses, while relations that were present in MariTerm, but missing in IWN, were penalized. This tailored method allowed for more accurate and precise alignment between the two lexical resources.

5.2.2. Synset update pipeline

As soon as the score computation was complete and its detailed breakdown saved in another CSV file, the expansion process began by selecting lemmas inside the spreadsheet that met certain similarity criteria. Subsequently, synsets are expanded with missing semantic relations.

To account for missing definition in synsets, a fallback mechanism was implemented, where a fallback definition is retrieved by examining in a predefined order the semantic relations associated with the given synset without gloss.

In case of discrepancies between glosses were detected (i.e., where glosses across resources vary

[9] A more refined approach for future work could involve checking for intersections between resources, e.g. using more shared lemmas to retrieve similar synset pairs, thus improving the accuracy and reliability of synset linkages.

for a synset or a target word) any definition from MariTerm inside IWN was replaced with the gloss from IWN where applicable. In the special case where the synset from IWN was the only one not having a definition, it inherited the gloss from MariTerm. In all other cases, no gloss substitution was carried out. Moreover, if a missing semantic relation pointed to a target word that did not feature its own synset inside of IWN, the automatic process ensures the creation of a new synset with a new identifier.

Finally, a key feature of all WordNet-like resources is consistency, where connections among WordNet synsets are reciprocal (i.e., if a synset shows an hyponymy relation to a certain target synset, the latter will contain, in its dedicated entry, a hyperonymy relation pointing to the first synset). These connections were also considered while designing the Python script and are consequently processed to maintain consistency within IWN.

After all expansions were applied, the system re-orders synsets for better navigation.

5.3 Post-expansion modifications

5.3.1 Manual edits and further gloss inconsistencies

Before proceeding with the linking, a manual check was carried out to validate the newest updates. Out of the approximately 400 synsets involved in the update, several modifications addressed issues in 20 synsets that were either incorrectly aligned or missed during the expansion process. This stage implied manually inserting or creating new synsets and resolving inconsistencies in definitions and semantic relations. Roughly 100 of the new synsets also had a numerical ID that was already taken from other synsets, and new numeric identifiers were checked and inserted manually. Moreover, 241 of the newly added synsets still presented gloss inconsistencies, where a synset displayed a definition when listed as a target synset, but not in its main entry. A small, dedicated script in Python was designed to resolve such conflict.

5.4. Linking stage

The linking step constituted the final stage of the whole pipeline. Since the original resources did not feature a suitable section or attribute to insert cross-resource links, the most viable solution seemed to be the creation of a custom node. This would be designed to store cross-resource connections (or plug-in relations) and would have the same structure of the section connected to PWN via the ILI index. Such an arrangement seemed to be the most suitable since the section connected to the ILI is defined inside of both resources and shows the same structure in each database.

The MariTerm introductory paper (Marinelli and Spadoni, 2007) described the node as being situated right between the internal links among resource synsets and the external links between the WordNet database and the ILI. Eventually, it was decided to mirror the description provided by Marinelli and Spadoni (2007) and place the node accordingly.

As for the linking process per se, an automatic mechanism for updating the plug-in nodes within the structure of the files was crucial. It started by clearing any existing plug-in nodes for each synset to ensure a clean state. For each synset, it matched corresponding synsets from MariTerm and IWN, creating new nodes for plug-in relations. Specifically, the nodes were populated with the newly added relations, which were slightly edited by the addition of a "plug-"prefix to differentiate them from ordinary semantic relations. Another kind of relation that populated the nodes is represented by "plug-synonym" relations. As described by Niero (2006), these are used for "overlapping synsets, i.e., synsets that have a similar meaning albeit belonging to different databases" (Niero, 2006).

During the linking process, all plug-relations were tracked to avoid duplicates, and any synset without a match was given an empty node to maintain structural consistency. Finally, the output files were saved with properly formatted entries, ensuring the newly integrated data was well organized and ready for future use.

6. Discussion

6.1 Results

Table 2 illustrates breakdown of results yielded by the semi-automated pipeline, both for the IWN synset expansion and cross-resource linking. In its turn, Table 3 provides insight into the content of the updated IWN versions, before and after manual post-hoc modifications. The final IWN version produced by the pipeline is intended to be the one that underwent manual changes and was enriched with the new synsets and the links to MariTerm concepts.

Data involved	**Count**
MariTerm > IWN expansion	
Preliminary candidate synsets	1157
Identified synset matches	747
IWN Word meanings updated	397
New synsets created in IWN	363
New Relations in IWN	1160
IWN <> MariTerm Linking	
IWN synsets linked to MariTerm	742
New IWN relations linked to MariTerm	843
MariTerm synsets linked to IWN	751
MariTerm relations linked to IWN	0

Table 1 - Results of the whole pipeline, divided by section

Resource	**Synsets**	**Lemmas**	**Internal Relations**
Automated, unedited IWN	49482	46425	133004
Post-hoc edited IWN	49477	46423	132983

Table 2 - Expanded versions of IWN (before and after manual edits)

The pipeline successfully matched 750 synsets from MariTerm into IWN. Of these, 397 ItalWordNet entries were successfully updated, resulting in the addition of 1160 missing relations and 363 new synsets. The lower number of updated entries should not be seen as discouraging, since the automatic process purposedly skips all matches that had no penalties, therefore needing no update whatsoever. As for the linking part, 742 IWN synsets were mapped as plug-synonyms to MariTerm, and 848 out of the 1160 new relations were linked back to the corresponding MariTerm synsets.

On the other hand, the mapping of IWN matched synsets and relations inside MariTerm was not as successful. While a total of 751 of synsets contained a very simple link to ItalWordNet, the updated file contains 1085 relations for plug-synonymy. The consequent implication is that some of the plug-synonyms are duplicates that refer to homonyms. Moreover, out of the 843 relations that were linked from ItalWordNet to MariTerm, the reversed linking did not work for any of the relations added to ItalWordNet. Such an outcome calls for urgent improvements in revising and automating the linking pipeline.

Theoretically, as described by Niero (2006), once the links are established between two overlapping synsets by means of plug-synonymy or plug-near synonymy, the following step is the creation of a new synset inheriting the hypernymy relations from the general lexical resource, with the hyponymy relations and synonyms being passed down from the specialized database. Since the creation of dedicated nodes provided a base for adding plug-ins, the creation of new synsets with these features represents a possible future advancement in enhancing the two resources.

Moreover, the mapping of IWN concepts inside MariTerm faced challenges, such as duplicate plug-synonym relations, suggesting that the automated pipeline needs refinement to better handle term overlap and ambiguity. Additionally, the manual evaluation of the new synsets inside IWN highlights the need for further improvement of the semi-automated pipeline.

6.2 Future advancements

Applications based on the proposed method are developable provided that two (or more) WordNet-based resources share the same representation, sets of semantic relations and same format standards, like in the described case.

Once the issues with the cross linking in the produced resources are resolved, the updated IWN and MariTerm could largely benefit from being fully converted in LOD format (e.g., RDF) or even by following the OnotoLex lemon format (McCrae et al., 2017). Given how Italian WordNet-like resources present potential issues for cross-lingual mapping of concepts due to their alignment to the relatively old EWN model, a future parallel advancement for long term interoperability with PWN could even consider a full conversion of LOD MariTerm to Open Multilingual WordNet, following the steps described in the work done by Quochi et al. (2017).

All in all, legacy resources like MariTerm have the potential to be integrated into broader frameworks like ItalWordNet, ensuring both the preservation and active use of specialized terminology. However, the degree of complexity of these kinds of resources raises important questions as to how much automation should be implemented to process, create and innovate WordNets.

6.3 Distribution

The data contained in the updated MariTerm with the plug-in extensions is currently available on the CLARIN4ILC repository at: `http://hdl.handle.net/20.500.11752/OPEN-1034`, where it will be stored for the long term. It is advisable to check the page regularly as license specifications and other metadata will be updated soon.

References

Yuri Bizzoni, Federico Boschetti, Harry Diakoff, Riccardo Del Gratta, Monica Monachini, and Gregory Crane. 2014. The Making of Ancient Greek WordNet. In *Proceedings of the Ninth International Conference on Language Resources and Evaluation* (LREC'14), pages 1140–1147, Reykjavik, Iceland. European Language Resources Association (ELRA). http://www.lrec-conf.org/proceedings/lrec2014/pdf/1071_Paper.pdf

Andrea Bocco, Luisa Bentivogli, and Emanuele Pianta, 2003. ArchiWordNet: Integrating WordNet with Domain-Specific Knowledge. In *Proceedings of the Second International WordNet Conference*. Pages 39-46, Brno, Czech Republic https://hdl.handle.net/11583/1917825

Christiane Fellbaum. 1998. *WordNet, an electronic lexical database.* MIT Press, Cambridge, Massachussets

Francesca Frontini, Riccardo Del Gratta and Monica Monachini 2016. GeoDomainWordNet: Linking the Geonames ontology to WordNet. In *Lecture notes in computer science*, pages 299-233. https://doi.org/10.1007/978-3-319-43808-5_18

Rita Marinelli and Giovanni Spadoni, 2007. Modeling a Maritime Domain Ontology, In *Tenth International Symposium on Social Communication,* pages 511–515, Santiago de Cuba, Cuba

John P. McCrae, Julia Bosque-Gil, Jorge Gracia, Paul Buitelaar, and Philipp Cimiano. 2017. "The Ontolex-Lemon model: development and applications." In *Proceedings of eLex 2017 conference*, pages 19-21.

Federica Niero. 2006. WordNet e sue applicazioni. Revisione e implementazione di un database di termini matematici [BSc. Thesis, Università degli Studi di Padova] pages 73-77. https://www.math.unipd.it/~laurap/grupponlp/TesiNieroFederica.pdf,

Umut Orhan, and Cagatay Neftali Tülü. 2021. A novel embedding approach to learn word vectors by weighting semantic relations: SemSpace. *In Expert Systems With Applications, 180*. Pages 1-3, 5-7 https://doi.org/10.1016/j.eswa.2021.115146

Emanuele Pianta, Luisa Bentivogli and Christian Girardi. 2002. *MultiWordNet: developing an aligned multilingual database*. In *Proceedings of the First International WordNet Conference* , pages 293-302. Mysore, India https://hdl.handle.net/11582/499

Valeria Quochi, Roberto Bartolini, and Monica Monachini. 2017. 'ItalwordNet goes open'. LiLT, Vol. 10, Issue 41

Adriana Roventini, Antonietta Alonge, Nicoletta Cazlolari, Bernardo Mangini, and Francesca Bretagna. 1998. ItalWordNet: Building a large semantic database for the automatic treatment of Italian. *In Linguistica Computazionale*, (XVIII-XIX), pages 745-791 https://hdl.handle.net/11582/2033

Cagatay Neftali Tülü, Umut Orhan, and Ehran Turan. 2019. Semantic Relation's Weight Determination on a Graph Based WordNet. In *Gümüşhane Üniversitesi Fen Bilimleri Enstitüsü Dergisi.* pages 67, 75-76 https://doi.org/10.17714/gumusfenbil.432582

Piek Vossen. 1998. *EuroWordNet: A multilingual database with lexical semantic networks.* Kluwer Academic

Mark Wilkinson, Michel Dumontier, IJsbrand Jan Aalbersberg, Gaby Appleton, Myles Axton, Arie Baak, Niklas Blomberg, Jan-Wiillem Boiten, Luiz Olavo Bonino da Silva Santos, Philip Bourne, Jildau Bouwman, Anthony Brookes, Tim Clark, Merce Crosas, Ingrid Dillo, Olivier Dumon, Scott Edmunds, Chris Evelo, Richard Finkers, and Barend Mons. 2016. The FAIR Guiding Principles for scientific data management and stewardship. *Scientific Data, 3.* https://doi.org/10.1038/sdata.2016.18

Expanding and Enhancing Derivational and Morphosemantic Relations in Princeton WordNet

Ivelina Stoyanova
Institute for Bulgarian Language
Bulgarian Academy of Sciences
Sofia, Bulgaria
iva@dcl.bas.bg

Svetlozara Leseva
Institute for Bulgarian Language
Bulgarian Academy of Sciences
Sofia, Bulgaria
zarka@dcl.bas.bg

Gianina Iordăchioaia
University of Graz
Graz, Austria
gianina.iordachioaia@uni-graz.at

Verginica Barbu Mititelu
RACAI
Bucharest, Romania
vergi@racai.ro

Abstract

We propose enhancements of the Princeton WordNet data by expanding and enriching the collection of verb – noun derivational pairs with additional linguistic information. We focus on: (i) assigning an explicit derivational affix to the verb or noun involved in each of the derivational relations defined in Princeton WordNet (both for the pairs in the provided standoff file and for those additionally extracted); (ii) determining the derivational direction, especially for zero-derived pairs; (iii) providing a morphosemantic relation for the non-annotated derivationally-related pairs along the lines already implemented in the annotated collection made available in the standoff file.

The RESULTING DATASET includes 5330 cases of zero derivation (2964 $zero_V$ and 2366 $zero_N$), 833 cases of direct noun-to-verb suffixal derivation, 15,801 cases of verb-to-noun suffixal derivation, as well as 1454 cases of either indirect derivation or derivation of both the verb and the noun from a third word.

1 Introduction

In this paper, we propose the enrichment of the Princeton WordNet (PWN) with morphological, derivational and semantic information for the verb – noun pairs that have an explicit derivational relation. Our objectives include: (i) enriching the derivational information in WordNet by assigning an explicit derivational affix to the verb and/or noun involved in each of the derivational relations starting with those pairs included in the PWN morphosemantic database made available as a standoff file and continuing with the derivationally related pairs additionally extracted from PWN; (ii) introducing the new feature of derivational direction within the description of the derivational relations, especially for zero-derived pairs; (iii) expanding the semantic relations by assigning morphosemantic relations to the identified derivationally related verb–noun pairs in PWN that have not yet been annotated with such a relation, along the lines adopted in the standoff file.

For the purpose of the work, we rely on several resources: (a) PWN (Miller et al., 1990b; Fellbaum, 1998), version 3.0, and the derivational relations defined in it; (b) the PWN morphosemantic database distributed as a standoff file[1] (Fellbaum et al., 2009), in which pairs of derivationally related nouns and verbs are labeled with one of 14 morphosemantic relations: Agent, Event, By-means-of, etc.; (c) the Oxford English Dictionary (OED) accessed through an API[2] and two lists of verb-to-noun zero-derived pairs and noun-to-verb zero-derived pairs provided by the OED team[3]; (d) lists of verbalising and nominalising suffixes compiled from theoretical literature, with a generalised invariant for each suffix.

Our contribution consists, first of all, in supplementing the derivational relations in WordNet with information about the nominalising and/or verbalising suffixes used in the derivation. The resulting dataset contains both originally provided verb–noun pairs supplied with morphosemantic relations from the standoff files, as well as additionally identified derivationally related pairs of literals. Second, not only pairs with overt suffixes, but also zero-derivation verb–noun pairs are supplied with information about the direction of derivation: verb-

[1] https://wordnetcode.princeton.edu/standoff-files/morphosemantic-links.xls

[2] https://developer.oxforddictionaries.com/

[3] We thank James McCracken and Emily Hoyland (the OED team) for providing us with the lists of zero nouns and zero verbs and API access.

to-noun or noun-to-verb. In this way, we are able to analyse the zero verb-to-noun suffix separately from the zero noun-to-verb suffix, and study the two comparatively. Moreover, we have attempted to develop methods for automatic detection of the direction of derivation based on lexicographic information from the OED (year of attestation, number of senses of the verb and the noun, frequency of usage). Third, we expand the number of pairs labeled with a morphosemantic relation by assigning them to the derivationally related pairs extracted from PWN.

Various subsets of the dataset can be used for a number of tasks: morphological and derivational analyses, validation of hypotheses on suffixal and zero-derivation, morphosemantic and other verb–noun relations in WordNet. We discuss our considerations on how such a dataset can help in identifying regular polysemy and in polysemy resolution. (Chalub et al., 2016) have shown that adding morphosemantic relations to a wordnet (in their case to the Portuguese Open WordNet (de Paiva et al., 2012)) helps to improve its quality.

Section 2 provides a summary of the recent research in derivational morphology, making a case for the need for large-scale empirical data as a testing ground for linguistic hypotheses. Section 3 describes the challenges and motivates the use of the PWN as a reliable resource in such a task. Section 4 centres on the methodology used in the annotation of the data, starting with how the derivational and semantic information in PWN can be combined towards the enhancement of the initial datasets, as well as outlining the procedures for expanding the data with new levels of description. Section 5 presents the final dataset, while Section 6 discusses the possibility to deepen the analysis by exploring some features of the dataset and PWN structural organisation. We finally outline the next steps of our research in Section 7.

2 Related work

Although polysemy in derivation has long been assumed to follow the general patterns of polysemy with lexical words (Rainer, 2004), recent research in lexical semantics recognizes that derivational processes contribute their share to polysemy and that affix polyfunctionality, in particular, poses a real challenge for lexical semantics (Grimshaw, 1990; Plag, 1999; Lieber, 2004, 2016; Bierwisch, 2009; Melloni, 2011; Bauer et al., 2013; Iordăchioaia and Melloni, 2023; Salvadori and Huyghe, 2022; Kawaletz, 2023; Valera, 2023).

Among the early attempts to model polysemy in derivation and affix polyfunctionality we find Plag (1999), who investigates the productivity of the different affixes involved in verb derivation in English, by looking at neologisms and using the OED for their meanings. Plag uses relations such as locative, ornative, causative, resultative, inchoative, performative and similative to describe derived verbs and argues that *-ify* and *-ate* are phonologically conditioned allomorphs of *-ise*, the most representative suffix, which systematically incorporates and expresses all the relations above. One important claim that Plag makes is that the variety of meanings that conversion/zero may express is so large that there cannot be any specific meaning attached to it (unlike for *-ise*; see also Clark and Clark (1979); Lieber (2004)). He argues that at least relations such as instrumental, privative and stative need to be added to those above to describe zero-derived verbs (Valera, 2023, for discussion on these relations in verbal derivation). This implies that the meaning of verbalising zero should be less predictable than that of the suffix *-ise* in relation to the derivational base.

The unpredictability of zero for verbal derivation, especially from noun bases, has been further confirmed by a large corpus-based study with distributional semantic methods by Kisselew et al. (2016), who predict the derivational direction of zero noun-verb pairs from semantic specificity (building on the assumption that derived words are more specific than their bases) and apply measures of information content (Entropy and Kullback-Leibler Divergence) to distributional representations of verbs and nouns in English. Their results show that information content is a good predictor for zero nouns derived from verbs but not for zero verbs derived from nouns. This means that the zero verbalising suffix is not predictable from the meaning of the base, while the zero nominalising suffix is. This further entails that zero is not necessarily less predictable than overt suffixes, but the derivational direction is crucial. In addition, the study presented by Kisselew et al. (2016) also makes the case for the need for both large-scale corpora for testing the linguistic hypotheses and gold-standard datasets against which the testing may be carried out.

Other quantitative studies with a computational approach such as Varvara (2017); Varvara et al. (2021, 2022) investigate nominalising suffixes in languages like Italian, German and French. Varvara (2017) focuses on event nominalisations in Italian and German with the aim to model the competition between different nominalising suffixes. The conclusion Varvara (2017) reaches is that the main difference between the competing nominalising suffixes in Italian is semantic, to the extent that they refer to different senses of their base verbs and disambiguate the vagueness of the base. For German, Varvara (2017); Varvara et al. (2021) argue that infinitive-based nominalisations are semantically more predictable from the base verb than those formed with the derivational suffix *-ung*, and that they are closer to inflectional processes like participial formation in this respect, while *-ung* is closer to proper derivation by means of the agentive suffix *-er*.

Varvara et al. (2022) develop and test an annotation scheme for derived nouns in context, by which they annotate the ontological type of their meaning and their relationship with the base (see this work also for further similar efforts on other languages). They annotate 4,500 corpus occurrences of 90 deverbal nouns ending with 6 different suffixes in French. For this, they develop an annotation sample that includes 23 ontological types (e.g. animate, artefact, event, etc.), 21 relational types (agent, beneficiary, result, etc.) and 62 complete types, the last of which is an attested combination of the other two. As a follow-up, these authors have enriched their work to include 42 derivational suffixes and 4 conversion forms in French (Varvara et al., 2024).

Lapesa et al. (2018) investigate the polysemy of deverbal nominalisations with the suffix *-ment* in English, by analysing a set of 55 types and 406 tokens extracted from the Corpus of Contemporary American English (Davies, 2010) and annotating them as eventive vs. non-eventive vs. ambiguous. To avoid possibly lexicalized readings and to extract productive polysemy patterns, they consider only low frequency neologisms of this kind. They build a distributional semantic model which can distinguish between eventive and non-eventive readings to a good extent and mostly needs only small context windows to identify the intended meaning. They find out that eventive readings are easier to classify than the non-eventive ones, which is usually due to the semantic similarity between abstract non-eventive and eventive nouns. While the study of Lapesa et al. (2018) does not make such fine distinctions as the one by Varvara et al. (2022), a question that arises for the latter is how viable the semantic distinctions they propose may be for other languages and how successfully they could be used for an automatic annotation.

Current research in derivational morphology, involving studies in both theoretical and computational or corpus linguistics, makes a strong claim for the need for constructing large-scale databases comprising rich derivational information that would enable reliable and possibly bias-free observations and conclusions.

The effort described in this paper and the resulting resource aim exactly at providing a database of derivationally and semantically related verb – noun pairs by building on an existing resource, increasing the amount of the data and enriching it with explicit suffixes and the direction of derivation.

3 Motivation and challenges

As previous literature shows (Plag, 1999; Fernández Alcaina, 2021; Lapesa et al., 2018; Varvara et al., 2022; Kawaletz, 2023; Lara Clares, 2023; Valera, 2023), work on the meaning and polyfunctionality of affixes involves large human annotation efforts. Unfortunately, such efforts often remain only locally exploited and are not further refined by other researchers because the methodology underlying the annotation is too specific to the purposes of the individual task. Indeed, these annotations are not free of possible bias due to the theoretical framework or practical assumptions adopted in the annotation guidelines. Ideally, human annotation efforts should target a more general lexical semantic description of a language, so that lexical semanticists would be able to employ such independently created and unbiased lexical resources to more objectively test their theoretical hypotheses.

This is precisely what the PWN project provides for English derivational morphology. WordNet is a rich lexical semantic resource that can be exploited to obtain new insights into affix polyfunctionality and develop automatic tools for disambiguation and polysemy resolution. Moreover, the PWN database was created on the basis of principles independent of the purpose of affix disambiguation, which makes it all the more reliable for such a task, unlike in the case of most databases created and annotated for this precise purpose.

Another advantage of the PWN is the organisation of the data along the concept of sense (represented by a synonym set) and not word. This allows a precise description and better understanding of the meaning relations that occur between derivationally-related words (in their different senses). In particular, the same or different morphosemantic relations may be found to hold between different senses of two derivationally-related words, a fine distinction that is not always captured by dictionaries. For instance, the verb *articulate* and the noun *articulation* occur as a pair several times and, depending on the meanings they enter the pairs, they are labeled with a different morphosemantic relation: Uses (for the meanings 'provide with a joint' and '(anatomy) the point of connection between two bones or elements of a skeleton (especially if it allows motion)' and for the meanings 'provide with a joint' and 'the shape or manner in which things come together and a connection is made'), Event (for the meanings 'speak, pronounce, or utter in a certain way' and 'expressing in coherent verbal form', for the meanings 'express or state clearly' and 'expressing in coherent verbal form', for the meanings 'provide with a joint' and 'the act of joining things in such a way that motion is possible' and for the meanings 'put into words or an expression' and 'expressing in coherent verbal form'), Property (for the meanings 'speak, pronounce, or utter in a certain way' and 'the aspect of pronunciation that involves bringing articulatory organs together so as to shape the sounds of speech').

Last but not least, the 14 morphosemantic relations in PWN are formulated to capture both derivational directions: from noun to verb and verb to noun. This leads to a more coherent and systematic ontology of the relations than in the previous literature, where, for instance, the diverse morphosemantic relations identified in verb formation (Plag, 1999; Valera, 2023) are entirely different from those in noun formation (Lieber, 2016; Varvara et al., 2022), without any evidence of the need to distinguish them. The PWN actually offers evidence for quite the opposite.

4 Methodology

The section presents the procedures for enhancing the original data supplied by the PWN project in terms of derivational and morphosemantic relations, by expanding their coverage, on the one hand, and adding new levels of description, on the other. We start with outlining some prerequisites that we rely on in the annotation procedures.

4.1 Prerequisites

We employ data derived from the PWN, and supplement it with information compiled from other resources.

Morphosemantic Database from PWN (MSD DATASET). This dataset is distributed by the PWN project[4] as a standoff file consisting of 17,739 derivationally related noun-verb pairs, which are labeled with a morphosemantic relation (such as Agent, Instrument, Event, etc.) (Fellbaum et al., 2009). Table 3 shows the set of morphosemantic relations with short definitions and examples.

Dataset of derivationally related verb–noun pairs in PWN (DERIV DATASET). This dataset covers 18,344 synset pairs in total, between whose members a derivational relation exists in PWN. Additionally, we identify automatically 23,418 pairs of literals within each pair of synsets which share a common base and use verbalising and nominalising suffixes.

In the DERIV DATASET there are 4,520 noun–verb pairs of literals that are not in the MSD DATASET and are linked by a derivational relation alone (i.e., with no morphosemantic relation assigned), e.g. *carbon* and *carbonate*.

Dataset from OED of zero derivation verb–noun pairs with the direction of derivation (OED ZERO DATASET). The dataset contains two lists derived from OED[5]:

- a list of 2,830 pairs of verb and noun OED lexical entries labeled as verb-to-noun zero derivation;
- a list of 5,921 pairs of verb and noun OED lexical entries labeled as noun-to-verb zero derivation.

Set of nominalising, verbalising and other suffixes (SUFFIX DATASET). This dataset comprises 7 verbalising and 26 nominalising suffixes in total, which are reduced to 5 and 11 invariant verbalising and nominalising suffixes, respectively. These represent direct noun-to-verb or verb-to-noun derivations, including also zero_N and zero_V suffixes.

There are further 36 suffixes which take part in more complex derivational patterns, such that both

[4]https://wordnetcode.princeton.edu/standoff-files/morphosemantic-links.xls
[5]https://www.oed.com

the noun and the verb are derived from a third word (e.g., *rigidify – rigidness* both derived from the adjective *rigid*; *criminalise – criminal* both derived from the adjective *criminal*) or they are derived in several steps (e.g., *argue – argumentation* with an intermediary step *argument*; *attract – attractiveness* with an intermediary *attractive*).

4.2 Identifying the suffixes in derivationally related pairs of literals

For each derivational pair in the combined data from MSD DATASET and DERIV DATASET, we identify the following categories: (a) zero derivational pairs both for the noun to verb (*bottle > to bottle*) and the verb to noun (*to walk > the walk*) direction; (b) cases of overt verbalising suffixes such as *-ise*, *-ify*, *-ate*, etc. involved in the derivation of verbs from nouns; (c) cases of overt nominalising suffixes such as *-ion*, *-ing*, *-ment*, etc. involved in the derivation of nouns from verbs; (d) cases of other derivational models.

Suffix identification was performed automatically by finding the common base of the noun and the verb and the endings, matching them to known suffixes. The allomorphs of suffixes are mapped to the canonical form of each suffix. For instance, *-ion*, *-tion* and *-ation* are treated as variants of the same suffix *-ion*. In this way, we provide a unified and more complete representation in terms of the derivational pairs and the morphosemantic relations each (abstract) suffix is involved in.

In such a way, the productivity and the polyfunctionality of each suffix is made explicit along with the relative probability for a suffix to be the exponent of a given relation.

4.3 Direction of conversion and affixal derivation

The overt suffixes are clearly associated with a particular direction of derivation since they are either verbalising (e.g., *-ise, -ify*, etc.) or nominalising (e.g., *-ment, -ion, -ing*, etc.). In our data, 833 pairs of verb–noun literals are identified with a verbalising suffix, thus assigned a noun-to-verb direction; and 15,801 pairs of verb–noun literals are identified with a nominalising suffix, thus assigned a verb-to-noun direction.

The dataset contains 5,330 cases of zero derivation. For these the OED ZERO DATASET and the OED API Service are used to determine the derivational direction. Via the OED API we obtain the definitions of the verb and noun zero derivatives and match them semi-automatically (automatic matching with manual validation) to PWN senses based on lexical and semantic similarity between OED sense definitions and PWN glosses. The identification of the closest match of OED entries to PWN synsets allows us to transfer the information about the direction of derivation from the OED ZERO DATASET to the zero derivational verb–noun pairs in PWN.

Incorporating information on the direction in zero derivation verb–noun pairs allows us to distinguish between verbalising and nominalising zero affixes, given the important differences between them (Kisselew et al., 2016), and to treat them uniformly with overt suffixes. Directionality in zero derivation is a long-known non-trivial task, especially for languages such as English with barely any morphological evidence (Marchand, 1964; Kiparsky, 1982; Plank, 2010; Bram, 2011). To ensure a high reliability of the derivational direction, we coded it on the basis of the OED ZERO DATASET lists.[6] Building further on our dataset, future research on directionality in conversion will be able to employ the morphosemantic relations specific to a derivational relation as a further directionality criterion (Barbu Mititelu et al., 2023).

There are further 1454 verb–noun derivationally related pairs of literals exhibiting more complex derivational patterns. These cases have not been assigned a direction of derivation.

4.4 Newly assigned morphosemantic relations

We develop procedures to expand the morphosemantic relations annotation in PWN. For this purpose, we explore several semantic features in the PWN description.

We analyse the synset gloss of the derived word and search for certain triggers which signal a particular morphosemantic relation. For instance, a noun synset gloss beginning with "the act of..." or "an event of..." indicates the existence of an Event relation between the noun and the verb in the pair under observation. Triggers such as "an instrument for...", "a device for...", "an implement for...", etc. correlate with an Instrument relation, and so forth.

[6] To determine directionality, OED lexicographers have reportedly considered the full history of each word, including date of attestation, early frequency of use, but also linguistic and etymological factors such as the behavior of cognate words, the donor in case of loanwords, and semantic properties to the extent that the more basic meaning would be associated with the base word (Philip Durkin, p. c.); see also Plag (2003) for directionality tests.

Another feature used in a complementary manner with the gloss, especially when the latter does not provide sufficient information, is the semantic class (defined as a semantic primitive or prime) assigned to each noun or verb synset in PWN. Semantic primes as presented in Miller et al. (1990a) define language-independent semantic classes, in particular 25 noun classes, e.g. noun.person, noun.artifact, noun.act, and 15 verb classes, e.g. verb.emotion, verb.motion, verb.communication. For instance, when considering the morphosemantic relation to be assigned to the pair *sink* "go under" (e.g., *The raft sank and its occupants drowned*) – *sinking* "a descent as through liquid (especially through water)", the annotator should be prompted by the prime of the nominal synset (noun.event) and the association between the Event relation and semantic class noun.event.

A third feature employed in the assignment of the morphosemantic relations is the membership of the related synsets in certain subtrees in which a morphosemantic relation occurs (frequently) between other pairs. Consider the case of *nickel*:1 – *nickel*:1, *silver*:1 – *silver*:1, *copper*:1 – *copper*:1 and *chrome*:1 – *chrome*:1. The verb synsets are hyponyms of *cover*:1, while the nouns are hyponyms of *metal*:1, and all the pairs are assigned the morphosemantic relation Uses, which in this case may be interpreted as a relation between (i) a noun denoting a metal, which is used to cover a surface or a thing so that it acquires some quality of the metal, and (ii) a verb denoting the action of covering with the metal. There are other pairs in PWN, e.g.: *aluminium*:1 – *aluminize*:1, where the verb is a hyponym of *cover*:1 and the noun is a hyponym of *metal*:1, but their derivational relation is not labeled morphosemantically. The semantics of the relationship between the members of the unlabeled pair is very likely the same as for the labeled ones above. After inspecting the glosses, one can confirm with certainty that the pair *aluminium*:1 – *aluminize*:1 is an instance of the Uses relation.

The judgments were made by trained annotators according to a methodology which is based on the linguistic features outlined above.

These criteria are applied on their own or in combination, as well as in consideration of the suffix and its distribution across relations in the available data. For instance, with nouns derived with the suffix *-er* and having the prime noun.person, the relation is unambiguously determined as Agent, while for those with the semantic prime noun.artifact, the relation is most likely Instrument. This conclusion becomes self-evident if one considers the very strong correlation between these primes and the respective relations established for the suffix.

Suffix	Base	Derivation	#
zero$_V$	*fake*	*to fake*	2964
-ise	*agony*	*to agonise*	463
-ate	*acetyl*	*to acetylate*	219
-ify	*city*	*to citify*	151
-en	*threat*	*to threaten*	16
-ion	*to admit*	*admission*	4330
-er	*to adjust*	*adjuster*	3442
zero$_N$	*to glide*	*the glide*	2366
-ing	*to play*	*the playing*	1987
-ment	*to replace*	*replacement*	699
-ance	*to occur*	*occurrence*	367
-ant	*to pollute*	*pollutant*	159
-age	*to parent*	*parentage*	145
-al	*to dispose*	*disposal*	135
-ure	*to press*	*pressure*	108
-ee	*to train*	*trainee*	83
Other	*rigid*.adj	*to rigidify – rigidness*	1454

Table 1: Distribution of verbalising and nominalising suffixes in the RESULTING DATASET with examples

5 Results

The resulting resource, RESULTING DATASET, presents a comprehensive description of derivationally related pairs of verb–noun literals including the suffixes, the direction of derivation (whenever available), as well as semantic information in the form of an assigned morphosemantic relation between the noun and the verb. While based on the derivational relation, in essence, the morphosemantic relation is semantic and thus extends beyond the particular pair of literals, and holds between the corresponding verb and noun synsets.

Table 1 shows the distribution of the data for each derivational direction and each suffix.

Less productive and unproductive suffixes such as *-th* in *grow - growth*, have also been included in the RESULTING DATASET, as they provide valuable data about the frequency of the respective derivational processes, their representation in comparison with derivations with other suffixes and the roots involved in them.

Along with derivational pairs obtained in a single derivational step, we also preserve the ones that involve a more complex process, such as a 2-step derivation or derivation from another base word. Although these pairs have no clear direction of derivation, a particular morphosemantic relation can be identified, and for this the direction is not mandatory.

The resulting resource also includes British/American spelling doublets such as *acclimatize – acclimatization* and *acclimatise – acclimatisation*, thus providing a fuller picture of the variants of English. In certain cases, e.g. for the purposes of machine learning and automatic identification of morphosemantic relations, these can be considered as duplicates and removed in order to avoid skew in the data.

Table 2 shows the association of each canonical suffix with different subsets of the 14 morphosemantic relations. While there is substantial ambiguity among suffixes, there are additional semantic features in PWN which can help to reduce ambiguity. For example, the suffix *-er* is associated with 12 out of the 14 morphosemantic relations, but the prevalent ones are Agent (in 76.8% of cases) and Instrument (in 11.7% of cases), which explains why *-er* is usually considered an agentive suffix and gives a strong indication as to the most likely relation. Moreover, when the noun semantic class is noun.person, it is associated with the agentive morphosemantic relation, while noun.artefact is associated with the instrument relation.

Table 3 presents the results of the expansion of the morphosemantic relations providing the initial number of the relations in MSD DATASET compared to the final number in the RESULTING DATASET. No relation is assigned in the cases where no suitable relation is identified among the set of 14 morphosemantic relations. The initial number of assigned relations has been increased by 20% up to 21,251.

The RESULTING DATASET (version 1.0) is distributed as a stand-alone resource that can be linked to PWN 3.0 or any other wordnet. The dataset is released under the Creative Commons Attribution-NonCommercial 4.0 International license.[7]

Suffix	# rel.	Morphosemantic relations
$zero_V$	12	Event (35.2%), Result (8.3%), By-means-of (8.3%)
-ise	9	Result (31.1%), By-means-of (15.2%), Event (10.5%)
-ate	11	Result (27.3%), Event (21.7%), By-means-of (16.8%)
-ify	8	Result (53.4%), By-means-of (18.4%), Uses (12.6%)
-en	4	Event (61.5%), Result (15.4%), Property (15.4%)
-ion	14	Event (71.3%), Result (9.7%)
-er	12	Agent (76.8%), Instrument (11.7%)
$zero_N$	12	Event (71.4%), Result (8.1%), By-means-of (8.1%)
-ment	12	Event (65.4%), State (11.2%), By-means-of (8.4%)
-ance	7	Event (67.3%), By-means-of (12.7%)
-ant	7	Agent (53.5%), By-means-of (14.9%), Material (8.9%), Uses (8.9%)
-age	9	Event (56.4%), Result (10.3%), Location (10.3%)
-al	6	Event (78.7%), Result (10.3%)
-ure	9	Event (51.0%), Result (14.3%), State (12.2%)
-ee	8	Undergoer (59.3%), Agent (19.8%), Destination (15.1%)

Table 2: Ambiguity of suffixes: number of morphosemantic relations (out of 14) covered by a particular suffix, and the most frequent of them.

6 Discussion

Regular polysemy is reflected in morphosemantic relations, especially since from a contemporary point of view a verb's sense may be considered related to more than one (closely) related noun senses or vice versa. Such an example is found with nouns of the class noun.artifact (mostly containers) and nouns denoting the quantity that the respective container holds, e.g. *barrel*:2, *cask*:2 ('a cylindrical container that holds liquids') and *barrel*:4, *barrelful*:1 ('the quantity that a barrel (of any size) will hold'). Each of the two synsets is related to *barrel*:1 ('put in barrels') by means of the relations Location and Undergoer, respectively. Regular polysemy reveals how regularities between related meanings in the nominal or the verbal domain are reflected in the semantics of the relation in verb-noun pairs.

Observations on structured parts of the lexicon, such as the ones discussed above, also enable us to predict missing relations, both morphoseman-

[7] https://github.com/WordNetMorhosemantics/SuffixalDerivation

Relation	Description	Example	Initial #	Result #
Agent	an entity that acts volitionally so as to bring about a result	*colonize – colonizer*	3,043	3,356
Body-part	a part of the body (e.g. of an Agent) involved in the situation	*extend – extensor*	43	46
By-means-of	something that causes, facilitates, enables the occurrence of	*decree – decree*	1,235	1,480
Destination	a recipient, an addressee or a goal	*patent – patentee*	17	19
Event	something that happens at a given place and time	*wash – washing*	8,158	10,015
Instrument	an object (rarely abstract) acting under the control of an Agent	*browse – browser*	813	875
Location	a concrete or an abstract place involved in the situation	*hospitalize – hospital*	288	394
Material	a substance or material used to obtain a certain effect or result	*polymerize – polymer*	114	116
Property	an attribute or a quality	*beautify – beauty*	318	486
Result	the outcome of the situation described by the verb	*syllabify – syllable*	1,439	1,784
State	an abstract entity, such as a feeling, a cognitive state, etc.	*anger – anger*	528	677
Undergoer	an entity affected by the situation described by the verb	*invite – invitee*	878	1006
Uses	a function an entity has or a purpose it serves	*cement – cement*	740	896
Vehicle	an artifact serving as a means of transportation	*fight – fighter*	87	101

Table 3: The set of morphosemantic relations and initial number of occurrences in the MSD DATASET compared to the final number in the RESULTING DATASET.

tic and derivational. Consider *jar*:5 ('place in a cylindrical vessel') and the noun synsets *jar*:1 ('a vessel (usually cylindrical') and *jar*:2, *jarful*:1 ('the quantity contained in a jar'). Although only the Undergoer relation is encoded, the Location relation is easily predictable on the basis of the *barrel* example above. Exploring further the hyponyms of the synset *containerful*:1 ('the quantity that a container will hold'), we discover that 25 out of its 67 hyponyms have corresponding verbs, but only 3 of the verbs are appropriately linked to the noun synsets denoting the respective quantity and artifact (in a like manner to *barrel*) – the remaining verbs lack one or both morphosemantic relations or even the derivational ones (e.g., *bag(ful) - bag*). In such a way, we are able to tackle the inconsistencies in derivational and morphosemantic relations throughout this and other parts of the PWN structure.

These observations can also be implemented into automatic procedures to discover morphosemantic and other semantic relations between single units in PWN, as well as between (sub)trees or semantic (sub)classes.

7 Conclusions and future work

We have presented here the creation of a large set of derivationally related word pairs, by enhancing the PWN morphosemantic database with new pairs of literals linked through derivation with the explicit suffixes involved, as well as with a morphosemantic relation. The RESULTING DATASET includes over 21,000 verb–noun pairs.

Our dataset seems to confirm previous insights according to which verbalising suffixes are more polyfunctional and less predictable than the nominalising suffixes (Kisselew et al., 2016; Barbu Mititelu et al., 2023). However, surprisingly, zero suffixes, although polyfunctional, are not less predictable than the overt ones, as claimed by Plag (1999); Lieber (2004). The zero and overt suffixes exhibit similar levels of polyfunctionality, and the developed dataset provides material for detailed analysis into these claims.

One of the directions to be further investigated is the development and improvement of various procedures for automatic analysis, identifications of derivational or semantic features (e.g., the suffix, the direction of derivation, the morphosemantic relation, etc.), in order to increase the scope of the data and the depth of the analysis.

A natural extension of the work would be to study the derivational relations for other languages using the corresponding (aligned) wordnets and taking as a point of departure the assumption that the semantic dimension of the morphosemantic relations is transferable across languages.

Acknowledgments

We thank our student assistants Anna-Lena Feichter and Mariya Kavaldzhieva for a first round of manual annotation of the data.

References

Rie Kubota Ando and Tong Zhang. 2005. A framework for learning predictive structures from multiple tasks and unlabeled data. *Journal of Machine Learning Research*, 6:1817–1853.

Galen Andrew and Jianfeng Gao. 2007. Scalable training of L1-regularized log-linear models. In *Proceedings of the 24th International Conference on Machine Learning*, pages 33–40.

Verginica Barbu Mititelu, Gianina Iordăchioaia, Svetlozara Leseva, and Ivelina Stoyanova. 2023. The meaning of zero nouns and zero verbs. In Sven Kotowski and Ingo Plag, editors, *The semantics of derivational morphology. Theory, methods, evidence*, pages 63–102. Walter de Gruyter, Berlin/Boston.

Laurie Bauer, Rochelle Lieber, and Ingo Plag. 2013. *The Oxford Reference Guide to English Morphology*. Oxford University Press, Oxford, UK.

Manfred Bierwisch. 2009. Nominalization – lexical and syntactic aspects. In Anastasia Giannakidou and Monika Rathert, editors, *Quantification, definiteness, and nominalization*, pages 281–320. Oxford University Press, Oxford, UK.

Barli Bram. 2011. *Major Total Conversion in English*. Ph.D. thesis, Victoria University of Wellington.

Fabricio Chalub, Livy Real, Alexandre Rademaker, and Valeria de Paiva. 2016. Semantic links for Portuguese. In *Proceedings of the Tenth International Conference on Language Resources and Evaluation (LREC'16)*, pages 885–891, Portorož, Slovenia. European Language Resources Association (ELRA).

Eve V. Clark and Herbert H. Clark. 1979. When nouns surface as verbs. *Language*, 55(4):767–811.

Mark Davies. 2010. The Corpus of Contemporary American English as the first reliable monitor corpus of English. *Literary and Linguistic Computing*, pages 447–464.

Valeria de Paiva, Alexandre Rademaker, and Gerard de Melo. 2012. OpenWordNet-PT: An open Brazilian Wordnet for reasoning. In *Proceedings of COLING 2012: Demonstration Papers*, pages 353–360, Mumbai, India. The COLING 2012 Organizing Committee.

Christiane Fellbaum, editor. 1998. *WordNet: An Electronic Lexical Database*. MIT Press.

Christiane Fellbaum, A. Osherson, and P. E. Clark. 2009. Putting semantics into WordNet's 'morphosemantic' links. In Z. Vetulani and H. Uszkoreit, editors, *Human Language Technology. Challenges of the Information Society. LTC 2007*, pages 350–358. Springer, Berlin, Heidelberg.

Cristina Fernández Alcaina. 2021. *Competition in the derivational paradigm of English verbs*. Ph.D. thesis, University of Granada.

Jane Grimshaw. 1990. *Argument Structure*. MIT Press, Cambridge, MA.

Gianina Iordăchioaia and Chiara Melloni. 2023. The zero suffix in english and italian deverbal nouns. *Zeitschrift für Sprachwissenschaft*, 42:1:109–132.

Lea Kawaletz. 2023. *The semantics of English -ment nominalizations*. Language Science Press, Berlin.

Paul Kiparsky. 1982. From cyclic phonology to lexical phonology. In Harry van der Hulst and Norval Smith, editors, *The structure of phonological representations*, pages 131–175. Foris, Dordrecht.

Max Kisselew, Laura Rimell, Alexis Palmer, and Sebastian Padó. 2016. Predicting the direction of derivation in English conversion. In *Proceedings of the ACL SIG-MORPHON workshop*, pages 93–98, Berlin.

Gabriella Lapesa, Lea Kawaletz, Ingo Plag, Marios Andreou, Max Kisselew, and Sebastian Padó. 2018. Disambiguation of newly derived nominalizations in context: A distributional semantics approach. *Word Structure*, 11:277–312.

Cristina Lara Clares. 2023. *Morphological competition in present-day English nominalisation*. Ph.D. thesis, University of Granada.

Rochelle Lieber. 2004. *Morphology and Lexical Semantics*. Cambridge University Press, Cambridge.

Rochelle Lieber. 2016. *English Nouns. The Ecology of Nominalization*. Cambridge University Press, Cambridge.

Hans Marchand. 1964. A set of criteria for the establishing of derivational relationship between words unmarked by derivational morphemes. *Indogermanische Forschungen [Indo-Germanic research]*, 69:10–19.

Chiara Melloni. 2011. *Event and result nominals*. Peter Lang, Bern.

George A. Miller, Richard Beckwith, Christiane. Fellbaum, Derek Gross, and Katherine Miller. 1990a. Introduction to Wordnet: an on-line lexical database. *International journal of lexicography*, 3(4):235–244.

George A. Miller, Richard Beckwith, Christiane Fellbaum, Derek Gross, and Katherine Miller. 1990b. Introduction to WordNet: An online lexical database. *International Journal of Lexicography*, 3(4):235–244.

Ingo Plag. 1999. *Morphological Productivity: Structural Constraints in English Derivation*. De Gruyter, Berlin/New York.

Ingo Plag. 2003. *Word-formation in English*. Cambridge University Press, Cambridge.

Frans Plank. 2010. Variable direction in zero-derivation and the unity of polysemous lexical items. *Word Structure*, 3.1:82–97.

Franz Rainer. 2004. Polysemy in derivation. In Rochelle Lieber and Pavol Štekauer, editors, *The Oxford Handbook of Derivational Morphology*, pages 338–353. Oxford University Press, Oxford.

Mohammad Sadegh Rasooli and Joel R. Tetreault. 2015. Yara parser: A fast and accurate dependency parser. *Computing Research Repository*, arXiv:1503.06733. Version 2.

Justine Salvadori and Richard Huyghe. 2022. Affix polyfunctionality in french deverbal nominalizations. *Morphology*, 33:1–39.

Salvador Valera. 2023. The semantics of noun-to-verb zero-derivation in english and spanish. *Zeitschrift für Sprachwissenschaft*, 42:1:153–180.

Rossella Varvara. 2017. *Verbs as nouns: empirical investigations on event-denoting nominalizations*. Ph.D. thesis, University of Trento.

Rossella Varvara, Gabriella Lapesa, and Sebastian Padó. 2021. Grounding semantic transparency in context a distributional semantic study on german event nominalizations. *Morphology*, 31:409–446.

Rossella Varvara, Justine Salvadori, and Richard Huyghe. 2022. Annotating complex words to investigate the semantics of derivational processes. In Harry Bunt, editor, *Proceedings of the 18th Joint ACL - ISO workshop on Interoperable Semantic Annotation (ISA-18)*, pages 133–141. European Language Resources Association (ELRA), Paris.

Rossella Varvara, Justine Salvadori, and Richard Huyghe. 2024. Creating and exploiting a lexical database of deverbal nouns in French. Talk given in the workshop *Data-based research in word formation*, within *The Biennial of Czech Linguistics*, Charles University, Prague.

The Impact of Age and Gender on Sensory Imagery: Insights from the IMAVIC Dataset

Simona Corciulo⋆**, Mario Alessandro Bochicchio**◇ **Rossana Damiano**⋆**, Viviana Patti**⋆
⋆ Computer Science Department, University of Turin, Turin, Italy
◇ Computer Science Department, University of Bari "Aldo Moro", Bari, Italy
{simona.corciulo|rossana.damiano|viviana.patti}@unito.it
mario.bochicchio@uniba.it

Abstract

With the advent of Large Language Models, conversational skills are no longer exclusive to humans, but human features such as senses and imagination remain a topic of debate in conversational systems. In this paper we describe the IMAVIC (IMAgery and Vividness In Context) dataset, annotated to investigate how linguistic context modulates sensory imagery, defined as the cognitive capacity to generate mental representations of sensory experiences across modalities (vision, hearing, touch, smell, and taste) in the absence of direct external stimuli. This study focuses on how linguistic stimuli, both in isolation and in context, elicit and modulate such imagery, and how these processes vary based on demographic factors. IMAVIC includes ratings from 909 native English speakers on the vividness of mental images and the intensity of sensory experiences evoked by adjectives, nouns, and adjective-noun pairs across five sensory modalities. The analysis of data reveals significant differences in sensory imagery across genders and age groups, suggesting that biological and sociocultural factors shape our imaginative abilities and providing a foundation for the development of models targeting sensory grounding.

1 Introduction

Sensory imagery, the ability to mentally recreate perceptual experiences without direct sensory input, plays an important role in cognition, influencing processes such as memory recall and language comprehension. Collecting data on sensory imagery, particularly in relation to linguistic context, can offer a more detailed understanding of how demographic factors, such as age and gender, influence this cognitive function. Insights from such studies are not only important for advancing theoretical knowledge but also have potential practical applications in domains where sensory experiences are central. For example, in conversational interfaces and healthcare or assistive technologies, a more precise understanding of sensory imagery could enhance communication by allowing greater personalization of interactions. Furthermore, these findings may inform the development of machine learning models aimed at simulating human sensory and cognitive processes with greater accuracy, thereby improving their applicability in real-world contexts.

This study focuses on how demographic factors, specifically age and gender, influence sensory imagery, which in this context refers to the cognitive ability to generate mental representations of perceptual experiences in response to linguistic stimuli. Building on the theory of embodied cognition, which suggests that language processing is closely tied to sensory and motor systems (Barsalou, 1999, 2008), previous research has shown how isolated words can evoke sensory representations (Lakoff, 2012). However, the effects of sentence context on sensory imagery remain less explored, particularly in relation to demographic differences. To address this gap, we created the Imagery and Vividness in Context (IMAVIC) dataset, which contains ratings on the vividness of mental representations, as well as the type and intensity of sensory imagery evoked by specific textual stimuli, focusing on adjectives and nouns presented both in isolation and within context. By examining the effects of the linguistic context, age and gender, this research seeks to provide information on how these factors shape sensory imagery in both conversational interfaces and healthcare/assistance systems, where it can be crucial to fully comprehend people's special needs and communicate about sensory experiences.

Motivation The motivation for this study stems from the need to better understand how age and gender influence sensory imagery in response to linguistic stimuli, particularly when considering the role of sentence context. The social relevance of this issue is related to the growing interest in conversational interfaces and the trend toward an aging population. Previous research has shown that age-related declines in sensory and cognitive processing can affect the vividness of mental images (Li and Lindenberger, 2002), while gender differences suggest that women may engage more deeply with sensory and emotional stimuli than men (Canli et al., 2002). Despite these insights, the role of sentence context in modulating sensory imagery across these demographic groups remains understudied. The IMAVIC dataset offers the opportunity to explore these issues. Earlier findings have shown that context can enhance sensory imagery, especially for adjective-noun pairs. This study seeks to extend these findings by examining how demographic factors further influence these effects, offering cautious hypotheses about how age and gender can interact with contextual modulation of sensory imagery. In this setting, our work aims to explore four research questions:

- How does phrasal context affect the vividness of sensory imagery in nouns and adjectives?
- How and to what extent does gender influence the vividness of sensory imagery?
- How does gender influence sensory imagery across different modalities?
- How does age affect the vividness of sensory imagery?

Understanding these interactions has potential applications beyond sensorial/cognitive aspects. For instance, insights gained could inform the development of assistive technologies that adapt to the sensory and cognitive needs of various users, particularly older adults and individuals with sensory impairments.

This paper is structured as follows: First, we introduce the concept of sensory imagery and its cognitive relevance, with a particular focus on how demographic factors such as age and gender can influence this process. We then present the Imagery and Vividness in Context (IMAVIC) dataset and detail the methodology used to collect and analyze sensory imagery ratings in both decontextualized and contextualized linguistic forms. In the results section, we examine the effects of age and gender, and linguistic context on sensory imagery, highlighting key patterns and demographic differences. Following this, we discuss the implications of these findings for fields such as conversational interfaces and healthcare or assistive technologies, where sensory experiences are essential for personalized interaction. Finally, we conclude by outlining future research directions, emphasizing the potential for further exploration on the integration of sensory imagery data into machine learning models and assistive systems.

2 Related Work

Previous studies on perception, imagination and language have revealed how sensory experiences and bodily interactions fundamentally shape cognitive processes. Three key frameworks - sensory grounding (Chalmers, 2024; Spendlove and Ventura, 2019), embodied cognition (Lakoff and Johnson, 2008; Lakoff, 2012; Leitan and Chaffey, 2014), and body grounding (Gallese and Lakoff, 2005) - have provided valuable insights into these relationships. The intrinsic meaning of these frameworks lies in their shared emphasis on the interconnectedness of sensory experiences and cognitive functions. Sensory grounding posits that our thoughts and mental representations are not purely abstract but are anchored in the physical sensations we experience. Embodied cognition suggests that cognition arises from active bodily interactions with the world, meaning our mental processes are deeply tied to our physical state and actions. Body grounding, a more specific component, focuses on how posture and movement directly shape cognitive activities such as memory, attention, and language.

A key extension of embodied cognition theory is its implication for language processing. Unlike traditional views that treat language as an abstract symbolic system, embodied cognition proposes that linguistic comprehension is closely intertwined with sensory and motor experiences. Rather than being processed in isolation as abstract symbols, language comprehension activates the same neural circuits involved in direct interaction with the environment and external stimuli. This means that understanding language involves not only symbolic processing but also the activation of perceptual representations, which are grounded in past sensory experiences. These neural activations enable the brain to recreate sensory patterns, allowing it to simulate or imagine experiences without direct stimuli, thus integrating sensory and semantic information (Kosslyn et al., 2001; Schacter and Addis, 2007). Such mental simulations, triggered by linguistic input, allow individuals to construct meaning based on the recreation of sensory experiences, contributing to a richer and more dynamic understanding of language. This process highlights how perception, imagination, and language are interdependent, working together through shared neural mechanisms that tie sensory experiences to linguistic and cognitive functions.

These principles directly relate to sensory imagery, the mental recreation of sensory experiences, as they highlight how imagination and perception share neural mechanisms. When we engage in sensory imagery, such as visualizing an object or imagining a sound, we activate the same brain regions involved in actual sensory perception. This overlap underscores the idea that our mental imagery is grounded in the same sensory systems that process real-world experiences, reinforcing the connection between body, mind, and environment.

While perception and imagination are universal cognitive processes, substantial research (Schacter et al., 2013; de Dieuleveult et al., 2017) has shown that they are influenced by demographic variables, particularly gender and age. Studies indicate that men and women exhibit notable differences in sensory processing and mental imagery, shaped by both biological and cultural factors.

Women have been found to outperform men in tasks involving olfactory and tactile sensitivity, suggesting a heightened perceptual acuity in these modalities. Research shows that hormonal variations play a key role in these differences. For example, estrogen levels have been linked to increased sensitivity in olfactory perception, leading to higher detection rates of odors (Doty and Cameron, 2009). Similarly, women generally exhibit superior performance in tactile discrimination tasks, potentially due to differences in skin receptor density and hormonal influences (Brand and Millot, 2001). Conversely, men often excel in visuospatial tasks, particularly those requiring mental rotation and spatial navigation. Studies have consistently shown that men tend to perform better on tasks involving the rotation of objects in three-dimensional space, an ability linked to enhanced activation in parietal regions of the brain (Halpern, 2000). These differences may be partly attributed to evolutionary pressures, where spatial navigation was crucial for survival in male-dominated activities such as hunting and exploration.

Age also profoundly affects both perception and imagination, with distinct developmental trajectories across the lifespan. In children, perceptual systems are highly plastic, rapidly adapting to new sensory stimuli and refining perceptual and imaginative abilities. For example, the capacity to visualize and manipulate mental images develops alongside increasing exposure to complex visual stimuli during childhood (Cascio et al., 2019). As cognitive and sensory functions peak in adulthood, individuals demonstrate highly efficient multisensory integration and rapid mental images generation (de Dieuleveult et al., 2017).

However, with advancing age, perceptual and imaginative abilities tend to decline. Older adults often experience reduced sensitivity in sensory modalities such as vision and hearing, alongside decreased vividness and accuracy of mental images. Studies suggest that this decline is associated with structural and functional changes in the brain, particularly in areas related to sensory processing and memory, such as the prefrontal cortex and hippocampus (Li and Lindenberger, 2002). Despite this, many older individuals compensate for sensory deficits through cognitive strategies and accumulated knowledge, maintaining a degree of perceptual and imaginative capacity well into old age (Baltes and Smith, 2003).

Gender differences persist across the lifespan, with some evidence suggesting that the decline in sensory and cognitive functions may manifest differently between men and women. For example, while both sexes experience age-related declines in sensory acuity, women tend to retain greater olfactory sensitivity and verbal memory, whereas men maintain a relative advantage in spatial tasks (Lindenberger and Baltes, 1994). These gendered patterns of cognitive aging highlight the importance of considering both biological and experiential factors in understanding the evolution of perceptual and imaginative abilities.

Cultural background also significantly influences how individuals perceive and imagine the world. Research by (Nisbett and Masuda, 2013) indicates that individuals from Western cultures tend to focus more on isolated objects in their environment, while those from Eastern cultures exhibit a greater sensitivity to context and relationships between objects. These cultural differences shape not only perceptual tendencies but also the content and structure of mental imagery. Additionally, educational background and socioeconomic status contribute to the variability in imaginative and perceptual skills, with greater exposure to diverse stimuli often enhancing these abilities (Wang, 2021).

In summary, while perception and imagination are universally shared processes, they are deeply influenced by factors such as gender, age, and culture. These differences underscore the importance of accounting for demographic variables in cognitive research, particularly in understanding how sensory experiences and mental imagination evolve across the human lifespan.

3 Methodology

This section provides a brief overview of the key methodological aspects here adopted. It includes a summary of the variables measured, task structure for annotators, and data processing techniques, focusing on the selection of sentences and target words.

Participant Recruitment and Sample Composition The study recruited a total of **903** native English-speaking participants, aged 18–80 years, through the Prolific crowdsourcing platform. The sample was balanced across genders, with 52.2% identifying as female and 47.8% as male, and showed the highest representation among participants aged 30–39 years, followed by 20–29 years. This distribution reflects a younger-skewed sample typical of online recruitment platforms. Of the recruited participants, 835 effectively completed the annotation tasks, providing a total of 5,611 valid responses across approximately 27,000 questions. Each target (adjective, noun, or adjective-noun pair) was rated by 3 annotators for both vividness and sensory imagery, ensuring robust data quality. Control questions were incorporated to identify and exclude incomplete or invalid responses, maintaining high reliability in the aggregated results.

Variables and Rating Scales Key variables include the vividness of mental imagery and the intensity of sensory imagery across different senses. Both variables measure the intensity of mental imagery: the first provides a general measure of the overall vividness of the mental image, while the second offers a detailed measure of intensity across individual sensory modalities - vision, hearing, touch, smell, and taste. Both are rated on a Likert scale from 0 to 4.

Task Structure for Annotators The annotation tasks are designed to optimize completion time and ensure reliable data. Tasks are divided into sections with and without context, and each target is evaluated by multiple annotators to ensure consistency.

Linguistic Data Selection and Processing The corpus was curated to include texts with high potential for sensory engagement, focusing on adjective-noun relationships. Data were sourced from reviews and comments, selected for their multisensory descriptions.

Validation Criteria and Analysis Appropriate statistical tests, including non-parametric methods and mixed linear regression models, were used to validate the results.

The IMAVIC dataset A corpus of 303 sentences, each containing at least one adjective and one noun. The initial corpus included a well-established dataset of wine reviews available on Kaggle[1], which was extended by scraping descriptions, reviews, and comments on consumer products (e.g., cosmetics, beverages, artworks) from platforms such as Fragrantica, Reddit, Google Art and Culture, and YouTube. The collection and selection of texts were automated using custom Python scripts to ensure the quality and variety of the dataset. The corpus was processed to select sentences following an adjective-noun structure, in which the adjective directly modifies the noun. This particular structure was chosen due to its relevance in studying synesthetic metaphors, which are often instrumental in examining how the human mind integrates and associates sensory experiences through language. To maintain consistency with the Lancaster Sensorimotor Norms (Lynott et al., 2020) and allow for meaningful comparisons, the analysis focused on singular nouns, as words in the reference corpora are annotated in this form. Each selected sentence also included at least two additional words from the reference dataset, in addition to the target adjective-noun pair, and sentences were limited to a maximum of 20 words. This constraint aimed to optimize annotation time while also enabling an assessment of how context affects linguistic interpretation. Following classification, 303 sentences were retained. A total of 303 adjectives and 303 nouns were annotated, as each sentence contained at least one of each. However, given that many target words appear multiple times, often functioning as both adjectives and nouns, the actual number of annotations exceeds this base count. Terms such as "light," "clean," "stone," and "wood" exhibit flexibility in meaning and grammatical role depending on context, which is particularly valuable for examining the influence of linguistic surroundings

[1] https://www.kaggle.com/datasets/zynicide/wine-reviews/data

on sensory interpretation. This repetition was considered beneficial, as it allows for a more in-depth investigation into how context, meaning, and grammatical function interact, laying a foundation for exploring linguistic and perceptual dynamics.

4 Results and Discussion

In this section the results are reported and discussed according to the above-defined research questions.

4.1 How and to what extent does gender influence the vividness of sensory imagery?

Our findings address this research question by revealing some gender differences in the vividness of mental imagery in response to textual stimuli, particularly as age increases. However, these differences are not uniformly substantial and may be influenced by other factors such as age-related cognitive changes and the type of targets. Overall, both men and women experience a decline in mental vividness with age, but this decline appears more pronounced in women, particularly for categories such as adjectives and nouns after the age of 50. Men, on the other hand, show an initial increase in the vividness of nouns between the ages of 50 and 60, followed by a sharp decline between the ages of 70 and 80 as reported in Fig. 1. These observations suggest that age and gender interact in shaping sensory imagery, with potential influences from cognitive aging and contextual cues. Despite the general decline with age, women tend to maintain higher mental vividness than men in some modalities, such as smell and, in certain cases, touch (Fig. 2). These differences in mental vividness are not always substantial, but they are consistent with the findings of (Canli et al., 2002), who reported greater activation of brain regions in women during the recall of emotional memories. This suggests a predisposition in women for processing and integrating sensory and emotional information. The more pronounced decline observed in women may indicate that, although they tend to exhibit greater mental vividness overall, aging affects their ability to sustain this vividness more significantly than it does for men.

Additionally, our results indicate that phrasal context differentially influences mental vividness across genders. Men show greater olfactory intensity when stimuli are presented with contextual support compared to women, as shown in Fig. 2, where men exhibit a peak in intensity in the 40–50 age range, followed by a sharp decrease after age 60. Conversely, women demonstrate more stable olfactory intensity across age groups, catching up to and surpassing men in the 60-70 age range. This suggests that context may play a more significant role in enhancing sensory imagery for men, while women maintain a steadier sensory response across conditions. These results align with the findings of Ehrlichman and Halpern (Ehrlichman and Halpern, 1988), who demonstrated that olfactory stimuli enhance the recall of emotional memories, with women typically showing a more intense response to such stimuli, especially at older ages.

In summary, while gender differences in sensory vividness are present, they are not uniformly substantial and may be mediated by factors such as age-related cognitive decline. Our data, alongside prior research, suggest that gender and age interact in complex ways to influence the vividness of sensory imagery. Although women generally exhibit greater mental vividness in certain modalities, particularly in smell and touch, aging appears to have a more significant impact on their ability to maintain this vividness over time. At the same time, contextual factors seem to amplify mental vividness for men, particularly in the olfactory domain, although this effect diminishes with age.

4.2 How does phrasal context affect the vividness of sensory imagination on nouns and adjectives?

Our findings indicate that context enhances sensory imagery for both men and women, although the effect is more pronounced in women. In terms of olfactory intensity without context, men exhibit an average score of 0.26, with a minimum of 0.20 and a maximum of 0.33 across age groups. For women, the average score is 0.24, with a minimum of 0.19 and a maximum of 0.33. When context is considered, the scores increase: for men, the average score is 0.62, with a minimum of 0.42 and a maximum of 0.74. For women, the average score is 0.57, with a minimum of 0.48 and a maximum of 0.70. This suggests that women may derive greater benefits from narrative or contextual cues, which help them form richer mental images, particularly in sensory modalities such as touch and smell, as reported in Fig.2. However, the degree to which context influences mental imagery varies with age, and this modulation may be influenced by age-related cognitive changes. For example, in

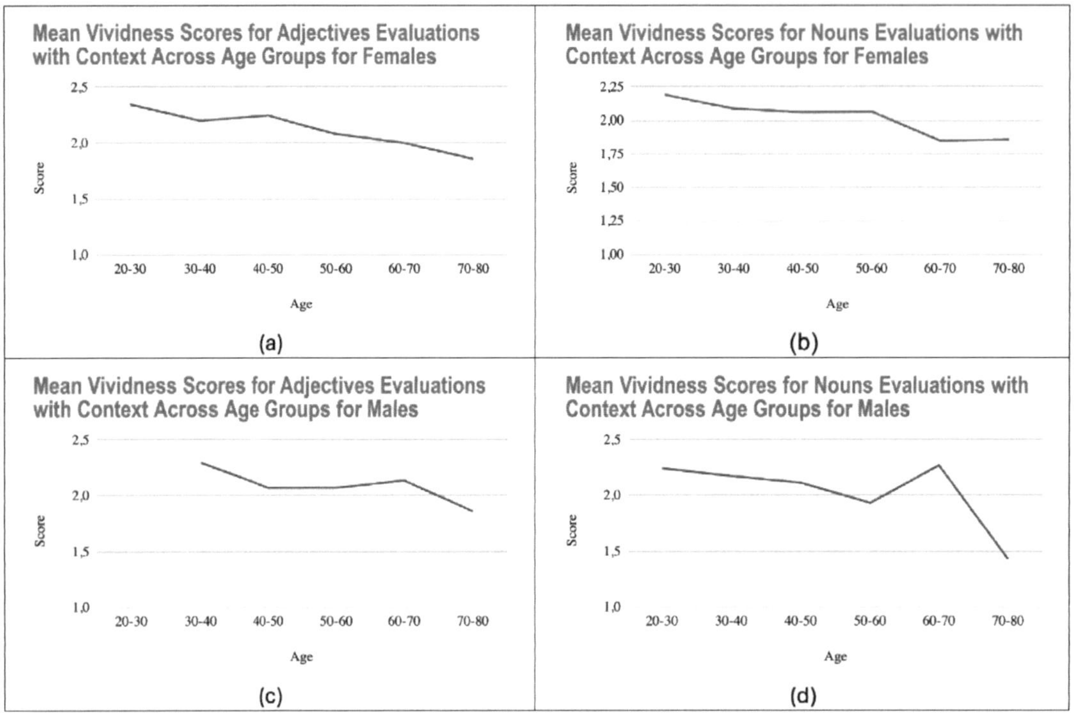

Figure 1: The graphs show age-related changes in mental vividness for adjectives and nouns with contextual support, comparing men and women. Both genders experience a decline in vividness with age, but the decline is steeper for women. Men show a temporary increase in the vividness of nouns between ages 50-60 before a sharp decline in the 70-80 range, while women demonstrate a more consistent decline.

the 60-70 age group, women exhibit more stable olfactory intensity scores, with an average of 0.33 without context and 0.70 with context, surpassing men whose scores are 0.20 without context and 0.70 with context. In contrast, men tend to respond more strongly to visual and auditory stimuli, often even without contextual support. As shown in Figure 4, men demonstrate a peak auditory response in early adulthood (20-30 years), followed by another increase between 50-60 years, after which the response declines sharply. These age-related variations may reflect deeper cognitive differences between genders in the processing of sensory information. Men's reliance on direct sensory stimuli, such as auditory and visual cues, supports previous findings by Kring and Gordon, who observed stronger male responses in these modalities compared to females (Kring and Gordon, 1998). Our interpretation aligns with research suggesting that women are more likely to integrate contextual details into their sensory experiences. Davis demonstrated that women tend to recall emotionally charged autobiographical events more vividly, confirming their propensity for processing emotional and sensory information (Davis, 1999). This is consistent with our findings, which show that women benefit more from context in enhancing mental vividness. Conversely, studies like that of Mann et al. suggest that men tend to favor more analytical, practical modes of information processing, particularly in visual and auditory domains, which could explain their stronger response to these modalities without the need for additional context (Mann et al., 1990).

In summary, the modulatory effect of context on sensory imagery varies between genders, with women showing a greater sensitivity to contextual cues that enrich sensory imagery, while men are more responsive to unembedded targets, particularly in the auditory and visual domains. These findings suggest that age and cognitive changes may further modulate how context impacts sensory imagery, with gender playing a critical role in shaping these dynamics.

4.3 How does gender influence sensory imagery across different modalities?

Our analysis of sensory modalities - taste, smell, touch, sight, and hearing - reveals notable gen-

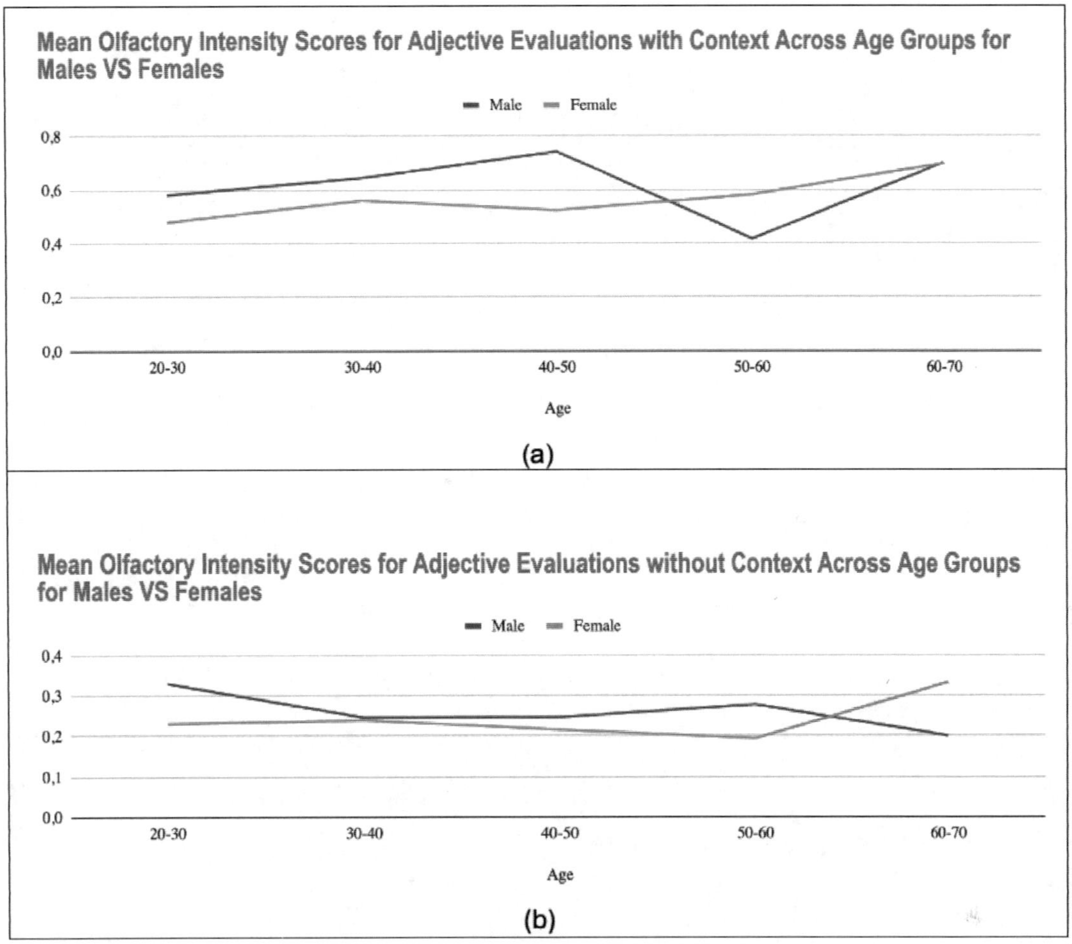

Figure 2: The graphs display mean olfactory intensity scores for adjective, both with and without context, across age groups. Men show higher olfactory intensity with context until the age of 50-60, after which females catch up and surpass them. Without context, men score higher in younger age groups, but women surpass them in the 60-70 range. Context has a greater impact on olfactory intensity for men, while women maintain steadier responses.

der differences in the vividness of sensory imagery. Here, women consistently exhibit stronger responses , particularly in sensory domains that are associated with intimate and personal experiences as reported in Fig. 2. This observation aligns with the findings of (Schaefer and Philippot, 2005), who showed that women tend to relive autobiographical memories with greater sensory vividness than men. In our study, women's olfactory intensity remains more stable across age groups, surpassing men in the 60-70 age range, particularly when context is not provided. Conversely, men show somewhat stronger responses than women to auditory stimuli. For instance, in the 60-70 age group, men have an average auditory score of 0.17, while women register a score of 0.00. This suggests a potential difference in auditory processing between the two groups, although further investigation is needed to confirm the extent of this variation, as reported in Fig 3. These findings support the results of Hofer et al. (Hofer et al., 2007), who observed that men exhibit greater brain activation in visual and auditory regions when processing emotional words. This suggests that these sensory modalities are more integral to men's cognitive processing of imagery. For example, as in Fig. 3, men's auditory load peaks in the 20-30 age range, followed by another increase between 50-60 years, before declining sharply after 60. Women, however, demonstrate a more stable auditory response across age groups, with less pronounced fluctuations.

In summary, gender plays a significant role in shaping how individuals experience and construct mental imagery across different senses. Women

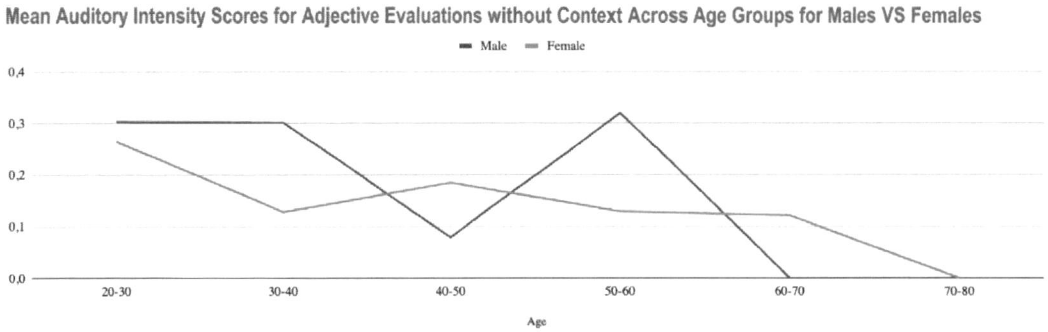

Figure 3: The graph illustrates the auditory load associated with nouns presented without context, across different age groups for male and female participants. Males show a stronger response initially, with a peak in the 20-30 age range and another in the 50-60 group, followed by a sharp decline after 60-70 years. Females, on the other hand, display a more stable auditory load across the age groups, with slight fluctuations and a steady decline starting from the 50-60 age range. These results suggest that, in the absence of contextual cues, auditory imagery for nouns varies more significantly with age in males than in females.

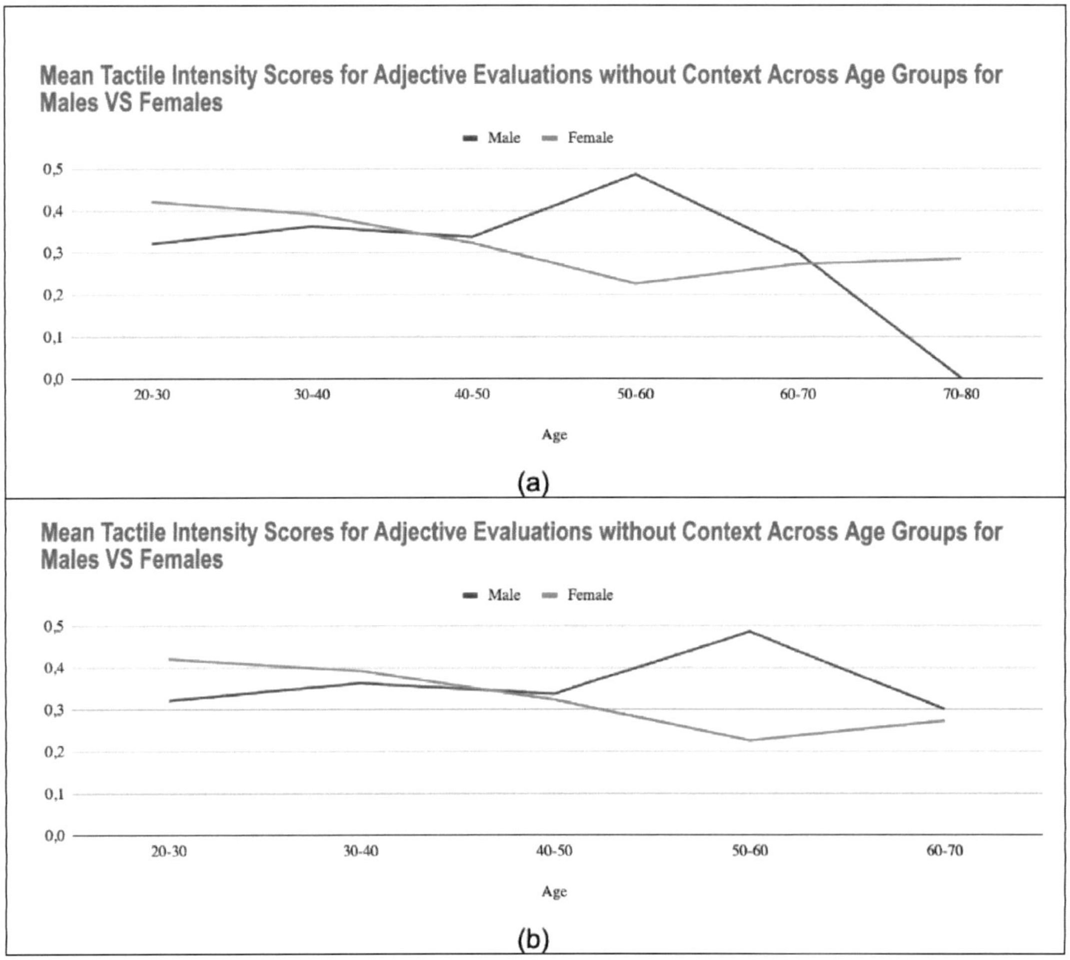

Figure 4: The graph shows tactile load variations by age for men and women in response to tactile stimuli. Both genders start with similar values, but men show a slight increase between 40-60, followed by a sharp decline after 60-70. By 70-80, men's tactile load drops to zero, while women maintain a more stable response, suggesting they sustain tactile vividness longer as they age.

tend to have a heightened response in modalities related to personal and emotional experiences, whereas men rely more on visual and auditory stimuli, particularly when context is absent. These findings align with prior research, suggesting deeper cognitive differences in how men and women process sensory information.

4.4 How does age affect the vividness of sensory imagery?

A relevant finding relates to the resilience of women's sensory responses in older age groups. Therefore, it is important to note that while the data suggest a trend, the limited sample size warrants further investigation to confirm it with greater certainty. Our data suggest that after the age of 50, women may maintain a slightly higher level of tactile sensory vividness compared to men. For instance, in the 60-70 age group, women have an average tactile score of 0.18, which is about 9% higher than the average score of 0.17 for men. However, given the small difference, further research is needed to confirm this trend (Fig. 4). This is particularly evident in modalities such as touch, where women show more stable tactile responses across age groups. In contrast, men experience a noticeable decline in tactile vividness after the age of 60, with their average score dropping from 0.32 in the 50-60 age group to 0.17 in the 60-70 age group. This reduction suggests a sharper decrease in tactile responses as they age. These results align with Uzer and Gulgoz (Uzer and Gulgoz, 2015), who found that older women tend to retain more vivid sensory and emotional memories than men, particularly in relation to olfactory and gustatory stimuli, which decline more rapidly in men. The observed differences in sensory processing and mental imagery between men and women may be influenced by social and cultural factors. Grossman and Wood (Grossman and Wood, 1993) suggest that women's socialization often encourages a focus on sensory experiences linked to physical contact and emotional intimacy. This emphasis on emotional expression and interpersonal sensitivity may contribute to the greater sensory vividness observed in women, as their mental representations are often more grounded in sensory and emotional experiences. Conversely, Halpern (Halpern, 2000) argues that men are generally socialized to be more emotionally detached and practical, with societal expectations emphasizing visual and auditory skills rather than proximal sensory experiences like touch. As a result, men may construct mental images that prioritize sight and hearing, while being less connected to emotional or intimate physical experiences. This could explain the steeper decline in sensory vividness observed in men, especially in tactile modalities, as they age. In summary, the data suggest that women maintain more stable sensory vividness into older age, particularly in tactile modalities, while men exhibit a sharper decline in sensory imagery after 60. These gender differences in sensory resilience may be shaped by socialization patterns, which influence how men and women process and prioritize different sensory experiences throughout their lives.

5 Conclusions and Future Work

In conclusion, this research has highlighted how sensory grounding - the anchoring of cognitive experiences in sensory systems — affects imagination and perception in response to textual stimuli. Age and gender play significant role in modulating the construction and understanding of sensory references, revealing meaningful differences in embodied simulation and mental imagination across demographic groups. These findings encourage further large-scale annotation efforts campaigns and the development of computational models for text generation that account for gender and age differences in human-computer communication. Future work will focus on using the collected data to analyze the influence of context on variations in vividness of the mental images and sensory imagery. This in-depth investigation will help delineate the neurocognitive mechanisms governing the interaction between perception and imagination, offering new insights for the development of advanced assistive devices based on language. Integrating these data will allow the design of personalized tools that dynamically adapt to patients' needs, promoting functional recovery and improving individual autonomy through advanced interfaces.

Acknowledgements

This publication was produced with the co-funding of European Union - Next Generation EU, in the context of The National Recovery and Resilience Plan, Investment Partenariato Esteso PE8 "Conseguenze e sfide dell'invecchiamento", Project Age-It (Ageing Well in an Ageing Society), CUP: B83C22004800006. The work of Viviana Patti and Rossana Damiano is partially supported by

"HARMONIA" project - M4-C2, I1.3 Partenariati Estesi - Spoke 2 Cascade Call - FAIR - CUP C63C22000770006 - PE PE0000013 under the NextGenerationEU programme.

References

P.B. Baltes and J. Smith. 2003. New frontiers in the future of aging: From successful aging of the young old to the dilemmas of the fourth age. *Gerontology*, 49(2):123–135.

L. W. Barsalou. 1999. Perceptual symbol systems. *Behavioral and Brain Sciences*, 22(4):577–660.

L. W. Barsalou. 2008. Grounded cognition. *Annual Review of Psychology*, 59(1):617–645.

G. Brand and J.L. Millot. 2001. Sex differences in human olfaction: between evidence and enigma. *The Quarterly Journal of Experimental Psychology: Section B*, 54(3):259–270.

T. Canli, J. E. Desmond, Z. Zhao, and John D. E. Gabrieli. 2002. Sex differences in the neural basis of emotional memories. *Proceedings of the National Academy of Sciences*, 99(16):10789–10794.

C.J. Cascio, D. Moore, and D McGlone. 2019. Social touch and human development. *Developmental cognitive neuroscience*, 35:5–11.

D. J. Chalmers. 2024. Does thought require sensory grounding? from pure thinkers to large language models. *arXiv preprints*, page arXiv:2408.09605.

P.J. Davis. 1999. Gender differences in autobiographical memory for childhood emotional experiences. *J. of personality and social psychology*, 76(3):498.

Alix L. de Dieuleveult, Petra C. Siemonsma, Jan B. F. van Erp, and Anne-Marie Brouwer. 2017. Effects of aging in multisensory integration: a systematic review. *Frontiers in aging neuroscience*, 9:80.

R.L. Doty and E. L. Cameron. 2009. Sex differences and reproductive hormone influences on human odor perception. *Physiology & behavior*, 97(2):213.

H. Ehrlichman and J.N. Halpern. 1988. Affect and memory: effects of pleasant and unpleasant odors on retrieval of happy and unhappy memories. *Journal of personality and social psychology*, 55(5):769.

V. Gallese and G. Lakoff. 2005. The brain's concepts: The role of the sensory-motor system in conceptual knowledge. *Cognitive neuropsychology*, 22(3-4):455–479.

M. Grossman and W. Wood. 1993. Sex differences in intensity of emotional experience: a social role interpretation. *Journal of personality and social psychology*, 65(5):1010.

D.F. Halpern. 2000. *Sex differences in cognitive abilities*. Psychology press.

A. Hofer, C. M. Siedentopf, A. Ischebeck, M. A. Rettenbacher, M. Verius, S. Felber, and W. Wolfgang Fleischhacker. 2007. Sex differences in brain activation patterns during processing of positively and negatively valenced emotional words. *Psychological medicine*, 37(1):109–119.

S.M. Kosslyn, G. Ganis, and W. L. Thompson. 2001. Neural foundations of imagery. *Nature reviews neuroscience*, 2(9):635–642.

A.M. Kring and A.H. Gordon. 1998. Sex differences in emotion: expression, experience, and physiology. *Journal of personality and social psychology*, 74(3):686.

G. Lakoff. 2012. Explaining embodied cognition results. *Topics in Cognitive Science*, 4(4):773–785.

G. Lakoff and M. Johnson. 2008. *Metaphors we live by*. University of Chicago Press.

N. Leitan and L. Chaffey. 2014. Embodied cognition and its applications: A brief review. *Sensoria: A Journal of Mind, Brain & Culture*.

K. Z. Li and U. Lindenberger. 2002. Relations between aging sensory/sensorimotor and cognitive functions. *Neuroscience and Biobehavioral Reviews*, 26(7):777–783.

U. Lindenberger and P.B. Baltes. 1994. Sensory functioning and intelligence in old age: a strong connection. *Psychology and aging*, 9(3):339.

D. Lynott, L. Connell, M. Brysbaert, J. Brand, and J Carney. 2020. The lancaster sensorimotor norms: multidimensional measures of perceptual and action strength for 40,000 english words. *Behavior research methods*, 52:1271–1291.

V.A. Mann, S. Sasanuma, N. Sakuma, , and S. Masaki. 1990. Sex differences in cognitive abilities: A cross-cultural perspective. *Neuropsychologia*, 28(10):1063–1077.

R.E. Nisbett and T. Masuda. 2013. Culture and point of view. In *Biological and cultural bases of human inference*, pages 49–70. Psychology Press.

D.L. Schacter and D.R. Addis. 2007. The cognitive neuroscience of constructive memory: remembering the past and imagining the future. *Philosophical Transactions of the Royal Society B: Biological Sciences*, 362(1481):773–786.

D.L. Schacter, B. Gaesser, and DR Addis. 2013. Remembering the past and imagining the future in the elderly. *Gerontology*, 59(2):143–151.

A. Schaefer and P. Philippot. 2005. Selective effects of emotion on the phenomenal characteristics of autobiographical memories. *Memory*, 13(2):148–160.

B. Spendlove and D. Ventura. 2019. Modeling knowledge, expression, and aesthetics via sensory grounding. In *Proc. of the Tenth Int. Conference on Computational Creativity, ICCC 2019, Charlotte, North Carolina, USA, June 17-21*, page 326. Association for Computational Creativity (ACC).

T. Uzer and S. Gulgoz. 2015. Socioemotional selectivity in older adults: Evidence from the subjective experience of angry memories. *Memory*, 23(6):888–900.

Q. Wang. 2021. Cultural pathways and outcomes of autobiographical memory development. *Child Development Perspectives*, 15(3):196–202.

Remedying Gender Bias in Open English Wordnet

John P. McCrae
Insight Centre & ADAPT Centre
University of Galway
john@mccr.ae

Haotian Zhu
University of Washington
haz060@uw.edu

Fei Xia
University of Washington
fxia@uw.edu

Al Waskow
Insight Centre
University of Galway
margaret.waskow@universityofgalway.ie

Kexin Gao
University of Washington
kexing66@uw.edu

Abstract

Open English Wordnet aims to improve and maintain a wordnet for English, based on the Princeton WordNet. In this context, we identify a number of gender biases in the existing wordnet and consider the challenges of remediating the biases in the resource. In particular, we look at structural, contextual and definitional biases in the resource and examine how changes to the structure of the wordnet and to the textual definitions can create a wordnet that more fairly represents reality. We propose a number of changes that introduce 317 new synsets as well as changing the definitions or relations of over 400 further synsets. We show that these changes reduce certain kinds of gender bias within the resource.

1 Introduction

English Wordnet, first introduced by Princeton as Princeton WordNet (Miller, 1995; Fellbaum, 2010, PWN) and more recently as an open-source project, Open English Wordnet (McCrae et al., 2019, OEWN)[1], is one of the primary resources for computational lexicography. Like many lexical resources, English Wordnet reflects some of the biases of when it was created and this has been criticised in general in lexicography (Pettini, 2021). Recently, Zhu et al. (2024) identified a number of challenges specifically with English Wordnet and in this work, we consider the challenges associated with removing or limiting these biases. To this extent, we aim to tackle three main forms of bias. Firstly, structural bias, which we interpret primarily by the inclusion of gendered role words (such as 'policeman') in the resource. We modify the resource such that gendered words are in a unique synset that is also marked as gendered by being a hyponym of the synset for 'male'[09647338-n] or 'female'[09642198-n]. Secondly, we look at the use of pronouns in definitions[2] and analysed those that represent a gender bias. We considered how to change this and decided to use the singular 'they'. Finally, we look at definitions and show that as a result of the changes we made, the definitions used for female terms are improved over PWN. These changes are all part of the 2024 release of Open English Wordnet. Finally, we note that distributional bias, as identified by Zhu et al. (2024), is still a major issue and we further identify ways in which English Wordnet under-represents women. In this paper, we only consider gender bias, but other kinds of bias exist in the resource and these techniques could be helpful in fixing these issues.

In this paper, we first consider related work in Section 2 and then provide a definition of bias in Section 3. We then introduce the Open English WordNet in Section 4 and describe our methodology for removing bias in Section 5 and the results of the work. In Section 6, we discuss some of the limitations and potential future work, before finishing with conclusions in Section 7.

2 Related Work

In this study, we focus on gender bias in English Wordnet. We first discuss a taxonomy of gender bias in human-generated text and then review previous research on gender bias in NLP research.

2.1 Taxonomy of Gender Bias

To meaningfully categorize various kinds of gender bias, Hitti et al. (2019) propose two types of gender bias in text: **structural** and **contextual** bias. **Structural** bias 'occurs when bias can be traced down from a specific grammatical construction,' including gender generalization (e.g., generic *he*) and explicit marking of sex (e.g.,

[1]'Wordnet' is the generic term for this kind of resource, 'WordNet' is a trademark of Princeton University. We use the term *English Wordnet* to encompass the wordnets released by Princeton along with those subsequently released as open-source resources

[2]We do not include the example text within definitions. These have been separated in an early version of OEWN

'*chairman*' vs. '*chairwoman*'). **Contextual** bias 'requires the learning of the association between gender marked keywords and contextual knowledge,' which includes societal bias, where societal norms reflect traditional gender roles, and behavioural bias, which is a generalization of attributes and traits onto a gendered person.

Based on Hitti et al. (2019), Doughman et al. (2021) and Doughman and Khreich (2022) provide a more fine-grained taxonomy with five types of gender bias, linking each type to possible real-world implications.

2.2 Gender Bias Study in NLP

The identification and quantification of gender bias have received increasing attention in the realm of NLP in recent years. There are various kinds of gender bias that researchers have examined: gender bias in text (Cryan et al., 2020; Li et al., 2020), in NLP systems (Zhao et al., 2018; Savoldi et al., 2021), in language models (Bordia and Bowman, 2019; Fatemi et al., 2023) and in word embeddings (Bolukbasi et al., 2016; Caliskan et al., 2017; May et al., 2019).

Another important aspect of studying gender bias lies in bias mitigation. To mitigate bias in text, Sczesny et al. (2016) explore the use of gender-fair language in overcoming gender stereotyping and discrimination. Dinan et al. (2020) propose a general-purpose technique to mitigate gender bias in human-generated dialogue utterances by leveraging data augmentation, positive-bias data collection and bias-controlled training. In this work, we focus on identifying and mitigating gender bias in human-generated text, namely, in English Wordnet.

3 Definition and Statement of Bias

We adopt the definition of gender bias as given in Doughman et al. (2021): '*an exclusionary, implicitly prejudicial, or generalized representation of a specific gender as a function of various societal stereotypes.*' To systematically understand what kinds of gender bias exist in English Wordnet, we adopt and extend the gender bias taxonomy from Hitti et al. (2019) and Doughman et al. (2021). In our study, we first consider **structural bias** and **contextual bias**. We also add two new types of bias: **distributional bias** and **definitional bias**. Table 1 lists all bias types and illustrative examples.

3.1 Structural Bias

Structural gender bias considers the association between various linguistic patterns and gender. Such bias can occur at different linguistic levels such as morphology, syntax, semantics, etc.

3.1.1 Explicit Marking of Sex (B1)

At the morphological level, explicit marking of sex appears when gender-neutral entities are denoted by gender markers such as '*-man*' and '*-woman.*' Here, the term 'gender marker' refers not to grammatical gender markers but to free morphemes such as '*-woman*' in '*needlewoman*'[3] or head nouns in compound phrases such as '*woman*' in '*slovenly woman*'. **B1** in Table 1 presents an example where '*policeman*' contains the marker '*-man*' whereas its definition denotes a gender-neutral meaning.

3.1.2 Generic *he* (B2)

We also examine the generic usage of the gendered pronoun '*he*' where the pronoun is co-indexed with a gender-neutral common noun. As shown in the example from **B2** of Table 1, the word *scientist* is gender neutral but is co-indexed with a male reflexive pronoun '*himself*'.

3.2 Contextual Bias (B3)

In the proposed gender bias taxonomy (Hitti et al., 2019), contextual bias has two subtypes: societal bias, where one gender is stereotypically assigned a social role, and behavioural bias, where certain attributes or traits associated with one gender can lead to generalized gender stereotypes. For example, in Wordnet, for the word entries '*slovenly woman*' and '*rich man*', each prescribes a specific trait to a gender, while the connotations related to the adjectival modifiers appear different.

3.3 Additional Bias

We add two gender bias types to the taxonomy:

3.3.1 Distributional Bias (B4)

Distributional bias is concerned with the uneven distribution of different genders. For example, in OEWN 2024, the number of male names (6,778) is significantly greater than that of female ones (845) as shown in Table 4.

3.3.2 Definitional Bias (B5)

The different definitions given to male and female words implicate the differentiated representation

[3]'needleman' is attested in the Oxford English Dictionary

Type	ID	Subtype	Example
Structural Bias	**B1**	Explicit Marking of Sex	*policeman*: a member of a police force
	B2	Generic *he*	*researcher*: a scientist_i who devotes himself_i to doing research.
Contextual Bias	**B3**	Contextual Bias	(1) *slovenly* woman vs. *rich* man (2) He made an *honest* woman of her.
Additional Bias	**B4**	Distributional Bias	For OEWN 2024, 6,778 male names and 845 female names.
	B5	Definitional Bias	*horseman*: a man skilled in equitation *horsewoman*: a woman horseman

Table 1: Taxonomy with types and subtypes of gender bias and examples. In the examples, red indicates male gender; blue female; green neutral. Mentions that refer to the same person are indicated by i. Examples in B1, B2, B3 (1) and B5 are the definitions of entries from WordNet. B3 (2) is from the example sentence in the word entry 'honest woman' in Wordnet.

of men and women in lexical resources, which we denote as 'definitional bias'. As shown in **B3** in Table 1, the definition given in PWN to '*horseman*' only refers to men and is detailed, whereas '*horsewoman*', in PWN, is defined solely based on the male version: '*horseman*'[4].

4 Open English Wordnet

Open English Wordnet (McCrae et al., 2019, 2020, OEWN) is a 'fork' of Princeton WordNet (Miller, 1995; Fellbaum, 2010, PWN) that aims to further develop a wordnet for English. The project is open-source and is hosted on GitHub. It has made 5 releases of its WordNet on an annual basis since 2019. These have been released in various formats including the original Princeton WordNet database format, allowing this resource to act as a 'drop-in' replacement for Princeton WordNet, as well as in the standard formats proposed by the Global WordNet Association (McCrae et al., 2021, GWA). The scope of this project has fixed a wide range of issues from simple typos up to identifying and merging duplicate synsets and introducing new synsets. In addition, the project aims to take feedback from other wordnet projects in other languages, such as plWordNet (Maziarz et al., 2016), and incorporate changes that are relevant to English. The project aims to evolve English Wordnet along the lines set up by Princeton WordNet, and to that extent has developed guidelines that describe how the English Wordnet can be constructed, for example on criteria for inclusion of terms or novel senses. Further, the project aims to keep the resource up-to-date with modern English, not only by including neologisms but also by ensuring that the resource matches modern lexicographic practices. It was in this context that the new guidelines on the use of gendered language have been developed.

[4]This definition along with a few others was changed in OEWN 2024 to be more balanced

	Phase 1	Phase 2
Hypernym Links for Missing Gender (1a)		
Male	0	61
Female	26	58
Both	84	0
New Synset from Neutral (1b)		
Male	13	13
Female	0	5
Both (1c)	17	209
New Synset from other Gender (1d)		
Male	26	0
Female	0	34

Table 2: Summary of changes to OEWN 2024 to fix structural bias. We show the number of new hypernym links created to add missing gender information as well as the new synsets created.

5 Methodology

We consider four kinds of bias and how we can mitigate these issues. Firstly, we consider structural bias in two aspects: the explicit marking of gender in terms such as 'mailman' and the usage of the male pronoun, 'he'. We then consider definitional bias in the length of definitions and finally, we consider distributional bias in the resource.

5.1 Structural Bias - Explicit Marking of Sex

In order to examine the structural biases in English Wordnet, we examined the usage of gendered words (**B1**). The first step was to compile a list of gendered words and this was done in two stages. In **Phase 1**, we extracted all gendered words in

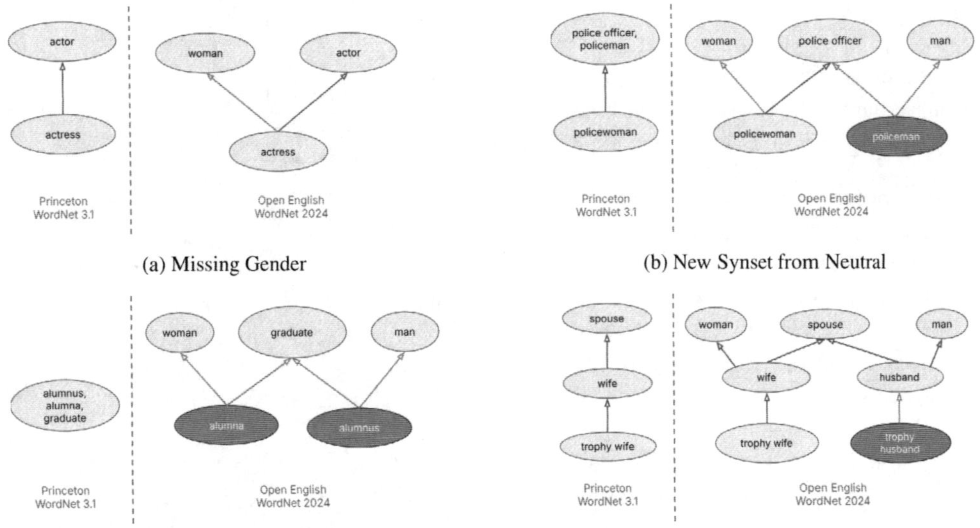

(a) Missing Gender

(b) New Synset from Neutral

(c) Both Synsets from Neutral

(d) New Synset from other Gender

Figure 1: Examples of structural biases found in English Wordnet and the proposed changes made in Open English Wordnet 2024. Changes made in Open English Wordnet are highlighted in blue.

English Wordnet based on a list in Wiktionary[5], which allowed us to identify words that have an unusual feminine morphological form (such as 'ladette' or 'dominatrix') or have no morphological clues (such as 'bride' or 'wife'). For **Phase 2**, we used words that end in words known to be gendered such as '-man' and '-woman'. This list was compiled by taking all the words in OEWN 2023 that were descended from the synset for 'man'[10306910-n] or 'woman'[10807146-n] with a few alterations[6]. For this second stage, we first manually classified whether the words represented a gender usage, as many terms like 'German'[09767053-n] or 'brahman'[09892023-n] were included. In total, 556/1092 words found this way were gendered terms. Then for each of these terms found, we examined the usage of the synset and how this can be changed to better represent gender. These can be divided into four main classes:

Missing Gender In these cases, the word was explicitly gendered but the direct hypernym was not gendered. We consider a word to be explicitly gendered if the definition contains a gendered term (such as 'a man who') or if all lemmas were gendered (for example by ending in '-man'). An example of this was 'actress'[09787123-n], which is a hyponym of 'actor'[09784701-n], which in this case was a gender-neutral term. For these cases, we simply added a second hypernym link to the synset for 'woman'[10807146-n] to indicate the gender, as depicted in Figure 1a.

Synset from Neutral In this case, there was an exclusively (normally female-gendered) term and the hypernym included a term that was of the opposite gender. For example, 'policewoman'[10468986-n] was a hyponym of a synset that included 'police officer' and 'policeman'[10468557-n]. In order to fix this, we introduced a new synset that had 'policeman'[80600405-n] as a member and was a hyponym of 'man'[10306910-n]. In addition, both of the gendered synsets were given links to the appropriate gender term as for the previous case, as depicted in Figure 1b.

New Synsets of both Genders We also discovered that there were cases where both male-gendered and female-gendered terms occurred in the same synset or where both a male and a female variant of the term should be introduced. For example, there was a single synset with the terms 'alumnus', 'alumna' and 'graduate'[09805779-n]. In this case, these are not true synonyms as you cannot substitute 'alumnus' in a sentence that uses

[5]https://en.wiktionary.org/w/index.php?title=Category:en:Female_people

[6]In particular, the words 'ex' and 'cat' were removed, although they had gendered usage.

'alumna'. As such, in this case, we introduced two new synsets ('alumnus'[80186365-n] and 'alumna'[86032704-n]) as well as links to gendered terms to arrive at the same modelling as the previous case, as in Figure 1c.

Synset from other Gender Finally, we encountered a number of terms that were clearly female-gendered but had no masculine-gendered term or vice versa. In these cases, we used corpus evidence and native-speaker intuition to decide if these terms had an equivalent and if so we introduced a new synset with the new term. In some cases, these terms were not generally linked to the synset for 'man'/'woman', but to another already gendered word. For example, we introduced 'trophy husband'[80620228-n]7 (from 'trophy wife'[10750477-n]) and linked it to 'husband'[10213586-n] as depicted in Figure 1d.

The summary of the changes is presented in Table 2 for both phases.

There were a number of challenges with this classification. Firstly, many gender-neutral terms have only become gender-neutral in recent usage, a particular example of this is 'actor' and 'actress', where the use of the female-specific term can be considered offensive (Duran, 2024). However, historically the term 'actor' only referred to males and referring to a woman as an 'actor' would have been offensive. In general, we chose to assume that terms that end in '-er'/'-or' are gender-neutral. One further exception to this was 'master', which may be used in a gender-neutral way, but also has some cases, where its use is gendered. In particular, 'schoolmaster' is marked as male in English Wordnet and in other dictionaries and would seem to be a gendered term, whereas other compounds (e.g., 'spymaster') are not gendered.

Another bias was found in that some male terms have more senses than their equivalent female terms. One particular example of this was 'viscountess'[10775729-n] defined as 'a wife or widow of a viscount' but there were two senses for 'viscount' as ' a son or younger brother or a count'[10775816-n] and 'a British peer who ranks below an earl and above a baron'[10775483-n] and, as such, a 'viscountess' should have had two senses depending on the kind of viscount the viscountess is a wife of. In general, it was noted that there were far more male-gendered terms in previous versions of English Wordnet.

7This is attested in the Cambridge Dictionary

	Male	Female
Gendered	839	157
Unbiased	37	3
Biased	181	2
Unclear	8	0
Incidental	4	2
Total	1,069	164

Table 3: Analysis of Pronoun Usage in OEWN 2023

As part of the work, we introduced many new terms into OEWN 2024, and this led to some key considerations. Firstly, we must be sure that these new terms are significant in that they have documented usage, for this, we relied on looking in corpora (primarily CoCA (Davies, 2010)) and other dictionaries to find usages of these terms. This meant that in some cases, such as for 'hodman'[10199158-n], we did not introduce a female equivalent even though the job could be done by a woman and the female term can be easily derived morphosyntactically. Secondly, we also noted that the creation of terms, especially in the case of novel masculine-gendered terms, would project biases about women onto men. As such, we did not introduce some male-gendered variants of terms such as 'slovenly woman' and in most cases removed these terms, mostly due to them being compositional terms8. This change also eliminated some contextual bias (**B3**).

5.2 Structural Bias - Generic 'he'

Another major source of bias is the use of pronouns in definitions (**B2**), in particular, the usage of 'he'/'him'/'his'/'himself' and 'she'/'her'/'hers'/'herself'. We classified the usage into the following groups, **gendered** was usage that clearly referred to a person that identifies as male/female; **unbiased** usage, where the definition used an expression such as 'his or her' to indicate both genders; **biased** usage was for the case where a male or female pronoun was used with an ungendered noun. It should be noted that the two cases where a female pronoun was used indicated a contextual bias as they were used for the terms 'shopper'[10612003-n] and 'teacher' (in the definition

8So, word sense disambiguation algorithms could tag the individual words in the composition

of the verb 'shepherd'[02555865-v]), which are traditionally female professions. Finally, we saw eight cases where the reference was to a word that was potentially gendered. This included words such as 'pope', a role that can currently only be held by a man[9]. Finally, in a few cases, denoted as **incidental**, the most appropriate gender cannot be deduced from the context, primarily due to an example being given within the definition. The distribution of these is given in Table 3. We also note that there were substantially more usages of male pronouns reflecting the distributional biases in English Wordnet.

In order to fix the issues of gender bias related to the use of pronouns, there are the following strategies:

Generic 'he' The masculine pronoun has a history of usage without referring to gender (Wagner, 2003), and as such, one option would be to simply keep all the references to 'he' as is and remove other styles (such as below). This however does not reflect modern usage and so would not be appropriate.

He or she The solution already adopted in several entries in English Wordnet is to use both male and female pronouns ('he or she'). This has a number of issues, not only is it more wordy, but also the ordering of the pronouns still puts the male pronoun first. Ordering the female pronoun first would not be less biased and sounds unnatural[10]. Further, the use of 'he' or 'she' is exclusionary to non-binary people who use other pronouns.

(s)he This option only works for the plain form of the pronoun and has most of the disadvantages of the above option.

Alternation Another option would be to randomly use one of the two pronouns (or 'his/her' and 'her/his'). While this could be made unbiased so that both pronouns have equal distribution, this would not be apparent to users of the wordnet, who do not read all definitions.

Singular 'they' Singular 'they' has been used in English for a long time and is widely accepted as a gender-neutral pronoun (Balhorn, 2004). The principle disadvantage is that it is not approved of by some style guides (most notably *The Elements of Style* (Strunk and White, 1999)). However, most style guides prefer this and it avoids the disadvantages discussed above.

As such, in discussion with the community[11] of OEWN, we adopted the use of the singular 'they' for most examples. For the cases, where the gender was unclear, we rewrote the definition in a way that avoids the use of pronouns.

5.3 Definitional Bias

In English Wordnet, a potential source of biases is shorter definitions when describing females as opposed to males (**B5**). In some cases, it may be appropriate to use a shorter definition, for example, 'a female actor' as the definition of 'actress'[09787123-n] is an efficient and complete definition. In order to investigate whether female definitions in general are shorter, we needed to establish whether a particular synset referred exclusively to males, females or neutrally to both genders. Our method to do this was to consider all non-instance hyponyms of 'doer'[09786620-n] (including indirect hypernyms) and check whether they are also hyponyms of 'male'[09647338-n] or 'female'[09642198-n]. Unfortunately, this information was very incomplete in previous versions of English Wordnet and in a few cases produced synsets that were erroneously both male and female. A large number of fixes were made[12] to ensure that the hierarchy is correct, and in addition, the gender of words was inferred for existing synsets as part of the changes discussed in Section 5.1. As a result, we raised the number of gendered role words from 248 (101 male, 147 female and 8 erroneously in both[13]) in Princeton WordNet 3.1 to 1,186 in OEWN 2024. Of these, 395 synsets in PWN were gendered due to definition or lemmas but not explicitly marked as such using a hypernym. In Table 4, we present the average definition length in OEWN 2024 and PWN 3.1[14] in terms of words and characters. We see that

[9]Although there are claims of a historical female pope, this is believed to be apocryphal and this pope would have used male pronouns

[10]It sounds unnatural to the native Anglophone authors of this article. In CoCA 'his or her' has 17,285 occurrences against 472 for 'her or his' suggesting this is a widely-shared opinion

[11]`https://github.com/globalwordnet/english-wordnet/issues/1058`

[12]OEWN Issues: #1073, #1075, #1078-#1082

[13]According to PWN's hypernyms

[14]As PWN's gender assertions are unreliable, we decided the gender based on the OEWN 2024 synset that is aligned to

	Average Word Count	Average Characters	Number of Synsets	Number of Lemmas
		Princeton WordNet 3.1		
Male Roles	9.61	51.50	309	489
Female Roles	8.08	42.83	324	523
Neutral Roles	9.52	55.11	6,023	9,683
		Open English Wordnet 2024		
Male Roles	9.52	50.75	585	815
Female Roles	8.67	46.83	601	851
Neutral Roles	9.53	55.12	6,061	9,736
Male Names	13.98	91.74	2,722	6,778
Female Names	13.54	85.38	398	845

Table 4: Length of Definitions in OEWN 2024 and PWN 3.1

female definitions are generally shorter, however, OEWN has slightly longer definitions than PWN for females with about the same for male and neutral definitions. We also see that there are in both resources more female synsets than male and this is due to cases like 'actress', where there is no specific male term.

5.4 Distributional Bias

We also examined the definitions of named people in the resource (**B4**). Again there was no direct information for most synsets in English Wordnet about gender, except in a few cases where the named person was an instance of a gendered word like 'queen'[10518940-n]. As such, we used a partial mapping to WikiData, where gender information is available (in particular using the `P21` property)[15] and we present the analysis of the lengths and frequency of definitions based on the gender given in WordNet also in Table 4[16]. We see that while there is a huge distributional bias in the number of male figures mentioned in WordNet, the definitions are of similar length, with definitions of female figures being only slightly shorter in general.

6 Discussion

In this work, we have laid out the changes we have made to reduce gender bias in Open English Wordnet. These changes should be relevant to wordnets for other languages as well as for other lexicographic projects targeting English. In fact, such initiatives are common in lexicography, with similar initiatives as far back as the 1980s (White, 1989), and the Oxford English Dictionary was even the subject of an online petition (Pettini, 2021). Lexicographers have a dual role, both to record and reflect language as it is used, but also they can be 'agents of change' as reference works (Müller-Spitzer, 2023; Fuertes-Olivera and Tarp, 2022) in society. Open English Wordnet is a resource that reflects modern English with the purpose of enabling NLP applications such as word sense disambiguation, while also providing a structured organisation of words that can power psycholinguistic investigation including those that use large language models. As such, the resource needs to reflect the biases that are inherent in society, but avoid forcing more bias into its applications by, for example, forcing a sense to be disambiguated to a male synset, when the entity in the context is clearly female.

When applied to cross-linguistically, we hope that some of these fixes can be used to help with other languages. Firstly, the Open English Wordnet project will contribute these changes to the Collaborative Inter-lingual Index (Bond et al., 2016) so that they may be useful to other wordnets. In particular, this would be useful for languages that have mandatory gender for most role words (this applies to most European languages) as there are now synsets for gender-specific as well as gender-neutral terms. In this way, the German 'Polizist' could be linked through policeman[80600405-n] to terms such as

this PWN synset.

[15]Two named figures in English Wordnet have a non-binary identity and are excluded from this analysis

[16]We present only the results for OEWN 2024 as the total number of proper noun synsets and their definitions has not changed substantially

'policier' in French, while the feminine 'Polizistin' would be linked through 'policewoman'[10468986-n] to 'policière' in French. We note the changes made in OEWN 2024 did not remove any synsets, and added gender to a synset if its definition explicitly marked the synset as male or if all lemmas were male-gendered, which may differ from the policy of other wordnets constructed using the EXTEND methodology (Vossen, 1998). For role words, our changes created both gender-neutral and gender-specific synsets, unless we could not find attestations of the terms in English, and aimed to cover all such role words in OEWN, but some may be missed if they were not in Wiktionary and did not follow a typical derivational pattern (such as '-man'/'-woman').

Finally, we note that the change of gendered pronouns relies on a fairly unique case of English having an animate, gender-neutral pronoun, whereas most other languages either lack gendered pronouns entirely (such as 'hän' in Finnish) or gender-neutral pronouns are neologisms that are not widely used (such as 'elle' in Spanish).

7 Conclusion

This work has presented a number of changes to Open English Wordnet that have made the resource more applicable and more fair for modern usage of English. While we managed to mostly remove or limit the structural biases in English Wordnet, other biases still exist. In particular, distributional biases are still a major issue in the resource with male figures being named more than seven times as frequently as female figures and a similar frequency for the use of female pronouns versus male. It is hard to fix these in a way that reflects a world where women have traditionally been excluded from roles where they would acquire notoriety to be included in the resource. Further, OEWN has a current moratorium on the introduction or removal of proper nouns that would prevent this. We also note that this work has approached gender as a binary, which excludes many non-binary people, and there is scope for improving this in future releases.

Acknowledgements

John P. McCrae is supported by Research Ireland under Grant Number SFI/12/RC/2289_P2 Insight_2, Insight SFI Centre for Data Analytics and Grant Number 13/RC/2106_P2, ADAPT SFI Research Centre.

References

Mark Balhorn. 2004. The Rise of Epicene They. *Journal of English Linguistics*, 32(2):79–104.

Tolga Bolukbasi, Kai-Wei Chang, James Zou, Venkatesh Saligrama, and Adam Kalai. 2016. Man is to computer programmer as woman is to homemaker? debiasing word embeddings.

Francis Bond, Piek Vossen, John McCrae, and Christiane Fellbaum. 2016. CILI: the collaborative interlingual index. In *Proceedings of the 8th Global WordNet Conference (GWC)*, pages 50–57, Bucharest, Romania. Global Wordnet Association.

Shikha Bordia and Samuel R. Bowman. 2019. Identifying and reducing gender bias in word-level language models. In *Proceedings of the 2019 Conference of the North American Chapter of the Association for Computational Linguistics: Student Research Workshop*, pages 7–15, Minneapolis, Minnesota. Association for Computational Linguistics.

Aylin Caliskan, Joanna J. Bryson, and Arvind Narayanan. 2017. Semantics derived automatically from language corpora contain human-like biases. *Science*, 356(6334):183–186.

Jenna Cryan, Shiliang Tang, Xinyi Zhang, Miriam J. Metzger, Haitao Zheng, and Ben Y. Zhao. 2020. Detecting gender stereotypes: Lexicon vs. supervised learning methods. *Proceedings of the 2020 CHI Conference on Human Factors in Computing Systems*.

Mark Davies. 2010. The Corpus of Contemporary American English as the first reliable monitor corpus of English. *Literary and Linguistic Computing*, 25(4):447–464.

Emily Dinan, Angela Fan, Adina Williams, Jack Urbanek, Douwe Kiela, and Jason Weston. 2020. Queens are powerful too: Mitigating gender bias in dialogue generation.

Jad Doughman and Wael Khreich. 2022. Gender bias in text: Labeled datasets and lexicons. *CoRR*, abs/2201.08675.

Jad Doughman, Wael Khreich, Maya El Gharib, Maha Wiss, and Zahraa Berjawi. 2021. Gender bias in text: Origin, taxonomy, and implications. In *Proceedings of the 3rd Workshop on Gender Bias in Natural Language Processing*, pages 34–44, Online. Association for Computational Linguistics.

Crystal Duran. 2024. Actor vs. actress. *Backstage*.

Zahra Fatemi, Chen Xing, Wenhao Liu, and Caiming Xiong. 2023. Improving gender fairness of pre-trained language models without catastrophic forgetting. In *Proceedings of the 61st Annual Meeting of the Association for Computational Linguistics (Volume 2: Short Papers)*, pages 1249–1262, Toronto, Canada. Association for Computational Linguistics.

Christiane Fellbaum. 2010. *WordNet*, pages 231–243. Springer Netherlands, Dordrecht.

Pedro A Fuertes-Olivera and Sven Tarp. 2022. Critical lexicography at work: reflections and proposals for eliminating gender bias in general dictionaries of Spanish. *Lexikos*, 32(2):105–132.

Yasmeen Hitti, Eunbee Jang, Ines Moreno, and Carolyne Pelletier. 2019. Proposed taxonomy for gender bias in text; a filtering methodology for the gender generalization subtype. In *Proceedings of the First Workshop on Gender Bias in Natural Language Processing*, pages 8–17, Florence, Italy. Association for Computational Linguistics.

Lucy Li, Demszky Dorottya, Bromley Patricia, and Jurafsky Dan. 2020. Content analysis of textbooks via natural language processing: Findings on gender, race, and ethnicity in texas u.s. history textbooks. *AERA Open*, 6.

Chandler May, Alex Wang, Shikha Bordia, Samuel R. Bowman, and Rachel Rudinger. 2019. On measuring social biases in sentence encoders. *ArXiv*, abs/1903.10561.

Marek Maziarz, Maciej Piasecki, Ewa Rudnicka, Stan Szpakowicz, and Paweł Kędzia. 2016. plWordNet 3.0 – a comprehensive lexical-semantic resource. In *Proceedings of COLING 2016, the 26th International Conference on Computational Linguistics: Technical Papers*, pages 2259–2268, Osaka, Japan. The COLING 2016 Organizing Committee.

John P. McCrae, Michael Wayne Goodman, Francis Bond, Alexandre Rademaker, Ewa Rudnicka, and Luis Morgado Da Costa. 2021. The GlobalWordNet formats: Updates for 2020. In *Proceedings of the 11th Global Wordnet Conference*, pages 91–99, University of South Africa (UNISA). Global Wordnet Association.

John P. McCrae, Alexandre Rademaker, Francis Bond, Ewa Rudnicka, and Christiane Fellbaum. 2019. English WordNet 2019 – an open-source WordNet for English. In *Proceedings of the 10th Global Wordnet Conference*, pages 245–252, Wroclaw, Poland. Global Wordnet Association.

John Philip McCrae, Alexandre Rademaker, Ewa Rudnicka, and Francis Bond. 2020. English WordNet 2020: Improving and extending a WordNet for English using an open-source methodology. In *Proceedings of the LREC 2020 Workshop on Multimodal Wordnets (MMW2020)*, pages 14–19, Marseille, France. The European Language Resources Association (ELRA).

George A. Miller. 1995. Wordnet: a lexical database for english. *Commun. ACM*, 38(11):39–41.

Carolin Müller-Spitzer. 2023. Gender stereotypes in dictionaries: the challenge of reconciling usage-based lexicography with the role of dictionaries as social agents. *Lexikos*, 33(2):79–94.

Silvia Pettini. 2021. "One is a woman, so that's encouraging too". the representation of social gender in "powered by Oxford" online lexicography. *Lingue e Linguaggi*, (44):275–295.

Beatrice Savoldi, Marco Gaido, Luisa Bentivogli, Matteo Negri, and Marco Turchi. 2021. Gender bias in machine translation. *Transactions of the Association for Computational Linguistics*, 9:845–874.

Sabine Sczesny, Magda Formanowicz, and Franziska Moser. 2016. Can gender-fair language reduce gender stereotyping and discrimination? *Frontiers in Psychology*, 7.

William Strunk and E. B. White. 1999. *The Elements of style*. Allyn and Bacon : Longman, Boston (USA).

Piek Vossen. 1998. *Introduction to EuroWordNet*, pages 1–17. Springer Netherlands, Dordrecht.

Susanne Wagner. 2003. *Gender in English pronouns: Myth and reality*. Ph.D. thesis, Freiburg (Breisgau), Univ., Diss., 2003.

Linda White. 1989. Feminism and lexicography: Dealing with sexist language in a bilingual dictionary. *Frontiers: A Journal of Women Studies*, pages 61–64.

Jieyu Zhao, Tianlu Wang, Mark Yatskar, Vicente Ordonez, and Kai-Wei Chang. 2018. Gender bias in coreference resolution: Evaluation and debiasing methods. In *Proceedings of the 2018 Conference of the North American Chapter of the Association for Computational Linguistics: Human Language Technologies, Volume 2 (Short Papers)*, pages 15–20, New Orleans, Louisiana. Association for Computational Linguistics.

Haotian Zhu, Kexin Gao, Fei Xia, and Mari Ostendorf. 2024. Disagreeable, slovenly, honest and un-named women? investigating gender bias in English educational resources by extending existing gender bias taxonomies. In *Proceedings of the 5th Workshop on Gender Bias in Natural Language Processing (GeBNLP)*, pages 219–236, Bangkok, Thailand. Association for Computational Linguistics.

Improving the lexicographic accessibility of WN through LLMs

Ágoston Tóth
Department of English Linguistics
University of Debrecen
toth.agoston@arts.unideb.hu

Esra Abdelzaher
Department of English Linguistics
University of Debrecen
esra.abdelzaher@gmail.com

Abstract

This paper reports the results of an ongoing research on the usability of neural language models to improve WordNet (WN) data for pedagogical lexicographic use. We test the efficacy of BERT-based methods for the selection of example sentences from SemCor and the addition of guidewords to WN senses. We probed our method in a series of time-measured classroom experiments that used WN data only and WN data after adding example sentences and guidewords. We compare two methods of the automatic selection of "good" examples for lexicographic use and discuss the value of BERT probability scores to the selection of useful guidewords. The gap between the pedagogical values of the SemCor extracted sentences and the handpicked examples in WN was reflected in the longer time students spent on the decoding tasks after adding examples and guidewords. However, the decoding performance, especially in the synonym selection task, significantly improved. We argue that the use of Large Language Models can help in improving the accessibility of WN information for educational purposes.

1 Introduction

Gouws (2018) proposed that the accessibility, clarity and retrieval of lexicographic information are the three determining factors that predict the success or failure of a dictionary. The outer access to the information is facilitated in WordNet (WN; Fellbaum, 1998) through a search engine that locates lemmas (co-)listed in synonym sets, similar to any online dictionary. However, the inner access to the information at the microstructure level (e.g. senses, glosses, examples) is practically obstructed – for nonprofessional users – in various ways, including the sophisticated hierarchical representation of sense relations, variety of hyperlinks, information overload, limited and sometimes lack of example sentences and absence of guidewords.

This study probes the usability of Large Language Models (LLMs) in facilitating the use of English WN 3.1 senses for pedagogical lexicography. We mainly targeted two lexicographic features that appear to be insufficient in or missing from the WN design (Miller, 1995; Fellbaum, 1998): example sentences and guidewords. We aim at answering the following questions:

1. Can BERT (Devlin et al., 2019) help in selecting useful examples for practical lexicographic use?
2. How typical or good are the sense-tagged sentences in Semantic Concordance (SemCor; Miller et al., 1993) for pedagogical lexicographic use?
3. How far can BERT's most probable words for a target word in a sense-tagged sentence function as a guideword for this sense?
4. Would BERT-based modifications significantly influence the decoding performance or the consultation time shown by English as a Second Language (ESL) learners consulting WN-modified entries?

The rest of this paper will discuss the importance of guidewords and example sentences in pedagogical lexicography (Section 2), overview the usability of LLMs in lexicographic practice in Section 3, describe the methods of utilizing LLMs in example and guideword selection and the collection of data in Section 4, display and discuss the most important findings in Section 5 and draw the conclusion in Section 6.

2 Access and microstructure of WN: missing features

Despite the uniqueness of the access and microstructure features of WN as a lexicographic resource, the database underrepresents two significant features to a lexicographic entry, namely guidewords and example sentences. Whereas the latter is limitedly represented for several senses, the former is totally missing from the database by design.

The importance of examples in a dictionary entry has been stressed since Dr. Johnson's plan for a dictionary (Atkins and Rundell, 2008). Lexicographic examples should tell the user about the standard and idiosyncratic behavior of a word (Kilgarriff, 2005, 2013) and they are particularly important to the explanation of abstract words and disambiguation of related word senses and near-synonyms (Abdelzaher, 2024; Fillmore and Atkins, 1992). Therefore, several proposals have been made to the selection of the best examples for lexicographic resources, e.g. using handcrafted examples by expert lexicographers, corpus-based citations without alternation (Ruppenhofer et al., 2016), automatic algorithmic selection from corpus sentences (Kilgarriff et al., 2008).

Guidewords, signposts or shortcuts are additional words or phrases preceding each sense to help dictionary users locate the required information faster and easily. Guidewords can be hypernyms, hyponyms or even brief glosses that improve the accessibility of information for users (Heuberger, 2016). They are currently present in leading pedagogical dictionaries such as the Oxford Advanced Learner's Dictionary. The importance of guidewords increases in longer dictionary entries as they shorten the consultation time (Abdelzaer, 2022; Lew and Pajkowvska, 2007; Ptasznik and Lew, 2014), increase the accuracy of sense selection (Dziemianko, 2016), their form also affects the accuracy of encoding performance (Dziemianko, 2017).

3 The usability of LLMs in lexicography

Lexicographers have been arguing for and against the usability of generative and non-generative LLMs, especially recent GPT models, in performing traditional lexicographic tasks which require the processing of large corpora given the large corpora involved in the training of such models. This may facilitate the lexicographic tasks such as updating lists of headwords, writing definitions and selecting examples, but at the same time imposes risks of reproducing linguistic bias and circulating hallucinations (McKean and Fitzgerald, 2024). Prominent lexicographers such as de Schryver participated in a Youtube-registered talk about the possibility of replacing lexicographers with ChatGPT. He explained how this AI-based model can translate strings of words, create dictionary entries for existing words, propose humorous fake entries for words and produce XML-formatted entries (De Schryver and Joffe, 2023). Similarly, Phoodai and Rikk (2023) attempted to compare lexicographic information in ChatGPT-generated entries to lexicographic information in OALD to show the effectiveness of AI models to date.

In contrast, Jakubíček and Rundell (2023) effectively responded to de Schryver's and Joffe's (2023) with a detailed evaluation of 99 entries that were generated using ChatGPT. They highlighted the lexicographic limitations of using such methods despite their outperformance of existing NLP technologies. First, the word sense induction task is limited by (a) generation of false polysemy of the same sense, (b) missing senses despite their frequency based on corpus analysis and (c) suggesting senses which are not evident to the authors without providing citation. Furthermore, they detected some syntactic errors in formulating the definitions and illustrated the lack of diversity in the example sentences suggested by the system which limited their pedagogical value. Moreover, they judged the examples as saliently formulaic and unnatural. However, they praised the system's ability to assign labels to marked uses, such as the "archaic" ones and acknowledged the definitions of general and technical words. Nichols (2023) referred to the model's improper handling of synonymy, frequent generation of syntactically erroneous responses and considerable change in the responses to the same question.

Therefore, the more human-supervised and corpus-centered approach of using the output of non-generative LLMs could be more helpful in lexicography. Tóth and Abdelzaher (2023), for instance, explored the combined use of dimensionality reduction algorithms and the output of neural word embeddings (BERT representations) in finding clusters of word senses. The results showed the usability of visualized clusters in detecting semantic and syntactic patterns of word uses, although the suggested clusters did not correspond to the sense categories in the studied dictionary.

In the present study, we argue for the use of non-generative LLMs in pedagogical lexicography as they let us use authentic corpus data rather than generated output, and they are directly trained to carry out token unmasking, which we will make use of (see Section 4). These characteristics make non-generative LLMs highly relevant for our purposes despite the fact that they tend to feature less parameters than modern generative models.

4 Methodology

We conducted three experiments focusing on sense and synonym selection tasks. The lexicographic entries in each experiment contained the same words (e.g. *appear*, *tell*, *development*) but included different lexicographic information cited from WN and Semantic Concordance (SemCor 3.0). We accessed SemCor 3.0 through Sketch Engine. The sense-annotated corpus was first announced by Miller et al. (1993) and it has been continuously updated based on the updated senses in WN. The version we use has been automatically mapped to the WN 3.0 senses by Rada Mihalcea (https://www.sketchengine.eu/semcor-annotated-corpus).

4.1 BERT-based selection of examples and guidewords

We used TPEX scoring (Tóth, forthcoming) to characterize SemCor sentences that contained the selected headwords. TPEX relies on large pretrained neural language models that natively support the word unmasking function to list the most probable tokens and the probability of their appearance in the masked position, the position which is originally occupied by the headwords in our experiments. Tóth tested 4 models (BERT, RoBERTa, ALBERT and BigBird) and discussed the use of two TPEX variants, TPEX-*abs* (which returns the probability with which BERT predicts the headword to appear in the masked position, disregarding other candidates and their probabilities) and TPEX-*rel* (the probability of the appearance of the headword in the masked position divided by the probability of the most probable token predicted for that position). TPEX returns values in the [0,1] interval.

In the present paper, we use TPEX-*abs* to characterize SemCor sentences. We also collect probability scores for other tokens predicted to hide behind the masks, and use these lists to select guidewords (see section 5.1 below). In every case, we use BERT (bert-large-uncased) from the Happy Transformer library available at happytransformer.com to carry out the unmasking procedure.

BERT (Bidirectional Encoder Representations from Transformers; Devlin et al., 2019) is directly trained on the task of revealing masked tokens in context, the same task that we use it for. Therefore, we do not rely on transfer learning and other techniques that equip GPT and other generative LLMs with AI (or AI-like) capabilities; instead, we employ a machine-learning system to perform a task it is originally trained on.

Since the networks that we use are known to create contextualized word embeddings, lexical ambiguity is not an issue with TPEX scoring; the tested sentences do not have to be disambiguated or annotated in any way, and we are not restricted to use SemCor sentences in future applications.

A limitation of our research is that we make predictions on BERT *tokens*. The token dictionary is restricted to about 30000 token types in BERT, and we compute the probability of appearance in the masked position for single tokens. It is possible to change the token dictionary and include the headwords that we need to cover, but this process is rather resource-hungry as it requires the training of a large neural network (albeit a much smaller one than those driving generative LLMs). It may not be an option in some lexicographical projects, which restricts them to tokens available in the token vocabulary. Whether this issue has a technical solution (perhaps a fine-tuning procedure with a modified vocabulary) or needs further fundamental research is an open question.

4.2 Designing WN-based lexicographic entries

We represented WN data in the conventional lexicographic entries ESL learners are familiar with. In the first experiment, we kept only the synset and the gloss, in the second experiment we added an example sentence selected using GDEX scoring (Kilgarriff et al., 2008) using the default GDEX configuration in Sketch Engine (https://www.sketchengine.eu), and in the – LLM-assisted – third experiment, we added a guideword and an example using the TPEX scoring explained in Subsection 4.1. We replaced the target word with a pseudo word to avoid the influence of previous exposure; replacing the target word with a coined or obsolete word to test the influence of a lexicographic variable on the decoding performance of learners is a common practice in lexicography (Chan, 2014; Dziemianko, 2016). We used words from the *Compendium of Lost Words*. Appendix 1 shows a sample of the modified lexicographic entries in the third experiment, which embeds the most modified entries.

4.3 User-based testing

We designed two decoding tasks to test the learners' ability to understand the meaning of the target sense from WN's original and modified data. The first task asked the students to read a lexicographic entry and respond to a grid-form question in which all the senses of the target word are present and four test sentences are provided. Participants are required to match each sentence with its correct sense in a one-to-one correspondence task. The task was scored according to binary values (0 for incorrect answers; 1 for correct answers) regardless of the similarities between the correct sense and the chosen sense by the participants.

In the second task, participants were asked to choose the word from six options that could replace the target word in each of the four sentences where they identified the correct sense. The options included synonyms, hyponyms and hypernyms of the target word in a sense other than the one instantiated in the target sentence We also included distractors in the options (i.e., words that are not semantically similar to the target word but they fit within the context of the test sentence). The test sentences have been cited from the WN database. The task has been graded according to the same grading method used in the sense selection task. Samples of task 1 and task 2 are present in Appendix 2.

The test has been conducted using Psytoolkit (Stoet, 2017) which allows automatic measuring of the time spent on each task, supports various question types (e.g. multiple choice, short and long text responses, voice recording) and allows the insertion of video, audio or graphic files in a question. The participants in the experiments were ESL learners in the 3rd and 4th year of English-major programs at a European higher educational institute. More information about the proficiency levels, frequency of using dictionaries and familiarity with the WN database are available in Appendix 3.

5 Results and discussion

5.1 Selection of examples and guidewords

There were salient differences between the scores of GDEX and the TPEX scores which is reflected in the anticorrelation (Pearson-r = -0.0225), but the differences were not statistically significant (P = 0.529284). On several occasions the highest TPEX scores corresponded to 0 GDEX scores and vice versa. Therefore, our suggested approach of multiplying the TPEX score by the GDEX score led to the discard of the examples which are judged as totally not good or atypical, and kept only the examples which are to some extent good and typical according to both algorithms. TPEX selected the following example as the most typical use of *tell*: *and grandma is n't strong enough to take on something like that, and to tell you the truth neither am I* (TPEX score = 0.9). On the contrary, the GDEX score assigned to the same sentence was 0, which led to its exclusion from the experiments. Similarly, GDEX scores were the highest for the sentence *He felt tired and full and calm* (Target sense = *full*_4, GDEX = 0.9), but – according to TPEX – the probability of the appearance of *full* in this context was 0. The sentence was accordingly excluded from the test. It was evident that GDEX scores reflected the overall readability of the sentence, but they were not sensitive to the typical or canonical occurrences of the headwords.

TPEX scores, in contrast, are primarily assigned according to the probability of the occurrence of the target word in the given sentence without considering other pedagogical factors such as the length of the sentence, the presence of pronouns or advanced (e.g. CEFR C1 and C2-level) vocabulary. Although the highest TPEX scores would recommend the most canonical uses of a target word from a corpus, they would not reflect other pedagogically relevant aspects (i.e. the features observed in the GDEX algorithm). It was not accordingly predictable which entries would be more valuable for the learners when they perform the tasks. The scores of the selected examples in the third experiment ranged from 0.8 for *tell* senses 1 and 2 to 0.1 for *development* according to our new, composite score (i.e., GDEX*TPEX).

The list of most probable words suggested by BERT included examples of multiple sense relations present in the WN database with all their pedagogical values and challenges. To elaborate, *be* was recorded as a hypernym for *appear* in WN and was also frequently suggested by BERT as the most probable word when *appear* was masked. Including *be* as a guideword may not be of any pedagogical value for the learners especially in our experiments (which already disguise the target word). The list of the most probable words included direct and indirect hypernyms, synonyms and near-synonyms, hyponyms and distributionally similar words. Whereas hypernyms and synonyms were usable as guidewords in several cases, the rest of the words were not suitable for the representation of WN senses. BERT probability scores do not seem to mirror the fine-granularity of WN senses even if sense-tagged sentences are processed. *Growth* and *improvement*, for example, appeared as the most probable words for sentences representing different senses of the target word *development*. While *improvement* is the direct hypernym of the first WN sense of development, *growth* is a synonym of the third sense. They cannot be used interchangeably as guidewords in a WN-based entry disregarding their respective senses. However, it is noteworthy that the senses of *development* were highly overlapping in SemCor, too, which led the annotators to assign two senses the same sentence more than once. In the third experiment, a guideword was successfully added to 54% of the senses collectively in all entries. Whereas the entry of *tell* had the highest number of guidewords (for 5 senses out of 7), the entry of *sound* had the least number of guidewords (for 2 senses out of 8) due to the high overlap of the most probable words for almost all senses.

5.2 Differences in the decoding performance and consultation time

Examining the differences in the time and performance among the three groups showed significant variations. First, the consultation time varied significantly between the three groups. Even though participants in the first experiment consulted the shortest entries which included only the synset and the gloss, they spent longer time on the sense selection task than participants in the second group. The consultation time decreased by 35 seconds on average per task for the second group if compared to the first group and increased by 20 seconds for the third group if compared to the first group. Time differences were statistically significant for the three groups (F = 3.51, P = 0.021). The Post Hoc Tukey test showed the significant differences were between the first and third groups (Q = 3.51, P = 0.036) and between the second and third groups (Q = 3.39, P = 0.045). The length of the entry (i.e., the total number of words in the entry) was negatively correlated with the time of sense selection for the three groups but the anti-correlation was statistically significant for the third group only (r = -0.1914, P = 0.00291).

Second, participants in the first group showed the poorest performance in synonym and sense selection tasks whereas participants in the third experiments showed the best performance but spent the longest time on the consultation process. There was a significant correlation between the time spent on the task and the accuracy of sense selection in the second (r = 0.2103, P = 0.001047) and third (r = 0.452, P = 0.00341) experiments. The differences in the sense selection task among the three groups were significant according to one-way ANOVA test (F = 6.812, P = 0.0011). The Post Hoc Tukey test showed the significant differences were between the first and third groups (Q = 5.19, P = 0.0007). The same applies to the accuracy of synonym selection task (F = 7.8055, P = 0.00454). The differences were significant between the first and third groups. Figure 1 shows the overall accuracy of sense and synonym selection among the three groups.

Third, the performance of the participants in the synonym selection task was better than their responses to the sense selection task in the three experiments. However, the difference was statistically significant in the third experiment only, according to ANOVA test (F = 7.12, P = 0.001). There was also a significant anti-correlation between the time spent on the sense and synonym selection tasks in the third experiment (r = -0.362, P = 0.0217).

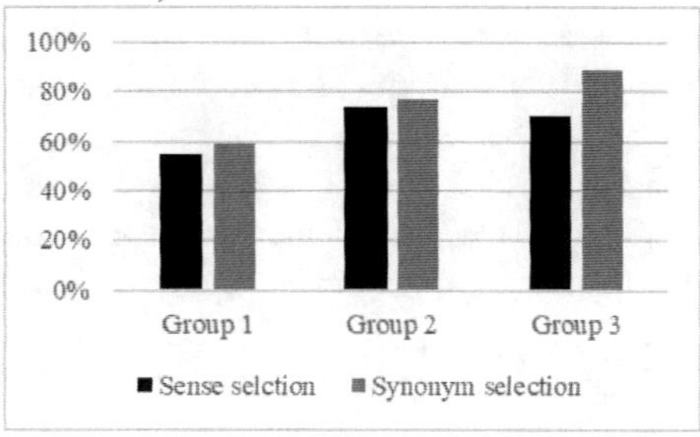

Figure 1: Accuracy of sense and synonym selection tasks

5.3 The influence of the new lexicographic features

It is evident that consulting the entries that included only the synset and the gloss was not effective in helping ESL learners decode the meaning of the target words in either of the tasks, despite spending the shortest time on the task. The addition of a single example sentence for each sense in the entry improved the performance of the participants in the two tasks and surprisingly shortened the consultation time. The examples added to the entries in the second experiment were generally short (average of 6 words) and had relatively low GDEX scores (0.450). They did increase the length of the entry but they did not prolong the consultation period.

The considerable improvement in the decoding performance was noticeable in the third experiment but also there was a considerable delay in the time of the responses to the two tasks. The example sentences added based on the TPEX*GDEX scores for SemCor citations were longer (average of 12 words) than the examples recommended by the GDEX scores for the sentences provided in the WN database in experiment 2. The differences in the length of the example sentences were statistically significant for all test words ($F = 23.278$, $P = 0.00001$). We argue that the presence of the guidewords had a positive effect on shortening the consultation time for long word entries as the shortest consultation time in the third group was associated with the words that had the most number of guidewords and vice versa. Participants spent an average of 4 minutes on the two tasks for the word *tell* (which was the shortest consultation time) and spent 7 minutes on the same tasks when they consulted the entries of *sound* and *development*.

6 Conclusion

This study explored the efficiency of LLMs in improving WN information for pedagogical lexicography. The selection of examples from the WN database or the SemCor corpus has been challenging for the limited number of examples and frequent use of incomplete sentences in the former and the run-on sentences, advanced words and overlapping senses in the latter. It should be noted that WN examples had not been added to the database for lexicographic or teaching purposes. They were, however, added to help in disambiguating one sense from another (Baker and Fellbaum, 2009). Therefore, in many cases they are phrases showing strong associations between the target word sense and another word. They can be beneficial for teaching collocations, but they are not as useful when it comes to explaining word senses for ESL learners (especially if the target word is replaced with a pseudo word). This imposes a challenge on the comprehensive use of WN's sense-tagged sentences in pedagogical lexicography. A combination of two example selection methods (i.e. GDEX and TPEX) appears to be an effective solution for choosing examples of a reasonable length, with accessible words and high probability of the occurrence of the target word in the specified sense. That is to say, the answer to the first question in the present study is yes, the proposed BERT-based method of the selection of examples is helpful in finding typical examples of word use.

Furthermore, enhancing TPEX scores with GDEX score facilitates the selection of more pedagogically valuable examples, which addresses the second question of the study. The SemCor corpus contains many examples that are lexicographically valuable according to the two scoring methods but, unfortunately, around 50% of the SemCor citations for the words tested in our experiments were assigned a score of 0 according to either or both of the scoring methods. Given the challenge of creating a sense-tagged corpus similar to SemCor, future research may consider (a) simplifying the TPEX-selected sentences through shortening their length, (b) replacing C2 words with B1–B2 synonyms or near-synonyms, or both (a) and (b). As annotations are not necessary for TPEX or GDEX scoring, any source of text can be used. Selecting or upscoring examples that only use lemmas that are listed in a controlled (defining) vocabulary, such as the Oxford 3000 list, may also be an option; several learner's dictionaries have already introduced the process of writing the *definitions* based on controlled defining vocabularies, too.

The results of the third experiment indicated the importance of the guidewords to improving the decoding performance of ESL learners, but the challenge of finding appropriate guidewords for the fine-grained senses in WN was also salient. Despite the richness of the sense relations in the database, none of these relations could be systematically used to find a guideword. Synonymy, which is the only relation that is consistently present across all POS is not available for all word senses, i.e. for single-member synsets. For instance, three of the eight senses of *appear* do not have any synonyms in WN. Moreover, sometimes WN records synonyms that are infrequently used in this sense and would, accordingly, perplex users for either the synonym's unfamiliarity or familiarity in another sense (e.g. *euphony* as a synonym of *music*). The same applies to the use of WN's hypernyms as guidewords. In many cases, the hypernym is too general to provide helpful information to learners (e.g. *process* as a hypernym of *development*). Moreover, the hypernym-hyponym relation is not applicable to the adjective net. In this regard, BERT's most probable words could partially address this challenge by suggesting high-frequency and most probable replacements. However, this does not solve the problem of overgeneralizing a sense by suggesting its direct or indirect hypernym (e.g. *be* for *appear* in several sentences) or further specifying it by suggesting a hyponym (e.g. *ring* or *jingle* for *sound*) or troponym. This shows the complexity of the issue, and we argue that human lexicographical expertise is still key to the success of the guideword-selection process.

Finally, the remarkable advancement in the participants' responses after consulting WN entries in the third experiment (with example sentences and guidewords) shows how the database can be successfully integrated in pedagogical lexicography. WN has already been included in the new types of dictionaries such as aggregators (e.g. *The fine dictionary*) and portals (e.g. *Onelook*) probably due to the accessibility of its structure which is less complicated if compared to other resources such as FrameNet.

Acknowledgments

This publication was supported by the Institute of English and American Studies at the University of Debrecen.

References

Esra M. Abdelzaher. 2022. A classroom-based study on the effectiveness of lexicographic resources. *Lexicography: AsiaLex*, 9(2):139–174.

Esra M. Abdelzaher. 2024. *Approaches of cognitive linguistics and ontologies in lexicographic sense delineation*. Ph.D. thesis, Debrecen University.

Sue Atkins and Michael Rundell. 2008. *The Oxford guide to practical lexicography*. Oxford University Press, Oxford, UK.

Collin F. Baker and Christiane Fellbaum. 2009. WordNet and FrameNet as Complementary Resources for Annotation. In *Proceedings of the Third Linguistic Annotation Workshop (LAW III)*. Association for Computational Linguistics, Suntec, Singapore, pages 125–129.

Alice Y. W. Chan. 2014. How can ESL students make the best use of learners' dictionaries? *English Today*, 30(3).

Gilles-Maurice de Schryver and David Joffe. 2023. The end of lexicography, welcome to the machine: on how ChatGPT can already take over all of the dictionary maker's tasks. In *The 20th CODH Seminar, Center for Open Data in the Humanities*, Research Organization of Information and Systems, National Institute of Informatics, Tokyo, Japan.

Jacob Devlin, Ming Wei Chang, Kenton Lee and Kristina Toutanova. 2019. BERT: Pre-training of deep bidirectional transformers for language understanding. In *NAACL HLT 2019 - 2019 Conference of the North American Chapter of the Association for Computational Linguistics: Human Language Technologies - Proceedings of the Conference, volume 1*.

Anna Dziemianko. 2016. An insight into the visual presentation of signposts in English learners' dictionaries online. *International Journal of Lexicography*, 39(4):490–524.

Anna Dziemianko. 2017. Dictionary entries and bathtubs: Does it make sense? *International Journal of Lexicography*, 30(3):263–284.

Christiane Fellbaum, editor. 1998. *WordNet: An Electronic Lexical Database*. Cambridge, MA, MIT Press.

Charles Fillmore and Sue Atkins. 1992. Towards a frame-based organization of the lexicon: the semantics of RISK and its neighbors. In A. Lehrer and E. Kittay, editors, *Frames, fields, and contrasts: New essays in semantic and lexical organization*, pages 75–102.

Rufus H. Gouws. 2018. Dictionaries and access. In Pedro A. Fuertes-Olivera, editor, *The Routledge Handbook of Lexicography*, pages 43–58.

Reinhard Heuberger. 2016. 'Learners' Dictionaries: History and Development; Current Issues'. In Philip Durkin, editor, *The Oxford Handbook of Lexicography*.

Miloš Jakubíček and Michael Rundell. 2023. The end of lexicography? Can ChatGPT outperform current tools for post-editing lexicography? In M. Medveď, M. Měchura, C. Tiberius, I. Kosem, J. Kallas, M. Jakubíček and S. Krek, editors, *Electronic lexicography in the 21st century (eLex 2023): Invisible Lexicography. Proceedings of the eLex*

2023 conference. Brno, 27–29 June 2023. Lexical Computing CZ s.r.o., Brno, pages 518–533.

Adam Kilgarriff. 2005. Putting the Corpus Into the Dictionary. *Proceedings of the Second MEANING Workshop*, Trento, Italy, 3-4 February 2005.

Adam Kilgarriff. 2013. Using Corpora as Data Sources for Dictionaries. In Howard Jackson, editor, *The Bloomsbury Companion to Lexicography*. Bloomsbury, London, pages 77–96.

Adam Kilgarriff, Katy Mcadam, Michael Rundell, and Pavel Rychlý. 2008. GDEX: Automatically Finding Good Dictionary Examples in a Corpus. In Elisenda Bernal and Janet DeCesaris, editors, *Proceedings of the 13th EURALEX International Congress*. Institut Universitari de Linguistica Aplicada, Universitat Pompeu Fabra, Barcelona, Spain, pages 425–432.

Robert Lew and Julita Pajkowska. 2007. The Effect Of Signposts On Access Speed And Lookup Task Success in Long And Short Entries. *Revista Horizontes de Linguistica Aplicada*, 6(2), 235-252.

Erin McKean and Will Fitzgerald. 2024. The ROI of AI in lexicography. *Lexicography: Journal of AsiaLex* 11 (1): 7–27.

George A. Miller. 1995. WordNet: A Lexical Database for English. *Communications of the ACM* 38 (11): 39–41.

George A. Miller, Claudia Leacock, Randee Tengi and Ross T. Bunker. 1993. A Semantic Concordance. In *Human Language Technology: Proceedings of a Workshop Held at Plainsboro, New Jersey, March 21-24, 1993.*

Wendalyn Nichols. 2023. Invisible lexicographers, AI, and the Future of the Dictionary. Youtube, uploaded by eLex conference, 26 July 2023.

Chayanon Phoodai and Richárd Rikk. 2023. Exploring the Capabilities of ChatGPT for Lexicographical Purposes: A Comparison with Oxford Advanced Learner's Dictionary within the Microstructural Framework. In M. Medveď, M. Měchura, C. Tiberius, I. Kosem, J. Kallas, M. Jakubíček and S. Krek, editors, *Electronic lexicography in the 21st century (eLex 2023): Invisible Lexicography. Proceedings of the eLex 2023 conference. Brno, 27–29 June 2023.* Lexical Computing CZ s.r.o., Brno, pages 345–375.

Bartosz Ptasznik and Robert Lew. 2014. Do menus provide added value to signposts in print monolingual dictionary entries? An application of linear mixed-effects modelling in dictionary user research. *International Journal of Lexicography*, 27(3).

Joseph Ruppenhofer, Michael Ellsworth, Myriam Schwarzer-Petruck, Christopher Johnson and Jan Scheffczyk. 2016. *FrameNet II: Extended theory and practice*. International Computer Science Institute, Berkeley, CA.

Gijsbert Stoet. 2017. PsyToolkit: A Novel Web-Based Method for Running Online Questionnaires and Reaction-Time Experiments. *Teaching of Psychology*, 44(1):24–31.

Ágoston Tóth and Esra Abdelzaher. 2023. Probing visualizations of neural word embeddings for lexicographic use. In M. Medveď, M. Měchura, C. Tiberius, I. Kosem, J. Kallas, M. Jakubíček and S. Krek, editors, *Electronic lexicography in the 21st century (eLex 2023): Invisible Lexicography. Proceedings of the eLex 2023 conference. Brno, 27–29 June 2023.* Lexical Computing CZ s.r.o., Brno, pages 545–566.

Ágoston Tóth. Forthcoming. TPEX: Neurális nyelvi modellek alkalmazása példamondatok kiválasztásában ['TPEX: The application of neural language models in selecting example sentences']

A Appendices

Appendix 1. The modified entry for *appear* in experiment 3.

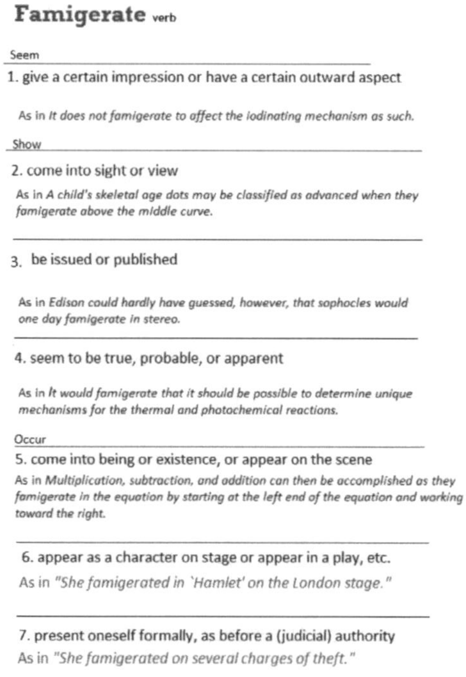

Famigerate verb

Seem

1. give a certain impression or have a certain outward aspect

As in *It does not famigerate to affect the iodinating mechanism as such.*

Show

2. come into sight or view

As in *A child's skeletal age dots may be classified as advanced when they famigerate above the middle curve.*

3. be issued or published

As in *Edison could hardly have guessed, however, that sophocles would one day famigerate in stereo.*

4. seem to be true, probable, or apparent

As in *It would famigerate that it should be possible to determine unique mechanisms for the thermal and photochemical reactions.*

Occur

5. come into being or existence, or appear on the scene

As in *Multiplication, subtraction, and addition can then be accomplished as they famigerate in the equation by starting at the left end of the equation and working toward the right.*

6. appear as a character on stage or appear in a play, etc.

As in *"She famigerated in `Hamlet' on the London stage."*

7. present oneself formally, as before a (judicial) authority

As in *"She famigerated on several charges of theft."*

Appendix 2. Samples of sense and synonym selection tasks

Sense selection task for the word *appear*

Choose the meaning of "famigerate" in the following sentences.

Item	1. give a certain impression or have a certain outward aspect	2. come into sight or view	3. be issued or published	4. seem to be true, probable, or apparent	5. come into being or existence, or appear on the scene	6. appear as a character on stage or appear in a play, etc.	7. present oneself formally, as before a (judicial) authority
They famigerate like people who had not eaten or slept for a long time.	○	○	○	○	○	○	○
The new Woody Allen film hasn	○	○	○	○	○	○	○
It famigerates that the weather in California is very bad.	○	○	○	○	○	○	○
A new star famigerated on the horizon.	○	○	○	○	○	○	○

Synonym selection task for the first sense of *appear*

Choose the most suitable word that can replace "famigerate" in the following sentences without making significant changes in the meaning

They famigerate like people who had not eaten or slept for a long time.

- ○ talk
- ○ look
- ○ perform
- ○ speak
- ○ show up
- ○ act

Appendix 3. Description of the participants in the three groups (till the date of submission)

	Ex 1	Ex 2	Ex 3
3rd year students	70%	0	100%
4th year students	30%	65%	0
5th year students	0	35%	0
Proficiency > B2	75%	100%	100%
Daily use of monolingual dictionaries	12%	37%	55%
Daily use of bilingual dictionaries	12%	80%	95%
Familiarity with WN data at the time of the test	0	10%	0

B Supplementary Material

TPEX scores for the sentences cited from SemCor and reported in this study are available through: https://github.com/WNTPEX/TPEX_WN/blob/main/supplementary%20data_TPEX%20scores.xlsx

Illustrating the Usage of Verbs in WordNet: the Class of Self-motion Verbs

Svetlozara Leseva
Institute for Bulgarian Language
Bulgarian Academy of Sciences
Sofia, Bulgaria
zarka@dcl.bas.bg

Ivelina Stoyanova
Institute for Bulgarian Language
Bulgarian Academy of Sciences
Sofia, Bulgaria
iva@dcl.bas.bg

Abstract

The paper presents an outline of the procedures for selection and annotation of examples illustrating the usage of verbs belonging to various semantic classes (focusing on verbs of self-induced motion) in WordNet and the use of the annotated examples to validate the semantic and syntactic descriptions of the respective verbs as represented by the FrameNet valence patterns. This is done by complementing the information encoded in the synsets with conceptual information from FrameNet through the assignment of FrameNet frames and the associated valence and syntactic patterns.

The examples are collected from semantically annotated corpora for English and Bulgarian, as well as from an aligned parallel corpus. The annotation includes: assignment of a FrameNet frame to the verb in the sentence (and to the synset as a whole), annotation of the boundaries of the frame elements, their type (Self mover, Path, Source, Goal, etc.), and their syntactic category according to the types and categories defined in FrameNet. The annotated examples are then matched to the valence patterns associated with the respective verb, thus confirming their validity in Bulgarian.

The results of our work are the annotated corpus itself and the enriched representation of the verb synsets, which enables various semantic labelling and extraction tasks, parallel study of the semantic and syntactic expression, etc.

1 Introduction

We present our ongoing efforts on developing a language resource built to serve as a dataset of usage examples for the conceptual description of verbs in WordNet and their lexical, semantic and syntactic realisation in text. In this paper we focus in particular on verbs denoting self-induced motion (as a subclass of motion verbs). The annotated examples are linked to WordNet synsets and illustrate verbs in Bulgarian and English.

The complex semantic description of verbs derived from lexical semantic resources such as WordNet and FrameNet contains complementary semantic information (Baker and Fellbaum, 2009). Our work involves two main resources: (a) the Princeton WordNet, PWN (Fellbaum, 1998) and the Bulgarian WordNet (Koeva, 2021) – and for that matter, any other wordnet aligned with PWN, and (b) FrameNet (Baker et al., 1998; Ruppenhofer et al., 2016). We focus in particular on the information each of the resources provides and how it is used towards their mutual enrichment and enlargement.

We explore the transferability of the information across languages, in particular between English and Bulgarian, while also taking into account the language-specific aspects of the conceptual description in view of its syntactic realisation aiming at comprehensive study of the behaviour of verbs.

The main objective of our work is to supplement WordNet with a dataset of annotated examples illustrating the usage of verbs, in particular verbs describing self-induced motion. Moreover, we establish: (a) language-independent principles of annotation relying on the notion of universality of conceptual description using FrameNet frames; (b) cross-language alignment in terms of verb translational equivalents based on WordNet, and in terms of participants in their conceptual structure.

The principles of information transfer across languages can be beneficial for low-resourced languages such as Bulgarian. The dataset can be used to study the syntactic expression and the validity of the valence patterns across languages, thus facilitating comparative studies on conceptual structure.

2 Related work

In addition to WordNet and FrameNet which will be touched upon in Section 3 below we sketch a number of possibly interrelated resources that provide semantic and syntactic description and/or have served in various annotation initiatives.

VerbNet (Kipper-Schuler, 2005) provides good coverage of the English verb inventory and defines syntactic-semantic relations in a more explicit way by means of predicate-argument structures (combinations of thematic roles) with one-to-one linking to the syntactic category (type of phrase) and grammatical function (subject, object, etc.) of each argument expressed in a relatively small number of syntactic frames. Selectional restrictions are defined for the thematic roles assigned to a verb's arguments; they describe the semantic/ontological classes of nouns that express the arguments. However, although the verb classes describe the syntactic behaviour of verbs, many of the traditional thematic roles employed may be too general for the semantic description. Moreover, the existing mappings between WordNet synsets and VerbNet classes are very limited and do not provide sufficient data for analysis.

VerbAtlas (Fabio et al., 2019) is a lexical-semantic resource covering the verb synsets in BabelNet. BabelNet is a very large multilingual (for over 500 languages) semantic network integrating lexicographic and encyclopaedic knowledge from WordNet and Wikipedia (Navigli and Ponzetto, 2010). In VerbAtlas, each verb synset is assigned to a frame corresponding to its prototypical predicate-argument structure. Obligatory components are described using 26 semantic roles and the semantic restrictions governing their compatibility (116 types). A semantic annotation API with the frames described in it is also provided with the resource.

Predicate Matrix (de Lacalle et al., 2014) is a lexical resource resulting from the integration of several sources of predicate information: FrameNet, VerbNet, PropBank and WordNet, that have been previously aligned in Semlink[1] (Palmer, 2009). Predicate Matrix is compiled using advanced graph-based algorithms to extend the mapping coverage between resources. Additionally, by exploiting SemLink new role mappings are inferred among the different predicate schemas.

More recently, the SynSemClass lexicon[2] has marked a distinguishable effort towards combining the rich semantic description in the Vallex dictionary family with conceptual and syntactic information from external semantic resources in order to create a multilingual contextually-based verb lexicon. The aim of the lexicon is to provide a resource of classes of verbs that compares their semantic roles as well as their syntactic properties (Urešová et al., 2020a). In addition, each entry is linked to FrameNet, WordNet, VerbNet, OntoNotes and PropBank, as well as the Czech VALLEX.

Efforts on mappings lexical semantic resources are also relevant to our work. Correlation of WordNet with FrameNet is proposed for different languages, e.g. Danish (Pedersen et al., 2018), Dutch (Horak et al., 2008), Korean (Gilardi and Baker, 2018), Bulgarian (Leseva and Stoyanova, 2020). One of the challenges in aligning resources based on different methodologies is the alignment between the units that are represented in them. When aligning lexical units evoking particular frames from FrameNet and literals from synonym sets in WordNet, a coverage of 30.5% was achieved (Leseva and Stoyanova, 2019). New methods have been proposed to increase the coverage by discovering suitable literals based on semantic relations with literals already described in semantic frames (Burchardt et al., 2005) or on the basis of the inheritance of conceptual features in hypernym–hyponym trees, i.e., by assigning frames from hypernyms to hyponyms where possible and implementing a number of validation procedures based on the structural properties of the two resources, primarily the relations encoded in them (Leseva and Stoyanova, 2020).

Combining the semantic description of verbs from different resources is proposed by Urešová et al. (2020a,b). The result is a multilingual dictionary with the comprehensive description of the semantic classes of verbs and the semantic roles and syntactic properties of their arguments. The project is also aimed at creating an ontology of events, processes and states, and for this purpose each dictionary entry is linked to its correspondences in FrameNet, WordNet, VerbNet, Ontonotes and PropBank, as well as the Valence Dictionary of Czech Verbs (Lopatková et al., 2016), which presents the predicate-argument structure of each verb, its semantic class and the syntactic transformations (diatheses) in which it participates.

3 Resources

Here, we outline the lexical-semantic, conceptual and corpus resources employed in the study.

[1] https://verbs.colorado.edu/semlink/
[2] https://ufal.mff.cuni.cz/synsemclass

3.1 WordNet

WordNet[3] (Miller, 1995; Fellbaum, 1998) provides extensive lexical coverage; the verbs represented in it are organised in 14,103 synsets (including verb synsets specific for Bulgarian). We use both Princeton WordNet and the Bulgarian WordNet (Koeva, 2021), which are aligned at the synset level using unique synset identifiers. WordNet provides the most coarsely-grained semantic division in terms of a set of language-independent semantic primitives (semantic classes) assigned to all the nouns and verbs in the resource. The verbs fall into 15 groups, such as verb.change (verbs describing change in terms of size, temperature, intensity, etc.), verb.cognition (verbs of mental activities or processes), verb.motion (verbs of change in the spacial position), verb.communication (verbs describing communication and information exchange), etc.[4]

Verb synsets are interrelated and form a hierarchical structure by a troponymy relation (a manner relation analogous to hypernymy in nouns); for example, in *talk – whisper* the second member of the pair refers to a particular, semantically more specified, manner of performing the action referred to by the first verb (Fellbaum, 1999).

3.2 FrameNet

FrameNet[5] (Baker et al., 1998; Baker, 2008) is a lexical semantic resource that couches lexical and conceptual knowledge using the apparatus of frame semantics. Frames are conceptual structures that describe types of objects, situations, or events along with their components (frame elements) (Baker et al., 1998; Ruppenhofer et al., 2016). Depending on their status, the frame elements (FE) can be core, peripheral, or extra-thematic (Ruppenhofer et al., 2016). In terms of the conceptual description, we deal primarily with core FEs, which instantiate conceptually necessary components of a frame and which in their particular configuration make a frame unique and different from other frames.

FrameNet frames are organised into a hierarchical network, using a number of frame-to-frame relations (Ruppenhofer et al., 2016, 81–84). Here we list the hierarchical relations that bear most relevance to the internal structure of thematic verb classes. These are: Inheritance – a relationship between a parent frame and a more specific (child) frame, such that the child frame elaborates the parent frame; Uses (also called 'weak inheritance') – a relationship between two frames where the first one makes reference in a very general kind of way to the structure of a more abstract, schematic frame; Perspective – a relation indicating that a situation viewed as neutral may be specified by means of perspectivised frames that represent different possible points-of-view on the neutral state-of-affairs; Subframe – a relation between a complex frame referring to sequences of states and transitions (each of which can be separately described as a frame), and the frames denoting these states or transitions.

FrameNet has been employed in various initiatives, most notably ones focused on: (i) the creation of FrameNet-like resources for other languages such as the efforts undertaken within the Multilingual FrameNet initiative (Gilardi and Baker, 2018); (ii) the annotation of data using these resources, which has been carried out within the Multilingual FrameNet Shared Annotation Task (Torrent et al., 2020). Both research venues have confirmed empirically the applicability of the FrameNet descriptions across languages.

3.3 Combining WordNet and FrameNet

The combination of the resources helps redeem some of their shortcomings regarding conceptual description. A particular deficiency to the optimal use of the rich semantic information provided by FrameNet is its relatively small coverage in terms of lexical units. One way to alleviate this is to expand the coverage of FrameNet against the WordNet sense inventory through procedures for mapping WordNet synsets whose members evoke an existing frame but have not been matched with one yet, as well as through defining new frames to describe parts of the lexicon that have not been described yet.

We use a mapping between WordNet and FrameNet obtained from several already available ones (Shi and Mihalcea, 2005; Tonelli and Pighin, 2009; Leseva and Stoyanova, 2020). The task essentially involves manual validation of the accuracy of the proposed automatic mapping for the lexical units selected for the study (i.e. lexemes describing motion and self-induced motion in particular) and correction of the frames assigned to them if necessary. The validation consists in checking whether the proposed definition for the frame, the configuration of frame elements and their syntactic expres-

[3] `https://wordnet.princeton.edu/`

[4] The list of semantic primes along with short definitions is available at: `https://wordnet.princeton.edu/documentation/lexnames5wn`.

[5] `https://framenet.icsi.berkeley.edu/fndrupal/`

sion are reflected by the semantics and syntactic properties of the respective verb.

We first inspect the verb senses that have counterparts in both FrameNet and WordNet, i.e. verbs that have been encoded in both resources and have been mapped to each other. If the alignment is correct, the two lexemes will describe (near-)identical senses. Compare, for instance, the verb synset {walk:1} ("use one's feet to advance; advance by steps") and the lexical unit *walk.v* ("move at a regular and fairly slow pace by lifting and setting down each foot in turn"). Although the phrasing differs, the two definitions clearly describe the same sense, as additionally confirmed by the usage examples and the verbs' place in the overall internal structure of the respective resource: {walk:1} is a hyponym of the synset {travel:1; move:1; go:1; locomote:1}, the root of the subtree which contains most of the self-induced motion verbs, and *walk.v* evokes the Self_motion frame (one of the principal frames describing motion); it is also a descendant of the Motion frame, the prototypical representative of this semantic domain (Johnson et al., 2001, 16).

At the next stage we move on to validating the assignment of frames to WordNet verbs that do not have a counterpart in FrameNet. We implement this step through exploring the system of semantic relations in the two resources, in particular the inheritance of semantic information between frames. For instance, the verb synset {gallop:4} ("go at galloping speed") does not have a correspondence in FrameNet, but its hypernym {pace:5} ("go at a pace") is assigned the Self_motion frame. After inspecting {gallop:4}, we are able to confirm the validity of the automatic assignment of the frame of its hypernym. Other procedures involving the internal structure of the resources are also applied in the process.

As a result of the validation of the synset-to-frame alignment of the verbs belonging to the domain of motion, we obtain a list of pairs of verb senses and FrameNet frames which describe the semantics of the verbs in the respective synsets. This list represents the collection of senses and the pertaining semantic descriptions derived from both resources that serves as an inventory for which to supply examples.

3.4 Corpora

In order to explore the syntactic expression of the verbs and their participants we study the use examples from various corpora. First, we rely on semantically annotated corpora – the English SemCor and its counterpart BulSemCor, both of which are annotated with WordNet senses.

SemCor (current version 3.0) (Miller et al., 1993, 1994; Landes et al., 1998) is compiled by the Princeton WordNet team and covers texts excerpted from the Brown Corpus. SemCor is supplied with POS and grammatical tagging and all open-class words (both single words and multiword expressions, as well as named entities) are semantically annotated by assigning each word a unique WordNet sense (synset ID). SemCor is the largest manually annotated corpus of this kind and amounts to 226,040 sense annotations.

BulSemCor (Koeva et al., 2006, 2011) is designed according to the general methodology of the original SemCor and criteria for ensuring an appropriate coverage of contemporary general lexis. In addition to open-class words, BulSemCor includes annotation of closed-class words such as preposition, conjunctions, particles, etc.; for that purpose the Bulgarian WordNet has been expanded with closed-class words (Koeva et al., 2011). The size of the corpus is close to 100,000 annotated units.

In addition, we employ parallel resources to extract bilingual examples that would be annotated and analysed in juxtaposition. In particular, we use the Bulgarian-English Sentence- and Clause-Aligned Corpus (**BulEnAC**)[6], a parallel corpus aligned at sentence- and clause level and containing annotations of the syntactic relations between the pairs of clauses and the lexical or other elements realising this relation (conjunctions, complementisers, punctuation). The corpus contains 366,865 tokens altogether – 176,397 tokens in Bulgarian and 190,468 tokens in English (Koeva et al., 2012a). BulEnAC is particularly suitable for both mono- and bilingual semantic annotation tasks as it provides aligned translation equivalents at sentence- and clause level, i.e. the context in which a predicate's semantic and argument structure is realised.

When the above corpora do not provide sufficient data, we could supplement the dataset with examples from the **Bulgarian National Corpus**, which consists of a monolingual (Bulgarian) part and 47 parallel corpora. The Bulgarian part amounts to 1.2 billion words of running text distributed in 240,000 samples, which reflect the language predominantly in its written modality from the mid-20th century (1945) until the present day (Koeva et al., 2012b).

[6]https://dcl.bas.bg/en/resources_list/bulenac/

4 Selection and annotation of examples

Below we outline the steps involved in the selection and annotation of examples.

Selection of verbs and verb senses. We focus on verbs expressing self-induced non-directed translational motion, in particular verbs that evoke the FrameNet frame Self_motion and their counterparts in WordNet.

In total, the class of motion verbs in WordNet covers 1,463 synsets. Out of this number, we have identified 248 verb synsets representing the subclass of self-motion evoking the Self_motion frame. There are 140 synsets assigned the Self_motion frame in the Bulgarian WordNet, including 6 language-specific synsets with no counterpart in English.

Automatic collection of examples from corpora. For each literal from the selected synset inventory, we perform automatic collection of usage examples in English and Bulgarian from the corpora described in Section 3.4.

We start by extracting sentences from SemCor and BulSemCor as the verbs in these corpora are assigned WordNet senses and can be used for the annotation task in a straightforward manner. As a result, we obtained 824 examples in English and 186 in Bulgarian.

In order to increase the number of examples and to provide more representative data in terms of the valence patterns covered and the variation in the syntactic expression of the frame elements, we supplement the collection of examples with ones from the Bulgarian National Corpus and the Bulgarian-English Clause-aligned Corpus. As these two resources are not word sense disambiguated, we apply additional manual filtering to make sure that the automatically collected sentences contain at least one of the verb senses selected for the study. As a result of this procedure, we were able to increase the data by 745 parallel Bulgarian–English sentence pairs. The bilingual examples are especially valuable as they allow for a direct comparison between the ways of expressing similar or equivalent linguistic content in the two languages.

The examples in both languages are POS-tagged, morphosyntactically annotated and lemmatised.

Assignment of valence patterns to English and Bulgarian synsets. FrameNet describes the semantic and syntactic properties of lexical units evoking a given semantic frame in terms of valence patterns: co-occurring combinations of frame elements attested in the FrameNet corpus, i.e. the actual realisations of a lexical unit in context. As these patterns are derived from the annotated data, they may not be exhaustive in the sense that they may not cover all the possible combinations of frame elements and different syntactic realisations, or may not be the most representative ones (i.e. the most frequent ones found in the language).

Semantic frames are relatively universal and language-independent by design as they are grounded in human cognition and experience. This assumption, while not explored here (but cf. (Boas, 2020)), has been implicitly taken for granted in previous and ongoing work, thus providing the motivation for adopting the FrameNet methodology in the creation of framenets for a number of typologically diverse languages where their cross-lingual application has been tested empirically in a satisfactory way (Tiago Torrent and Matos, 2018). Our own experience with Bulgarian has shown that the frames are comprehensive enough to enable a detailed description of the Bulgarian lexical units studied so far, and sufficiently general to allow for further refinements, if needed. As valence patterns describe the combinations of co-occurring frame elements in actual data, they are also quite applicable across languages. The observed variations in the attested configurations cross-linguistically or among same-language verbs may point to important contrasts and are thus all the more interesting to study.

The greatest differences are found at the level of syntactic expression as different languages have different inventories of grammatical and lexical devices. While being more language-specific, syntactic expression in one language may also be used as a point of departure for analysis and comparison in another language (at least in the case of English and Bulgarian), especially in the scenario where annotated data are lacking or scarce as is the case for Bulgarian. We have thus started with the syntactic descriptions provided for English through the FrameNet system of frames and annotated examples and have confirmed, rejected, modified or elaborated on them if necessary.

In certain cases, the original patterns attested in FrameNet have been generalised in order to match the Bulgarian data. For example, patterns involving finite and non-finite clauses have been clustered together and labelled as `Clause` to account for the fact that Bulgarian lacks non-finite clauses and such clauses will have as counterparts finite clauses or will be rendered in another way. Prepositional phrases realising the same frame element with PPs headed by different prepositions (e.g. PP[of], PP[from] when used to introduce the frame element COMPONENTS in the frame `Building`) have also been grouped together.

Particular attention is paid to examples which cannot be matched to any available pattern as this might signal that the respective pattern is specific to Bulgarian.

Below we illustrate some of the patterns attested for the lexical units evoking the frame Self_motion as identified in the FrameNet data. For the sake of easier understanding, we give only English examples adapted from the FrameNet corpus.

[NP.Ext]$_{\text{SELF\_MOVER}}$ [PP]$_{\text{PATH}}$
[She]$_{\text{SELF\_MOVER}}$ **walked** [along the beach]$_{\text{PATH}}$.

[NP.Ext]$_{\text{SELF\_MOVER}}$ [PP]$_{\text{AREA}}$
[He]$_{\text{SELF\_MOVER}}$ **ran** [about the room]$_{\text{AREA}}$.

[NP.Ext]$_{\text{SELF\_MOVER}}$ [PP]$_{\text{GOAL}}$
[They]$_{\text{SELF\_MOVER}}$ **walked** [to the entrance]$_{\text{GOAL}}$

[NP.Ext]$_{\text{SELF\_MOVER}}$ [AdvP]$_{\text{AREA}}$
[Pelicans]$_{\text{SELF\_MOVER}}$ **were flying** [about]$_{\text{AREA}}$.

[NP.Ext]$_{\text{SELF\_MOVER}}$ [AdvP]$_{\text{GOAL}}$
[The boy]$_{\text{SELF\_MOVER}}$ **sneaked** [home]$_{\text{GOAL}}$.

[NP.Ext]$_{\text{SELF\_MOVER}}$ [AdvP]$_{\text{MANNER}}$ [PP]$_{\text{PATH}}$
[The two guards]$_{\text{SELF\_MOVER}}$ **were strolling** [leisurely]$_{\text{MANNER}}$ [around the fence]$_{\text{PATH}}$.

[NP.Ext]$_{\text{SELF\_MOVER}}$ [PP]$_{\text{SOURCE}}$ [PP]$_{\text{GOAL}}$
[The toddler]$_{\text{SELF\_MOVER}}$ **jumped** [from the boulder]$_{\text{SOURCE}}$ [into the shallow water]$_{\text{GOAL}}$.

[NP.Ext]$_{\text{SELF\_MOVER}}$ [PP]$_{\text{PATH}}$ [PP]$_{\text{GOAL}}$
[Jenny]$_{\text{SELF\_MOVER}}$ **dashed** [down the bank]$_{\text{PATH}}$ [to the river]$_{\text{GOAL}}$.

[NP.Ext]$_{\text{SELF\_MOVER}}$ [AdvP]$_{\text{MANNER}}$ [AdvP]$_{\text{AREA}}$
[The men]$_{\text{SELF\_MOVER}}$ **danced** [merrily]$_{\text{MANNER}}$ [around]$_{\text{AREA}}$.

Annotation of the frame elements. At this stage, the annotation of frame elements is performed predominantly manually in order to ensure better precision and analysis. For a part of the syntactic components, more specifically the the subject, some preliminary annotation has been performed automatically, followed by manual post-editing.

We have adopted the Berkeley FrameNet approach to annotation. The process consists of the identification and labelling of the syntactic constituents that realise each frame element. Hence, the projection of frame elements into syntactic positions is implemented in a straightforward manner by associating each frame element with a syntactic category that may be further specified for its grammatical function – specifically for subject (NP.Ext) and object (NP.Obj) phrases. Object and adverbial PPs are not explicitly distinguished, but this information is recoverable from the semantics of the respective frame element; for instance, PLACE, TIME, SPEED, FREQUENCY, etc. are adverbial PPs, while other frame elements qualify as prepositional objects. This declarative linking enables the direct observation of the syntactic properties and behaviour of lexical units.

The aggregation of the examples annotated for each target Lexical Unit provides empirical data about the attested valence patterns in terms of the combinations of overtly expressed frame elements (and possibly non-overt elements understood from the context, see next paragraph) and the specific ways in which they are realised syntactically.

An important feature of the FrameNet methodology and by extension of the annotation adopted in our corpus, is the labelling of syntactically non-overt but semantically obligatory frame elements, the so-called null instantiations (NIs) cf. Ruppenhofer et al. (2016, 28–30). Null instantiations have different status depending on whether the referent of the respective frame element is retrievable from the previous context. A definite null instantiation (DNI) stands for a non-expressed frame element that has a definite reference, e.g. the non-overt subject in the case of pro-drop languages such as Bulgarian. An indefinite null instantiation (INI) is observed where a frame element represents a generalised non-specific entity understood from the broader context by virtue of some convention or habitual interpretation: for instance, the frame element INGESTIBLE in the following sentence is not expressed, but is understood to be some kind of food or meal: *[She]*$_{\textit{INGESTOR}}$ ***ate*** *[hastily]*$_{\textit{MANNER}}$ *[_]*$_{\textit{INGESTIBLE:INI}}$. A constructional null instantiation (CNI) is observed when the lexical omission is licensed by the grammatical construction in which the frame element is found, e.g. the subject of an imperative sentence in both Bulgarian and English.

In such a way the annotated data provide information about the regularities and dependencies

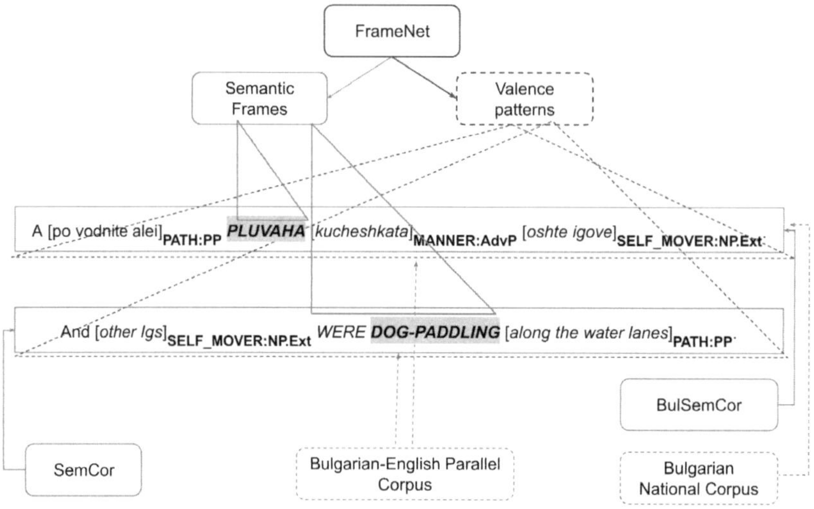

Figure 1: Interaction between the various resources

existing with respect to the co-occurrence or, oppositely, the competition between certain frame elements, including the possibility to leave some of them implicit under certain conditions.

Figure 1 summarises the interaction among the different resources and the information encoded in them. The dotted lines stand for data that need to be validated manually (examples from corpora lacking sense annotation and requiring additional filtering), while the solid lines denote verified examples, such as sentences extracted from sense-annotated corpora. Solid lines are also used to mark semantic frames since they provide relatively universal descriptions, while dotted lines are reserved for valence patterns (and syntactic realisations), which need to be verified for each language and for each verb individually.

The Self_motion frame. Self_motion describes the self-induced and self-controlled motion of an entity along a trajectory. More precisely, a SELF_MOVER, a living being (or by metaphorical extension a self-directed entity such as a vehicle) moves under its own direction along a PATH – any trajectory of motion confined between a starting point, the SOURCE, and an end point, the GOAL. An AREA covered may be mentioned when the motion does not occur along a single linear trajectory, as can be the DIRECTION – i.e. the general spatial orientation of the motion from the deictic centre towards a (possibly implicit) reference point.

Not all core-elements need to be expressed simultaneously. In particular, due to the fact that DIRECTION, GOAL, PATH and SOURCE define a linear trajectory together, they form a single coreness frame element set (Ruppenhofer et al., 2016, 25–26), meaning that it is usually sufficient to realise only one of them in order to satisfy the semantic valence of the verb; in other terms, each of them on its own evokes the entire notion of motion along a trajectory. In addition, as the AREA defines motion that cannot be described along a single coherent route, it can only be expressed when none of the frame elements in the above core set is realised.

In addition to the core frame elements, a number of others may also be expressed, specifying various circumstances or aspects of the situation, such as TIME, DURATION, SPEED, MANNER, PLACE, etc.

We annotate both core and non-core frame elements. Examples 1–3 include annotated sentences along with the patterns to which they are matched. Note that Example 1 illustrates a mismatch in the patterns for each language since the English verb *dog-paddle* incorporates a component describing the manner of swimming, while the Bulgarian sentence employs a MANNER frame element realised as an adverbial – *kucheshkata* (doggy-style) – to render the same meaning in conjunction with the verb *pluvam* (swim). In fact, this would be the conventional way of translating the English verb as it does not have a straightforward equivalent in Bulgarian. Example 3 illustrates a difference in the syntactic expression of the frame element DIRECTION in the two languages, resulting in different valence patterns, although consisting of the same configuration of frame elements.

Example 1. FrameNet frame: `Self_motion`

BG: [NP.Ext]$_{\text{SELF\_MOVER}}$ [AdvP]$_{\text{MANNER}}$ [PP]$_{\text{PATH}}$
EN: [NP.Ext]$_{\text{SELF\_MOVER}}$ [PP]$_{\text{PATH}}$

A [*po vodnite alei*]$_{\text{PATH:PP}}$ ***pluvaha*** [*kucheshkata*]$_{\text{MANNER:AdvP}}$ [*oshte igove*]$_{\text{SELF\_MOVER:NP.Ext}}$.
And [*other Igs*]$_{\text{SELF\_MOVER:NP.Ext}}$ ***were dog-paddling*** [*along the water lanes*]$_{\text{PATH:PP}}$.

Example 2. FrameNet frame: `Self_motion`

[NP.Ext]$_{\text{SELF\_MOVER}}$ [PP]$_{\text{PATH}}$

[_]$_{\text{SELF\_MOVER:DNI:NP.Ext}}$ ***varvyahme*** [*v neshto kato ledena zala*]$_{\text{PATH:PP}}$.
[*We*]$_{\text{SELF\_MOVER:NP.Ext}}$ ***were walking*** [*through a kind of ice hall*]$_{\text{PATH:PP}}$.

Example 3. FrameNet frame: `Self_motion`

BG: [NP.Ext]$_{\text{SELF\_MOVER}}$ [PP]$_{\text{DIRECTION}}$ [PP]$_{\text{PATH}}$
EN: [NP.Ext]$_{\text{SELF\_MOVER}}$ [AdvP]$_{\text{DIRECTION}}$ [PP]$_{\text{PATH}}$

[*Toy*]$_{\text{SELF\_MOVER:NP.Ext}}$ ***tichashe*** [*na zapad*]$_{\text{DIRECTION:PP}}$ [*prez lozyata*]$_{\text{PATH:PP}}$.
[*He*]$_{\text{SELF\_MOVER:NP.Ext}}$ ***was running*** [*west*]$_{\text{DIRECTION:PP}}$ [*through the vineyards*]$_{\text{PATH:PP}}$.

5 Results

While in this paper we focus on self-motion verbs, the principles and methodology adopted here are applied to the description of verbs belonging to other semantic classes as well.

There are two principle results from our work: (i) a corpus of examples illustrating the use of a given class of verbs in Bulgarian annotated according to the methodology proposed by the Berkeley FrameNet project, in which some of the sentences are paired with their annotated English counterparts if the examples are extracted from the Bulgarian-English Sentence- and Clause-Aligned Corpus; (ii) a collection of verb synsets from the Princeton WordNet and the Bulgarian WordNet aligned with a number of FrameNet frames relevant for the studied class of verbs and the semantic and syntactic information that can be derived from the frame's description and the annotated examples.

More specifically, for each verb that has a counterpart in FrameNet, we list the patterns attested in the FrameNet Corpus that meet several criteria: appear in three or more examples; contain at least one core frame element; appear in their canonical form (and not in alternations, e.g. preferring active-voice rather than passive-voice examples).

For the verbs in WordNet which are assigned a given frame but do not have a correspondence denoting a (near-)equivalent sense in FrameNet, we assign the aggregate of valence patterns attested for all the verbs evoking the relevant frame. As part of them may not be relevant for the particular verb, the need for providing examples confirming the valence patterns is tantamount.

As a result each of the verbs in the studied inventory is supplied with a list of valence patterns. While for the verbs in the Princeton WordNet the patterns are confirmed by the FrameNet corpus examples, they are not necessarily valid for the equivalent Bulgarian verbs and need to be validated against corpus evidence.

At the next stage, for each annotated sentence in our corpus we extract the configuration of frame elements in order to identify the valence pattern realised in it and match the pattern to the identical one in the FrameNet frame. The patterns confirmed by examples are marked in bold.

As some patterns are more frequent than others, the annotated examples would help to obtain a more comprehensive and accurate picture of the combinatorial properties of verbs and the typical syntactic realisation of their frame elements. While we focus on Bulgarian and English, the valence patterns should be applicable to other languages.

Language	EN	BG	Aligned
# Verbs	65	32	26
# WordNet Synsets	31	16	15
# Valence patterns	40	32	30
# Sentences	254	228	50
# Annotated FEs	541	508	–

Table 1: Distribution of annotated examples for self-motion verbs.

Table 1 shows the distribution of the annotated examples across synsets and patterns. The English dataset covers 254 fully annotated examples of self-motion verbs, while the Bulgarian dataset contains 228 examples. The total number includes 50 parallel pairs of sentences.

The self-motion subset is part of a larger corpus of annotated examples of verbs in WordNet, which covers several semantic classes involving motion and includes so far over 1,200 examples for

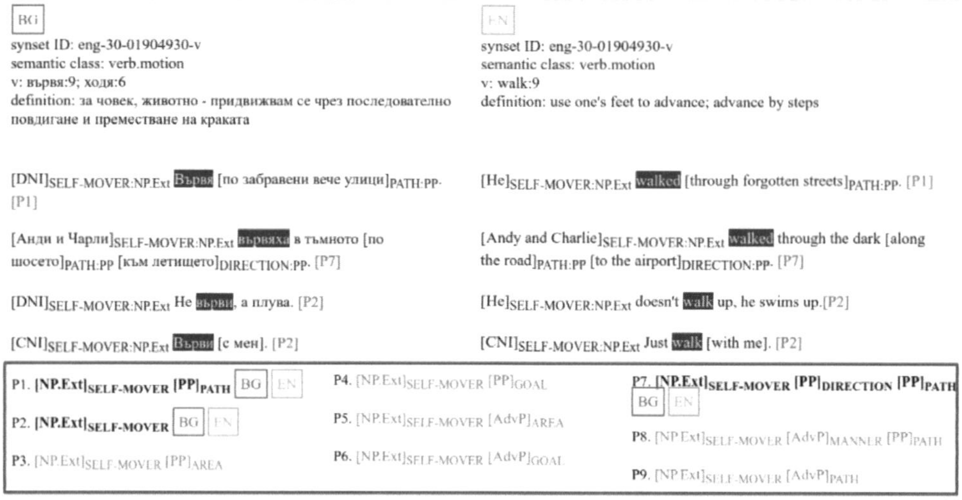

Figure 2: Visualisation of annotated examples for the verbs in a synset in Bulgarian and English.

Bulgarian and over 1,500 examples in English.

A possible application of the corpus is the cross-lingual analysis aiming to match the pairs of literals within corresponding synsets for Bulgarian and English that exhibit the same set of valence configurations and syntactic patterns. On this basis we can identify closer translational pairs as opposed to verbs that share only part of the valence patterns or differ significantly in their syntactic realisation despite their similar meaning.

In the current version of the dataset, all patterns attested for Bulgarian are matched to patterns attested in FrameNet. Moreover, the data show a considerably low degree of variation in terms of the syntactic realisation of the frame elements in the two languages.

The Bulgarian dataset needs to be further extended to provide sufficient data that would enable us to make reliable conclusions on the pattern correspondences. This includes the annotation of examples exhibiting language-specific syntactic patterns that are not found (or are rare) in English.

6 Conclusions and future work

The compiled dataset of annotated examples is part of an ongoing effort on the semantic, syntactic and aspectual analysis of several large semantic classes of verbs – verbs of motion, verbs of communication, and verbs of change. Our next task will be to expand the data further by covering more verbs, verb classes and peculiarities of the semantics and syntactic behaviour of the studied predicates. Extending the scope of annotation systematically beyond core frame elements is also a research venue to be pursued, especially as the expression of some frame elements such as GOAL, MANNER or PURPOSE, among others, may be correlated to changes in the aspectual interpretation of verbs.

The empirical data enable the study of the two languages under discussion individually, as well in comparative or contrastive terms. The linking of the annotated examples to lexical resources such as WordNet and FrameNet facilitates the applicability of the corpus for various research tasks.

The dataset can be employed in the training of semantic role labelling, semantic disambiguation, syntactic pattern analysis, as well as in extracting parallel valence patterns, translation equivalents of verb phrases, etc. The proposed approach can also be extended to other languages, in particular to ones that have their own wordnets linked to PWN, thus resulting in the creation of a multilingual and more universally applicable resource.

The resources created as part of this work are made available to the community under the Creative Commons Attribution 4.0 International license.[7]

Acknowledgements

This research is carried out as part of the project *An Ontology of Activity Predicates – Linguistic Modelling with a Focus on Bulgarian* funded by the Bulgarian National Science Fund, Grant Agreement No KP–06–N80/9 from 8.12.2023.

[7] https://dcl.bas.bg/corpus-data-semantic-frames-2024/

References

C. F. Baker and C. Fellbaum. 2009. WordNet and FrameNet as Complementary Resources for Annotation. In *Proceedings of the Third Linguistic Annotation Workshop (ACL-IJCNLP '09), Association for Computational Linguistics, Stroudsburg, PA, USA*, pages 125–129.

Collin F. Baker. 2008. FrameNetPresent and Future. In *The First International Conference on Global Interoperability for Language Resources*, Hong Kong. City University, City University.

Collin F. Baker, Charles J. Fillmore, and John B. Lowe. 1998. The Berkeley FrameNet project. In *COLING-ACL '98: Proceedings of the Conference. Montreal, Canada*, pages 86–90.

Hans C. Boas. 2020. *A roadmap towards determining the universal status of semantic frames*, pages 21–52. De Gruyter Mouton, Berlin, Boston.

Aljoscha Burchardt, Katrin Erk, and Anette Frank. 2005. A WordNet detour to FrameNet. In *Sprachtechnologie, mobile Kommunikation und linguistische Resourcen*, volume 8 of *Computer Studies in Language and Speech*. Lang, Frankfurt, Germany.

Maddalen Lopez de Lacalle, Egoitz Laparra, and German Rigau. 2014. Predicate Matrix: extending SemLink through WordNet mappings. In *Proceedings of the Ninth International Conference on Language Resources and Evaluation (LREC'14)*, pages 903–909, Reykjavik, Iceland. European Language Resources Association (ELRA).

Andrea Di Fabio, Simone Conia, and Roberto Navigli. 2019. VerbAtlas: a Novel Large-Scale Verbal Semantic Resource and Its Application to Semantic Role Labeling. In *Proceedings of the 2019 Conference on Empirical Methods in Natural Language Processing and the 9th International Joint Conference on Natural Language Processing (EMNLP-IJCNLP)*, pages 627–637, Hong Kong, China. Association for Computational Linguistics.

C. Fellbaum. 1999. The Organization of Verbs and Verb Concepts in a Semantic Net. In P. Saint-Dizier, editor, *Predicative Forms in Natural Language and in Lexical Knowledge Bases*, volume 6 of *Text, Speech and Language Technology*, pages 93 – 110. Springer, Dordrecht.

Christiane Fellbaum, editor. 1998. *WordNet: an electronic lexical database*. MIT Press, Cambridge, MA.

Luca Gilardi and Collin F. Baker. 2018. Learning to Align across Languages: Toward Multilingual FrameNet. In *Proceedings of the International FrameNet Workshop 2018: Multilingual FrameNets and Constructicons*, pages 13–22.

Ales Horak, Piek Vossen, and Adam Rambousek. 2008. The Development of a Complex-Structured Lexicon based on WordNet. In *Proceedings of the Fourth International Global WordNet Conference (GWC 2008), Szeged*, pages 200–208, Szeged, Hungary. University of Szeged, Department of Informatics.

Christopher R. Johnson, Charles J. Fillmore, Esther J. Wood, Margaret Urban, Miriam R. L. Petruck, Collin F. Baker, and et al. Charles J. Fillmore. 2001. The FrameNet Project: Tools for Lexicon Building. `https://citeseerx.ist.psu.edu/pdf/0ece390b6f4e6b38c5733248992ff73f846d91aa`.

Karin Kipper-Schuler. 2005. *VerbNet: A broad-coverage, comprehensive verb lexicon. PhD Thesis*. Computer and Information Science Dept., University of Pennsylvania. Philadelphia, PA.

Svetla Koeva. 2021. The Bulgarian WordNet: Structure and specific features. *Papers of Bulgarian Academy of Sciences*, 8(1):47–70.

Svetla Koeva, Svetlozara Leseva, Borislav Rizov, Ekaterina Tarpomanova, Tsvetana Dimitrova, Hristina Kukova, and Maria Todorova. 2011. Design and development of the Bulgarian sense-annotated corpus. In *Information and communications technologies: present and future in corpus analysis: Proceedings of the III International Congress of Corpus Linguistics*, pages 143 – 150.

Svetla Koeva, Svetlozara Leseva, and Maria Todorova. 2006. Bulgarian sense tagged corpus. In *Proceedings of LREC 2006*, pages 79 – 86.

Svetla Koeva, Borislav Rizov, Ekaterina Tarpomanova, Tsvetana Dimitrova, Rositsa Dekova, Ivelina Stoyanova, Svetlozara Leseva, Hristina Kukova, and Angel Genov. 2012a. Bulgarian-English Sentence- and Clause-Aligned Corpus. In *Proceedings of the Second Workshop on Annotation of Corpora for Research in the Humanities (ACRH-2)*, page 51–62. Lisboa: Colibri.

Svetla Koeva, Ivelina Stoyanova, Svetlozara Leseva, Rositsa Dekova, Tsvetana Dimitrova, and Ekaterina Tarpomanova. 2012b. The Bulgarian National Corpus: theory and practice in corpus design. *Journal of Language Modelling*, 0(1):65–110.

Shari Landes, Claudia Leacock, and R. Tengi. 1998. Building Semantic Concordances. In *WordNet: An Electronic Lexical Database*.

Svetlozara Leseva and Ivelina Stoyanova. 2019. Enhancing conceptual description through resource linking and exploration of semantic relations. In *Proceedings of 10th Global WordNet Conference, 23 – 27 July 2019, Wroclaw, Poland*, pages 229–238.

Svetlozara Leseva and Ivelina Stoyanova. 2020. Beyond lexical and semantic resources: linking WordNet with FrameNet and enhancing synsets with conceptual frames. In *Towards a Semantic Network Enriched with a Variety of Semantic Relations*. Prof. Marin Drinov Academic Publishing House of the Bulgarian Academy of Sciences.

Markéta Lopatková, Václava Kettnerová, Eduard Bejček, Anna Vernerová, and Zdeněk Žabokrtský. 2016. *Valenční slovník českých sloves VALLEX*. Karolinum, Praha.

George A. Miller. 1995. WordNet: A lexical database for English. *Commun. ACM*, 38(11):39–41.

George A. Miller, Martin Chodorow, Shari Landes, Claudia Leacock, and Robert G. Thomas. 1994. Using a Semantic Concordance for Sense Identification. In *Human Language Technology: Proceedings of a Workshop held at Plainsboro, New Jersey, March 8-11, 1994*.

George A. Miller, Claudia Leacock, Randee Tengi, and Ross T. Bunker. 1993. A Semantic Concordance. In *Human Language Technology: Proceedings of a Workshop Held at Plainsboro, New Jersey, March 21-24, 1993*.

Roberto Navigli and Simone Paolo Ponzetto. 2010. BabelNet: Building a Very Large Multilingual Semantic Network. In *Proceedings of the 48th Annual Meeting of the Association for Computational Linguistics*, pages 216–225, Uppsala, Sweden. Association for Computational Linguistics.

Martha Palmer. 2009. Semlink: linking PropBank, VerbNet and FrameNet. In *Proceedings of the Generative Lexicon Conference*. 9–15.

Bolette Pedersen, Sanni Nimb, Anders Søgaard, Mareike Hartmann, and Sussi Olsen. 2018. A Danish FrameNet Lexicon and an Annotated Corpus Used for Training and Evaluating a Semantic Frame Classifier. In *Proceedings of the Eleventh International Conference on Language Resources and Evaluation (LREC 2018)*, Miyazaki, Japan. European Language Resources Association (ELRA).

Josef Ruppenhofer, Michael Ellsworth, Miriam R. L. Petruck, Christopher. R. Johnson, Collin. F. Baker, and Jan Scheffczyk. 2016. *FrameNet II: extended theory and practice*. International Computer Science Institute, Berkeley, California.

Lei Shi and Rada Mihalcea. 2005. Putting pieces together: combining FrameNet, VerbNet and WordNet for robust semantic parsing. In A. Gelbukh, editor, *Computational Linguistics and Intelligent Text Processing. CICLing 2005. Lecture Notes in Computer Science*, volume 3406. Springe, Berlin, Heidelbergr.

Collin Baker Tiago Torrent, Michael Ellsworth and Ely Matos. 2018. The multilingual framenet shared annotation task: a preliminary report. In *Proceedings of the Eleventh International Conference on Language Resources and Evaluation (LREC 2018)*, Paris, France. European Language Resources Association (ELRA).

Sara Tonelli and Daniele Pighin. 2009. New Features for Framenet – Wordnet Mapping. In *Proceedings of the Thirteenth Conference on Computational Natural Language Learning (CoNLL'09), Boulder, USA*.

Tiago T. Torrent, Collin F. Baker, Oliver Czulo, Kyoko Ohara, and Miriam R. L. Petruck, editors. 2020. *Proceedings of the International FrameNet Workshop 2020: Towards a Global, Multilingual FrameNet*. European Language Resources Association, Marseille, France.

Zdenka Urešová, Eva Fucíková, Eva Hajičová, and Jan Hajič. 2020a. SynSemClass Linked Lexicon: Mapping Synonymy between Languages. In *Proceedings of the Globalex Workshop on Linked Lexicography, Language Resources and Evaluation Conference (LREC 2020), Marseille, 11–16 May 2020*, pages 10 – 19.

Zdenka Urešová, Eva Fučíková, Eva Hajičová, and Jan Hajič. 2020b. Syntactic-Semantic Classes of Context-Sensitive Synonyms Based on a Bilingual Corpus. In *Human Language Technology. Challenges for Computer Science and Linguistics*, pages 242–255. Springer International Publishing.

plWordNet 5.0 – challenges of a life-long wordnet development process

Ewa Rudnicka, Bartłomiej Alberski, Maciej Piasecki
Department of Artificial Intelligence
Wrocław University of Science and Technology
ewa.rudnicka, bartlomiej.alberski, maciej.piasecki@pwr.edu

Abstract

The construction of plWordNet began in 2005 and has been continued since then. In this paper we present the latest 5.0 version and describe the challenges connected with a life-long wordnet development process. These involve changes in the procedures and lexicographers' teams, the necessity to extend the lexical description and the need to link to external resources (Princeton WordNet, sense-tagged corpora, valence dictionary). We describe different strategies and diagnostics implemented to improve the quality of the resource.

1 Introduction

The most burning question for wordnets today is whether we still need them in the large language models (LLMs) era? With the advent of the Chat GPT and other dialogue models, more and more language data is automatically generated recently. The quality of such data varies. This creates a danger of affecting the actual language use by its native speakers. Also, once it is fed to the models as training data we end in a kind of a vicious circle (Baloccu et al., 2024). Therefore, high-quality manually crafted and curated lexical resources remain a valuable source of data for different purposes of AI and NLP, both development and evaluation. In this paper we present the newest version of plWordNet, 5.0., as the core of a system of inter-linked language resources.

plWordNet is a large, manually constructed, corpus-based wordnet of Polish, but over the years it has become more than that. Now it is the heart of a complex system of language resources encompassing sense-annotated corpora (KPWr, KPWr 100, Sherlock Holmes corpus, Wiki-GLEX, EmoGLEX, KGR10, Składnica, the corpus of examples from the valence dictionary Walenty, and a knowledge graph VeSNet – a network of interlinked thesauri, encyclopedias, ontologies and dictionaries. Moreover, it is linked to the Polish valence dictionary Walenty. Sense-annotated corpora constitute crucial resources for word-sense disambiguation systems and, currently, LLMs. Knowledge graphs like VeSNet provide reliable information both about language including its specialist domain and the world.

The paper will focus on three main directions of the latest plWordNet development, all of which are intertwined: reviewing the granularity of plWordNet senses, acquiring new (glosses) and usage examples from the external inter-linked resources such as the sense-annotated corpus KPWr and the valence dictionary Walenty, and verifying and modifying plWordNet relational structure.

2 Background

Born in the 80-ties, no longer developed, with gaps and flaws, Princeton WordNet remains a basic reference to English sense inventory in the NLP (Miller et al., 1990) (Miller and Fellbaum, 2007). One of the reasons for this fact is that it is linked to hundreds, if not thousands of other resources in English and other languages. These include ontologies (e.g. SUMO), corpora (SemCor, WordNet Gloss Tag) (Vial et al., 2017)), valence dictionaries (VerbNet, FrameNet) (Baker et al., 1998) (Ryant and Kipper, 2004), and, above all, wordnets of other languages (EuroWordNet, OpenMultiLingual WordNet) (Vossen, 1998a)(Vossen, 1998b)(Bond and Paik, 2012). In this way, a multi-lingual, multi-dimensional system of interlinked language resources was created, with great potential of use in the NLP. To name the main use cases, sense-anotated corpora are explored in word sense disambiguation systems, knowledge graphs in named entity recognition tasks. All of the above resources can be used as reliable sources of data in the validation of the workings of large language models.

Sense annotated corpora are very special, valuable type of corpora, because they combine the data of the actual word use with the information of their dictionary meaning. Building a good-quality resource of this type requires time and means. The first corpus anotated with WordNet senses was SemCor (Miller et al., 1993).

plWordNet started off in 2005 (Piasecki, 2009), while its mapping to Princeton WordNet in 2012 (Rudnicka et al., 2012). It had a deep corpus connection from the very beginning, since the KGR corpus served as its crucial source of information on the frequency of words, their senses and relations between them. This was possible due to a custom-designed method of (semi)-automatic extraction of lexico-semantic information from a corpus developed by (Piasecki, 2009). One of the perks of the method was a number of corpus examples added to plWN senses. Nevertheless, this process was still lemma, not sense based leaving the user find the appropriate example for a given sense. At a later stage of work, corpus examples were manually disambiguated by linguists and added to the proper LUs. The first Polish corpus annotated with plWN sense was the KPWr corpus (The Corpus of Wrocław University of Science and Technology) (Broda et al., 2012).

3 Verification and LU description enrichment process

In this section we describe the key stages of the latest plWordNet development and improvement process involving the selection of lexical units for manual verification and description enrichment.

Originally, plWordNet was built of lexical units, synsets and relations between them. Additional elements of lexical description such as glosses, registers and usage examples were scarce. Examples and glosses were added only in the case of polysemous and hard to distinguish senses in order to clarify their meanings. However, at some point, purely relational description became insufficient for many, especially users, e.g. researchers from Social Sciences and Humanities (SS&H) who began to treat plWN as a kind of electronic dictionary. Furthermore, the presence of glosses and examples improves the quality of NLP (Bevilacqua et al., 2020)(Janz and Piasecki, 2023)(Banerjee et al., 2003). With the growing awareness of the role of glosses, registers and usage examples, they started to be systematically added to the description of lexical units (ver. 3.0, (Maziarz et al., 2016).

Lemmas	194 107
LUs	294 842
Glosses	160 937
Examples	240 741
LUs relations	275 367
Synsets	228 308
Synset relations	427 921

Table 1: plWordNet 4.2 statistics

Still, knowing the plWN size, it was clear that it was going to be a long-term task.

3.1 Selection of lexical units for verification

The starting point for our work was plWordNet 4.2 version. The essential statistics for this version are given in Table 1.

When we juxtapose the number of LUs (ca 290k) with the number of glosses (ca 170k glosses), we observe that only slightly above a half of LUs have glosses. The number of examples (ca 241k) is comparably higher, but it still does not cover all LUs. In addition, some LUs may have more than one usage example, while other ones none at all. Therefore, in our recent work we set off to fill in at least the part of the missing glosses and examples. To that end we decided to capitalise on the existing connections between plWordNet senses and different corpora.

Bearing in mind the size and complexity of plWordNet database as well as the time of its development, choosing the subset of units for verification and description enrichment has been a non-trivial task. In the latest stage of the plWordNet improvement process, we made a systematic selection of lexical units for verification and description enrichment. We decided to focus on the following four groups of lexical units:

1. LUs with a direct link to sense-tagged corpora, yet without glosses or examples (ca 13k);
2. LUs without glosses and examples and not attested in the sense-tagged corpora (ca 23k);
3. LUs with glosses, but without examples and not attested in the sense-tagged corpora (ca 46.5k)
4. verbal LUs with a direct link to the Walenty valence dictionary (ca 3.1k).

The detailed numbers are given in Table 2.

LUs in sense-tagged corpora without glosses and examples	13 233
LUs without glosses and examples and with no attestation in the corpora	22 724
LUs with glosses, but without examples	46 523
Verbal units linked to Walenty	3096

Table 2: Selected LUs

Alongside those four main groups, we have been working on the so called 'problematic cases' tagged as 'to be verified' in the WordNetLoom editing system. They originally came from our internal worksheets produced during other works, such as, for instance, corpus annotation with senses. The problems were related to the suspected wrong granularity of senses, wrongly directed relations, wrong usage example(s) or a mistake in the gloss (too wide or too narrow), wrong collocation provided for a given sense, or improper semantic domain ascribed. There were about 1k of such problematic LUs marked in the internal worksheets and about 6.5k marked directly in the database using the WordNet Loom 2.0 application. Still, it must be emphasized that the signal for verification did not necessarily mean that correction was needed in each case.

Having chosen a subset of lexical units for description enrichment and verification, we decided to work from the lemma level going two directions. On the one hand, we were checking the granularity of senses for each lemma. On the other hand, we were adding glosses and usage examples to individual lexical units which allowed us to verify the credibility of their sense granularity.

3.2 Reviewing the granularity of selected plWordNet senses

The primary source of mistakes in plWordNet is the wrong granularity of senses that is distinguishing too many or too few senses for a given lemma. The effect of such mistake is too narrow or too broad meaning of a given lexical unit which results in senses overlapping the scope of their meanings. Therefore, the verification of a potential mistake always needs to start from checking all the existing senses of a given lemma, especially with reference to the corpus data. The next step is to provide the gloss, register and at least two usage examples for a given sense. Lexical units with all those elements present will be classified as units with the higher description standard. In the course of work, we added almost 60k new usage examples and 8K new glosses as shown in Table 3.

Lexical units for whose senses no corpus attestation was found were marked for an extra verification at the later stages of plWN development. Currently, there are 1.2k of such units, that can be divided into the following groups:

1. imprisoned meanings, e.g. *etylowy*.1 'ethyl [alcohol]';
2. non-lexicalised multi-word expressions, e.g. *poczucie własnej godności*.1 'sense of self-dignity';
3. borrowings, e.g. *blezer*.1 'blazer';
4. contractions, *TB*.3 'terabite';
5. typos in lemmas, e.g. *leiszmania*.1 'Leishmania';
6. some participles, e.g. *dorastający*.1 'growing up';
7. nominalised adjectives, e.g. *małowierny*.1 'unfaithful';
8. gerunds, e.g. *obudzenie*.2 'waking up';
9. neologisms, e.g. *odsetka*.1 'percentage';
10. archaisms, e.g. *dębnik*.2 'tan'.

As for the verbal units, our works are carried out on the whole derivational nests, aspectual pairs and reflexive verbs with the reflexive particle *się*. We further process only such forms and senses that are attested in corpora. For example, the analysis of the verbal lemma *stawiać* will not only cover its 25 senses, but also its derivatives such as *postawić* 'put on', *ustawiać* 'put', *ustawić* 'put', *wystawać* 'stick out', *przedstawiać* 'present', *przedstawić* 'present', *przeciwstawiać* 'contrast', *przeciwstawić* 'contrast', *przeciwstawiać się* 'resist' and *przeciwstawić się* 'oppose'.

3.3 In search of new glosses and usage examples

The procedure of adding glosses and examples was fully manual. The senses selected for verification (see Table 2, Sect. 3.1) were divided according to their part of speech and the number of meanings of a lemma. After a given sense was identified and attested in the corpora, missing glosses and/or usage examples were added. The work of the lexicographers was supervised by a coordinator. Verified usage examples were automatically added to the database (in three stages). Examples that were directly added to the database were verified and corrected in the database (in the WordNetLoom system). The most common mistakes included:

1. wrongly identified meaning, e.g. *we własnym sosie* 2 – oppressively 1, that is 'w zaduchu' 'in the chokehold', while the found usage example as its illustration corresponds to the different senses: *we własnym sosie* 1 – unalterably;

2. an improper member of the aspectual pair, e.g. *wtargać* 1 – bring 1, while the usage example includes the verb *wtargnąć*;

3. the absence of the actually described LU in the usage example, e.g. in the case of *rozbójnictwo* 1 – banditry 1, the provided examples include *rozbójnik* 1 – bandit 1 or *rozbój1* – mugging 1;

4. improper verbal form, e.g. *wykwitnąć* 3 – pop out 1 – an infinitive, while in the usage example a participial form is used "były wykwitającymi kwiatami" – 'were blooming flowers' or e.g. *zesłodować* 1 – malt 3 – an infinitive, while the usage example includes *zesłodowanie* — a gerund form;

5. metalanguage in usage examples, e.g. *świński trucht* 2, while the example goes:
Pierwszy raz słyszę, by ktoś, narzekając na wolny przebieg spraw, mówił o "świńskim truchcie".
'It is the first time that I hear somebody complaining about the slow pace of process and speaking about "(*approx.*) jog trot"'
– in this particular case, the expression *świński trucht* is used in a metalanguage function, not literally as a part of the sentence. It is even emphasised by the use of quotation marks and the introduction "speaking about".

The results of the work are described in Table 3.

To conclude, we set the required standard of description at the level of lexical units so that each lexical unit is assigned its register, definition, and also minimum two use examples. All lexical units verified to meet this standard receive the status of partially processed. As a result of recent work, the number of units with the highest description standard has almost tripled, and almost 30k (precisely 29 367) lexical units have achieved it. This resulted in the manual addition of almost 60k (56 641) examples and almost 8k (7 561) definitions to the lexicon. Before this phase of work had been started, glosses sometimes were one-word only, and many lexical units had no definition at all. It was especially common practice in the case of monosemous lemmas.

LUs in sense-tagged corpora without glosses and examples	5768
LUs without glosses and examples and with no attestation in the corpora	19 523
LUs with glosses, but without examples	46 523
Verbal units linked to Walenty	864
New examples	56979
New glosses	7561
LUs in new standard	29518
LUs to be verified in the next stage of work	1274

Table 3: Results of the verification and enrichment process

4 Verification and improvement of the plWordNet sense and synset relational structure

4.1 Verifying the hypo and hypernymy relation structure

The backbone of the plWordNet (hierarchical) vertical structure is mainly formed by hyponymy and hypernymy relations. They form a bidirectional pair and are as the main *constitutive relations* (Piasecki, 2009)(Maziarz et al., 2013) for all parts of speech. In short, constitutive relations are a subset of lexico-semantic relations that determine by definition the wordnet structure and serve as a basis for defining synsets, i.e. lexical units sharing relation structures are grouped into synsets, see (Maziarz et al., 2013). Thus, analysis of the local structure of constitutive relations reveals if a given word sense, represented by a lexical unit, is correctly described. Further more, comparison of such local constitutive relation structures for the lexical units of a given lemma provides insight into proper identification of the different senses. Thus, in order to properly characterise a lexical unit it is necessary to recognise and describe its relations with other lexical units that results in its inclusion into a synset (one lexical unit belongs to one synset only).

The set of required relations of plWordNet has been slightly evolving over years, and its contemporary state is presented below (Dziob et al., 2019):

1. for all parts of speech: hypo/hypernymy, mero/holonymy and inter-register synonymy;
2. in addition, for adjectives and adverbs: value of the attribute;
3. verbs, see (Dziob and Piasecki, 2018): presupposition, preceding, meronymy/holonymy, inchoativity, causality, pro- cessuality and state.;
4. for proper nouns only: type/instance.
5. relational adjectives are described only by relacyjność
6. feminine nouns are described by the femininity relation.

During the verification of the correctness of constitutive relations it often turns out that the hypernym for a given synset is semantically too wide, i.e. too high in the hypernymy structure (too close to top level), or too narrow (too deep in a subtree). A consequence of the incorrect hypernymy scope is wrong sense description of the hyponyms of a lexical unit. In the case of too high hypernymy location of a lexical unit too general meaning specification may be ascribed to its hyponyms, especially when their remaining relation structure is poor or even does not exist. Such a situation would be a hypernym: człowiek ze względu na swoje zajęcie1 for kaletnik 1 – skinner 4. A much better hypernym for kaletnik 1 is rzemieślnik 1 – craftsman.3. Careful inspection of the hypo/hypernymy structure resulted in 115 473 changes introduced in plWordNet 5.0 in comparison to the previous version.

4.2 Increasing the relation structure density

In addition to the verification of the existing relation structure, another important direction in improving the wordnet quality is increasing the relation structure density – the structure is the primary means for expressing knowledge about word senses. In the earlier versions of plWordNet, at least one constitutive relation was considered satisfactory for a minimal description of an lexical unit. However, recently we aim at increasing the number of relations per a single LU. Literature studies show that the quality of text processing increases with the increase in the number of relations per lexical unit in a lexical resource used for the purposes of processing (Bevilacqua et al., 2020) (Janz and Piasecki, 2023). Therefore, during the verification of selected nodes of the wordnet graph we add new relations from a wide spectrum of relations available in plWordNet. These involve both synset and sense-level relations. The results of our work are shown in Table 4 where we juxtapose relation counts for 4.2 and 5.0 versions of plWordNet. The number of sense relations have grown by 3.5k, while the number of synset relations by 43k.

Number of relations	plWN 4.2	plWN 5.0
LUs	275 367	278 934
Synsets	567 871	610 806

Table 4: plWordNet 4.2 and 5.0 sense and synset relation counts

5 Verification and improvement of interlingual links

The manual mapping of plWordNet onto Princeton WordNet has been carried out since 2012 (Rudnicka et al., 2012, 2021). It was a dynamic process with mapping procedures refined or modified in response to results of the earlier mapping or new mapping challenges. At the beginning, lexicographers had to mainly rely on the internal relation structures of plWordNet and Princeton WordNet as well as glosses and usage examples if such were available. As the network of interlingual relations was growing they gained additional information – the existing interlingual relations whose input also needed to be taken into account while establishing new relations. Throughout this time, there has been also many changes in plWordNet itself. Thus, there are certainly nodes or fragments of the bilingual wordnet graph which could be improved.

Therefore, to address these issues, we have designed a series of automatic diagnostics of the interlingual relation system that were run through the database. Next, their results in the form of the produced lists of synsets and lexical units were presented to lexicographers in the Tracker system (Naskręt et al., 2018). They manually analysed them and, in consequence, some links were deleted, other ones altered.

5.1 Synsets

The first series of diagnostics was designed to eliminate the obvious mistakes, the kind of 'slips of the tongue' or 'typos', which bearing in mind the time and scope of manual work were bound to happen occasionally. Those involved the following:

1. links between synsets of improper parts of speech (e.g. I-mero/I-holonymy between non-noun synsets);
2. wrong direction of a relation (PL-ENG/ENG-PL);
3. missing bidirectional relations (e.g. I-hypo/I-hypernymy).

Since the beginning of synset mapping, we have followed (Vossen, 1998b) in assuming one interlingual synonymy relation per synset. This restriction was lifted for verbal synsets due to essential differences in lexicalising aspect in English and Polish (lexical aspect in Polish vs grammmatical aspect in English). Consequently, the pairs of Polish perfective and imperfective verbal synsets were allowed to be mapped to the same English verbal synset (covering perfective and imperfective senses of a given verb) (Rudnicka et al., 2021). Still, our first diagnostic test was to check if there were any instances of multiple synonymy links between Polish and English synsets and verify them manually. We deleted 1 167 mistakes and left 2 712 links between verbal synsets that were correct. 1 079 new links were added. The number of deleted links is very small in comparison to the overall number of I-synonymy links which amounts to 943k.

Another diagnostic directly linked to the mapping procedure was checking the cases of a simultaneous interlingual synonymy and interlingual hyponymy links for a single synset. Interlingual synonymy was always treated as a priority relation in the mapping procedure. If it could be established no further relation was necessary. Interlingual hyponymy was only introduced when no interlingual synonym could be found in the other wordnet. However, since the mapping was extended in time and carried out by partially different lexicographers' teams at different stages there could appear situations when both relations existed for the same synset linking it to two different other language synsets. For example, the Polish synset *farsowość*.1 was linked to the English synset *comicality*.1 via interlingual hyponymy relation and to *farcicality*.1 via interlingual synonymy relation. Since I-synonymy is more detailed than the I-hyponymy we deleted the latter. Nevertheless, there may be cases where such pairs of relations are justified. This happens when the hyponymy relation is the only interlingual relation describing its hypernym. For example the English synset *interactive kiosk*.1 is the I-synonym of *infokiosk*.1, but also I-hyponym for *kiosk*.4, which is the only interlingual relation of the latter. All in all, as a result of verifying this diagnostic we deleted 1 737 relations and added 735 new ones.

Interlingual relations	deleted	added
verbal synsets	1 065	19 816
non-verbal synsets	14 868	23 972
Sum	15 933	43 788

Table 5: interlingual synset relations for verbs and other POS

Certain changes were connected with introducing new interlingual relations at further stages of work, such as, for instance interlingual inter-register synonymy for synsets sharing the meaning but differing in register. This relation started to be systemically introduced for Polish synsets which were stylistically marked and thus inter-register synonyms to neutral Polish synsets otherwise linked via I-synonymy to neutral English synsets. Before introducing this relation I-hyponymy was used, but it was later replaced with I-inter-register synonymy. We replaced 1 168 instances of such relation, i.e. to improve consistency of application of different relations.

Apart from analysing the results of our diagnostic tests, we have been also continuing the works on filling in the missing links between plWordNet and Princeton WordNet synsets. These mainly focused on verbal synsets and on Princeton WordNet synsets. Verbs were the last of all parts of speech that we started to map, while for a very long time we were going from plWordNet to Princeton WordNet direction which left a number of English synsets unmapped. The summary results of our work are shown in Table 5.

5.2 Lexical units

Equivalence relations between lexical units form an extra layer of interlingual mapping between plWordNet and Princeton WordNet (Rudnicka et al., 2019). They link pairs of Polish and English lexical units that display strong equivalence in meaning and use and thus function as (mutual)

domains	LU pairs	Right links	Wrong links	Deleted links	Changed links
location	35	31	0	1	3
activity	93	64	7	19	1
property	96	78	18	6	12
artefact	156	145	0	8	0
natural object	94	86	8	3	7
body part	93	86	0	6	3
thinking	81	68	13	0	13
group	37	29	0	6	4
plant	31	28	3	0	3
state	53	46	0	4	3
communication	64	51	0	11	2
relation	41	32	0	9	1
food	30	23	7	1	6
natural phenomenon	39	34	5	0	6
possession	54	46	0	8	0
event	38	33	5	0	5
natural proc.	43	33	2	8	0
quantity	43	39	0	3	0
substance	31	29	1	1	0
emotion	24	10	1	1	1
system	13	11	0	1	0
animal	8	7	0	1	0
time	8	8	0	0	0
shape	13	12	1	0	1
person	6	2	1	0	2
h. hierarchy	3	3	0	0	0
purpose	4	2	1	0	0
SUM	1231	978	73	97	73

Table 6: Manual verification of equivalence mapping across domains

translational equivalents. This applies especially to strong and regular equivalence links. In addition, weak equivalents links hold between units that can function as translational equivalents, even descriptive ones (Rudnicka et al., 2019).

The number of equivalence links is much smaller than that of interlingual relations for two reasons. First, it was not the goal to introduce such links for all lexical units, because this would not be possible due to substantial differences between languages (Polish and English). Second, the mapping procedure was even more demanding than that for the interlingual mapping between synsets, hence very time consuming. Currently, the equivalence mapping exists for almost 27k pairs of Polish and English noun lexical units.

In establishing so strong type of interlingual links as equivalence links one would expect the correspondence in semantic domains of the Polish and English lexical units. However, lexical unit assignment to both Princeton WordNet lexicographer's files and plWordNet domains is to some extent arbitrary and cannot be treated as a decisive factor in establishing a link. Still, some domains tend to correlate, others do not (Maziarz et al., 2014). Therefore, we have checked the distribution of domains between Polish and English lexical units linked by equivalence links and selected for manual verification such pairs of domains that occur five or less times in the mapping.

	deleted	added	sum
Equivalence relations	810	13 623	14 433

Table 7: Equivalence relations

The results of the manual verification of equivalence links across plWordNet domains are presented in Table 6. We observe that most of the analysed connections were right links. The exact shares vary across domains. This finding corroborates the prediction that domain assignment is arbitrary, especially across two wordnets of two very different languages. It can also be treated as a kind positive validation/re-evaluation of the equivalence mapping procedure used in linking plWordNet and Princeton WordNet senses. On the other hand, for each domain we have discovered some number of links that had to be altered, either deleted altogether or changed to a different type of equivalence link. In some cases the change also involved the change of the interlingual relation between the plWordNet and Princeton WordNet synsets the lexical units in question were the components of.

In addition to the verification of the earlier existing links, we have also continued with introducing new equivalence links. The summary results of our work are shown in Table 7.

6 Conclusion and future work

We plan to further increase the quality of plWordNet and provide each lexical unit with a higher standard of description that is a gloss and minimum two usage examples.

Other planned work is to continue work on the density of the relation network by increasing the number of instances and supplementing the list of relations with new types, e.g., the masculinity relation describing at the unit level masculine derivations derived from feminine word-forming bases, e.g., *wdowiec* 'widower' ⇒ *wdowa* 'widow', zodiakarz 'zodiacarius' ⇒ *zodiakara* 'zodiacara', or the compression relation linking at the unit level univerbisms with their word bases, e.g., *starówka* 'old town' ⇒ *stare miasto* 'old town'. It is also important to supplement the resource with new lexical units, as well as to verify and possibly correct selected parts of the graph.

It is also planned to integrate with the parallel Polish-English corpus Paralela (Pęzik, 2016), as well as with the Wielki Otwarty Korpus (WOK, Large Open Corpus of Polish) (Broda et al., 2012). The idea is that linking plWordNet to these resources will result in a very large sense-tagged corpus (for the purposes of word sense disambiguation). Another task is to create domain subwordnets, e.g., a subwordnet of musicological terms, which will be a separate domain resource, but will also be linked to plWordNet. First we will start with an experimental task that will test the theoretical assumptions and technical capabilities of such a solution. Ultimately, it will facilitate the NLP of domain texts.

Due to the technical possibilities of the WordNet-Loom 2.0 editor (Naskręt et al., 2018) we plan to build test resources in a form of sub-wordnet. The current form of the tool makes it possible not only to add headwords that form a separate resource from plWordNet, but even to create your own types of relations or edit the existing ones. The planned sub-wordnets will be test wordnets including specialist vocabulary. The resource will be distinct from plWordNet, but connected to it via selected nodes consisting of common synsets. The enterprise has an experimental character.

Acknowledgments

References

Collin F Baker, Charles J Fillmore, and John B Lowe. 1998. The berkeley framenet project. In *COLING 1998 Volume 1: The 17th International Conference on Computational Linguistics*.

Simone Balloccu, Patrícia Schmidtová, Mateusz Lango, and Ondřej Dušek. 2024. Leak, cheat, repeat: Data contamination and evaluation malpractices in closed-source llms. *arXiv preprint arXiv:2402.03927*.

Satanjeev Banerjee, Ted Pedersen, et al. 2003. Extended gloss overlaps as a measure of semantic relatedness. In *Ijcai*, volume 3, pages 805–810.

Michele Bevilacqua, Roberto Navigli, et al. 2020. Breaking through the 80% glass ceiling: Raising the state of the art in word sense disambiguation by incorporating knowledge graph information. In *Proceedings of the conference-Association for Computational Linguistics. Meeting*, pages 2854–2864. Association for Computational Linguistics.

Francis Bond and Kyonghee Paik. 2012. A survey of wordnets and their licenses. In *proceedings of the 6th global WordNet conference (GWC 2012)*, pages 64–71. Matsue.

Bartosz Broda, Michał Marcińczuk, Marek Maziarz, Adam Radziszewski, and Adam Wardyński. 2012. Kpwr: Towards a free corpus of polish. In *Proceedings of LREC*, volume 12.

Agnieszka Dziob and Maciej Piasecki. 2018. Implementation of the verb model in plWordNet 4.0. In *Proceedings of the 9th Global Wordnet Conference*, pages 113–122, Nanyang Technological University (NTU), Singapore. Global Wordnet Association.

Agnieszka Dziob, Maciej Piasecki, and Ewa Rudnicka. 2019. plWordNet 4.1 - a linguistically motivated, corpus-based bilingual resource. In *Proceedings of the 10th Global Wordnet Conference*, pages 353–362, Wroclaw, Poland. Global Wordnet Association.

Arkadiusz Janz and Maciej Piasecki. 2023. Word sense disambiguation based on iterative activation spreading with contextual embeddings for sense matching. In *Proceedings of the 12th Global Wordnet Conference*, pages 140–149.

Marek Maziarz, Maciej Piasecki, Ewa Rudnicka, and Stan Szpakowicz. 2014. Registers in the system of semantic relations in plWordNet. In *Proceedings of the Seventh Global Wordnet Conference*, pages 330–337, Tartu, Estonia. University of Tartu Press.

Marek Maziarz, Maciej Piasecki, Ewa Rudnicka, Stan Szpakowicz, and Paweł Kędzia. 2016. plWordNet 3.0 – a comprehensive lexical-semantic resource. In *Proceedings of COLING 2016, the 26th International Conference on Computational Linguistics: Technical Papers*, pages 2259–2268, Osaka, Japan. The COLING 2016 Organizing Committee.

Marek Maziarz, Maciej Piasecki, and Stanisław Szpakowicz. 2013. The chicken-and-egg problem in wordnet design: synonymy, synsets and constitutive relations. *Language Resources and Evaluation*, 47(3):769–796.

George A Miller, Richard Beckwith, Christiane Fellbaum, Derek Gross, and Katherine J Miller. 1990. Introduction to wordnet: An on-line lexical database. *International journal of lexicography*, 3(4):235–244.

George A Miller and Christiane Fellbaum. 2007. Wordnet then and now. *Language Resources and Evaluation*, 41:209–214.

George A Miller, Claudia Leacock, Randee Tengi, and Ross T Bunker. 1993. A semantic concordance. In *Human Language Technology: Proceedings of a Workshop Held at Plainsboro, New Jersey, March 21-24, 1993*.

Tomasz Naskręt, Agnieszka Dziob, Maciej Piasecki, Chakaveh Saedi, and António Branco. 2018. WordnetLoom – a multilingual Wordnet editing system focused on graph-based presentation. In *Proceedings of the 9th Global Wordnet Conference*, pages 190–199, Nanyang Technological University (NTU), Singapore. Global Wordnet Association.

Piotr Pęzik. 2016. Paralela corpus and search engine.

M Piasecki. 2009. A wordnet from the ground up. *Oficyna Wydawnicza Politechniki Wroclawskiej*.

Ewa Rudnicka, Marek Maziarz, Maciej Piasecki, and Stan Szpakowicz. 2012. A strategy of mapping Polish WordNet onto Princeton WordNet. In *Proceedings of COLING 2012: Posters*, pages 1039–1048, Mumbai, India. The COLING 2012 Organizing Committee.

Ewa Rudnicka, Maciej Piasecki, Francis Bond, Łukasz Grabowski, and Tadeusz Piotrowski. 2019. Sense equivalence in plwordnet to princeton wordnet mapping. *International Journal of Lexicography*, 32(3):296–325.

Ewa Rudnicka, Wojciech Witkowski, and Maciej Piasecki. 2021. A (non)-perfect match: Mapping plWordNet onto PrincetonWordNet. In *Proceedings of the 11th Global Wordnet Conference*, pages 137–146, University of South Africa (UNISA). Global Wordnet Association.

Neville Ryant and Karin Kipper. 2004. Assigning xtag trees to verbnet. In *Proceedings of the 7th International Workshop on Tree Adjoining Grammar and Related Formalisms*, pages 194–198.

Loïc Vial, Benjamin Lecouteux, and Didier Schwab. 2017. *UFSAC: Unification of Sense Annotated Corpora and Tools*. Ph.D. thesis, UGA-Université Grenoble Alpes.

Piek Vossen. 1998a. Introduction to eurowordnet. *EuroWordNet: A multilingual database with lexical semantic networks*, pages 1–17.

Piek Vossen. 1998b. A multilingual database with lexical semantic networks. *Dordrecht: Kluwer Academic Publishers. doi*, 10:978–94.

Word Sense Disambiguation with Large Language Models: Casing Bulgarian

Nikolay Paev, Kiril Simov, Petya Osenova
Artificial Intelligence and Language Technology
Institute of Information and Communication Technologies
Bulgarian Academy of Sciences
Bulgaria
nikolay.paev@iict.bas.bg, kivs@bultreebank.org, petya@bultreebank.org

Abstract

The paper presents two approaches to Word Sense Disambiguation in Bulgarian with the usage of Large Language Models (in our case - our own pre-trained BERT models). The knowledge from a Bulgarian WordNet (BTB-WordNet) has been used in the fine-tuning stages. As far as we know, the presented results are the SOTA in Word Sense Disambiguation task for Bulgarian. In addition, we experimented with various ways in dividing the data into training, development, and test datasets.

1 Introduction

The Word Sense Disambiguation (WSD) task is still an open NLP task, especially for the less-resourced and undertrained languages with respect to the semantic parsing and knowledge extraction. In this paper, we present an approach for WSD using Large Language Models (LLM). LLMs were fine-tuned on a dataset produced through compiled examples that are related to the WordNet synsets. We explored not only how well can LLMs be fine-tuned to the tasks of WSD, but also how well the knowledge learned by the model interacts with the knowledge encoded within the WordNet itself. The interaction between the two sources of knowledge was performed during the fine-tuning. It largely depends on the selection of elements in the training, development, and test datasets.

For example, let us consider the following Bulgarian sentence: "Нашата статия беше приета за конференцията Global WordNet в Италия." "Nashata statiya beshe prieta za konferenciyata Global WordNet v Italia." ("Our paper was accepted for the Global WordNet Conference in Italy.") The lemma 'статия' (statiya) is part of two synsets connected through a hyperonym relation: a) 'статия' (statiya) (as a paper, synset: oewn-06280609-n[1], gloss: a scholarly article describing the results of observations or stating hypotheses), and b) its hyponym 'статия' (statiya) (as an article, synset: oewn-06278749-n, gloss: nonfictional prose forming an independent part of a publication). Thus, when we annotate the occurrence of the word 'статия' (statiya) in the above sentence in the first sense, it is an exact annotation and thus classified as a positive example of a correct annotation. But using the second sense, which in the Bulgarian WordNet (which we use) is related to the same word 'статия' (statiya) as a negative example for the annotation in the same sentence, results in a false statement. Adding such examples within the dataset for WSD makes the dataset contain contradictory statements. LLMs very easily recognize such contradictions. Similar contradictions could also arise from more subtle interactions of relations within the WordNet. Thus, the selection of examples for the WSD dataset has to be done carefully.

For our experiments, Bulgarian BTB-WordNet (BGWN) is used (Simov and Osenova, 2023). The corpus of annotated examples of Bulgarian is composed of data selected to reflect the senses within BGWN. Each example contains at least one word form annotated with a sense of BGWN. Some examples might be related to more than one sense. Also, in some of the examples all non-functional words happen to be annotated. The number of different sentences is 86 755, the number of the annotations amounts to 111 272. The senses were assigned to 27 597 lemmas and these lemmas are part of 20 615 synsets. Thus, we consider the resulted corpus large enough for fine-tuning of LLMs with respect to Bulgarian WSD. The corpus allows us to perform experiments with different settings according to these characteristics.

[1]The Synset identifier was taken from the Open English Wordnet — https://en-word.net/lemma/paper

To our knowledge, here we present the SOTA for Bulgarian in the WSD task.

The structure of the paper is as follows. In the next section, we present some focused related work. Section 3 describes the approaches that we implemented for fine-tuning of LLMs to the WSD task. The first is a binary classification of a context-gloss pair, where the context is the candidate word form within the text, and the gloss is the definition of the candidate sense. The second approach is the evaluation of all candidate senses with respect to their appropriateness for a given context. In Section 4 we report on the experiments with BGWN data. The last section concludes the paper and outlines some future directions of research.

2 Related Work

For the various types of WSD tasks, already LLMs started to be explored. For example, (Kibria et al., 2024) test four LLMs for English - ChatGPT-3.5, Mistral, Llama, Gemini Pro. The last one performed the best on the nine selected WSD datasets. However, no fine-tuning was performed in the experiments. The goal of the research reported in the paper is to evaluate the different LLMs with respect to their knowledge necessary for the task of WSD. The main difference with our work is that our aim is to train a WSD model using fine-tuning on our annotated corpus.

(Sumanathilaka et al., 2024) approach the improvement of WSD through the usage of LLMs and more precisely, of various prompt techniques. The authors suggest a method that combines a knowledge graph, a Part-of-Speech tagging and few-shot prompting as a guide to LLMs. Similarly to the above work this is not using fine-tuning. We plan to explore some of the proposed approaches in combination with the approach we present in this paper. Especially, combination with knowledge graphs, POS tagging, and Named Entity Recognition.

In (Bevilacqua et al., 2021) the recent trends in WSD have been described. Among other points, the authors note that 'different kinds of knowledge are orthogonal to each other and can be exploited in conjunction' and that adding more quality data improves the results. However, they also argue that at the moment the knowledge-based WSD is not so crucial as it was before due to the existence of many and multilingual pre-trained models.

Concerning WSD in other languages, in (Laba et al., 2023) a supervised fine-tuning of a pre-trained LLMs (mostly BERT-based) was employed on a dataset of Ukrainian, generated in an unsupervised way. The aim was to obtain better contextual embeddings for ambiguous words. We support authors' conclusion that 'WSD involves not just the knowledge of language but world knowledge and the capability of piecing together facts from multiple sources — in other words, functional competence.'

In our work, we started with a set-up very close to the one described in (Huang et al., 2019). Table 1 presents their construction methods for *context-gloss* pairs. In the first case, the target element (usually a word form) in the relevant context (usually a sentence) is coupled with all glosses for the target element. The glosses are taken from a Wordnet. For the context-gloss pairs, a binary classification has been performed (Yes/No) reflecting whether the gloss describes the correct sense for the target element in the context, or not. These pairs are called *Context-Gloss Pairs*. The specific examples of such pairs are given in the first part of the table. Additionally, the authors introduced a modification called *Context-Gloss Pairs with Weak Supervision*. In this case, the context part of the pair has been modified by highlighting the target element in quotation marks. The gloss part has also been modified by placing the lemma of the target element in front of the gloss. In Table 2 the prefix of the target element is highlighted by underlining. These modifications are shown in the second part of Table 1. Both types of context-gloss pairs have been constructed for all the senses related to the target element in the WordNet. Then these pairs were used for the fine-tuning of a BERT language model[2]. There are three fine-tuned models: (1) the model performs a classification of the target element in the context-gloss pair (the model is called **GlossBERT(Token-CLS)**); (2) the model performs a classification of [CLS] token in the context-gloss pair, and in this way the whole sentence is classified (the model is called **GlossBERT(Sent-CLS)**); and (3) the model performs a classification of [CLS] token in the context-gloss pair with weak supervision, and in this way the whole sentence is classified but with a stress on the target element (the model

[2]BERT model was introduced by Devlin et al. (2018)

Sentence with four targets:
Your research stopped when a convenient assertion could be made.

Context-Gloss Pairs of the target word [research]	Label	Sense Key
[CLS] Your research ... [SEP] systematic investigation to ... [SEP]	Yes	research%1:04:00::
[CLS] Your research ... [SEP] a search for knowledge [SEP]	No	research%1:09:00::
[CLS] Your research ... [SEP] inquire into [SEP]	No	research%2:31:00::
[CLS] Your research ... [SEP] attempt to find out in a ... [SEP]	No	research%2:32:00::

Context-Gloss Pairs with weak supervision of the target word [research]	Label	Sense Key
[CLS] Your "research" ... [SEP] research: systematic investigation to ... [SEP]	Yes	research%1:04:00::
[CLS] Your "research" ... [SEP] research: a search for knowledge [SEP]	No	research%1:09:00::
[CLS] Your "research" ... [SEP] research: inquire into [SEP]	No	research%2:31:00::
[CLS] Your "research" ... [SEP] research: attempt to find out in a ... [SEP]	No	research%2:32:00::

Table 1: The construction methods for training examples. The sentence is taken from SemEval-2007 WSD dataset. The ellipsis "..." indicates the remainder of the sentence or the gloss. The table is copied from (Huang et al., 2019), page 3510.

is called **GlossBERT(Sent-CLS-WS)**). The reported experiments show that the results improve from the first model to the last one (with some small exceptions).

In our own work, we start directly with the context-gloss pairs with weak supervision. Since in our case the context examples are directly included within the synsets of BGWN, the division of a context-gloss dataset in training, development, and test sets is not performed on the basis of the whole annotated texts, but on the individual context-gloss pairs. During the development and test evaluation phases, positive and negative cases were taken into account. We performed experiments by using different divisions of the context-gloss dataset in training, development, and test sets, and these divisions demonstrate different results, respectively.

Song et al. (2021) implemented an approach to semantically extend the sense representation in context-gloss pairs. This approach is called **Enhancing Sense Representations** (**ESR**). The idea is to add related words to the gloss of the synset. The motivation for this is the observed fact that the definitions within the synsets are usually short sentences, and thus do not provide enough information about the sense of the synset. This is especially true when the definitions were written for human understanding. The related words are constructed by first concatenating the words from the following three sources in order: (i) all the lemmas belonging to the synset (synonyms); (ii) WordNet example phrases or sentences of the synset; (iii) the hypernym gloss of the synset. All textual elements are concatenated and cleaned. The cleaning step is performed by deleting all the stop words and all the repeated words except the first occurrence. Another extension is on the context in the pair — the neighboring sentences of the context sentence are concatenated to it. In this way, the example consists of a larger context (more than one sentence) and a large sense description — the definition and related words. The paper demonstrates an improvement of the performance models trained over such extended context-gloss pairs.

In our work, we also enlarge the example, but only with lemmas from related synsets. We use more relations from WordNet, but we do not use the textual elements of the neighboring synsets.

In (Wahle et al., 2021) the authors propose some supervised methods that integrate WordNet knowledge for WSD in LM during the pre-training phase. In our case, we inject this knowledge into the fine-tuning phase. Interestingly, the authors also find that XLNet is more suitable for WSD than BERT. However, we used BERT in our current experiments.

3 LLM Word Sense Disambiguation Models

In this section, we present the models that were implemented in order to fine-tune LLMs to the task of Word Sense Disambiguation. We have performed experiments with three models - two binary classification models and one multiple choice model.

Pre-trained Language Models. For our experiments, we used our own pre-trained BERT models of two different sizes: 355M parameters (BERT-Large (**BERT-L**) with 24 layers and embedding dimension of 1024) and one with 657M parame-

Sentence with a single target:	
След приключването на курса има възможност за продължение ...	
... на работата с менторите, по същата схема на провеждане на занятията.	
Context-Gloss Pairs with weak supervision of the target word [продължение]	Label
[CLS] След приключването на курса има възможност за "продължение" ...	
... [SEP] продължение: Увеличаване на периода от време, в което нещо се ... [SEP]	**Yes**
[CLS] След приключването на курса има възможност за "продължение" ...	
... [SEP] продължение: Част от нещо (книга, пиеса, филм и други) ... [SEP]	**No**
Multiple choice disambiguation	
[CLS] След приключването на курса има възможност за продължение ...	
... [SEP] продължение: Увеличаване на периода от време, в което нещо се случва. ...	(1)
... [SEP] продължение: Част от нещо (книга, пиеса, филм и други) незавършено, ...	(2)
... [SEP] продължение: В спорта - допълнителното време, назначено за определяне ... [SEP]	(3)
Glosses with additional related lemmas (application of ESR)	
Увеличаване на периода от време, в което нещо се случва. ... [продължаване, продължение, ...]	
Част от нещо (книга, пиеса, филм и други) незавършено, ... [дял, клон, ...]	
В спорта - допълнителното време, назначено за определяне ... [времеви период, продължение, ...]	

Table 2: The construction methods for training examples in both setups. The first setup is similar to **GlossBERT**. The second setup presents multiple choice disambiguation where the embedding of the target word in the example is passed through a linear layer and compared with a dot product to the embeddings of the target word in each glosses passed through a separate linear layer. In this way the model assigns some probability to each candidate sense — (1), (2), or (3). The last part of the table demonstrates the addition of the list of lemmas by application of an ESR procedure.

ters (which we call BERT-ExtraLarge (**BERT-XL**) with 24 more layers — 48 in total). These BERT models were pre-trained on 20B Bulgarian tokens. Our pre-training dataset consists of mainly Web data, literature, administrative and scientific documents, as well as Wikipedia articles. The models were trained for 3 and 5 epochs, respectively, and a single epoch of pre-training took 23 and 60 hours on 16 Nvidia A100s. We plan to upload the models on Huggingface in the near future.

Fine-tuning Data Models. For our fine-tuning experiments with *Context-Gloss Pairs* we opted for the second setup (**GlossBERT(Sent-CLS)**) where the [CLS] token is passed through a classification layer. The model is trained on the binary classification task of predicting whether the gloss matches the target word. We explored the idea for *Context-Gloss Pairs with Weak Supervision* - the target word is enclosed in special tokens. Another modification which we studied is enriching the glosses with a list of lemmas related to the same sense of the gloss. (similar to **Enhancing Sense Representations** Song et al. (2021)). The lemmas are concatenated to the end of the gloss. We suppose that expanding the context can leverage the ability of the pre-trained model to recognize similar words.

We also explored a second setup — multiple choice disambiguation. We suppose that providing more glosses as options helps the model select the best one by excluding the others. The context contains the example and an arbitrary number of glosses prepended by the target word and separated with [SEP] tokens. The embedding of the first token of the target word in the example as well as the embedding of the first token of the target word in each gloss are passed through separate linear layers and then the dot product score is calculated between the results. The model is trained with *Cross Entropy Loss* to assign a high score to the correct glosses and low scores to the wrong ones. We considered two setups: (i) a list of glosses containing a single correct one, and (ii) a setup where a part of the inputs have no correct glosses, and in that case the model must assign the highest score to the last [SEP] token.

Examples of these setups are given in Table 2. The upper part of the table depicts two examples for binary classification — one positive (Yes) and one negative (No). The lower part of the table shows an example for the multiple choice classification, which contains three senses related to the same lemma.

Task 01:	Binary classification of context-gloss pairs with weak supervision			
	BERT Model	**ESR**	**Size Training**	**Accuracy**
Split: by examples				
01.	BERT-L	ESR -	88996	87.57
02.	BERT-L	ESR +	88996	89.22
03.	BERT-XL	ESR -	88996	89.57
04.	BERT-XL	ESR +	88996	**91.17**
Split: by synsets				
05.	BERT-L	ESR -	85254	72.77
06.	BERT-L	ESR +	85254	78.05
07.	BERT-XL	ESR -	85254	73.64
08.	BERT-XL	ESR +	85254	**81.88**
Task 02:	**Binary classification of context-gloss pairs with weak supervision Gloss with target word prefix:** *target word:gloss*			
Split: by examples				
09.	BERT-L	ESR -	88996	87.97
10.	BERT-L	ESR +	88996	90.31
11.	BERT-XL	ESR -	88996	89.60
12.	BERT-XL	ESR +	88996	**91.83**
Split: by synsets				
13.	BERT-L	ESR -	84840	73.26
14.	BERT-L	ESR +	84840	81.62
15.	BERT-XL	ESR -	84840	77.53
16.	BERT-XL	ESR +	84840	**82.75**

Table 3: The results from the experiments with binary classification.

Selection of Datasets. For the binary classification task, both positive and negative context-gloss pairs are necessary. Consider the synset s. A positive pair is made by taking a single example e and pairing it with the definition def_s of s — (e, def_s). Negative pairs are made in a more complex way. Consider all lemmas related to the synset. Some of them are related to more than one synset. Let l be one such lemma related to both s and $\hat{s}$ and $s \neq \hat{s}$. Then the negative pair is taken to be $(e, def_{\hat{s}})$.

As mentioned previously in the introduction section, a problem with negative examples could arise if we use a definition from a synset that shares the same lemma as another synset whose definition is used for a positive example and the two synsets are semantically related. (If s and $\hat{s}$ are connected by the *hypernym* relation, for example.) In the sentence discussed above, the contradiction follows from the fact that the positive example claims that the sense for the target word is 'paper' as a scientific paper, while the negative example states that it is not the case, and that the same target word is an article being any type of non-fictional prose and thus forming an independent part of a publication (in Bulgarian the lemma is the same). Obviously, such a negative claim is not true for the target word. Thus, if the negations are selected completely random the resulting dataset could contains contradictions. Therefore, we have to control the selection of negative examples in order to escape from such contradictions.

Thus, the GlossBERT method as described above can lead to undesired data elements in the dataset for the fine-tuning step. The hyperonimy relation between the synsets is not the only relation in a wordnet that could couse introduction of such contradictory examples. Other relations in BGWN include also *causes, entails, mero_member, mero_part, mero_substance, instance_hypernym, similar, sem-derives-to, sem-derives-to-p, sem-derives-to-v, sem-derived-from-adj, sem-derived-from, sem-derives-to-adj, sem-derived-from-v*. In addition, the related synsets are not necessarily directly connected by some of these relations. Thus, we add one more constraint to the selection of the negative synset $\hat{s}$ — not only it must share a lemma with s but it must not belong to the transitive closure starting from the synset s over some of these relations: *causes, entails, hypernym, mero_member, mero_part, mero_substance, instance_hypernym, similar, sem-derives-to, sem-derives-to-p, sem-derives-to-v, sem-derived-from-adj, sem-derived-from, sem-derives-to-adj, sem-derived-from-v*.

In addition to ruling out possible contradictory negative examples, we require that each target word has exactly one positive pair and exactly one negative pair in the fine-tuning dataset. In this way, the classes are kept balanced. The total number of context-gloss pairs in the fine-tuning dataset is 111 272.

The dataset for the multiple choice is constructed in a similar manner. The senses that could lead to contradiction with the correct sense of the target word are not included in the list of potential senses. The resulting fine-tuning dataset in this case has 55 636 entries in total.

In order to perform a step of enriching the gloss similar to *Enhancing Sense Representations*, described above, we selected the related synsets following the relations mentioned above, because they implied synsets that follow logically from the target synset. In addition, we selected not only the immediately connected synsets, but also those that were on the transitive closure of the relations. We restricted the number of synsets from which we select lemmas to be up to 10.

Partitioning of the Datasets. The choice of training, validation, and test sets also matters for fine-tuning. Since most of the synsets have more than one example and we construct an example-gloss pair for each example, the same glosses are repeated across the datasets. This enables the model to overfitting with respect to the glosses. This means that the model becomes very well tuned to the glosses it observed, but it is not able to deal easily with a sense that it did not observe during the fine-tuning. In addition this overfitting adjusts the model to the features that were explicated within the examples. Therefore, such potential overfitting restricts the application of the model to the annotated examples that are related to the senses in the training set. If we consider using the model for disambiguation with the synsets of the same wordnet, the overfitting to the glosses does not cause big problems, and thus it can be ignored. In this case, a simple data split over the examples in the dataset is good enough. We denote this split as *split by examples*.

However, it is clear that the disambiguation model should work well not only over the senses within the training set, but also over new, unseen glosses. For such cases the overfitting should be stopped beforehand. Thus, we use a validation set that does not contain the same glosses for early stopping. We achieve this by splitting the dataset in such a way that examples from the same synset cannot be part of different partitions of the fine-tuning dataset. We call such a division of the fine-tuning dataset a *split by synsets*. The choice for a negative synset is also restricted to the synsets of the same set, which makes the context-gloss pairs totally independent. The new restrictions slightly lower the size of the fine-tuning dataset — it totals to 92 958 for the pairs, and to 46 479 for the multiple choice set.

Our intuition behind such a split is that fine-tuning with it forces the model to generalize over the context-gloss pairs in a better way. Thus, it makes the inference during the exploitation of the model more independent from the actual glosses the model observed during the fine-tuning step. Making the validation set independent leads to an earlier increase in the validation loss during training. This way the training process can be stopped earlier avoiding potential overfitting over the glosses and the resulting model should be better suited for disambiguation over new glosses.

4 Experiments and Results

In this section, we report our findings from several experiments that follow the approaches described in the previous section.

We fine-tuned the models on 8 Nvidia A100s. The training was the same for both – the binary classification of the example-gloss pairs, and the multiple choice disambiguation. We trained for 3 epochs with a learning rate of 2e-05 with linear decay and batch size of 32x8 and 8x8 for the two tasks, respectively. The validation loss was calculated on every 100 steps (out of roughly 1000 for the 3 epochs) and the best model was chosen. The best model performance was usually achieved midway through training, with slightly increasing validation loss thereafter.

We performed Binary classification experiments with both pre-trained models - **BERT-L** and **BERT-XL**. The results are given in Table 3. We organized the experiments in two tasks: **Task 1** includes experiments for a binary classification of context-gloss pairs with weak supervision. In this task, we do not add the target word in front of the gloss; **Task 2** is similar, but the target word is added to the gloss as a prefix. For both tasks, the experiments use the two splits of the pairs — "split by examples" and "split by synsets". Furthermore,

Task 03:	Multiple choice disambiguation			
	BERT Model	**ESR**	**Size Training**	**Accuracy**
Split: by examples				
17.	BERT-XL	ESR -	44556	83.82
18.	BERT-XL	ESR +	44556	**89.78**
Split: by synsets				
19.	BERT-XL	ESR -	42627	72.09
20.	BERT-XL	ESR +	42627	**86.82**
Task 04:	**Multiple choice disambiguation Gloss with target word prefix:** *target word:gloss*			
Split: by examples				
21.	BERT-XL	ESR -	44336	85.03
22.	BERT-XL	ESR +	44336	**89.96**
Split: by synsets				
23.	BERT-XL	ESR -	42420	74.14
24.	BERT-XL	ESR +	42420	**89.24**
Task 05:	**Multiple choice disambiguation using binary classification model Gloss with target word prefix:** *target word:gloss*			
Split: by examples				
21.	BERT-XL	ESR -	44336	75.47
22.	BERT-XL	ESR +	44336	81.52
Split: by synsets				
23.	BERT-XL	ESR -	42420	83.07
24.	BERT-XL	ESR +	42420	87.71

Table 4: The results from the experiments with multiple choice disambiguation.

the experiments were performed over pairs with added lemmas from related synsets (ESR column). The results show that the exploration of a larger model produces better results. This is evident from the comparison of experiments 01, 02, 05, 06, 09, 10, 13, 14 with experiments 03, 04, 07, 08, 11, 12, 15, 16 respectively. This observation is similar to the results in other NLP tasks. Thus, for the other setups we use only the larger pre-trained model (BERT-XL).

The addition of lemmas from related synsets also improves the results. Here, the observation is that the added value from the application of ESR is much higher in the cases of "split by synsets" than "split by examples". In our view, this is due to the overfitting in the case of "split by examples". In the other case, the impact of the model generalization over the glosses and the related information is much bigger. The last improvement of the results arises from the addition of the target word to the glosses in the context-gloss pairs. This is visible by comparing the experiments in Task 01 and Task 02.

The results from our second setup — multiple choice disambiguation — are given in Table 4. The results here are parallel to the ones reported above for the binary classification ones. Thus, all the methods for expanding the semantic content in the senses work in the same way. The main difference is the result produced by the multiple choice disambiguation — distribution over the glosses that are candidates for the sense of the target word. In our view, this approach could be useful for many more applications than the binary classification approach. One such application is, for example, finding new senses for a given lemma.

The results from both setups are not comparable. The binary classification accuracy shows how confident the model is that the word in the example is used with a specific sense. If we would like to use the binary classification for disambiguation, the model should be inferred with all possible senses of the target word separately, and then the senses can be ranked according to the confidence of the model predicting label Yes. The multiple choice disambiguation model does that process in a single step. Thus, a more suitable comparison of the binary classification model to the multiple choice model should be the result from the above-mentioned setup, which is given in Table 4 as Task 05. The data show that the multiple choice model performs better for disambiguation overall.

5 Conclusion and Future Work

In this paper, we describe several LLM-based models for the WSD task in Bulgarian. We provide two setups for solving the problem. The two approaches complement each other. The binary classification setup provides a better result but requires several applications in order for the best solution to be found. It is not easy to recognize the cases where there is a gap in the lexical resource with respect to senses. The multiple choice approach solves the problem at once. It is also relatively easy to add an option for the missing senses. Last but not least, among our models there are such that are a SOTA in WSD for Bulgarian.

We also demonstrate that the proper selection of training, development, and test sets from a dataset of all context-gloss pairs is important for the quality and behavior of the model. Then the application of the models will depend on the task that we would like to solve. We recognize these differences because we started with examples for the senses within BGWN. We think that such problems arise also when it comes to whole texts annotated with senses.

One direction of future work is to improve the knowledge resource that we use – BGWN. It can be improved through the incorporation of more and diverse semantic information within the synsets. This might be done, for example, by improving the informativeness of the definitions by requiring a more complex structure for them, where various characteristics of the lemma meanings are made explicit. Also, through the addition of more examples and relations among the synsets. To sum up, more information has to be added in the direction of a more dense and versatile hierarchy, as well as in the direction of definitions and related examples.

Acknowledgments

The reported work has been supported by CLaDA-BG, *the Bulgarian National Interdisciplinary Research e-Infrastructure for Resources and Technologies in favor of the Bulgarian Language and Cultural Heritage, part of the EU infrastructures CLARIN and DARIAH.* We also acknowledge the provided access to *the e-infrastructure of the Centre for Advanced Computing and Data Processing* (the Grant No BG05M2OP001-1.001-0003).

References

Michele Bevilacqua, Tommaso Pasini, Alessandro Raganato, and Roberto Navigli. 2021. Recent Trends in Word Sense Disambiguation: A Survey. In *International Joint Conference on Artificial Intelligence*.

Jacob Devlin, Ming-Wei Chang, Kenton Lee, and Kristina Toutanova. 2018. BERT: Pre-training of Deep Bidirectional Transformers for Language Understanding. *CoRR*, abs/1810.04805.

Luyao Huang, Chi Sun, Xipeng Qiu, and Xuanjing Huang. 2019. GlossBERT: BERT for Word Sense Disambiguation with Gloss Knowledge. In *Proceedings of the 2019 Conference on Empirical Methods in Natural Language Processing and the 9th International Joint Conference on Natural Language Processing (EMNLP-IJCNLP)*, pages 3509–3514. ACL.

Raihan Kibria, Sheikh Intiser Uddin Dipta, and Muhammad Abdullah Adnan. 2024. On Functional Competence of LLMs for Linguistic Disambiguation. In *Proceedings of the 28th Conference on Computational Natural Language Learning*, pages 143–160, Miami, FL, USA. Association for Computational Linguistics.

Yurii Laba, Volodymyr Mudryi, Dmytro Chaplynskyi, Mariana Romanyshyn, and Oles Dobosevych. 2023. Contextual Embeddings for Ukrainian: A Large Language Model Approach to Word Sense Disambiguation. In *Proceedings of the Second Ukrainian Natural Language Processing Workshop (UNLP)*, pages 11–19, Dubrovnik, Croatia. Association for Computational Linguistics.

Kiril Simov and Petya Osenova. 2023. Recent Developments in BTB-WordNet. In *Proceedings of the 12th Global Wordnet Conference*, pages 220–227, University of the Basque Country, Donostia - San Sebastian, Basque Country. Global Wordnet Association.

Yang Song, Xin Cai Ong, Hwee Tou Ng, and Qian Lin. 2021. Improved Word Sense Disambiguation with Enhanced Sense Representations. In *Findings of the Association for Computational Linguistics: EMNLP 2021*, pages 4311–4320. ACL.

Deshan Sumanathilaka, Nicholas Micallef, and Julian Hough. 2024. Assessing GPT's Potential for Word Sense Disambiguation: A Quantitative Evaluation on Prompt Engineering Techniques. *2024 IEEE 15th Control and System Graduate Research Colloquium (ICSGRC)*, pages 204–209.

Jan Philip Wahle, Terry Ruas, Norman Meuschke, and Bela Gipp. 2021. Incorporating Word Sense Disambiguation in Neural Language Models. *ArXiv*, abs/2106.07967.

Automatic Detection of Coptic Text Reuse: Applying Coptic Wordnet to Intertextuality Studies in Selected Coptic Monastic Writings

So Miyagawa
University of Tsukuba
miyagawa.so.kb@u.tsukuba.ac.jp

Luis Morgado da Costa
Vrije Universiteit Amsterdam
lmorgado.dacosta@gmail.com

Laura Slaughter
University of Oslo
l.a.slaughter@dscience.uio.no

Heike Behlmer
Georg-August-Universität Göttingen
hbehlme@uni-goettingen.de

Abstract

This study explores the application of Coptic Wordnet to intertextuality studies in Coptic literature, focusing on works of the 4th/5th century Egyptian abbots Shenoute and Besa, and on the Bible in Coptic. Using the semantic relations captured in Coptic Wordnet, we enhance the automatic detection of text reuse, including quotations, allusions, and paraphrases. Our findings demonstrate that incorporating Coptic Wordnet data enables the identification of previously undetected intertextual relationships, providing a more comprehensive understanding of the interconnected nature of Coptic texts. This research highlights the potential of wordnets in tracing the traveling of words, phrases, and concepts from authoritative texts into the wider language, offering new insights into the linguistic and conceptual landscape of Coptic-speaking Egyptian Christianity in Late Antiquity.

1 Introduction

Intertextuality studies in the Coptic literature have traditionally relied on manual analysis and expert knowledge to identify text reuse. However, the advent of digital tools and resources has opened up new possibilities for automating and enhancing this process. This study explores the application of Coptic Wordnet to intertextuality studies, focusing on works of the 4th/5th century Egyptian abbots Shenoute and Besa, and on the Bible in Coptic. Coptic Wordnet, a lexical database that captures semantic relations beyond direct synonymity between Coptic words, serves as a powerful tool to improve automatic detection of text reuse. By leveraging this resource, we aim to uncover not only verbatim quotations but also more subtle forms of intertextuality, such as allusions and paraphrases.

The significance of this research lies in its potential to enhance our understanding of the intertextual relationships within Coptic literature, provide insights into the transmission of religious and cultural concepts in Late Antique Egypt, and demonstrate the value of computational approaches in the study of ancient languages and literatures. Through this work, we seek to bridge the gap between traditional philological methods and modern computational techniques, offering new perspectives on the rich tapestry of Coptic literary production.

2 Background

2.1 Intertextuality in Coptic Literature

Coptic literature, particularly the works of prominent monastic leaders like Shenoute (4--5th century) and Besa (5th century), is characterized by its rich intertextual relationships with the Bible and other authoritative texts by patristic authors such as Athansius, or earlier monastic writings. These connections offer valuable insights into the religious, cultural, and linguistic landscape of Coptic-speaking Egyptian Christianity in Late Antiquity. Intertextuality in Coptic literature manifests itself in various forms, including direct quotations, allusions, paraphrases, thematic parallels, and structural echoes.

Previous studies, such as Karl Heinz Kuhn's work on Besa's *Letters and Sermons* (Kuhn, 1956), have provided attestations of these intertextual relationships. However, the manual nature of these studies limits their scalability and the ability to uncover more subtle forms of text reuse. Our approach aims to complement and extend these traditional methods by applying computational techniques to a wider corpus of texts, potentially revealing patterns and connections that might otherwise remain hidden.

2.2 The Coptic Language

Coptic, the final stage of the Egyptian language, has a recorded history spanning over 5,000 years.

Written in a script derived from the Greek alphabet supplemented with characters from Demotic Egyptian, Coptic was primarily used from the 2nd to the 14th centuries CE. It served as the language of Christian Egypt during the Roman, Byzantine, and early Islamic periods, playing a crucial role in the preservation and transmission of early Christian literature.

The Coptic language is characterized by several key features that make it both fascinating and challenging to study. It comprises multiple dialects, with Sahidic being the main literary dialect in the first millennium CE and the focus of the Coptic Wordnet. Coptic's morphology is primarily agglutinative, with some fusional features, allowing for complex word formations. Its lexicon is a rich blend of native Egyptian words and Greek loanwords, reflecting the cultural and linguistic interactions between Greeks and Egyptians starting with the conquest of the country by Alexander the Great in 332 BCE. The verbal system is particularly complex, with numerous tenses, aspects, and moods expressed through a combination of auxiliaries and affixes. Syntactically, Coptic employs a system of bound groups[1] and converbs, which can pose challenges for automatic analysis and translation.

Understanding these linguistic features is crucial for developing effective tools and resources for Coptic language processing, including the construction and application of Coptic Wordnet. Our work takes into account these unique characteristics of Coptic to ensure that our computational approaches are sensitive to the language's specific structures and nuances.

2.3 Coptic Wordnet

Coptic Wordnet (Slaughter et al., 2019) is a lexical database that organizes Coptic words into synsets (synonym sets) and captures various semantic relations between them. It is part of the larger family of Wordnets, which originated with the development of Princeton Wordnet for English in the mid-1980s. The core structure of Coptic Wordnet comprises synsets, senses, as well as semantic relations established by the Princeton Wordnet. This rich semantic network enables the identification of conceptual connections beyond simple synonymity relations, making it a valuable resource for intertextuality studies.

The development of Coptic Wordnet represents a significant step forward in the digital humanities approach to Coptic studies. By providing a structured representation of the Coptic lexicon and its semantic relationships, it opens up new possibilities for computational analysis of Coptic texts. This resource not only aids in the automatic detection of intertextuality but also serves as a valuable tool for linguists, historians, and scholars of early Christianity studying the Coptic language and its literature.

2.3.1 Construction of Coptic Wordnet

A team of Coptologists and computer scientists built Coptic Wordnet automatically and evaluated it manually. Its construction was a complex process that drew upon multiple data sources and linguistic resources, leveraging them through an algorithm based on multilingual sense intersection.

It used lemma alignments from three primary sources: the Coptic Dictionary Online (CDO) (Feder et al., 2018), the MySQL version of Crum's *Coptic Dictionary* (Crum, 1939) in Milan Konvicka's Marcion Software,[2] and the Database and Dictionary of Greek Loan Words in Coptic (DDGLC).[3] These sources provided a rich foundation of Coptic words with translations in multiple languages, including English, French, German, Czech, and Greek.

The construction of the Coptic Wordnet followed the 'expand' approach, using other wordnets as a foundation for its structure. These wordnets included the Princeton Wordnet (English; Fellbaum, 2017), GermaNet and Odenet (German; Hamp and Feldweg, 1997; Siegel and Bond, 2021), WOLF (French; Sagot and Fišer, 2008), Greek Wordnet (Bizzoni et al., 2014), Ancient Greek Wordnet (Bizzoni et al., 2014) and Czech Wordnet (Pala and Smrž, 2004).

This automated process was followed by a manual evaluation phase, where Coptic scholars reviewed a sample of the automatically generated senses to assess accuracy and refine the results. Based on this evaluation, the Coptic Wordnet has data distributed over four levels of confidence, based on the number of interesected language dur-

[1] A Coptic bound group is a sequence of morphs, likely connected by a shared stress, that consists of structural elements with grammatical meaning and lexical elements, and the order of constituents within the group is fixed based on dependency classes Layton, 2011, 22--27, Haspelmath, 2014, 123--126.

[2] `http://marcion.sourceforge.net/` (accessed October 16, 2024)

[3] `https://www.geschkult.fu-berlin.de/en/e/ddglc/index.html` (accessed October 16, 2024)

ing its construction phase (for more details, see Slaughter et al., 2019). For this expriment, we used the wordnet as a whole (i.e. without filtering by levels of confidence). The size of the Coptic Wordnet used for this experiment can be see in Table 1.

POS	No. synsets	No. senses
nouns	13,904	97,527
verbs	7,491	92,019
adjectives	3,488	20,723
satellite adj	229	587
adverbs	737	7,373
non-referential	22	448
Total	25,871	218,677

Table 1: Coptic Wordnet Coverage (taken from: Slaughter et al., 2019)

3 Methodology

Our approach combines the text reuse detection capabilities of the text reuse detection tool TRACER (see 3.1) with the semantic richness of Coptic Wordnet to enhance the identification of intertextual relationships in Coptic literature. This integration allows us to move beyond simple string matching and consider the semantic context and relationships between words, thereby improving our ability to detect non-verbatim text reuse.

3.1 Text Reuse Detection with TRACER

TRACER, developed by the eTRAP research group at the University of Göttingen (Büchler et al., 2018; Büchler et al., 2014), is a versatile tool for detecting text reuse. Its workflow consists of text preprocessing, feature selection, link generation, scoring, and post-processing steps. While effective at identifying verbatim quotations and idiomatic expressions, TRACER initially struggled with more subtle forms of intertextuality (Büchler, 2013). This limitation prompted us to explore ways to enhance its capabilities through the integration of semantic information from Coptic Wordnet.

3.2 Integration of Coptic Wordnet

To address the limitations of purely lexical matching, we integrated Coptic Wordnet into TRACER's workflow. TRACER relies on word-to-word mappings to find text reuse. We used the Coptic Wordnet to create these mappings in several steps. We started by collecting standard synonymity mappings based on synsets. We then expanded these word sets based on the semantic relations captured in the Wordnet including hypernymy/hyponymy, and co-hyponymy. Details on the generation of word pairings are provided below, for each semantic relation:

- **Synonymy:** All senses belonging to a synset were paired with all other senses belonging to the same synset.
- **Hypernymy/hyponymy:** All senses belonging to a synset were paired with all senses belonging to its hypernyms/hyponyms (multiple inheritance allowed); Hypernym/hyponym chains were limited to 12 levels of recursion. This creates mappings of the type "dog ↔ animal" (and vice versa).
- **Co-hyponymy:** All senses belonging to a synset were paired with all senses belonging to hyponym of the first synset's hypernym. Hypernym chains were limited to 3 level of recursion. This creates mappings of the type "dog ↔ cat" (and vice versa), because both share a hypernym.

This greatly expanded semantically related words incorporated into TRACER's feature selection process. A summary of the number of relations extracted can be see in Table 2.

Relation	No. pairs
synonymy	4,103,650
hypernymy	9,797,575
hyponymy	9,867,688
cohyponymy	164,789,665
Total	188,558,578

Table 2: Lexical pairs provided to TRACER

TRACER's similarity calculation algorithm was adjusted to consider these semantic relationships when comparing text segments. This allowed us to detect potential text reuse even when the exact wording differed, as long as the concepts expressed were semantically related. Finally, we adjusted the thresholds for identifying potential text reuse to accommodate this expanded feature set, striking a balance between sensitivity and precision in our detection of intertextual relationships.

4 Results and Discussion

4.1 Improved Intertextual Detection

Previously, TRACER had been employed to detect text reuse from the Psalms in works of the two monastic authors mentioned above: Shenoute and Besa (Miyagawa, 2022). The choice had focused on Shenoute's *Canon* 6, a collection of writings on monastic discipline, and Besa's letters to monks and nuns, because these works exist in digital editions. The size of the corpora are follows: Shenoute, *Canon* 6 (49,412 words), Besa, *Letters and Sermons* (60,628 words), and the Sahidic Coptic translation of the Psalms (104,815 words).[4]

The integration of Coptic Wordnet with TRACER significantly enhanced our ability to detect non-verbatim text reuse. Table 3 shows the number of text reuse candidates generated by TRACER with and without the use of Coptic Wordnet (CWN) for various works.

	With CWN?	
Work	**No**	**Yes**
Besa		
Letters and Sermons	629	42,542
Shenoute, *Canon* 6 works		
He Who Sits Upon His Throne	84	5,535
Remember, O Brethren	31	2,582
I Am Not Obliged	207	11,293
Is It Not Written	98	8,235
People Have Not Understood	3	115

Table 3: TRACER's Text Reuse Candidates between Shenoute/Besa's Works and Psalms

As evident in Table 3, the use of Coptic Wordnet dramatically increased the number of candidate text reuse identified by TRACER. For instance, in Besa's *Letters and Sermons*, the number of candidates increased from 629 to 42,542 when using CWN.

Our analysis of the works of Shenoute's *Canon* 6 and Besa's *Letters and Sermons*, and the Sahidic Coptic translation of the Psalms revealed a rich tapestry of intertextual relationships that had previously gone unnoticed.

For this paper, our evaluation focused on the candidates generated for Psalm 1:1 in Besa's *Letters and Sermons*. We identified 18 possible text reuses out of 82 candidates. These allusions were not direct quotations, but rather semantic echoes that our enhanced system was able to capture through the recognition of related concepts and themes. Checking candidates of text-reuse is time-consuming and requires a high level of expertise. For this same reason, there is no gold standard against which we can evaluate our results. Regardless, in our expert point of view, we deem our work of great value to support the detection of text reuse.

In Shenoute's works, we discovered semantic clusters that shed light on the author's conceptual framework. For example, we found that the concept of "righteousness / justice" (ⲇⲓⲕⲁⲓⲟⲥⲩⲛⲏ *dikaiosunê* was frequently associated with related ideas such as "judgement" (ϩⲁⲡ *hap* or ⲕⲣⲓⲥⲓⲥ *krisis*) and "truth" (ⲙⲛⲧⲙⲉ *mntme*). This clustering of concepts provides insights into Shenoute's theological and ethical thinking, revealing patterns that might not be immediately apparent through traditional close reading methods.

4.2 Discussion and Limitations

The construction and application of Coptic Wordnet revealed several challenges specific to working with ancient languages. The limited textual evidence available for Coptic means that certain word senses or usage patterns are difficult to verify. By using an automatically created resource, such as the Coptic Wordnet, we are also constrained by the limitations of this resource. We know, for example, that many of the pairings used in this study are of low confidence. This means that other parameters, such as TRACER's sensibility, had to be tuned to filter out many other potentially interesting instances. We understand the value that human curation would bring to the Coptic Wordnet. But, at the same time, the lack of Coptic native speakers eliminates the possibility of intuition-based verification, a method often employed in developing Wordnets for modern languages.

One problem that most certainly arises from the automatic methods used to create the Coptic Wordnet is the challenge of capturing diachronic changes in word meanings over the many centuries of Coptic's use. Another problem posed by the current version of the Coptic Wordnet is the cultural and conceptual gaps between the ancient Coptic-speaking world and our modern context assumed by most wordnets. Many concepts in Coptic texts are deeply rooted in ancient Egyptian, Hellenis-

[4] The corpora were processed using the Coptic NLP Service (available at https://tools.copticscriptorium.org/coptic-nlp/, accessed October 18, 2024). For our analysis, we utilized the "word" unit as defined by this tool.

tic, and early Christian cultures, making them difficult to map onto modern conceptual frameworks. We had to contend with dialectal variations within Coptic, although our current focus on Sahidic Coptic mitigated this issue to some extent.

4.3 Future Work

Looking to the future, we have identified several key areas for improvement and expansion of our work. Refinement of Coptic Wordnet through manual curation and expansion will be a priority, as will enhancing our text reuse detection methods using more advanced NLP techniques. We plan to develop a larger, manually annotated corpus of Coptic texts, which will provide valuable training data for machine learning approaches and allow for more robust evaluation of our methods.

Generating and comparing different types of word-to-word mappings would be important to explore in future experiments. This could be done, for example, by filtering mappings by confidence level (which would likely generate much fewer but higher quality candidates of text reuse). It would also be worth exploring how different methods or thresholds for hypernym/hyponym recursion would affect TRACER's performance. For this experiment, we opted for a broad coverage (up to 12 levels of recursion) -- which should help detect less literal instances of text reuse -- such as allusions and paraphrases. However, this comes with the cost of generating many spurious text reuse candidates.

Another exciting avenue for future research would be exploring cross-linguistic intertextual relationships, particularly between Coptic and contemporaneous languages like Greek and Syriac. This comparative approach could shed light on the transmission and adaptation of ideas across linguistic and cultural boundaries in the Late Antique world.

Finally, we aim to integrate our work with other digital humanities resources, creating a more comprehensive ecosystem of tools and data for Coptic studies. This integration will not only enhance the utility of Coptic Wordnet but also contribute to the broader goal of making Coptic literature more accessible to researchers and the public alike.

5 Conclusion

This research demonstrates the potential of applying Coptic Wordnet to intertextuality studies in Coptic literature. By integrating semantic relations from Coptic Wordnet into text reuse detection tools, we have significantly enhanced our ability to identify and analyze intertextual relationships in Coptic texts. This approach not only advances our understanding of Coptic literature but also provides a model for similar studies in other ancient languages, showcasing the value of digital humanities approaches in classical and religious studies.

Our work bridges the gap between traditional philological methods and modern computational techniques, offering new perspectives on the rich tapestry of Coptic literary production. As we continue to refine our methods and expand the scope of our research, we anticipate that this approach will yield further insights into the interconnected nature of ancient texts and the transmission of ideas in the early Christian world. The development and application of Coptic Wordnet represents a significant step forward in the digital study of Coptic, opening up new possibilities for research and analysis. As we move forward, we hope that this work will not only contribute to Coptic studies but also inspire similar efforts in other areas of historical linguistics and digital humanities.

References

Yuri Bizzoni, Federico Boschetti, Harry Diakoff, Riccardo Del Gratta, Monica Monachini, and Gregory Crane. 2014. The making of Ancient Greek WordNet. In *Proceedings of the Ninth International Conference on Language Resources and Evaluation (LREC-2014)*, pages 1140--1147, Reykjavik, Iceland. European Languages Resources Association (ELRA).

Marco Büchler. 2013. Informationstechnische Aspekte des Historical Text Re-use.

Marco Büchler, Philip R Burns, Martin Müller, Emily Franzini, and Greta Franzini. 2014. Towards a historical text re-use detection. In *Text Mining*, pages 221--238. Springer.

Marco Büchler, Greta Franzini, Emily Franzini, Maria Moritz, and Kirill Bulert. 2018. TRACER-a multilevel framework for historical text reuse detection.

Walter Ewing Crum. 1939. *A Coptic Dictionary*. Oxford University Press, Oxford.

Frank Feder, Maxim Kupreyev, Emma Manning, Caroline T Schroeder, and Amir Zeldes. 2018. A linked coptic dictionary online. In *Proceedings of the Second Joint SIGHUM Workshop on Computational Linguistics for Cultural Heritage, Social Sciences, Humanities and Literature*, pages 12--21.

Christiane Fellbaum. 2017. Wordnet: An electronic lexical resource. *The Oxford Handbook of Cognitive Science*, pages 301--314.

Birgit Hamp and Helmut Feldweg. 1997. GermaNet-a lexical-semantic net for German. In *Proceedings of the ACL workshop Automatic Information Extraction and Building of Lexical Semantic Resources for NLP Applications*, Madrid, Spain.

Martin Haspelmath. 2014. A grammatical overview of Egyptian and Coptic. In Eitan Grossman, Tonio Sebastian Richter, and Martin Haspelmath, editors, *Egyptian-Coptic Linguistic in Typological Perspective*, Empirical Approaches to Language Typology 55, pages 103--144. De Gruyter Mouton, Berlin.

K. H. Kuhn. 1956. *Letters and Sermons of Besa*. Corpus Scriptorum Christianorum Orientalium, vol. 157. Scriptores Coptici, tomus 21. Imprimerie Orientaliste L.Durbecq, Louvain.

Bentley Layton. 2011. *A Coptic grammar: With chrestomathy and glossary: Sahidic dialect*, 3 edition. Harrassowitz Verlag, Wiesbaden.

So Miyagawa. 2022. *Shenoute, Besa and the Bible Digital Text Reuse Analysis of Selected Monastic Writings from Egypt*. SUB Göttingen.

Karel Pala and Pavel Smrž. 2004. Building Czech WordNet. *Romanian Journal of Information Science and Technology*, 7(1-2):79--88.

Benoît Sagot and Darja Fišer. 2008. Building a free French wordnet from multilingual resources. In *Proceedings of the Sixth International Language Resources and Evaluation (LREC'08)*, Marrakech, Morocco.

Melanie Siegel and Francis Bond. 2021. OdeNet: Compiling a German wordnet from other resources. In *Proceedings of the 11th Global Wordnet Conference (GWC 2021)*, pages 192--198.

Laura Slaughter, Luis Morgado Da Costa, So Miyagawa, Marco Büchler, Amir Zeldes, and Heike Behlmer. 2019. The making of coptic wordnet. In *Proceedings of the 10th Global Wordnet Conference*, pages 166--175.

Adding Audio to Wordnets

Francis Bond
Dept. of Asian Studies and Sinofon Project
Faculty of Arts
Palacký University
bond@ieee.org

Abstract

This paper explores the integration of sound files into wordnets, transforming them from static lexical databases into multimodal tools for linguistics, language learning and maintenance. Traditionally, wordnets focus on textual representations. Adding sound improves usability for language learners and linguists, especially in less-documented or endangered languages.

We extracted sound data for basic vocabulary in 24 languages from the TUFS Basic Vocabulary Modules, link them to senses and make them available as small wordnets. We also discuss the issues involved with merging the data into an existing wordnet, looking at the Open English Wordnet. In addition, this paper outlines the process of integrating audio, discusses potential use cases, and evaluates the technical challenges involved. Finally we suggest an extension to the wordnet formats to allow sound for examples and definitions as well.

1 Introduction

Wordnets are powerful lexical databases that organize words into synsets (sets of synonyms), which are linked by various semantic relations. Originally developed for English, wordnets have been created cover many languages, providing a valuable resource for natural language processing (NLP) tasks and lexicographic applications (Miller, 1995; Fellbaum, 1998; Vossen, 1998; Vossen et al., 1999; Bond and Foster, 2013). Despite their utility, wordnets, like most lexicographical resources, traditionally focus on textual representations of lexical knowledge, lacking multimodal components such as sound, which limits their usability as comprehensive dictionaries.

The addition of sound files to wordnets has the potential to transform them from static lexical databases into more dynamic, user-friendly resources. By associating sound files with specific synsets or lexical entries, wordnets can provide users with the ability to hear pronunciations, which is especially valuable for language learners, phoneticians, and researchers focusing on dialectology or sociolinguistics. This is particularly important for less well-known or endangered languages, where wordnets might serve as the primary lexicon, if not the only resource available. Several projects involved with language documentation and maintenance have noted that they would like to add audio files to their wordnets (Sio and Costa, 2019; Morgado Da Costa et al., 2023). The African Wordnet project (AWN) noted that pronunciation (in this case information about tones) is essential for disambiguating some words, although it is not shown in the standard orthography (Bosch and Griesel, 2018). In these cases, sound files help preserve and make available phonetic information, supporting both pronunciation accuracy and the documentation of spoken forms where orthographies may be underdeveloped or nonstandardized. Sinha et al. (2020) went as far as synthesizing audio for the Hindi WordNet, which underscores the value of sound. And of course, sound has been incorporated into many online dictionaries beyond wordnets with most online dictionaries of English having audio recordings of entry words, and a few even adding audio for example sentences (Fuertes-Olivera and Bergenholtz, 2011, p254). Some lexicons even include *sound effects* to present an ostensive definition of sounds.

While audio files are still not widely integrated into wordnets, there have been related efforts to enhance wordnets with pronunciation data. The 2021 release of Open English WordNet included pronunciation information for nearly 35,000 entries.[1] Efforts have also been made to extract pronunciation data from Wiktionary for use in word-

[1] https://github.com/globalwordnet/english-wordnet/releases/tag/2021-edition

nets (Declerck et al., 2020; Declerck and Bajčetić, 2021) but to the best of our knowledge this has not yet been incorporated into any actual wordnets. For general users, particularly non-linguists, sound files offer a straightforward way to learn correct pronunciations without requiring knowledge of phonetic transcriptions like the International Phonetic Alphabet (IPA). This makes wordnets more accessible to the average person, removing potential barriers created by complex orthographies or regional phonetic variations. Additionally, for languages with significant dialectal diversity, sound files can capture and preserve different regional variations, providing a richer and more comprehensive resource that reflects the full linguistic diversity of the language community.

In this paper, we explore the technical and linguistic considerations involved in adding sound files to wordnets, focusing on the challenges of linking audio data to synsets, managing multilingual and dialectal variation, and ensuring the quality of the recordings. We present a case study of a wordnet that has incorporated sound files, showcasing the process and reflecting on user feedback. By doing so, we aim to demonstrate that sound-enriched wordnets offer a significant improvement in both educational and research contexts, expanding their role beyond traditional text-based lexical databases.

2 Resources

In this section describe the main resources we use.

2.1 TUFS

The TUFS Basic Vocabulary Modules (Kawaguchi et al., 2007) are a resource developed for online language learning, containing vocabulary words and example sentences across 24 languages. This dataset, particularly focused on Asian languages, serves as a foundational tool for learners by providing vocabulary, grammar sketches, dialogues and example sentences in a formal conversational register. The vocabulary is designed to cover commonly used words, using words selected according to the Japanese Language Proficiency Test (N5). Additionally, the dataset provides translations across different languages, some of which introduce nuanced differences, such as gender distinctions in languages like German and Vietnamese.

Bond et al. (2020b) linked the TUFS data with the Open Multilingual Wordnet (OMW). This gave new resources for evaluating and enriching existing wordnets, created new wordnets for languages such as Khmer, Korean, Lao, Mongolian, Tagalog, Urdu, and Vietnamese. The linking process identifies multilingual connections between vocabulary items, improving cross-linguistic understanding and data integration across languages. However, they did not take advantage of the fact that the TUFS modules include good quality audio data for all of the vocabulary and example sentences.

2.2 Cantonese Wordnet

Recent work on the Cantonese wordnet (Sio and Costa, 2019) has focused on adding pronunciation, in the form of both transliterations and audio. The most recent release (Sio et al., 2025, this volume) includes over 2,000 pronunciations. Each pronunciation has a phonemic transcription using jyutping (the Linguistic Society of Hong Kong Cantonese Romanization Scheme), and an audio file, either reused from wikimedia commons or newly recorded.

2.3 Open Multilingual Wordnet

We use (and extend) the software for reading and displaying wordnets for the Open Multilingual Wordnet 2.0 (Bond et al., 2020a). This open-source software handles global wordnet association WordNet Lexical Markup Framework (WN-LMF) a standard format for representing wordnet-style lexical databases (Vossen et al., 2016; Bond et al., 2016; McCrae et al., 2021).

3 Creating and displaying

Since 2021 (WN-LMF 1.1) has had the capability to represent the pronunciation of lemmas (McCrae et al., 2021). This is in the <Pronunciation> element, which gives the IPA text. It has the following attributes:

- **variety** encodes the language variety, for example by using the IETF language tags to indicate dialect, where British English in IPA would be `en-GB-fonipa`. We do not have a general standard for how these are labelled, each wordnet can decide on its own.

- **notation** can encode further information such as indicating the speaker particular dialect (this was **notes** in McCrae et al. (2021))

- **phonemic** indicates whether the transcription

is phonemic, **true**, or phonetic, **false**, defaulting to **true** (phonemic)

  - Phonemic transcription represents the phonemes (distinctive sounds) of a language. It is more abstract and focuses on the sounds that change the meaning of words. Typically it is presented with sounds enclosed in slashes, e.g., /kæt/.
  - Phonetic transcription represents the exact pronunciation of speech, including fine details of how each sound is produced. It is more detailed and is typically shown in brackets, e.g., [kʰæt̚].

  Phonemic transcription is generally more suitable for dictionaries, because dictionaries aim to represent how words are typically pronounced in the language without overwhelming users with excessive phonetic detail. Phonemic transcription balances simplicity and accuracy by focusing on sounds that change meaning, which is important for learners to distinguish between words.

  For example, in a dictionary, users usually need to know whether a word starts with a /b/ or /p/ to distinguish *bat* from *pat*, but they don't necessarily need to know that in some dialects the t in *cat* might be unreleased.

- **audio** gives the URL of an audio file of the pronunciation

An example of encoding is given in Figure 1. Here we show the pronunciation under the lemma, it is also possible to store the pronunciation under the variant forms.

We have extended the OMW format (Bond and Foster, 2013) to read the pronunciation and store it in the database. The schema for the table for pronunciation is shown in 2. This is similar to how it is stored in the Python WN module (Goodman and Bond, 2021), which can also read and access the pronunciation.

3.1 Display

We display the pronunciation when we look at the sense of a word. If there is audio, then we show a loudspeaker (🔊), clicking on which plays the audio file. If there is a `value` then we show this, either between // if phonemic is true, or between [] if it is false.

For the TUFS wordnets, most of them have only audio. For the Open English Wordnet, entries with pronunciation generally only have the `value`, we have created a hybrid example here to show both (Figure 3). The Cantonese Wordnet has both pronunciation and audio, but has chosen to add them to the variants. Figure 4 shows two variants with different pronunciations, one showing the 'lazy' pronunciation (Chen, 2018; Cheng et al., 2022).

4 Discussion

We have shown that the current GWA format can usefully represent audio for wordnet words. In addition we have extracted audio from TUFS and linked it to senses for 24 languages, for a total of 10,945 pronunciations. These are all common words from a beginners vocabulary and thus useful for early learners. A release of this data will be made available at `https://github.com/fcbond/tufs`.

They can be loaded as wordnets, but are not full wordnets — they have no internal links, or definitions (except for Japanese). Our hope is that the audio links (and example sentences and new senses) will be taken up by existing projects and merged. This can be done fully automatically for TUFS nodes that map to only one ILI link, if there is not existing information about the pronunciation. If there is already pronunciation (as there is in the Open English WordNet), and there are multiple variants, then they must be disambiguated. For example, *fall* "autumn" has three pronunciations in the OEWN: /fɔːl/ (GB) and /fɔl/ (US) and /fɑl/ (unmarked). The pronunciation in TUFS is closest to /fɔːl/.[2] To be safe, even words with only one pronunciation shown should be checked, in case the pronunciation is not the same.

We compared the pronunciations in OEWN (2024 release candidate) and TUFS (English). Most words in OEWN have no pronunciation (0), for those that do, over a third have two or more pronunciations (Table 1).

When we looked at TUFS, 454 English words have associated audio. Of these, 381 have a pronunciation in OEWN (the other 63 do not). 126 have only one pronunciation. We plan to cooperate with the OEWN to merge this data.

To merge the pronunciations requires a competent speaker of the language in question. We do not

[2] `https://www.coelang.tufs.ac.jp/mt/en/vmod/sound/word/word_1142.mp3`

```
<LexicalEntry id="ex-rabbit-n">
    <Lemma writtenForm="rabbit" partOfSpeech="n"/>
        <Pronunciation variety="en-GB-fonxsamp en-US-fonxsamp"
            audio ="https://path/rabbit.flac">'r\{bIt</Pronunciation>
    <Pronunciation variety="en-AU-fonxsamp" notation="weak vowel merger"
            audio ="https://path/rabbit1.flac">'r\{b@t</Pronunciation>
     </Lemma>
 </LexicalEntry>
```

Figure 1: WN-LMF representation of pronunciation

```
CREATE TABLE pronunciations
  (id INTEGER PRIMARY KEY ASC,
   w_id INTEGER NOT NULL,     -- id of the linked word
   value   TEXT,              -- phonemic or phonetic realization
   variety TEXT,              -- encoding of the realization
   phonemic BOOLEAN NOT NULL CHECK (mycolumn IN (0, 1)) DEFAULT 1,
   notation TEXT,             -- any comments
   src_id INTEGER NOT NULL, -- which wordnet it came from
   t TIMESTAMP DEFAULT CURRENT_TIMESTAMP,
   FOREIGN KEY(w_id) REFERENCES w(id));
```

Figure 2: SQL representation of the pronunciation

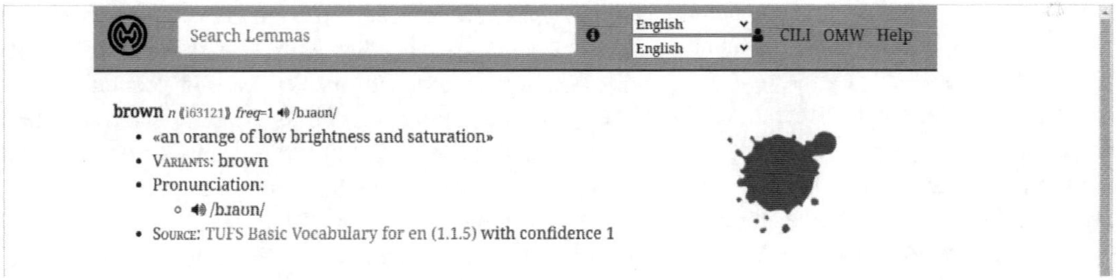

Figure 3: Pronunciation for *brown*, showing the pronunciation and an image from ARASAAC

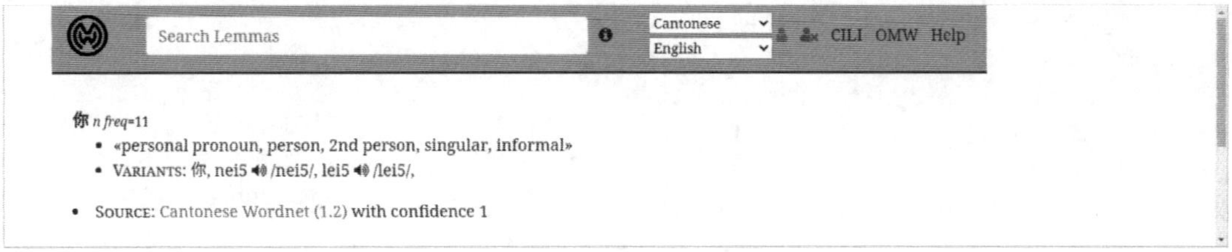

Figure 4: Pronunciation for 你 *nei5* showing a variant with the lazy l

Pronunciations	Number	Example
0	128,313	heel
1	22,606	brown
2	10,202	dog
3	479	fall
4	45	wolf
5	6	croissant
6	2	scallop

Table 1: Distribution of Pronunciations in OEWN (2024)

speak all 24 languages in the TUFS collection, but are happy to work with existing wordnet projects who wish to use his data.

4.1 Extending the GWA formats

Currently `Pronunciation` is only defined for lemmas. However, it would be easy to also add it to `Example` and possibly even `Definition`. Having pronunciation, especially audio, available for example sentences provides significant advantages for language learners. One of the most important reasons is that pronunciation in isolation can differ from pronunciation in context. Words often change due to natural speech phenomena such as connected speech, assimilation, or elision. By hearing how words sound in full sentences, learners can better understand how they flow together and how stress and rhythm work in natural speech, improving their fluency and pronunciation (Lew, 2011, pp255–266).

Additionally, example sentences demonstrate important aspects of prosody, such as intonation and sentence stress, which affect meaning and convey emotion. In many languages, the intonation pattern of a sentence can alter its meaning, such as rising intonation in questions or stress on certain words to indicate emphasis. Learners benefit from hearing these subtleties, which helps them sound more natural and better interpret the nuances of spoken language in real conversations.

For language documentation, where the orthography may not be fully standardized, having audio recordings of example sentences is even more crucial. The audio preserves the authentic pronunciation and prosody of the language, especially in cases where writing systems might not fully capture the phonetic details or where different writing systems coexist. This ensures that even if the orthography changes or develops over time, the spoken language, as documented in audio form, remains accessible and accurately represented for future researchers and learners.

Lastly, providing pronunciation for sentences aids listening comprehension. In connected speech, words may be pronounced differently than in isolation, and learners need exposure to such variations to understand real-world speech. Moreover, hearing sentences in context allows learners to grasp common collocations, idiomatic expressions, and how prosody affects meaning, which enriches their vocabulary and overall understanding. By including sentence-level pronunciation, learners can bridge the gap between theoretical knowledge and everyday spoken language. For these reasons, the TUFS modules includes the pronunciation for example sentences, and it would be good to take advantage of this.

4.2 Images

In addition, researchers have been trying to associate images with wordnet since at least Bond et al. (2008). We are now using illustrations from the Aragonese Center of Augmentative and Alternative Communication (Arasaac) to illustrate the OMW. The pictographic symbols are the property of the Government of Aragón and have been created by Sergio Palao, under a Creative Commons License BY-NC-SA.[3] These illustrations have several advantages for illustrating lexicons. First, they are designed for communicative purposes and widely used. Secondly, the symbols have been augmented with many localised versions for different cultures, such as Arabic, Bulgarian, SEA and Urdu.[4] Thirdly, the symbols are line drawings, which have been shown to be more effective for dictionary users (Dziemianko, 2022). Finally, they have been linked to Princeton WordNet 3.1 by Schwab et al. (2020), and so can be linked to CILI.

8,402 ili concepts are linked to illustrations. We further extend the coverage by illustrating a concept with an illustration of its direct hypernym if it exists. We show an example in Figure 3.

5 Conclusion

Incorporating audio into wordnets is the next step towards creating more comprehensive and user-friendly linguistic tools, enhancing both educational and research potential. This paper has outlined practical methods for linking sound files with

[3] `https://arasaac.org/`

[4] Global Symbols CIC

synsets, unlocking new possibilities for both linguistic research and language education. While challenges remain in ensuring broad accessibility and accurate audio representation, the benefits for language preservation and phonetic research are clear. Future research should focus on improving audio integration and scaling its application in collaborative, multilingual wordnets, further enhancing their utility. In particular, we would like to make the interface better suited for use on a smaller device like a telephone.

5.1 Acknowledgments

ChatGPT (4o) was used to copyedit the paper and help with the LaTeX formatting. ChatGPT (4o) and Claude (3.5 Sonnet) were used to debug the code for extracting the data from TUFS and formatting it for OMW.

References

Francis Bond and Ryan Foster. 2013. Linking and extending an open multilingual wordnet. In *51st Annual Meeting of the Association for Computational Linguistics: ACL-2013*, pages 1352–1362, Sofia.

Francis Bond, Hitoshi Isahara, Kyoko Kanzaki, and Kiyotaka Uchimoto. 2008. Boot-strapping a WordNet using multiple existing WordNets. In *Sixth International Conference on Language Resources and Evaluation (LREC 2008)*, Marrakech.

Francis Bond, Luis Morgado da Costa, Michael Wayne Goodman, John Philip McCrae, and Ahti Lohk. 2020a. Some issues with building a multilingual wordnet. In *Twelth International Conference on Language Resources and Evaluation (LREC 2020)*, Marseilles.

Francis Bond, Hiroki Nomoto, Luís Morgado da Costa, and Arthur Bond. 2020b. Linking the TUFS basic vocabulary to the open multilingual wordnet. In *Twelth International Conference on Language Resources and Evaluation (LREC 2020)*, Marseilles.

Francis Bond, Piek Vossen, John McCrae, and Christiane Fellbaum. 2016. CILI: The collaborative interlingual index. In *Proceedings of the 8th Global Wordnet Conference (GWC 2016)*, pages 50–57.

Sonja Bosch and Marissa Griesel. 2018. African Wordnet: facilitating language learning in African languages. In *Proceedings of the 9th Global Wordnet Conference*, pages 306–313, Nanyang Technological University (NTU), Singapore. Global Wordnet Association.

Katherine Hoi Ying Chen. 2018. Ideologies of language standardization: The case of Cantonese in Hong Kong. In *The Oxford Handbook of Language Policy and Planning*. OUP.

Lauretta Cheng, Molly Babel, and Yao Yao. 2022. Production and perception across three Hong Kong Cantonese consonant mergers: Community- and individual-level perspectives. *Laboratory Phonology*, 13.

Thierry Declerck and Lenka Bajčetić. 2021. Towards the addition of pronunciation information to lexical semantic resources. In *Proceedings of the 11th Global Wordnet Conference*, pages 284–291, University of South Africa (UNISA). Global Wordnet Association.

Thierry Declerck, Lenka Bajcetic, and Melanie Siegel. 2020. Adding pronunciation information to wordnets. In *Proceedings of the LREC 2020 Workshop on Multimodal Wordnets (MMW2020)*, pages 39–44, Marseille, France. The European Language Resources Association (ELRA).

Anna Dziemianko. 2022. The usefulness of graphic illustrations in online dictionaries. *ReCALL*, 34(2):218–234.

Christine Fellbaum, editor. 1998. *WordNet: An Electronic Lexical Database*. MIT Press.

Pedro A. Fuertes-Olivera and Henning Bergenholtz, editors. 2011. *e-Lexicography: The Internet, Digital Initiatives and Lexicography*. A&C Black.

Michael Wayne Goodman and Francis Bond. 2021. Intrinsically interlingual: The Wn Python library for wordnets. In *11th International Global Wordnet Conference (GWC2021)*.

Yuji Kawaguchi, Toshihiro Takagaki, Nobuo Tomimori, and Yoichiro Tsuruga, editors. 2007. *Corpus-Based Perspectives in Linguistics*, volume 6 of *Usage-Based Linguistic Informatics*. John Benjamins Publishing Company, Amsterdam.

Robert Lew. 2011. Multimodal lexicography: The representation of meaning in electronic dictionaries. *Lexicos*, 20.

John P. McCrae, Michael Wayne Goodman, Francis Bond, Alexandre Rademaker, Ewa Rudnicka, and Luís Morgado da Costa. 2021. The global wordnet formats: Updates for 2020. In *11th International Global Wordnet Conference (GWC2021)*.

George A. Miller. 1995. WordNet: A lexical database for English. *Commun. ACM*, 38(11):39–41.

Luís Morgado Da Costa, František Kratochvíl, George Saad, Benidiktus Delpada, Daniel Simon Lanma, Francis Bond, Natálie Wolfová, and A.l. Blake. 2023. Linking SIL semantic domains to wordnet and expanding the Abui wordnet through rapid words collection methodology. In *12th International Global Wordnet Conference (GWC2023)*.

Roberto Navigli and Simone Paolo Ponzetto. 2012. BabelNet: The automatic construction, evaluation and application of a wide-coverage multilingual semantic network. *Artificial Intelligence*, 193:217–250.

Didier Schwab, Pauline Trial, Céline Vaschalde, Loïc Vial, Emmanuelle Esperanca-Rodier, and Benjamin Lecouteux. 2020. Providing semantic knowledge to a set of pictograms for people with disabilities: a set of links between WordNet and arasaac: Arasaac-WN. In *Proceedings of the Twelfth Language Resources and Evaluation Conference*, pages 166–171, Marseille, France. European Language Resources Association.

Shikha Sinha, Kalika Bali Narayan, and Prabhakar Singh. 2020. Synthesizing audio for hindi wordnet. In *Proceedings of the 10th Global WordNet Conference*, pages 230–235.

Joanna Ut-Seong Sio and Luis Morgado Da Costa. 2019. Building the Cantonese Wordnet. In *Proceedings of the 10th Global Wordnet Conference*, pages 206–215, Wroclaw, Poland. Global Wordnet Association.

Piek Vossen, editor. 1998. *Euro WordNet*. Kluwer.

Piek Vossen, Francis Bond, and John McCrae. 2016. Toward a truly multilingual global wordnet grid. In *Proceedings of the 8th Global Wordnet Conference (GWC 2016)*. 419–426.

Piek Vossen, Wim Peters, and Julio Gonzalo. 1999. Towards a universal index of meaning. In *Proceedings of ACL-99 Workshop, Siglex-99, Standardizing Lexical Resources*, pages 81–90, Maryland.

Enhancing Linguistic Resources for Diachronic Analysis via Linked Data

Eleonora Ghizzota and Pierpaolo Basile and Claudia d'Amato and Nicola Fanizzi
Department of Computer Science, University of Bari Aldo Moro, Italy
e.ghizzota@phd.uniba.it, {name.surname}@uniba.it

Abstract

The Linked Linguistic Knowledge Graph (LLKG) is a language-independent linguistic resource designed for diachronic analysis set on well-known ontologies for linguistics. LLKG is suitable for holding information from various collections by interconnecting the entities with external resources to expand the reachable knowledge. The resources involved in this study are the Linguistic Knowledge Graph, a time-sensitive graph database for linguistic knowledge, and Etymological WordNet, a lexical resource for describing word origins. Except for the significance of the data they hold, these resources were considered aligned with the objectives of this work due to their design choices, which hinder the contribution to the cloud of Linguistic Linked Open Data and prevent the discovery of new knowledge. Figuratively speaking, we intend to burst the bubble of their isolation. To this purpose, this work focuses on translating the Labelled Property structure into Resource Description Framework Schema and adopting the lexicon model for ontologies LEMON. This work also illustrates how to enrich the graph by manually linking its entities to resources on the Web, e.g., Universal WordNet, LiLa and Wikidata.

1 Introduction and Motivations

Words originate and evolve in several scenarios: different pronunciations diverge in different languages; changes occur within the same language as historical events unfold; distinct languages come into contact and borrow words from one another. Similarly, the meanings associated with words should not be regarded as static over time, as they are dynamic and constantly evolving to reflect cultural changes. This vitality of language causes the semantics of words to undergo considerable mutations (Traugott, 2005), ranging from an utter transformation of their core to a slight shift; in particular, they can experience *pejoration* or *amelioration* when meanings become respectively more negative or more positive, or they can *broaden* or *narrow* their scope. Such mutations are often tightly correlated with the culture of the period they occur in. Consider the Latin adjective *beatus*, annotated in McGillivray et al. (2022) with five senses: "happy", "fortunate", "rewarded", "rich" and "blessed". When considering the period in which these senses occur, it is noticeable that the sense "blessed" only emerged later with the advent of Christianity, overshadowing the other senses.

Recent years have seen a rising interest in computational *Lexical Semantic Change Detection* (LSCD) (Basile and McGillivray, 2018; Tsakalidis et al., 2021; Kutuzov et al., 2018; Tahmasebi et al., 2021; Castano et al., 2022); the availability of large corpora and the development of computational semantics have stimulated numerous initiatives for capturing semantic change in a data-driven fashion. In Armaselu et al. (2022), authors have encouraged the integration of distributional approaches for Natural Language Processing (NLP) with Linked Open Data[1] (LOD) technologies, emphasising how these external resources better support the heterogeneous nature of the data relevant to this phenomenon, which include linguistic knowledge but also information on historical events and entities, as well as bibliographical and geographical data. Particularly, such technologies could be leveraged in linguistics to investigate word histories, conduct etymological research, and analyse quantitative patterns in the distribution of word senses across time and according to the authors of the texts and other textual features. The knowledge attainable from external resources can also be valuable in explaining the motives behind a change in semantics, which is often tightly bound to social and cultural aspects. This type of information can not be acquired via observing and analysing a corpus, but requires the support and involvement of external knowledge. LOD are

[1] w3.org/DesignIssues/LinkedData

based on ontologies and Knowledge Graphs (KG) (Hogan et al., 2021), graphs of data intended to convey knowledge of the real world, allowing the modelling of complex domains. Knowledge Graphs offer several advantages: *(i)* they hold semantically structured, potentially very large, machine-readable data collections; *(ii)* they can be enhanced with schemas and ontologies to define and reason about the semantics of nodes and edges, making it possible to discover implicit knowledge; *(iii)* a KG and its schema are not language-specific; *(iv)* LOD principles encourage interlinking ontologies and data, therefore it is possible to discover even more knowledge by traversing these external links. Despite these advantages, integrating LOD to help diachronic analysis has not yet been thoroughly investigated.

This work intends to *(RQ1)* design a knowledge graph for diachronic analysis *(i)* set on well-grounded ontologies for linguistics, i.e., LEMON, and *(ii)* fit for holding information coming from diverse datasets; *(RQ2)* link the entities to external resources to enrich knowledge.

The paper is structured as follows: Section 2 introduces the resources at issues while Section 3 illustrates in detail the design and the linking process behind the LLKG. Finally, Section 4 summarises our contribution and proposes future works.

2 Resources

This section briefly illustrates the resources involved in the construction of the LLKG.

2.1 Etymological WordNet

Etymological WordNet[2] (De Melo, 2014) (EtymWN) is a lexical resource for describing word origins as relationships between two terms, even from different languages, in a machine-readable network. It is intended as a network of words that can capture etymological and word synchronic and diachronic information in a lexical network; however, no word sense-specific information is considered. Relations are reported in a triple format, $\langle \texttt{lang}_a\texttt{:t}_1\texttt{, rel:relation, lang}_b\texttt{:t}_2\rangle$, where $\texttt{t}_1$ and $\texttt{t}_2$ are terms, $\texttt{lang}_a$ and $\texttt{lang}_b$ are (not necessarily) different languages.

The EtymWN graph has been mined from the 2013-09-07 version of English Wikitionary, obtaining a network of 3,000,000 terms. EtymWN models 500,000 etymological origin links, 500,000 etymological relatedness links, and 2,300,000 derivational and compositional links. Thanks to the graph representation, EtymWN makes navigating and uncovering connections between words, even unexpected ones, much more explicit; besides, network-like graphs are machine-readable and language-neutral. Nevertheless, EtymWN Achilles' heel is its own source: as a matter of fact, Wikitionary allows *anyone* to contribute, thus it is sensible to suppose that some contributions might be inaccurate or false. That is why both Wikitionary and Etymological WordNet are not to be considered indisputable sources, still they are very useful as exploratory tools.

[2] `etym.org`

2.2 Linguistic Knowledge Graph

Linguistic Knowledge Graph (Basile et al., 2022) (LKG) aims at capturing different aspects of lexical resources, such as relations between words and concepts, morphological and syntactical information. Moreover, it can cover diachronic aspects of language: the date of publication of a document and the birth and death of an author. The LKG models time-sensitive linguistic knowledge using a graph database. Its purpose is to lay the foundations for the study of word histories, for etymological research and, finally, for the analysis of the distribution of word senses not only over time but also according to the authors of the text and other textual features.

The LKG schema was designed by taking inspiration from the ontology-lexicon model LEMON (McCrae et al., 2012) and semantic networks such as WordNet and BabelNet. This graph model has been developed with the intent of modelling *(i)* relations between concepts and words, *(ii)* information about word occurrences, *(iii)* diachronic information of concepts and words. Conversely to LEMON built on RDF-S and OWL, the structure of LKG is based on the Labelled Property Graph (LPG) model, ensuring great flexibility and expressive power. In LPG both nodes and arcs are associated with unique identifiers, can be labelled and can store property values as `attribute-value` maps. Section 3 will illustrate the details of the process for converting the schema from LPG to RDF-S.

2.2.1 Data sources

LKG imports (McGillivray et al., 2023a,b) a portion of the LatinISE corpus (McGillivray and Kilgarriff, 2013; McGillivray et al., 2022), which gathers ten million word tokens that have been lemmatised and PoS-tagged. In addition, 40 selected Latin lemmas were included, of which 17 have undergone a semantic shift and 23 have maintained their original meaning. For each lemma, 60 fragments were randomly extracted from the corpus, 30 dated BCE and 30 CE, and have been manually annotated by 10 scholars with a high-level knowledge of Latin, following the DuReL framework (Schlechtweg et al., 2018) which measures the semantic relatedness of a word usage with respect to its dictionary definitions. The motivations behind the choice of LatinISE are three: *(i)* data in LatinISE are not compliant with the Linked Data principles, therefore we took on the challenge of translating it from Labelled Property Graph to Resource Description Framework; *(ii)* besides manual annotated senses, LatinISE includes metadata for each fragment valuable in a diachronic analysis setting, i.e., the author, his or her date of birth and death, and occupation, the opus it occurs in and its publishing date; *(iii)* LatinISE is the dataset of choice for Latin in the SemEval-2020 Task 1 (Schlechtweg et al., 2020), in view of assessing the contribution of LLKG to the lexical semantic change detection task.

In a Lexical Semantic Change setting, it is crucial to have a language-specific model available, as well as access to extensive corpora covering several periods. Among historical languages, Latin is one of the most represented thanks to several factors: *(i)* accessible digital data covering two thousand years of history, e.g., LiLa (Passarotti et al., 2020, 2019b), Latin WordNet (Minozzi, 2017) and LatinISE, *(ii)* extensive computational language resources specially designed for Latin are available, e.g., Classical Language Toolkit (Johnson et al., 2021), UDPipe (Straka et al., 2016; Straka and Straková, 2017), *(iii)* ancient languages offer the opportunity to study long-term lexical semantic change and Latin itself is a prime example of a language that is not only ancient but has also continued to be actively used long after the end of antiquity, undergoing various diachroinc evolution observable in a wealth of textual data (Stroh, 2007; Leonhardt, 2013).

Refinements. After comparing the schema and the graphical representation followed by a qualitative analysis of the dataset, several discrepancies were revealed, especially in the naming of classes, relations and attributes. Moreover, a few relations and classes from the schema are missing from the dataset and vice versa. A comprehensive and compact list mapping schema, graph and dataset is available in the project documentation[3].

It was noticed that eleven lemma nodes had an incorrect part-of-speech tag: they were labelled as nouns whilst, according to the list provided in (McGillivray et al., 2022), they are verbs or adjectives. To avoid downstream inaccuracies, the PoS-tags of the following words were manually corrected: *acerbus*, *adsumo*, *beatus*, *credo*, *dubius*, *fidelis*, *itero*, *licet*, *necessarius*, *oportet*, *simplex*. Finally, it was observed that four lemmas in the dataset were spelled differently, once again w.r.t. the above mentioned list: *civitas*, *jus*, *virtus* and *voluntas* were replaced with *ciuitas*, *ius*, *uirtus* and *uoluntas*, respectively.

Integration. Due to the incompleteness of the author's mapping to Wikidata, 586 sentences out of 2,398 were missing. After a manual mapping, all the 586 missing sentences, together with 82 authors, respective Wikidata entities, and 114 works, have been included in the dataset; if an author Wikidata entity was not available, `None` was used. There are cases in which the author is uncertain or unknown, but these notations were not shared among annotators (e.g., `unknown`, `[Auctor incertus]`, `No Author`, `[Anonymous]`), therefore every different notation would result in a different entity in the graph. In order to unify these notations placeholder entities `Unknown author`, `Uncertain author`, `Anonymus`, and `Various authors` have been introduced. See Table 1.

Entity	Count
`Unknown author`	79
`Uncertain author`	81
`Anonymus`	10
`Various authors`	14

Table 1: Count of each placeholder entity, for a total of 184.

Additionally, during the mapping process, it became clear that many authors were occurring in the dataset with different notations, leading to multiple separated entities in the graph when there should be just one instead. Examples are "Plautus" and "Plautus Titus Maccius", "Ovidius", "Ouidius" and "Ovidius Naso Publius", which have been unified in "Plautus Titus Maccius" and "Ovidius Naso Publius", respectively.

[3]https://anonymous.4open.science/r/LLKG-2C87/

On the other hand, there are distinct works presenting the exact same title. Consider, for instance, Ovidius's "Metamorphoses", 8 AD, and Apuleius' "Metamorphoses", 2 AD. This conflict has been solved using one of the many alternative titles of Apuleius' work, "Asinus aureus".

The code for integrating the original dataset with missing authors and fragments is available on GitHub[4].

3 Linked Linguistic Knowledge Graph

The principal objectives of *Linked Linguistic Knowledge Graph* (LLKG) are to *reorganise* and *link* the contents of LKG (§2.2) and EtymWN (§2.1). Although existing semantic networks and ontologies heavily inspire the design of LKG, it defines its custom schema instead of reusing an already existing one violating the Linked Data principles[5]. Similarly, EtymWN does not provide a reusable definition of its relations. As a consequence, these design choices hinder the contribution of the resource to the Web of Linked Data, in particular to the cloud of Linguistic Linked Data (Chiarcos et al., 2011, 2012), and, conversely, prevent the discovery of new knowledge. To put this figuratively, we intend to burst the bubble of LKG and EtymWN.

As for the former objective (3.1), this work focuses on the translation of the LPG structure into RDF-S, in conformity with the state-of-the-art method described in (Hogan et al., 2021) and adopts the lexicon model for ontologies LEMON; on the other hand, entities have been manually linked to a variety of resources on the Web (3.2). From a technical perspective, the RDFLib 7.0.0 Python package[6] was used to generate a graph in Turtle syntax. The resource is freely available on Zenodo[7].

3.1 Schema

The schema has been informally divided into five sub-graphs, namely LINGUISTIC, EXAMPLE, AUTHOR, CORPUS, DATE. The figures of the graph, a detailed report of the mapping of each sub-graph from LPG to RDF-S and the employed vocabularies are available on GitHub[8]. The following sections highlight the necessary mappings from LKG to LLKG for converting the LPG format to RDF-S in the schema description.

3.1.1 Linguistic Sub-graph.

LEMON, short for *lexicon model for ontologies*[9] (McCrae et al., 2012), makes an effort to provide rich linguistic grounding for ontologies; it includes the representation of morphological and syntactic properties of lexical entries as well as the syntax-semantics interface[10], i.e., the meaning of these lexical entries with respect to an ontology or vocabulary.

Traditional vocabularies like those offered by OWL and RDF-S do not support the definition of linguistic and lexical entities and relationships such as inflected forms, varied genders, usage notes, or the creation of a comprehensive lexical resource due to their general nature. Consequently, LEMON aims to bridge this gap by providing a vocabulary that enriches ontologies with linguistic details.

Due to the conformation with the LEMON model and the underlying translation from an LPG to RDF-S structure, the schema of the LINGUISTIC sub-graph has undoubtedly experienced the most substantial alterations with respect to its original structure. This structure adaptation is mainly grounded on ONTOLEX and VARTRANS modules: the former models the lexical entries and senses, while the latter introduces vocabulary for representing relations between them.

LEXICALENTRY. Starting from the core of this sub-graph, the lexical entry is represented in LKG by the `LexiconEntry` class, which can be specialised into `Lemma` or `WordForm`, suggesting that lemmas and entries are in some way related. On the other hand, LEMON separates these entities: `ontolex:LexicalEntry` has three sub-classes, `ontolex:Word`, which corresponds to `WordForm` in LKG, `ontolex:Affix` and `ontolex:MultiwordExpression`, whereas a lemma is an `ontolex:Form` entity linked to an `ontolex:LexicalEntry` through the `ontolex:canonicalForm` relation; the actual lemma string is a literal connected to `ontolex:Form` via `ontolex:writtenRep`.

`ontolex:Form` represents one generic grammatical realisation of a lexical entry, thus its instance alone is not enough to represent the concept

[4]github.com/pippokill/GraphLatinISE
[5]w3.org/DesignIssues/LinkedData
[6]rdflib.readthedocs.io/en/stable/index.html#
[7]zenodo.org/records/14623212
[8]github.com/Midorilly/STKG-LLKG/

[9]w3.org/2016/05/ontolex/
[10]w3.org/2016/05/ontolex/#syntax-and-semantics-synsem

of lemma and requires ontolex:canonicalForm to translate the :HAS_LEMMA from LKG. As for the lemma properties posTag and mwe, they have been converted into two distinct entities according to LEMON; in LLKG, the former is a lexinfo:PartOfSpeech entity linked to ontolex:Form via lexinfo:partOfSpeech, the latter is represented with the aforementioned ontolex:MultiwordExpression.

ontolex:LexicalEntry is connected to dct:LinguisticSystem via dct:language; even though this structure may appear identical to LKG, it is to be noted that since Lemma is a sub-class of LexiconEntry, it can be connected to Language via :HAS_LANGUAGE. This is not reflected in LLKG, where only an ontolex:LexicalEntry is associated with its respective language entity. Properties of Language iso639-1 and iso639-2 in LKG have been transposed into relations iso6391 and iso6302 as sub-properties of dct:identifier connected to dct:LinguisticSystem; additionally, relation iso6393 was included.

:{LEX_RELATION} between two LexiconEntry has found its counterpart in vartrans:lexicalRel between two ontolex:LexicalEntries. As suggested in the vartrans documentation[11], it would be preferable to introduce more specific sub-properties in place of vartrans:lexicalRel, which relates two lexical entries that stand in some unspecified lexical relation; however, LKG lacks the necessary information.

As for Etymological WordNet, an extension of ONTOLEX-LEMON vocabulary for modelling etymology, LEMONETY[12], has been designed by Khan. However, the information in EtymWN does not provide a deep understanding of the etymologies (e.g., etyma, cognate forms, respective lemmas), which is instead required by LEMONETY; furthermore, considering *(i)* the reification of every etymological link, etymology and etymon necessary according to the schema of LEMONETY, and that *(ii)* EtymWN graph counts 3,000,000 terms and approximately 6,000,000 etymological relations, it would result in a very considerable number of additional nodes. Therefore, for the time being the following relations were defined: llkg:etymology, llkg:etymologicalOriginOf, llkg:etymologicallyRelated, llkg:hasDerivedForm, llkg:isDerivedFrom, llkg:orthographyVariant. They all relate to two ontolex:LexicalEntry entities and are sub-properties of vartrans:lexicalRel, except for llkg:orthographyVariant. Notwithstanding, in light of the *do not reinvent the wheel* cornerstone, LEMONETY offers a finer modelling solution to be considered in future works.

[11]lexinfo.net/ontology/2.0/lexinfo#

[12]github.com/anasfkhan81/lemonEty

LEXICALSENSE. The second cornerstone of the LINGUISTIC sub-graph is represented by lexical senses. In LKG, they are LexiconConcept, whereas LLKG employs ontolex:LexicalSense. Lexical senses are word senses gathered into synsets, expressed in LKG as Concept and in LLKG as ontolex:LexicalConcept. The :REFER_TO link between a sense and a synset in LKG has been replaced with ontolex:isLexicalizedSenseOf. An additional relation introduced by LEMON, ontolex:evokes between a lexical entry and a concept was included in the schema.

Whilst LKG defines the :HAS_DEFINITION relation between LexiconConcept and Text to embody the gloss of the sense, LLKG employs dct:description between ontolex:LexicalSense and rdfs:Literal. This choice was made to define a more straightforward and disjoint schema since in LKG, the Text entity is used for representing both sense glosses and textual excerpts, resembling a datatype more than an actual class.

Although this is not specified in the LKG schema and graph visualisation, a SAME_AS relation occurs in the dataset; following a qualitative analysis, we concluded that it is used for relating equivalent senses from different resources, e.g., Latin WordNet and Lewis-Short Dictionary. LLKG adopts owl:sameAs. From the LatinISE dataset structure, it was clear that lexical entries are linked to senses extracted from the Lewis-Short Dictionary only, pointing to their Latin WordNet corresponding sense. Attribute resource was converted into relation dct:source linking ontolex:LexicalSense and rdfs:Resource. In the case of senses from Latin WordNet, two additional properties, llkg:wn30ID and llkg:wn31ID, were included to hold the WordNet 3.0 and 3.1 sense identifiers; a supplementary relation rdfs:seeAlso connects each sense with the LatinWordNet 3.1 URI retrieved from LiLa (see Section 3.2.2).

As concerns relations between senses, e.g., hyponymy and hypernymy, they were expressed in LKG via a generic :{SEM_RELATION}, without providing further details. With the WordNet Interface provided by NLTK[13], it was possible to reconstruct the specific relation between synsets using their WordNet identifiers. Therefore, the LLKG schema leverages the wn:hypernym and wn:hyponym relations from the WordNet schema.

At last, the "glue" relation between words and their senses :HAS_CONCEPT has its LEMON counterpart in ontolex:sense linking an ontolex:LexicalEntry entity to one or more ontolex:LexicalSense entities.

3.1.2 Example Sub-graph

The EXAMPLE sub-graph is the joining link between the LINGUISTIC and CORPUS sub-graphs and contains crucial information for the study of semantic shift of words. An example is a fragment of text in which a specific word occurs with a particular sense.

The LKG schema does not specify an example as an entity but expresses this concept with the relation :HAS_EXAMPLE between LexiconConcept and Text, with attributes begin, end and grade; similarly, LKG expresses the concept of a word occurring in a text with the relation :HAS_OCCURRENCE between LexiconEntry and Text. In LLKG the originally merged usage of entity Text for representing both a fragment from a text and the actual definition of a word sense has been split, obtaining two distinct classes: wn:Example from the GLOBAL WORDNET RDF SCHEMA and schema:Quotation from SCHEMA.ORG, linked via dct:isPartOf. As concerns the :HAS_EXAMPLE relation, the WordNet Schema defines wn:example as "an example usage of a sense or synset", connecting an ontolex:LexicalSense with a wn:Example and making the translation rather direct. Conversely, no definition of a relation between a lexical entry and an example is available, therefore :HAS_OCCURRENCE has become dct:isPartOf from an ontolex:LexicalEntry to a wn:Example. Attributes indicating the offset of a word string in an example, begin and end of :HAS_OCCURRENCE and :HAS_EXAMPLE, were collapsed into two relations powla:start and powla:end, linking wn:Example to an unsigned integer. Considering that the offset of word sense corresponds to the offset of the word form conveying it, duplicating these two properties as LKG does would result in an unnecessary redundancy.

Finally, :HAS_EXAMPLE is characterised by the grade attribute, which carries the annotation score of a sense when its word form occurs in a fragment, essential information for diachronic analysis. In LLKG, grade is a relation llkg:grade between wn:Example and a rdfs:Literal of type float.

Below is an example of the lexical entry dubious.

```
<http://lexvo.org/id/term/eng/dubious> a
     ontolex:Word ;
    rdfs:label "dubious"^^xsd:string ;
    llkg:etymologicallyRelated <http://lexvo.
        org/id/term/eng/doubt>,
       <http://lexvo.org/id/term/eng/
           dubitation> ;
    llkg:etymology <http://lexvo.org/id/term/
        lat/dubius> .

<http://lexvo.org/id/term/lat/dubius> a
     ontolex:Word ;
    rdfs:label "dubius"^^xsd:string ;
    llkg:hasDerivedForm <http://lexvo.org/id/
        term/lat/dubiam> ;
    llkg:llkgID 4161225 ;
    dct:language <http://lexvo.org/id/iso639-3/
        lat> .

<http://lexvo.org/id/term/lat/dubiam> a
     ontolex:Word ;
    rdfs:label "dubiam"^^xsd:string ;
    llkg:isDerivedFrom <http://lexvo.org/id/
        term/lat/dubius> ;
    dct:isPartOf llkg:example_4102 ;
    dct:language <http://lexvo.org/id/iso639-3/
        lat> ;
    ontolex:canonicalForm <http://lila-erc.eu/
        data/id/lemma/100177> ;
    ontolex:sense llkg:dubius-0, llkg:dubius-1,
         llkg:dubius-2 .

<http://lila-erc.eu/data/id/lemma/100177> a
     ontolex:Form ;
    rdfs:label "dubius"^^xsd:string ;
    llkg:llkgID 4039 ;
    lexinfo:partOfSpeech lexinfo:adjective ;
    ontolex:writtenRep "dubius"@la .
```

3.1.3 Date Sub-graph.

Plenty of schemata are already available for modelling persons and corpora entities; for the DATE, AUTHOR and CORPUS sub-graphs we opted for SCHEMA.ORG because of its considerably extended vocabulary, which made the translation quite direct.

LKG concretely distinguishes a TemporalSpecification in sub-classes TimePoint and TemporalInterval; the former contains the actual information about a

[13]nltk.org/

date, i.e., attributes year, month and day, the latter is related to two TimePoint nodes via startTime and endTime relations. LLKG leverages schema:Date datatype for representing both TimePoint and TemporalInterval; dates were converted according to the ISO-8601 standard date format as required by SCHEMA.ORG: YYYY-MM-DD for TimePoint and YYYY-MM-DD/YYYY-MM-DD for TemporalInterval. As a result, in LLKG schema:Date is intended as the datatype of rdfs:Literal, not a class.

3.1.4 Author Sub-graph.

LKG Person is now schema:Person, and the properties name and surname are relations schema:givenName and schema:familyName, respectively. :BORN and :DIED are schema:birthDate and schema:deathDate. Although it is not specified in the schema of LKG, nodes of class Occupation and relation HAS_OCCUPATION occur in the dataset. To this purpose, the schema:Occupation class and the schema:hasOccupation relation were employed. Additionally, the schema:Organization class was included in order to model the concept of corpora authors, which usually are research teams or organisations.

3.1.5 Corpus Sub-graph.

Finally, Text, Document and Corpus were transposed into schema:Quotation, schema:Book and schema:Collection respectively, and they are all sub-classes of schema:CreativeWork. As mentioned earlier, schema:Quotation is the result of the split of Text class: this means that for each Text node in LKG there are a schema:Quotation and a wn:Example nodes in LLKG, connected by dct:isPartOf. schema:Quotation is the class that actually holds the string of the fragment via schema:text. LKG Sentence sub-class of Text was discarded since we felt this was an unnecessary specialisation. Relation :BELONG_TO between Text and Document, Document and Corpus was translated into schema:isPartOf.

As for the :HAS_AUTHOR relation, SCHEMA.ORG provides schema:author linking a schema:CreativeWork and a schema:Person or schema:Organization; in LKG, all three classes are linked to their author. However, we found that specifying the author of both a fragment and the document it belongs to is excessive; consequently, in LLKG only schema:Book and schema:Collection utilise the schema:author relation since they most likely differ. :PUBLISHED_IN is now schema:datePublished. All three classes are also connected to dct:LinguisticSystem via dct:language, as in LKG.

3.2 Linking

After determining the resources of interest, we settled on proceeding with a manual linking via SPARQL endpoints. This section briefly describes the resources and illustrates the queries. Below an overview of which classes are linked to which resource: *Lexvo.org* for ontolex:LexicalEntry and dct:LinguisticSystem; *Universal WordNet* for ontolex:LexicalSense; *LiLa* for ontolex:Form and ontolex:LexicalSense rdfs:seeAlso; *Wikidata* for ontolex:Form rdfs:seeAlso, schema:Person, schema:Occupation and schema:Book.

3.2.1 Lexvo.org and Universal WordNet

Lexvo.org (de Melo, 2015) is a service that publishes information about numerous aspects of human language online in both human-readable and machine-readable form, contributing to the Web of Linked Data and the Semantic Web. It defines URIs for terms, languages, scripts, and characters, which are not only highly interconnected but also linked to a variety of resources on the Web. Lexvo.org also includes Universal WordNet (UWN)[14] (de Melo and Weikum, 2009). UWN is a large knowledge graph that aims at describing words, entities, and concepts in over 200 different languages in a large network structure. For each entry, UWN provides a corresponding list of meanings and shows how such meanings are semantically related. UWN includes the Princeton's WordNet lexical database (Fellbaum, 1998).

For instancing ontolex:LexicalEntry nodes, the URI of lexical entries is obtained by concatenating lexvo.org/id/term/ with the ISO 6391-3 code of the language and the entry itself, for example: ⟨lexvo.org/id/term/lat/dubius a ontolex:Word⟩.

As for ontolex:LexicalSense entries of Latin WordNet, to lexvo.org/uwn/entity/s/ was appended a string with the PoS-tag the WordNet 3.0

[14] mpi-inf.mpg.de/departments/databases-and-information-systems/research/yago-naga/uwn

identifier: ⟨lexvo.org/uwn/entity/s/a960629 a ontolex:LexicalSense⟩.

Regarding the dct:LinguisticSystem nodes, Lexvo.org provides a dump from which the URIs of entities of type lvont:Language, the preferred label and ISO 639-1, 639-2 and 639-3 codes (if defined) were fetched.

3.2.2 LiLa

The LiLa project[15] (Passarotti et al., 2020, 2019b) has built a Linked Data-based Knowledge Base of Linguistic Resources and Natural Language Processing tools for Latin. The core of LiLa is an extensive collection of Latin lemmas that serves as its foundation. Interoperability among the resources is facilitated by connecting all lexical resource entries and corpus tokens to a common lemma. LiLa also offers a SPARQL endpoint for access[16].

To fetch the URI of a Lemma node, its written representation ?written and its PoS-tag ?pos are bound to its value and posTag attributes, respectively. Since the written representation alone might point to more than one lemma, the PoS-tag is leveraged to disambiguate. Nevertheless, there are some cases in which the PoS-tag is not enough, e.g., salus: the query returns two lemmas, lila-erc.eu/data/id/lemma/123273, 2nd masculine declension of *salus, -i*, "high tide; sea; wave", and lila-erc.eu/data/id/lemma/123276, 3rd feminine declension of *salus, -utis*, "health; salutation; Salvation". Only if manually analysed it is possible to notice that the lexical entries related to the lemma *salus* in the dataset are declined forms of *salus, -utis*. Therefore, additional information such as the inflection type and the gender would make the query results more accurate. Currently all the returned URIs are retained.

```
SELECT ?lemma
WHERE {
    ?lemma ontolex:writtenRep ?written ;
    lila:hasPOS ?pos .
}
```

Regarding the sense URIs, if the attribute resource of LexiconConcept is "Latin WordNet", it is possible to retrieve its WordNet 3.0 and 3.1 alpha-numeric identifier by giving in input the alias attribute, e.g., "sour.a.02", to the NLTK WordNet interface, obtaining "02368787-a" and "02377355-a" respectively. In order to have an actual URI to bind ?lemmaURI to, this query is performed later on in the graph creation, after all the nodes and relations ontolex:canonicalForm and ontolex:sense have already been created, allowing us to navigate the graph.. ?resource is bounded to lila-erc.eu/data/lexicalResources/LatinWordNet/Lexicon. Finally, only the ?senseURI containing the aforementioned WordNet 3.1 identifier is retained.

```
SELECT ?senseURI
WHERE {
    ?resource lime:entry ?lexentry.
    ?lexentry ontolex:canonicalForm ?
        lemmaURI ;
    ontolex:sense ?senseURI .
    FILTER(regex(?senseURI,"{}")). }
}
```

In the case of attribute resource having value "Lewis-Short Dictionary," retrieving a URI was not possible: the authors of LatinISE performed a manual selection of the senses, in some cases simplifying the gloss and not providing identifiers.

3.2.3 Wikidata

Wikidata is a collaborative, multilingual knowledge graph. Serving as a shared repository of open data, it is freely accessible to everyone and can be queried via its SPARQL endpoint. Wikidata is a document-oriented database whose pivotal elements are the items encapsulating topics, concepts, or objects. Although mapping of authors and occupations to Wikidata items is provided with the LatinISE dataset, not all the authors occurring in the dataset were mapped. Therefore, an attempt was made to fill possible gaps. The listings below illustrates the queries.

The first query retrieves the Wikidata Lexeme URI ?lexeme of a lemma, given its LiLa URI mentioned in 3.2.2, wdt:P11033 ?lila.

```
SELECT ?lexeme
WHERE {
?lexeme a ontolex:LexicalEntry ;
    wdt:P11033 ?lila .
FILTER(regex(?lila,"{}"))
}
```

As concerns the query for the author, first and foremost, ?authorURI must be an instance (wdt:P31) of human (wd:Q5); then rdfs:label or skos:altLabel should match ?label because it was noticed that in many cases the name of the author provided in the dataset, ?label, does not match the label of the Wikidata item.

[15] lila-erc.eu

[16] lila-erc.eu/sparql/lila_knowledge_base/sparql

```
SELECT ?authorURI
WHERE {
    ?authorURI wdt:P31 wd:Q5 .
    { ?authorURI skos:altLabel ?label .}
    UNION
    { ?authorURI rdfs:label ?label . }
FILTER (regex(str(?label), "{}", "i"))
} LIMIT 1
```

For instance, ⟨wd:Q2039 a schema:Person⟩ refers to "Titus Livius".

On the other hand, for obtaining a ?documentURI, instead of looking at all the instances of written work (wd:Q47461344) and then filtering by label, an operation that might take too much time, the SPARQL pattern takes advantage of the information about the author to narrow the field. In this query, the author (wdt:P50) is bound to the ?authorURI value retrieved from the graph. Since in many cases the title values of Document nodes correspond to the original Latin title, they rarely match with the preferred label of the Wikidata corresponding item. Therefore, likewise author query, a check for both rdfs:label and skos:altLabel to match ?label is performed. However, several items correspond to this pattern; we are interested only in the original work. To avoid this situation, the retrieved URIs are limited to the ones having the same language (wdt:P407) as the author's language (wdt:P6886).

```
SELECT ?documentURI ?languageISO
WHERE {
    BIND (wd:{} AS ?authorURI)
    ?documentURI wdt:P50 ?authorURI .
    ?authorURI wdt:P6886 ?language.
    ?language wdt:P220 ?languageISO .
    { ?documentURI skos:altLabel ?label ;
        wdt:P407 ?language }
    UNION
    { ?documentURI rdfs:label ?label ;
        wdt:P407 ?language }
FILTER (regex(str(?label), "{}", "i"))
} LIMIT 1
```

For instance, ⟨wd:Q1155892 a schema:Book⟩ refers to "Ab Urbe condita" written by "Titus Livius", whilst the actual label of the Wikidata item is "History of Rome".

4 Conclusions and Future Work

We have introduced the *Linked Linguistic Knowledge Graph* (LLKG), a linguistic resource for supporting the diachronic analysis of language, reorganising and linking the contents of Linguistic Knowledge Graph and Etymological WordNet.

Etymological WordNet is a lexical resource that undertakes the effort of describing word origins in terms of relationships between two terms, even from different languages, in a machine-readable network. *Linguistic Knowledge Graph* captures different aspects of lexical resources, such as relations between words and concepts, morphological and syntactical information. Moreover, it covers diachronic aspects of language: the date of publication of a document, the birth and death of an author.

To this purpose, we have focused on translating the Labelled Property Graph structure into Resource Description Framework Schema and have adopted the lexicon model for ontologies LEMON. Etymological WordNet and a portion of LatinISE were loaded into our resource, and missing fragments have been integrated. Upon completion, the LLKG includes 194 authors, 406 literary works, 108 occupations, 527 senses, 7,908 languages and 2,879,193 lexical entries. Regardless of the data LLKG contains at the moment, it is important to highlight that the resource is language independent.

On the other hand, entities have been linked to various resources on the Web, e.g., Wikidata, resulting in more than 2,897,000 unique external links. Missing or incorrect Wikidata identifiers of authors were manually adjusted.

Future works include analysing the lexical and semantic relations in the LLKG to define more specific ones and integrating information about the lemmas, lexical entries, and fragments for more precise disambiguation when querying external sources. The necessity for a deeper analysis of etymological relations arose, together with the necessity of a more fine-grained vocabulary to represent them, i.e., LEMONETY (Khan, 2018). In addition to this, the integration of other annotated corpora, e.g., the LASLA Corpus and the Index Thomisticus Treebank already imported in LiLa (Fantoli et al., 2022; Passarotti et al., 2019a), can only benefit the LLKG resource.

Finally, studies on semantic change can leverage knowledge into LLKG to improve performance and provide explainability capabilities.

References

Florentina Armaselu, Elena-Simona Apostol, Anas Fahad Khan, Chaya Liebeskind, Barbara McGillivray, Ciprian-Octavian Truică, Andrius Utka, Giedrė Valūnaitė Oleškevičienė, and Marieke van Erp. 2022.

Ll (o) d and nlp perspectives on semantic change for humanities research. *Semantic Web*, 13(6):1051–1080.

Pierpaolo Basile, Pierluigi Cassotti, Stefano Ferilli, and Barbara McGillivray. 2022. A new time-sensitive model of linguistic knowledge for graph databases. In *Proceedings of the 1st Workshop on Artificial Intelligence for Cultural Heritage co-located with the 21st International Conference of the Italian Association for Artificial Intelligence (AIxIA 2022)*, page 69. CEUR Workshop Proceedings.

Pierpaolo Basile and Barbara McGillivray. 2018. Exploiting the web for semantic change detection. In *Discovery Science: 21st International Conference, DS 2018, Limassol, Cyprus, October 29–31, 2018, Proceedings 21*, pages 194–208. Springer.

Silvana Castano, Alfio Ferrara, Stefano Montanelli, Francesco Periti, et al. 2022. Semantic shift detection in vatican publications: a case study from leo xiii to francis. In *CEUR WORKSHOP PROCEEDINGS*, volume 3194, pages 231–243. CEUR-WS.

Christian Chiarcos, Sebastian Hellmann, and Sebastian Nordhoff. 2011. Towards a linguistic linked open data cloud: The open linguistics working group. *Traitement automatique des langues*, 52(3):245–275.

Christian Chiarcos, Sebastian Hellmann, Sebastian Nordhoff, Steven Moran, Richard Littauer, Judith Eckle-Kohler, Iryna Gurevych, Silvana Hartmann, Michael Matuschek, and Christian M. Meyer. 2012. The open linguistics working group. In *Proceedings of the Eighth International Conference on Language Resources and Evaluation (LREC'12)*, pages 3603–3610, Istanbul, Turkey. European Language Resources Association (ELRA).

Gerard De Melo. 2014. Etymological wordnet: Tracing the history of words. In *LREC 2014*, pages 1148–1154.

Gerard de Melo. 2015. Lexvo.org: Language-related information for the Linguistic Linked Data cloud. *Semantic Web*, 6(4):393–400.

Gerard de Melo and Gerhard Weikum. 2009. Towards a universal wordnet by learning from combined evidence. In *Proceedings of the 18th ACM Conference on Information and Knowledge Management*, CIKM '09, page 513–522, New York, NY, USA. Association for Computing Machinery.

Margherita Fantoli, Marco Passarotti, Francesco Mambrini, Giovanni Moretti, and Paolo Ruffolo. 2022. Linking the LASLA corpus in the LiLa knowledge base of interoperable linguistic resources for Latin. In *Proceedings of the 8th Workshop on Linked Data in Linguistics within the 13th Language Resources and Evaluation Conference*, pages 26–34, Marseille, France. European Language Resources Association.

Christiane Fellbaum. 1998. *WordNet: An electronic lexical database*. MIT press.

Aidan Hogan, Eva Blomqvist, Michael Cochez, Claudia d'Amato, Gerard de Melo, Claudio Gutiérrez, Sabrina Kirrane, José Emilio Labra Gayo, Roberto Navigli, Sebastian Neumaier, Axel-Cyrille Ngonga Ngomo, Axel Polleres, Sabbir M. Rashid, Anisa Rula, Lukas Schmelzeisen, Juan F. Sequeda, Steffen Staab, and Antoine Zimmermann. 2021. *Knowledge Graphs*. Number 22 in Synthesis Lectures on Data, Semantics, and Knowledge. Springer.

Kyle P. Johnson, Patrick J. Burns, John Stewart, Todd Cook, Clément Besnier, and William J. B. Mattingly. 2021. The Classical Language Toolkit: An NLP framework for pre-modern languages. In *Proceedings of the 59th Annual Meeting of the Association for Computational Linguistics and the 11th International Joint Conference on Natural Language Processing: System Demonstrations*, pages 20–29, Online. Association for Computational Linguistics.

Anas Fahad Khan. 2018. Towards the representation of etymological data on the semantic web. *Information*, 9(12):304.

Andrey Kutuzov, Lilja Øvrelid, Terrence Szymanski, and Erik Velldal. 2018. Diachronic word embeddings and semantic shifts: a survey. *arXiv preprint arXiv:1806.03537*.

Jürgen Leonhardt. 2013. *Latin: Story of a world language*. Harvard University Press.

John McCrae, Guadalupe Aguado-de Cea, Paul Buitelaar, Philipp Cimiano, Thierry Declerck, Asunción Gómez-Pérez, Jorge Gracia, Laura Hollink, Elena Montiel-Ponsoda, Dennis Spohr, et al. 2012. Interchanging lexical resources on the semantic web. *Language Resources and Evaluation*, 46:701–719.

Barbara McGillivray, Pierluigi Cassotti, Pierpaolo Basile, Davide Di Pierro, and Stefano Ferilli. 2023a. Using graph databases for historical language data: Challenges and opportunities. In *Proceedings of the 19th Conference on Information and Research Science Connecting to Digital and Library Science (IRCDL 2023)*.

Barbara McGillivray, Pierluigi Cassotti, Davide Di Pierro, Paola Marongiu, Anas Fahad Khan, Stefano Ferilli, and Pierpaolo Basile. 2023b. Graph databases for diachronic language data modelling. In *Proceedings of the 4th Conference on Language, Data and Knowledge*, pages 86–96, Vienna, Austria. NOVA CLUNL, Portugal.

Barbara McGillivray and Adam Kilgarriff. 2013. Tools for historical corpus research, and a corpus of latin. *New methods in historical corpus linguistics*, 1(3):247–257.

Barbara McGillivray, Daria Kondakova, Annie Burman, Francesca Dell'Oro, Helena Bermúdez Sabel, Paola Marongiu, and Manuel Márquez Cruz. 2022. A new corpus annotation framework for latin diachronic lexical semantics. *Journal of Latin Linguistics*, 21(1):47–105.

Stefano Minozzi. 2017. Latin wordnet, una rete di conoscenza semantica per il latino e alcune ipotesi di utilizzo nel campo dell'information retrieval. *Strumenti digitali e collaborativi per le Scienze dell'Antichita*, (14):123–134.

Marco Passarotti, Eleonora Litta, Flavio Massimiliano Cecchini, Matteo Pellegrini, Giovanni Moretti, Paolo Ruffolo, and Giulia Pedonese. The lila knowledge base of interoperable linguistic resources for latin. architecture and current state.

Marco Passarotti, Francesco Mambrini, Greta Franzini, Flavio Massimiliano Cecchini, Eleonora Litta, Giovanni Moretti, Paolo Ruffolo, and Rachele Sprugnoli. 2020. Interlinking through lemmas. the lexical collection of the lila knowledge base of linguistic resources for latin. *Studi e Saggi Linguistici*, 58(1):177–212.

Marco Passarotti et al. 2019a. The project of the index thomisticus treebank. *Digital classical philology. Ancient Greek and Latin in the digital revolution*, 10:299–319.

Marco Carlo Passarotti, Flavio Massimiliano Cecchini, Greta Franzini, Eleonora Litta, Francesco Mambrini, and Paolo Ruffolo. 2019b. The lila knowledge base of linguistic resources and nlp tools for latin. In *LDK (Posters)*, pages 6–11.

Dominik Schlechtweg, Barbara McGillivray, Simon Hengchen, Haim Dubossarsky, and Nina Tahmasebi. 2020. Semeval-2020 task 1: Unsupervised lexical semantic change detection. *Preprint*, arXiv:2007.11464.

Dominik Schlechtweg, Sabine Schulte im Walde, and Stefanie Eckmann. 2018. Diachronic usage relatedness (durel): A framework for the annotation of lexical semantic change. *arXiv preprint arXiv:1804.06517*.

Milan Straka, Jan Hajic, and Jana Straková. 2016. Udpipe: trainable pipeline for processing conll-u files performing tokenization, morphological analysis, pos tagging and parsing. In *Proceedings of the Tenth International Conference on Language Resources and Evaluation (LREC'16)*, pages 4290–4297.

Milan Straka and Jana Straková. 2017. Tokenizing, pos tagging, lemmatizing and parsing ud 2.0 with udpipe. In *Proceedings of the CoNLL 2017 shared task: Multilingual parsing from raw text to universal dependencies*, pages 88–99.

Wilfried Stroh. 2007. Latein ist tot, es lebe latein!: kleine geschichte einer grossen sprache. *(No Title)*.

Nina Tahmasebi, Lars Borin, and Adam Jatowt. 2021. Survey of computational approaches to lexical semantic change detection. *Computational approaches to semantic change*, 6(1).

Elizabeth Closs Traugott. 2005. Semantic change: Bleaching, strengthening, narrowing, extension. In Keith Brown, editor, *Encyclopedia of Language and Linguistics*, pages 124–31. Elsevier.

Adam Tsakalidis, Pierpaolo Basile, Marya Bazzi, Mihai Cucuringu, and Barbara McGillivray. 2021. Dukweb, diachronic word representations from the uk web archive corpus. *Scientific Data*, 8(1):269.

Leveraging LLMs to Automatically Construct WordNets as Bilingual Resources

Johann Bergh
yovisto GmbH
Potsdam, Germany
johann@yovisto.com

Jörg Waitelonis
yovisto GmbH
Potsdam, Germany
joerg@yovisto.com

Melanie Siegel
Darmstadt University
of Applied Science
melanie.siegel@h-da.de

Abstract

The Princeton WordNet (OEWN[1]) is widely recognized as the gold standard for both the quality and quantity of synsets it contains, with over 120,000 manually curated entries, making it one of the most comprehensive WordNets available. In contrast, non-English WordNets within the Open Multilingual WordNet (OMW) project contain significantly fewer synsets, highlighting a substantial disparity. This gap poses challenges for researchers, particularly when working in multilingual settings or with under-resourced languages, where WordNets are often unavailable. This shortfall also limits the applicability of WordNets in multilingual and minority language contexts. In this paper, we propose automated methods to construct high-quality WordNets to bridge these gaps. Specifically, we introduce a method leveraging large language models (LLMs) to generate missing lemmas. Our approach was evaluated using a manually compiled dataset, demonstrating its potential to address the synset shortfall in non-English and low-resource languages.

1 Introduction

OEWN is a hand-curated WordNet that contains more than 120,000 synsets. Most other WordNets, especially those in the OMW project, contain far fewer synsets, and some of them were constructed by means of automation, or they were only partly hand-curated. Table 1[2] gives a brief summary of the number of synsets for OEWN and some of the other important European languages. Most of them have fewer than a third of the number of synsets that OEWN has. This poses a problem not only for researchers who want to work with these languages, but also for those who are interested in using WordNets as bilingual resources. Automated methods for addressing this problem have thusfar proved to be inadequate, mainly due to stumbling blocks encountered when using machine translations. Especially for languages with fewer resources, the effort of manually creating a WordNet is often too high and the need for automatic methods is urgent.

WordNet	Language	No. Synsets
OEWN	English	120,135
WOLF	French	59,091
OpenWN-PT	Portuguese	43,895
Multil. Central Repos.	Spanish	38,512
OdeNet	German	36,268
MultiWordNet	Italian	35,001
Open Dutch WordNet	Dutch	30,177

Table 1: Details of European WordNets in OMW

The Interlingual Index (ILI) is an identifier (Bond et al., 2016) that was introduced to the OMW project to enable a synset from one language to be linked to an equivalent synset of another language. It is very important for the usage of WordNets in bilingual contexts. We have tested various ways of automatically creating new and hybrid WordNets and propose a method that allows WordNets for new languages to be created with help of Large Language Models (LLMs) with reasonable quality within 2–3 days.

The advent of LLMs and Prompt Engineering has brought many advancements in solving lexical semantic tasks. WordNets are still relevant, however, and complement LLMs in several ways. With its explicit structure and fine-grained lexical relations, WordNets can complement LLMs by offering a precise semantic network that can help models reason about language. The explainability and transparency of WordNets, which allows for the referencing of explicit semantic relationships and traceable logic, provide an advantage over the black-box nature of LLMs. Researchers have started to use LLM technology for the construction and expansion of WordNets. For example, (Wojtasik et al., 2023) generated definitions for synsets in the Polish WordNet with an LLM. (Oliveira, 2023) have added synonym, antonym, hypernym, and hyponym relations to the Portuguese WordNet prompting BERT models.

In this paper, we address the current challenges in the automatic construction of WordNets. In addition to discussing machine-translated and hybrid WordNets, we

[1]The Open English WordNet (OEWN) is a copy of the Princeton WordNet and forms part of the Open Multilingual WordNet Project. When referring to OEWN in this article, it can also be interpreted as the Princeton WordNet.

[2]Taken from `https://github.com/goodmami/wn/tree/v0.9.5` on 2024-10-11

introduce several methods in LLMs for automating the creation of high-quality WordNets. We demonstrate that the 'LLM as a judge' technique achieves a 93% success rate in predicting lemmas, highlighting its effectiveness in improving the accuracy and efficiency of WordNet construction.

The paper is structured as follows: Section 2 introduces and discusses the current challenges in automatic WordNet construction, along with related work in the field. Sections 3 and 4 elaborate on machine translation and hybrid approaches. In Section 5, we present the automated WordNet creation using large language models (LLMs). Section 6 provides a comprehensive evaluation of the proposed method, where the results generated by the LLM are compared against a ground truth.

2 WordNet Automation, the Current State

Vossen (1998) outlines two approaches for creating WordNets:

- The *merge* approach: all senses for an applicable word is compiled from scratch, with synsets that then contain all the words for a given sense.
- The *expansion* approach: synsets from an existing WordNet are used to create equivalent synsets in another WordNet.

Neale (2018) gives an outline of WordNet construction methods and best practices. The *merge* or *expansion* methods can be used independently to create WordNets, or they can be used in combination. In general, the *merge* approach is used to create higher quality WordNets, with more manual intervention, and takes longer. The expansion approach seems to be more suitable to create automated WordNets in a shorter time span, albeit at a lower quality. This approach also often uses OEWN as a base WordNet since it is of high quality, and with its more than 120,000 synsets also one of the most complete WordNets available. With the advent of the ILI, it also makes sense to work with OEWN as a base, so that the benefit of connecting equivalent synsets in different languages can be realized easily.

Machine translation plays a central role in creating automated WordNets quickly, but comes with some stumbling blocks, as reported by Siegel and Bergh (2023). Most notably, problems arise with machine translations when translating homographs (words with similar spelling but different meanings) and polysemes (words with similar spelling and closely related meanings). For example, the words 'washer' and 'bank' in English can have different meanings depending on the context, and if these words are converted into another language with machine translation, the result will not necessarily be correct, because of the missing context. Siegel and Bergh (2023) proposed a method for getting better machine translations, by providing additional context. All synsets in OEWN have a short, concise definition, and this can be used to provide the additional context for improving machine translations. This might be achieved by concatenating the synset lemma and definition before doing the machine translation. The translation of the word 'washer' from English to German is shown below:

- EWN ID: `ewn-10788571-n`
ILI: `i94042`
Lemma-Definition combination:
`washer: someone who washes things for a living`
Machine translation:
`Wäscher: jemand, der beruflich Dinge wäscht`
- EWN ID: `ewn-04562157-n`
ILI: `i60971`
Lemma-Definition combination:
`washer: seal consisting of a flat disk placed to prevent leakage`
Machine translation:
`Unterlegscheibe: Dichtung, die aus einer flachen Scheibe besteht, um ein Auslaufen zu verhindern`
- EWN ID: `ewn-04561970-n`
ILI: `i60970`
Lemma-Definition combination:
`washer: a home appliance for washing clothes and linens automatically`
Machine translation:
`Waschmaschine: ein Haushaltsgerät zum automatischen Waschen von Kleidung und Wäsche`

Though the original intention with this method was to find the most suitable ILI from OEWN for OdeNet (Siegel and Bond, 2021), the German WordNet from OMW, it can also be used to create high-quality WordNets.

As an example, the Japanese WordNet (Kaji and Watanabe, 2006)(Isahara et al., 2008) was created through a non-context-aware translation of the synset lemmas from the English WordNet, and thereafter a word-sense disambiguation method was applied to resolve possible false translations due to the missing context. In these publications an explicit measurement of the success was not given, and in a consequent publication in 2009 (Bond et al., 2009) it is reported that the WordNet has only 51,000 synsets compared to the circa 120,000 found in OEWN. Romanyshyn et al. (2024) worked on methods for adding Hypo-Hypernym Relations for the recently created Ukrainian WordNet by Siegel et al. (2023). They also experimented with a form of context-aware machine translation as part of a process of identifying Hypo-Hypernym relations for the Ukrainian WordNet, but the focus of their work was not to create a complete WordNet by automated means. Recently, some attempts have been made to compile electronic dictionaries with LLMs in non-English languages, such as in the work of Chow et al. (2024). They worked on a Singlish dictionary that contains 1,783 entries. This work was not done within the context of WordNets though, and is still very limited in scope.

3 Automated Creation of a WordNet with Context-Aware Machine Translation

To create a non-English WordNet by automated means from scratch using OEWN as a base, the only requirement is a machine translation API from English to the target language of your choice. Similar to the process described by Siegel and Bergh (2023), Figure 1 depicts the WordNet creation process. The first step would be to translate all the lemma-definition combinations in OEWN to the target language and save it to a database.

- For each lemma in each synset in OEWN:
  - combine the lemma and the synset definition with a colon
  - then translate it with translation API to obtain the corresponding translated lemma-definition pair
  - save the original as well as translated pair with the corresponding ILI and WordNet ID (of the original in OEWN) in database table

As an example, let us take the OEWN synset ewn-05933552-n:

- lemmas: `criterion` and `standard`
- definition: `the ideal in terms of which something can be judged`

The target language that we are translating into is Afrikaans (a minority Germanic language of South Africa with Dutch roots), and we use the Google Translate API [3]. After applying the algorithm, an extract of the database for this synset is displayed in Table 2. The version of OEWN we used had about 211,000 lemmas, meaning that the complete database will also have 211,000 entries after the algorithm and machine translation have been applied to all the OEWN synsets. We now have all the data necessary to construct the complete Afrikaans WordNet. WordNets are published in various file formats (McCrae et al., 2021), including the XML-based WN-LF format[4] and RDF, but we will take the WN-LF WordNet file for OEWN which can be downloaded from the OEWN website[5] or through the wn python package (Goodman and Bond, 2021) on pypi[6]. We will refer to the WordNet we are about to create as an *inferred WordNet*. Inferred WordNets are always created using the *expansion* approach. We now have to go through a series of steps to replace the data contained in the OEWN WN-LF file with the data contained in our database table with the machine translations:

- Each synset in OEWN has an ILI and a synset ID. We do not want to change the ILI, since it should stay the same across WordNets so that synsets with similar meanings in different languages can stay connected to each other. We do want to change the synset ID though, since this is language specific. Synset IDs in OEWN start with `ewn-`. We replace this with the prefix `in` with stands for inferred WordNet plus the language code; for the Afrikaans WordNet, `ewn-` would be replaced with `inaf-`. For example, `ewn-05933552-n` becomes `inaf-05933552-n`.
- Lemmas or `Lexical Entries` in WordNets are connected to synsets via `Senses`. They also have IDs starting with a prefix; in OEWN it is also `ewn-`. These IDs also needs to be replaced with `inaf-`.
- Now that we have created suitable IDs for all the WordNet elements (Lemmas, Senses and Synsets) in our target language, we also need to copy and replace the machine translated values for the Lemmas and the synset definitions to the correct places in the file. This process is a simple find and replace operation that is done by looking up the correct values in the database table with the machine translations.
- If all the above steps have been followed, we will have a valid WordNet that can be used, but one final clean-up step is still required to make it optimal. There will be some synsets in the target language that have duplicate lemmas. This is because two lemmas that form part of a synset in OEWN, might be translated into the target language as the same lemma. As an example, the OEWN Synset `ewn-05623283-n` which means 'knowing how to avoid embarrassment or distress' has two lemmas, prudence and circumspection, which are both translated into 'versigtigheid' in Afrikaans. To clean this up, the duplicate lemmas must be removed, and the `Senses` that connect the lemmas with the synsets must be restructured, so that the duplicate lemmas are not connected to the synsets any more.

The inferred Afrikaans WordNet is available online[7]. Similarly, inferred WordNets can also be created for other languages. As part of this project, Deepl[8] was used to create inferred WordNets for the most important European languages[9], and Google Translate was

[3]`https://translate.google.com`

[4]`https://globalWordNet.github.io/schemas/`

[5]`https://en-word.net/`

[6]`https://pypi.org/project/wn/`

[7]`https://github.com/pssvlng/open-afrikaans-wordnet`

[8]`https://www.deepl.com`

[9]`https://github.com/pssvlng/open-european-wordnets-inferred`

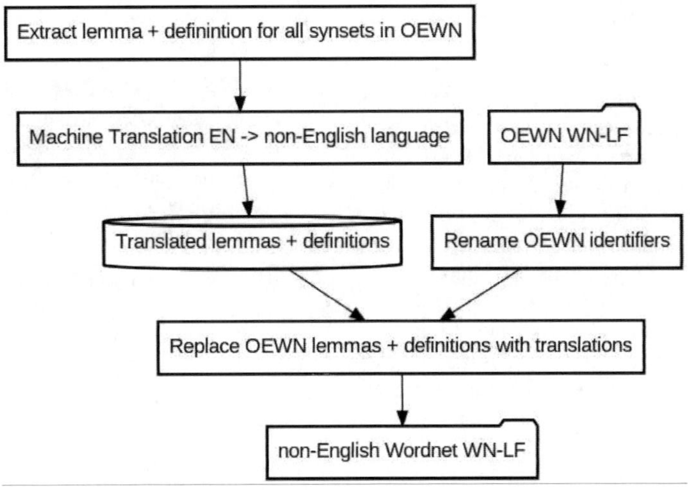

Figure 1: Creation of an Inferred WordNet

ILI	WordNet ID	Source Lemma-Definition	Target Lemma-Definition
i67968	ewn-05933552-n	criterion: the ideal in terms of which something can be judged	kriterium: die ideaal op grond waarvan iets beoordeel kan word
i67968	ewn-05933552-n	standard: the ideal in terms of which something can be judged	norm: die ideaal waarteen iets getoets kan word

Table 2: Context Aware Machine Translation for `ewn-05933552-n` into Afrikaans

used to create WordNets for some of the most important indigenous South African languages[10] and Ukrainian[11]. In theory, with this method, it would be possible to create a WordNet in any language that has machine translation support.

4 Automated Creation of Hybrid WordNets

As mentioned in the introduction, there are many existing non-English WordNets that form part of the OMW project, but have significantly fewer synsets than OEWN. Though lacking in quantity, these existing WordNets are mostly hand-curated, and therefore are of high quality. Consequently, the idea is to merge an inferred WordNet, as described in Section 3, with one of the existing WordNets in the OMW project, thereby creating a complete bilingual resource (i.e. the resulting WordNet in the target language has just as many synsets as OEWN). An inferred WordNet can also be said to be a complete bilingual resource, in the sense that it has the same number of synsets than OEWN, but merging a WordNet from OMW into the inferred WordNet will result in higher quality. A WordNet, formed as a result of merging an inferred WordNet with a WordNet from OMW, will be referred to as a *hybrid WordNet*.

As an example, we take OdeNet, and then the process of creating a hybrid WordNet can be described as follows:

- create an inferred German WordNet $inferred_1$ using the methods described in Section 3
- get a list of ILIs $list_1$ for all the synsets in OdeNet
- remove all the synsets in $inferred_1$ with ILIs in $list_1$, resulting in a modified WordNet $inferred_2$ which will have fewer synsets than $inferred_1$
- insert all synsets from OdeNet into $inferred_2$, resulting in a new WordNet $hybrid_1$ which has the same number of synsets as OEWN and $inferred_1$

Hybrid WordNets were created for the most important European languages, and are available online[12], as is an interface for browsing the Hybrid German WordNet[13].

Hybrid WordNets is a good way to retain the high quality of hand-curated WordNets, but also supplementing it with additional synsets from inferred WordNets in order to create a complete bilingual resource. Since hand-curated synsets are of higher quality, the idea is that the synsets taken from inferred WordNets to supplement hybrid WordNets will become fewer over time as more synsets are added to the hand-curated, non-English OMW WordNet; consequently improving the quality of hybrid WordNets as time progresses.

[10]`https://github.com/pssvlng/open-african-wordnets`
[11]`https://github.com/pssvlng/ua-wordnet`
[12]`https://github.com/pssvlng/open-european-wordnets-hybrid`
[13]`https://edu.yovisto.com/wordnet/`

5 Automated WordNet Creation with LLMs

Though the quality of WordNets created with context-aware machine translation is good for certain languages, there are also a few challenges. Firstly, the quality depends on the language and the machine translation API used. The quality for widely-spoken languages such as German, French and Spanish are much better than those of minority languages. Minority languages done with Google Translate such as Afrikaans proved to be of lower quality. In many instances, the machine translations are correct but use inefficient grammatical structures and repetitions. For example, the OEWN synset `ewn-05622811-n` has the following Lemma-Definition combination in English, followed by the translated Afrikaans and German:

- logic: reasoned and reasonable judgment
- logika: redelike en redelike oordeel
- Logik: begründetes und vernünftiges Urteil

In the Afrikaans translation we see the unnecessary duplication of the word `redelike`, since the machine translation was unable to find suitable words for both `reasoned` and `reasonable`. The German translation fares better and has two unique words in this case, namely `begründetes` and `vernünftiges`. By crafting suitable prompts with LLMs, better results can be obtained for the non-optimal Afrikaans translation. For example, consider the following prompt and result obtained by using GPT4[14]:

- Prompt: The word 'logic' is a noun in English, with the definition 'reasoned and reasonable judgment'. Translate the definition into Afrikaans, making sure that the correct meaning in context is conveyed. Give only the translation in your answer.
- Result: beredeneerde en redelike oordeel

Here we see that GPT4 fared much better than the machine translation and was able to find two suitable words for `reasoned` and `reasonable`, namely `beredeneerde` and `redelike`.

As mentioned previously, there is also the issue that the inferred WordNet constructed from the context-aware machine translations will always have fewer lemmas than OEWN (even though the number of synsets will be the same). This is because two lemmas that form part of a synset in OEWN, might be translated into the target language as the same lemma. Well-crafted LLM prompts can be used to 'recover' some of the lost lemmas as a result of the machine translation. Consider the example of the Afrikaans word 'versigtigheid', mentioned previously, that has the meaning 'prudence' with the definition 'knowing how to avoid embarrassment or distress'. The following prompt with GPT4 helps us to achieve our goal:

- Prompt: The Afrikaans word 'versigtigheid' is a noun that has the meaning 'prudence', with the definition being 'knowing how to avoid embarrassment or distress'. Give synonyms for the word 'versigtigheid'. Your answer should only contain a list of comma-separated words in Afrikaans.
- Result: omsigtigheid, bedagsaamheid, behoedsaamheid, waaksaamheid, sorgsaamheid, verskrokkenheid, voorbedagtheid

We also observed that machine translations do not seem to do well with slang and neologisms. For example, the English neologism 'staycation', referring to a vacation spent at home, is merely translated into 'Urlaub' in German, meaning 'vacation' in English, when using Deepl. GPT4, on the other hand, does a better job. Observe the following prompt and result:

- Prompt: Translate the English word 'staycation' into German, making sure to convey the correct meaning in context. Give only the correct word in your answer.
- Result: Heimurlaub

Here 'Heimurlaub' correctly encoded the semantic meaning in German of a vacation spent at home.

Some languages, especially Germanic languages, are very rich in compound words and other deducible linguistic patterns. LLMs can be used to 'harvest' the most significant compound words in these languages. Consider the following prompt and result in GPT4 for the German word 'Bank', which, as in English, means a financial institution:

- Prompt: The German word 'Bank' refers to a financial institution. In your answer, give only a comma-separated list of the most import compound German words for 'Bank'
- Result: Bankkonto, Bankangestellter, Bankfiliale, Banküberweisung, Bankgeheimnis, Bankkarte, Bankomat, Bankeinzug, Bankkredit, Bankkunde, Banknote, Bankverbindung, Bankwesen, Bankenkrise, Bankenaufsicht

Follow-up prompts can also be crafted to determine if one of these compound words have a connection to 'Bank' in the context of a WordNet. For example, some of these words could either be hypernyms, hyponyms, meronyms or holonyms of 'Bank'.

Finally, a word goes to the non-deterministic nature of LLMs. Non-determinism in LLMs is often criticized, since results are not always reproducible. We can use this to our advantage though, to optimize quality. To illustrate, let us take another example from the Afrikaans WordNet. The OEWN synset `ewn-05625839-n` has a lemma 'brainpower' with a definition of 'mental ability'. The machine translation into Afrikaans looks as follows:

[14] `https://openai.com/index/gpt-4/`

- breinkrag: geestelike krag

The translation of 'mental ability' into 'geestelike krag' is very clumsy and even partially incorrect, as it rather conveys the meaning of 'spiritual power' instead of mental ability. Now consider the following prompt with GPT4 that was run 3 times, obtaining different results:

- Prompt: The word 'brainpower' is a noun in English with the definition of 'mental ability.' Translate the definition into Afrikaans, making sure that the correct meaning in context is conveyed. Give only the translation in your answer.
- Result 1: mentale vermoë.
- Result 2: geestelike vermoë.
- Result 3: verstandelike vermoë.

All three of the results correctly translated the English word 'ability' as 'vermoë' instead of 'krag'. The correct translation of 'mental' is in `Result 3`, namely 'verstandelike'. In `Result 1` 'mentale' is a suboptimal anglicization, and 'geestelike' in `Result 2` is incorrect. As the second step in this process, we now craft another prompt to try and extract the correct result:

- Prompt: Which one of the following three Afrikaans phrases refering to 'Brainpower' is grammatically the most correct: 1) metale vermoë, 2) geestelike vermoë, 3) verstandelike vermoë. Give only the most correct phrase in your answer.
- Result: verstandelike vermoë

With this additional prompting, the LLM acts as a judge of the before generated information. To verify and compare the effectiveness of the different methods, we conducted an evaluation.

6 Evaluation

For the above-mentioned implementations, an evaluation was done to verify the success rate for German and Afrikaans. A selection of 697 synsets was taken from OdeNet. Hand-curated synsets in OdeNet, where the quality has been verified manually, are marked with a confidence score of 1.0 in the metadata. For each of these synsets we took the ILIs and extracted the first lemma and definition of the corresponding OEWN synset. We then obtained a translated lemma and definition in German using context-aware machine translation, and also using LLM prompts in GPT4. For example, the prompt for getting the translated English adjective 'drunk' (ILI: i5040) in German, looks as follows:

- Prompt: The word 'drunk' is an adjective in English with the definition 'as if under the influence of alcohol'. Translate the word 'drunk' into German, making sure that the correct meaning in context is conveyed. Give only the translated word in your answer.

In addition, a non-context-aware machine translation has been done, using only the lemma.

OdeNet is quite synonym-rich (with many lemmas per synset on average), and as the next step we now try to find out if our translated lemmas for LLM prompts, context-aware machine translation and non-context-aware machine translation are found in the lemma list of the corresponding OdeNet synset. For example, let us take the result we get from the prompt example above (English adjective 'drunk' - ILI: i5040) and compare it with the lemma list of the corresponding OdeNet synset:

- Prompt result: **betrunken**
- OdeNet lemma list (ILI: i5040): ['voll', 'zu', 'berauscht', 'dicht', 'voll wie eine Haubitze', 'alkoholisiert', 'breit', 'strunz', 'unter Alkohol', 'besoffen', 'blau', 'hackevoll', 'trunken', 'im Rausch', 'abgefüllt', **'betrunken'**, 'stoned', 'bezecht', 'hacke', 'strack']

Here we can see that the prompt result is found in the OdeNet lemma list and therefore verified as correct. The results in Table 3 show the number of matches (lemma found in the OdeNet synset) for each of the above-mentioned options for our selected dataset of 697 synsets. Here we can clearly see that the LLM-prompt approach fares the best with 488 matches (or 70%), meaning that these translations are verified as correct because they were found in the lemma list of the corresponding OdeNet synset. As expected, the context-aware machine translations does better than the non-context-aware machine translation, with 437 (63%) vs. 398 (57%) matches in the lemma list of the corresponding OdeNet synset. The remaining entries, which were not found in the lemma list of the corresponding OdeNet synset, are not necessarily incorrect, so these were evaluated manually. For the LLM prompts, 142 of its remaining entries were judged to be correct, while there still remained 67 errors. The context-aware translations had 140 correct results of its remaining entries, with 120 errors. Finally, for the non-context aware translations, 135 of its remaining entries were correct, with 164 errors. Therefore, for the LLM-prompt approach a total of 630 entries were correct, translating to an overall success rate of 90%. The context-aware translations has 577 correct entries with an overall success rate of 83%. Finally, the success rate for the non-context aware translations was 76%, with 533 correct entries.

As a final test, we also took all the 697 synsets, and used the approach as described in the final part of Section 5, i.e. run the prompt 3 times and then ask for the best result in a follow-up prompt (LLM as a Judge). Of the 697 synsets, 430 results were verified as correct, because they were found in the lemma list of the corresponding OdeNet synset. We also found another 86 correct entries from the manual evaluation that has already been done. In the same way, we were also able to

	LLM Prompts	Context-aware Trans.	Non-context Aware Trans.	LLM as a Judge
Automated Matches (exists in OdeNet)	488	437	398	430
Manually Verified Matches	142	140	135	215 (86 + 129)
Manually Verified Errors	67	120	164	52 (32 + 20)
Success Rate	630 (90%)	577 (83%)	533 (76%)	645 (93%)

Table 3: Matches for German (of 697 synsets)

	LLM Prompts	Context-aware Trans.	LLM as a Judge
Matches for Overlapping Subset	348	348	339 (260 + 79)
Errors for Overlapping Subset	4	4	14
Matches for Non-overlapping Subset	272	197	291 (136 + 155)
Errors for Non-overlapping Subset	73	148	53 (19 + 34)
Success Rate	620 (89%)	545 (78%)	630 (90%)

Table 4: Matches for Afrikaans (of 697 synsets)

confirm 32 errors. The remaining 149 entries were also evaluated manually, and 129 were judged to be correct, with a further 20 errors. The overall success rate for LLM as a Judge amounts to 93%, and can be seen in the rightmost column of Table 3.

For the evaluation of Afrikaans, we followed a different approach, since we do not have a hand-curated, manually verified WordNet for Afrikaans, as was the case for German. We used the same set of 697 ILIs as for the German. If the context-aware machine translation and the LLM prompts produced the same result, we suspected that the probability of correctness would be quite high, seeing that it has been confirmed by two different approaches. The 354 overlapping entries, and the remaining 343 entries were evaluated manually as two subsets. The results are presented in Table 4. In the subset with the 354 overlapping entries, 348 (or 99%) were correct, thereby confirming our hypothesis. Of the 343 entries in the second subset, 272 LLM prompt results were correct, and 197 correct for the context-aware translations. In summary, the LLM prompts did much better than the context-aware machine translations, with an overall success rate of 89% vs. 78%. Interesting to note is that of the 148 incorrect context-aware machine translations, 24 were close to correct, but had part of speech inconsistencies. This means that the translation was often correct, but, for example, was given in the noun form instead of the verb form. This problem did not occur with the LLM prompt results, and it also makes sense, since the prompts give more detailed instructions about the part of speech to the LLM, as can be seen from the example prompt shown earlier in this section.

Similar to the German, we also did a LLM as a Judge evaluation on all the synsets for Afrikaans to do a comparison. In the overlapping subset, we were able to confirm 260 correct entries from the manual evaluation already done. The remaining 93 entries were also evaluated manually, with 79 correct results and 14 errors. Similarly, for the non-overlapping subset, 136 entries were confirmed to be correct, and 19 were confirmed to be errors. Of the remaining 189 entries, a manual evaluation showed that 155 were correct, with 34 errors. The overall success rate translates to 90%; making it slightly better than the LLM-prompt approach, as can be seen in the final column of Table 4. The result sets are available online[15].

7 Conclusion

In this paper, we discussed methods for improving the quality and quantity of synsets in WordNets created by automatic means. The ILI allows us to link synsets with similar meaning in different languages to each other. Consequently, we used the OEWN WordNet from the OMW project as a base WordNet from which WordNets in other languages could be created, allowing us to also retain the link between the synsets with the ILI; therefore the resulting WordNet also is a complete bilingual resource.

Inferred WordNets created for languages other than English are realized by doing context-aware machine translations of OEWN. We referred to the usage of machine translation API for getting context-aware machine translations to construct inferred WordNets. In practice, though, we chunked WordNet lemma-definition combinations into a set of documents, which were translated and decoded, to get the results quicker. It enabled us to create inferred WordNets for any language in about 2–3 days. The lemma-definition combinations of the synsets in OEWN were chunked into 26 files and passed through machine translation, which

[15] `https://github.com/pssvlng/gwc-2025-results`

takes less than a day. The remaining part of the process is managed by automated scripts, with minor manual intervention required. This method was used to create inferred WordNets for Afrikaans, Dutch, French, German, Italian, Portuguese, Spanish, Romanian, Ukrainian, as well as some indigenous South African languages, namely, Northern Sotho, Sesotho, Tsonga, Xhosa and Zulu.

A hybrid WordNet takes synsets from a hand-curated, non-English WordNet in OMW, and synsets from an inferred WordNet of the same language, merging them into one WordNet. The high quality, hand-curated synsets from OMW are used, and the supplementation of additional synsets from an inferred WordNet results in a complete bilingual resource. In the context of this project, hybrid WordNets were created for Dutch, French, German, Italian, Portuguese, Spanish. Recently, Siegel et al. (2023) also started working on a Ukrainian WordNet (using the *merge* approach) in the context of the OMW project, using more conventional sources, such as electronic dictionaries. This development opens up the possibility of creating a hybrid Ukrainian WordNet in the foreseeable future.

We introduced some techniques that can be used with LLMs to improve the quality of existing WordNets, but indeed also to construct WordNets from scratch. The commercial LLM models, such as GPT4, provide the best quality for minority languages such as Afrikaans, but it comes at a cost. Constructing a non-English WordNet from scratch with LLMs will require well over a million prompts, and therefore might not be viable for everyone. Open Source LLM models found on platforms such as hugging-face[16] are rapidly improving in quality, while also providing more affordable pricing options. Therefore, the creation of high-quality WordNets for minority languages with LLMs is a definite possibility in the near future.

Acknowledgement

This work has partially been funded by German Federal Ministry of Education and Research (BMBF) under FKZ 16INBI001.

References

Francis Bond, Hitoshi Isahara, Sanae Fujita, Kiyotaka Uchimoto, Takayuki Kuribayashi, and Kyoko Kanzaki. 2009. Enhancing the Japanese WordNet. In *Proceedings of the 7th Workshop on Asian Language Resources (ALR7)*, pages 1–8, Suntec, Singapore. Association for Computational Linguistics.

Francis Bond, Piek Vossen, John McCrae, and Christiane Fellbaum. 2016. CILI: the collaborative interlingual index. In *Proceedings of the 8th Global WordNet Conference (GWC)*, pages 50–57, Bucharest, Romania. Global Wordnet Association.

[16]https://huggingface.co/

Siew Yeng Chow, Chang-Uk Shin, and Francis Bond. 2024. This word mean what: Constructing a Singlish dictionary with ChatGPT. In *Proceedings of the 2nd Workshop on Resources and Technologies for Indigenous, Endangered and Lesser-resourced Languages in Eurasia (EURALI) @ LREC-COLING 2024*, pages 41–50, Torino, Italia. ELRA and ICCL.

Michael Wayne Goodman and Francis Bond. 2021. Intrinsically interlingual: The wn python library for wordnets. In *Proceedings of the 11th Global Wordnet Conference*, pages 100–107, University of South Africa (UNISA). Global Wordnet Association.

Hitoshi Isahara, Francis Bond, Kiyotaka Uchimoto, Masao Utiyama, and Kyoko Kanzaki. 2008. Development of the Japanese WordNet. In *Proceedings of the Sixth International Conference on Language Resources and Evaluation (LREC'08)*, Marrakech, Morocco. European Language Resources Association (ELRA).

Hiroyuki Kaji and Mariko Watanabe. 2006. Automatic construction of Japanese WordNet. In *Proceedings of the Fifth International Conference on Language Resources and Evaluation (LREC'06)*, Genoa, Italy. European Language Resources Association (ELRA).

John P. McCrae, Michael Wayne Goodman, Francis Bond, Alexandre Rademaker, Ewa Rudnicka, and Luis Morgado Da Costa. 2021. The GlobalWordNet formats: Updates for 2020. In *Proceedings of the 11th Global Wordnet Conference*, pages 91–99, University of South Africa (UNISA). Global Wordnet Association.

Steven Neale. 2018. A survey on automatically-constructed WordNets and their evaluation: Lexical and word embedding-based approaches. In *Proceedings of the Eleventh International Conference on Language Resources and Evaluation (LREC 2018)*, Miyazaki, Japan. European Language Resources Association (ELRA).

Hugo Gonçalo Oliveira. 2023. On the acquisition of wordnet relations in portuguese from pretrained masked language models. In *Proceedings of the 12th Global Wordnet Conference*, pages 41–49.

Nataliia Romanyshyn, Dmytro Chaplynskyi, and Mariana Romanyshyn. 2024. Automated extraction of hypo-hypernym relations for the Ukrainian WordNet. In *Proceedings of the Third Ukrainian Natural Language Processing Workshop (UNLP) @ LREC-COLING 2024*, pages 51–60, Torino, Italia. ELRA and ICCL.

Melanie Siegel and Johann Bergh. 2023. Connecting multilingual wordnets: Strategies for improving ILI classification in OdeNet. In *Proceedings of the 12th Global Wordnet Conference*, pages 363–368, University of the Basque Country, Donostia - San Sebastian, Basque Country. Global Wordnet Association.

Melanie Siegel and Francis Bond. 2021. OdeNet: Compiling a GermanWordNet from other resources.

In *Proceedings of the 11th Global Wordnet Conference*, pages 192–198, University of South Africa (UNISA). Global Wordnet Association.

Melanie Siegel, Maksym Vakulenko, and Jonathan Baum. 2023. Towards UkrainianWordNet: Incorporation of an existing thesaurus in the domain of physics. In *Proceedings of the 19th Conference on Natural Language Processing (KONVENS 2023)*, pages 121–126, Ingolstadt, Germany. Association for Computational Lingustics.

Piek Vossen, editor. 1998. *Euro WordNet*. Kluwer.

Konrad Wojtasik, Arkadiusz Janz, and Maciej Piasecki. 2023. Wordnet for definition augmentation with encoder-decoder architecture. In *Proceedings of the 12th Global Wordnet Conference*, pages 50–59.

Extracting WordNet links from dictionary glosses – Latvian Wordnet example

Elīza Gulbe and **Agute Klints** and **Gunta Nešpore-Bērzkalne** and
Laura Rituma and **Madara Stāde** and **Ilze Lokmane** and **Pēteris Paikens**
Institute of Mathematics and Computer Science, University of Latvia
Raiņa bulvāris 29, Riga, Latvia
Correspondence: peteris@ailab.lv

Abstract

This paper presents a project report on methods for extending the Latvian WordNet by automated extraction of candidate semantic links. We describe our experiments with neural network classifiers applied to extract, score and rank potential synonymy and hypernymy links between senses based on the sense glosses in the Tezaurs.lv online dictionary, and provide a manual evaluation of these candidates, demonstrating 72% and 67% accuracy for synonymy and hypernymy links respectively. As the methods used are language-independent, we hope that this research would be applicable to other wordnets as well.

Keywords – Latvian WordNet, machine learning, semantic link detection, hypernymy, synonymy

1 Introduction

In this paper we describe our experiments with automated WordNet link candidate extraction to support the enlargement of Latvian WordNet (Paikens et al., 2023). The current version of Latvian WordNet consists of 11 399 words that are linked in 8 768 synsets by manually curated links. However, potential NLP applications of this data require a high coverage and motivate a search for approaches that could significantly extend this resource without excessive amount of manual linguist labor. As the underlying lexical resource – Tezaurs.lv digital dictionary (Grasmanis et al., 2023) – contains more than 400 000 entries, their sense definition gloss data is a valuable potential source for further WordNet links. While the earlier development of Latvian WordNet focused on the most frequent core words, which often are highly polysemous and required careful restructuring of the sense inventory to ensure clear separation of senses and appropriate granularity, the senses for the less common words usually are usable as-is. Motivated by the recent advances in applying language models and embeddings to link extraction, as described in the next chapter, we investigated options to automatically identify the 'low hanging fruit' of potential new WordNet links based on this data.

2 Related Work

There are several strategies for detecting semantic links between words or synsets automatically. The first strategy is to create semantic relations based on Princeton WordNet. For example, (Bakay et al., 2021) mapped eight different semantic relations semi-automatically for Turkish WordNet KeNet by finding corresponding synset and its relation to other synsets in English WordNet PWN which were then checked by human annotators.

The second strategy for detecting semantic relations is to use word embeddings. For example, (Oliveira, 2023) applied masked patterns on BERT models to identify semantic relationship between words. (Tseng and Hsieh, 2019) attempted to identify hypernymy-hyponymy relationship in Chinese by building binary classifier based on the assumption that there is a semantic relationship between a word and its composing character. A similar approach was also taken by (Berend et al., 2018) where logistic regression model was trained for hypernymy discovery, which output the likelihood of two words being hypernyms for a given query. The highest ranked candidates were then selected as the most suitable hypernyms.

Whereas (Pocostales, 2016) approached the hypernymy-hyponomy detection problem by computing an average embedding offset of 200 known hypernym-hyponym pairs to then predict the hypernyms of new words. This approach was also studied by (Kafe, 2019) showing that none of the tested offset calculations methods were able to detect symetric relations (synonymy and antonymy), whereas for asymetric relations (hyperonymy/hyponymy and meronymy) this method was able to detect semantic relationship for Skip-Gram and GloVe embeddings (Tan et al., 2020).

The third strategy is to use existing lexical resources, such as dictionaries or corpora, as the basis for the detection of semantic links. For example, earlier work on compiling lexical resources directly from monolingual dictionaries includes DanNet, a Danish WordNet, which reused sense distinctions and hypernym-hyponym relationships explicitly available in the Den Danske Ordbog to semi-automatically construct a WordNet, with missing information supplemented manually to ensure a consistent semantic hierarchy.(Pedersen et al., 2009) Whereas, in the construction of plWordNet for Polish, a hybrid method combining automated and semi-automated techniques was used.(Broda et al., 2009) Distributional methods, leveraging co-occurrence patterns in texts, and pattern-based methods, utilizing linguistic templates, were employed to extract semantic relations.

Many of the described methods focus solely on semantic relations at the word level. However, in WordNet, a synset encompasses both words and their specific senses, each linked to the same underlying concept. Building on existing approaches, we aim to leverage lexical resources, such as dictionaries, and pattern-based recognition methods to generate candidate word pairs with potential semantic relationships. To address the challenge of polysemy, this research introduces a mechanism that compares words along with their respective senses to other words and senses, enabling the detection of semantic relations at a sense level by training a neural network classifier trained on already existing Latvian WordNet dataset.

3 Candidate Extraction

Table 1 shows the unique counts of relationship types in the current Latvian WordNet dataset for nouns. For example, if a synset contains *n* records, the unique synonymy links within the synset is calculated by:

$$C(n,2) = \frac{n!}{2!(n-2)!} \qquad (1)$$

The sums of unique synonymy links are then accumulated for all synsets. For other links we calculate the unique count by multiplying the number of senses within two synsets - if $synset_1$ has *n* entries and $synset_2$ has *m* entries, we obtain **n * m** unique relationships in total which are later accumulated for the whole Latvian WordNet for nouns.

For the purpose of this research we focused only on hypernym and synonym detection because the sample count for other relation types was insufficient for the selected solution implementation as shown in Table 1.

Relation type	Unique count
synonymy	18 682
hypernymy	11 802
similar	919
holonym	811
see-also	659
antonym	274

Table 1: Unique counts of relationship types recorded in the Latvian WordNet dataset for nouns

3.1 Hypernymy

To get hypernym candidates we applied one of the rule-based extraction principles using Tēzaurs database previously studied in (Grūzītis et al., 2007) - if the principal clause consists of a noun in the nominative case, the noun is usually a hypernym of the word being explained. This approach does not map specific hypernym senses together, therefore, if $sense_1$ has a hypernym candidate $word_2$ with *n* senses, we generate *n* potential hypernym sense candidates. This approach was applied to 8000 most frequent words in the corpora for words with four or less senses thus generating 12000 hypernym candidate senses in total. The word frequency data was calculated based on the Latvian National Corpora Collection (Saulite et al., 2022)

For example, the word *lidaparāts* 'aircraft' has only one sense - *ierīce, transportlīdzeklis, kas spēj pārvietoties pa gaisu vai kosmosā* 'device, vehicle capable of moving through air or space'. In this case the extracted hypernymy candidate words are *ierīce* 'device' and *transportlīdzeklis* 'vehicle' because both of these words are included in the definition in the nominative case and belong to the principal clause of the sentence. Both *ierīce* 'device' and *transportlīdzeklis* 'vehicle' have only one meaning in their respective glosses, therefore, we generate two sense pairs as potential hypernym candidates that are later evaluated by our method.

3.2 Synonymy

For synonymy we had an unstructured data source available for the candidates - an older synonym dictionary (Grīnberga et al., 1972) that was digitized, which included both absolute and near synonyms for 5839 words. This allowed to generate potential synonym candidates using Tēzaurs database. For example, if $word_1$ has *n* senses and $word_2$ has *m* senses, in total **n * m** synonym candidates are generated. As this is a first prototype for semantic link extraction, headings with four or less senses were selected. Additionally, as the selected dictionary consisted also of less popular words we chose 7000 synonym candidates with most popular words based on the Latvian National Corpora Collection (Saulite et al., 2022).

4 Relation Detection

To detect hypernym and synonym relations between two word senses, we trained a single hidden layer neural network. We created the vector embedding representation of the dataset using a pretrained monolingual encoder-only BERT model for Latvian, provided by the HPLT project (de Gibert et al., 2024). For each relationship type in the dataset (hypernymy, synonymy, or other) **we embedded both the sense and its respective word** for the training process. Therefore, when training the model we use the candidate pair senses, their respective word and class they belong to.

During the experimentation phase, we tested different model architectures, using 20% of the entire dataset as a validation set to compare performance. We explored variations in hidden layer sizes, activation functions, and optimizers. Additionally, we performed hyperparameter tuning on parameters such as the number of epochs, batch size, and learning rate to maximize model's performance. The tuning process involved systematic experimentation with different values for each parameter to identify the optimal configuration for our dataset.

The highest validation dataset results, shown in Table 2, were obtained by training a single hidden layer neural network with the following architecture:

- Input layer - a concatenation of $word_1$ embedding, $sense_1$ embedding, $word_2$ embedding, $sense_2$ embedding of size 3072;
- Hidden layer of size 512 followed by ReLU activation function;
- Output layer of size 3 (to predict if the given input layer is synonym, hypernym or other) followed by Softmax activation function to convert logits into probabilistic distribution.

The best performance was achieved with a hyperparameter configuration of 140 epochs, a batch size of 32, and a learning rate of 1.62×10^{-5}.

After training the model, we applied it to data retrieved from the candidate extraction phase, described in Section 3, to obtain probabilities for each candidate's relationship type: synonymy, hypernymy, or other. We specifically focused on candidates with potential synonym or hypernym relations, passing them through the model to identify the highest probability of synonymy or hypernymy for each word pair. In this task, we concentrated on the highest probability sense pair within each word pair, and even if the probabilities were close, only the sense pairs with the highest probability were considered as candidates for a potential semantic link that were later evaluated manually as described in Section 5.1.

4.1 Dataset

A subset of labeled nouns from the Latvian WordNet data was used as examples for training and evaluating the classifier. The dataset includes three classes: *synonyms* (18 682 samples), *hypernyms* (11 802 samples), and *negative examples* (40 000 samples). Negative examples are derived from the Latvian Wordnet data specifically for nouns and include **(1) random negatives**: senses not classified as synonyms or hypernyms; **(2) higher-level hypernyms**: those not falling under direct hypernyms; **(3) close embeddings without relations**: word pairs with small Euclidean distances but no labeled relations; **(4) unrelated senses of related words**: instances where a word has multiple senses, with only one being a hypernym or synonym of another word, while the unrelated senses are used as negatives; and **(5) similar/also/antonyms/holonyms**: pairs not qualifying as synonyms or hypernyms, included to differentiate other relations from hypernyms and synonyms.

5 Evaluation

The evaluation of the provided solution consists of automatic validation after the completion of training process and manual evaluation of generated semantic links analyzed by linguists followed by analysis of systematic errors produced by the selected implementation method.

5.1 Methodology for manual evaluation

We conducted a manual evaluation of 400 sense pairs identified as synonyms or hypernyms. Each

Class	Precision	Recall	F1-score
Hypernymy	0.87	0.68	0.77
Synonymy	0.91	0.93	0.92
Other	0.91	0.93	0.92

Table 2: Validation dataset results

dataset was independently evaluated by three linguists. Each rater was presented with an Excel spreadsheet where each row contained a word with its gloss, as well as a candidate link target word with its gloss, highlighting the proposed specific synonym or hypernym candidate sense. The raters were instructed to evaluate each pair based on whether the senses shared either an interchangeable (synonym) or a hierarchical (hypernym) relationship. They provided a definitive "yes" or "no" for each candidate pair. We define "complete rejection" as an instance when all the raters responded with "no" and "partial rejection" as an instance when 1 or 2 raters responded with "no". Whereas "complete approval" is defined as an instance when all three raters responded with "yes".

5.2 Results

Comparing the results of the validation dataset shown in Table 2 and from manual review in Table 3 we see a substantial discrepancy between the automatic validation results from the validation dataset and the manual evaluation results where the automatic validation shows a more optimistic outcome, - 87% precision in automatic validation versus average precision of 72% for hypernyms and 91% precision in automatic validation opposed to average precision of 67% for synonyms. This discrepancy likely arises because the validation dataset consists of preprocessed entries, where meanings have been refined to ensure similar granularity, facilitating accurate link prediction. In contrast, the manually reviewed data lacks this level of pre-processing, meaning definitions are less aligned in granularity, which makes it more challenging to confirm links and leads to lower precision.

5.3 Observations

As mentioned above, there were two types of negative results: complete rejection and partial rejection (Figure 1). Approximately 20 % of proposed candidates were rejected outright in both (synonymy and hypernymy) cases. 15% of synonym candidates and 27% of hypernym candidates were partially

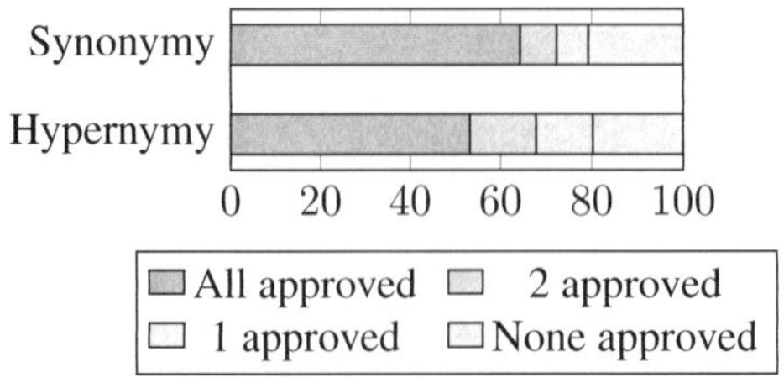

Figure 1: Approval rates based on number of approvals

rejected - at least one linguist would have approved the candidate.

The first observation of the **complete rejection** of proposed synonym pairs is that the proposed words were correct, but the senses were mismatched. However, it can be inferred that the validation tool should enable linguists to assess alternative meaning pairs when a word has multiple interpretations.

Among the completely rejected hyperonym candidates, there were cases where one of the coordinated elements of the sentence was chosen from the definition as a candidate, for example, in definition *mutācijas rezultātā radies dzīvnieks, augs, tā pazīme* 'animal, plant or the feature as a result of mutation' the first conjunct "animal" is chosen as the candidate. That indicates that the principle mentioned in the section 3.1 can give negative results in the case of coordination.

Fully or partially rejected candidates also include senses of derivatives which in Tēzaurs are often explained with schematic definitions like *ļaunprātība – 'Vispārināta īpašība –> ļaunprātīgs'* ('malice - generalized quality –> malicious') with a reference to its base word. In these examples hypernym *īpašība* 'quality' was proposed. But *īpašība* 'quality' in this gloss indicates derivation's semantic role in relation to its base word rather than names a hypernym, therefore such schematic definitions should be excluded from candidate extraction.

The **partial rejection** of proposed hypernyms and synonyms can be attributed to several factors.

First of all, a different granularity of word sense and the resulting ambiguity of definitions - the word's meaning is not sufficiently detailed to encompass the proposed hypernym. In many cases some linguists could detect these details as a reason to reject proposed hypernym, some may not. For example, the case of *ceptuve* 'bakery' where the gloss includes both a company and a building where this company acts, had a proposed hypernym *uzņēmums* 'company'. Some approved this as hy-

	Rater 1	Rater 2	Rater 3	Average	Fleiss' Kappa
Synonymy	77.50%	65.75%	72.75%	72.00%	0.76
Hypernymy	69.00%	60.50%	71.75%	67.08%	0.59

Table 3: Acceptance rate of synonym and hypernym candidates, including average score and Fleiss' Kappa

pernym, but some didn't, because of the more narrow semantic element 'building' in the hyponym's definition.

The same goes for synonym candidates - the senses of one of the candidates are separated in more detail, while the other one is given only a synonym in the definition, for example, the synonym candidates *tracis*, *troksnis*, *strīds*, *kņada*, *drūzma* ('ruckus', 'argument', 'quarrel') all can be applied both to the noise made by several living beings together, often quarreling, and to the quarrel itself, which can be obtained through active actions, speeches that create noise. The meaning of noise is not synonymous with the meaning of arguing. However, only some of these dictionary entries explicitly separate these senses, and thus proper WordNet links can not be made without restructuring the senses to ensure the same granularity.

Another reason for the rejection of candidates can be that the proposed hypernym is at a higher level, and some of the linguists thought of a more accurate direct hypernym for the hyponym. For example for *vieglatlēts* '(track and field) athlete' the proposed hypernym was *sportists* 'sportsman'. Some accepted this as its hypernym, but one considered that direct hypernym for *vieglatlēts* is *atlēts* 'athlete', whereas its hypernym is *sportists* 'sportsman'. Additionally, some proposed hypernyms may seem overly broad — such as *auklīte* 'nanny' being categorized under *sieviete* 'woman' — leading to ambiguity about whether a lower-level hypernym, such as *speciāliste* 'specialist' or other, should apply in between.

The third reason is the linguist's subjective sense of language and knowledge of the world. This leads to differences in linguists' understanding of how well a hypernym fits. For example, there may be disagreement over whether *kājsargs* 'leg guard' and *rāvējslēdzējs* 'zipper' qualify as a form of a device (the proposed hypernym for both was *ierīce* 'device'), because they are not the prototypical devices. In some cases it may differ in how literally linguists interpret sense definitions, as seen in examples like *bļitka* which means certain very low-valued paper money that was used in World War I, and the proposed hypernym *sīknauda* 'small change' where the sense definition explicitly mentions coins and technically excludes paper money.

Likewise, the candidate's evaluation can be influenced by the linguist's knowledge of the meaning of words - if they do not know the word, they will rely only on the definition, but if the other rater has more specific personal knowledge of the essential nuances of the meaning of the word, the evaluations can differ.

A lot of disagreements were observed in pairs of abstract concepts. The perception and interpretation of such concepts are strongly influenced by individual linguistic intuition, which is why some linguists may feel that the candidates are appropriate in the case of abstract concepts, while others may feel they are not.

6 Conclusions

The observed accuracy of identified candidate links means that all the links do need manual review, however, they are useful to speed up the Latvian WordNet extension as the significant number of unambiguously acceptable links can be rapidly annotated, and the manual verification of the candidate sense pairs took much less effort than annotating a similar quantity of synsets from scratch.

We identified that the addition of targeted negative examples and exclusion o certain word groups was valuable in improving the accuracy of selected candidates.

It is relevant to note that even after putting significant effort in the evaluation process, we still observe a major accuracy difference between the automatic evaluation on the previously annotated WordNet links and the manual evaluation on truly new, unseen data. Apparently the selection of dictionary entries used for the initial core Latvian WordNet and also the manual restructuring of their sense inventory means that their 'linkability' is substantially different than the rest of the dictionary. Most of the disagreements between the raters about the proposed candidates arose due to inconsistencies and imperfections in the underlying dictionary data. In several cases, a single sense in the entry should be divided into multiple senses. The manually reviewed data lacks the degree of pre-processing that is put in current Latvian WordNet development, resulting in definitions that are less consistent in granularity, thus making it more difficult to verify connections and reducing precision.

Acknowledgments

This research was funded by Latvian Council of Science project "Advancing Latvian computational lexical resources for natural language understanding and generation" (LZP2022/1-0443).

References

Özge Bakay, Özlem Ergelen, Elif Sarmış, Selin Yıldırım, Bilge Nas Arıcan, Atilla Kocabalcıoğlu, Merve Özçelik, Ezgi Sanıyar, Oğuzhan Kuyrukçu, Begüm Avar, and Olcay Taner Yıldız. 2021. Turkish WordNet KeNet. In *Proceedings of the 11th Global Wordnet Conference*, pages 166–174, University of South Africa (UNISA). Global Wordnet Association.

Gábor Berend, Márton Makrai, and Péter Földiák. 2018. 300-sparsans at SemEval-2018 task 9: Hypernymy as interaction of sparse attributes. In *Proceedings of the 12th International Workshop on Semantic Evaluation*, pages 928–934, New Orleans, Louisiana. Association for Computational Linguistics.

Bartosz Broda, Maciej Piasecki, and Stan Szpakowicz. 2009. A wordnet from the ground up. *Oficyna Wydawnicza Politechniki Wroclawskiej.*

Ona de Gibert, Graeme Nail, Nikolay Arefyev, Marta Bañón, Jelmer van der Linde, Shaoxiong Ji, Jaume Zaragoza-Bernabeu, Mikko Aulamo, Gema Ramírez-Sánchez, Andrey Kutuzov, Sampo Pyysalo, Stephan Oepen, and Jörg Tiedemann. 2024. A new massive multilingual dataset for high-performance language technologies. In *Proceedings of the 2024 Joint International Conference on Computational Linguistics, Language Resources and Evaluation (LREC-COLING 2024)*, pages 1116–1128, Torino, Italia. ELRA and ICCL.

M. Grasmanis, P. Paikens, L. Pretkalnina, L. Rituma, L. Strankale, A. Znotins, and N. Gruzitis. 2023. Tēzaurs.lv – the experience of building a multifunctional lexical resource. In *Electronic lexicography in the 21st century (eLex): Invisible Lexicography*, pages 400–418.

E. Grīnberga, O. Kalnciems, G. Lukstiņš, and J. Ozols, editors. 1972. *Latviešu valodas sinonīmu vārdnīca.* Liesma, Rīga.

Normunds Grūzītis, Gunta Nešpore, and Baiba Saulīte. 2007. Hierarhisku attieksmju izgūšana no latviešu valodas skaidrojošās vārdnīcas. *Vārds un tā pētīšanas aspekti*, 11:147–159.

Eric Kafe. 2019. Fitting semantic relations to word embeddings. In *Proceedings of the 10th Global Wordnet Conference*, pages 228–237, Wroclaw, Poland. Global Wordnet Association.

Hugo Gonçalo Oliveira. 2023. On the acquisition of WordNet relations in Portuguese from pretrained masked language models. In *Proceedings of the 12th Global Wordnet Conference*, pages 41–49, University of the Basque Country, Donostia - San Sebastian, Basque Country. Global Wordnet Association.

Peteris Paikens, Agute Klints, Ilze Lokmane, Lauma Pretkalniņa, Laura Rituma, Madara Stāde, and Laine Strankale. 2023. Latvian WordNet. In *Proceedings of the 12th Global Wordnet Conference*, pages 187–196, University of the Basque Country, Donostia - San Sebastian, Basque Country. Global Wordnet Association.

Bolette Sandford Pedersen, Sanni Nimb, Jørg Asmussen, Nicolai Hartvig Sørensen, Lars Trap-Jensen, and Henrik Lorentzen. 2009. DanNet: The challenge of compiling a wordnet for danish by reusing a monolingual dictionary. *Language Resources and Evaluation*, 43(3):269–299.

Joel Pocostales. 2016. NUIG-UNLP at SemEval-2016 task 13: A simple word embedding-based approach for taxonomy extraction. In *Proceedings of the 10th International Workshop on Semantic Evaluation (SemEval-2016)*, pages 1298–1302, San Diego, California. Association for Computational Linguistics.

Baiba Saulite, Roberts Darģis, Normunds Gruzitis, Ilze Auzina, Kristīne Levāne-Petrova, Lauma Pretkalniņa, Laura Rituma, Peteris Paikens, Arturs Znotins, Laine Strankale, Kristīne Pokratniece, Ilmārs Poikāns, Guntis Barzdins, Inguna Skadiņa, Anda Baklāne, Valdis Saulespurēns, and Jānis Ziediņš. 2022. Latvian national corpora collection – korpuss.lv. In *Proceedings of the Thirteenth Language Resources and Evaluation Conference*, pages 5123–5129, Marseille, France. European Language Resources Association.

Yixin Tan, Xiaomeng Wang, and Tao Jia. 2020. From syntactic structure to semantic relationship: hypernym extraction from definitions by recurrent neural networks using the part of speech information. *CoRR*, abs/2012.03418.

Yu-Hsiang Tseng and Shu-Kai Hsieh. 2019. Augmenting Chinese WordNet semantic relations with contextualized embeddings. In *Proceedings of the 10th Global Wordnet Conference*, pages 151–159, Wroclaw, Poland. Global Wordnet Association.

An Experiment in CILI-Based Validation: The Case of the Estonian Wordnet

Ahti Lohk[1] and **Heili Orav**[2]

[1]Department of Software Science, Tallinn University of Technology, Tallinn, Estonia
[2] Department of Computer Science, University of Tartu, Tartu, Estonia

<ahti.lohk@taltech.ee,
heili.orav@ut.ee>

Abstract

This paper presents a novel approach to validating wordnet structure by leveraging cross-lingual comparison through the Collaborative Interlingual Index. Focusing on the Estonian Wordnet, we hypothesize that the absence of a CILI-linked English synset between two consecutive Estonian synsets in a hypernymy chain may indicate a structural or semantic inconsistency. We propose a method for automatically detecting such inconsistencies and apply it to the Estonian Wordnet, analyzing the results to identify potential areas for improvement. Our findings contribute to the ongoing efforts to enhance the quality and reliability of language-specific wordnets and offer valuable insights for the development and maintenance of these resources.

1 Introduction

In the rapidly evolving field of natural language processing, resources that provide structured lexical-semantic information remain invaluable. Wordnets, as lexical databases that organize words into sets of synonyms (synsets) connected through semantic relations like hypernymy (is-a) and hyponymy (is-a-kind-of), offer a hierarchical network of concepts that support various language-related applications (Fellbaum, 1998). While large language models (Zhao et al., 2023; Naveed et al., 2023) have transformed NLP by enabling machines to generate and understand text with remarkable fluency, wordnets continue to play a critical role in tasks that require explicit semantic relationships and structured knowledge. Ensuring the quality and completeness of wordnets is therefore essential for enhancing the effectiveness of these applications and for integrating structured semantic information into advanced NLP systems.

Cross-lingual comparison offers a valuable approach to validating wordnet structure and identifying potential inconsistencies. The Collaborative Interlingual Index (CILI) provides a framework for this purpose by linking wordnet-like resources across multiple languages (Bond et al., 2016). This interconnectedness allows for the examination of synset correspondences and the detection of potential discrepancies in semantic relations across different language editions. CILI has been instrumental in enabling the integration of multiple wordnets and addressing challenges like **structural issues** such as loops or cycles in hypernymy chains, **duplicate senses** where the same concept is represented multiple times, and **semantic misalignments** between synsets in different wordnets (Bond et al., 2020). Furthermore, CILI can help identify **non-lexicalized synsets**, where a concept exists in one language but not in another, thereby supporting better multilingual alignment.

Researchers have explored various ways to utilize CILI for wordnet validation and enhancement. For instance, (Lohk et al. 2023) employed CILI to identify and potentially rectify "parentless" synsets in the Estonian Wordnet (Orav et al., 2019), highlighting the potential of cross-lingual analysis in improving wordnet structure. (Slaughter et al., 2018) demonstrated how CILI can be leveraged for cross-linguistic analysis in specific domains, showcasing its versatility in addressing domain-specific inconsistencies.

This paper builds upon our previous experiment (Lohk et al. 2023), which focused on utilizing CILI and other wordnets to validate semantic relations within the Estonian Wordnet. While our prior work aimed to automatically identify and potentially rectify "parentless" synsets by finding missing relations, this study shifts the focus to identifying existing relations that might require modification or replacement. In essence, we aim to determine whether certain established connections within the Estonian Wordnet's structure should be broken and replaced with more accurate alternatives.

This paper presents an experiment aimed at identifying potential structural inconsistencies in the Estonian Wordnet by leveraging its connections to the Open English WordNet (Oewn) through the Collaborative Interlingual Index (CILI) (McCrae et al., 2019). The focus of this experiment is on identifying cases where two consecutive Estonian synsets, connected via an IS-A (hypernym) relationship and both mapped to CILI identifiers (CILI: i1 and CILI: i2), do not have an intermediate synset between them in the Estonian Wordnet, although such a synset does exist in the Open English WordNet (see Figure 1).

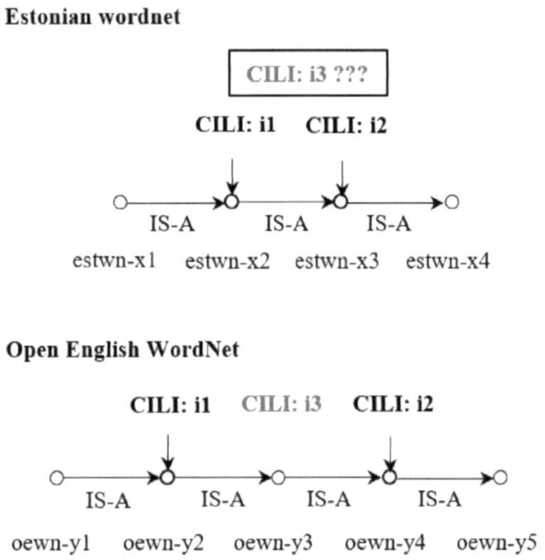

Figure 1: Identifying structural misalignments in hypernymy chains between the Estonian Wordnet and Open English WordNet via CILI

Specifically, we are interested in cases where an intermediate synset (CILI: i3), present between CILI: i1 and CILI: i2 in the Open English WordNet, is also present in the Estonian Wordnet but is not positioned between these two synsets. This indicates that while the synset corresponding to CILI: i3 exists in both wordnets, its placement in the IS-A hierarchy differs. We hypothesize that such discrepancies could reveal structural or semantic inconsistencies within the Estonian Wordnet.

The following sections of this paper will delve into the methodology employed for this analysis, present the statistical findings, and discuss the types of inconsistencies observed in the Estonian Wordnet. The insights gained from this study contribute to the ongoing efforts to improve the quality and reliability of the Estonian Wordnet and offer valuable lessons for the development and maintenance of other language-specific wordnets.

2 Methodology

2.1 Research Questions

This study investigates the potential of using the Collaborative Interlingual Index for identifying structural inconsistencies within the Estonian Wordnet. Specifically, we examine the following hypothesis:

The presence of a CILI-linked English synset between two consecutive Estonian synsets in a hypernymy chain, where this intermediate synset(s) also exists in the Estonian Wordnet but is not positioned between these two synsets, may indicate a structural or semantic misalignment in the Estonian Wordnet (see Figure 1)**. This misalignment could suggest incomplete or incorrect modeling of hierarchical relationships within the Estonian Wordnet.**

This research aims to explore this hypothesis by developing and applying a method for automatically detecting such inconsistencies within the Estonian Wordnet. The findings will be analyzed to identify potential areas for improvement in the Estonian Wordnet's structure and to assess the broader applicability of CILI-based validation for language-specific wordnets.

2.2 Data

This experiment utilizes data from two wordnets:

- **Open English WordNet (version 2023)**[1] (McCrae et al., 2019)

[1] **Open English WordNet**, version 2023. Available at: https://en-word.net/ (downloaded file: *english-wordnet-2023.xml.gz*).

- **Estonian Wordnet (version 2.6.0)**[2] (Orav et al., 2019)

2.3 Methodological Approach

To identify potential inconsistencies in the Estonian Wordnet, this study employs a systematic, CILI-driven approach. The methodology comprises the following steps:

Data Extraction and Preparation: Synset data is extracted from the XML-formatted datasets of both the Open English WordNet and the Estonian Wordnet. This includes parsing synsets to obtain their associated words, definitions, hypernym relations, and CILI identifiers.

Hypernymy Chain Construction: Hypernymy chains are constructed for each Estonian synset, tracing the "is-a" relationships between synsets from specific concepts to more general concepts. This step maps the hierarchical structure within the Estonian Wordnet.

CILI-Based Inconsistency Detection: The core of the methodology lies in identifying structural gaps in CILI linkages within the hypernymy chains of the Estonian Wordnet. For each Estonian synset's IS-A chain, we compare it against its corresponding English counterpart in the Open English WordNet (if available through CILI). Specifically, we flag cases where an English synset (linked via CILI) exists between two consecutive Estonian synsets but does not occupy the same position in the Estonian Wordnet. These cases are treated as potential structural or semantic inconsistencies, as the intermediate synset is present in both wordnets but misaligned within the Estonian hierarchy.

Lexicographical Review and Correction: The flagged inconsistencies are reviewed by a professional lexicographer to assess their validity. This step involves manual examination and correction of the identified issues within the Estonian Wordnet, ensuring that any structural or semantic problems are accurately addressed.

Result Analysis: The identified inconsistencies are collected and analyzed to pinpoint specific areas within the Estonian Wordnet that may require further examination and potential refinement.

This hybrid methodology leverages automated cross-lingual comparisons facilitated by CILI alongside manual lexicographical review to provide insights into the structural integrity of the Estonian Wordnet and to suggest targeted improvements.

2.4 Tools

The Python programming language, along with the xml.etree.ElementTree module, was used for reading the wordnets data and traversing the hierarchical structures. All codes developed for this experiment are available in the GitHub repository[3].

2.5 Limitations

This study operates under several limitations that may impact on the comprehensiveness and generalizability of the findings.

Word-net	Synset Cate-gory	Total Synsets	CILI-Linked Synsets	CILI Cove-rage (%)
OEWN	Overall	120,135	120,135	100.0%
	Used synsets	98,299	98,299	100.0%
	- Nouns	84,463	84,463	100.0%
	- Verbs	13,836	13,836	100.0%
EstWN	Overall	92,214	25,798	29.1%
	Used synsets	84,377	22,150	26.2%
	- Nouns	77,610	19,979	25.7%
	- Verbs	6,767	3,171	46.9%

Table 1: CILI coverage in OEWN and EstWN

Firstly, the coverage of the Collaborative Interlingual Index (CILI) within the Estonian Wordnet (EstWN) is notably incomplete. Out of 92,214 total synsets in EstWN, only 25,798 synsets (29.06%) are equipped with CILI links. Focusing exclusively on noun and verb synsets, the dataset comprises 84,377 synsets, of which 77,610 are nouns and 6,767 are verbs. Among these, 19,979 noun synsets (25.7%) and 3,171 verb synsets (46.9%) have associated CILI links. In contrast, the Open English WordNet (OEW) exhibits complete CILI coverage for its noun and verb synsets, with all 120,135 synsets (100%) fully linked. Specifically, the subset of noun and verb synsets

[2] **Estonian Wordnet**, version 2.6.0. Available at: `https://gitlab.keeleressursid.ee/avalik/data/-/tree/master/estwn/estwn-et-2.6` (downloaded file: *estwn-et-2.6.0.xml*).

[3] `https://github.com/ahtilohk/GWC2025`

used in this experiment includes 98,299 synsets, consisting of 84,463 nouns (85.9%) and 13,836 verbs (14.1%), all of which are CILI-equipped.

The limited CILI coverage in EstWN restricts the analysis to a subset of synsets, potentially overlooking inconsistencies present in the unlinked portions of the network. Additionally, the focus on only noun and verb synsets excludes other parts of speech.

3 Results and Discussion

3.1 Overview of Detected Inconsistencies

The application of our CILI-based methodology to the Estonian Wordnet (EstWN) revealed several types of inconsistencies within the hypernymy chains. These inconsistencies can be categorized into four main areas:

- **Imprecise Hypernyms**: Instances where a synset's hypernym is overly general and can be refined to a more specific concept (see Appendix A).
- **Cultural and Linguistic Divergences**: Differences arising from cultural or societal perspectives that affect the alignment between Estonian and English synsets (see Appendix B).
- **Taxonomic Hierarchy Issues**: Confusions within biological classifications, leading to incorrect hierarchical representations (see Appendix C).
- **Translation Challenges:** Concepts that are not lexicalized in Estonian, making direct translation or alignment inappropriate (see Appendix D).

3.2 Statistical Findings

A total of 650 Estonian synsets were reviewed using our methodology[4]. This analysis led to the identification and correction of inconsistencies in 77 synsets, thereby improving approximately 11.8% of the examined hierarchies. The corrections are detailed as follows:

- **Hypernym Refinement**: In 63 cases, the existing hypernym was refined to a more precise concept (see Appendix A). For example, refining the hypernym of "amphibolite" from "rock" to "metamorphic rock" enhances the accuracy of geological classifications within the wordnet.
- Hypernym Replacement: In 14 cases, a completely new hypernym was identified and assigned (see Appendix A). This replacement ensures that the synsets more accurately reflect the intended meanings and relationships.
- **Adjustments to English Connections**: Corrections were made to some English synset associations where errors were found, ensuring better alignment between Estonian and English WordNets (see Appendix A).

These findings demonstrate the effectiveness of our methodology in detecting and addressing specific inconsistencies. However, they also highlight areas, such as biological taxonomies, where further improvements are necessary to achieve comprehensive accuracy.

3.3 Examples of Inconsistencies and Corrections

Each example provided in the appendices illustrates the nature of the inconsistency and the corresponding correction applied. The appendices present detailed synset paths and CILI identifiers to facilitate a deeper understanding of each case.

Appendix Structure Explanation:

- **Focus path** refers to the chain of synsets in the wordnet under observation, which in our case is the Estonian Wordnet (EstWN). This path illustrates the hierarchy leading from the specific synset up to its root within EstWN.
- **Reference path** refers to the chain of synsets in the wordnet through which potential errors are attempted to be identified. For this purpose, we use the Open English WordNet (OEWN). The Reference Path includes OEWN synsets linked via CILI to corresponding EstWN synsets, aiding in pinpointing discrepancies.

[4] Out of 2052 synsets, 1959 were nouns and 93 were verbs.

- **Arrow (→)** indicates a potential problem area through a range of arrows.

- **CILI identifiers** provide a unique reference to each synset, facilitating easy navigation and cross-referencing between EstWN and OEWN.

- **Path continuation (...)** indicates that the full path from the synset to the root is not displayed in the appendices to conserve space. In actual results, the complete hierarchical path is available to provide context for each inconsistency.

3.3.1 Example 1: Refinement of Hypernyms

- **Concept**: Amphibolite (*amfiboliit*)

- **Original hypernym**: Rock, Stone

- **Refined hypernym**: Metamorphic Rock

- **Discussion**: The initial hypernym "rock" was too broad, encompassing a wide range of geological materials. By refining it to "metamorphic rock," we provide a more accurate classification that benefits applications requiring detailed geological information. This refinement aligns the EstWN more closely with precise scientific terminology, enhancing its utility for specialized fields. (See Appendix A for detailed paths)

3.3.2 Example 2: Cultural and Linguistic Divergences

- **Concept**: Riesling (*riisling*); baba (*baaba*); muffin (*muffin*)

- **Original English hypernym**: Rhine Wine, Rhenish; cake; quick bread

- **Estonian consideration**: The term "Rhine wine" is not commonly used in Estonian. Instead, Estonians classify Riesling primarily by grape variety rather than region. Additionally, distinctions such as savory versus sweet pastries are handled differently – *baba* is under baked goods and muffin is kind of pie in EstWN.

- **Discussion**: Those divergences underscore the importance of cultural context in wordnet alignment. There always are some nuances what are differently made or understood in vocabulary of edible stuff. (See Appendix B for detailed paths)

3.3.3 Example 3: Taxonomic Hierarchy Issues

- **Concept**: Ocelot (*otselot*)

- **OEWN hierarchy**:

  Ocelot > Wildcat > True Cat, Cat > Feline, Felid

- **Issue**: In Estonian, "cat" is primarily associated with domestic cats rather than the broader category of felines. This misalignment incorrectly suggests that an ocelot is a type of domestic cat.

- **Discussion**: This example highlights the necessity for standardized taxonomic terms within EstWN. Correcting the hierarchy to accurately place "ocelot" within the broader category of felines, rather than domestic cats, ensures that biological classifications are both accurate and meaningful within the Estonian context. (See Appendix C for detailed paths)

3.3.4 Example 4: Translation Challenges

- **Concepts**: Change of Magnitude, Animal Tissue, Popular Music Genre, Imperial Decree

- **Issue**: These concepts lack direct lexical equivalents in Estonian, complicating their translation and alignment within the Open English WordNet.

- **Discussion**: The absence of direct Estonian equivalents for these terms indicates a need for careful consideration when incorporating such concepts into EstWN. It may be necessary to omit certain concepts that do not align well with Estonian linguistic and cultural contexts to maintain the relevance and accuracy of the wordnet for Estonian users. (See Appendix D for detailed paths)

3.4 Hypernym Refinement

The identification of imprecise hypernyms often results from the historical development of EstWN, which has been under continuous improvement since 1998. Early contributors may have selected the best available hypernym at the time, even if a more precise term existed but was not yet included in the database. Our methodology facilitated the revisitation and refinement of these hypernyms, thereby enhancing the accuracy and utility of the wordnet. For instance, updating the hypernym of "amphibolite" from "rock" to "metamorphic rock" not only corrects the classification but also supports applications requiring detailed geological information. (Refer to Appendix A for specific examples)

3.5 Cultural and Linguistic Specificities

Discrepancies between the Estonian WordNet (EstWN) and the Open English WordNet often highlight deeper cultural and linguistic differences. These differences are particularly evident in the domains of food and drink, which serve as clear demonstrations of cultural specificities. For instance, the classification of "Riesling" illustrates how wine categories vary across cultures. While English speakers might group Riesling under the broader category of "Rhine wine," Estonians typically classify it based on the grape variety, irrespective of the production region. The classification of Riesling in the English WordNet appears problematic, as its definition states that it can originate from California, yet its hypernym is restricted to German wines.

Similarly, other examples underscore divergences in the conceptualization of everyday items. In Estonian, *baba* is categorized as a type of pie rather than a cake, diverging from the English understanding. Additionally, distinctions such as savory versus sweet pastries are handled differently in the respective wordnets.

Beyond food, cultural differences extend to other domains: for example, a "beretta" is understood in Estonian as a headdress, not simply a hat, and a "rock group" is not equated with a "dance orchestra."

These examples illustrate the importance of cultural context in aligning wordnets across languages. A straightforward one-to-one mapping is often inadequate and may fail to capture the nuances of language-specific conventions. Adaptations must respect the linguistic and cultural frameworks of individual languages to ensure classifications are both meaningful and accurate. For instance, while "country music" is invariably associated with American folk traditions in the English WordNet, it holds far less cultural relevance in Estonian contexts.

These findings underscore the necessity of culturally informed approaches when integrating or comparing wordnets. Without such considerations, the resulting classifications risk being misaligned or culturally irrelevant, undermining their utility and coherence. (Refer to Appendix B for detailed instances)

3.6 Taxonomic Hierarchies in EstWN

Biological classifications within EstWN revealed significant inconsistencies, particularly in the representation of animal hierarchies. Traditional taxonomic principles, as established by Carl von Linné, emphasize hierarchical categorization. However, EstWN's current representation often lacks this standardization. The "ocelot" example demonstrates this issue, where the hierarchy incorrectly places the ocelot within the category of domestic cats rather than the broader felines. The OEWN synset for 'cat' refers to all domestic and wild cats. Felis catus denotes the name of a group of animals in zoology and is therefore not an exact match. Establishing standardized taxonomic terms and structures within EstWN is essential for accurate biological representation and to avoid confusion in hierarchical relationships. (Refer to Appendix C for detailed paths)

3.7 Translation and Lexicalization Challenges

Certain concepts present in the Open English WordNet are not lexicalized in Estonian, posing significant translation and alignment challenges. Terms such as "change of magnitude," "imperial decree," and "popular music genre" are compositional terms and those are not frequent in Estonian. Making their inclusion in the hierarchy of hypernymy of EstWN seems too artificial. This finding suggests the need for a selective approach when incorporating concepts into EstWN, potentially omitting those that do not align with the Estonian linguistic and cultural context. Careful consideration is required to maintain the relevance and accuracy of the wordnet for Estonian users. (Refer to Appendix D for detailed examples)

4 Conclusion

This study demonstrates the potential of leveraging the Collaborative Interlingual Index (CILI) for detecting and addressing structural inconsistencies in wordnets. By applying a cross-lingual comparison methodology to the Estonian Wordnet

(EstWN), we identified and corrected various types of inconsistencies, thereby improving the wordnet's accuracy and reliability.

Key contributions of this research include:

- **Enhanced Precision**: Refining hypernyms to more specific concepts improve the semantic accuracy of EstWN.
- **Cultural and Linguistic Nuance**: Acknowledging and respecting the unique cultural contexts of different languages ensures that synset relationships are appropriately mapped, recognizing that concepts in one language may not directly correspond to those in another.
- **Standardized Taxonomies**: Highlighting the need for consistent biological classifications within EstWN.
- **Methodological Framework**: Providing a systematic approach that can be applied to other language-specific wordnets.

Our CILI-based methodology proved effective in identifying and correcting structural inconsistencies in EstWN. By refining hypernyms, adjusting for cultural and linguistic differences, addressing taxonomic misalignments, and considering translation challenges, we improved approximately 11.8% of the reviewed synsets. These findings suggest that while the methodology addresses key inconsistencies, there is room for further refinement, particularly in areas such as biological classifications and cultural-specific synsets.

4.1 Limitations and Future Work

Despite these advancements, the study is constrained by the incomplete coverage of CILI in EstWN, as illustrated in Figure 1 and detailed in the appendices. Specifically, within the Open English WordNet (OEWN), a synset must exist between arrows that is also present in EstWN. Removing this constraint could reveal additional synsets in OEWN that exist in EstWN but are currently unlinked due to incomplete CILI coverage. Our experiment identified 1,052 initial cases out of 10,056, representing approximately 10%, indicating that many potential inconsistencies remain undetected.

Future work should focus on semi-automatically identifying new CILI links for EstWN and assigning them to the appropriate synsets. One promising approach involves utilizing multilingual embedding models, such as LaSBE (Chen et al., 2020) or mBERT,(Devlin et al., 2018) to vectorize both EstWN and OEWN synsets along with their definitions. Additionally, CILI identifiers can serve as confirmatory indicators to ensure that assigning a CILI to an EstWN synset is semantically appropriate.

4.2 Final Remarks

Our findings support ongoing efforts to enhance wordnet quality and suggest that cross-lingual comparison, when thoughtfully applied, is a valuable tool for wordnet maintenance and development. By addressing both existing inconsistencies and expanding the methodological framework, this research contributes to the broader goal of creating robust and semantically accurate lexical resources.

References

Fellbaum, D. C. 1998. WordNet: An Electronic Lexical Database. Cambridge: MIT Press

Bond, F., Da Costa, L.M., Goodman, M.W., McCrae, J.P. and Lohk, A., 2020, May. Some issues with building a multilingual wordnet. In Proceedings of the Twelfth Language Resources and Evaluation Conference (pp. 3189-3197).

Bond, F., Vossen, P., McCrae, J.P. and Fellbaum, C., 2016. Cili: the collaborative interlingual index. In *Proceedings of the 8th Global WordNet Conference (GWC)* (pp. 50-57).

Chen, Y.-C., Markov, K., Yao, Y., Wei, F., Duh, K., & Lei, J. (2020). *LaBSE: Language-agnostic BERT Sentence Embedding*. arXiv preprint arXiv:2007.09405.

Devlin, J., Chang, M.-W., Lee, K., & Toutanova, K. (2018). *BERT: Pre-training of Deep Bidirectional Transformers for Language Understanding*. arXiv preprint arXiv:1810.04805.

Lohk, A. 2015. A System of Test Patterns to Check and Validate the Semantic Hierarchies of Wordnet-type Dictionaries. Tallinn, Estonia: TalTech Press.

McCrae, J.P., Rademaker, A., Bond, F., Rudnicka, E. and Fellbaum, C., 2019, July. English WordNet 2019 – An Open-Source WordNet for English. In Proceedings of the 10th Global WordNet Conference (GWC2019), pp 245-252.

Naveed, H., Khan, A. U., Qiu, S., Saqib, M., Anwar, S., Usman, M., ... & Mian, A. (2023). A comprehensive overview of large language models. *arXiv preprint arXiv:2307.06435*.

Orav, H., Vare, K. and Zupping, S., 2018, January. Estonian Wordnet: Current State and Future Prospects. In Proceedings of the 9th Global Wordnet Conference, pp. 347-351.

Slaughter, L., Wang, W., da Costa, L.M. and Bond, F., 2018. Enhancing the Collaborative Interlingual Index for Digital Humanities: Cross-linguistic analysis in the domain of theology.

Zhao, W. X., Zhou, K., Li, J., Tang, T., Wang, X., Hou, Y., ... & Wen, J. R. (2023). A survey of large language models. *arXiv preprint arXiv:2303.18223*.

Appendix A. Refinement of Hypernyms

1591. Difference found (Noun):
Focus path:
→ estwn-et-65507-n (amfiboliit) - CILI: i114043
→ estwn-et-3300-n (kivim, kivi) - CILI: i114224
...
Reference path:
→ oewn-14690548-n (amphibolite) - CILI: i114043 [Focus: estwn-et-65507-n (amfiboliit)]
oewn-14722859-n (metamorphic rock) - CILI: i114233 [Focus: estwn-et-39141-n (metamorfiit, moondekivim)]
→ oewn-14720954-n (stone, rock) - CILI: i114224 [Focus: estwn-et-3300-n (kivim, kivi)]
...

Appendix B. Cultural and Linguistic Divergences

1137. Difference found (Noun):
Focus path:
→ estwn-et-3888-n (reinvein) - CILI: i78749
→ estwn-et-497-n (vein) - CILI: i78715
...
Reference path:
→ oewn-07913175-n (Rhine wine, Rhenish, hock) - CILI: i78749 [Focus: estwn-et-3888-n (reinvein)]
oewn-07908788-n (white wine) - CILI: i78718 [Focus: estwn-et-44240-n (valge vein)]
→ oewn-07907701-n (vino, wine) - CILI: i78715 [Focus: estwn-et-497-n (vein)]
...

Appendix C. Taxonomic Hierarchy Issues

1557. Difference found (Noun):
Focus path:
→ estwn-et-63224-n (otselot) - CILI: i46619
→ estwn-et-11491-n (kaslane, kaslased) - CILI: i46591
...
Reference path:
→ oewn-02128146-n (ocelot, panther cat, Felis pardalis) - CILI: i46619 [Focus: estwn-et-63224-n (otselot)]
oewn-02127275-n (wildcat) - CILI: i46615
oewn-02124272-n (cat, true cat) - CILI: i46593 [Focus: estwn-et-11490-n (kodukass, kiisu, kass)]
→ oewn-02123649-n (feline, felid) - CILI: i46591 [Focus: estwn-et-11491-n (kaslane, kaslased)]
...

Appendix D. Translation Challenges

1530. Difference found (Noun):
Focus path:
→ estwn-et-61361-n (aktsiatükeldus) - CILI: i37705
→ estwn-et-1299-n (jaotamine, jagamine) - CILI: None
...
Reference path:
→ oewn-00439983-n (split up, stock split, split) - CILI: i37705 [Focus: estwn-et-61361-n (aktsiatükeldus)]
oewn-00364086-n (step-up, increase) - CILI: i37323 [Focus: estwn-et-662-n (rohkendamine, rohkendus, suurendus, kasv, suurendamine)]
oewn-00352311-n (change of magnitude) - CILI: i37257
→ oewn-00191991-n (change) - CILI: i36418 [Focus: estwn-et-534-n (muutmine)]
...

Everybody Likes to Sleep: A Computer-Assisted Comparison of Object Naming Data from 30 Languages

Alžběta Kučerová
MCL Chair
University of Passau
Passau, Germany
alzbeta.kucerova@uni-passau.de

Johann-Mattis List
MCL Chair
University of Passau
Passau, Germany
mattis.list@uni-passau.de

Abstract

Object naming – the act of identifying an object with a word or a phrase – is a fundamental skill in interpersonal communication, relevant to many disciplines, such as psycholinguistics, cognitive linguistics, or language and vision research. Object naming datasets, which consist of concept lists with picture pairings, are used to gain insights into how humans access and select names for objects in their surroundings and to study the cognitive processes involved in converting visual stimuli into semantic concepts. Unfortunately, object naming datasets often lack transparency and have a highly idiosyncratic structure. Our study tries to make current object naming data transparent and comparable by using a multilingual, computer-assisted approach that links individual items of object naming lists to unified concepts. Our current sample links 17 object naming datasets that cover 30 languages from 10 different language families. We illustrate how the comparative dataset can be explored by searching for concepts that recur across the majority of datasets and comparing the conceptual spaces of covered object naming datasets with classical basic vocabulary lists from historical linguistics and linguistic typology. Our findings can serve as a basis for enhancing cross-linguistic object naming research and as a guideline for future studies dealing with object naming tasks.

1 Introduction

We all choose particular names for objects when using language in daily communication (Silberer et al., 2020). Psychologists have been interested in the topic of object naming since the late 19th century (see e.g. Catell 1886), with object recognition considered a key function of the human brain (Rossion and Pourtois 2004; Hummel 2013; Wardle and Baker 2020). Beyond psychology, researchers have previously also studied its mechanisms in psycholinguistics, computational linguistics, or language and vision research (Silberer et al., 2020).

Figure 1: Object naming datasets use picture stimuli similar to this one as a visual cue. The concept BED was used in all of our datasets.

Most scholars to date conduct research monolingually and rarely attempt to explore cross-linguistic perspectives. When they do, they stumble upon issues in replicability, as the concepts they include often do not exist in all languages. Many datasets also include unique, culture-specific items, which pose a bottleneck for low-resource languages or generally any language outside of the Indo-European language family. Time and again, researchers must update or adapt their word lists for each newly tested language, which increases not only the workload but also diminishes the chance of true comparative research (see e.g. Bangalore et al. 2022; Tsaparina et al. 2011; van Dort et al. 2007), and ultimately, the generalizability of any effect across different languages (Blum et al., 2024).

The main idea of this study is to take the first steps towards making current object naming data more transparent and comparable across individual object naming datasets. We address this problem by using a computer-assisted approach to integrate object naming data from various sources into a multilingual dataset. We compare a large multilingual sample of commonly cited object naming datasets (including datasets like Snodgrass and Vanderwart 1980 and Moreno-Martínez and Montoro 2012). In this way, we can obtain insights into commonalities and differences of the semantic space covered by object naming studies. Currently, our sample consists of datasets on object naming from 30 languages and 10 language families. To allow for a systematic comparison, they are linked to norm datasets on concepts in comparative linguistics (Concepticon, `https://concepticon.clld.org`, List et al. 2025) and can therefore be directly linked to concept norms in psycholinguistics (NoRaRe, `https://norare.clld.org`, Tjuka et al. 2020).

2 Background

2.1 Object Naming

When communicating, we often encounter situations in which we want to refer to objects that surround us. While simply pointing to them is possible, we typically use language to refer to these objects, that is, we *name* them. This way, we introduce them into the conversation or direct our conversation partners to them. In disciplines such as psycholinguistics or language and vision research, object naming is an important task that scientists use to gain insights into how humans access and select names for objects in their environment. To study the cognitive processes of converting visual stimuli into semantic concepts, pictures are often used as a visual cue (Ghasisin et al., 2015) – for an example see Figure 1. Scholars in this field of research construct concept lists along with picture-pairings and use them to investigate various research questions such as language production and processing (Tomaschek and Tucker, 2023), aging of the human brain (Connor et al., 2004), aphasia (Paradis, 2011), developmental language disorders (Araújo et al., 2011), or also as a tool for the development and fine-tuning of models in natural language processing (Krishna et al., 2016; Silberer et al., 2020). The extensive use of object naming datasets across a broad range of fields shows that this kind of data might deserve more widespread attention by scholars interested in meaning and semantics.

2.2 Concepticons and WordNets

WordNets represent one of the most widespread computer-assisted approaches to meaning and have proven extremely useful in handling various problems in lexical semantics (Rudnicka et al., 2019). When dealing with cross-linguistic resources aiming to compare words and their meanings across multiple languages, however, the use of *Concepticons* (Gaizauskas et al., 1997) presents a straightforward alternative. While a WordNet can be understood as a collection of words in a given language that are assigned to a given number of senses, with the senses being linked to each other by an ontology, a Concepticon seeks to link concepts across multiple languages. The concepts themselves are usually taken from questionnaires or concept lists that are traditionally compiled in historical linguistics, linguistic typology, or language documentation, in order to assemble lexical items for a given language that can be easily compared with lexical items from other languages that express similar or identical meanings.

2.3 The CLLD Concepticon

With the CLLD Concepticon (List et al. 2025, `https://concepticon.clld.org`), a large Concepticon has been compiled that links several hundred concept lists and questionnaires that are used in historical linguistics (Swadesh, 1955), cognitive linguistics (Nicholas et al., 1989), and psycholinguistics (Snodgrass and Vanderwart, 1980) to a common concept space. This space consists of more than 4000 different *concept sets* that are individually defined and linked to individual *elicitation glosses* in individual concept lists. Apart from the data and the web application that can be used to browse through the datasets, the CLLD Concepticon has also established a workflow for the linking of concept lists, which makes use of computer-assisted techniques, providing automatic methods that can be used for the mapping of concept lists to the CLLD Concepticon (List, 2022), and guidelines for individual and collaborative annotation (Tjuka 2020, see also Tjuka et al. 2023).

2.4 Norms, Ratings, and Relations

Apart from being useful for the design and investigation of cross-linguistic questionnaires, the CLLD Concepticon can also be used as the basis to increase and enrich all datasets that can be represented in the form of a concept list. An

#	Language	Dataset	Reference
1	Arabic	Boukadi-2015-348, Dunabeitia-2022-500	Boukadi et al. 2015, Duñabeitia et al. 2022
2	Hindi	Ramanujan-2019-158	Ramanujan and Weekes 2019
3	Russian	Tsaparina-2011-260, Dunabeitia-2022-500	Tsaparina et al. 2011, Duñabeitia et al. 2022
4	Catalan	Dunabeitia-2022-500	Duñabeitia et al. 2022
5	German	Dunabeitia-2018-750, Dunabeitia-2022-500	Duñabeitia et al. 2018, Duñabeitia et al. 2022
6	Hungarian	Dunabeitia-2022-500	Duñabeitia et al. 2022
7	Slovak	Dunabeitia-2022-500	Duñabeitia et al. 2022
8	Czech	Dunabeitia-2022-500	Duñabeitia et al. 2022
9	Japanese	Nishimoto-2005-359	Nishimoto et al. 2005
10	Turkish	Raman-2013-260, Dunabeitia-2022-500	Raman et al. 2013, Duñabeitia et al. 2022
11	Croatian	Rogic-2013-346	Rogić et al. 2013
12	Welsh	Dunabeitia-2022-500	Duñabeitia et al. 2022
13	Norwegian	Dunabeitia-2022-500	Duñabeitia et al. 2022
14	Basque	Dunabeitia-2022-500	Duñabeitia et al. 2022
15	Cantonese	Zhong-2024-1286	Zhong et al. 2024
16	Serbian	Dunabeitia-2022-500	Duñabeitia et al. 2022
17	Korean	Hwang-2021-60, Dunabeitia-2022-500	Hwang et al. 2021, Duñabeitia et al. 2022
18	Malay	vanDort-2007-50, Dunabeitia-2022-500	van Dort et al. 2007, Duñabeitia et al. 2022
19	Dutch	Shao-2016-327,Dunabeitia-2018-750, Dunabeitia-2022-500	Shao and Stiegert 2016, Duñabeitia et al. 2018, Duñabeitia et al. 2022
20	Greek	Dimitropoulou-2009-260	Dimitropoulou et al. 2009
21	Mandarin	Liu-2011-435	Liu et al. 2011
22	Hebrew	Dunabeitia-2022-500	Duñabeitia et al. 2022
23	Spanish	MorenoMartinez-2012-360, Dunabeitia-2018-750, Dunabeitia-2022-500	Moreno-Martínez and Montoro 2012, Duñabeitia et al. 2018, Duñabeitia et al. 2022
24	Kannada	Bangalore-2022-180	Bangalore et al. 2022
25	French	Dunabeitia-2018-750, Dunabeitia-2018-750	Duñabeitia et al. 2018
26	English	Snodgrass-1980-260, Dunabeitia-2018-750, Dunabeitia-2022-500	Snodgrass and Vanderwart 1980, Duñabeitia et al. 2018, Duñabeitia et al. 2022
27	Polish	Dunabeitia-2022-500	Duñabeitia et al. 2022
28	Finnish	Dunabeitia-2022-500	Duñabeitia et al. 2022
29	Italian	Dunabeitia-2018-750, Dunabeitia-2022-500	Duñabeitia et al. 2022
30	Portuguese	Dunabeitia-2022-500	Duñabeitia et al. 2022

Table 1: Languages covered in our multilingual sample and their corresponding datasets.

example for this reuse potential is the Database of *Norms, Ratings, and Relations of Words and Concepts* (NoRaRe, Tjuka et al. 2022, `https://norare.clld.org/`). This database builds on the CLLD Concepticon to harvest various kinds of speech norms, ratings, and additional kinds of semantic metadata (including data from the Open Multilingual Wordnet project, Bond and Foster 2013), that are typically compiled in psycholinguistics and computational linguistics, but barely integrated across individual languages (Tjuka et al., 2020).

While a full integration of WordNet resources has not been approached so far, neither within the CLLD Concepticon, nor within the NoRaRe database, it is important to emphasize that the lack of integration is not due to the impossibility to integrate WordNets and Concepticons, but rather due to the lack of resources to carry out this task.

3 Materials and Methods

3.1 Materials

For our analysis, we compiled and investigated 17 distinct object naming datasets of various sizes featuring 30 languages from 10 different language families. A detailed overview can be found in Table 1, with a comprehensive list of all covered languages.

3.2 Methods

We mapped all concepts present in our object naming datasets onto existing Concepticon *concept sets* using the standard workflow accessible to everybody using the `PyConcepticon` library (Forkel et al. 2021, `https://pypi.org/project/pyconcepticon`, for a detailed description and further requirements see Tjuka 2020). After the initial automatic mapping was finished, we manually

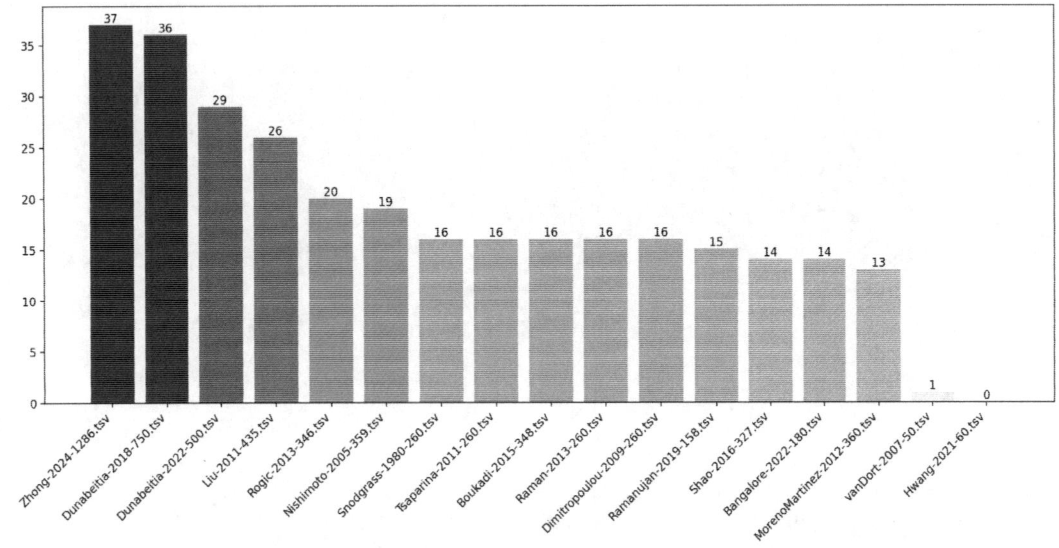

Figure 2: Overlap of our object naming datasets with the Swadesh (1955) list in historical linguistics.

checked all entries. In cases, where concepts were matched to incorrect or multiple *concept sets*, we corrected them. Similarly, if no *concept set* was found for certain concepts, but they appeared frequently across our datasets, a new *concept set* was introduced – e.g. PIANO (INSTRUMENT) and TOP (TOY), alongside a short definition. In total, we have introduced 42 new *concept set* to Concepticon, and once this was done, we submitted all of the datasets and new *concept sets* to the public repository of the Concepticon project (`https://github.com/concepticon/concepticon-data`) and had them reviewed by a team of Concepticon editors for inclusion in the version 3.3 of the CLLD Concepticon (List et al., 2025).

Subsequently, we conducted multiple exploratory analyses of the data. Firstly, we ran a frequency analysis of concepts from all languages, that appeared across all or most datasets. This helped us to identify to which degree concepts differ regarding their suitability for object naming across languages. Secondly, we were interested to see which of the concepts included in our datasets belong to the realm of *basic vocabulary* (Swadesh, 1955). Using the nouns in the 100 item concept list that Swadesh (1955) proposed for the purpose of historical language comparison, we tried to identify which basic concepts recur in object naming studies. Lastly, we assessed all datasets for concepts that only appeared once within the sample in order to get a better understanding regarding the amount of idiosyncratic items in object naming studies.

3.3 Implementation

All comparisons, frequency analyses, and visualizations were conducted with the help of Python scripts. All data and code needed to replicate the studies have been curated on GitHub (Version 0.3, `https://github.com/calc-project/object-naming-data`) and archived with Zenodo (`https://doi.org/10.5281/zenodo.14628417`).

4 Examples

In the following, we illustrate how the linked concept lists can be put to direct use, by assessing the amount of basic vocabulary items in object naming data and by discussing recurring and unique concepts in object naming questionnaires.

4.1 Basic Vocabulary

Most object-naming datasets strive to be applicable and relevant across many different cultures and as many languages as possible, to facilitate comparative research. To achieve this, one should elicit words for such concepts that exist in all of the chosen languages. Our analysis, however, revealed that this is not always the case in object naming datasets (for more detail, see Sections 4.2 and 4.3). In historical linguistics, concepts that are expressed regularly by individual words across as many languages as possible have been investigated for a long time in the context of the so-called *basic vocabulary*. Popularized by Morris Swadesh (1909–1967), the

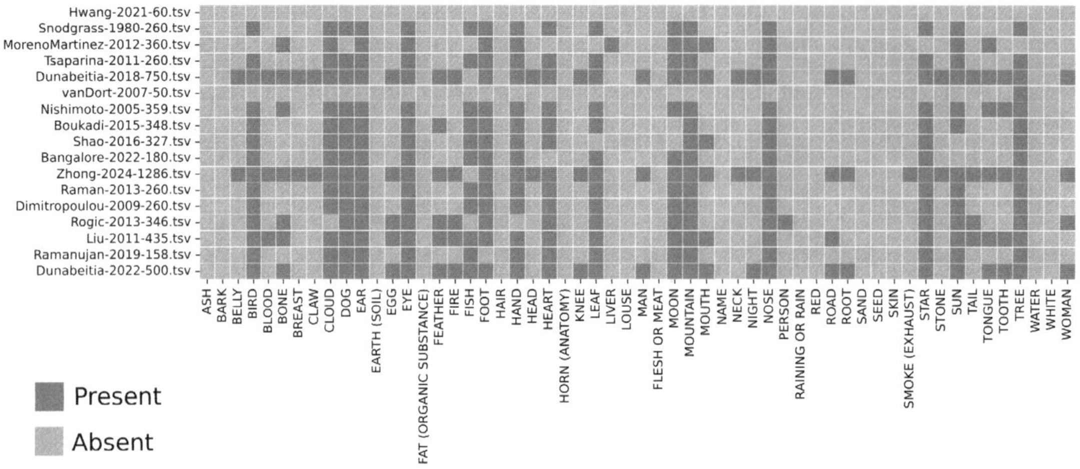

Figure 3: Swadesh concepts in the object-naming datasets (nouns). The y-axis represents the ID of each individual dataset, while the x-axis displays all 56 nouns extracted from the Swadesh (1955) list.

idea "that certain parts of the lexicon of human languages are universal, stable over time, and rather resistant to borrowing" (List et al., 2016, 2393) has been fascinating historical linguists for a long time. When dealing with object naming data derived from object naming studies, it may therefore be interesting to test to which degree the basic concepts proposed by historical linguists overlap with the concepts selected by psychologists conducting object namings studies. To answer this question, we compared all our datasets with the basic concepts in Swadesh's list of 100 items (Swadesh, 1955), from which we selected all 56 nouns, given that object naming uses primarily nouns as stimuli. We assessed our datasets for overlap with this list of supposedly stable and universally expressed concepts, looking at the number of basic concepts used across object naming datasets, as well as investigating the particular basic concepts employed by particular datasets. The results show that most datasets employ very few basic concepts. With a decreasing amount of concepts in the dataset in general, the amount of basic concepts also declines. The largest included dataset, Zhong et al. 2024, with a total of 1286 items, contained only 37 of Swadesh's basic concepts. The regularly cited Snodgrass and Vanderwart (1980) dataset, and datasets inspired by it, yielded between 14 and 16 basic concepts from the list of 56 nouns. One dataset in our sample did not include any of Swadesh's basic concepts at all (Hwang et al., 2021). To further elaborate on our analysis, we also looked into the specific basic concepts that the lists include. The results of both analyses are presented in Figures 2 and 3.

Figure 4: A total of 42 recurring concepts in at least 15 out of 17 datasets - we find BED in all 17 of them.

4.2 Recurring Concepts Across Languages

Having mapped such a large number of datasets from as many as 30 languages, we sought to determine whether there was any common ground or standard in the authors' choice of concepts. We hypothesized that this would be the case. Early investigations have shown that this overlap would, however, be much smaller than expected. At the end, we compared all of our 17 datasets with each other and discovered that the overlap consists of exactly one word: BED – hence our title. We therefore decided to estimate two further benchmarks for the assessment of shared concepts, specifically words that appear in at least 16 out of the 17 datasets and words that appear in at least 15 out of the 17 datasets. This has proven rather useful and the result of this can be seen in Figure 4.

With the first benchmark, our lists had an overlap of 11 concepts: ANT, SAW, AIRPLANE, TABLE, CAMEL, BUTTERFLY, HOUSE, SNAIL, RHINOCEROS, APPLE, and BED, but with the

Concept	Absent	Concept	Absent	Concept	Absent	Concept	Absent	Concept	Absent	Concept	Absent
AIRPLANE	9	CAT	9, 8	GLOVE	9, 10	MOUNTAIN	9, 8	SNAIL	8	TRAIN	9, 8
ANT	9	COW	9, 8	GRAPE	9, 13	NOSE	9, 8	TREE	14, 8	TURTLE	9, 8
APPLE	9	DUCK	9, 8	GUITAR	2, 15	OWL	9, 8	SOCK	9, 8		
BALL	9, 8	EAR	9, 8	GUN	9, 8	PEAR	9, 8	SPECTACLES	9, 14		
BANANA	9, 8	ELEPHANT	9, 8	HAMMER	9, 8	POT	9, 8	SPIDER	9, 8		
BED	–	EYE	9, 8	HORSE	9, 8	RHINOCEROS	6	SQUIRREL	10, 14		
BUTTERFLY	9	FINGER	9, 8	HOUSE	8	SAW	8	TABLE	9		
CAMEL	8	FLAG	14, 8	LION	9, 8	SHEARS	15, 14	TIGER	9, 15		

Table 2: Recurring concepts in at least 15 out of 17 datasets with a specification of the dataset, in which they are absent. BED is the only concept that is present in all of them. For number references, see Table 1.

second, slightly larger one, this number increased to 42 items. We were interested to see, which datasets were the ones that did not include certain concepts. An overview is shown in Table 2, for the numbers of datasets, please refer to Table 1. One can observe that it is mostly two datasets that often lack certain concepts. These are Hwang et al. (2021) and van Dort et al. (2007), two monolingual datasets on Korean and Malay, respectively. Both of these languages are, however, included within other datasets as well. The reason behind them not featuring these concepts is likely their size. In comparison to the other datasets, they only feature 60 and 50 items and have therefore *fewer spaces to fill*. In the case of other larger datasets, such as e.g. Ramanujan and Weekes, 2019 (Hindi) and Bangalore et al., 2022 (Kannada), missing items might not be featured because they are not native to the area, e.g. GUITAR. This is something a researcher attempting to create a multilingual dataset should always keep in mind.

4.3 Unique Concepts

Not all *concept sets* recur in object naming datasets. We find that many researchers include highly specific or niche items, which can act as a constraint when it comes to later application of a dataset in low-resource languages, or generally any language that falls outside the Indo-European language family. Examples of such concepts include items like: DANDELION, EUCALYPTUS, POLAR BEAR, or culturally specific items, such as CHURRERA or FOOTBALL HELMET. On the other hand, some authors incorporate otherwise underrepresented concepts from Swadesh (1955), such as LIVER and SMOKE (EXHAUST), which would be advantageous in cross-linguistic, comparative studies.

5 Conclusion

Object naming is a growing and relevant field in many scientific disciplines. New datasets are produced, adapted, or updated every year. Through a computer-assisted analysis of 17 datasets from 30 languages and 10 language families, our study demonstrates that transparency and cross-linguistic comparability of object naming data can be achieved, for example, by mapping existing concept lists onto *concept sets* in Concepticon. By applying computational methods, we have assessed, compared, and evaluated an extensive multilingual dataset, providing insights into the general strategies and patterns, as well as the covered semantic space. We have shown that object naming datasets employ some basic concepts as per Swadesh (1955), even though the number is smaller than expected. Additionally, we found that although object naming datasets differ greatly, there appear to be several recurring concepts – 42 in total. Lastly, we showed that some concepts appear exclusively in certain datasets and often introduce overly specific, niche or cultural items that pose a bottleneck for low-resource languages. Because most of the covered object naming datasets include valuable psycholinguistic norms, they will be linked to NoRaRe in the future. Our study can serve as a basis for enhancing comparative and transparent cross-linguistic object naming research and as a guideline for future studies in the field.

Limitations

Our study by now follows a concept-based approach, using the CLLD Concepticon. However, in the future, our findings can be extended using additional semantic technologies. Thus, as suggested by one of our reviewers, the integration with the Open Multilingual WordNet should be explored, as it might provide new insights and prove useful for resources that could build on our object naming data. We would also like to explore the integration with Interlingual Indices (Bond et al., 2016, Vossen et al., 1999), as a WordNet technology that offers services similar to a Concepticon.

Supplementary Material

Data and code have been curated on GitHub (Version 0.3, `https://github.com/calc-project/object-naming-data`) and archived with Zenodo (`https://doi.org/10.5281/zenodo.14628417`).

Acknowledgements

This project was supported by the ERC Consolidator Grant ProduSemy (PI Johann-Mattis List, Grant No. 101044282, see `https://doi.org/10.3030/101044282`). Views and opinions expressed are, however, those of the authors only and do not necessarily reflect those of the European Union or the European Research Council Executive Agency (nor any other funding agencies involved). Neither the European Union nor the granting authority can be held responsible for them. We would like to thank the anonymous reviewers for their helpful comments. We also thank Frederic Blum and Annika Tjuka for their assistance with the collaborative review of our data for the inclusion in the Concepticon project. We further express our gratitude to all people who share their data openly, so we can use them in our research.

References

Susana Araújo, Luís Faísca, Ines Bramão, Filomena Inácio, Karl Magnus Petersson, and Alexandra Reis. 2011. Object naming in dyslexic children: more than a phonological deficit. *J. Gen. Psychol.*, 138(3):215–228.

Shrilekha Bangalore, Holly Robson, and Arlene J. Astell. 2022. Standardizing norms for 180 coloured Snodgrass and Vanderwart pictures in Kannada language. *PLOS ONE*, 17(4):e0266359.

Frederic Blum, Ludger Paschen, Robert Forkel, Susanne Fuchs, and Frank Seifart. 2024. Consonant lengthening marks the beginning of words across a diverse sample of languages. *Nat. Hum. Behav.*, 8(11):2127–2138.

Francis Bond and Ryan Foster. 2013. Linking and extending an open multilingual wordnet. In *Proceedings of the 51st Annual Meeting of the Association for Computational Linguistics*, pages 1352–1362, Stroudsberg. Association for Computational Linguistics.

Francis Bond, Piek Vossen, John McCrae, and Christiane Fellbaum. 2016. CILI: the Collaborative Interlingual Index. In *Proceedings of the 8th Global WordNet Conference (GWC)*, pages 50–57, Bucharest, Romania. Global Wordnet Association.

Mariem Boukadi, Cirine Zouaidi, and Maximiliano A. Wilson. 2015. Norms for name agreement, familiarity, subjective frequency, and imageability for 348 object names in Tunisian Arabic. *Behavior Research Methods*, 48:585–599.

James McKeen Catell. 1886. The time it takes to see and name objects. *Mind*, os-XI(41):63–65.

Lisa Tabor Connor, Avron Spiro, 3rd, Loraine K Obler, and Martin L Albert. 2004. Change in object naming ability during adulthood. *J. Gerontol. B Psychol. Sci. Soc. Sci.*, 59(5):P203–9.

María Dimitropoulou, Jon Andoni Duñabeitia, Panagiotis Blitsas, and Manuel Carreiras. 2009. A standardized set of 260 pictures for Modern Greek: Norms for name agreement, age of acquisition, and visual complexity. *Behavior Research Methods*, 41:584–589.

Jon Andoni Duñabeitia, Ana Baciero, Kyriakos Antoniou, Mark Antoniou, Esra Ataman, Cristina Baus, Michal Ben-Shachar, Ozan Can Çağlar, Jan Chromý, Montserrat Comesaña, Maroš Filip, Dušica Filipović Đurđević, Margaret Gillon Dowens, Anna Hatzidaki, Jiří Januška, Zuraini Jusoh, Rama Kanj, Say Young Kim, Bilal Kırkıcı, Alina Leminen, Terje Lohndal, Ngee Thai Yap, Hanna Renvall, Jason Rothman, Phaedra Royle, Mikel Santesteban, Yamila Sevilla, Natalia Slioussar, Awel Vaughan-Evans, Zofia Wodniecka, Stefanie Wulff, and Christos Pliatsikas. 2022. The Multilingual Picture Database. *Science Data*, 9(431).

Jon Andoni Duñabeitia, David Crepaldi, Antje S. Meyer, Boris New, Christos Pliatsikas, Eva Smolka, and Marc Brysbaert. 2018. Multipic: A standardized set of 750 drawings with norms for six European languages. *Quarterly journal of experimental psychology (2006)*, 71(4):808–816.

Robert Forkel, Christoph Rzymski, and Johann-Mattis List. 2021. *PyConcepticon [Python library, Version 2.8.0]*. Zenodo, Geneva.

Robert Gaizauskas, Kevin Humphreys, Saliha Azzam, and Yorick Wilks. 1997. Concepticons vs. lexicons: An architecture for multilingual information extraction. In *Information Extraction A Multidisciplinary Approach to an Emerging Information Technology*, pages 28–43, Berlin, Heidelberg. Springer Berlin Heidelberg.

Leila Ghasisin, Fariba Yadegari, Mehdi Rahgozar, Ali Nazari, and Niloufar Rastegarianzade. 2015. A new set of 272 pictures for psycholinguistic studies: Persian norms for name agreement, image agreement, conceptual familiarity, visual complexity, and age of acquisition. *Behav. Res. Methods*, 47(4):1148–1158.

John E. Hummel. 2013. *Object Recognition*. Oxford University Press.

Yu M. Hwang, Na Yoonhye, and Sung-Bom P. 2021. A categorical naming test, set of 60 pictures from two main semantic categories: living and artificial objects. *PLOS ONE*, 16(2).

Ranjay Krishna, Yuke Zhu, Oliver Groth, Justin Johnson, Kenji Hata, Joshua Kravitz, Stephanie Chen, Yannis Kalantidis, Li-Jia Li, David A. Shamma, Michael S. Bernstein, and Fei-Fei Li. 2016. Visual genome: Connecting language and vision using crowdsourced dense image annotations. *arXiv preprint*.

Johann-Mattis List. 2022. How to map concepts with the PySem library. *Computer-Assisted Language Comparison in Practice*, 5(1):1–5.

Johann-Mattis List, Michael Cysouw, and Robert Forkel. 2016. Concepticon. a resource for the linking of concept lists. In *Proceedings of the Tenth International Conference on Language Resources and Evaluation*, pages 2393–2400, Luxembourg. European Language Resources Association (ELRA).

Johann-Mattis List, Annika Tjuka, Frederic Blum, Alžběta Kučerová, Carlos Barrientos, Christoph Rzymski, Simon Greenhill, and Robert Forkel. 2025. *CLLD Concepticon [Dataset, Version 3.3.0]*. Max Planck Institute for Evolutionary Anthropology, Leipzig.

Youyi Liu, Hao Meiling, Ping Li, and Hua Shu. 2011. Timed picture naming norms for Mandarin Chinese. *PLOS ONE*, 6(1).

Francisco Javier Moreno-Martínez and Pedro R. Montoro. 2012. An ecological alternative to Snodgrass & Vanderwart: 360 high quality colour images with norms for seven psycholinguistic variables. *PLOS ONE*, 7(5):1–9.

Linda E. Nicholas, Robert H. Brookshire, Donald L. MacLennan, James G. Schumacher, and Shirley A. Porrazzo. 1989. The Boston Naming Test: Revised administration and scoring procedures and normative information for non-brain-damaged adults. In *Clinical Aphasiology Conference*, pages 103–115, Boston. College-Hill Press.

Takehiko Nishimoto, Kaori Miyawaki, Takashi Ueda, Yuko Une, and Masaru Takahashi. 2005. Japanese normative set of 359 pictures. *Behavior Research Methods*, 37:398–416.

Michel Paradis. 2011. Principles underlying the Bilingual Aphasia Test (BAT) and its uses. *Clinical Linguistics & Phonetics*, 25(6–7):427–443.

Ilhan Raman, Evren Raman, and Biran Mertan. 2013. A standardized set of 260 pictures for Turkish: Norms of name and image agreement, age of acquisition, visual complexity, and conceptual familiarity. *Behavior Research Methods*, 46:588–595.

Keerthi Ramanujan and Brendan S. Weekes. 2019. Predictors of lexical retrieval in Hindi–English bilingual speakers. *Bilingualism: Language and Cognition*, 23(2):265–273.

Maja Rogić, Ana Jerončić, Marija Bošnjak, Ana Sedlar, Darko Hren, and Vedran Deletis. 2013. A visual object naming task standardized for the Croatian language: a tool for research and clinical practice. *Behavior Research Methods*, 45(4):1144–1158.

Bruno Rossion and Gilles Pourtois. 2004. Revisiting Snodgrass and Vanderwart's object pictorial set: The role of surface detail in basic-level object recognition. *Perception*, 33(2):217–236.

Ewa Rudnicka, Maciej Piasecki, Francis Bond, Łukasz Grabowski, and Tadeusz Piotrowski. 2019. Sense equivalence in plWordNet to Princeton WordNet mapping. *International Journal of Lexicography*, 32(3):296–325.

Zeshu Shao and Julia Stiegert. 2016. Predictors of photo naming: Dutch norms for 327 photos. *Behavior Research Methods*, 48:577–584.

Carina Silberer, Sina Zarrieß, and Gemma Boleda. 2020. Object naming in Language and Vision: A survey and a new dataset. In *Proceedings of the Twelfth Language Resources and Evaluation Conference*, pages 5792–5801, Marseille, France. European Language Resources Association.

Joan G. Snodgrass and Mary Vanderwart. 1980. A standardized set of 260 pictures: Norms for name agreement, image agreement, familiarity, and visual complexity. *Journal of Experimental Psychology: Human Learning and Memory*, 6(2):174–215.

Morris Swadesh. 1955. Chemakum lexicon compared with Quileute. *International Journal of American Linguistics*, 21(1):60–72.

Annika Tjuka. 2020. Adding concept lists to Concepticon: A guide for beginners. *Computer-Assisted Language Comparison in Practice*, 3(1).

Annika Tjuka, Rober Forkel, and Johann-Mattis List. 2023. Curating and extending data for language comparison in Concepticon and NoRaRe [version 2; peer review: 2 approved]. *Open Research Europe*, 2(141).

Annika Tjuka, Robert Forkel, and Johann-Mattis List. 2020. *NoRaRe. Cross-Linguistic Database of Norms, Ratings, and Relations of Words and Concepts. Version 0.1.0*. Max Planck Institute for the Science of Human History, Jena.

Annika Tjuka, Robert Forkel, and Johann-Mattis List. 2022. Linking norms, ratings, and relations of words and concepts across multiple language varieties. *Behavior Research Methods*, 54(2):864–884.

Fabian Tomaschek and Benjamin V. Tucker. 2023. Where does morphology fit? In Davide Crepaldi, editor, *Linguistic Morphology in the Mind and Brain*, pages 80–95. Routledge.

Diana Tsaparina, Patrick Bonin, and Alain Méot. 2011. Russian norms for name agreement, image agreement for the colorized version of the Snodgrass and Vanderwart pictures and age of acquisition, conceptual familiarity, and imageability scores for modal object names. *Behavior Research Methods*, 43(4):1085–1099.

Sandra van Dort, Etain Vong, Rogayah A. Razak, Rahayu Mustaffa Kamal, and Hooi Poh Meng. 2007. Normative data on a malay version of the boston naming test. *Jurnal Sains Kesihatan Malaysia*, 5(1):27–36.

Piek Vossen, Wim Peters, and Julio Gonzalo. 1999. Towards a universal index of meaning. In *Proceedings of ACL-99 Workshop, Siglex-99, Standardizing Lexical Resources*, pages 81–90. University of Maryland, College Park, Maryland USA.

Susan G. Wardle and Chris I. Baker. 2020. Recent advances in understanding object recognition in the human brain: deep neural networks, temporal dynamics, and context. *F1000Research*, 9:590.

Jing Zhong, Weike Huang, Keyi Kang, Jon Andoni Duñabeitia, Christos Pliatsikas, and Haoyun Zhang. 2024. Standardizing norms for 1286 colored pictures in Cantonese. *Behavior Research Methods*, 56:6318–6331.

A Semi-Automated Approach to the Annotation of Argument Structures in Turkish Datasets

Neslihan Cesur[1], Sabri İnce[2], Ali Hakkı Aydın[3], Ece Su Eren[2], Deniz Gücükçavuş[2], Murat Papaker[3], Kaan Bayar[2], Deniz Baran Aslan[2], Yelda Fırat[4], Olcay Taner Yıldız[1]

[1]Özyeğin University, [2]Boğaziçi University, [3]Galatasaray University, [4]Mudanya University

Correspondence: neslihan.cesur@ozu.edu.tr; olcay.yildiz@ozyegin.edu.tr

Abstract

This paper presents a PropBank annotation project for Turkish, focusing on core arguments in matrix clauses. Our dataset comprises of five different corpora with 25,580 sentences labeled for verbal predicates and core arguments. Using a semi-automatic approach, we leveraged a dependency layer to pre-assign some ARG0s and ARG1s, followed by manual corrections. Our work will be used in the development of Abstract Meaning Representations (AMRs), enhancing Turkish NLP resources for semantic parsing and higher-level language tasks.[1]

1 Introduction

Understanding argument structure is essential to the study of syntax and semantics in natural language processing (NLP). In linguistic theory, argument structure refers to the way a predicate, typically a verb, organizes its participants (arguments). These arguments can vary depending on the predicate, including roles such as the agent (who performs the action), the patient (who undergoes the action), or additional participants that further specify the event or action (e.g., a location, instrument, or beneficiary). Correctly representing the argument structure of a sentence is crucial as the arguments contain syntactic and semantic information concerning the participants of the event. This information is is used for higher-level NLP tasks such as information extraction, machine translation, question answering, and text summarization.

This understanding of argument roles has been formalized in the PropBank project (Kingsbury and Palmer, 2002, 2003; Palmer et al., 2005; Bonial et al., 2014), which provides a layer of semantic role annotations over syntactically parsed texts. It has been widely used as a resource for developing supervised machine learning models in NLP, contributing to syntactic-semantic integration. PropBank captures the relationship between predicates and their core arguments using a numbered argument schema. Each label in the schema is intended to represent generalized semantic functions: ARG0 typically corresponds to the agent or causer, while ARG1 corresponds to the theme or patient of the verb. Adjuncts and other modifiers are marked with various ARGM labels such as temporal (ARGM-TMP) or locational (ARGM-LOC) modifiers. Bonial et al. (2012) elaborates on the annotation guidelines in detail.

For our project, we conducted verbal predicate selection and argument labeling across five different datasets, comprising a total of 25,580 sentences. The annotation of our datasets was carried out as part of a broader multi-layer NLP project. Each dataset had already been labeled for various linguistic information: morphological analysis using an automatic analyzer (Yıldız et al., 2019), morphological disambiguation, and word sense disambiguation using definitions from the Turkish WordNet (KeNet) (Bakay et al., 2019, 2021). Additionally, the sentences were annotated with Universal Dependencies (UD)-style dependency relations. Before labeling the arguments, we tagged all sentences which had verbal predicates, leaving out nominal predicates and noun phrases. With the availability of a manually-annotated dependency layer, we were able to automatically assign some agents (ARG0) and direct objects (ARG1). This automatic process was followed by the manual annotation of missing arguments and the correction of automatically labeled arguments.

Since this PropBank annotation is part of a larger project aimed at constructing Abstract Meaning Representations (AMRs), we focused solely on the core arguments while excluding modifiers. The argument labeling of subordinate clauses will be conducted at the AMR stage. The labeling of ad-

[1]This work is supported by the Scientific and Technological Research Council of Turkey (TÜBİTAK) under Project No. 123E027, titled *Learning Abstract Meaning Representation for Turkish and Building A Question Answering System*.

juncts and modifiers will be addressed right before AMR annotations, using frame elements from the Turkish FrameNet (Marsan et al., 2021).

2 Previous PropBank Datasets

Several projects have been carried out in an effort to adapt PropBank to typologically diverse languages. These projects include PropBanks for Arabic (Palmer et al., 2008; Zaghouani et al., 2010), Basque (Agirre et al., 2006; Aldezabal et al., 2010), Chinese (Xue, 2006; Xue and Palmer, 2009) and Finnish (Haverinen et al., 2015) among others.

The annotation of the first dataset, along with several studies on semantic role labeling and the development of a Turkish PropBank (Sahin, 2016; Şahin and Adalı, 2018), was carried out using the IMST Dataset (Sulubacak et al., 2016). In a related effort, Şahin (2018) conducted a verb sense annotation project using crowd-sourced annotators to create an initial PropBank resource.

Ak et al. (2018) further advanced Turkish PropBank development by using the Turkish Penn TreeBank to semantically label over 9,500 sentences and map predicate-argument structures for 1,914 Turkish verb senses. Subsequently, Ak and Yıldız (2019) introduced a method to automatically generate PropBank annotations using an English-Turkish parallel corpus.

For our annotation efforts, we utilized the frame files developed in TRopBank v2.0 (Kara et al., 2020). This version contains frame files for 17,691 Turkish verbs. A key feature of TRopBank v2.0 is that its predicate-argument structures are based not on individual verbs but on the synsets defined in Turkish WordNet (Ehsani et al., 2018; Bakay et al., 2019). While this approach is efficient in terms of time and resource management, it occasionally introduces challenges during the labeling of specific predicates.

3 Data and Annotation

The datasets used in this project are diverse in nature. Turkish ATIS (Cesur et al., 2024) and Turkish Penn Treebank (Kuzgun et al., 2020) are the adaptations of well-known NLP benchmarks, with ATIS focusing on flight-related queries (Hemphill et al., 1990) and Penn Treebank offering syntactically annotated sentences from the Wall Street Journal (Marcus et al., 1993). The Tourism dataset consists of user comments from a tourism website, reflecting informal, real-world language. FrameNet contains example sentences crafted for the Turkish FrameNet project (Marsan et al., 2021) to illustrate semantic frames. Finally, KeNet (Ehsani et al., 2018) includes example sentences extracted from the Turkish Language Association (TDK) dictionary, providing formal and structured language samples.

Figure 1: The interface for word sense disambiguation. The light verb construction *ilişkili olmak* (to be related) appears as a collocation in Turkish WordNet. In this context, both words are assigned the same ID.

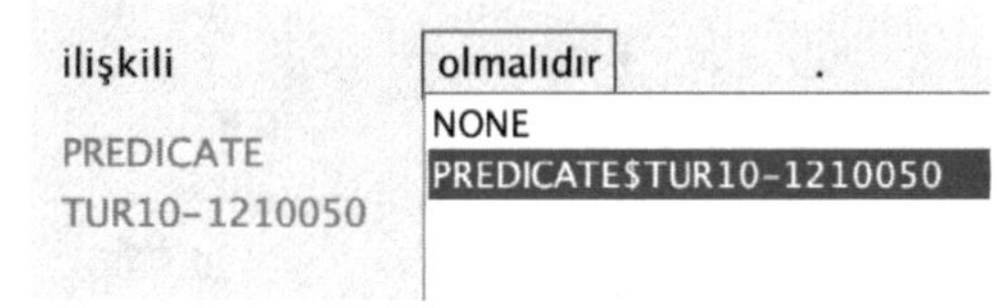

Figure 2: The interface for predicate selection. Both components of the construction *ilişkili olmak* can be marked as predicates, as they share the same WordNet ID.

3.1 Predicate selection

The first step in our annotation process was to identify and label verbal predicates across the datasets. Sentences containing only noun phrases or nominal clauses were excluded from annotation. For example, the Tourism and ATIS datasets included several instances of such structures. Sentences like *Otel iyiydi* ("The hotel was good") or *San Francisco'ya uçuşlar* ("Flights to San Francisco") were omitted because they do not contain verbal predicates.

In cases where predicates appeared as multi-word constructions, each word was labeled as a predicate only if all components shared the same WordNet ID in the word sense disambiguation layer. This ensured consistency in labeling across complex predicates. Figure 1 shows the word sense disambiguation layer for the light verb construction *ilişkili olmak* ("to be related"), where both words share the same WordNet ID, resulting in a single unified definition. Since this construction is recognized as a collocation, both words are marked as predicates in the predicate selection layer, as demonstrated in Figure 2.

Another factor influencing predicate selection is the morphological layer. Errors in morphological disambiguation can prevent the word sense layer from displaying appropriate verb definitions. If a noun sense is incorrectly selected, the predicate layer offers no options beyond "NONE." Figure 3 illustrates a case where a word has two valid morphological analyses. The word *açtı* can be interpreted either with the adjectival root *aç* ("hungry") or the verbal root *aç-* ("to open"). When combined with the past tense suffix *-DI*, the first analysis forms a nominal predicate ("he/she was hungry"), while the second forms a verbal predicate ("he/she opened (it)").

The choice made at the morphological layer directly determines the available word senses in the word sense disambiguation layer, which subsequently affects predicate selection. If the adjectival interpretation is selected, the annotator is unable to label the word as a predicate and must revise both the morphological analysis and the word sense disambiguation.

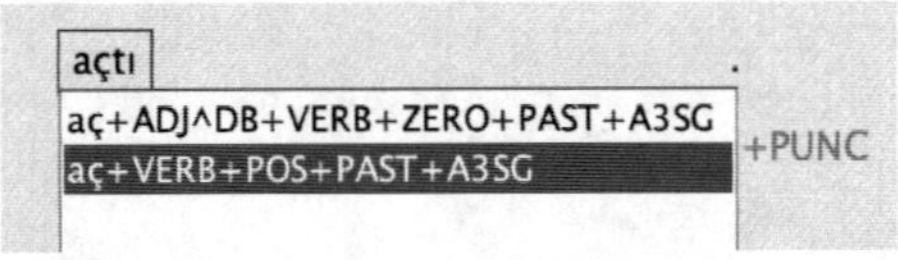

Figure 3: The interface for morphological disambiguation. The word *açtı* can either have an adjectival root and or a verbal root depending on the linguistic context.

In this phase of our project, we focused exclusively on annotating predicates and core arguments within matrix clauses, meaning that predicates appearing in embedded clauses were not labeled. However, when multiple clauses were connected through coordination, whether by a conjunction (e.g., *ve* "and," *ama* "but") or a punctuation mark (e.g., a comma or semicolon), each predicate within those coordinated structures was annotated independently. This approach ensures that all main predicates across conjoined clauses receive proper labeling, even though only the primary predicate of the matrix clause was prioritized in simpler sentence structures.

3.2 Pre-processing with the dependency layer

After predicate selection, sentences containing verbal predicates underwent an automatic labeling process, where ARG0s and ARG1s were assigned based on their dependency analysis. We assumed that most subjects would function as agents (ARG0) and therefore assigned ARG0 to tokens marked with the NSUBJ dependency relation, along with any dependents tied to them. This approach allowed entire phrases to be labeled efficiently. Figure 4 illustrates the dependency relations that result in multiple words being labeled as a single argument unit.

One challenge with this assumption arises with unaccusative predicates, whose subjects are marked as NSUBJ but semantically correspond to ARG1 rather than ARG0. Since the identification of unaccusative predicates followed the definitions in TRopBank v2.0, the algorithm ensured that for verbs which do not receive ARG0 arguments, the NSUBJ marked words would be labeled ARG1 instead of ARG0. Later the annotators corrected any exceptional cases during the manual review.

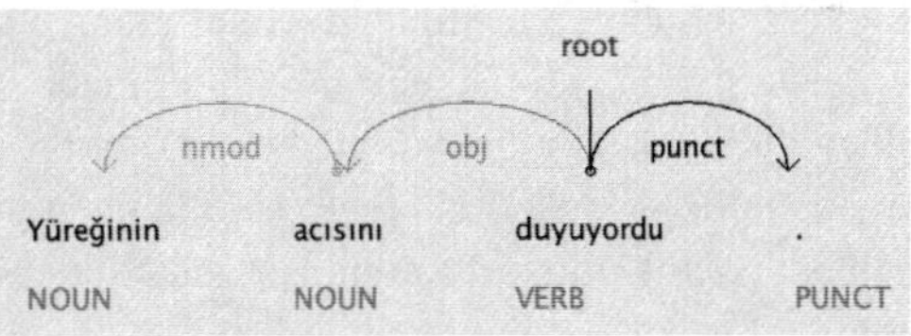

Figure 4: Dependency relations for the sentence meaning *(He/She) felt the pain in his/her heart.* The head of the noun phrase (*acısını*) is connected to the root with the OBJ tag, leading it to be labeled as ARG1. Since *yüreğinin* is attached to the head via the NMOD tag, it also inherits the ARG1 label.

Similarly, passive predicates posed another challenge. Although passive subjects should be marked as ARG1, they are often labeled NSUBJ in the dependency layer. While Universal Dependencies (UD) provides the NSUBJ:pass tag for passive subjects, inconsistencies in the datasets meant many passive subjects were marked with NSUBJ. In such cases, ARG0 was manually corrected to ARG1.

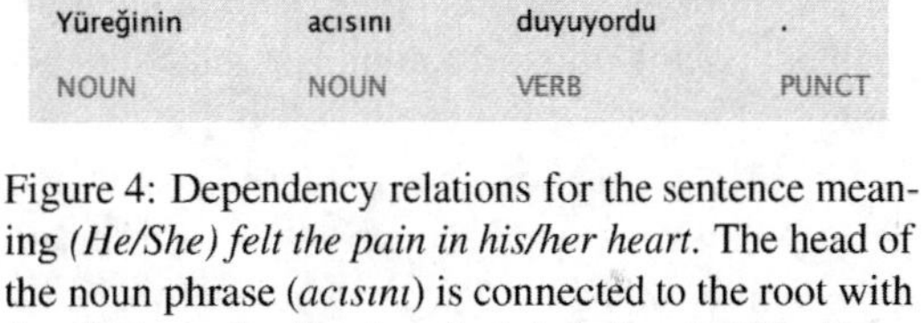

Figure 5: Dependency relations for the sentence meaning *Flowers bloomed wherever you stepped.* The noun marked as the subject (*güller*) automatically receives the ARG0 label. As there are no dependents linked to it, the other tokens are not assigned any argument labels.

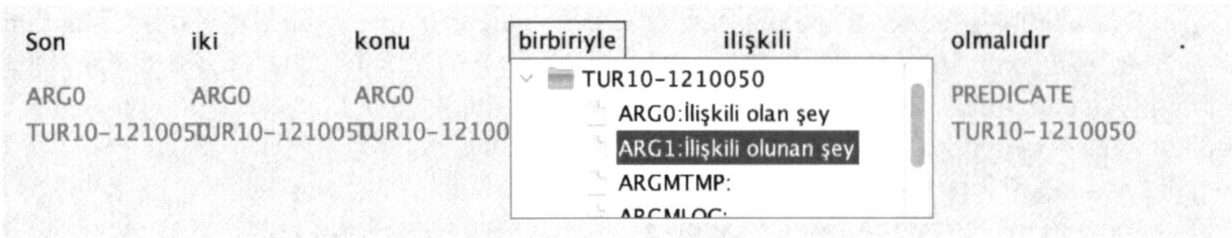

Figure 6: Interface for manual argument selection. Clicking on a word reveals frame file annotations from TRopBank v2.0 for each predicate. Annotators assign the appropriate argument label, displayed beneath the word along with its corresponding WordNet ID. To remove an argument label, the annotator clicks the predicate's ID, marking the word as "NONE."

For objects, tokens connected to the predicate with the OBJ relation were automatically labeled as ARG1. While this approach rarely resulted in over-generation, it sometimes caused under-generation. In PropBank, the scope of what constitutes an argument is more semantically driven, often including elements marked as OBL (oblique) or ADV/ADVCL (adverbial/adverbial clause) in the dependency layer. However, our automatic labeling algorithm was not designed to capture these cases comprehensively, and these arguments were manually added during the argument selection process.

Although automatic labeling reduced the amount of manual work, it was not entirely foolproof due to several challenges. The first issue arose from errors in the dependency layer: faulty dependency relations led to incorrect argument tags, which had to be corrected during manual annotation. Additionally, when the dependents of long noun phrases were not correctly linked to the head, only part of the phrase was labeled automatically, making the task of argument labeling more tedious for annotators.

Another challenge involved coordinated sentences. The algorithm only processed phrases directly linked to the predicate marked as the ROOT, resulting in automatic labeling for the arguments of only one predicate. The remaining arguments in the coordinated structure had to be annotated manually.

3.3 Argument selection

Following the automatic labeling of ARG0 and ARG1, annotators manually reviewed each sentence to identify and annotate missing arguments and correct any errors introduced by the automatic labeling algorithm. As discussed earlier, errors in lower layers—such as morphological and semantic disambiguation—also required manual correction. Since the same annotation interface, StarDust (Yenice et al., 2022), was used across all layers, the correction process was relatively straightforward for the annotators.

Figure 6 presents the interface used for manual argument selection. Clicking on a word displays the relevant frame file annotations from TRopBank v2.0 for each predicate in the sentence. Annotators open the frame file with the matching ID and assign the appropriate argument label. Both the selected label and the corresponding WordNet ID are then displayed beneath the word. If an argument label needs to be removed, the annotator clicks on the predicate's ID in the selection panel, marking the word as "NONE."

Following our choice explained earlier, in this iteration, only matrix clauses were annotated for arguments. The arguments of coordinated sentences were included in the annotation, while embedded clauses, even those with finite verbs, were not annotated separately. This decision aimed to avoid confusion, minimize time loss, and eliminate the need to modify the interface to accommodate cases where a single word plays multiple roles. Specifically, phrases often function as part of a larger constituent in the matrix clause while simultaneously carrying a distinct role in an embedded clause, which would complicate the annotation process. We plan to overcome this issue in the final phase of our project, which will be the construction of AMR structures for each sentence annotated for predicates and arguments. The arguments from the main clauses will be automatically integrated into the AMRs, while the arguments from embedded clauses will be added manually using the AMR interface.

Another decision we made was to exclude non-core arguments from our annotation process. This choice aimed to prevent redundancy, as a FrameNet layer will be incorporated before the construction

Dataset	ARG0	ARG1	ARG2	ARG3
Atis	995	16,090	698	0
Tourism	1,279	6,259	142	0
FrameNet	1,211	3,001	159	8
Penn TreeBank	18,283	31,359	756	25
KeNet	11,811	24,797	1,267	42
Total	**32,542**	**76,983**	**2,853**	**73**

Table 1: Distribution of core arguments (ARG0–ARG3) across the datasets. ARG0 typically marks agents or causers, while ARG1 often denotes patients or themes. ARG2 and ARG3 represent more specialized roles depending on the verb's semantics, with fewer occurrences in most datasets.

of the AMRs. The ARGM arguments typically convey information related to time, location, manner, and purpose, all of which are also captured within frame elements. Given that we have expanded upon the previous Turkish FrameNet project (Marsan et al., 2021) to encode frame information for each predicate, we opted to integrate this information at a later stage.

While Table 1 presents the number of annotated core arguments in each dataset, Table 2 details the counts of sentences labeled with verbal predicates, alongside those further annotated for arguments. Notably, across all datasets, a significant portion of sentences lacks core arguments. This is particularly evident in the Tourism dataset, which exhibits a lower ratio of arguments compared to predicates.

Among the labeled arguments, ARG1 is the most prevalent category. This trend highlights the frequent omission of subjects in Turkish, as indicated by the lower counts of ARG0s. The occurrences of ARG2 and ARG3 are comparatively minimal, aligning with linguistic expectations. This distribution may also be influenced by the limitations associated with missing argument specifications in the TRopBank frame files.

Dataset	argument	predicate
Atis	2,568	3,036
Tourism	3,717	7,166
Penn TreeBank	9,322	12,152
FrameNet	1,877	2,484
KeNet	9,385	11,839

Table 2: Number of sentences labeled for verbal predicates and core arguments across five datasets. The "predicate" column shows the total number of sentences with an identified verbal predicate, while the "argument" column indicates how many of those were further annotated with core arguments.

This issue encountered during this process was due to an annotation choice in the TRopBank project, which constructed frame files based on the definitions of WordNet synsets rather than on individual verbs. This approach resulted in numerous exceptional cases where certain verbs were missing specific argument definitions. While these issues could be addressed by incorporating the missing arguments for each verb, we opted not to implement these changes in this iteration due to time constraints. However, refining the previous project is essential for large-scale annotation projects like this one.

4 Discussion

This paper presented a semi-automated approach to annotating argument structures in Turkish datasets, focusing on verbal predicates and core arguments. Five datasets were annotated with a total of 25,580 sentences, with ARG0 and ARG1 assignments facilitated through dependency-based pre-labeling. Some challenges arose from dependency errors, passive structures, and unaccusative predicates, which required careful manual review to ensure alignment with TRopBank v2.0's frame files. We suggest that these frame files are updated to accommodate specific argument requirements of some Turkish verbs.

As stated earlier, this PropBank annotation is part of a larger, multi-layer NLP project aimed at enhancing Turkish semantic resources. In future work, each sentence will be annotated for frame elements according to the semantic frame of its predicate. Later on, the annotated core arguments will be integrated into AMR structures with additional layers, including subordinate clauses.

By focusing on precise predicate and core argument labeling in matrix clauses, this project lays the foundation for building high-quality AMRs for Turkish. These resources will not only support advanced NLP tasks such as semantic parsing but will also contribute to broader research efforts in multilingual natural language understanding.

References

Eneko E Agirre, Izaskun Aldezabal, Jone Etxeberria, and Eli Pociello. 2006. A preliminary study for building the basque propbank. In *Proceedings of the 5th International Conference on Language Resources and Evaluations (LREC)*.

Koray Ak, Cansu Toprak, Volkan Esgel, and Olcay Taner Yildiz. 2018. Construction of a turkish proposition bank. *Turkish Journal of Electrical Engineering and Computer Sciences*, 26(1):570–581.

Koray Ak and Olcay Taner Yıldız. 2019. Automatic Propbank generation for Turkish. In *Proceedings of the International Conference on Recent Advances in Natural Language Processing (RANLP 2019)*, pages 33–41, Varna, Bulgaria. INCOMA Ltd.

Izaskun Aldezabal, María Jesús Aranzabe, Arantza Díaz de Ilarraza Sánchez, and Ainara Estarrona. 2010. Building the basque propbank. In *LREC*. Citeseer.

Özge Bakay, Özlem Ergelen, Elif Sarmış, Selin Yıldırım, Bilge Nas Arıcan, Atilla Kocabalcıoğlu, Merve Özçelik, Ezgi Sanıyar, Oğuzhan Kuyrukçu, Begüm Avar, et al. 2021. Turkish wordnet kenet. In *Proceedings of the 11th global wordnet conference*, pages 166–174.

Özge Bakay, Özlem Ergelen, and Olcay Taner Yıldız. 2019. Integrating turkish wordnet kenet to princeton wordnet: The case of one-to-many correspondences. In *2019 Innovations in Intelligent Systems and Applications Conference (ASYU)*, pages 1–5. IEEE.

Claire Bonial, Julia Bonn, Kathryn Conger, Jena D Hwang, and Martha Palmer. 2014. Propbank: Semantics of new predicate types. In *LREC*, pages 3013–3019.

Claire Bonial, Jena Hwang, Julia Bonn, Kathryn Conger, Olga Babko-Malaya, and Martha Palmer. 2012. English propbank annotation guidelines. *Center for Computational Language and Education Research Institute of Cognitive Science University of Colorado at Boulder*, 48.

Neslihan Cesur, Aslı Kuzgun, Mehmet Kose, and Olcay Taner Yıldız. 2024. Building annotated parallel corpora using the atis dataset: Two ud-style treebanks in english and turkish. In *Proceedings of the 17th Workshop on Building and Using Comparable Corpora (BUCC)@ LREC-COLING 2024*, pages 104–110.

Razieh Ehsani, Ercan Solak, and Olcay Taner Yildiz. 2018. Constructing a wordnet for turkish using manual and automatic annotation. *ACM Transactions on Asian and Low-Resource Language Information Processing (TALLIP)*, 17(3):1–15.

Katri Haverinen, Jenna Kanerva, Samuel Kohonen, Anna Missilä, Stina Ojala, Timo Viljanen, Veronika Laippala, and Filip Ginter. 2015. The finnish proposition bank. *Language Resources and Evaluation*, 49:907–926.

Charles T Hemphill, John J Godfrey, and George R Doddington. 1990. The atis spoken language systems pilot corpus. In *Speech and Natural Language: Proceedings of a Workshop Held at Hidden Valley, Pennsylvania, June 24-27, 1990*.

Neslihan Kara, Deniz Baran Aslan, Büşra Marşan, Özge Bakay, Koray Ak, and Olcay Taner Yıldız. 2020. Tropbank: turkish propbank v2. 0. In *Proceedings of the Twelfth Language Resources and Evaluation Conference*, pages 2763–2772.

Paul Kingsbury and Martha Palmer. 2003. Propbank: the next level of treebank. In *Proceedings of Treebanks and lexical Theories*, volume 3. Citeseer.

Paul R Kingsbury and Martha Palmer. 2002. From treebank to propbank. In *LREC*, pages 1989–1993.

Aslı Kuzgun, Neslihan Cesur, Bilge Nas Arıcan, Merve Özçelik, Büşra Marşan, Neslihan Kara, Deniz Baran Aslan, and Olcay Taner Yıldız. 2020. On building the largest and cross-linguistic turkish dependency corpus. In *2020 Innovations in Intelligent Systems and Applications Conference (ASYU)*, pages 1–6. IEEE.

Mitch Marcus, Beatrice Santorini, and Mary Ann Marcinkiewicz. 1993. Building a large annotated corpus of english: The penn treebank. *Computational linguistics*, 19(2):313–330.

Büsra Marsan, Starlang Yazılım Danısmanlık, Neslihan Kara, Merve Ozçelik, Bilge Nas Arıcan, Neslihan Cesur, Aslı Kuzgun, Ezgi Sanıyar, Oguzhan Kuyrukçu, and Olcay Taner Yıldız. 2021. Building the turkish framenet. *South African Centre for Digital Language Resources (SADiLaR) Potchefstroom, South Africa*, page 118.

Martha Palmer, Olga Babko-Malaya, Ann Bies, Mona T Diab, Mohamed Maamouri, Aous Mansouri, and Wajdi Zaghouani. 2008. A pilot arabic propbank. In *LREC*.

Martha Palmer, Daniel Gildea, and Paul Kingsbury. 2005. The proposition bank: An annotated corpus of semantic roles. *Computational linguistics*, 31(1):71–106.

Gözde Gül Sahin. 2016. Framing of verbs for turkish propbank. *Turkish Computational Linguistics*, pages 3–9.

Gözde Gül Şahin. 2018. Verb sense annotation for turkish propbank via crowdsourcing. In *Computational Linguistics and Intelligent Text Processing: 17th International Conference, CICLing 2016, Konya, Turkey, April 3–9, 2016, Revised Selected Papers, Part I 17*, pages 496–506. Springer.

Gözde Gül Şahin and Eşref Adalı. 2018. Annotation of semantic roles for the turkish proposition bank. *Language Resources and Evaluation*, 52:673–706.

Umut Sulubacak, Tugba Pamay, and Gülsen Eryigit. 2016. Imst: A revisited turkish dependency treebank. *Proceedings of TurCLing*, pages 1–6.

Nianwen Xue. 2006. A chinese semantic lexicon of senses and roles. *Language resources and evaluation*, 40:395–403.

Nianwen Xue and Martha Palmer. 2009. Adding semantic roles to the chinese treebank. *Natural Language Engineering*, 15(1):143–172.

Arife B Yenice, Neslihan Cesur, Aslı Kuzgun, and Olcay Taner Yıldız. 2022. Introducing stardust: A ud-based dependency annotation tool. In *Proceedings of the 16th Linguistic Annotation Workshop (LAW-XVI) within LREC2022*, pages 79–84.

Olcay Taner Yıldız, Begüm Avar, and Gökhan Ercan. 2019. An open, extendible, and fast turkish morphological analyzer. In *Proceedings of the International Conference on Recent Advances in Natural Language Processing (RANLP 2019)*, pages 1364–1372.

Wajdi Zaghouani, Mona Diab, Aous Mansouri, Sameer Pradhan, and Martha Palmer. 2010. The revised arabic propbank. In *Proceedings of the fourth linguistic annotation workshop*, pages 222–226.

Can you hear me now?
Towards talking Wordnets: A Cantonese Case Study

Joanna Ut-Seong Sio
Palacký University
joannautseong.sio@upol.cz

Luis Morgado da Costa
Vrije Universiteit Amsterdam
lmorgado.dacosta@gmail.com

Francis Bond
Palacký University
bond@ieee.org

Kamila Liedermannova
Palacký University
kamila.liedermannova01@upol.cz

Abstract

This paper describes an expansion of the Cantonese Wordnet with a special focus on hand-checked audio recordings containing the pronunciaton of Cantonese senses. To achieve this we explored an open dataset from Wikimedia Commons and also developed our own dataset targeting Cantonese L2 learners. We added audio recordings to 2,859 senses. This work also led to a considerable improvement in the coverage of this wordnet increasing its number of concepts by 18%.

1 Introduction

1.1 Intro to Cantonese Wordnet

The Cantonese Wordnet (Sio and Morgado da Costa, 2019) is a small but growing wordnet project for Cantonese.[1] It started in 2019 with a core set of synsets, and it has been expanding since. In 2022 it received the first update (Sio and Morgado da Costa, 2022), receiving an example corpus of of 3,570 example sentences, and expanding its coverage by both adding more senses and by moving beyond the structure of the Princeton Wordnet (Fellbaum, 1998) concept inventory to include Cantonese specific concepts such as classifiers. In 2023, the Cantonese Wordnet received another round of attention with the creation of the Open Cantonese Sense-Tagged Corpus (Sio and Morgado da Costa, 2023), a method known to help identify problems in the lexicon, such as missing or indistinguishable senses, while also contributing to attestation of language use (Miller et al., 1993).

1.2 Motivation

From its inception, the Cantonese Wordnet has been committed to being a high quality, hand-curated resource designed to support linguistic research, teaching and learning of Cantonese.

The potential to use this wordnet for educational purposes was one of the main motivations to include hand-curated romanized transcriptions for each sense since its first release. The Cantonese Wordnet uses the Jyutping (粵拼) romanization system, developed by the Linguistic Society of Hong Kong (LSHK) in 1993 – which is widely used in Cantonese L2 Education. The creation of the Open Cantonese Sense-Tagged Corpus was also partially motivated by its usefulness to L2 learners of Cantonese – which can reliably get translations for all sense annotated words in a variety of languages using multilingual links provided by CILI – the Collaborative Interlingual Index (Bond et al., 2016), currently under development by the Global Wordnet Association.

This paper moves further in this direction, and follows through on previous plans to provide, alongside romanized transcriptions, audio recordings with pronunciations for individual senses. Audios of wordnet lemmas are an important addition, given that Cantonese is a tonal language predominantly used in speech. Furthermore, Cantonese has interesting phonetic variations. One example would be what commonly known by laymen as *laan5 jam1* "lazy pronunciations" (or more neutrally, Principle of Least Effort, or Principle of (Maximum) Ease of Articulation) (Ladefoged and Johnson, 2006; Bauer, 2016). Some examples of "lazy pronunciations" include /n/ and /l/ alternation (alveolar nasal alternates with lateral approximant, e.g., *naam4* and *laam4* (both mean "male")), or /ng/ and /∅/ alternation (velar nasal alternates with zero initial, e.g., *ngaa4* and *aa4* (both mean "tooth")) (Bauer, 2016). We include phonetic variations in our audio files whenever possible.

In its role as a resource to support teaching and learning of Cantonese, we believe audio recordings to be quite important. This is also evidenced by the fact that many learner dictionaries (in many languages) often include pronunciations. Specif-

[1] https://github.com/lmorgadodacosta/CantoneseWN

ically for Cantonese, e.g., CantoWords[2] provides such recordings. And while this is commendable and a great service to the Cantonese speaking and learning community, dictionaries like these have their limitations. An important limitation concerns its license. While less restrictive than others, its non-commercial license limits its use and integration in other research projects with a more permissible license (as is the case for the Cantonese Wordnet). Another problem is its quality. For words with multiple characters, CantoWords provides audio recordings that are the concatenation of multiple recordings. This is most certainly better than no recordings, but this type of recording is not able to capture the pronunciation, prosody and tonal nuances of complex words (e.g., tone sandhi).

We believe Cantonese should have an open dataset of high-quality recordings. Such a dataset would be a valuable resource to support linguistic research, the learning community, but also the development of Cantonese tools (including commercial ones).

2 Extending the Cantonese Wordnet

The work presented in this paper focuses on two complementary datasets: i) Cantonese audio extracted from Wikimedia Commons[3] and ii) a new dataset created for Cantonese L2 education.

2.1 Wikimedia Commons Data

We were first made aware of this dataset when we were contacted by Wikimédia France[4] to raise awareness of Lingua Libre[5] – an online platform that allows users to preserve linguistic diversity by allowing users to record words, phrases and proverbs in their own language. This tool is integrated with Wikimedia Commons, which is where the audio recordings are stored.

There was one particular user (Luilui6666)[6] who was actively helping record Cantonese audio, and who was happy to help the Cantonese Wordnet project. In total, this user shared 6,198 audio recordings, 1,645 of them explicitly marked as Cantonese (i.e., by using the language code 'yue'). Unfortunately, the information provided about these files includes only simplified Chinese characters. This is problematic for two reasons: i) Cantonese in Hong Kong uses traditional characters (using simplified characters likely hinders their discoverability); and ii) the conversion between simplified characters is not lossless. A classic example is the conversion of 发 *faat3* meaning "to send" or "hair" , the former is expressed by the traditional form 發 and the latter 髮.

Status	No. of Recordings
Rejected	297
Failed Links	57
Linked to New Senses	648
Linked to Existing Senses	643
Total	1,645

Table 1: Wikimedia Commons Data Summary

Since the Cantonese Wordnet is still a small project, we knew that many of these recordings could include words still missing from the wordnet. We proceeded to convert the file names from simplified to traditional characters (so they could be matched with the wordnet).[7] The full list of recordings was then matched against existing senses based on their written form. Out of the total number of recordings, 643 were found in the Cantonese wordnet, and 1002 were missing.

We proceeded to automatically produce Jyutping transcriptions for each missing lemma[8] and to link them by hand to the wordnet when it was possible and desirable. We found the data contained three main choices: i) the lemma was rejected (i.e., either was not a single lemma or were not strictly Cantonese); ii) the lemma was deemed fit to be added to the wordnet but we were not able to do so (this can happen for a variety of reasons, which will be discussed in greater detail below); and iii) the lemma was added to the Cantonese wordnet. Table 1 shows a summary of the results.

2.2 Cantonese L2 Data

As a complement to the Wikimedia Commons Data, we also started collecting our own recordings. We employed the help of a Cantonese L2 lecturer and native speaker to create a list of common words used in Cantonese L2 teaching. The same individual recorded high quality readings of this list using professional grade equipment. If a word had more

[2] `https://cantowords.com/`

[3] `https://commons.wikimedia.org`

[4] `https://www.wikimedia.fr/`

[5] `https://lingualibre.org/`

[6] `https://commons.wikimedia.org/wiki/User:Luilui6666`

[7] `https://pypi.org/project/chinese-converter`

[8] `https://pypi.org/project/pinyin-jyutping`

Status	No. of Recordings
Failed Link	112
Linked to New Senses	349
Linked to Existing Senses	406
Total	867

Table 2: Cantonese L2 Data Summary

than one possible pronunciation, multiple recordings were made. This generated 867 recordings.

We followed the same procedure described above. The 867 recordings were matched against the Cantonese Wordnet linking 406 recordings to existing senses. Of the 461 remaining recordings, 349 were hand-linked to the wordnet with new links, and 112 failed to be linked (see discussion below). A summary is shown in Table 2.

3 Discussion

3.1 Wikimedia Commons Data

There are a few hurdles in incorporating all the Wikimedia Commons audio recordings into the Cantonese Wordnet. The main problem is that not all of the items are Cantonese, but rather Hong Kong "Chinese", a distinction that requires some discussion.

All literate Cantonese speakers use two different varieties of Chinese in Hong Kong. Cantonese is used at home, in everyday conversation and to a more limited extent, in informal writing (e.g., social media, tabloid magazines, etc.). Cantonese is not taught in school. Standard written Chinese (Mandarin) is also used in Hong Kong. It is taught in schools and is used in formal writings. This is Hong Kong "Chinese". Hong Kong "Chinese" is generally not spoken, except in cases like poetry recital or reading out loud from books.

All standard written Chinese lexical items can be pronounced in Cantonese. For example, the lemma for "umbrella" in standard Chinese is 雨傘, pronounced as *yǔsǎn* in Mandarin. The term is not used in Cantonese, but can be pronounced in Cantonese as *jyu5 saan3*. [9] Furthermore there is a substantial overlap between the lexical items in standard written Chinese and Cantonese. As a result, it is not always easy to distinguish the two varieties (Bauer, 2016). The Cantonese Wordnet, as of now, only contains items that belong to Cantonese as a spoken variety. The rule of thumb is that we only include items that we think would appear in spoken Cantonese (including both informal conversation and more formal contexts, such as news reports).

The Wikimedia Commons recordings contain mostly (possibly only) items that are used in standard Chinese (Mandarin). The recordings are items pronounced in Cantonese. Many of these items are also used in Cantonese, but not all. Thus, not all of the items are usable (e.g., 沸騰 *fèiténg* "to boil" is used in Mandarin but would instead be expressed as 滾 *gwan2* in Cantonese). Furthermore, the recordings do not only contain single lemmas but also phrases (e.g., 在…時候 " during...the time") and sentences (e.g., 他的褲子和他的襯衣不相配 "His pants and his shirt don't match"). These are not entries suitable for the Cantonese Wordnet, as they can be decomposed further. At any rate, the audio recordings of the longer chunks, phrases and sentences are all standard Chinese (Mandarin) pronounced in Cantonese. These phrases and sentences contain non-Cantonese constructions and lexical items, e.g., the Mandarin 的, *de* "of", which should be 嘅 *ge3* in Cantonese; the Mandarin 在 *zài*, "be at", which should be 喺 *hai2* in Cantonese; the Mandarin 喝, *hē*,"drink", which should be 飲, *jam2*, in Cantonese. The audio recordings of these longer phrases also seem to be put together with smaller chunks in such a way that the sound segments overlap, rendering them unintelligible. Despite these challenges, the Wikimedia Commons dataset offers a valuable resource for expanding Cantonese word coverage, provided careful attention is paid to the distinction between Hong Kong "Chinese" and spoken Cantonese usage, and checking of the individual audio files.

Among lemmas (in the recordings) that we would like to include in the Cantonese wordnet but do not yet exist in the Princeton WordNet, they are mainly idioms (e.g., 供不應求 *gung1 bat1 ying3 kau4* "demand is greater than supply"), which do not correspond to single lemmas, and culturally (Chinese) specific items (e.g., 繁體字 *faan4 tai2 zi6* "(Chinese) traditional characters", 拜年 *baai3 nin4* "going to visit relatives during Chinese New Year holidays").

3.2 Cantonese L2 data

The second set of audio recordings was recorded and compiled by a native Cantonese speaker (who was also a lecturer of Cantonese). There was no problem with the Cantonese-ness of the data. However, we still have to exclude some of the data for

[9] The word for umbrella in Cantonese is 遮 *ze1*.

now because they are arguably phrases. For example, 煲劇 *bou1 kek6* "to binge-watch a series", which contains both the verb 煲 *bou1* "to cook/boil" and the noun 劇 *kek6* "TV series". The syntactic status of these V-O sequences (compound words vs. phrases) are controversial in Cantonese grammar because on the one hand, they allow the insertion of aspectual particles in-between the two characters (V and O), e.g., the progressing aspectual particle 緊 *gan2* can be added in the middle of 煲劇 *bou1 kek6*: 煲緊劇 *bou1 gan2 kek6*, meaning the binge-watching of some series is in progress. On the other hand, their combinations are partially idiomatic in nature. For 煲劇 *bou1 kek6*, the verb 煲 *bou1* means "to cook/boil", not "watch". It only means "watch" in 煲劇 *bou1 kek6*. Furthermore, the metaphorical usage of the verb 煲 *bou1* "to cook/boil" is semi-productive. It can be used in a limited number of phrases like 煲電話粥 *bou1 din6 waa2 zuk1*, literally it means "to boil telephone congee', which means "to talk on the phone for a very long time"). At this moment, we have decided to not include such examples in the Cantonese Wordnet, though these are items that would be very useful for L2 learners. In the future, we would like to explore using two level of annotation for these idiomatic but compositional items, mapping them to both multi-word expressions and also decompositionally (Sio and Morgado da Costa, 2023).

Among lemmas (in the recordings) that we would like to include in the Cantonese wordnet but which do not have appropriate concepts in the Princeton WordNet, these include (i) locations in Hong Kong (e.g., 尖沙咀 *ziml saa1 zeoi2*, a waterfront area famous for shopping and views of Victoria Harbour), (ii) culturally (Hong Kong) specific items (e.g., 叮叮 *ding1 ding1*, Hong Kong trams) [10] and, (iii) Cantonese language specific phrases (e.g., 冚家鏟 *ham4 gaa1 caan2*, a swear word that literally means "whole family drop dead", meaning "bastard" or "jerk").

So far we have delayed adding new contentful concepts to the Cantonese Wordnet. In the future we will work with CILI (Bond et al., 2016) to create and share these concepts.

4 Release

Before the release of this paper, the Cantonese Wordnet had just over 5,250 concepts, lexified with around 16,300 senses. The work presented in this paper increased the sense inventory with 1050 new senses (695 new senses from the Wikimedia Commons dataset and 355 new senses from Cantonese L2 dataset). These new senses are distributed across 964 new concepts (665 from the Wikimedia Commons dataset and 308 from Cantonese L2 dataset) – an increase of 18%.

In addition to expanded coverage, the Cantonese Wordnet now also includes recordings for 2,138 unique pronunciations (combining both datasets), 15 of which have two sets of recordings (one male and one female voice). Each of these recordings corresponds to a hand checked (phonemic) Jyutping pronunciation.

Based on Jyutping matching , and given the occurrence of homophones, 1,809 senses previously included in the Cantonese Wordnet can now be linked to an audio recording. This is in addition to 1,050 new senses that were added as part of the work presented in this paper. In total, the Cantonese Wordnet currently has 2,859 senses linked to audio recordings.

4.1 Audio Recordings

The audio files for both datasets were originally encoded with Waveform Audio File Format (WAVE). We re-encoded the files using FLAC (Free Lossless Audio Codec),[11] which is lossless, so keeps all the information about the sound, and an open standard, therefore it is well supported. Because the snippets are single words, the audio files are sufficiently small (typically around 30kB).

These and all future audio recordings will become part of the standard release of the Cantonese Wordnet. Given their lightweight, the audio recordings will be released as part of the Cantonese Wordnet's original Github repository.[12]

4.2 Pronunciations in the Wordnet LMF

Similar to previous releases, this new version of the Cantonese Wordnet will be released in the Wordnet LMF format.[13]. Pronunciation was added to this LMF in McCrae et al. (2021, WN-LMF 1.1).

An example of its encoding is given in Figure 1. It uses the `<Pronunciation>` element. `<Pronunciation>` elements can currently be used as subelements of lemmas and forms. For the time

[10] The nickname 叮叮 *ding1 ding1* originates from the warning sounds of the bell, rung when the tram is in motion.

[11] `https://xiph.org/flac/index.html`

[12] `https://github.com/lmorgadodacosta/CantoneseWN`

[13] `https://github.com/globalwordnet/schemas`

```
<LexicalEntry id="cantown-yue-lex4">
    <Lemma writtenForm="你" partOfSpeech="n"/>
    <Form writtenForm="nei5">
        <Pronunciation variety="jyutping"
         audio ="https://path/nei5.flac">nei5</Pronunciation>
    </Form>
    <Form writtenForm="lei5">
        <Pronunciation variety="jyutping" notation="n/l lazy"
            audio ="https://path/lei5.flac">lei5</Pronunciation>
    </Form>
    </Lemma>
    <Sense id="cantown-yue-77000021-n-lex4"
    synset="cantown-yue-77000021-n"></Sense>
</LexicalEntry>
```

Figure 1: WN-LMF representation of pronunciation: the Cantonese lemma 你 has two forms *nei5* and *lei5*. Each form has a single pronunciation element (although multiple would be possible), linking it to the respective file.

being, we decided to keep it under form to allow clustering of multiple pronunciations by its Jyutping form. For example, in Figure 1, we currently have a single pronunciation for the Jyutping form *nei5*, but we see a future where we will have multiple recordings (e.g., using male and female voices, or representing regional variation). Another benefit of keeping Jyutping as a form, is the fact that many existing tools, such as the Open Multilingual Wordnet (Bond and Foster, 2013), display and even search over these fields. The `<Pronunciation>` element has 4 attributes:

- **audio**: provides the URL for the recording.
- **variety** encodes the language variety, for example by using the IETF language tags to indicate dialect, where Cantonese in jyutping would be `zh-yue-jyutping`. There is no general standard for how these are labelled, each wordnet can decide on its own — in our case `zh-yue` is redundant, so we omit it.
- **phonemic**: indicates whether the transcription is phonemic (**true**) or phonetic (**false**), with the default being **true** (phonemic).
- **notation**: can capture any additional details.

More detail of the audio support in the LMF is given in Bond (2025).

5 Future Work

The work presented in this paper is a step in a specific direction. As noted above, there are still many senses that do not have linked pronunciations. We would like to continue this work by exploring other open resources and continuing producing our own recordings to ensure that the majority of Cantonese senses, or at least those in common use, have a linked pronunciation. Of interest to this goal, is the fact that after inspecting the remainder of the data we extracted from Wikimedia Commons, it became clear many other recordings are pronounced in Hong Kong "Chinese". We believe that we can semi-automatically check which recordings may be of use to the Cantonese Wordnet – exploring homophones between Cantonese and Hong Kong "Chinese" to get additional recordings for the wordnet.

Another interesting avenue we would like to explore is exploring the new available recordings in the field of gamification of Cantonese learning and teaching. We believe the Cantonese Wordnet can soon be served as a learner's dictionary. And we would like to develop companion online apps to help Cantonese learners, gamifying the learning process of lexical and tonal knowledge.

6 Conclusion

This paper presents significant advancements in the Cantonese Wordnet, with the addition of 1,050 new senses across 964 new synsets and 2,138 new audio recordings, substantially improving its utility for both linguistic research and L2 Cantonese education. By incorporating pronunciations and linking them to specific senses, we have made the resource more accessible, especially in the context of Cantonese's tonal phonology. Moving forward, we plan to expand the dataset further, incorporating more educational and culturally specific lemmas, and explore ways to use this data in language-learning applications.

Acknowledgments

We would like to thank WikiCommons user Luilui6666 for changing the license of her recordings to accommodate the Cantonese Wordnet's license. We would also like to thank Dennis Lam for recording the the list of Cantonese L2 common lexical items for us.

Kamila Liedermannova would like to thank the IGA student grant funded by Palacký University (IGA_FF_2033_063 SPP: 432105081/31) for supporting this research study.

References

Robert S Bauer. 2016. The hong kong cantonese language: Current features and future prospects. *Global Chinese*, 2(2):115–161.

Francis Bond. 2025. Adding audio to wordnets,. In *13th International Global Wordnet Conference (GWC 2025)*. (this volume).

Francis Bond and Ryan Foster. 2013. Linking and extending an open multilingual wordnet. In *Proceedings of the 51st Annual Meeting of the Association for Computational Linguistics*, pages 1352–1362.

Francis Bond, Piek Vossen, John Philip McCrae, and Christiane Fellbaum. 2016. Cili: the collaborative interlingual index. In *Proceedings of the 8th Global WordNet Conference (GWC)*, pages 50–57.

Christiane Fellbaum, editor. 1998. *WordNet: An Electronic Lexical Database*. MIT Press, Cambridge, MA.

Peter Ladefoged and Keith Johnson. 2006. A course in phonetics (5th). *Thomson Wadsworth*, pages 133–236.

John P. McCrae, Michael Wayne Goodman, Francis Bond, Alexandre Rademaker, Ewa Rudnicka, and Luís Morgado da Costa. 2021. The global wordnet formats: Updates for 2020. In *11th International Global Wordnet Conference (GWC2021)*.

George A Miller, Claudia Leacock, Randee Tengi, and Ross T Bunker. 1993. A semantic concordance. In *Human Language Technology: Proceedings of a Workshop Held at Plainsboro, New Jersey, March 21-24, 1993*.

Joanna Sio and Luis Morgado da Costa. 2023. The open cantonese sense-tagged corpus. In *Proceedings of the 12th Global Wordnet Conference*, pages 263–268.

Joanna Ut-Seong Sio and Luis Morgado da Costa. 2019. Building the cantonese wordnet. In *Proceedings of the 10th Global Wordnet Conference (GWC 2019), Wroclaw, Poland*.

Joanna Ut-Seong Sio and Luis Morgado da Costa. 2022. Enriching linguistic representation in the cantonese wordnet and building the new cantonese wordnet corpus. In *Proceedings of the 13th Conference on Language Resources and Evaluation*, Marseille, France. European Language Resources Association (ELRA).

Challenges and Solutions in Developing Low-Resource Wordnets: Insights from Assamese and Bodo

Shikhar Kumar Sarma, Ratul Deka, Bhatima Baro, Vaskar Deka, Umesh Deka, Mirzanur Rahman, Satyajit Sarmah, Kuwali Talukdar, Kishore Kashyap, Department of Information Technology, Gauhati University, India

sks001@gmail.com, rdeka8258@gmail.com, bhatimaishaan@gmail.com, vaskardeka@gauhati.ac.in, humeshdeka@gmail.com, mr@gauhati.ac.in, ss@gauhati.ac.in, kuwalitalukdar@gmail.com, kb.guwahati@gmail.com

Abstract

This paper explores the challenges and solutions encountered in the development of wordnets for low-resource languages, specifically Assamese and Bodo. As critical linguistic resources, wordnets enhance natural language processing (NLP) applications by providing structured semantic relationships in a strong lexical resource. However, the development process for these wordnets faced significant obstacles, including limited linguistic data, the absence of trained native experts for annotation, and the need for language-specific adaptations. This study details the methodologies employed to address these challenges, including collaborative efforts with local linguists, the use of computational techniques for data enrichment, and the integration of community feedback to refine the wordnets. We also present a comparative analysis of the Assamese and Bodo wordnets, highlighting their unique characteristics and commonalities. Our findings justify the importance of strategic planning and community involvement in creating effective lexical resources for low-resource languages, paving the way for future advancements in NLP applications.

1 Introduction

Wordnets are invaluable linguistic resources that provide a structured representation of lexical relationships among words, facilitating various natural language processing (NLP) applications, including semantic analysis, machine translation, and information retrieval. However, the development of wordnets for low-resource languages like Assamese and Bodo poses unique challenges that differ significantly from those faced in high-resource languages. Assamese and Bodo are indigenous languages spoken in the northeastern region of India. Despite their rich linguistic heritage, both languages lack extensive digital resources, which hinders computational linguistic research and development. The absence of established wordnets for these languages not only limits access to language technology but also affects the preservation and promotion of their linguistic and cultural identity. This paper aims to provide insights into the challenges encountered during the development of Assamese and Bodo wordnets, including issues related to data scarcity, linguistic diversity, and the involvement of native speakers in the annotation process. We will also discuss the innovative solutions implemented to overcome these challenges, such as collaborative projects with local linguistic communities and the application of computational techniques for data enhancement. By sharing our experiences and methodologies, we hope to contribute to the broader discourse on developing wordnets for low-resource languages, ultimately supporting the advancement of NLP technologies that are inclusive of diverse linguistic contexts.

2 Related Works

The concept of wordnets, introduced by Miller (1995), serves as a crucial resource for natural language processing tasks across various languages. Their extensive application has paved the way for developing similar lexical databases in low-resource languages. For instance, Bhattacharyya (2010) discusses the adaptation of wordnet for Indian languages, highlighting the potential for cross-linguistic applications in machine translation and semantic analysis. Navigli and Velardi (2005) emphasize the importance of wordnets in word sense disambiguation, demonstrating their utility in improving computational linguistics tasks. Kumar and Rao (2012) further explore this aspect, illustrating how wordnet can enhance machine translation systems specifically for low-resource languages. Recent studies have focused on the challenges and strategies for constructing wordnets in low-resource contexts. Huang and Wang (2019) examine the construction process for the Uighur language, providing insights that may apply to other languages facing similar limitations. Bharati and Reddy (2013) present a lexicon-based approach to wordnet construction for Telugu, while Rao and Kumar (2020) discuss the broader challenges and opportunities in building low-resource wordnets. In the context of Indian languages, Reddy and Kumar (2018) analyze the specific challenges encountered in developing wordnets for languages like Hindi and Kannada. Jain and Gupta (2019) extend this discussion to Hindi and Bengali, underscoring the shared obstacles and potential methodologies applicable to low-resource languages. The development of Assamese wordnet has been an area of active research. Sarmah et al. (2012) present a novel document classification approach using Assamese wordnet, highlighting its practical applications. Additionally, Sarma et al. (2012) analyze the processes involved in building the Assamese wordnet, shedding light on the linguistic implications and methodologies. Sarma et al. (2010) provide foundational insights into the structural aspects of developing Assamese wordnet, while their subsequent work on the Bodo wordnet (Sarma et al., 2010) offers a comprehensive overview of its organization and development. Furthermore, Das and Sarma (2021) explore semantic dimensions in Assamese and Bodo using their respective wordnets, enriching the understanding of linguistic relationships in these languages. This body of work collectively emphasizes the significance of wordnets in advancing linguistic resources for low-resource languages, thereby enhancing natural language processing capabilities and fostering further research in the field.

3 Methodology

The development of wordnets for Assamese and Bodo involved a systematic approach to address the unique challenges presented by these low-resource languages. This section outlines the key methodologies employed in the creation of the wordnets, focusing on data collection, linguistic analysis, and community involvement.

3.1 Data collection

The first step in developing the wordnets was to gather existing lexical resources, including dictionaries, thesauri, and language corpora. Given the scarcity of digital resources for Assamese and Bodo, we relied on both primary and secondary sources.

Primary Sources: Collaborations with local linguists and university language departments facilitated access to unpublished lexicons and linguistic data. Fieldwork was conducted to document vernacular usage and regional variations.

Secondary Sources: We utilized available online dictionaries and existing databases, such as the Indo Wordnet, to use relevant lexical entries and synsets. These resources provided a foundational structure for the wordnets.

3.2 Linguistic analysis

Following data collection, a thorough linguistic analysis was conducted to identify semantic relationships and hierarchical structures among the lexical items. The analysis focused on-

Synonymy: Identifying synonyms to establish relationships within the same semantic field.

Antonymy and Hypernymy: Recognizing antonyms and hypernyms to enrich the semantic network and provide a comprehensive representation of word meanings.

Part-of-Speech Tagging: Each word was tagged for its part of speech to facilitate accurate semantic categorization.

3.3 Community involvement

Engaging with native speakers and local linguistic communities played a pivotal role in the development process. This involved-

Annotation Workshops: We organized workshops where community members participated in annotating lexical entries, ensuring cultural and contextual relevance in the wordnets.

Feedback Mechanisms: Continuous feedback loops were established to refine the wordnets based on community input, helping to address issues of ambiguity and regional dialects.

3.4 Integration and validation

The final step involved integrating the gathered data into a cohesive wordnet structure. We utilized software tools designed for wordnet development to create the final databases for Assamese and Bodo. Validation of the wordnets was carried out through Expert Reviews. Linguistic experts reviewed the wordnets to ensure accuracy and comprehensiveness. We also performed Cross-Linguistic Comparison. The Assamese and Bodo wordnets were compared against existing wordnets of other languages to identify potential gaps and areas for improvement.

4 Results

The development process for the Assamese and Bodo wordnets yielded significant results, showcasing both the successes and challenges encountered along the way. This section presents the key outcomes of our efforts, including the size and structure of the wordnets, examples of lexical relationships, and insights gained from community involvement.

Wordnet Structure and Size:

The final Assamese and Bodo wordnets were constructed with attention to their unique linguistic features.

The key metrics are as follows-

Assamese Wordnet:

Total Synsets: 14,500

Total Lexical Entries: 55,300

Coverage of Parts of Speech: Nouns, Verbs, Adjectives, and Adverbs

Bodo Wordnet:

Total Synsets: 13,600

Total Lexical Entries: 42,250

Coverage of Parts of Speech: Nouns, Verbs, Adjectives, and Adverbs

Both wordnets exhibit a hierarchical structure, with hypernyms and hyponyms clearly defined, allowing for intuitive navigation of semantic relationships.

Community Involvement Insights: Community involvement was instrumental in the development of both wordnets. Feedback from native speakers highlighted several key insights.

Cultural Relevance: Community workshops revealed regional dialects and culturally specific terms that were not initially included, ensuring the wordnets are more reflective of everyday language use.

Validation of Relationships: Community feedback helped validate semantic relationships, particularly in cases of synonyms and antonyms, leading to a more robust representation of lexical semantics.

Challenges Faced:

While the results are promising, several challenges were encountered.

Data Scarcity: Limited availability of comprehensive linguistic resources for Assamese and Bodo posed significant hurdles during the initial stages of development.

Complex Dialectal Variation: The presence of diverse dialects within both languages, particularly for Assamese, complicated the process of establishing a unified wordnet structure.

Engagement with Communities: Maintaining consistent engagement with native experts proved challenging, affecting the pace of annotation and feedback collection.

Discussion

The development of wordnets for Assamese and Bodo has significant implications for natural language processing and the preservation of linguistic diversity. This section discusses the key findings from our research, reflecting on the methodologies employed, the impact of community involvement, and the broader relevance of our work. The successful establishment of Assamese and Bodo wordnets highlights the critical role of linguistic resources in advancing NLP for low-resource languages. By providing structured semantic information, these wordnets facilitate a range of applications, including machine translation, information retrieval, and sentiment analysis. Integrating wordnets in the NLP pipelines can bridge the gap in NLP capabilities for underrepresented languages, ultimately fostering greater inclusivity in technology. Engaging local linguistic experts and native communities proved to be a booster of our development process. The insights gained from workshops and feedback sessions not only enriched the wordnets but also empowered native experts by involving them in linguistic documentation and language technology efforts. This collaborative approach fosters a sense of ownership and ensures that the linguistic resources developed are culturally and contextually relevant. Despite the positive outcomes, challenges such as data scarcity and dialectal variation remain prevalent in the development of low-resource wordnets. Continuous efforts are necessary to continually update and refine the wordnets as language evolves and new linguistic data become available. Moving forward, the development of Assamese and Bodo wordnets can be enhanced by incorporating advancements in computational linguistics, such as machine learning techniques for automated data enrichment and validation. Expanding collaboration with academic institutions and linguistic communities will further strengthen the sustainability and relevance of these resources.

Conclusion

This study presents the challenges and solutions encountered in developing wordnets for Assamese and Bodo, two low-resource languages. The establishment of these wordnets is a critical step toward enhancing natural language processing capabilities and preserving linguistic diversity in the face of globalization. Our findings highlight the importance of linguistic resources that could potentially facilitate various NLP applications, from machine translation to semantic analysis. The successful engagement of local linguistic experts has proven to be invaluable, not only enriching the wordnets with culturally relevant data but also empowering native linguists to participate actively in the preservation of their languages and in the language technology sphere. Despite the hurdles faced such as data scarcity and dialectal variations, the methodologies employed have laid a strong foundation for future advancements. Continuous refinement of the Assamese and Bodo wordnets will be essential to accommodate evolving linguistic landscapes. Future work may focus on integrating emerging computational techniques to enhance the quality and usability of these resources, ultimately contributing to the broader goal of fostering inclusivity in language technology.

References

Miller, G. A. (1995). WordNet: A lexical database for English. Communications of the ACM, 38(11), 39-41. doi:10.1145/219905.219938.

Navigli, R., & Velardi, P. (2005). Evaluating wordnet-based measures for word sense disambiguation. In Proceedings of the 43rd Annual Meeting of the Association for Computational Linguistics (ACL), 2005, 48-55. doi:10.3115/1219840.1219849.

Bhattacharyya, P. (2010). WordNet for Indian languages. In Proceedings of the 7th Global WordNet Conference, 2010, 81-90.

Kumar, A., & Rao, M. (2012). A study on the role of WordNet in improving machine translation for low-resource languages. International Journal of Computer Applications, 46(21), 32-36. doi:10.5120/7101-9772.

Huang, Y., & Wang, L. (2019). Exploring the construction of WordNet for low-resource languages: A case study of Uighur. Language Resources and Evaluation, 53(4), 659-674. doi:10.1007/s10579-019-09429-5.

Bharati, A., & Reddy, P. (2013). A lexicon-based approach to wordnet construction for low-resource languages: The case of Telugu. In Proceedings of the 10th International Conference on Natural Language Processing (ICON 2013), 152-159.

Rao, M., & Kumar, A. (2020). Building low-resource wordnets: Challenges and opportunities. In Proceedings of the 12th Global WordNet Conference, 237-244.

Reddy, S., & Kumar, S. (2018). Challenges in developing WordNets for Indian languages: The case of Hindi and Kannada. International Journal of Linguistics, 10(1), 1-12. doi:10.5296/ijl.v10i1.12773.

Jain, S., & Gupta, S. (2019). Developing WordNets for low-resource languages: A case study of Hindi and Bengali. Journal of Natural Language Engineering, 25(1), 123-141. doi:10.1017/S1355770X18000058.

Sarmah, J., Saharia, N., & Sarma, S. K. (2012). A Novel Approach for Document Classification using Assamese WordNet. In Global Wordnet Conference (GWC), Japan.

Sarma, S. K., Saikia, U., Mahanta, M., & Bharali, H. (2012). Assamese Vocabulary and Assamese Wordnet Building: An Analysis. In Global Wordnet Conference (GWC), Japan.

Sarma, S. K., Gogoi, M., Medhi, R., & Saikia, U. (2010). Foundation and Structure of Developing an Assamese Wordnet. In Global Wordnet Conference, IIT Bombay.

Sarma, S. K., Gogoi, M., Brahma, B., & Ramchiary, M. B. (2020). A Wordnet for Bodo Language: Structure and Development. In Proceedings of the Eighth Global Wordnet Conference.

Das, B., & Sarma, S. K. (2021). Semantic Analysis of Assamese and Bodo using WordNet. Journal of Language Modelling, 9(1), 65-85.

Assamese WordNet based Quality Enhancement of Bilingual Machine Translation System - ACL Anthology](https://aclanthology.org/W14-0135/)

Shikhar Sarma, Dibyajyoti Sarmah, Ratul Deka, Anup Barman, Jumi Sarmah, Himadri Bharali, Mayashree Mahanta, and Umesh Deka. 2014. A Quantitative Analysis of Synset of Assamese WordNet: Its Position and Timeline. In Proceedings of the Seventh Global Wordnet Conference, pages 246–249, Tartu, Estonia. University of Tartu Press.

Himadri Bharali, Mayashree Mahanta, Shikhar Kr. Sarma, Utpal Saikia, and Dibyajyoti Sarmah. 2014. An Analytical Study of Synonymy in Assamese Language Using WorldNet: Classification and Structure. In Proceedings of the Seventh Global Wordnet Conference, pages 250–255, Tartu, Estonia. University of Tartu Press.

Anup Barman, Jumi Sarmah, and Shikhar Sarma. 2014. Assamese WordNet based Quality Enhancement of Bilingual Machine Translation System. In Proceedings of the Seventh Global Wordnet Conference, pages 256–261, Tartu, Estonia. University of Tartu Press.

Shikhar Kr. Sarma, Dibyajyoti Sarmah, Biswajit Brahma, Himadri Bharali, Mayashree Mahanta, and Utpal Saikia. 2012. Building Multilingual Lexical Resources using Wordnets: Structure, Design and Implementation. In Proceedings of the 3rd Workshop on Cognitive Aspects of the Lexicon, pages 161–170, Mumbai, India. The COLING 2012 Organizing Committee.

Extracting Conceptual Differences between Translation Pairs Using Multilingual WordNet

Ikkyu Nishimura[1,2], Yohei Murakami[1,3], Mondheera Pituxcoosuvarn[1,4],
[1] Faculty of Information Science and Engineering,
Ritsumeikan University, Ibaraki, Osaka, Japan
[2] is0368xk@ed.ritsumei.ac.jp [3] yohei@fc.ritsumei.ac.jp [4] mond-p@fc.ritsumei.ac.jp

Abstract

The concepts expressed by words and their translations in different languages do not always align. Despite advancements in machine translation, such differences can still lead to misunderstandings. Therefore, we proposed a method to extract conceptual differences in translation pairs from WordNet and Open Multilingual WordNet. We applied the proposed method to Japanese, Chinese, and Indonesian WordNets to investigate how many translation pairs with conceptual differences they have. Furthermore, we validated the extracted conceptual differences using human evaluators.

1 Introduction

Improvements in machine translation (hereinafter, this is called "MT") are reducing language barriers in multilingual communication. However, since languages evolve with their unique cultures and histories, their conceptual systems can differ, leading to misunderstandings. In particular, Asian languages tend to have lower similarity to English compared to European languages (Chiswick and Miller, 2005). This may result in a correct translation, but with differences in the concepts expressed between words. In this study, we propose a method to quantify the concepts represented by words using WordNet and Open Multilingual WordNet (hereinafter, this is called "OMW") to identify such conceptual differences across languages. We focus on Japanese, Chinese, and Indonesian, detecting conceptual differences across the three languages based on WordNet Synsets.

The following two challenges can be identified:

Quantification of the range of concepts
It is challenging to articulate the meanings and ranges of concepts associated with words because concepts are abstract. Therefore, we extract the linked concepts of each word as a set using a conceptual dictionary, allowing us to quantify the concepts of each word.

Detection of conceptual differences
Due to the unique conceptual systems of each language, comparing concepts expressed by words across languages is challenging. To address this, we utilize WordNet for the English concept system and OMW for aligning other languages, allowing us to compare and extract conceptual differences based on the English system.

2 Conceptual Differences in Multilingual Communication

2.1 Conceptual Difference

The advent of MT is making communication with people from different cultures and languages easier. However, communication through MT carries the potential for misunderstandings due to differences in the concepts expressed by words. For example, Yamashita and Ishida (2006) analyzed communication between speakers of different languages, observing that in conversations using MT, dialogues sometimes broke down when the meaning of a polysemous word changed during translation. In that case, the difference in concepts arose because the word had multiple meanings, but even words with the same meaning can express different concepts. For example, in the Japanese and English translation pair "団子 (dango)" and "dumpling", the latter broadly refers to boiled, ball-shaped foods, while Japanese distinguishes " 団子 (dango)" as items without fillings, categorizing stuffed foods like "餃子 (gyoza)" and "小籠包 (xiao long bao)" differently. In translation, there is no exact equivalent for the word "団子 (dango)" in the English conceptual system, so the translation result becomes "dumpling".

This issue is also present in the construction of Multilingual WordNet. Fellbaum and Vossen

Table 1: Conceptual differences between English and other languages

Lang	Total Word Pair	Concept Difference	Ratio
ja	477,031	33,190	7.0%
zh	199,724	12,327	6.1%
id	220,128	20,587	9.4%
nl	245,068	15,857	6.5%
fr	313,473	14,974	4.8%
es	165,224	8,705	5.3%
it	228,055	144,36	6.3%

※ja:Japanese, zh:Chinese, id:Indonesian, nl:Dutch, fr:French, es:Spanish, it:Italian

(2012) pointed out that even words deemed synonymous between different languages often only partially overlap in their meanings and concepts. Multilingual WordNet is created based on the synsets of the English WordNet. As a result, in non-English languages, a word may not correspond to a single synset but may instead be linked to multiple adjacent synsets (hypernyms and hyponyms). This happens because the conceptual system of the target language may differ from that of English. Table.1 illustrates the number of translation pairs where non-English words appear across adjacent synsets. It reveals that less than 10% of word pairs exhibit such differences. In this study, we define such variations in the concepts expressed by words as conceptual differences and focus on detecting these differences.

2.2 Related Works

2.2.1 Cross-Language WordNet

In addition to the initiatives related to the Japanese, Chinese, and Indonesian WordNets, which are the focus of this study, we introduce research efforts on cross-lingual WordNets.

Fellbaum and Vossen (2012) analyzed the challenges of aligning WordNets across different languages from a linguistic perspective. Isahara et al. (2008) developed the Japanese WordNet by translating words within WordNet into Japanese. Wang and Bond (2013) aligned Chinese with WordNet. Additionally, Choi et al. (2004) developed a cross-linguistic WordNet that aligns Korean, Japanese, and Chinese. Putra et al. (2008) proposed the development of the Indonesian WordNet through manual annotation by human annotators. Additionally, Open WordNet Bahasa, which aligns with both Indonesian and Malay, was developed by Noor et al. (2011). Rudnicka et al. conducted a study aimed at mapping the Polish WordNet to the English Princeton WordNet. In addition, they proposed a system to detect gaps and mismatches between the Polish and English WordNets (Rudnicka et al., 2023).

These studies focused on the development of WordNets in various languages and their alignment with other languages.

2.2.2 Conceptual Difference Detection

Next, we discuss research on detecting conceptual differences between languages caused by cultural and linguistic variations.

Yoshino et al. (2015) proposed a method to detect conceptual differences between Japanese and Chinese using Wikipedia category information and descriptions. We detected conceptual differences between languages due to cultural variations, using image similarity and an optimized threshold for automatic detection (Pituxcoosuvarn et al.; Nishimura et al., 2020). Li et al. (2019) conducted research on measuring semantic similarity between texts in different languages. In this study, they calculated the similarity between Chinese and Lao texts using WordNet. Stoyanova et al. (2013) proposed a method for identifying relationships between English and Bulgarian concepts by using word similarity within WordNet.

These studies detect interpretation differences among speakers of different languages. This research aims to automatically identify conceptual differences among Japanese, Chinese, and Indonesian, using WordNet and OMW based on the English conceptual system.

3 Extraction Method of Conceptual Difference

3.1 Quantification of the Concept Range

To extract the conceptual differences between translation pairs, quantifying the range of concepts for each word is necessary. We propose a method for quantifying the conceptual range of words using WordNet and OMW[1]. Our method's feature is that by leveraging the structure of OMW, which links various languages to the conceptual system represented by English WordNet, it allows for the comparison of word concepts based on WordNet

[1]OMW version 1.4

synsets across different languages with distinct conceptual systems (Bond and Foster, 2013).

We target the languages Japanese (ja), Chinese (zh), and Indonesian (id) to extract word pairs with conceptual differences across these three languages. Asian languages, in comparison to European languages, tend to show lower similarity to English. Therefore, in WordNet, which is based on the English conceptual framework, these languages are mapped to a different conceptual system. By comparing Asian languages using WordNet as the reference point, we can detect a greater number of conceptual differences.

The first step of our proposal is to quantify the range of concepts for each word. The synsets in the WordNet and their superordinate-subordinate relationships are represented by a graph G, as in Equation 1.

$$G = (V, E) \tag{1}$$

A graph G has a set V of synsets and a set E whose edges are is-a relations between synsets.

$$V = \{v_1, v_2, v_3, \cdots, v_l\} \tag{2}$$

Also, a graph G is a directed graph using an is-a relation called hypernym, which identifies upper-level synsets from lower-level synsets.

If v_i be the upper synset and v_j the lower synset, the edges are represented as (v_j, v_i). Due to the structure of WordNet, each synset has a word representing its concept because synsets are defined by a collection of synonymous words, and there is a set of words W as in Equation 3.

$$W = \{w_1, w_2, w_3, \cdots, w_n\} \tag{3}$$

Some synset v_i as in Equation 4 is a set of words as in Equation 5.

$$v_i \in V \tag{4}$$

$$v_i \subset W, w_k \in v_i \tag{5}$$

We define the set of synsets C_{w_k} that is the range of the concept of a word w_k. First, C_{w_k} has v_i ($v_i \in C_{w_k}$) because $w_k \in v_i$. For any synset $v \in C_{w_k}$, the parent node v_p, child node v_c, and sibling node v_b are used to obtein the set of synsets associated with the word w_k (Equation 6). In this paper, this set C_{w_k} is the concept range of word w_k.

$$\begin{aligned} C_{w_k} = {} & C_{w_k} \cup \\ & \{v_p \mid v \in C_{w_k}, (v, v_p) \in E, w_k \in v_p\} \cup \\ & \{v_c \mid v \in C_{w_k}, (v_c, v) \in E, w_i \in v_c\} \cup \\ & \{v_b \mid v \in C_{w_k}, (v, v') \in E, (v_b, v') \in E, \\ & \qquad w_k \in v_b\} \end{aligned} \tag{6}$$

3.2 Extraction of Conceptual Difference

The second step of our proposal is to extract word pairs with different conceptual ranges between words in one language and its translation in another. Specifically, we compare the concept ranges $C_{w_k^{l_1}}$ and $C_{w_k^{l_2}}$ for words $w_k^{l_1}$ in language l_1 and $w_k^{l_2}$ in different language l_2 contained on the same synset. If $C_{w_k^{l_1}} \neq C_{w_k^{l_2}}$ then $w_k^{l_1}$ and $w_k^{l_2}$ are as word pairs with conceptual difference. We get concept-differential word pairs in three languages: Japanese, Chinese and Indonesian.

There are seven patterns of conceptual differences obtained between the two languages depending on how the conceptual ranges are combined. First, the common set (ComSet) of concept ranges of words ($w_k^{l_1}$, $w_k^{l_2}$) in the two languages (l_1, l_2) is Equation 7 .

$$ComSet(w_k^{l_1}, w_k^{l_2}) = C_{w_k^{l_1}} \cap C_{w_k^{l_2}} \tag{7}$$

The symmetric difference set (DiffSet) of concept ranges of words ($w_k^{l_1}$, $w_k^{l_2}$) in the two languages (l_1, l_2) is Equation 8. For word pairs with conceptual difference $C_{w_i^{l1}} \neq C_{w_i^{l2}}$, so $DiffSet \neq \emptyset$.

$$\begin{aligned} & DiffSet(w_k^{l_1}, w_k^{l_2}) = \\ & \qquad (C_{w_k^{l_1}} - C_{w_k^{l_2}}) \cup (C_{w_k^{l_2}} - C_{w_k^{l_1}}) \end{aligned} \tag{8}$$

We classify as horizontal types the cases in which the synsets in the common set and the synsets in the symmetric difference set are siblings, as in Equation 9.

$$\begin{aligned} & \forall v_x \forall v_y ((v_x \in ComSet(w_k^{l_1}, w_k^{l_2}) \\ & \qquad \wedge v_y \in DiffSet(w_k^{l_1}, w_k^{l_2})) \Rightarrow \\ & \exists v (v \in V \wedge (v_x, v) \in E \wedge (v_y, v) \in E))) \end{aligned} \tag{9}$$

In addition, we define a horizontal (part common) type as one that satisfies the 10 equation.

$$((C_{w_k^{l_1}} - C_{w_k^{l_2}}) \neq \emptyset) \wedge ((C_{w_k^{l_2}} - C_{w_k^{l_1}}) \neq \emptyset) \tag{10}$$

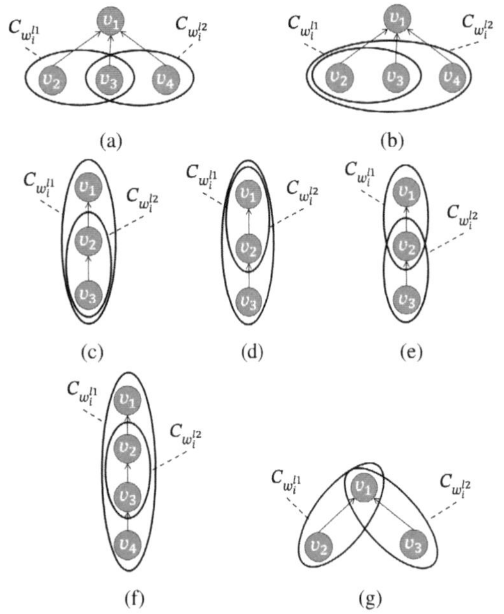

Figure 1: Type of conceptual difference

Figure 1a is an example of the horizontal-(part common) type. In Figure 1a, the nodes v_1, v_2, v_3 and v_4 are each synset and the edges between the nodes are Hypernym. The conceptual range $C_{w_k^{l_1}}$ of a word $w_k^{l_1}$ in language l_1 is the circle enclosing node v_2 and node v_3, the conceptual range $C_{w_k^{l_2}}$ of a word $w_k^{l_2}$ in language l_2 is the circle enclosing node v_3 and node v_4, which is the circle enclosing v_4. $C_{w_k^{l_1}} = \{v_2, v_3\}$ and $C_{w_k^{l_2}} = \{v_3, v_4\}$ as shown in Figure 1a, the common set is $ComSet(w_k^{l_1}, w_k^{l_2}) = \{v_3\}$, the symmetric difference set is $DiffSet(w_k^{l_1}, w_k^{l_2}) = \{v_2, v_4\}$. They satisfy the Equation 9 and Equation 10. The two concept ranges are partially common because $w_k^{l_1}$ and $w_k^{l_2}$ overlap the concept of node v_3 and have concepts (nodes v_2 and v_4) that can only be represented by their respective concept ranges.

On the other hand, among the horizontal types, those satisfying the Equation 11 are considered horizontal (inclusive). Figure 1b is an example of the horizontal (inclusive) type, the concept ranges of w1 and w2 are $C_{w_k^{l_1}} = \{v_2, v_3\}$ and $C_{w_k^{l_2}} = \{v_2, v_3, v_4\}$. Since $C_{w_k^{l_2}}$ encompasses $C_{w_k^{l_1}}$, $w_k^{l_2}$ expresses a broader meaning than $w_k^{l_1}$ and is an inclusion relation.

$$((C_{w_k^{l_1}} - C_{w_k^{l_2}}) = \emptyset) \vee ((C_{w_k^{l_2}} - C_{w_k^{l_1}}) = \emptyset) \tag{11}$$

As in the Equation 12, we classify the conceptual difference as vertical type if there exists at least one parent-child relationship between the synset in the common set and the synset in the symmetric difference set.

$$\exists v_x \exists v_y ((v_x \in ComSet(w_k^{l_1}, w_k^{l_2}) \wedge v_y \in DiffSet(w_k^{l_1}, w_k^{l_2})) \Rightarrow ((v_x, v_y) \in E \vee (v_y, v_x) \in E) \tag{12}$$

Among the vertical types, the vertical (lower inclusive) type is the one that satisfies the Equation 13. As in the example in Figure 1c, the vertical (lower inclusive) type is the case where the synset in the symmetric difference set is the upper synset of the synset in the common set.

$$\forall v_x \in ComSet(w_k^{l_1}, w_k^{l_2}), \forall v_y \forall v_z (((v_x, v_y) \in E \wedge (v_z, v_x) \in E) \Rightarrow (v_y \in (ComSet(w_k^{l_1}, w_k^{l_2}) \cup DiffSet(w_k^{l_1}, w_k^{l_2})) \wedge v_z \notin DiffSet(w_k^{l_1}, w_k^{l_2})) \tag{13}$$

There are vertical types that satisfy the Equation 14. The synset in these symmetric difference sets is a subsynset of the synset in the common set. As shown in Figure 1d, the one satisfying the Equation 10 and the Equation 14 is the vertical (upper common) type. The others are the vertical (upper inclusive) type (as shown in Figure 1g).

$$\forall v_x \in ComSet(w_k^{l_1}, w_k^{l_2}), \forall v_y \forall v_z (((v_x, v_y) \in E \wedge (v_z, v_x) \in E) \Rightarrow (v_y \notin DiffSet(w_k^{l_1}, w_k^{l_2}) \wedge v_z \in (ComSet(w_k^{l_1}, w_k^{l_2}) \cup DiffSet(w_k^{l_1}, w_k^{l_2})) \tag{14}$$

As in the Equation 15, there is at least one parental relationship and at least one child relationship between the synset of the symmetric difference set and the synset of the common set here. Among them, those satisfying the Equation 10 are the vertical (part common) type, and those satisfying the Equation 11 are the vertical (inclusive) type. An example of the vertical (part common) type is shown in Figure 1e and an example of the vertical (inclusive) type is shown in Figure 1f.

In these inclusion relation, the conceptual range of one word is broader than that of the other, so there can be a discrepancy in communication in one direction, as in dumpling and dumpling, but

Table 2: Number of word pairs extracted

Lang	Word Pair	Concept Difference
ja - zh	236,590	27,005
ja - id	398,048	60,581
zh - id	111,450	14,175
Word Triplets	**11,571**	**1,375**

※ja:Japanese, zh:Chinese, id:Indonesian

not in the other. On the other hand, partial or superordinate commonality may lead to discrepancies in conversation in either orientation.

$$\exists v_w \, \exists v_x \, \exists v_y \, \exists v_z ((v_w, v_x \in ComSet(w_k^{l_1}, w_k^{l_2}) \wedge v_y, v_z \in DiffSet(w_k^{l_1}, w_k^{l_2})) \Rightarrow ((v_w, v_y) \in E \wedge (v_z, v_x) \in E)) \quad (15)$$

4 Human Judgements of Conceptual Differences

The creation of the correct labels is the result of manually determining the conceptual differences between words using a questionnaire.

4.1 Creating Word Triplets

In this section, we describe a method for manually creating the correct labels in order to evaluate the accuracy of the proposed method. Our proposal could find word pairs with conceptual differences between the Japanese, Chinese and Indonesian. As a result, 27,005 word pairs were obtained out of 236,590 total word pairs in ja-zh, 60,581 out of 398,048 word pairs in ja-id and 14,175 out of 111,450 word pairs in zh- id (Table 2) Word triplets are Japanese-Chinese-Indonesian word combinations that are filtered in two steps for word pairs, and they are created from the remaining word pairs (Table 2). The first filtering is to remove abstract concepts that are difficult to determine conceptual differences. The top-level concepts of synsets on WordNet: physical entity, abstraction and thing, which are located one level below entity, and word pairs extracted from the lower-level concepts of abstraction are excluded. The second filtering is to check the bilingual relationship between word pairs. In order to target word pairs that are most likely to appear as translation results in MT, word pairs where neither translation result was the other when each word was translated by MT are deleted. In the word pairs $w_k^{l_1}$ and $w_k^{l_2}$, word pairs where the Google MT of $w_k^{l_1}$ does not result in $w_k^{l_2}$ and the translation of $w_k^{l_2}$ does not result in $w_k^{l_1}$ are removed.

Figure 2: Images and queries in questionnaires

The next step is to create word triplets from the filtered Japanese-Chinese, Japanese-Indonesian and Chinese-Indonesian word pairs. Word pairs with words in common between any two languages are retrieved. If the three words in the two word pairs have a common part of the concept range, the three words are a word triplet. For example, there is a word pair w_k^{ja} and w_k^{zh} in ja-zh, and a word pair w_k^{ja} and w_k^{id} in ja-id. If the concept range $C_{w_k^{ja}} \wedge C_{w_k^{zh}} \wedge C_{w_k^{id}} \neq \emptyset$, then $(w_k^{ja}, w_k^{zh}, w_k^{id})$ is a word triplet. There are 11,571 word triplets created from word pairs between all languages (Table 2). Of these, 1,375 are from word pairs with conceptual differences.

4.2 Design of the Questionnaire and Collection of Images

In one task of the questionnaire, respondents were asked to select images that matched a word in their mother tongue from a group of images corresponding to the word triplet. The subjects were Japanese, Chinese and Indonesian, and we checked whether there were differences in responses between languages.

The image groups used in the questionnaire are the images obtained by image retrieval using the synsets in each concept range, if the word triplet of words are ja:w_k^{ja}, zh:w_k^{zh} and id:w_k^{id}. We make the query for Image Search from an English word

Table 3: Sample word triplet and image selection results for Japanese (ボート), Chinese (船), and Indonesian (kapal)

	Answer				
	1	2	3	4	5
Japanese	A,B,G	C,G	Non	D,F	G,H,I
Chinese	G,H,I	H,I	I	G,H,I	G,H

Table 4: The tallyed table generated from the query 「"boat"」 in Table 3

	matching image found	no matching image found
Japanese	3	2
Chinese	5	0

that is randomly selected from a synset in $C_{w_k^{ja}} \cup C_{w_k^{zh}} \cup C_{w_k^{id}}$. It is necessary to differ between higher and lower level synsets. the query was created so that it was an AND search with the higher synset words minus the lower concept words. The query is an AND search based on the relationship between synsets in $C_{w_k^{ja}} \cup C_{w_k^{zh}} \cup C_{w_k^{id}}$, where the higher concept words are subtracted from the lower concept words. For example, there is a word triplet (ボート (bo-to), 船 (chuan), kapal). If union of the concept range of these words has $\{v_1, v_2, v_3\}$, we get one word at random from the English words in $v_1, v_2 and v_3$: (v_1:craft, v_2:vessel ship, v_3:boat). If the parent relation $((v_2, v_1) \in E) \wedge ((v_3, v_2) \in E)$ holds in the order v_1, v_2, v_3, then query for v_1 is 「"craft"-"vessel ship" -"boat"」, the query for v_2 is 「"vessel ship" - "boat"」 and the query for v_3 is 「"boat"」. The "-" in the query means NOT and words with "-" are deleted. We use the top three images (Figure 2) that are got from Image Search with these query in the questionnaire.

4.3 Judgements of the Conceptual Difference

Judgement of the conceptual difference is to totaling up of the questionnaire answer by language and is to check if there is a difference in the answer between languages. If there is a difference in the aggregated answers, it is judged as having a conceptual difference; if there is no difference in the answers, it is judged as having no conceptual difference. This process involves evaluating each tally table generated from the query by applying Fisher's exact test to identify conceptual differences. Tasks with significant differences in any of the tallied tables are a conceptual difference. As an example, to judge the conceptual differences between (ボート (bo-to), 船 (chuan), kapal) in Japanese and Chinese, responses from Japanese and Chinese speakers will be collected based on the following categories: 「"craft" -"vessel ship" -"boat"」, 「"vessel ship" -"boat"」, and 「"boat"」. Fisher's exact test will be performed on each of the three generated contingency tables to determine if there is a statistically significant difference between the responses of Japanese and Chinese speakers. The contingency tables will be created based on whether the respondents judged that one or more images matched the keyword. For each language, the tables will count the number of people who determined 'matching image found' and 'no matching image found.' In the case of the contingency table for 「"boat"」 from the (ボート (bo-to), 船 (chuan), kapal) set, selecting one or more images from Image G, Image H, or Image I (Figure 2) will be classified as 'matching image found', while selecting none will be classified as 'no matching image found.' For example, in the (ボート (bo-to), 船 (chuan), kapal) task, if the responses follow Table 3, the contingency table for 「"boat"」 appears as in Table 4. I will create similar contingency tables for other queries, and if any show statistically significant differences, I will conclude that this task reflects a conceptual difference. We used the 1,375 word triplets identified by the proposed method as having conceptual differences (Table 2) as analysis data. Fifteen participants (5 Japanese, 5 Chinese, and 5 Indonesian) manually judged the conceptual differences. The results showed 528 triplets with differences between Japanese and Chinese, 476 between Japanese and Indonesian, and 471 between Chinese and Indonesian.

Table 5: Assessment results

	ja-zh	ja-id	zh-id
Accuracy	0.81	0.70	0.69
Precision	0.43	0.44	0.32
Recall	0.87	0.80	0.71
F-Score	0.58	0.57	0.44

※ja:Japanese, zh:Chinese, id:Indonesian

Table 6: Classification of conceptual differences and breakdown of data

Type of Conceptual Difference	ja-zh		ja-id		zh-id	
	Pair	Ratio of the Conceptual Difference	Pair	Ratio of the Conceptual Difference	Pair	Ratio of the Conceptual Difference
horizontal (part common)	43	**(+) 72.0%**	105	**(+) 49.5%**	81	**(+) 56.8%**
horizontal (inclusive)	637	35.5%	758	34.4%	758	33.2%
vertical (lower inclusive)	280	39.6%	248	40.8%	278	35.6%
vertical (upper inclusive)	634	34.7%	575	32.7%	621	35.3%
vertical (part common)	26	26.9%	62	38.7%	59	44.1%
vertical (inclusive)	27	**(+) 63.0%**	52	25.0%	89	**(-) 11.2%**
vertical (upper common)	62	**(+) 51.6%**	111	**(+) 45.0%**	109	29.4%
Equivalence	24	33.3%	13	23.1%	17	29.4%

5 Evaluation and Analysis

5.1 Evaluation

We evaluated the proposed method using four metrics: accuracy, precision, recall, and F-score. As the evaluation dataset, we use 100 randomly selected triplets from the total of 11,571 word triplets in Table 2. These are assigned as correct labels based on the results of human judgments of conceptual differences. Table 5 presents the results. In the evaluation dataset between Japanese and Chinese (85 cases without conceptual difference, 15 with), the proposed method classified 30 out of 100 data points as having a conceptual difference. For Japanese and Indonesian (75 cases without, 25 with), 45 out of 100 were determined to have a conceptual difference. In the Chinese and Indonesian comparison (83 cases without, 17 with), 38 out of 100 were classified as having a conceptual difference. The proposed method demonstrates a consistently high recall across all languages, with a precision of approximately 43%. This indicates that the method tends to over-detect conceptual differences. Consequently, the F-score hovers around 50%. However, since conceptual differences can serve as a root cause of misunderstanding, over-detection is arguably less problematic than failing to detect such differences. Therefore, the relatively low precision and F-score of the proposed method are not considered critical shortcomings.

5.2 Discussion

Based on the classification of conceptual differences, we categorize the analysis data and analyze the detection accuracy of conceptual differences for each type.

Table 6 shows the breakdown of data by classification in the analysis dataset. The "Equivalence" classification refers to data where no conceptual difference was found between the languages, though differences were observed between other language pairs. Conversely, the remaining seven types are cases where the proposed method detected conceptual differences. We examined the independence of classification and detection accuracy for each language using the Chi-squared test. To perform the test, a contingency table was created based on the breakdown of data by the seven classifications, and the test was conducted. The results indicated that for all language pairs, the p-value was less than the significance level of 0.01, suggesting that there was a significant difference in detection accuracy based on the classification of conceptual differences. Further residual analysis was conducted to identify which classifications showed significant differences. (+) or (-) marks indicate where the adjusted residuals exceeded an absolute value of 1.96. The results of the residual analysis suggest that for all language pairs, the detection accuracy was high for the horizontal (part common) type of conceptual differences. On the other hand, for the zh-id pair, the detection accuracy was low for the vertical (inclusion) type. An example of the horizontal (part common) type is the triplet (容器, 容器, bekas). The Japanese term "容器" refers to small containers used in daily life, while the Chinese term "容器" encompasses containers in general. As a result, in the survey, Japanese respondents chose images of items like bowls and garbage bins, whereas Chinese respondents selected images of not only bottles but also large containers used on container ships. This indicates that, in the case of the horizontal (part common) type, there are differences in conceptual range at the same level, making it easier for human raters to perceive conceptual differences.

6 Conclusion

Translation pairs can have differing concepts expressed by words across languages, potentially leading to misunderstandings in multilingual communication. This study used WordNet and OMW to quantify concepts and extract conceptual differences by comparing ranges across language pairs. From the three languages of Japanese, Chinese, and Indonesian, we formed word pairs based on the same synset, detecting conceptual differences in 27,005 pairs (Japanese-Chinese), 60,581 pairs (Japanese-Indonesian), and 14,175 pairs (Chinese-Indonesian) out of the total 236,590, 398,048, and 111,450 pairs, respectively. We also classified the differences in conceptual ranges topologically and found significant differences in detection accuracy based on classification type among the three languages.

Acknowledgments

This research was partially supported by a Grant-in-Aid for Scientific Research (B) (23K21730,2024) from the Japan Society for the Promotion of Sciences (JSPS).

References

Francis Bond and Ryan Foster. 2013. Linking and extending an open multilingual wordnet. In *Proceedings of the 51st Annual Meeting of the Association for Computational Linguistics (Volume 1: Long Papers)*, pages 1352–1362.

Barry R Chiswick and Paul W Miller. 2005. Linguistic distance: A quantitative measure of the distance between english and other languages. *Journal of Multilingual and Multicultural Development*, 26(1):1–11.

Key Sun Choi, Hee Sook Bae, Wonseok Kang, Juho Lee, Eunhe Kim, Hekyeong Kim, Donghee Kim, Youngbin Song, and Hyosik Shin. 2004. Korean-chinese-japanese multilingual wordnet with shared semantic hierarchy. In *4th International Conference on Language Resources and Evaluation, LREC 2004*, pages 1131–1134.

Christiane Fellbaum and Piek Vossen. 2012. Challenges for a multilingual wordnet. *Language Resources and Evaluation*, 46:313–326.

Hitoshi Isahara, Francis Bond, Kiyotaka Uchimoto, Masao Utiyama, and Kyoko Kanzaki. 2008. Development of the japanese wordnet. In *Proceedings of the Sixth International Conference on Language Resources and Evaluation (LREC'08)*.

Sizhuo Li, Lanjiang Zhou, Jianan Zhang, Feng Zhou, Jianyi Guo, and Wenjie Huo. 2019. Chinese-lao cross-language test similarity computing based on wordnet. In *Proceedings of International Conference on Mechatronics and Intelligent Robotics (ICMIR2018)*, pages 459–464.

Ikkyu Nishimura, Yohei Murakami, and Mondheera Pituxcoosuvarn. 2020. Image-based detection criteria for cultural differences in translation. In *International Conference on Collaboration Technologies and Social Computing*, pages 81–95.

Nurril Hirfana Bte Mohamed Noor, Suerya Sapuan, and Francis Bond. 2011. Creating the open wordnet bahasa. In *Proceedings of the 25th Pacific Asia Conference on Language, Information and Computation*, pages 255–264.

Mondheera Pituxcoosuvarn, Donghui Lin, and Toru Ishida. A method for automated detection of cultural difference based on image similarity.

Desmond Darma Putra, Abdul Arfan, and Ruli Manurung. 2008. Building an indonesian wordnet. In *Proceedings of the 2nd International MALINDO Workshop*, pages 12–13.

Ewa Rudnicka, Łukasz Grabowski, Maciej Piasecki, and Tomasz Naskręt. 2023. In search of gaps between languages and wordnets: the case of polish-english wordnet. *International Journal of Lexicography*, 36(1):68–92.

Ewa Rudnicka, Marek Maziarz, Maciej Piasecki, and Stan Szpakowicz. A strategy of mapping polish wordnet onto princeton wordnet.

Ivelina Stoyanova, Svetla Koeva, and Svetlozara Leseva. 2013. Wordnet-based cross-language identification of semantic relations. In *Proceedings of the 4th Biennial International Workshop on Balto-Slavic Natural Language Processing*, pages 119–128.

Shan Wang and Francis Bond. 2013. Building the chinese open wordnet (cow): Starting from core synsets. In *Proceedings of the 11th Workshop on Asian Language Resources*, pages 10–18.

Naomi Yamashita and Toru Ishida. 2006. Automatic prediction of misconceptions in multilingual computer-mediated communication. In *Proceedings of the 11th International Conference on Intelligent User Interfaces*, pages 62–69.

Takashi Yoshino, Mai Miyabe, and Tomohiro Suwa. 2015. A proposed cultural difference detection method using data from japanese and chinese wikipedia. In *Proceeding of 2015 International Conference on Culture and Computing (Culture Computing)*, pages 159–166.

Kinship Terms: Intercultural Linguistic Markers of Teknonymy

Esra Abdelzaher
Department of English Linguistics
University of Debrecen
esra.abdelzaher@gmail.com

Bacem Essam
Department of Computer Science
Cairo University
literaryartrans@gmail.com

Abstract

This study proposes that teknonymy (i.e., the act of referring to someone by relating them to a kinship, dominantly a father or a mother) is more than an anthropological practice that varies across cultures. We argue that teknonymy and teknonymy-like are well-structured relations that take different patronymic, matronymic and charactonymic patterns in Semitic, Germanic, Slavic and Romance languages. We analyze the semantics, polarity and sociolinguistic aspects of kinship terms in 3K constructions in Arabic to build an automatic classifier that separates teknonyms (e.g. Abu Ahmed/father of Ahmed) from near teknonyms (Abu Alfasad/father of corruption) and sub-classify the usage of the kinship as patronym, matronym or charatonym, among others. We also provide a user-friendly web-based version of the most frequent 1k kinship constructions in Arabic (https://arabic-studies.com/TI/index.html). Our results reveal both universal and cultural-specific patterns in teknonymic structure and significant cross-linguistic variations, providing insights into the interface between language, culture, and cognition and implications for including teknonymic structures in multilingual wordnets.

1 Introduction

Teknonyms, a type of naming convention that begins with a kinship term such as *father*, *mother* or *son*, are prevalent in many cultures but vary in form and function across languages. Classical Arabic, for instance, incorporated teknonyms into its metaphorical framework, allowing things to be referred to without using their original given names (Alenizi, 2019; Ebraheme, 2016; Salamh et al., 2022). These designations encompassed the anthroponymic (e.g. *Abu Lahab* for a man named *Abd Al-Ozza*), zoological (e.g. *Abu Al-Harith* [lions], *Umm Amer* [hyenas]), topographical (e.g. *Umm Al-Qura* [Mecca]), and conceptual (e.g. *Umm Qashaam*, epitomizing warfare) (Almuhanna, 2023) names. Contemporary Arabic lexicographers prioritize the consideration of teknonyms as a cornerstone of the Arabic naming system over consideration of their generic metaphorical usage. Arabic nomenclature incorporates proper nouns, teknonyms, and epithets (Ebraheme, 2016).

Old English also used forms of teknonyms in the naming system, such as "Fitzwilliam" or "Fitzwilliam" (son of William), to denote lineage, evolving in Middle English into the form of "Williamson" (Tait, 2006). In the Renaissance era (1500–1660), English borrowed teknonyms from Gaelic; for example, Macbeth, stemming from Mac Bethad (son of life) (Davis, 2012), which is similar to the contemporary usage of McDonald or McMahon in American English, and to O'Connor or O'Brien in Irish English (Tait, 2006; Tucker, 2006). In modern British and American English, informal parental sobriquets are employed to reference offspring (e.g. Johnny's mum, Susie's dad). However, they are not frequently used as addressing terms. The use of kinship terms in teknonym-like constructions, such as "father of modern Philosophy" is currently prevalent in English and other languages. A sample of Arabic and English teknonyms is available in Appendix 1.

We argue that teknonymy and near-teknonymy are integral to using kinship terms in different languages. The scope of the current study is limited to the Arabic language. Our study aims at:

(a) proposing an annotation schema to separate teknonyms and near-teknonyms from each other and from standard uses of kinship terms in Arabic
(b) exploring the possibility of automatically classifying the uses of kinship terms in

teknonyms, near-teknonyms and non-teknonyms
(c) introducing a browsable database of the most frequent uses of Arabic kinship terms

2 Teknonymy: A multilingual kinship-based relation

The use of kinship terms in addressing and naming constructions has been studied in different Semitic, Slavic and Romance languages. Teknonyms exhibit remarkable universality and diversity across languages and cultures, as a fundamental linguistic feature identifying individuals through their familial roles. This concept manifests in various forms, from the complex Korean system of address (incorporating kinship terms, honorifics, and pronouns, with teknonyms often using birth-order designations among parents) to the extensive use in Arabic naming conventions (employing "Abu" for father and "Umm" for mother, alongside patronymics and epithets). Other languages demonstrate related practices, such as Icelandic (using patronymic and sometimes matronymic naming), Spanish (incorporating both paternal and maternal surnames), and even constructed languages like Klingon (deliberately including patronymic elements). Semitic languages similar to Arabic also utilize teknonyms or related concepts, as seen in Hebrew (using "Avi" for father and "Em" for mother, often as given names), Aramaic (employing "Abba" for father and "Imma" for mother in teknonym formation), and Amharic (using a patronymic system where a person's name is followed by their father's name). Maltese, a Semitic language with significant Romance influence, offers an interesting example of teknonymic evolution. While it retains some Arabic-origin patronymic forms, these have primarily transitioned into surnames rather than active teknonyms. For instance, surnames like "Bencini" (from "Bin Cini," meaning "son of Cini") demonstrate the historical use of teknonyms in Maltese culture, even as their current function has shifted.

In the present study, we differentiate between teknonyms and near-teknonyms based on the original function of the relation in Arabic (i.e. further specification of the referent). Therefore, constructions like Ibn Misr/Son of Egypt which can be generically used to refer to anyone born in Egypt or of Egyptian origin will be considered teknonym-like, mainly if they have frequently used cross-lingual equivalents (e.g., son of Rome, Son of England).

3 Creating Arabic teknonymy dataset

3.1 Data compilation

We collected Arabic teknonyms from classical and contemporary resources, whereas other constructions embedding kinship terms were retrieved from corpora and databases using lists of Arabic kinship terms. The collection of classical Arabic teknonyms was the easiest because there are multiple classical biographical lexica, and dictionaries which are sorted according to the uses of patronyms and matronyms (e.g. the book of the proper names of people known by their teknonyms, the book of poets' matronym teknonyms). For Modern Standard Arabic (MSA), we bootstrapped constructions starting with kinship terms in contemporary Arabic dictionaries, newspapers, and literary works such as ArTenTen (a web-crawled Arabic corpus available through Sketch Engine). For contemporary Arabic dialects, sources include dialect-specific crowdsourced dictionaries (e.g. http://ar.mo3jam.com), social media corpora (e.g. Refaee & Rieser, 2014, Essam et al., 2019; Essam & Abdo, 2021), and databases (e.g. Bouamor, Habash, et al., 2019; Bouamor, Hassan, et al., 2019). The raw lists of teknonyms and other kinships, including constructions, included more than 7K constructions. After removing the duplicates and false positive constructions (e.g. words sharing the same form with one of the kinship terms), the list included 4K constructions, which were further classified manually during the annotation process. A sample of teknonymic patterns, their frequency and a cross-linguistic reference to English examples are presented in Appendix 2.

3.2 Linguistic annotation

Each construction was annotated by 3 native speakers of Egyptian, Tunisian and Saudi Arabic. The annotation schema included the number of words in the construction, the identification of the kinship terms and their number, the detection of their literal or metaphoric use, the identification of the proper and common nouns, the selection of a literal or metaphoric use of the common word, the identification of the singularity, plurality and gender of the referent, the documentation of the polarity of the construction, its frequent association with a specific dialect, the patronymic, matronymic or charactonymic use of the kinship term and, finally, its label as a teknonym, near-teknonym or non-teknonym. A sample of the annotated dataset is viewable as supplementary material. Our annotation schema showed variation in the distribution of kinship patterns in the categories of teknonyms and near-teknonyms. Table 1 shows a sample of the patterns associated with teknonyms (Tek.) and near-teknonyms (N.Tek) in our dataset.

Table 1. Dichotomy of teknonymic constructions

Pattern	**Tek.**	**N.Tek**
Kinship term (literal) + proper noun	√	×
Kinship term (literal) + definite common noun	×	√
Kinship term (metaphoric) + proper noun	×	√
Kinship term(metaphoric) + indefinite common noun	√ less frequent	√
Kinship term + definite common noun + definite common noun	×	√
Kinship term (literal) + indefinite common noun	×	√
Kinship term (metaphoric) + definite common noun	√	√
Kinship term (literal) + kinship term (literal) + proper noun	√	×
Kinship term (literal) + kinship term (metaphoric) + definite common noun	√	√ less frequent

Abbreviations: **N.Tek**: Near-teknonym; **Tek**: Teknonym

3.3 Automatic classification of teknonyms

We trained a classifier to predict the type of construction and the use of the kinship term in the construction. We used cross-validation to train a classifier to predict the type of the construction as teknonym, near-teknonym or non-teknonym. The results of the classification task are reported in Table 2. Whereas the Area Under Curve (AUC) is comparable for the three classifiers, the Classification Accuracy (CA) was highest for the Random Forest (RF) algorithm, followed by Logistic Regression (LR) and Naïve Bayes (NB). The Precision (P) and Recall (R) were also the highest for the RF classifier, which was also associated with the highest Matthews Correlation Coefficient (MCC).

Table 2. Results of the classification task

	AUC	**CA**	**F1**	**P**	**R**	**MCC**
RF	0.99	0.97	0.97	0.97	0.97	0.94
LR	0.99	0.94	0.94	0.95	0.94	0.86
NB	0.98	0.94	0.94	0.94	0.94	0.86

Unlike the successful prediction of the teknonymy labels, the classifier was far less successful in predicting the use of the kinship term. Table 3 shows the average results of the automatic classification of the kinship term across 12 classes.

Table 3. Mean values for classifying kinship terms

	AUC	**CA**	**F1**	**P**	**R**	**MCC**
RF	0.94	0.86	0.83	0.81	0.86	0.80
LR	0.94	0.85	0.81	0.80	0.85	0.78
NB	0.92	0.74	0.76	0.80	0.74	0.65

The misclassified cases were mostly associated with the female gender of the referent (OffspringF) which ended up in male counterpart category in 99% of the cases. Also 48% of the matronymic uses appeared in the patronym category. Figure 1 shows the scatter plot of the misclassified cases.

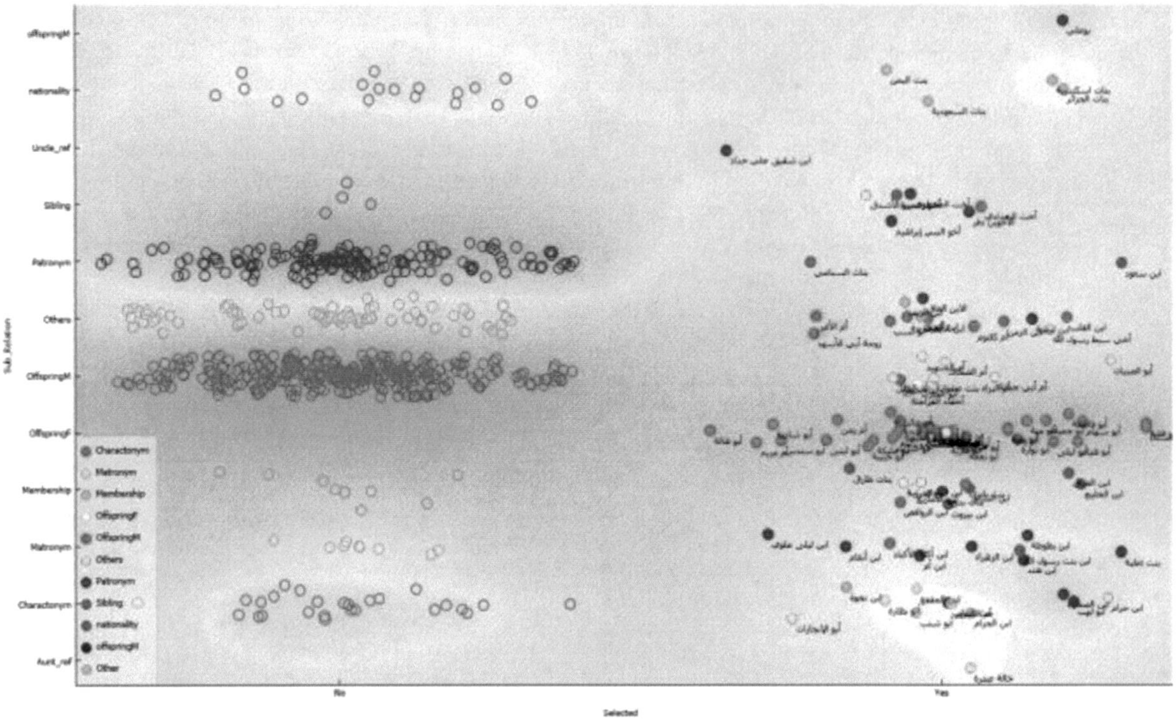

Figure 1. Scatter plot of the misclassified cases

4 Browsable database of teknonyms

We developed a web-based searchable version of the annotated dataset. The web version currently contains the most frequent 1K constructions embedding kinship terms.

The database can be browsed using any Arabic kinship term. The results retrieve the possible constructions in which this term can be used and recall the annotated semantic, pragmatic and sociolinguistic information recorded for the construction in the dataset. For each restored construction, the retrieved information includes the kinship term, which is the head of the construction and the total number of kinship terms in the construction for cases like *the son of the mother of x*. Based on identifying the head kinship term, further information about the gender and countability of the referent are provided. Including a proper noun, such as the father of Ahmed or a common noun, such as the father of virtue, is also clarified in the recalled information. Additional information about the category of the construction as a teknonym, near-teknonym or non-teknonym is also provided in the user-friendly interface, as well as the relation holding between the kinship term and the rest of the words in the construction, e.g. patronymy, matronymy, offspring in cases of the literal use of the kinship term or nationality, membership or charactonym in cases of the metaphoric uses of the head kinship term. Figure 2 shows the interface of the web version of the database.

Figure 2. Searchable Web-based Interface

5 Conclusion

We proposed an annotation schema to separate teknonyms and near-teknonyms from each other and from standard uses of kinship terms in Arabic. Our schema depended on identifying the head kinship term and its literal or metaphoric use, classifying the following noun into proper or common, and deciding whether it was used literally or metaphorically, too. We included other corpus-based information about the association of the construction with a specific dialect or sentimentality. We also explored the possibility of the automatic classification of the uses of kinship terms into three broad categories (i.e. teknonyms, near-teknonyms and non-teknonyms) and more specific classes (e.g. matronym, charactonym, membership). Our results showed promising results for most classification algorithms at the broad level, but the classification accuracy significantly dropped for the sub-classification. The gender factor appeared to be the most influential in the misclassified cases as most of the matronym patterns were classified as patronym, and several offspring_female cases were misplaced in the offspring_male.

Finally, we proposed a browsable database of Arabic teknonyms, which is a valuable resource for both linguistic research and cultural studies, potentially inspiring similar projects for other languages to enable the analysis of comparable constructions in different languages. Teknonyms demonstrate linguistic universality while maintaining cultural specificity, suggesting a common human tendency to identify individuals through kinship terms that can adapt and persist even as their primary function changes. The successful automatic inter/intra-language classification of teknonyms, near-teknonyms, and non-teknonyms can advance syntagmatic relationships in NLP for identifying and categorizing kinship-based naming conventions.

Acknowledgements

None

References

Michael Adams. 2013. *From Elvish to Klingon: Exploring invented languages*. Oxford: Oxford University Press

Reima Al-Jarf. 2023. The Interchange of Personal Names in Muslim Communities: An Onomastic Study. *Journal of Gender, Culture and Society*, 3(1):42–56. https://doi.org/10.32996/jgcs.2023.3.1.5

Aied Alenizi. 2019. The Norms of Address Terms in Arabic: The Case of Saudi Speech Community.

International Journal of English Linguistics, 9(5). https://doi.org/10.5539/ijel.v9n5p227

Amin Almuhanna. 2023. On the Origin of Kuwaiti Surnames. *Al-'Arabiyya*, 55–56:175–221.

Houda Bouamor, Nizar Habash, Mohammad Salameh, Wajdi Zaghouani, Owen Rambow, Dana Abdulrahim, Ossama Obeid, Salam Khalifa, Fadhl Eryani, Alexander Erdmann, and Kemal Oflazer. 2019. The madar Arabic dialect corpus and lexicon. *In LREC 2018 - 11th International Conference on Language Resources and Evaluation.*

Lucien Brown and John Whitman. 2015. Honorifics and politeness in Korean. *Korean Linguistics*, 17(2). https://doi.org/10.1075/kl.17.2.001int

Frans Ciappara. 2010. Religion, kinship and godparenthood as elements of social cohesion in Qrendi, a late-eighteenth-century Maltese parish. *Continuity and Change*, 25(1). https://doi.org/10.1017/S0268416010000019

Madison Davis. 2012. *The Shakespeare Name and Place Dictionary*. Routledge

Kenneth Dimaggio. 2016. From Egypt to the Arizona desert to places still to come: The ongoing meta-literary journey of eliza's escape to freedom in uncle Tom's Cabin. *International Journal of Literary Humanities*, 14(3):41–49.

Barahmi Ebraheme. 2016. The semiotics of the proper nouns: The case of teknonyms (in Arabic). *Dyrassat.*

Miseon Lee, Sorin Huh, and William O'Grady. 2017. Korean subject honorifics: An experimental study. *Journal of Pragmatics*, 117. https://doi.org/10.1016/j.pragma.2017.06.001

Eshrag Ali Refaee. 2022. Detecting Hadith *Authenticity Using a Deep-learning Approach. Scientific Journal of King Faisal University Basic and Applied Sciences*, 23(1):80–84.

Eshrag Refaee and Verena Rieser. 2014. Evaluating Distant Supervision for Subjectivity and Sentiment Analysis on Arabic Twitter Feeds. *In ANLP 2014 - EMNLP 2014 Workshop on Arabic Natural Language Processing, Proceedings*, pages 174–179. https://doi.org/10.3115/v1/W14-3624

Sami Ben Salamh, Zouheir Maalej, and Mohammed Alghbban. 2022. To be or not to be your son's father/mother. *Pragmatics. Quarterly Publication of the International Pragmatics Association* (IPrA). https://doi.org/10.1075/prag.00001.ben

Clodagh Tait. 2006. Namesakes and nicknames: Naming practices in early modern Ireland, 1540-1700. *Continuity and Change*, 21(2):313–340. https://doi.org/10.1017/S0268416006005935

Kenneth Tucker. 2006. A comparison of Irish Surnames in the United States with those of Eire. *A Journal of Onomastics* (54)1: 55-75 https://doi.org/10.1179/nam.2006.54.1.55

A Appendices

Appendix 1. Sample of Arabic and English Teknonyms

Teknonym	Variety	Meaning	Source
Abu Abed	Syrian Arabic	Father of Abed	Dialect database
Abu Adnan	Gulf Arabic	Father of Adnan	Dialect database
Abu Alaa'	Egyptian Arabic	Father of Alaa'	Social media corpus
Abu Al-Duhhak	Classical Arabic	Father of the beaming person	Biographical lexica
Abu Al-Kasim	Modern Standard Arabic	Father of Kasim	Literary texts
Addison	Middle English	Adam's son	Biographical lexica
Son of King Charles III	Contemporary British English	Son of King Charles III	General reference corpora
The son of Marcus Cato	Early Modern English	The son of Marcus Cato (Cato the Elder)	Literary corpus

Appendix 2. A cross-linguistic sample of teknonymic patterns

Teknonym pattern	Example	Trend	
Patronymic teknonym	Ibn/ben Mousa Williamson	Maintained (Ar)	Diminished (Br En)
Matronymic teknonym	Ibn Angham Mollison	Increasing (Ar)	Diminished (Br En)
Father of x(daughter)	Father of Helen Keller Abu Fatima	Increasing (Ar)	Decreasing (Br En)
Father of x(son)	Abu Ahmed Father of Boris	Maintained (Ar)	Decreasing (Br En)
Three- to four-word teknonyms	Ibn Abu Al-No'man Mother of Queen Elizabeth	Decreasing (Ar)	Decreasing (Br En)
Charactonymic teknonym	Um Al-Noor Grayson	Maintained (Ar)	Diminished (Br En)

B Supplementary Material

The most frequent usages of kinship terms in Arabic, according to our dataset, are accessible at https://arabic-studies.com/TI/index.html .

Wordnet Enhanced Neural Machine Translation for Assamese-Bodo Low Resource Language Pair

Kuwali Talukdar, Shikhar Kumar Sarma, Kishore Kashyap, Ratul Deka, Bhatima Baro, Mirzanur Rahman, Farha Naznin
Department of Information Technology, Gauhati University, India
kuwalitalukdar@gmail.com, sks001@gmail.com, kb.guwahati@gmail.com, rdeka8258@gmail.com, bhatimaishaan@gmail.com. mr@gauhati.ac.in, farha.gu@gmail.com

Abstract

Neural Machine Translation (NMT) for low-resource language pairs, such as Assamese-Bodo, is hindered by the limited availability of parallel corpora. In this work, we enhance the NMT process by integrating WordNet resources specifically developed for Assamese and Bodo. The WordNet resources consist of parallel synsets mapped via synset IDs, where each synset contains synonymous words. Additionally, concept sentences tied to each synset provide high-quality, semantically equivalent parallel sentence pairs, which are directly utilized as training data. Our approach explores two methods: (1) injecting parallel synsets into the NMT training pipeline and (2) augmenting the training dataset with the WordNet-derived parallel corpus. We evaluate the effectiveness of these approaches using BLEU scores on Assamese-Bodo translations. The results demonstrate significant improvements in translation accuracy when incorporating WordNet resources, achieving BLEU score gains of up to 2-3 points compared to baseline models. This study highlights the potential of leveraging structured lexical databases like WordNet to improve NMT for low-resource languages.

1 Introduction

Neural Machine Translation has made significant progress in improving translation quality for widely spoken languages with abundant parallel corpora. However, for low-resource language pairs such as Assamese and Bodo, the scarcity of large-scale parallel datasets poses a substantial challenge to developing well performed and reliable NMT systems. Both Assamese and Bodo are prominent languages in Northeast India, with unique linguistic structures and limited digital resources. The lack of well-aligned, high-quality parallel corpora leads to lower translation performance when using standard NMT approaches. In an effort to address this issue, we explore the integration of WordNet resources into the NMT pipeline. WordNet is a lexical database that organizes words into sets of synonyms (synsets), each representing a unique concept. Assamese and Bodo WordNets contain parallel synsets, with synonymous words in both languages mapped to a shared synset ID. In addition, each synset is accompanied by concept sentences, which are direct translations of one another. These concept sentences form a high-quality, semantically aligned parallel corpus, which can significantly enhance the training process of NMT models. This paper presents a novel approach where Assamese-Bodo WordNet resources are utilized to enrich the NMT training pipeline. Specifically, we inject parallel synsets into the NMT model and augment the training dataset with WordNet-derived concept sentences. Our experiments show that these enhancements lead to notable improvements in translation accuracy, as measured by BLEU scores. By leveraging structured lexical databases, we aim to bridge the resource gap for Assamese and Bodo and demonstrate the broader applicability of WordNet resources in low-resource NMT scenarios.

2 Related Works

Neural Machine Translation (NMT) for low-resource languages has been an active area of research, but significant challenges persist due to the lack of parallel corpora. Various strategies have been developed to address this issue, such as transfer learning, data augmentation, and the use of linguistic resources like WordNet. This section reviews relevant works, focusing on the development of WordNet for Assamese and Bodo, and recent advances in NMT for these languages.
The Assamese and Bodo WordNets were developed as part of efforts to create structured lexical databases for these underrepresented languages. Previous works on Assamese WordNet [Shikhar et al., 2010] and Bodo WordNet [Sarma et al., 2010] documented the creation of synsets that include synonymous words in Assamese and Bodo, linked by shared synset IDs. These resources have been expanded to cover a wide range of concepts, along with concept sentences that provide high-quality parallel sentences for both languages. The creation of these WordNets marked a significant milestone in digital linguistic resources for the Assamese-Bodo language pair, laying the groundwork for further applications in machine translation and NLP tasks.

The development of Assamese WordNet laid the groundwork for creating linguistic resources essential for natural language processing tasks. Shi8khar et al. (2010) discussed the design and implementation of the Assamese WordNet, focusing on building synsets and their application in enhancing bilingual machine translation quality. The integration of parallel synsets across languages has proven to be a useful technique to improve translation accuracy in Assamese-English bilingual systems. Similarly, the Bodo WordNet has undergone extensive research, providing a well-mapped synset structure in Bodo, contributing significantly to linguistic analysis. The development of the Bodo WordNet, as discussed in Sarma's paper on its design and structure, plays a critical role in the preservation and computational representation of this low-resource language.

Recent advancements in NMT for low-resource languages include work on translation models for Assamese-English and Bodo-English language pairs. Prior research on English-Assamese NMT [Talukdar et al., 2023] demonstrated the effectiveness of sequence-to-sequence models in translating between these languages, albeit with the challenges of limited parallel corpora. Similarly, work on English-Bodo NMT [Parvez et al., 2023] showed improvements in translation quality by leveraging transfer learning from larger resource pairs such as English-Hindi, but further enhancements were needed to improve Bodo translation accuracy. Building on these efforts, another study on Assamese-Bodo NMT [Sarma et al., 2023] highlighted the complexities of translating between two low-resource languages that share lexical and syntactic similarities but lack a sufficient parallel corpus. This work showed that while conventional NMT models can achieve reasonable results, there is considerable potential for improvement by incorporating linguistic resources such as WordNet. Although much of the work on NMT has focused on training models with large datasets, integrating lexical databases like WordNet is a relatively unexplored approach, particularly for low-resource language pairs. Prior research on using WordNet for machine translation has shown promising results for resource-rich languages, where synsets and semantic relations help resolve ambiguities and improve translation quality [Fellbaum, 1998]. However, the application of WordNet to NMT for low-resource languages remains limited. In this context, our current work proposes to leverage the Assamese and Bodo WordNets to improve NMT performance by injecting parallel synsets and high-quality concept sentences into the training pipeline. This approach aligns with recent trends in NMT that focus on enriching training data with structured linguistic knowledge to overcome the limitations of small parallel corpora.

Two different NMT models were built using transformer encoder-decoder architectures, with varying numbers of layers and attention heads. Preprocessing techniques like normalization, tokenization, and subword tokenization (BPE, Sentencepiece, and Wordpiece) were applied to optimize performance. These models were trained on around 92,410 parallel sentence pairs, with evaluations showing BLEU scores for both English-to-Bodo and Bodo-to-English translations. The Bodo-to-English translations generally performed better, achieving a BLEU score of 14.62 using the Wordpiece method for an 8k vocabulary. The models highlighted the importance of selecting appropriate subword tokenization and vocabulary sizes for low-resource language translation tasks. A work on Assamese WordNet based Quality Enhancement of Bilingual Machine Translation, presented at the Global Wordnet Conference 2014, discusses the use of Assamese WordNet to improve bilingual translation quality, which serve as a foundational reference for our current research. In terms of Neural Machine Translation (NMT), recent work by Talukdar et al. explored NMT for Assamese-Bodo translation using transformer-based architectures. Talukdar's research highlighted the challenges of low-resource language translation and emphasized the need for effective preprocessing techniques like normalization, tokenization, and subword tokenization (BPE, Sentencepiece, and Wordpiece). The models were trained on large datasets, including 92,410 parallel sentence pairs, with promising BLEU scores demonstrating the potential for high-quality translation between Assamese and Bodo. This current research extends these efforts by integrating WordNet resources into the NMT pipeline, aiming to improve translation accuracy for Assamese-Bodo translations. By leveraging parallel synsets and concept sentences, this study introduces a novel approach to enhance the existing translation systems.

3 Methodology

In this section, we describe the methodology used to integrate WordNet resources into the neural machine translation (NMT) pipeline for the Assamese-Bodo language pair. Our approach involves two main steps: parallel synset injection and the inclusion of WordNet-based parallel datasets in the training process.

3.1 Data sources and preprocessing

WordNet Data: The Assamese and Bodo WordNets are crucial resources for this study. Each synset in these WordNets consists of a set of synonymous words that are mapped to the synsets in the other language. Additionally, the concept sentences provided in both WordNets are exact translations of each other, forming a high-quality parallel corpus that serves as a gold-standard dataset for NMT training. The synset mapping and concept sentences allow for the creation of a bilingual lexicon, which provides important semantic alignments between the two languages. These resources were integrated into the NMT pipeline at various stages to enrich the model's understanding of semantic relationships.

Parallel Corpus: We utilized an existing parallel Assamese-Bodo dataset containing approximately 92,410 sentence pairs, as mentioned in earlier works by Talukdar et al. This corpus is composed of sentences from a wide range of domains such as administration, law, agriculture, education, and tourism. The dataset was preprocessed using normalization and tokenization techniques before being fed into the model. We used the IndicNLP library for Bodo and the Moses decoder for Assamese to perform tokenization, followed by subword tokenization using three techniques: BPE (Byte Pair Encoding), SentencePiece, and WordPiece.

3.2 NMT architecture

Base Model: We used the OpenNMT-py framework to build two transformer-based models, referred to as Model 1 and Model 2. Model 1 features 3 layers each in the encoder and decoder, while Model 2 uses 6 layers. Both models employ multi-head attention mechanisms, with 4 attention heads in Model 1 and 8 in Model 2. The models are configured with the following hyperparameters:

Encoder hidden size: 256 (Model 1), 512 (Model 2)
Decoder hidden size: 256 (Model 1), 512 (Model 2)
Word vector size: 256 (Model 1), 512 (Model 2)
Transformer feedforward size: 1024 (Model 1), 2048 (Model 2)

WordNet Integration: We experimented with two strategies for incorporating the WordNet resources into the NMT training process:

Parallel Synset Injection: Parallel synsets from the Assamese and Bodo WordNets were injected into the encoder-decoder process. 14000 parallel sysnsets consists of total 43450 tokens in Assamese side and 32300 tokens in Bodo side. This step was intended to enrich the model's contextual understanding of synonyms, enabling it to generalize better across different sentence structures.

WordNet-based Dataset Augmentation: 14000 parallel synset dataset and concept sentence pairs were added to the NMT training corpus. By expanding the training set with high-quality, semantically rich sentences from WordNet, we aimed to improve translation accuracy.

3.3 Experimental setup

Training and Validation: The models were trained using a batch size of 256 tokens (Model 1) and 512 tokens (Model 2) with the Assamese-Bodo dataset and WordNet-augmented data. We validated the models every 10,000 steps using a randomly selected subset of 600 sentences from the corpus. Each model was trained for a total of 100,000 steps, and the best checkpoint based on validation accuracy was selected for final testing.

Evaluation Metrics:
We used the BLEU (Bilingual Evaluation Understudy) score to evaluate the performance of the translation models. The models were tested on unseen sentence pairs, and BLEU scores were calculated using the SacreBLEU library. We compared the BLEU scores of both models across the different tokenization strategies and vocabulary sizes (8,000 and 16,000).

4 Results and analysis

In this section, we present the experimental results of integrating WordNet resources into the Assamese-Bodo Neural Machine Translation (NMT) system. We assess the performance of the models across various tokenization methods and vocabulary sizes and compare the impact of WordNet-enriched data.

Baseline Model Performance: Before integrating WordNet resources, we trained baseline transformer models using the Assamese-Bodo parallel corpus. Both Model 1 (3-layer transformer) and Model 2 (6-layer transformer) were trained and evaluated using three different tokenization methods: Byte Pair Encoding (BPE), SentencePiece, and WordPiece. The results are summarized in Table 1.

Model	Tokenization Method	Vocabulary Size	BLEU Score (Assamese to Bodo)	BLEU Score (Bodo to Assamese
Model 1	BPE	8,000	10.42	11.35
Model 1	SentencePiece	8,000	10.83	12.05
Model 1	WordPiece	8,000	11.14	12.50
Model 2	BPE	16,000	12.75	13.65
Model 2	SentencePiece	16,000	13.40	14.20
Model 2	WordPiece	16,000	14.02	14.62

Table 1: Baseline BLEU Scores for Assamese-Bodo Translation (without WordNet)

Model	Tokenization Method	Vocabulary Size	BLEU Score (Assamese to Bodo)	BLEU Score (Bodo to Assamese
Model 1	BPE	8,000	12.31	13.45
Model 1	SentencePiece	8,000	12.88	13.98
Model 1	WordPiece	8,000	13.05	14.30
Model 2	BPE	16,000	15.11	16.12
Model 2	SentencePiece	16,000	15.54	16.60
Model 2	WordPiece	16,000	16.35	17.02

Table 2: BLEU Scores for Assamese-Bodo Translation (with WordNet)

Figure 1: Training Loss Progress Over Time & Validation BLEU Scores Over Epochs

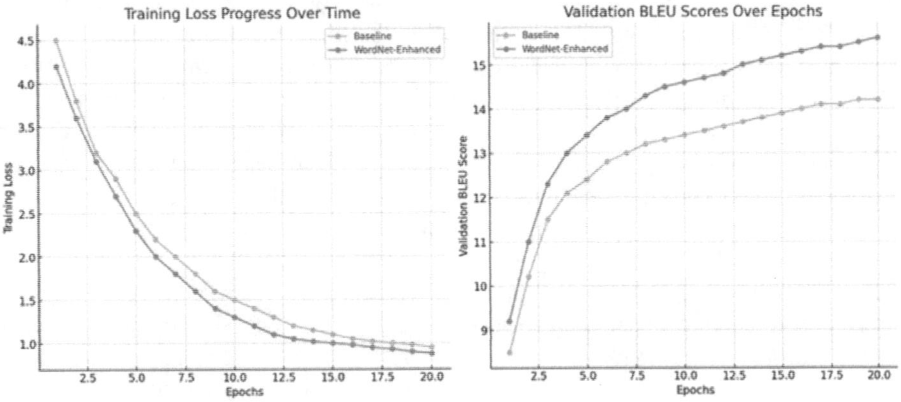

Figure 2: Comparison of different BLEU scores

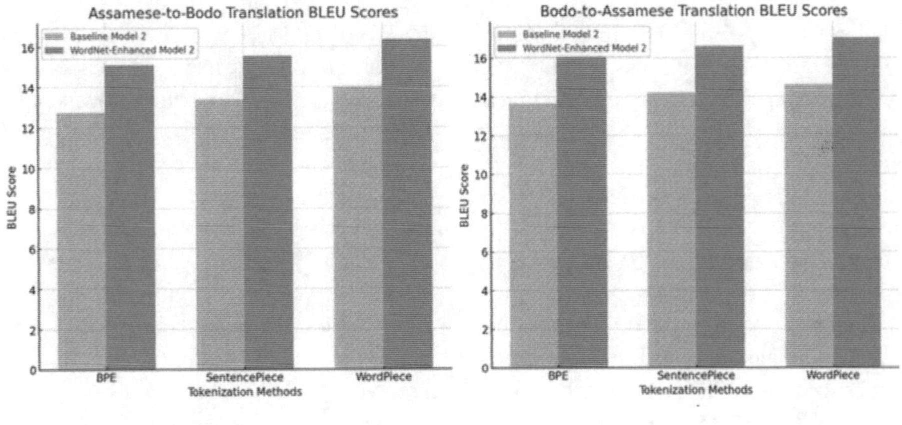

From the baseline results, we observed that Model 2 consistently outperformed Model 1, particularly in the Bodo-to-Assamese translation direction. Among the tokenization methods, WordPiece performed the best, achieving a BLEU score of 14.62 for Bodo-to-Assamese translation.

WordNet-Enhanced Model Performance: Next, we integrated the WordNet parallel synsets and concept sentences into the NMT training process as described in the methodology section. The performance of the models trained with WordNet-enriched data is shown in Table 2.

The incorporation of WordNet data into the NMT training process led to substantial improvements in translation quality across all models and tokenization methods. For the Bodo-to-Assamese direction, the best performing model achieved a BLEU score of 17.02, while the Assamese-to-Bodo direction saw a maximum BLEU score of 16.35. The integration of WordNet resources improved the BLEU scores by approximately 2-3 points compared to the baseline.

Comparative Analysis:
Impact of Tokenization: Across all models, the WordPiece tokenization method consistently

outperformed BPE and SentencePiece, especially in low-resource settings with a vocabulary size of 8,000. This aligns with previous research, which suggests that WordPiece tokenization tends to produce better segmentation for low-resource languages.

Effect of WordNet Integration: The most significant impact was observed in Model 2 (6-layer transformer) with WordNet-enhanced training. The integration of parallel synsets and concept sentences allowed the model to make better semantic associations, leading to improvements in both translation directions. The improvements were especially noticeable in the Bodo-to-Assamese direction, where WordNet-enriched data helped the model better capture the nuances of this morphologically rich language.

The Training Loss Progress Over Time Graph shows the reduction in training loss over 20 epochs for both the baseline and WordNet-enhanced models. The WordNet-enhanced model converges slightly faster, indicating better learning efficiency.

The Validation BLEU Scores Over Epochs Graph tracks the improvement in translation quality over time, as measured by BLEU scores. The WordNet-enhanced model consistently outperforms the baseline, showing more substantial gains after the initial epochs.

The two bar graphs based on the BLEU scores for both Assamese-to-Bodo and Bodo-to-Assamese translations, comparing the performance of the baseline and WordNet-enhanced models across different tokenization methods show the BLEU scores for Model 2 using BPE, SentencePiece, and WordPiece tokenization methods, with and without WordNet enrichment. Right Graph (Bodo-to-Assamese Translation) displays the BLEU scores for Model 2 under the same conditions, demonstrating the improvements from WordNet integration.

Conclusion

This study presented a novel approach to enhancing neural machine translation (NMT) for low-resource languages by integrating WordNet resources, using the Assamese-Bodo language pair as a case study. By injecting parallel synsets and concept sentences from the Assamese and Bodo WordNets into the NMT pipeline, we aimed to address the key challenges associated with low-resource machine translation. The integration of WordNet resources significantly improved translation performance, with BLEU scores increasing by approximately 2-3 points compared to the baseline models. The best-performing model, which utilized WordPiece tokenization and WordNet-enhanced training, achieved a BLEU score of 17.02 for Bodo-to-Assamese translation. By using parallel synsets, the NMT system was able to make better semantic associations across Assamese and Bodo. The concept sentences, which serve as high-quality parallel data, contributed directly to the model's improved generalization capabilities. The WordPiece tokenization method was the most effective for both translation directions, particularly in settings with a smaller vocabulary size of 8,000. This tokenization method appeared to strike a balance between segmentation quality and model training efficiency.

Despite the improvements, challenges remain, particularly in handling complex syntactic structures and idiomatic expressions not covered by WordNet. Moreover, the relatively limited size of the WordNet synsets and concept sentences restricted the system's ability to generalize further. This research demonstrates the potential for WordNet-enriched NMT systems, particularly for low-resource languages that lack substantial parallel corpora. Future work could focus on expanding WordNet resources for Assamese and Bodo, as well as applying this methodology to other low-resource language pairs. Additionally, exploring techniques such as contextual embeddings and pre-trained language models could further improve translation accuracy and reduce errors in challenging linguistic contexts. Overall, this study lays the groundwork for using lexical resources like WordNet to enhance machine translation systems, offering a promising path for improving translation quality in low-resource scenarios.

References

Shikhar Kr Sarma, M. Gogoi, B. Brahma, and Mane BalaRamchiary. 2010. A Wordnet for Bodo language: Structure and development. Global Wordnet Conference (GWC10), Mumbai, India.

Shikhar, Dr & Gogoi, Moromi & Medhi, Rakesh & Saikia, Utpal. (2010). Foundation and Structure of Developing an Assamese Wordnet.

Assamese WordNet based Quality Enhancement of Bilingual Machine Translation System - ACL Anthology](https://aclanthology.org/W14-0135/)

Shikhar Sarma, Dibyajyoti Sarmah, Ratul Deka, Anup Barman, Jumi Sarmah, Himadri Bharali, Mayashree Mahanta, and Umesh Deka. 2014. A Quantitative Analysis of Synset of Assamese WordNet: Its Position and Timeline. In Proceedings of the Seventh Global Wordnet Conference, pages 246–249, Tartu, Estonia. University of Tartu Press.

Himadri Bharali, Mayashree Mahanta, Shikhar Kr. Sarma, Utpal Saikia, and Dibyajyoti Sarmah. 2014. An Analytical Study of Synonymy in Assamese Language Using WorldNet: Classification and Structure. In Proceedings of the Seventh Global Wordnet Conference, pages 250–255, Tartu, Estonia. University of Tartu Press.

Anup Barman, Jumi Sarmah, and Shikhar Sarma. 2014. Assamese WordNet based Quality Enhancement of Bilingual Machine Translation System. In Proceedings of the Seventh Global Wordnet Conference, pages 256–261, Tartu, Estonia. University of Tartu Press.

Shikhar Kr. Sarma, Dibyajyoti Sarmah, Biswajit Brahma, Himadri Bharali, Mayashree Mahanta, and Utpal Saikia. 2012. Building Multilingual Lexical Resources using Wordnets: Structure, Design and Implementation. In Proceedings of the 3rd Workshop on Cognitive Aspects of the Lexicon, pages 161–170, Mumbai, India. The COLING 2012 Organizing Committee.

Parvez Aziz Boruah, Kuwali Talukdar, Mazida Akhtara Ahmed, and Kishore Kashyap. 2023. Neural Machine Translation for a Low Resource Language Pair: English-Bodo. In Proceedings of the 20th International Conference on Natural Language Processing (ICON), pages 295–300, Goa University, Goa, India. NLP Association of India (NLPAI).

Kuwali Talukdar, Shikhar Kumar Sarma, Farha Naznin, Kishore Kashyap, Mazida Akhtara Ahmed, and Parvez Aziz Boruah. 2023. Neural Machine Translation for Assamese-Bodo, a Low Resourced Indian Language Pair. In Proceedings of the 20th International Conference on Natural Language Processing (ICON), pages 714–719, Goa University, Goa, India. NLP Association of India (NLPAI).

Mazida Ahmed, Kuwali Talukdar, Parvez Boruah, Prof. Shikhar Kumar Sarma, and Kishore Kashyap. 2023. GUIT-NLP's Submission to Shared Task: Low Resource Indic Language Translation. In Proceedings of the Eighth Conference on Machine Translation, pages 935–940, Singapore. Association for Computational Linguistics.

Deriving semantic classes of Italian adjectives via word embeddings: a large-scale investigation

Ivan Lacić
University of Bologna
ivan.lacic2@unibo.it

Ludovica Pannitto
University of Bologna
ludovica.pannitto@unibo.it

Abstract

This paper investigates the application of word embeddings to derive semantic classes for Italian adjectives. Adjectives were clustered using UMAP for dimensionality reduction and K-means for clustering. Semantic categories such as "Relational", "Descriptive", "Evaluative", "Membership", and "Physical/Health-Related" were tested by employing predefined prototypical adjectives for each class. The precision and recall of the classification were analyzed, revealing high accuracy for some classes (e.g., "Evaluative"), but challenges in distinguishing more nuanced categories such as "Descriptive". Furthermore, cluster overlaps were visualized using KDE and quantified using KNN, , highlighting semantic intermingling between groups, especially between the "Descriptive" and "Evaluative" categories. Finally, a comparison with Wordnet's adjective categories was provided.

1 Introduction

Meaning is a fundamental aspect of language, making semantics essential for all levels of linguistic analysis. However, incorporating semantics into such analysis presents challenges due to the complexity and labor-intensive nature of semantic annotation. It is widely acknowledged that, unlike nouns and verbs, adjectives exhibit non-trivial semantic behavior, resulting from the intricate interaction between their semantic and syntactic properties. The meaning of adjectives is particularly fluid, often shifting based on linguistic context. Consider, for example, the adjective *heavy*, that can refer to physical weight in the sentence "The box is heavy", but takes on a different meaning in "It has been a heavy week", where it signifies emotional or mental strain rather than physical weight. As a result, analyzing and representing the semantics of adjectives is far from straightforward. WordNet (Miller, 1995) traditionally lacks a comprehensive semantic hierarchy for adjectival meanings, offering only a coarse classification with three labels derived from `lexfiles`: *adj.all* for descriptive adjectives, *adj.pert* for pertainyms, and *adj.ppl* for adjectival participles. Given the significant influence of linguistic context on adjectival meaning, this study explores the possibility of deriving a semantic classification of Italian adjectives through word embeddings, leveraging distributional semantics (Lenci and Sahlgren, 2023). By providing an empirical framework for categorizing adjectives based on their semantic similarities, this analysis highlights the advantages of using word embeddings for semantic classification while also identifying the limitations of current clustering techniques when applied to highly polysemous word classes.

The paper is structured as follows. Section 2 provides a concise overview of the current state of the art. Section 3 details the dataset used to construct the vector space. In Section 4, three case studies are introduced, along with their respective results. Section 5 compares the semantic classes derived from word embeddings with those in WordNet's classification. Lastly, Section 6 summarizes the key findings and offers recommendations for future research.

2 Related work

To the best of our knowledge, the only WordNet-derived resources that organize adjectival synsets into a hierarchy are GermaNet (Hamp and Feldweg, 1997; Henrich and Hinrichs, 2010), which divides adjectives into 16 semantic classes based on those proposed by Hundsnurscher and Splett (1982), and the Bulgarian WordNet (Dimitrova and Stefanova, 2018), which largely follows the German approach. In addition to WordNet, several other feature-based semantic classification systems are available (Schweinberger and Luo, 2024). Typology-based approaches, such as those proposed by Dixon

(1977), offer language-independent classifications of adjectives based on their syntactic and morphological properties. Corpus-based classification systems, like the one in Biber et al. (2007), categorize adjectives based on frequency patterns in the Longman Spoken and Written English Corpus. Additionally, automated classification, such as the UCREL semantic analysis system (USAS, Piao et al. 2005), assigns words and MWEs to 21 semantic fields using resources such as lexical databases and thesauri. Although the aforementioned approaches provide valuable insights, they often rely on predefined structures or patterns that may not fully capture the semantic nuances of adjectives, particularly given their contextual variability. Furthermore, while some of these resources have been adapted for Italian (e.g., Python Multilingual UCREL Semantic Analysis System[1] , Songlin Piao et al. 2016), a comprehensive, Italian-specific semantic classification is still lacking.

Distributional approaches have been extensively applied to adjectival meaning, for example, to derive adjectival scales (Kim and de Marneffe, 2013) or their negated meaning (Aina et al., 2019). However, more focused works on the semantic classification of adjectives are scarcer. One such example is Montes and Geeraerts (2022), which explore the application of distributional methods to the semantic analysis of Dutch adjectives. The work also addresses the difficulties in aligning distributionally derived senses with lexicographic inventories, emphasizing how distributional models offer empirically founded categories that can be quantitatively described, explained in terms of contextual elements, and interpreted in terms of, at least, *aspects* of senses. Additionally, given their syntactic functions, Baroni and Zamparelli (2010) distributionally represent adjectives as matrices rather than vectors, interpreting them as linear maps that can be applied over nouns to shift their meaning. However, none of the above studies specifically focus on Italian adjectives.

3 Data

In order to test our intuition, we built a Distributional Space Model using the itWaC corpus (Baroni et al., 2009), a fairly large corpus (2 billion tokens) constructed by crawling the web from medium-frequency words from the Repubblica corpus (Baroni et al., 2004) and basic Italian vocabulary lists as seeds. The corpus comes already lemmatized and POS-tagged, which allowed us to directly isolate lexemes for representation in the distributional space, without requiring additional preprocessing steps. We utilized the `gensim`[2] (Řehřek and Sojka, 2010) implementation of the `word2vec` algorithm (Mikolov, 2013) to build the embeddings.More specifically, after evaluating model performance on Multilingual SimLex-999 and WS-353 (Vulić et al., 2020), we opted for the Skip-gram architecture over a 5-dimensional window to build 500-dimension vectors (see Appendix A). Out of a total of $12,812$ lemmas tagged as `ADJ` in the corpus, we filtered down to $8,348$ types by applying several filtering steps. We excluded adjectives with a frequency lower than 10 and removed non-existent and non-Italian adjectives, identified using criteria such as word length and cross-referencing the dataset with the `kaikki.org` machine-readable Italian dictionary (Ylonen, 2022). While this filtering approach may have result in the exclusion of some relevant adjectives, the benefits of this process were deemed to outweigh the potential drawbacks. This filtered space formed the basis for the subsequent clustering steps.

4 Experiments and results

This chapter presents the key analyses and findings of the study. We begin by investigating the construction of meaning clusters using dimensionality reduction techniques, as outlined in Section 4.1. Next, we evaluate the semantics of these clusters by comparing them with predefined categories of adjectives, as detailed in Section 4.2. Finally, Section 4.3 examines the overlap between clusters to assess the degree of semantic intermingling between groups.

4.1 Looking for meaning clusters

The first step of the analysis involved exploring the constructed distributional space by reducing the high-dimensional vector space to a two-dimensional plane using Uniform Manifold Approximation and Projection (UMAP, Leland et al. 2018) with default parameters (*n-neighbors* $= 15$, *min-dist* $= 0.1$). UMAP, like the widely employed t-SNE algorithm, generates a high-dimensional graph representation of the data and optimizes a low-dimensional graph to closely match the

[1] `https://github.com/UCREL/pymusas?tab=readme-ov-file`

[2] `https://radimrehurek.com/gensim/`

original structure. However, compared to t-SNE, UMAP is generally more effective at preserving the global structure in the final projection. Figure 1 displays the UMAP projection, where denser areas indicate groups of adjectives with similar distributional patterns, while more isolated points represent adjectives with unique distributional characteristics.

Figure 1: UMAP dimensionality reduction

To determine the optimal number of clusters, i.e. groups, into which the dataset should be divided, the `NbClust` package (Charrad et al., 2014) was used. `NbClust` computes up to 30 indices to determine the appropriate number of clusters and recommends the best clustering solution based on a majority vote among these indices. For this study, the index argument was set to "all", resulting in the calculation of 26 indices (excluding *Gamma*, *Tau*, *Gap*, and *Gplus* due to their high computational costs). Based on 10 indices[3], including the D-index (Figure 2), it was shown that 5 clusters represent the optimal clustering solution. The D-index (Lebart et al., 1995) showed a marked improvement up to 5 clusters, with diminishing returns beyond that point. The D-index is based on clustering gain on intra-cluster inertia, namely the degree of homogeneity among data pertaining to a cluster. It is computed for each step P_k, consisting of k clusters, as the average distance between each point assigned a cluster and the cluster centroid. Given two partitions P_{k-1} and P_k, composed of $k-1$ and k clusters respectively, the gain in intra-cluster inertia is defined as (with $d(P_k)$ being the value of the index at k clusters):

$$G = d(P_{k-1}) - d(P_k) \tag{1}$$

The optimal number of clusters can, therefore, be visually identified by the sharp knee in the graph, which corresponds to a significant decrease in inertia gain. The noticeable drop in D-index (Figure 2 – left plot) and a large spike in the second differences plot (Figure 2 – right plot) suggest the point of the most significant improvement in clustering.

[3]KL, CCC, Scott, TraceW, Friedman, Rubin, DB, Ratkowsky, Dunn, SDindex.

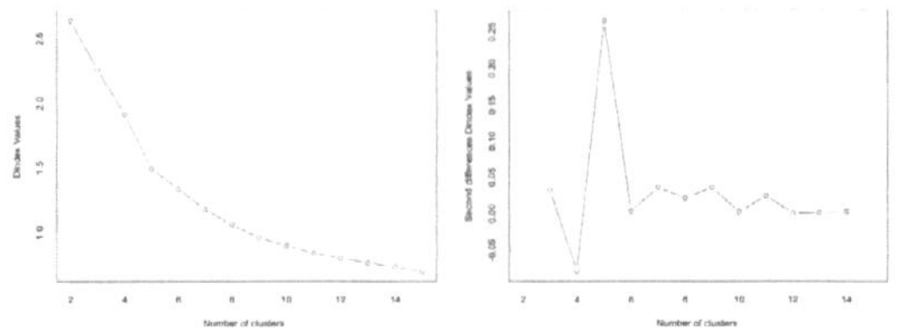

Figure 2: D-index: the left side of the panel shows the D-index itself while the right side shows the gain in intra-cluster inertia.

Consequently, the UMAP-reduced data was clustered into 5 groups using *K-means*, as shown in Figure 3. K-Means partitions a set of n observations into K clusters, with each observation assigned to the cluster whose centroid is nearest, serving as the representative instance of that cluster. Table 1 presents the distribution of the $8,348$ adjectives across the clusters.

Cluster	# of adjectives	Label
1	467	Relational
2	2436	Descriptive
3	2709	Evaluative
4	1038	Physical/Health related
5	1698	Membership

Table 1: Distribution of adjectives in five clusters. Labels in the third column are discussed in Section 4.2

Figure 3: K-Means clustering: in the plot, each dot represents and adjective colored according to its cluster

The quality of the clustering was evaluated using the Davies-Bouldin Index (Davies and Bouldin, 1979) and the Calinski-Harabasz Index (Caliński and Harabasz, 1974), with scores of 0.92 and 7119.29, respectively, indicating satisfactory and distinct clusters.

4.2 Evaluation of the semantics of clusters

We now turn to examining the adjectives within these clusters to establish five labels that represent semantic categories for the classification of adjectives

The initial approach involved extracting the top 50 most representative adjectives for each cluster, based on their Euclidean distance to the cluster centroid. This analysis revealed that Cluster 1 predominantly includes environmental and agricultural adjectives (e.g., *meteoclimatico* 'meteoroclimatic', *orticolo* 'horticultural') adjectives, while Cluster 2 mainly features adjectives expressing temporal and relational relationships (e.g., *indiretto* 'indirect', *futuro* 'future'). Cluster 3 is characterized by emotional and evaluative adjectives (e.g., *indemoniato* 'possessed', *soffocante* 'suffocating'). In Cluster 4, technical adjectives, mainly related to chemistry, are prevalent (e.g., *chimico* 'chemical', *inorganico* 'inorganic'). Finally, Cluster 5 is centered around historical and cultural adjectives, such as *aristocratico* 'aristocratic' and *feudale* 'feudal'. However, such approach was deemed overly fine-grained and influenced by the specificity of the 50 adjectives extracted. Consequently, a larger random sample of adjectives from each cluster was manually examined to refine the classification. Upon careful analysis, the refined labels presented in Table 2 were proposed, along with examples of adjectives for each label.

Cluster	Adjectives	Label
1	*primo* 'first', *ambientale* 'environmental', *idrico* 'aquatic'	Relational (Rel)
2	*nuovo* 'new', *specifico* 'specific', *rotondo* 'round'	Descriptive (Des)
3	*bello* 'nice', *difficile* 'hard', *eccessivo* 'excessive'	Evaluative (Eva)
4	*sanitario* 'healthcare', *cronico* 'chronic', *chimico* 'chemical'	Physical/Health-Related (Phy/H)
5	*italiano* 'Italian', *musulmano* 'Muslim', *democratico* 'democratic'	Membership (Mem)

Table 2: Adjective clusters and suggested labels

Recognizing the contextual flexibility of adjectives, it is evident that certain adjectives may be associated with multiple labels, as the proposed labels are not rigid but interconnected. For instance, *Membership* and *Physical/Health-Related* classes can be considered sub-classes of *Relational adjectives*, as they share inherent relational traits. However, distinct clusters in the visualization highlight unique contextual patterns that differentiate these groups. Additionally, while the suggested labels reflect the predominant themes of each cluster, it is important to note that not every adjective within a cluster will strictly conform to the assigned category. This is because *K-means* clustering, applied to general-purpose word embeddings, captures patterns of co-occurrence and contextual similarity rather than rigid or strictly contextual semantics. To validate the consistency of the semantic categories, each adjective was compared with a set of representative examples for each identified semantic category, assigning the adjective to the most pertinent label. We manually identified six highly prototypical adjectives (by asking fellow expert linguists) for each target category ($p_i^1, ...p_i^6$ for clusters $C_i \in [1, 5]$) based on the five aforementioned semantic classes. These six adjectives per category are presented in Table 3.

Cluster	Adjectives
Rel	*primo* 'first', *ultimo* 'last', *notturno* 'nocturnal', *architettonico* 'architectural', *costiero*, 'coastal', *idrico* 'water-related'
Des	*nuovo* 'new', *vecchio* 'old', *rotondo* 'round', *silenzioso* 'quiet', *grande* 'big', *verde* 'green'
Eva	*bello* 'nice', *buono* 'good', *orrendo* 'horrible', *cattivo* 'mean', *stupido* 'stupid', *fantastico* 'fantastic'
Phy/H	*chimico* 'chemical', *biologico* 'biological', *ospedaliero* 'hospital-related', *genetico* 'genetic', *visivo* 'visual', *malato* 'sick'
Mem	*italiano* 'Italian', *americano* 'American', *democratico* 'democratic', *straniero* 'foreign', *domestico* 'domestic', *cristiano* 'Christian'

Table 3: Six prototypical adjectives per category

From each of the 5 clusters C_i, 250 adjectives $a_i^1, ...a_i^{250}$ were selected to assess their alignment with predefined semantic categories. For each adjective a_i^n, we retrieved its 30 nearest neighbors $N(a_i^n, 30)$ in the vector space and calculated the cosine similarity between these neighbors and each of the six prototypical adjectives $p_j^{\{1,...,6\}}$. Each adjective a_k^n was then assigned to the semantic class C_s that maximized the cumulative similarity between its 30 nearest neighbors $N(a_k^n)$ and the prototypical adjectives $p_s^1, ..., p_s^6$ in each semantic class.

In formula, this can be expressed as:

$$C(a_k^n) = \arg\max_s \left(\sum_{x \in N(a_k^n)} \sum_{p \in \{p_s^1, \dots p_s^6\}} \cos(x, p) \right) \quad (2)$$

This scoring system aims to match each adjective with the semantic category that most accurately reflects its typical usage based on vector space relationships. After identifying the most probable category for each adjective, we evaluated the overall alignment of each cluster with the semantic category represented by the prototype adjectives. This evaluation focused on how well the clustering-based labels aligned with the semantic themes identified by human informants. The results of the validation are summarized in Table 4. Categories such as *Evaluative* and *Relational* are predominantly represented by adjectives that align with their initial cluster label. Others, like *Descriptive*, exhibit a broader distribution of adjectives across multiple clusters.

	Rel	Des	Eva	Phy/H	Mem	TOT
Rel	**189**	8	7	37	9	250
Des	56	**69**	51	28	46	250
Eva	5	20	**216**	0	9	250
Phy/H	10	23	30	**179**	8	250
Mem	23	13	19	21	**174**	250
TOT	283	133	323	265	246	

Table 4: Confusion matrix presenting the validation results

To quantify the agreement between the cluster-assigned labels and the prototype-derived semantic categories, Precision, Recall, and F1-Score were calculated (Table 5). As observed, precision varies considerably across the clusters. The *Evaluative* cluster achieves the highest precision (0.864), indicating accurate classification with few false positives. In contrast, the *Descriptive* cluster exhibits the lowest precision (0.276), reflecting the challenges in distinguishing descriptive adjectives from other classes. Recall, on the other hand, is moderate to high for most clusters, with the *Membership* cluster performing the best (0.702).

Overall, the metrics suggest that the clustering strategy is effective, while also revealing challenges in distinguishing overlapping or subtly distinct categories. This is reflected in a Normalized Mutual Information (NMI) score of 0.3724 and an Adjusted Rand Index (ARI) of 0.3756, suggesting moderate agreement between the prototype-derived categories and the cluster-derived labels. Additionally, the similarity between the two metrics suggests that the clusters are not significantly affected by the chance agreement, thereby strengthening the overall validity of the clustering results. The relatively lower NMI and ARI scores may be attributed to semantic overlaps (adjectives may belong to multiple categories), cluster ambiguity (clusters contain mixed or overlapping semantic categories), or the limitations of the *K-means* algorithm when applied to complex linguistic data.

4.3 Cluster overlap

To further investigate one potential cause, viz. overlap between clusters, Kernel Density Estimation (KDE, Silverman 1998) was employed to visualize regions of high density within the clusters. KDE generates a continuous density surface, highlighting areas where adjectives are densely packed and where clusters overlap. Dense regions represent the core areas of each cluster, most indicative of each cluster's semantic space, while overlapping contours indicate shared or closely positioned adjectives. The resulting density plot is shown in Figure 4.

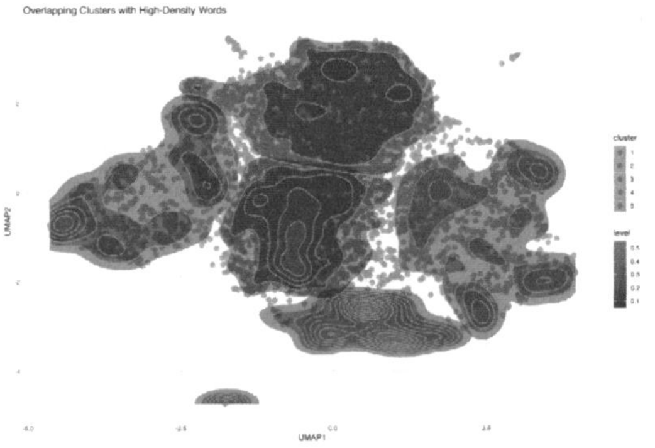

Figure 4: Kernel Density Estimation (KDE) plot

The high-density contours in the plot demonstrate that the clusters generally maintain their distinct boundaries, with little overlap between them. While clusters may touch or be adjacent, their core high-density areas remain separate, indicating clear semantic distinctions. To further investigate the overlap between clusters, we proceed by quantifying it, using spatial indexing with a *K-nearest neighbor* (KNN) approach[4], provided by the `Fast`

[4]A combined approach using KNN and Gaussian Mixture Models (GMM) with Bhattacharyya distance was tested to quantify overlap based on probability distributions, incorporating weighted averages. However, it was determined that the KNN values alone provided more interpretable and straightforward results

Cluster	TP	FP	FN	TN	Precision	Recall	F1-Score
Relational	189	61	88	912	0.756	0.682	0.717
Descriptive	69	181	63	937	0.276	0.522	0.361
Evaluative	216	34	110	890	0.864	0.663	0.750
Physical/Health	179	71	88	912	0.716	0.670	0.692
Membership	174	76	74	926	0.696	0.702	0.699

Table 5: Classification metrics for each cluster

`Nearest Neighbor` (FNN) package[5]. The overlap between two clusters was operationalized as the number of points in the first cluster that have a nearby point in the second cluster (within a distance threshold 0.5 units in the UMAP space). The overlap counts are presented in Table 6.

	Rel	Des	Eva	Phy/H	Mem
Rel	x	x	x	x	x
Des	131	x	x	x	x
Eva	0	399	x	x	x
Phy/H	0	233	209	x	x
Mem	127	144	113	0	x

Table 6: Overlaps between clusters – K-Nearest Neighbors

The greatest overlap was observed between the *Descriptive* and *Evaluative* cluster (399 points). These findings corroborate the classification results from the 250 adjective samples (see Table 4), where a substantial portion of the adjectives intended for the *Descriptive* cluster was frequently misclassified as *Evaluative*. The substantial number of shared points between these two clusters emphasizes that adjectives assigned to the *Evaluative* and *Descriptive* categories are not only close in semantic space but are often intermingled, making it difficult to separate them in a reduced-dimensional representation. The overlap detected using the KNN approach thus serves as a validation of the classification confusion observed, confirming that the semantic boundaries between *Descriptive* and *Evaluative* adjectives are porous, leading to a blending of meanings that complicates their discrete categorization.

Following the cluster evaluation, we put the annotation scheme to the test and proceed with the annotation of a sample of 500 adjectival lexemes extracted from itWaC. Unlike the highly prototypical adjectives used in the previous tests, this sample was not controlled, containing both frequent, unambiguous adjectives and those with lower frequencies and less straightforward semantics. The labeling results are presented in Table 7.

Label	TOT
Relational	7 (1.40%)
Descriptive	143 (28.60%)
Evaluative	285 (57.00%)
Physical/Health	31 (6.20%)
Membership	34 (6.80%)

Table 7: Results of word-embedding based semantic annotation

It can be observed that the majority of adjective types were classified as *Evaluative* and *Descriptive* adjectives, while only seven types were categorized as *Relational* adjectives. Following the initial automated clustering, a manual review was conducted to assess the accuracy of the labels assigned to the adjectives during the annotation process. Although the overall classification was generally satisfactory, the review revealed some instances of misclassification. In certain cases, it was determined that an alternative classification might more accurately reflect the semantic nature of the adjectives. Given that both the word embeddings and the chosen clustering method reflect patterns of co-occurrence and contextual similarity rather than strict semantic similarity, such results are not entirely unexpected. For instance, the assignment of the Membership class to the adjective *criminale* 'criminal' can be explained by the fact that the most strongly associated nouns (according to log-likelihood ratio) of the adjective in question in the itWaC corpus – *organizzazione* 'organization', *banda* 'gang', and *gruppo* 'group' – are all closely tied to concepts of membership and community. Despite these occasional discrepancies, we argue that the classification has provided a solid foundation and yielded valuable insights.

5 Wordnet comparison

Finally, we compared the proposed classification with the labels available in Wordnet, namely *adj.all* and *adj.pert*, as our dataset did not include any adjectival participles, categorized as verbs in itWaC.

By examining data in OpenMultilingualWordnet

[5]https://cran.r-project.org/web/packages/FNN/index.html

Cluster \ # Synsets	0	1	2	3	4	5	6	8	TOT
Relational	167	92	12	2	3	/	/	1	277
Descriptive	53	50	13	9	7	1	/	/	133
Evaluative	83	152	64	13	6	4	2	1	325
Physical/Health	116	131	16	2	1	/	/	/	267
Membership	89	134	20	3	/	/	/	/	246
TOT	508	559	125	30	16	6	3	1	1250

Table 8: Distribution of the number of synsets across clusters

(omw-1.4, Bond and Paik 2012; Bond et al. 2016), we annotated a sample of 250 adjectives randomly extracted from each cluster. As far as Italian is concerned, data in omw is derived from MultiWordNet (Pianta et al., 2002), a version of the Italian WordNet aligned with Princeton WordNet 1.6. Coverage was incomplete, as 507 out of 1250 adjectives were not associated with any synset in the database. Of the remaining adjectives, 559 were linked to a unique synset, while the others resulted ambiguous (≥ 2 synsets) . Table 8 displays the distribution of the number of synsets associated with each adjective across the five clusters.

For each retrieved synset, we used the `nltk`[6] to extract the semantic label (i.e., *all* or *pert*), which, in the case of adjectives, corresponds to the `lexname`.

First, a strong correlation was observed between Wordnet's *pert* label and our relational macro-category, which encompasses the Relational, Physical/Health-Related, and Membership classes. Specifically, of the 272 types labeled as *pert*, 258 (94.85%) fell within this macro-category (46 Relational, 102 Physical/Health-Related, and 110 Membership), highlighting both the embeddings' ability to capture relational meanings and the interconnectedness of these three semantic labels. Second, for the *all* label, another interesting pattern emerged. Among 149 adjective types with more than one synset, 116 (77.85%) were found in the Descriptive and Evaluative classes, reinforcing the higher polysemy in these clusters. This aligns with the earlier analysis, which showed that these two clusters exhibited the greatest overlap.

6 Conclusion and future work

The paper explored the possibility of deriving semantic classes for Italian adjectives using word embeddings. While adjectives belonging to certain categories were easily identifiable and demonstrated high accuracy (e.g., the *Evaluative* class), others (e.g., the *Descriptive* class) proved more difficult to categorize and lacked consistency. Furthermore, it was observed that, as shown in previous literature, the collocational context of adjectives, particularly with regard to the nouns they modify, has a significant influence on their classification in semantic classes. A holistic approach, which considers the bidirectional relationship between adjectives and nouns, is hence essential (for the so-called *composition method* to account for polysemy effects, see, e.g., Baroni and Zamparelli 2010, who treat adjectives as data-induced (linear) functions over nominal vectors).

To sum up, the semantic classification of Italian adjectives using word embeddings is feasible but not without challenges. Besides the issues with cluster coherence, adjective polysemy must also be addressed, as semantic class categorization may also depend on the specific sense of an adjective (cf., for instance, *raffreddato* which, depending on the context, can mean both 'cooled/chilled', hence belong to a *Descriptive* class, as well as 'have a cold', thus belong to *Physical/Health related* class). In this regard, the choice of embeddings could impact the results. Although POS-tagging enables our static model to differentiate between senses with different parts of speech, senses that share the same POS are still merged into a single vector. Therefore, it would be valuable to explore vectors based on syntactic collocates rather than a linear window, such as those produced by `word2vecf` (Levy and Goldberg, 2014), or natively contextual embeddings like those generated by BERT (Devlin et al., 2019), as they might perform better than static, general-purpose ones (see, *inter alia*, Soper and Koenig 2022 for a discussion on this topic). In addition, tests with alternative classifiers should be run. Finally, it would be beneficial to explore different (higher) values for K, as the five clusters used in this study represent a relatively coarse-grained grouping. For studies requiring more precision (fine-grained classification), this may not be suffi-

[6] `https://www.nltk.org/howto/wordnet.html`

cient. Regarding WordNet, while the nominal side of WordNet is deeply structured (with a lot of levels), in this proposal we suggest adding just one additional level to the hierarchy.

Acknowledgments

The authors are grateful to Dr. Matteo Pascoli for his support in the creation of the vector spaces.

References

Laura Aina, Raffaella Bernardi, and Raquel Fernández. 2019. Negated adjectives and antonyms in distributional semantics: not similar? *IJCoL. Italian Journal of Computational Linguistics*, 5(5-1):57–71.

Marco Baroni, Silvia Bernardini, Federica Comastri, Lorenzo Piccioni, Alessandra Volpi, Guy Aston, Marco Mazzoleni, et al. 2004. Introducing the La Repubblica corpus: A large, annotated, tei (xml)-compliant corpus of newspaper Italian. In *LREC*.

Marco Baroni, Silvia Bernardini, Adriano Ferraresi, and Eros Zanchetta. 2009. The wacky wide web: a collection of very large linguistically processed web-crawled corpora. *Language resources and evaluation*, 43:209–226.

Marco Baroni and Roberto Zamparelli. 2010. Nouns are vectors, adjectives are matrices: Representing adjective-noun constructions in semantic space. In *Proceedings of the 2010 Conference on Empirical Methods in Natural Language Processing*, pages 1183–1193.

Douglas Biber, Stig Johansson, Geoffrey Leech, Susan Conrad, and Edward Finegan. 2007. *Grammar of spoken and written English*. Longman.

Francis Bond and Kyonghee Paik. 2012. A survey of wordnets and their licenses. In *Proceedings of the 6th global WordNet conference (GWC 2012)*, pages 64–71. Matsue.

Francis Bond, Piek Vossen, John Philip McCrae, and Christiane Fellbaum. 2016. Cili: the collaborative interlingual index. In *Proceedings of the 8th Global WordNet Conference (GWC)*, pages 50–57.

Tadeusz Caliński and Jerzy Harabasz. 1974. A dendrite method for cluster analysis. *Communications in Statistics-theory and Methods*, 3(1):1–27.

Malika Charrad, Nadia Ghazzali, Véronique Boiteau, and Azam Niknafs. 2014. Nbclust: an R package for determining the relevant number of clusters in a data set. *Journal of statistical software*, 61:1–36.

David L Davies and Donald W Bouldin. 1979. A cluster separation measure. *IEEE transactions on pattern analysis and machine intelligence*, (2):224–227.

Jacob Devlin, Ming-Wei Chang, Kenton Lee, and Kristina Toutanova. 2019. BERT: Pre-training of deep bidirectional transformers for language understanding. In *Proceedings of the 2019 Conference of the North American Chapter of the Association for Computational Linguistics: Human Language Technologies, Volume 1*, pages 7–12.

Tsvetana Dimitrova and Valentina Stefanova. 2018. The semantic classification of adjectives in the Bulgarian wordnet: Towards a multiclass approach. *Cognitive Studies*, (18).

Robert MW Dixon. 1977. Where have all the adjectives gone? *Studies in Language*, 1:19–80.

Birgit Hamp and Helmut Feldweg. 1997. GermaNet - a Lexical-Semantic Net for German. In *Proceedings of the ACL Workshop on Automatic Information Extraction and Building of Lexical Semantic Resources for NLP Applications*, Madrid.

Verena Henrich and Erhard Hinrichs. 2010. GernEdiT - The GermaNet Editing Tool. In *Proceedings of the Seventh Conference on International Language Resources and Evaluation (LREC 2010)*, pages 2228–2235, Valletta, Malta.

Franz Hundsnurscher and Jochen Splett. 1982. *Semantik der Adjektive des Deutschen: Analyse der semantischen Relationen*. Springer.

Joo-Kyung Kim and Marie-Catherine de Marneffe. 2013. Deriving adjectival scales from continuous space word representations. In *Proceedings of the 2013 Conference on Empirical Methods in Natural Language Processing*, pages 1625–1630.

Ludovic Lebart, Alain Morineau, and Marie Piron. 1995. *Statistique exploratoire multidimensionnelle*. Dunod.

McInnes Leland, Healy John, and Melville James. 2018. Uniform manifold approximation and projection for dimension reduction. *arXiv preprint arXiv:1802.03426*.

Alessandro Lenci and Magnus Sahlgren. 2023. *Distributional semantics*. Cambridge University Press.

Omer Levy and Yoav Goldberg. 2014. Dependency-based word embeddings. In *Proceedings of the 52nd Annual Meeting of the Association for Computational Linguistics (Volume 2: Short Papers)*, pages 302–308.

Tomas Mikolov. 2013. Efficient estimation of word representations in vector space. *arXiv preprint arXiv:1301.3781*.

George A Miller. 1995. Wordnet: a lexical database for english. *Communications of the ACM*, 38(11):39–41.

Mariana Montes and Dirk Geeraerts. 2022. How vector space models disambiguate adjectives: A perilous but valid enterprise. *Yearbook of the German Cognitive Linguistics Association*, 10(1):7–32.

Emanuele Pianta, Luisa Bentivogli, and Christian Girardi. 2002. Multiwordnet: developing an aligned multilingual database. In *First international conference on global WordNet*, pages 293–302.

Scott Songlin Piao, Paul Rayson, Dawn Archer, and Tony McEnery. 2005. Comparing and combining a semantic tagger and a statistical tool for MWE extraction. *Computer Speech Language*, 19(4):378–397. Special issue on Multiword Expression.

Radim Řehřek and Petr Sojka. 2010. Software framework for topic modelling with large corpora. In *Proceedings of the LREC 2010 Workshop on New Challenges for NLP Frameworks*, pages 45–50. University of Malta.

Martin Schweinberger and Chang-Hao (Howard) Luo. 2024. Automated, corpus- and usage-based semantic classification of word class using word embeddings. Presentation delivered at ICAME 45 "Interlocking corpora and register(s): Diversity and innovation". Vigo, 18–22 June 2024.

Bernard W Silverman. 1998. *Density estimation for statistics and data analysis*. Routledge.

Scott Songlin Piao, Paul Edward Rayson, Dawn Archer, Francesca Bianchi, Carmen Dayrell, Mahmoud El-Haj, Ricardo-María Jiménez-Yáñez, Dawn Knight, Michal Křen, Laura Lofberg, et al. 2016. Lexical coverage evaluation of large-scale multilingual semantic lexicons for twelve languages. In *LREC 2016, Tenth International Conference on Language Resources and Evaluation*.

Elizabeth Soper and Jean-Pierre Koenig. 2022. When polysemy matters: Modeling semantic categorization with word embeddings. In *Proceedings of the 11th Joint Conference on Lexical and Computational Semantics*, pages 123–131.

Ivan Vulić, Simon Baker, Edoardo Maria Ponti, Ulla Petti, Ira Leviant, Kelly Wing, Olga Majewska, Eden Bar, Matt Malone, Thierry Poibeau, et al. 2020. Multi-simlex: A large-scale evaluation of multilingual and crosslingual lexical semantic similarity. *Computational Linguistics*, 46(4):847–897.

Tatu Ylonen. 2022. Wiktextract: Wiktionary as machine-readable structured data. In *Proceedings of the 13th Conference on Language Resources and Evaluation (LREC)*, pages 1317–1325.

A Distributional models

Models were created both with `CBoW` and `SkipGram` algorithms, with (linear) windows of 2 and 5 tokens and embedding dimensions of 200, 300, 500. Table 9 summarizes the results of the correlation with the popular dataset of Word Similarity and Relatedness.

Algorithm	CBOW						SkipGram					
Window		win2			win5			win2			win5	
Dimension	200	300	500	200	300	500	200	300	500	200	300	500
SimLex-999	0,343	0,353	0,370	0,342	0,349	0,364	0,354	0,373	**0,398**	0,334	0,352	0,370
WS353	0,519	0,524	0,519	0,558	0,554	0,555	0,559	0,562	0,565	0,569	0,571	**0,576**
WS353-Rel	0,402	0,408	0,396	0,455	0,447	0,444	0,466	0,473	0,459	0,486	**0,487**	**0,487**

Table 9: Correlation of cosine similarity with scores in Italian SimLex-999 and WS-353. Coverage was 924 out of 999 items for SimLex, and 287 out of 350 items for WS-353.

AUTHOR INDEX